SALINGER

DAVID SHIELDS SHANE SALERNO

SIMON & SCHUSTER
NEW YORK LONDON TORONTO SYDNEY NEW DELHI

Simon & Schuster
1230 Avenue of the Americas
New York, NY 10020

This Simon & Schuster export edition September 2013

Interior design by Nancy Singer
Jacket design by Christopher Lin
Back cover photograph courtesy of Denise Fitzgerald

Manufactured in the United States of America

10 9 8 7 6 5 4 3 2 1

ISBN 978-1-4767-4703-3
ISBN 978-1-4767-4484-1 (ebook)

FOR MY MOTHER

—Shane Salerno

FOR LAURIE AND NATALIE

—David Shields

CONTENTS

PART II
GARHASTHYA
HOUSEHOLDER DUTIES

PART III
VANAPRASTHYA
WITHDRAWAL FROM SOCIETY

PART IV

SANNYASA

RENUNCIATION OF THE WORLD

I was with the Fourth Division during the war. I almost always write about very young people.

—*J. D. Salinger*

What a low and specious thing "religion" would be if it were to lead me to negate art, love.

—*J. D. Salinger*

INTRODUCTION

J. D. Salinger spent ten years writing *The Catcher in the Rye* and the rest of his life regretting it.

Before the book was published, he was a World War II veteran with Post-traumatic Stress Disorder; after the war, he was perpetually in search of a spiritual cure for his damaged psyche. In the wake of the enormous success of the novel about the "prep school boy," a myth emerged: Salinger, like Holden, was too sensitive to be touched, too good for this world. He would spend the rest of his life trying and failing to reconcile these completely contradictory versions of himself: the myth and the reality.

The Catcher in the Rye has sold more than 65 million copies and continues to sell more than half a million copies a year; a defining book for several generations, it remains a totem of American adolescence. Salinger's slim oeuvre—four brief books—has a cultural weight and penetration nearly unmatched in modern literature. The critical and popular game over the past half-century has been to read the man through his works because the man would not speak. Salinger's success in epic self-creation, his obsession with privacy, and his meticulously maintained vault—containing a large cache of writing that he refused to publish—combined to form an impermeable legend.

Salinger was an extraordinarily complex, deeply contradictory human being. He was not—as we've been told—a recluse for the final fifty-five years of his life; he traveled extensively, had many affairs and lifelong friendships, consumed copious amounts of popular culture, and often embodied many of the things he criticized in his fiction. Far from being a recluse, he was constantly in conversation with the world in order to reinforce its notion of his reclusion. What he wanted was privacy, but the literary silence that reclusion brought became as closely associated with him as *The Catcher in the Rye*. Much has been made of how difficult it must have been for Salinger to live and work under the umbrella of the myth, which is undeniably true; we show the degree to which he was also invested in perpetuating it.

Other books about Salinger tend to fall into one of three categories: academic exegeses; necessarily highly subjective memoirs; and either overly reverential or overly resentful biographies that, thwarted by lack of access to the principals, settle for perpetuating the agreed-upon narrative. Previous biographies have tended to rely on the relatively small collections of Salinger papers and unpublished manuscripts found at Princeton University and the University of Texas, Austin. The result is the recycling of the same information from a very shallow well and the republication of inaccurate information. The letters we excerpt, ranging from 1940–2008, are from Salinger to his closest friends, lovers over many decades, World War II brothers-in-arms, spiritual teachers and others; the overwhelming majority of the letters have never been seen before.

We began with three goals: we wanted to know why Salinger stopped publishing; why he disappeared; and what he had been writing the last forty-five years of his life. Over nine years and across five continents, we interviewed more than two hundred people, many of whom had previously refused to go on the record and all of whom spoke to us without preconditions. We aim to provide a multilayered perspective on Salinger, offering first-person accounts from Salinger's fellow World War II counterintelligence agents with whom he maintained lifelong bonds, lovers, friends, caretakers, classmates, editors, publishers, *New Yorker* colleagues, admirers, detractors, and many prominent figures who discuss his influence on their lives, their work, and the broader culture.

By reproducing material that has never been published before—more than one hundred photographs and excerpts from journals, diaries, letters, memoirs, court transcripts, depositions, and recently declassified military records—we hope to deliver many factual clarifications and significant revelations. We particularly illuminate the last fifty-five years of his life: a period that, until now, had remained largely dark to biographers.

Still, we faced two major obstacles: The first was that key people had died before we began this project, and the second was that while certain members of the Salinger family initially cooperated, the Salinger family ultimately did not participate in formal interviews. Although they didn't speak directly to us, they had spoken, and through a careful dissection of their public statements and our obtaining of private letters and never-before-published documents, their voices appear throughout this book. In addition, many people unwilling to talk on the record directed us to crucial information and passed on photographs, letters, and diaries they had kept secret their entire lives; half a dozen of our most important interviewees spoke to us only after Salinger's death.

We also provide twelve "conversations with Salinger": revealing encounters over half a century between journalists, photographers, seekers, fans, family members, and the man who never stopped living his life like a counterintelligence agent. These episodes place the reader on increasingly intimate terms with an author who had been adamantly inaccessible for more than half a century.

—

There were two emphatic demarcation points in Salinger's life: World War II and his immersion in the Vedanta religion. World War II destroyed the man but made him a great artist. Religion provided the comfort he needed as a man but killed his art.

This is the story of a soldier and writer who escaped death during World War II but never wholly embraced survival, a half-Jew from Park Avenue who discovered at war's end what it meant to be Jewish. This is an investigation into the process by which a broken soldier and a wounded soul transformed himself, through his art, into an icon of the twentieth century and then, through his religion, destroyed that art.

Salinger was born with an embarrassing congenital deformity that shadowed his entire life. A college dropout, mercurial talent, wise-guy dandy out of an F. Scott Fitzgerald novel, he was ferociously determined to become a great writer. He dated Oona O'Neill—the gorgeous daughter of arguably America's greatest playwright, Eugene O'Neill—and published short stories in the *Saturday Evening Post* and other "slicks." After the war, Salinger refused to allow any of these stories to be republished. The war had killed that author.

A staff sergeant in the 12th Infantry, Salinger served through five bloody campaigns of the European Theater of 1944–45. His job, as a counterintelligence agent, involved interrogating prisoners of war; working the shadow war, the no-man's-land between Allies and Germans;

gathering information from civilians, the wounded, traitors, and black marketers. He saw firsthand the war's destruction and devastation. When the end was near, he and other soldiers entered Kaufering IV, an auxiliary of the Dachau concentration camp. Soon after witnessing Kaufering, Salinger checked himself into a Nuremberg civilian hospital, a psychic casualty of the war's final revelation.

Throughout the war and during his postwar hospitalization, Salinger had carried a personal talisman for survival inside the war's corpse machine: the first six chapters of a novel about Holden Caulfield. Those chapters would become *The Catcher in the Rye*, which redefined postwar America and can best be understood as a disguised war novel. Salinger emerged from the war incapable of believing in the heroic, noble ideals we like to think our cultural institutions uphold. Instead of producing a combat novel, as Norman Mailer, James Jones, and Joseph Heller did, Salinger took the trauma of war and embedded it within what looked to the naked eye like a coming-of-age novel. So, too, in *Nine Stories*, the ghost in the machine is postwar trauma: a suicide begins the book, is barely averted in the middle of the book, and ends the book.

Profoundly damaged (not only by the war), he became numb; numb, he yearned to see and feel the unity of all things but settled for detachment toward everyone's pain except his own, which first overwhelmed and then overtook him. During his second marriage, he steadily distanced himself from his family, spending weeks at a time in his detached bunker, telling his wife, Claire, and children, Matthew and Margaret, "Do not disturb me unless the house is burning down." Toward Margaret, who dared to embody the rebellious traits his fiction canonizes, he was startlingly remote. His characters Franny, Zooey, and Seymour Glass, despite or because of their many suicidal madnesses, had immeasurably more claim on his heart than his flesh-and-blood family.

A drowning man, grasping desperately for life rafts, drifting farther away from the taint of the everyday, occupying increasingly abstract realms, he disappeared into the solace of Vedantic philosophy: you are not your body, you are not your mind, renounce name and fame. "Detachment, buddy, and only detachment," he wrote in *Zooey*. "Desirelessness. 'Cessation from all hankerings.'" His work tracks exactly along this physical-metaphysical axis; book by book, he came to see his task as the dissemination of doctrine.

Salinger's vault, which we open in the final chapter, contains character-

and career-defining revelations, but there is no "ultimate secret" whose unveiling explains the man. Instead, his life contained a series of interlocking events—ranging from anatomy to romance to war to fame to religion—that we disclose, track, and connect.

Creating a private world in which he could control everything, Salinger wrenched immaculate, immortal art from the anguish of World War II. And then, when he couldn't control everything—when the accumulation of all the suffering was too much for a human as delicately constructed as he to withstand—he gave himself over wholly to Vedanta, turning the last half of his life into a dance with ghosts. He had nothing anymore to say to anyone else.

PART I

BRAHMACHARYA

APPRENTICESHIP

Landing at Utah Beach on D-Day, June 6, 1944.

1

WE'RE GOING TO START THE WAR FROM RIGHT HERE

UTAH BEACH, NORMANDY, JUNE 6, 1944;
SAINT-LÔ, MORTAIN, CHERBOURG, FRANCE, JUNE–AUGUST 1944

Salinger's 12th Infantry Regiment lands on Utah Beach on D-Day, June 6, 1944, with not quite 3,100 soldiers; by the end of June it will have lost about 2,500. Salinger comes face-to-face with oblivion in the massive aggregate and at the intimate level of his unit.

J. D. SALINGER: I landed on Utah Beach on D-Day with the Fourth Division.

MARGARET SALINGER: "I landed on D-Day, you know," he'd say to me darkly, soldier to soldier, as it were, as if I understood the implications.

EDWARD G. MILLER: Of all the days for someone to be initiated in combat, Jerome David Salinger's was D-Day.

ABLE SEAMAN KEN OAKLEY: On the evening prior to the D-Day landings, the senior arms officer gave us a briefing, and I will always remember his final words. "Don't worry if all the first wave of you are killed," he said. "We shall simply pass over your bodies with more and more men." What a confident thought to go to bed on.

SHANE SALERNO: Salinger was a privileged, sheltered twenty-five-year-old from Park Avenue who thought war would be an adventure—glamorous, romantic. He imagined himself the protagonist of a Jack London novel and hoped military service would explode the bubble in which he was raised. Salinger wrote, "My mind is stocked with some black neckties, and though I'm throwing them out as fast as I find them, there will always be a few left over." He wondered whether he lacked the requisite pain to become a writer. He wanted the war to toughen him, deepen him as a person and a writer. The next year would change him forever.

DAVID SHIELDS: Salinger told Whit Burnett, his writing teacher at Columbia University and the editor of *Story* magazine, that on D-Day he was carrying six chapters of *The Catcher in the Rye*, that he needed those pages with him not only as an amulet to help him survive but as a reason to survive.

WERNER KLEEMAN: Jerry was just a nice little boy then. He was kind of quiet. I could see he was a little bit of an eight ball. He was different. He didn't close the straps of his helmet. He did what he wanted to do.

ALEX KERSHAW: Salinger's serial number was 32325200, the same number he gave many years later to his fictional character Babe Gladwaller in "Last Day of the Last Furlough."

SHANE SALERNO: John Keenan served with Salinger in the Counter Intelligence Corps [CIC]. Salinger, Keenan, Jack Altaras, and Paul Fitzgerald were together throughout the war, calling themselves the "Four Musketeers"; they remained close friends all their lives. Altaras and Fitzgerald have never been identified before.

JOHN KEENAN: I guess about 3 a.m. the frogmen [naval combat demolition units] left. None of us could sleep, so we knew what was going on. There was a lot of small talk and a lot of fake bravado, too. I don't think anybody thought this was going to be the great adventure of our lives. Thank God they all got back. Five-ish the infantrymen left. They were the first wave.

EBERHARD ALSEN: Salinger was assigned to the 12th Infantry Regiment. I thought he landed with the regiment at 1030, almost four hours after H-Hour. But the U.S. Army's official *History of the Counter Intelligence Corps* states that the "4th CIC Detachment went in with the 4th Infantry Division when it stormed Utah Beach at 0645." This means that Salinger's CIC detachment went ashore at that time with the 8th Regiment, which spearheaded the landing of the 4th Division.

DAVID SHIELDS: An eyewitness, Werner Kleeman, who was serving as an interpreter for the 12th Infantry and who was friends with Salinger, reported that Salinger landed in the second wave of the D-Day assault.

ALEX KERSHAW: On D-Day, Salinger was in a landing craft, coming in toward Utah Beach, crammed in tight with his friends and fellow soldiers, some of whom would be dead shortly.

WERNER KLEEMAN: Shells were flying over our head. The small arms were still coming in. The artillery shells were coming in.

"The Four Musketeers": (L–R) J. D. Salinger, Jack Altaras, John Keenan, Paul Fitzgerald.

EDWARD G. MILLER: Most of these guys were nineteen, twenty, twenty-one years old. Salinger was twenty-five, an old man.

PAUL FITZGERALD (excerpt from an unpublished poem): Glamor and bravado were not a part of this. The beach was just ahead of us. Floating in the tide I saw my first casualty.

JOHN KEENAN: The battleships were firing at the coast, aiming at the pillboxes [fortified concrete structures from which German soldiers operated machine guns].

STEPHEN E. AMBROSE: The waves were pitching the landing craft around, coming over the gunwales to hit the troops smack in the face, making many of the men so miserable they could not wait to get off.

PRIVATE RALPH DELLA-VOLPE: The boats were going around like little bugs jockeying for position. I had had an extra, extra big breakfast, thinking it would help, but I lost it.

STEPHEN E. AMBROSE: So did many others. Seaman Marvin Perrett, an 18-year-old Coast Guardsman from New Orleans, was coxswain on a New Orleans–built Higgins boat. The 30 members of the Twelfth Regiment of the Fourth Division he was carrying ashore had turned their heads toward him to avoid the spray. He could see concern and fear on their faces. Just in front of him stood a chaplain. Perrett was concentrating on keeping his place in the advancing line. The chaplain upchucked his breakfast, the wind caught it, and Perrett's face (and everyone else on the boat) was covered with undigested eggs, coffee, and bits of bacon.

STAFF SERGEANT DAVID RODERICK: The beach at Utah Beach had a long and gentle upward slope. We surprised the Germans by assaulting Utah at low tide when the obstacles would be exposed. However, that gave our troops over one hundred yards of exposure in addition to approximately 100 yards of water. Our 4th Infantry Division troops were debarked in 3 feet to 6 feet of water and struggled the approximate 200 yards to the seawall. The seawall was 3 feet to 8 feet high with sand dunes behind them as high as 10 feet. Fortifications along the beach could sweep it with small arms fire, machine guns, and artillery.

My opinion is that the only question Salinger had—the only question any of us had—was "Am I gonna make it? Am I gonna make it to the beach?" I was particularly anxious about that because I wasn't a good swimmer. The life preservers that they gave you were a single wide strip that went around your waist, and you had all this heavy equipment on your back. If you weren't careful, if you fell in the water and inflated that thing, it might just turn you upside down and you'd drown.

PRIVATE ALBERT SOHL: "Get ready!" the coxswain shouted above the laboring engine. He skillfully swerved our craft inland between the milling maritime traffic. Sporadic explosions from inland artillery marched along the water's edge on invisible seven-league boots. My heart was pounding faster, but I still could not see anyone on shore resembling our foe. Approximately fifty yards from the beach, our pilot shoved the screws into reverse. As the boat hove to, he abruptly released the forward ramp. Guns blasted from afar. Planes zoomed overhead. Ragged shards of black smoke from swift-moving destroyers drifted across the chaotic scene. "This is the end of the line!" the coxswain shouted above the din. "Move your asses, I gotta go back for more passengers."

COLONEL GERDEN F. JOHNSON: The men felt their muscles tighten as the word was whispered back that the coast was just ahead. As they raced toward the shore, the skipper yelled for more blankets. That meant there were wounded on the beach, which scared the hell out of everyone. The immediate problem of every man came sharply into focus. Everyone knew that if they were going to get through that day alive, they would first have to survive the run into the beach. Nothing else mattered now. It was the all-important thing. If they made it, somehow they would have to live through what would seem an eternity of wading through water from the ramp to the landing craft to the beach—wading while held back by the burden of heavy equipment—an eternity when they would feel nakedly exposed to the murderous fire of someone behind the beach.

GENERAL MATTHEW RIDGWAY: For the first time I saw the loneliest and most ominous of all landscapes, a battlefield. And I knew for the first time that strange exhilaration that grips a man when he knows that somewhere out there in the distance, hostile eyes are watching him and that at any moment a bullet he may never hear, fired by an enemy he cannot see, may strike him.

CAPTAIN GEORGE MAYBERRY: Never before in my life had I wanted so badly to run, but I could only wade slowly forward. It was approximately a hundred yards to the edge of the shore and it took me two minutes to reach the shallow water. Those two minutes were extremely long. Even on the beach I couldn't run, as my uniform was sodden and heavy and my legs were numb and cramped.

Heavy shells commenced exploding on the beach, as well as sporadic mortar fire from a short distance inland. A soldier just ahead of me was blown to pieces by a direct hit. The instant it happened, something small hit me in the stomach—it was the man's thumb.

STAFF SERGEANT DAVID RODERICK: I noticed equipment, life preservers, lumber from a boat that hit a mine, floating in the water. Two hundred yards away I heard a loud explosion; B Battery, artillery, hit a mine and its landing craft blew up, a tremendous explosion. There were four artillery pieces and 60 men in the landing craft. We all watched in horror as bodies and metal flew into the air: 39 of the 60 men were killed.

—

STAFF SERGEANT DAVID RODERICK: We moved fast. Everyone's goal was the same: Get off and get to the seawall as quickly as possible. We were directly exposed to enemy fire. I remember one guy who went in with the first wave, struggling to stay afloat once he got off the landing craft. Some big guy grabbed him by the seat of the pants, lifted him up, and said, "Hey, Shorty, you better get your feet on the ground." Before Shorty could thank the guy, his rescuer took a bullet through the head.

Artillery poured down on us and snipers picked off my friends. In fact, the first man killed under my command was shot between the eyes on the beach by a German sniper. I could hear machine guns further down the beach where one battalion was attacking an enemy fortification.

JOHN McMANUS: There was a photo of an American soldier killed by a sniper on Utah, right before he got to the seawall. His body looked

U.S. soldiers behind a seawall at Utah Beach.

pristine, killed by a single shot to the head. It was one of the long-term images of Utah Beach.

WERNER KLEEMAN: Once we were on the beach we saw hundreds of little flags bearing the warning "Achtung, Minen!" (Attention! Mines!), but the mines turned out to be dummies. We saw that some soldiers had already been killed and were lying in a ditch before the seawall.

JOSEPH BALKOSKI: The 4th Division's entire first wave, consisting of more than 600 infantrymen in 20 landing craft, had come ashore considerably south of its intended landing point.

[Brigadier-General Theodore Roosevelt Jr.] was one of the first soldiers to discern this disturbing mistake. His command—"We're going to start the war from right here!"—would become the defining moment of the Utah Beach invasion.

EDWARD G. MILLER: The landmarks that Salinger had trained to spot, to orient himself once ashore, weren't there. The only fortunate thing was that the German defenses were a bit weaker there than they might've been had Salinger and his unit landed farther to the north on the Cherbourg Peninsula, but nonetheless the bullets were the same. The explosions, the artillery, the churning sand, the surf, the confusion, the rain, the smoke, the seasickness.

Salinger saw an introduction to combat that I don't think he or, for that matter, anyone in the army was prepared for. Day One ashore for Salinger would've been sheer terror. The urgency of getting himself ashore, getting set up ashore, protecting himself, the soldiers around him. Fire. Smoke. Yelling. No amount of training could've prepared him for that. The experience was brutal and sudden and shocking. It was simply burned into his soul.

DAVID SHIELDS: Salinger's only story that directly evokes war, "The Magic Foxhole," was written shortly after D-Day and is clearly based on that experience. It was never published. Cynical toward even the idea of war, the story relates the battle fatigue suffered by two soldiers, one of whom, Gar-

Advancing on Utah Beach, D-Day.

Wounded soldier on Utah Beach.

rity, tells the story in rapid-fire monologue. In the opening scene, a chaplain who is trying to find his glasses beneath dead bodies on Normandy beach gets killed. God is now not only sightless but dead. Salinger will spend the rest of his life trying to find a replacement vision, a replacement for God.

J. D. SALINGER ("The Magic Foxhole," unpublished):

> We come in twenty minutes before H-Hour on D-Day. There wasn't nothing on the beach but the dead boys of "A" and "B" Company, and some dead sailor boys, and a Chaplain that was crawling around looking for his glasses in the sand. He was the only thing that was moving, and eighty-eight shells were breaking all around him, and there he was crawling around on his hands and knees, looking for his glasses. He got knocked off. . . . That's what the Beach was like when I come in.

EBERHARD ALSEN: Many of the passages in "The Magic Foxhole" are autobiographical and exactly what Salinger witnessed. A similar account comes from Private Ray A. Mann, who landed on Utah Beach with the 8th Regiment.

PRIVATE RAY A. MANN: Our team rushed out of the craft and headed across the beach in small groups[. Just like that,] about 15 to 20 feet across the beach, shells started to fall. The first few landed in a group just ahead of me. Up to that point, I felt like that was almost like previous manoeuvres in Florida, even Slapton Sands. But when I saw our wounded men agonizing in pain and heard them scream, I knew that we were playing for keeps. A second group of shells landed near my group and hit apparently our First Sergeant. Never saw him again. The company clerk was also hit. . . . I finally reached the seawall and the German pillbox and paused to get my bearings. Even in the short time between my landing and the time we got to the seawall, I was shocked by the number of men who were landing and the number of wounded that I saw spread out over the beach. I saw a chaplain here and there praying over dead men.

ALEX KERSHAW: Only combat can teach you what fear does to the human body and the mind. All Salinger wanted to do is stay alive.

JOHN McMANUS: The D-Day veterans that I have interviewed told me they were thinking, "I can't wait to shoot somebody," and just a second later, "I don't want to shoot somebody."

—

STAFF SERGEANT DAVID RODERICK: Our artillery made a swishing sound going out. One of the things Salinger would have learned very quickly was what was incoming mail [German artillery] and what was outgoing mail [American artillery]. Our artillery made a swishing sound going out. Incoming mail—he would have tensed up and taken cover. He would have learned very quickly the difference in sounds, especially the German .88, which was the best artillery piece in the war, and it shot like a rifle. There wasn't much time between when you heard it and when it landed. It was just bang and on top of you. It was a great weapon for the Germans. They also had what we called Screaming Meemies, which was mortar rocket fire that went up real high before coming down. You could hear them screech, and that brought a chill to your bones. It didn't have an artillery shell, so it didn't spin like one in the air, which made the noise a little different, more eerie than normal artillery. I lost eight men on the second day from Screaming Meemies.

ALEX KERSHAW: Salinger knew that what was going to kill him was shrapnel, machine-gun fire, and artillery pieces. And the best way for him to stay alive was to get down, preferably with his head below ground; if not below ground, then as close to the ground as possible at all times.

JOHN CLARK: I had seen many terrible sights: pieces of bodies lying on the beach, guys blown all to hell. I think the thing that bothered me most was seeing a tank with a blade moving up the road and shoving the bodies into the ditch so they wouldn't be run over by the advancing tanks and trucks.

EDWARD G. MILLER: Once ashore, the first object for Salinger and the rest of his regiment was to organize and secure the beachhead. Some of the worst of the fighting wasn't at the beaches. That was over and done with in the first few hours, but the utter grind, the sheer hell of grueling infantry combat, came once they cleared the beach.

A wounded soldier receiving first aid at Les Dunes de Madeleine.

ALEX KERSHAW: Utah Beach was not the bloodiest beach on D-Day. There were two-hundred-odd casualties suffered by the 4th Infantry Division on Utah, and these were men Salinger knew and had trained with. The issue about Utah and D-Day is not one of casualties sustained on D-Day but the casualties sustained in the days immediately after. Because Utah was not the bloodiest beach on D-Day, there was a false sense of security among the 4th Division, certainly among Salinger and his comrades, as to what was to come next.

—

COLONEL GERDEN F. JOHNSON: Following the breakout from the beachhead, the American Third Army . . . sent six divisions racing

Soldiers on Utah Beach after initial assault.

toward Brittany in order to surround the Germans and open a route to Paris. These divisions had to be funneled through a narrow corridor east of Avranches, formed when the Germans flooded an area as large as Rhode Island.

STEPHEN E. AMBROSE: Colonel Russell "Red" Reeder was CO [Commanding Officer] of the 12th Infantry. . . . Reeder led his men through a hole in the seawall to the top of the dune, where he saw [Theodore] Roosevelt. "Red, the causeways leading inland are all clogged up," Roosevelt yelled. "Look at it! A procession of jeeps and not a wheel turning." To Reeder, "Roosevelt looked tired and the cane he leaned on heightened the impression." . . . Reeder made his decision. "We are going through the flooded area," he yelled.

COLONEL RUSSELL REEDER: The Germans had flooded the surrounding lowlands and meadows by damming streams, making a lake a mile wide. We had to cross the lake. We knew from spies and loyal Frenchmen that before the Germans made the lake, they had bulldozed furrows so that every now and then the water, instead of being chest high, was about ten feet deep. Back in England our general had told us we might have to ford it. He equipped us with inflatable life preservers, and we had paired men who could not swim with swimmers. I gave an arm signal and 3,000 heavily burdened infantrymen walked into the man-made lake. . . . When I saw non-swimmers near me in the lake struggling to go forward, hanging on to their weapons and equipment, I knew that we would win the war.

DAVID SHIELDS: Colonel Reeder's men struggled to cross the inundated fields. Later, Reeder recalled that moment: "Just before we departed England, the division commander said to me, 'Spies have informed us that the Germans have a way to put flammable material on the flooded areas. Tell the men what to do if this happens.'" In a 1958 letter to Cornelius Ryan, Reeder remarked, "I'm still searching for an answer."

STAFF SERGEANT DAVID RODERICK: There were only four causeways—we called them "causeways" or "exits"—that ran through those flooded areas toward Sainte-Mère-Église. Salinger would have had to get across the beach, over the seawall and the sand dune, onto the exits, and across the exits, where he would have begun to make his struggle inland. The 82nd Airborne and the 101st Airborne were responsible for being sure that we were able to cross the causeways. The 101st was to drop inland and attack and control the inward entrances. The 82nd was to protect the whole landing on the other side of Sainte-Mère-Église.

At this time, my hope, Salinger's hope—all of our hopes—was that rather than our just being shot or killed on the beach, Airborne would be able to control those exits so we wouldn't get caught out in the open, because if we got caught in the causeways or the flooded area, we were gonna be slaughtered.

We went six miles inland the first day, didn't stop until about midnight. We'd had to walk across the flooded area, and when we came onto a dry road, there were a couple villages where they gave us some wine.

ALEX KERSHAW: Salinger probably thought landing on D-Day was going to be the hardest thing, but in the days after he landed, when he went into a series of fields and hedgerows, he would have learned that everything he'd been taught in basic training didn't apply. Every field was going to cost twenty, thirty guys. One field of one hundred yards would sometimes cost a whole platoon. They had to advance day after day. Sometimes a whole company, two hundred guys, would spend a day taking one field of a hundred yards.

COLONEL GERDEN F. JOHNSON: In choosing their defensive positions, the Germans had wisely taken advantage of an area soon to become famous as the hedgerow country. The hedgerows of Normandy, according to local legend, were planted by the Romans to protect their small fields from half-civilized local tribes. Hedgerows are mounds of earth with stone and twisted roots imbedded in them, packed tight by the centuries into tough, steep-sided walls. They surround small, irregular fields called "bocages" by the Norman peasants, the earth and stone ramparts themselves being from three to seven feet high, often in double rows with a ditch between them. . . . The hedgerows made excellent fortifications. A handful of Germans with a few machine-guns hiding behind the hedges could hold off a regiment of infantry. The summer foliage concealed them from the air. A few tanks, strategically placed in the corners of fields under overhanging branches, gave terrific firepower to the enemy infantry.

The infamous hedgerows.

CLYDE STODGHILL: Bodies were lying in a field, and there were cries for help. Some who had fallen were moving a little and some lay still. Several of those who moved would jerk as aimed shots from German riflemen found their mark. Some men had taken shelter behind dead cows, but none dared rise up to fire. No one was still running toward the German hedgerow. The frontal attack had been doomed from the start, of course. Our ranks were considerably thinner, and one German was dead; that was all that had been accomplished.

COLONEL GERDEN F. JOHNSON: We ran into elements of the 82nd Airborne Division, bloody but tough. They told us how the Nazis had slit the throats of their paratroopers as they dangled helplessly from the shrouds of their parachutes caught in trees, of deliberate murder on the ground before the men could get clear of their chutes. Our men listened with rising anger—mingled with admiration for these comrades of the 82nd who had paved the way for us. Fear and doubt melted into one unanimous passion of hate.

STAFF SERGEANT DAVID RODERICK: Happy Birthday to me, 22 today. How nice it would be to be at home instead of here on the coast of France.

BILL GARVIN: During the days that followed, we became hardened to the realities of war. [The Germans] had the advantage of concealment, position selection, and withdrawal routes. We, the aggressors, had no choice but to advance into their gun sights if we were to take ground. We began losing heavily from snipers, constant artillery, and high concussion *Nebelwerfers* or Screaming Meemies fired in salvoes with grinding and wailing sound. The concussion from the close explosion of these rockets was so great that with helmet chinstraps fastened, one's neck could easily break.

DEBORAH DASH MOORE: Salinger had to keep going through the hedgerow fighting, which was very difficult fighting. He would have barely moved a couple of feet, and he would have seen a lot of guys go down. He would have seen men he cared about wounded, killed.

ALEX KERSHAW: Salinger would have experienced hedgerow fighting at its worst. A hundred yard gain on a three hundred yard front took an entire day for a battalion. German gunners were dug in every few yards. Forward movement brought certain fire. The Germans used this terrain to their great advantage. The fields were incredibly well mined by the Germans. One was called the "S" Mine, otherwise known as the "Bouncing Betty," which filled every single soldier, including Salinger, with immense fear. When a GI hit the trigger device on [a Bouncing Betty], a small charge would shoot up a canister. A Bouncing Betty had 360 ball bearings in it and was timed to explode just as it reached your genitals. The effect was devastating.

PRIVATE ALBERT SOHL: It was at the hedgerows, in some deep grass alongside a cow path, that we came upon our first casualty. A dead American soldier was lying grotesquely on his side. His helmet was askew, and he was still clutching his M-1 rifle. A thick, hardened crust of dried blood formed a dark red mask where his face had once been. His trousers and underwear were down below his knees. Obviously he had been in the process of relieving himself when a stray fragment of shrapnel brought a profane ending to his last living act.

CORPORAL ALTON PEARSON: While we were in our position behind hedgerows, I could hear the roars of bombers. They came in one squadron at a time, each one dropping bombs where the other ended and so on. The ground was shaking . . . so bad that it would knock out your breath if you lay on the ground.

PAUL FUSSELL: During the bombing, some German troops, literally driven insane, blew out their brains rather than remain in the noise, the flame, the smoke, the screams, the shaking earth, the flying bodies, and parts of bodies. Ordered from on high to "hold in position," General Fritz Bayerlein [commander of the Panzer Lehr Division] replied, "My grenadiers and the pioneers, my anti-tank gunners, they're holding. None of them have left their positions, none. They're lying in the holes

American troops fighting in the hedgerows.

still and mute, because they are dead. Dead. Do you understand?" A bit later, he reported, "After an hour I had no communication with anybody, even by radio. By noon nothing was visible but dust and smoke. My front lines looked like the face of the moon and at least 70 percent of my troops were out of action—dead, wounded, crazed, or numb."

LIEUTENANT ELLIOT JOHNSON: We were surrounded by hedgerow fences. One corner would be cut down so cattle could go and drink. In one such corner, there was a sniper. He was shooting at us. Every time, I'd stick my head out of the foxhole, I'd get shot at. I called two very dear friends on the [field] telephone. We fanned out, each of us with a grenade. At a given point, we pitched our grenades and accomplished what we had to do. I avoid using words like "kill a man" because I like to divorce myself from that.

CAPTAIN JOHN SIM: While we were being mortared, this lone German soldier had come down toward us, from the castle fence carrying a rifle. I quietly said to my batman, "Harris, you see that soldier coming down? Shoot him." And he did. Much later I thought, "How could I have given such an order?"

—

EDWARD G. MILLER: The drive to Cherbourg—what the 12th Infantry Regiment went through and what Salinger saw—can be summed up in casualty figures. The 12th Infantry landed on D-Day with not quite 3,100 soldiers. By the end of June, it had lost more than two thousand. The army hadn't anticipated infantry losses like this. Soldiers were being wounded and killed by the truckload.

JOHN McMANUS: The 12th Infantry, wedged in between the 8th on the left and the 22nd on the right, was making equally slow progress. The regiment's objective was the high ground northeast of Montebourg, but first it needed to capture Edmondeville.

To get even near Edmondeville, the 12th had to fight its way through these honeycomb-like, tree-rooted berms that were five, six feet high. It was small-unit fighting, nasty, intimate, and up close. There was one group of Americans on this side of the hedgerow and a group of Germans on

the other side, and only one of them was going to be alive to keep going the next day. The entrenched German machine guns were slaughtering Americans in droves. The fighting around Edmondeville was some of the bitterest combat of the Normandy campaign. Colonel Reeder's command post was almost overrun several times, which tells you the German and American front and rear lines were all mixed up: deadly chaos reigned.

DAVID SHIELDS: Three days after D-Day, Salinger's regiment was wedged between an enemy strongpoint at the village of Edmondeville and the guns of the fortress of Azeville. Here the Germans bombarded them on two sides. Salinger found himself on his belly, his regiment pinned down before Edmondeville. Under unrelenting machine-gun and mortar fire, desperate to withdraw, the soldiers were forced to rush the German defenses, regardless of the odds. They were cut down each time. After scrambling to collect the dead and wounded, they would storm the position yet again, only to gain a few feet at tremendous cost. For over two days and nights, Salinger's company repeatedly attacked until the Germans silently withdrew. This is one of the battles that Salinger details in "The Magic Foxhole."

J. D. SALINGER ("The Magic Foxhole," unpublished):

> The Air Corps finally smartened up and come around with some dive bombers to give us a hand, but we was—I mean our Company—was pinned down on this side of the swamp nearly two days. Out of around two hundred and eight of us only about thirty-five of us come through. The Swamp was a widow maker, all right.
>
> It was only about a few thousand yards across it, but the Front itself was real narrow—only about five hundred yards wide. Water on both flanks—grassy rivers, like. So you had to cross the damn thing, and they give the job to "C" company because we was the hottest outfit in the battalion, and because the C.O. asked for it, the bastard; he was bucking for his Captaincy.
>
> On the other side of the Swamp the Krauts had two goddamn companies, damn near full strength, and four twelve-centimeter mortars—four that we could count, anyways. Them mortars sure gave us hell.

SHANE SALERNO: In order to take a village whose population numbered fewer than a hundred, the 12th regiment had lost three hundred

men. Outnumbered two to one, the Germans finally came out with a white flag to surrender.

LIEUTENANT JOE MOSES: After much discussion, Lt. Everett decided to go forward with a few men to take . . . prisoners. All prisoners in sight were moving toward us with arms raised overhead. While we were moving to receive these men a German machine gun crew whom we had not spotted, but was a part of the unit, opened fire when Lt. Everett and guards were within 20 yards of his enemies. Lt. Everett was riddled through the head and down the right cheek across the chest. One enlisted man was also killed and two wounded.

JOHN McMANUS: The Americans who witnessed the false surrender became what I call "kill-crazy." Salinger's 12th determined that no Germans, even those who tried to surrender, would survive. They killed any and all. They hunted down and killed all the Germans they could find. We honestly don't know what happened from a German perspective because they were wiped out.

CAPTAIN FRANK P. BURK: [They] made the enemy pay dearly for their treachery.

SHANE SALERNO: Edmondeville scorched itself into the memories of Salinger and his fellow soldiers.

PAUL ALEXANDER: On June 12, not a week after D-Day, Salinger revealed his general feeling about what he was doing when he wrote [Whit] Burnett a brief postcard in which he mentioned conducting interrogation work. Most citizens, he said, were anxious about the shelling but thrilled the Allied troops had come to defeat the Germans.

COLONEL GERDEN F. JOHNSON: As we went into our eighth day, it was clear that the enemy, despite vicious counterattacks again and again, had been unable to drive us back even so much as a foot, and that the beachhead was thus fairly secure for the moment. Troops and supplies were pouring in over Utah Beach and spreading over the hard-gained ground that [the 12th Infantry] had fought so valiantly for. This under-

Paul Fitzgerald and J. D. Salinger with their beloved dogs.

scored the necessity for pushing the attack even harder to secure the vital port of Cherbourg in the minimum possible time.

ALEX KERSHAW: Salinger witnessed brutal street fighting in the Cotentin Peninsula as the 12th headed toward Cherbourg. The German failure to separate the American forces at Mortain was a turning point in this battle on the Western Front. On August 23, the 12th Regimental Combat Team started the 165-mile march toward Paris.

SHANE SALERNO: There has been a lot of misinformation about what J. D. Salinger actually did in the war. These inaccurate stories have been repeated for decades in numerous books and articles. The most recent offender is Kenneth Slawenski's *J. D. Salinger: A Life* (2010), which has dozens of errors about Salinger's war record. Slawenski claims that "once on the field of battle, he [Salinger] was forced to become a leader of men, responsible for squadrons and platoons." For starters, squadrons are only in the Air Force. Furthermore, members of the Counter Intelligence Corps didn't lead men; they weren't combat soldiers. Salinger's close friend John Keenan, who served with him in the CIC, explains their actual duties.

JOHN KEENAN: Our job was support for assault troops, working in German command posts and communication posts and communications terminals, telephone exchanges, also telegraph. We also had lists of people identified as German collaborators. We were to seize records, interrogate. A lot of it was aborted because a lot of the targets had been blown apart. For instance, the telephone exchange in Ste.-Marie-Eglise [had been destroyed]. We did get some prisoners, but we didn't have time to interrogate them; we had to send them back to England.

An American soldier looking upon a dead German soldier in Cherbourg.

ALEX KERSHAW: As a member of counterintelligence, Salinger had a lot of freedom, a lot of latitude. In some ways, it was a more intellectual, probing war for him than the average grunt. He, for example, would not have to reply to an officer with his rank because he was in counterintelligence. He could actually order a major or a colonel to do something, and yet he was a sergeant. He had a lot of latitude to move behind and near the enemy lines, to understand the culture, to understand the people, to understand what war did to the local people, how it strained the relationships between soldiers and locals, how it had corrupted and infected and damaged these great European cultures and traditions and peoples.

He would have understood what it was like to be a civilian and be bombed, what it was like to be a collaborator, to be a young, attractive female whose only opportunity for bread and to feed her family was to have a relationship with a German soldier.

He would have understood that level of complexity, not only of combat, but more importantly of the relationships that are strained and come into connection with combat and how war poisons everything. It spreads from the battlefield and poisons everything. He would have had a very complete picture of what war did to ordinary people in the Second World War.

JOHN McMANUS: The fighting the 4th Division did in Cherbourg was building by building, block by block. They advanced through building basements if they could, because being out in the street was too dangerous. Basements are very valuable in that environment. But once you encounter Germans, it's very close fighting, just like in the hedgerows. The killing with automatic weapons would be so close—Browning automatics, Thompson machine guns—ammo would literally tear a jagged hole in a person. Shots to the head would tear off pieces of skull. The 4th and two other divisions were fighting their way through the town to get to the German harbor defenses. The Allies needed to control the harbor to land supplies for the drive across Europe.

PAUL FUSSELL: The point of the whole operation was to obliterate that part of the German army holding up the Allied advance, and that advance had to proceed, regardless of any humane complications.

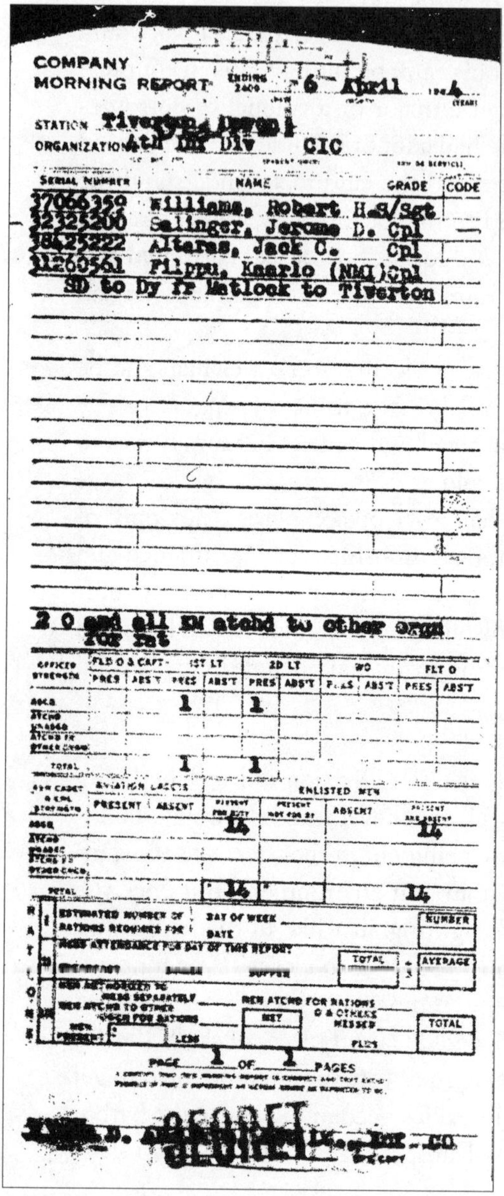

COMPANY MORNING REPORT ENDING 2400 6 April 1944

STATION Tiverton, Devon

ORGANIZATION 4th Inf Div CIC

SERIAL NUMBER	NAME	GRADE	CODE
37066359	Williams, Robert H.	S/Sgt	
32325200	Salinger, Jerome D.	Cpl	
38425222	Alteras, Jack C.	Cpl	
31260561	Filppu, Kaarlo (NMI)	Cpl	
	SD to Dy fr Matlock to Tiverton		

2 O and all EM atchd to other orgn for rat

PAGE 1 OF 1 PAGES

SECRET

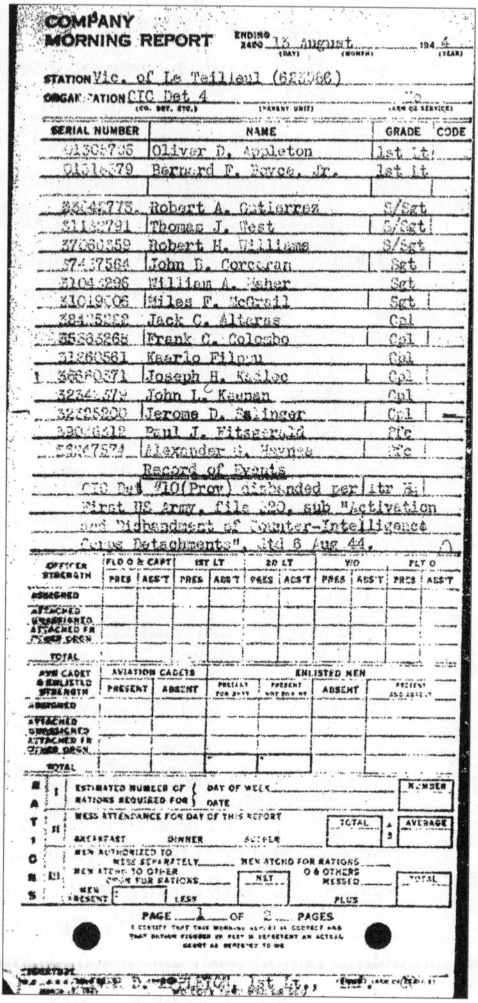

COMPANY MORNING REPORT ENDING 2400 13 August 1944

STATION Vic. of Le Teilleul (625966)

ORGANIZATION CIC Det 4

SERIAL NUMBER	NAME	GRADE	CODE
01305705	Oliver D. Appleton	1st Lt	
01016079	Bernard F. Boyce, Jr.	1st Lt	
38042775	Robert A. Gutierrez	S/Sgt	
31132791	Thomas J. West	S/Sgt	
37060359	Robert H. Williams	S/Sgt	
37437564	John D. Corcoran	Sgt	
31043296	William A. Maher	Sgt	
31019006	Miles F. McGrail	Sgt	
38425222	Jack C. Alteras	Cpl	
35365268	Frank C. Colombo	Cpl	
31260561	Kaarlo Filppu	Cpl	
36660571	Joseph H. Kadlec	Cpl	
32341579	John L. Keenan	Cpl	
32325200	Jerome D. Salinger	Cpl	
39026412	Paul J. Fitzgerald	Pfc	
38247574	Alexander G. Haynes	Pfc	

Record of Events

CIC Det #10(Prov) disbanded per ltr Hq First US Army, file 320, sub "Activation and Disbandment of Counter-Intelligence Corps Detachments", dtd 6 Aug 44.

PAGE 1 OF 2 PAGES

Company Morning Reports.

DAVID SHIELDS: The countless losses of U.S. staff officers as the 12th pushed from the beaches toward and into Cherbourg forced individual units to improvise with personnel. Salinger's role may have mutated from noncommissioned staff sergeant intelligence to unofficial combat officer status to infantryman to a combination of all these during reconnaissance operations. He is mute on the subject, but there are other accounts that give us a very good idea of the deadly, fluid situation that he and the 12th found themselves in.

CLYDE STODGHILL: Following the bombing and breakthrough at Saint-Lô, our battalion, perhaps the entire 12th Infantry Regiment, was assigned the job of cleaning out pockets of Germans left behind during the rapid advance. We hiked from place to place, frequently covering the same ground two or more times. Sometimes there were Germans waiting and a firefight ensued. . . . It was a grueling assignment that allowed little time for rest or sleep and left us in a state of weariness beyond mere exhaustion.

LEILA HADLEY LUCE: In the beginning Jerry felt very patriotic, that they were doing good in the world. I remember he said it was extraordinary to feel that he was part of something good. But when he saw people who were wounded or killed, when he saw death and mutilated people, this distressed him terribly. And then he didn't want anything to do with the war at all.

DEBORAH DASH MOORE: There isn't much time to reclaim who you were before the battle. You've been changed in ways that you can't quite fathom.

EDWARD G. MILLER: It was a long way from a Park Avenue apartment to Normandy and to war.

2

SLIGHT REBELLION OFF PARK AVENUE

NEW YORK CITY, 1919–1936; VIENNA, AUSTRIA, 1937–1938; COLLEGEVILLE, PENNSYLVANIA, 1938; VARIOUS ARMY BASES, 1941–1943

Born into Park Avenue affluence, the young Salinger is a contrarian, a loner, an actor, a poor student, a military academy student, and a college dropout artist, anything but his parents' son. Or so he needs to believe in order to become the writer he wants to be.

DAVID SHIELDS: Salinger grew up in a bubble. He loved his mother, who loved him. He adored his sister, Doris, who adored him. His father was conventional, stern, and, despite being a Jew whose business was importing hams, religious. Jerome David Salinger didn't want to be any of those things. Growing up the coddled son of a wealthy family, he was against whatever they were for—the values of upper-middle-class Manhattan; or rather, he was deeply conflicted about these values. His initial woe was, in a way, absence of woe.

IAN HAMILTON: His father, Sol Salinger, was born [March 16, 1887] in Cleveland, Ohio.

DAVID SHIELDS: Solomon Salinger, twenty-two, a Jew from Chicago, met Marie Jillich, seventeen, a Catholic born on August 26, 1893, in Atlantic, Iowa. When they married, she changed her name to the more Jewish-sounding "Miriam." It's in the very contradictions and confusions between his father's Judaism and his mother's Catholicism that Salinger will wind up finding himself; that's the gap he'll shoot.

SHANE SALERNO: Salinger's sister, Doris, told his daughter, Margaret, that in Chicago Sol and Miriam ran a movie theater, but it was unsuccessful. Sol found his niche with a meat-and-cheese importing business, J. S. Hoffman. The owner was so impressed by Sol he asked him to relocate to New York and manage the East Coast office.

EBERHARD ALSEN: After Salinger's sister, Doris, was born on December 17, 1912, his mother, Miriam, suffered two miscarriages.

SHANE SALERNO: Miriam's doctors didn't expect her second pregnancy to come to fruition, because during the second month she was ill with pneumonia. However, on January 1, 1919, at the New York Nursery and Child's Hospital on West 61st Street in Manhattan, Jerome David Salinger was born. He was nicknamed "Sonny" at birth.

WILLIAM MAXWELL: So far as the present population is concerned, there is a cleavage between those who have come to the city as adults and those who were born and raised there, for a New York childhood is a special experience. For one thing, the landmarks have a very different connotation. As a boy Jerry Salinger played on the steps of public buildings that a non-native would recognize immediately and that he never knew the names of. He rode his bicycle in Central Park. He fell into the Lagoon. Those almost apotheosized department stores, Macy's and Gimbel's, still mean to him the toy department at Christmas. Park Avenue means taking a cab to Grand Central at the beginning of vacation.

EBERHARD ALSEN: When Salinger was born, his family lived at 500 West 113th Street, then in North Harlem at 3681 Broadway, moved back to Morningside Heights—511 West 113th Street—down to the Upper West Side at 215 West 82nd, and finally—from the fall of 1932 onward—on the Upper East Side: Park Avenue and East 91st Street, 1133 Park Avenue, in the same general neighborhood where Holden Caulfield's affluent parents live.

MICHAEL CLARKSON: An introverted, polite child, Salinger liked to act and write and go for long walks by himself.

SHANE SALERNO: Doris Salinger told her niece, Margaret Salinger, "Your father and I were the best of friends growing up."

DORIS SALINGER: Did Mother ever tell you the Little Indian story about Sonny? One afternoon I was supposed to be taking care of Sonny while Mother was out shopping. He couldn't have been older than three or four at the most. I was about ten. We had a big fight about something—I forget what—but Sonny got so mad he packed his suitcase and ran away. He was always running away. When Mother came home from shopping a few hours later, she found him in the lobby. He was dressed from head to toe in his Indian costume, long feather headdress and all. He said, "Mother, I'm running away, but I stayed to say goodbye to you." When she unpacked his suitcase, it was full of toy soldiers. . . . They were very close. It was always Sonny and Mother, Mother and Sonny. Daddy always got the short end of the stick.

DAVID SHIELDS: One of the few anecdotes we have about Salinger's relationship with his father is echoed in the title of perhaps his most famous short story. At the beach, Sol would hold Jerry in the water and ask him to look for "bananafish."

MARK HOWLAND: In so many of Salinger's stories and novellas, the parents are effectively absent. We hear that there's so much love in these [Glass] stories, but we never meet Les, and we never see Les and Bessie, the patriarch and matriarch, interacting in any way.

SHANE SALERNO: Shortly after his bar mitzvah, Jerry and Doris were informed that Miriam was not born Jewish. The Salingers celebrated both Christmas and Chanukah.

JEAN MILLER: I think he had a lot of trouble with his father. He never told me his father was in the meat business. He always told me his father was in the cheese business, and his father very much wanted him to join him in the cheese business, which he had no intention of doing, and I think that caused a lot of friction.

He wasn't getting his father's approval. That brings me back to Jerry saying in a letter, "Sometimes you have to rely on your own approval. Sometimes you'll never get approval from people. It'll either come very late or never at all." I'm certain he was talking about his father. He told me the bare outline of how his father wanted him to go into this business. How he was not going to do that. How his father thought it was ridiculous that he was going to write. How his mother thought it was fine. That Jerry could do anything he set his mind to, according to his mother. His mother approved of everything he did. He never asked me to meet them. He never talked about defying his father as a youth. He never talked about those years.

DAVID SHIELDS: Throughout his life and writing career, Salinger and his alter egos (Holden, Buddy, et al.) rail against the hypocrisies of the bourgeoisie. A likely genesis was the criminal behavior of the J. S. Hoffman Company.

SHANE SALERNO: Sol Salinger was vice president of J. S. Hoffman when the company was indicted for violations of U.S. antitrust laws and price-fixing. In March 1940 the company was charged with conspiracy to monopolize the supply of "foreign-type cheese" made in the United States. Later that year the Federal Trade Commission issued an order to the company to "cease and desist from fixing or maintaining" prices that were offered to Wisconsin producers of Swiss and limburger cheese.

In 1941 a federal judge accused Hoffman of "knowingly and continuously" being "engaged in conspiracy to fix prices to be paid at cheese factories . . . during a period of approximately eight years [i.e., all of J. D. Salinger's Park Avenue childhood]. As a result of this conspiracy, the defendants suppressed the competition among themselves." In 1942 a federal grand jury charged Hoffman with "conspiracy to fix prices of American and brick cheeses."

Sol Salinger's and Hoffman's legal troubles continued. In September 1944 Hoffman pleaded no contest and paid a fine of $2,000 for conspiracy to fix the price paid by dealers of "foreign-type cheeses" manufactured in Wisconsin. And later that year Hoffman agreed to stop using insignia that implied their Swiss cheese was imported from Switzerland.

To the oversensitive son of a judgmental father who presented himself as an upholder of all things conventional and respectable, such misconduct must have landed with the force of revelation. Indeed, Salinger once referred to his father as a "crook," according to one of our interviewees.

JOHN C. UNRUE: There was an estrangement between Jerry and his father. He commented far less about his mother. He once joked, "My mother walked me to school until I was twenty-six years old. Typical of mothers."

JOYCE MAYNARD: Jerry told me almost nothing about his family. There were no photographs of him as a boy, of his family, of his sister. There was nothing.

LEILA HADLEY LUCE: I asked him if *Franny and Zooey* was autobiographical, if he had brothers and sisters, and if Bessie was modeled on his mother. He was totally evasive.

DAVID SHIELDS: Salinger's daughter, Margaret, points out that especially when growing up, Salinger was very conflicted about being half-Jewish, not because of his beliefs but because he was in a difficult social position. Many people in the 1940s held an open bias against Jews; the Ivy League, for instance, restricted the number of Jews they would accept. Being embraced by high society required not just money, education, and connections but also gentile status. As Salinger grew older, he frequently wanted what he claimed to despise: money, interest from Hollywood, the stamp of approval from the Ivy League. The wires got crossed from the very beginning.

CHILDHOOD FRIEND: He wanted to do unconventional things. For hours, no one in the family knew where he was or what he was doing. He just showed up for meals. He was a nice boy, but he was the kind of kid who, if you wanted to have a card game, wouldn't join in.

—

ERNEST HAVEMANN: [Salinger] was anything but a prodigy; he struggled along painfully in the New York City elementary schools. He was known as Sonny . . . in those days.

MARK HOWLAND: Salinger was a terrible student. His grades were atrocious.

JOHN SKOW: Unlike Zooey and the rest, [Salinger] was anything but a Quiz Kid. His grades at public schools[, which he attended through eighth grade on] Manhattan's Upper West Side,] were mostly B's, but arithmetic baffled him. The tall, skinny boy had a better time of it at Camp Wigwam in Harrison, Maine, where, at eleven, he played a fair game of tennis and made friends readily.

DAVID SHIELDS: The camp was attended by upper-middle-class Jewish children.

EBERHARD ALSEN: Young Jerry Salinger was a good mixer and participated fully in the camp's activities; he even helped put on a play.

ERNEST HAVEMANN: He was interested in dramatics as a boy: the 1930 annual of Camp Wigwam . . . listed him as everybody's "Favorite Actor."

PAUL ALEXANDER: In 1932, Sol Salinger set up an interview for his son at McBurney Preparatory, an exclusive private school on West 63rd Street on Manhattan's Upper West Side. Records suggest that at that interview Sonny was anything but impressive. Awkward and ambivalent, he created the impression of being what he was—a distracted, unfocused, smart-alecky kid who had no idea of what he wanted to do with his life. During the enrollment interview at the prep school, Sonny flippantly stated that he was interested in two subjects: "drama and tropical fish," demonstrating a hint of his defensive attitude.

SHANE SALERNO: Salinger attended McBurney for his freshman and sophomore years.

ERNEST HAVEMANN: His record as a freshman shows an IQ of 111, a shade above average, and grades of 80 in English, 77 in biology, 66 in Algebra, and 66 in Latin.

PHOEBE HOBAN: Salinger was a poor student. McBurney's files also show that Salinger shared some interests with Holden. He managed the fencing team, acted in school plays (often portraying women), and worked on the school newspaper, the *McBurneian*.

DAVID SHIELDS: A review in the school paper of a play called *Mary's Ankle* noted, "Some think Jerome Salinger gave the best performance."

SHANE SALERNO: Accused of being "hard-hit" by adolescence and not knowing the meaning of the word "industry," Salinger flunked out of McBurney in spring 1934. He performed no better at a private school, Manhasset, on Long Island.

HARVEY JASON: Salinger's father decided that his son needed structure, and he was whisked away to a military school.

Salinger at McBurney Prep School.

SHANE SALERNO: Sol initiated contact with Valley Forge Military Academy in Wayne, Pennsylvania, but he didn't accompany his son to the interview. Many people speculate that Sol didn't attend the interview to prevent his son's being rejected due to anti-Semitism.

DAVID SHIELDS: Salinger's mother was extremely overprotective. When Salinger's own daughter was being sent off to boarding school at twelve, Salinger mentioned how eager he had been to get away from his mother's blanketing warmth when he went to boarding school. His mother took him to the Valley Forge entrance interview. He was accepted, enrolled a few days later, and spent his junior and senior years there.

WILLIAM MAXWELL: At the age of fifteen, Salinger was sent to military school, which he not very surprisingly detested.

Salinger, second row, second from left, Valley Forge Military Academy.

LEILA HADLEY LUCE: He did say that he'd gone to a military school and, strangely enough, he said he liked it.

SHANE SALERNO: One can easily imagine Salinger sincerely believing both sentiments: proving his artistic bona fides to Maxwell by condemning military school and demonstrating that he was a hail-fellow-well-met by telling a date that he loved it.

DAVID SHIELDS: His sister, Doris, still called him "Sonny," but everyone else he asked to call him "Jerry." "J.D." was too formal, and "David" was too Jewish.

THE NEW YORK TIMES: (May 19, 1935) Miss Doris Jane Salinger, daughter of Mr. and Mrs. Sol Salinger of 1,133 Park Avenue, was married to William Seeman Samuels, son of Mrs. Maurice S. Samuels and the late Mr. Samuels, yesterday at the home of her parents. The ceremony was performed by Dr. John Lovejoy Elliott in the presence of relatives.

MARK HOWLAND: Valley Forge was a good place for Salinger because it got him out of New York and away from his father. A military school is a very structured environment. And at that time in his life, that seemed to be something that he needed and wanted.

DAVID SHIELDS: He was a man who hated ever being told what to do by anyone ever, and Valley Forge Military Academy was very strict, and yet he thrived here. He loved military school and, later, the military. He would do anything he had to do to become a writer, and he knew serving in the military would help him burn down to the ground the Park Avenue apartment in which he grew up. He wanted experience. He had no idea what it would cost him.

SHANE SALERNO: Salinger took all the required courses and participated in many extracurricular activities, such as ROTC and Glee Club, but his major love on campus was Mask and Spur, the drama club. He acted in every play in his two years there, most of the time playing the role of women, which by then was nothing new to him. He had played women in many, many plays.

One of his classmates owns a *Crossed Sabres* yearbook in which, instead of signing his name, Salinger signed the names of the characters he had played that year. He wasn't Jerome Salinger; he wasn't Sonny Salinger; he was a series of characters in a variety of plays, and that's how he wanted to be known to his classmates.

PAUL ALEXANDER: As a devoted member of the Mask and Spur Dramatic Club, Jerry appeared in R. C. Sherriff's *Journey's End*, playing the part of Young Raleigh.

SHANE SALERNO: His first year, he was a member of the staff of *Crossed Sabres*, the school yearbook; the second year, when he edited *Crossed Sabres*, it had photographs of Salinger in theatrical costume and in military uniform, including one of him on the opening pages. On one page, he tries to predict what all of his classmates will be doing in several years; he predicts that he'll be a great playwright and that one of his classmates will be playing strip poker with Mahatma Gandhi. Typical Salinger, mixing up sex, games, and celebrity.

PAUL ALEXANDER: Things began to go well for Jerry at Valley Forge, where besides being a member of Mask and Spur, the Glee Club,

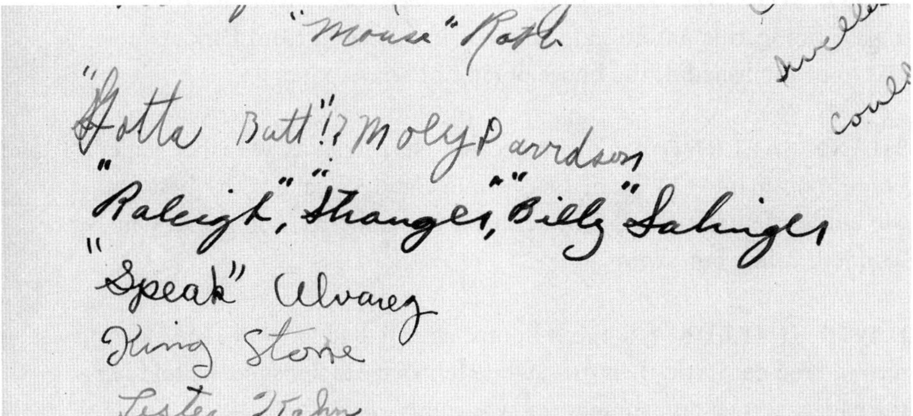

Salinger signed this Valley Forge yearbook with the names of the characters he portrayed in various plays.

and the Noncommissioned Officers Club, he joined the Aviation Club and the French Club.

HARVEY JASON: Valley Forge Military Academy is important for two reasons: number one, that's where Salinger really got his act together; and number two, that's where Salinger began to write.

EBERHARD ALSEN: Classmates remember that after lights out he would always be writing by the light of a flashlight under his bed covers.

SHANE SALERNO: From Valley Forge he gained a lot of discipline, and he learned French and German, which would help him tremendously during his service in the Army and the CIC. He also came away from Valley Forge with a passion for both acting and writing.

BEN YAGODA: In high school Salinger announced that his ambition was to succeed Robert Benchley as the theater critic for the *New Yorker*. Once he decided he wanted to be a writer, it wasn't much of a leap for him to covet publication in [his favorite magazine]. In the early '40s it had a cult following; it was read by literary insiders and sophisticates. You acquired a WASP badge of honor by being a *New Yorker* reader.

DAVID SHIELDS: His goal in life at fifteen was to write for the *New Yorker*. The searing ambition for the boy in full flight from Park Avenue was to be published in the house organ of Park Avenue.

SHANE SALERNO: Salinger became close friends with his Valley Forge roommates—William Dix, whom Salinger called "the best and the kindest," and Richard Gonder, who remembered Salinger as being "condescending but loving."

DAVID SHIELDS: Salinger's humor already had an edge. The cadets received red merits on their caps; when Jerry's mother visited, he told her the badges were a punishment for swearing.

RICHARD GONDER: Jerry's conversation was frequently laced with sarcasm about others and the silly routines we had to obey and follow at school. The school in those days was on a strictly military basis: up at

Salinger at Valley Forge Military Academy.

six, endless formations, marching from one activity to another, meals and classes at set hours, taps at ten. Jerry did everything he could do not to earn a cadet promotion, which he considered childish and absurd. His favorite expression for someone he didn't care for was "John, you really are a prince of a guy." What he meant by this, of course, was "John, you really are an SOB." Jerry and I hated the military aspects of the school. Everything was done in a row, and at fifteen you don't want to do things in a row.

Jerry was the delight of the English teachers, but he got only passing marks in his other subjects. He had a great sense of humor and was more sophisticated than the rest of us. He would read [us] the letters he sent home to his mother, whom he was very close to, and we were all astonished. He was very slight in build because he hadn't shot up yet, and he was worldly as far as his mind was concerned. He was a rather nice-looking guy. I liked him immensely. I enjoyed his wit and humor. He was so sure of himself as far as his writing went. He knew he was good.

JAMES LUNDQUIST: One of his classmates at Valley Forge, Alton McCloskey . . . did remember going along with Salinger to hit the local beer taps after lights out at the academy.

SHANE SALERNO: Other modest examples of Salinger's prep school rebellion included stealing off campus now and then for a swim on private property or breakfast in town.

JAMES LUNDQUIST: As literary editor of *Crossed Sabres*, the school yearbook, he wrote a poetic tribute to the school that is still sung at Last Parade.

J. D. SALINGER (Valley Forge Class Song, 1936):

The last parade, our hearts sink low:
Before us we survey—
  Cadets to be, where we are now
  And soon will come their day.
  Though distant now, yet not so far,
Their years are but a few.
Aye, soon they'll know why misty are
Our eyes at last review.
The lights are dimmed, the bugle sounds
  The notes we'll ne'er forget.
  And now a group of smiling lads:
  We part with much regret.
  Goodbyes are said, we march ahead
  Success we go to find.
  Our forms are gone from Valley Forge
  Our hearts are left behind.

SUBHASH CHANDRA: Salinger spent two years at Valley Forge and graduated in 1936, securing his only diploma. His final grades there . . . were: English: 88; French: 88; German: 76; History: 79; and Drama: 88.

DAVID SHIELDS: Colonel Milton G. Baker—Valley Forge's superintendent, an aggressive fund-raiser and promoter—would become the model for the headmaster of Pencey in *The Catcher in the Rye*.

EBERHARD ALSEN: There are many parallels between Salinger's experiences at Valley Forge and Holden Caulfied's experiences at Pencey Prep: Being managers of the fencing team and losing the team's equipment on the subway. In *The Catcher in the Rye,* James Castle, harassed by bullies, jumps to his death.

SHANE SALERNO: At Valley Forge, the student who fell off the roof above Salinger's dorm was named William Walters.

Salinger's graduation from Valley Forge; he is second from left.

EBERHARD ALSEN: Also, both Salinger and Holden are six feet two and a half and both are loners.

—

SHANE SALERNO: Salinger enrolled as a freshman at New York University, Washington Square College, for the 1936–37 academic year.

PAUL ALEXANDER: Complicating Salinger's return to New York was his dismay at having to live at home again. Herbert Kauffman, a friend from military school, stayed in the Salinger home for a time and remembered heated arguments between Jerry and his father. However, Sol was not the belligerent one; Kauffman said that it was Jerry who was sarcastic and unfair to his father. Sol wasn't insensitive to Jerry; he just didn't want him to become a writer. In the midst of the Great Depression, Solomon felt that the profession of neither writer nor actor would do his son any good. Nonetheless, Jerry and his friend Herb made a stab at being actors, going from theater to theater hoping for a big break.

MARK HOWLAND: The professions that Jerry was interested in were acting and writing, neither of which were legitimate fields, according to his father.

SHANE SALERNO: Salinger didn't "apply himself" and dropped out in the spring. His father couldn't have been too happy, especially when Salinger then took a job that summer aboard a Caribbean cruise ship while America was muddling through the Depression.

PAUL ALEXANDER: When nothing panned out, Jerry either agreed to or was pressured to accompany his father to Europe to learn the family business.

SHANE SALERNO: Salinger spent eight months in Europe in '37 and '38, mainly in Vienna, learning his father's meat-and-cheese business and writing advertising copy. Sol also thought his son's rudimentary high school knowledge of German and French might make him useful as a translator for the company.

DAVID SHIELDS: In a contributor's note to "The Heart of a Broken Story," published in *Esquire* in September 1941, Salinger mentions that when he was in Vienna he won "high honors in beer hoisting."

J. D. SALINGER (contributor's note for "Once a Week Won't Kill You," *Story*, November–December 1944):

> Spent a year in Europe when I was eighteen and nineteen, most of the time in Vienna. . . . I was supposed to apprentice myself to the Polish ham business. . . . They finally dragged me off to Bydgoszcz for a couple of months, where I slaughtered pigs, wagoned through the snow with the big slaughter-master, who was determined to entertain me by firing his shotgun at sparrows, light bulbs, fellow employees.

PAUL ALEXANDER: The apprenticeship was so disturbing to Salinger that as late as 1951 he still complained about it to friends like William Maxwell, who was his first editor at the *New Yorker*.

WILLIAM MAXWELL: He lived in Vienna, with an Austrian family, and learned some German and a good deal about people, if not about the exporting business. Eventually he got to Poland and for a brief while went out with a man at four o'clock in the morning and bought and sold pigs. He wrote and sent what he wrote to magazines in America—and learned, as well as this ever can be learned, how not to mind when the manuscripts came back to him.

EBERHARD ALSEN: One of the most autobiographical stories in all of Salinger's fiction is "A Girl I Knew" (1948). The story lightly fictionalizes Salinger's experiences in Europe before and right after the war, in 1937 and 1945. Like Salinger, the narrator of the story, John, has flunked out of college and his father has decided to apprentice him to his business. He sends him first to Vienna and then to Paris to study German and French. Like young Jerry Salinger, John is very tall—six foot two and a half—chain-smokes, and dabbles at writing stage plays. Also like Jerry Salinger, John falls in love with a Jewish girl in Vienna. Moreover, like Salinger, John returns to Europe during the war as a sergeant in the Counter Intelligence Corps and decides that he would like to go to Vienna after the war. We know about Salinger's crush on a Viennese girl from a letter to Ernest Hemingway that he wrote in 1945. In that letter he says he hopes to get a chance to return to Vienna because he wants to "put some ice skates on some Viennese girl's feet again."

RICHARD STAYTON: That moment when he tied that young lady's ice skates was one of the most beautiful experiences of his life. Then he experienced horrific warfare, and at the end of the war he discovered that the young lady whose ice skates he put on had been taken to a concentration camp and killed.

J. D. SALINGER ("A Girl I Knew," *Good Housekeeping*, February 1948):

> Leah was the daughter in the Viennese-Jewish family who lived in the apartment below mine—that is, below the family I was boarding with. She was sixteen, and beautiful in an immediate yet perfectly slow way. She had very dark hair that fell away from the most exquisite pair of ears I have ever seen. She had immense eyes that always seemed in danger of capsizing in their own innocence. Her hands were very pale brown, with slender, actionless fingers. When she sat down, she did the only sensible thing with her beautiful hands there was to be done: she placed them on her lap and left them there. In brief, she was probably the first appreciable thing of beauty I had seen that struck me as being wholly legitimate.

EBERHARD ALSEN: Like the narrator of "A Girl I Knew," Salinger went back to college after he returned from Europe.

DAVID SHIELDS: In September 1938, Salinger enrolled at Ursinus College in Collegeville, Pennsylvania, only fifteen miles from Valley Forge. This became a lifelong pattern: instant nostalgia, the attempt to replicate childhood experience. Salinger also said that he liked Ursinus and its obscurity; he claimed to appreciate that it wasn't in the Ivy League, the repository of overt snobbery and anti-Semitism. Which is a fascinating reason to like a school: because it's not like another kind of school. It suggests that you're more interested in this other kind of school.

FRANCES THIEROLF: When this handsome, suave, and sophisticated New Yorker in the black Chesterfield coat (complete with velvet collar) hit the campus in 1938, we had never seen anything quite like it. . . . Most of the girls were mad about him at once—including me—and the boys held him slightly in awe with a trace of envy thrown in. He declared openly that he would one day produce the Great American Novel. Jerry and I became special friends, mostly, I am sure, because I was the only one who believed he would do it.

DAVID SHIELDS: When Frances Thierolf got married, her name became "Frances Glassmoyer," the inspiration for the name of one of Salinger's most memorable fictional characters, Franny Glass.

SHANE SALERNO: Another Ursinus classmate said that Salinger looked on the college and students with "disdain," that he "seemed dissatisfied" and "never smiled, gave a friendly greeting, or responded to overtures of acceptance."

ANABEL HEYEN: He felt he had come down from New York and didn't really fit in. When I saw him around campus, he was very standoffish. It was hard to have a conversation with him. He was almost a recluse.

IAN HAMILTON: Salinger found an outlet for his true interest by writing a column, "The Skipped Diploma: Musings of a Social Soph," for the Ursinus College newspaper. He reviewed plays, movies, and books and took opportunities to function as a wit at large, often mocking Hollywood stars and lampooning theater productions and radio shows. Salinger's column of October 10, 1938, includes an especially telling statement concerning his frustrations and deep conflict with his father: "Once there was a young man who was trying to grow a mustache. This same young man did not want to work for his Daddykins—or any other unreasonable man. So the young man went back to College."

J. D. SALINGER (contributor's note for "Heart of a Broken Story," *Esquire*, September 1941):

On returning to America he went to a small college in Pennsylvania where, he says, he wrote a smug little column for the weekly paper.

DAVID SHIELDS: For his column "The Skipped Diploma," he used the byline JDS. The column was a vehicle to talk about whatever came to mind: movies, books, train rides, glib satires. His writing already displays talent, rancor, and wit, and he introduces a character named Phoebe.

J. D. SALINGER, ("The Skipped Diploma," October 10, 1938):

Letter: Dear Mother—You and your husband have failed to raise me properly. I can neither Begin the Beguin nor identify Joe Oglemurphey's torrid trumpet. In short, college life for me is not too peachy—Dolefully yours, Phoebe Phrosh.

Men bore me; / Women abhor me; / Children floor me; / Society stinks. . . . Book Dept.: For Hollywood's sake, it would be well for the authoress of *Gone with the Wind* to rewrite same, giving Miss Scarlett O'Hara either one slightly crossed eye, one bucked tooth, or one size-nine shoe.

J. D. SALINGER ("The Skipped Diploma," October 17, 1938):

Act One: Franklin:—I hate war. Eleanor hates war. James, Franklin, Elliot, and John hate war. War is hell! . . . Lovelorn Dept.: Question—I go with a boy who is so very confusing. Last Wednesday night I refused to kiss him good-night, and he became very angry. For nearly ten minutes he screamed at the top of his voice. Then suddenly he hit me full in the mouth with his fist. Yet, he says he loves me. What am I to think?? Answer—Remember, dearie. No one is perfect. Love is strange and beautiful. Ardor is to be admired.

J. D. SALINGER ("The Skipped Diploma," December 12, 1938):

Mr. X: College feller? Us: (cautiously) Yes. Mr. X: Thought so. Heh! heh! Larry—that's my oldest boy—he goes to college, too. Plays football. You play? Us: N-no. Mr. X: Well, I guess ya need a little weight. Heh! heh! Us: Heh! heh! . . . Mr. X: (after a bit, but with the same determination) Ya really wanna gain some weight, though. Us: (between gritted young, strong teeth) Can you suggest a plan? I refuse to eat breakfast foods. Mr. X: (happily) Well, why don't ya drop my oldest boy, Larry, a line? He'll be able to tell ya. Us: (momentarily struck with brilliance) You have been so kind that you don't deserve to be kept in the dark. The truth is, unfortunately, that for generations our family has suffered from beriberi. Mr. X: (retreating slightly) Oh.

DAVID SHIELDS: Salinger's voice is already in, if not full cry, beginning cry: his adroit mixture of high and low diction, his eye for satiric detail, his ear for revealing speech. What was still missing, of course, was what became the signature of his work: a heart in free fall.

—

PAUL ALEXANDER: Early one evening, not too deep into the fall semester, Jerry sat on the bed in the third-floor dormitory room to which he had been assigned without a roommate and spoke, in animated, energetic language, to the group of half a dozen fellow students who had gathered in his room. Tonight Jerry was telling the boys, as he had done on previous occasions, stories about his experiences in Europe. In the claustrophobic dorm room, with its impersonal, industrial feel, Jerry crafted his stories about his voyage to Europe, his adventures in Paris, and the disturbing events he witnessed on his predawn pig-slaughtering expeditions in Poland.

RICHARD DEITZLER: He wasn't what I'd call social, but he was an interesting person. He was a perfectly normal, attractive young man—an ordinary student. The thing that surprised us, of course, was the way he could tell stories.

DAVID SHIELDS: Salinger told tales and joked about other people, amusing classmates, but when they headed out drinking, he typically stayed in his dorm.

CHARLES STEINMETZ: I was in the same English class with him. We had to write different things—a piece of a description, a scene from a play, a narration. He wrote very well, so well the professor would read his compositions to the class. You could tell even then that he had a talent for writing. But Jerry didn't enjoy the course, because it wasn't what he wanted. He told me once, "I'm not satisfied. This is not what I want. . . . Charlie, I have to be a writer. I have to. Going here is not going to help me." He wanted a course that would teach him to write better and he felt he wasn't getting it out of this course. He was looking for more of an instructional approach to writing—an analytical approach. This professor just wanted us to write for effect. He didn't want to break down the process of writing.

SHANE SALERNO: When Salinger heard about a course in Columbia University's Extension Division that offered just such an approach, he quickly left Ursinus.

RICHARD DEITZLER: He didn't say goodbye to anyone. He just left [before the start of the second semester of his freshman year]. One day he was there, going to classes, writing for the school newspaper, telling stories to his dorm mates. The next day he was gone.

SHANE SALERNO: Ursinus registrar Barbara Boris later wrote, "Salinger had an average record; he did not 'flunk out.' I have no information on why he left the college."

—

DAVID SHIELDS: In January 1939 Salinger enrolled in two Columbia extension courses: short-story writing and poetry writing. The poetry class was taught by Charles Hanson Towne, whose 1919 poem "Of One Self-Slain" eerily foreshadows many of the key aspects (despair, alienation, suicidal ideation, religion, unfinished work) of Salinger's life and work to come:

> When he went blundering back to God,
> His songs half written, his work half done,
> What hills of peace or pain he won?
> I hope God smiled and took his hand,
> And said "Poor truant, passionate fool!

Life's book is hard to understand:
Why couldst thou not remain at school?"

Salinger's poem "Early Fall in Central Park," written for the course, begins, "Slobber and swarm, you condemned brown leaves." The elegiac note, struck early.

JOHN C. UNRUE: Salinger enrolled in Whit Burnett's short story class at Columbia University [in spring 1939]. It was a very important move for Salinger. Burnett was a professor at Columbia, but he was also editor of *Story* magazine.

Whit Burnett, Salinger's writing teacher at Columbia University.

JAY NEUGEBOREN: *Story* was started in Vienna in 1931, by Martha Foley, who was then a foreign correspondent, and her husband, Whit Burnett. During their first ten years, they published the very first work of a remarkable coterie of writers: John Cheever, William Saroyan, Erskine Caldwell, Carson McCullers, Jean Stafford.

Burnett and Foley read every submitted story. As Martha always said, "I publish the best stories I can find," which was tremendously enticing and encouraging for young writers sending their work. Their office also became a writers' hangout. It was just a little Manhattan storefront, but people like Malcolm Lowry and Nelson Algren would chat with the Burnetts and whoever else crossed the threshold. What seems to me extraordinary is that Martha Foley and Whit could pick out of thousands of stories by these writers and see something that nobody else had seen. These writers were submitting to a variety of magazines, and mostly they were rejected. *Story* gave many of them their first published start. How do you account for Martha and Whit's high rate of success? I think you account for it by the fact they truly loved short stories. They had a very simple aim: to publish the best short stories they could find. And that's what they did.

In that course at Columbia, there would have been a wide range of students: eighteen-year-olds, twenty-one-year-olds, but also thirty-, forty-, fifty-year-old people—businesspeople who wanted to learn how to write. The first semester he was in Whit Burnett's class, Salinger sat in the back of the room and did nothing.

WHIT BURNETT: There was one dark-eyed, thoughtful young man who sat through one semester of a class in writing without taking notes, seemingly not listening, looking out the window.

J. D. SALINGER ("A Salute to Whit Burnett"):

> Mr. Burnett simply and very knowledgeably conducted a short-story course, never mugwumped over one. Whatever personal reasons he may have had for being there, at all, he plainly had no intentions of using fiction, short or long, as a leg up for himself in the academic or quarterly-magazine hierarchies. He usually showed up for class late, praises on him, and contrived to slip

> out early—I often have my doubts whether any good and conscientious short-story-course conductor can humanly do more. Except that Mr. Burnett did. I have several notions how or why he did, but it seems essential only to say that he had a passion for good short fiction, strong short fiction, that very easily and properly dominated the room. It was clear to us that he loved getting his hands on anybody's excellent story . . . no particular pets, no fashionable prejudices. He was there, unmistakably, and however reechy it is almost sure to sound, in the service of the Short Story.

JOHN C. UNRUE: Initially, Salinger did not seem special as a writing student, showing little interest or enthusiasm while Burnett spoke.

WHIT BURNETT: He was a silent fellow. Almost never a question. Never a comment. I thought he was nothing.

DAVID SHIELDS: Burnett's marriage to Martha Foley would end in 1941 and she would leave the magazine. A student in Burnett's class, Hallie Abbett, whom he would marry and who would work with him on the magazine and various anthologies, described Salinger as a "grave, charming young man with an almost Egyptian quality of reserve."

JAY NEUGEBOREN: Salinger even apologized to Burnett for being lazy and shut off emotionally during the first semester of the class; he was blocked, he said, because of psychological problems.

JOHN C. UNRUE: Salinger returned the next fall to take the course a second time.

JAY NEUGEBOREN: The second semester, pretty much the same thing.

PAUL ALEXANDER: On September 6, 1940, Salinger told Whit Burnett that he had decided to use the initials "J. D." instead of "Jerome," because he was afraid readers would confuse him with the writer Jerome Faith Baldwin. In mid-September Salinger submitted a story called "The Survivors" to *Story* and Burnett turned it down.

SHANE SALERNO: Burnett read William Faulkner's "That Evening Sun Go Down" to the class.

J. D. SALINGER ("A Salute to Whit Burnett"):

> In class, one evening, Mr. Burnett felt himself in the mood to read Faulkner's "That Evening Sun Go Down" out loud, and he went right ahead and did it. . . . Almost anybody picked at random from a crowded subway car would have given a more dramatic or "better" performance. But that was just the point. Mr. Burnett very deliberately forbore to perform. He abstained from reading beautifully. It was as if he had turned himself into a reading lamp, and his voice into paper and print. By and large, he left you on your own to know how the characters were saying what they were saying. You got your Faulkner story straight, without any middlemen between.

JAY NEUGEBOREN: Toward the end of the second semester, Burnett noticed that his silent student was interested. He was engaged. He was animated.

WHIT BURNETT: He suddenly came to life. He began to write. Several stories seemed to come from his typewriter at once, and most of these were published.

PAUL ALEXANDER: Salinger turned in three stories, and Burnett was impressed; they were polished, sophisticated. They were the kind of stories that he didn't often get from students at that level. Now remember, Salinger was only twenty years old, but even at that point Burnett realized that if Salinger was willing to make the kind of commitment that he would have to make to the craft of writing, his future was limitless. Based on Burnett's encouragement, Salinger went home and wrote a story called "The Young Folks," which he submitted to Burnett, and much to Salinger's surprise, Burnett accepted it for his magazine and paid him twenty-five dollars. It was the first money J. D. Salinger ever made as a writer.

SHANE SALERNO: When, on January 15, 1940, "The Young Folks" was accepted, Salinger wrote gratefully to Burnett, "I'm two cold sweaty hands. . . . I can draw a rejection slip with both hands tied behind me. Writing has been important to me since I was seventeen. I could show you a lot of nice faces I have stepped on to illustrate the point."

PAUL ALEXANDER: "The Young Folks" has two hallmarks for which Salinger would become famous: an absolute dead-on accurate use of dialogue and a fascination, some might even say obsession, with the thinking and actions of young people.

J. D. SALINGER ("The Young Folks," *Story*, March–April 1940):

> "What do you do most of the time when you're home week ends, anyway?" Edna asked.

Whit Burnett and his wife, Martha Foley, who together edited *Story* magazine.

"Me? I don't know."
"Sow the old wild oats, I guess, huh?"
"I don't getcha," Jameson said.
"You know. Chase around. Joe College stuff."
"Naa. I don't know. Not much."

DAVID SHIELDS: Salinger told Burnett that if "The Young Folks" became a play, he wanted to portray the character William Jameson, since he was good at underacting.

JAY NEUGEBOREN: For a writer to be published in *Story* at that time, especially for a young writer who'd never been published before, gave the writer a self-confidence that we (and I think of myself as one of them) need to keep going. It validated them. It said, "You are a writer. You will be published. Keep going."

J. D. SALINGER ("The Young Folks," *Story*, March–April 1940):

> Edna shifted her position at the railing. She lighted the remaining cigarette in her case. Inside, somebody had turned on the radio, or the volume suddenly had increased. A girl vocalist was huskying through the refrain from that new show, which even the delivery boys were beginning to whistle. No door slams like a screen door.

DAVID SHIELDS: When the story appeared, Salinger's contributor's note read, "J. D. Salinger, who is twenty-one years old, was born in New York. He attended public grammar schools, one military academy, and three colleges, and has spent one year in Europe. He is particularly interested in playwriting."

SHANE SALERNO: In spring 1940, Salinger said that he "tried acting for a while . . . but I stopped because my writing is more important."

PAUL ALEXANDER: Salinger had found the subject matter about which he was supposed to write. He'd been searching for a special character or milieu; much of this process of discovery was unspoken, even accidental. Then he came to understand that his unique vehicle for analyzing the world and making distinctive fiction was Holden Caulfield.

Just before the summer of 1940, Salinger realized he needed to get away. In the early days of the summer of 1940, Salinger headed out of Manhattan. On August 8, he mailed a postcard to Whit Burnett from Murray Bay, a charming resort in Quebec, telling him he was working on a long short story—a departure for Salinger, since his stories tended to be relatively short. On [September] fourth, he wrote Burnett to say he had decided to try an autobiographical novel; naturally, he would show it to Burnett first.

DAVID SHIELDS: In a September 6, 1940, letter to Elizabeth Murray, from a hotel in Murray Bay, Salinger wrote, "From the people I've met in my petty wanderings I've come to the conclusion that there must be a God. So many magnificent monsters could never perform so many magnificent blunders so regularly and eternally, etc—by sheer accident."

SHANE SALERNO: "Slight Rebellion Off Madison" was Salinger's first story focused on Holden Caulfield. Holden has not been expelled; he has just come home from Christmas vacation. He has a middle name, Morrisey, that never surfaces again.

IAN HAMILTON: In a letter to a friend, he admits without equivocation that the boy-hero Holden Caulfield is a portrait of himself when young.

PAUL ALEXANDER: As he had with "The Young Folks," he wanted to write about rich, jaded teenagers from Manhattan. This time Salinger had come up with a new character around whom to focus the story, an animated yet neurotic teenage boy from the Upper East Side with the unusual name Holden Caulfield.

J. D. SALINGER ("Slight Rebellion Off Madison," *The New Yorker*, December 21, 1946):

> "Hey, Carl," Holden said, "you're one of these intellectual guys. Tell me something. Supposing you were fed up. Supposing you were going stark, staring mad. Supposing you wanted to quit school and everything and get the hell out of New York. What would you do?" . . .

"I'm in bad shape. I'm in lousy shape. Look, Sally. How would you like to just beat it? Here's my idea. I'll borrow Fred Halsey's car and tomorrow morning we'll drive up to Massachusetts and Vermont and around there, see? It's beautiful. I mean it's wonderful up there, honest to God. We'll stay in these cabin camps and stuff like that till my money runs out. I have a hundred and twelve dollars with me. Then, when the money runs out, I'll get a job and we'll live somewhere with a brook and stuff."

SHANE SALERNO: A little more than ten years later, Salinger had his New Hampshire cabin and brook and stuff.

—

DAVID SHIELDS: In the summer of 1941, Salinger was living with his parents in their Park Avenue apartment. His friend from prep school William Faison took him to Brielle, New Jersey, to visit his older sister, Elizabeth Murray, who introduced Salinger to Oona O'Neill. Salinger was floored by her beauty. He soon told Elizabeth that he was "crazy about Oona."

OONA O'NEILL: I knew he'd be a writer. I could smell it.

JANE SCOVELL: When she walked into a room, she just took people's breath away.

Salinger had a lot of things going for himself, too. He was handsome. He was well-spoken. He was intelligent. He was published. He was everything. One thing's for sure: they would have been damned attractive as a couple.

DAVID SHIELDS: Oona was impressed that Salinger was an up-and-coming writer who had published in *Story, Esquire,* and *Collier's.*

SHANE SALERNO: Oona O'Neill was the daughter of playwright Eugene O'Neill, who had won the Nobel Prize in Literature five years earlier.

Oona O'Neill, age sixteen, New York City.

DAVID SHIELDS: She had grown up with a writer who was a friend of Whit Burnett—Salinger's teacher at Columbia and the editor of *Story*.

LEILA HADLEY LUCE: She was original. She wasn't like everyone else. I think this is why Salinger liked her so much, because the one thing she was never guilty of was any clichés or any banalities. She was totally original.

A. SCOTT BERG: It must have been a living hell to be a child or spouse of Eugene O'Neill. I can hardly imagine what that would have been like—to have lived with what was clearly an extremely dark soul.

Oona O'Neill's father, the Nobel Prize–winning playwright Eugene O'Neill, and family.

JANE SCOVELL: Eugene O'Neill was a genius—completely dedicated to his work—and a really rotten father. He wasn't interested in children and he always said his real children were the characters in his plays.

ARAM SAROYAN: When Oona was very young, Eugene O'Neill, who had been drinking heavily, went off with a woman named Carlotta Monterey, who would become his lifelong amanuensis and manager. O'Neill essentially left Oona, along with Shane, her older brother.

JANE SCOVELL: Oona's father walked out on her when she was three. She was crazy about him, and when she saw his picture in newspapers, she'd start crying. Her mother would try to console her, but the child was almost inconsolable. Being the daughter of a celebrated person, especially someone celebrated for his art like O'Neill, is pretty burdensome. For Oona, it wasn't, "Oh, Daddy's home, I can run and hug him and kiss him." It was, "Daddy's locked up in his room. He's working. Keep quiet." It was a rather tortured and not very happy childhood, I'm afraid.

SHANE SALERNO: Jerry Salinger and Oona agreed to see each other when they returned to Manhattan. They went to museums, movies, and plays; they met for dinner at cafés and restaurants and took long walks through Central Park, past the ducks that Salinger would immortalize a decade later in *The Catcher in the Rye*. That summer Salinger fell deeply in love with Oona.

JOYCE MAYNARD: Jerry talked a lot about New York, the New York of his youth and his time with Oona O'Neill. He had quite a time in New York for a person who ultimately disavowed it.

Oona O'Neill.

LEILA HADLEY LUCE: Salinger and O'Neill made a gorgeous couple. He cut a dashing figure, with his dark good looks, his perfect posture, his thin athletic build. She was a radiant, classic beauty with extraordinary grace.

JANE SCOVELL: One of the things that attracted Oona to Salinger was the fact that he was a deep thinker and was interested in the problems adolescents have. Her adolescence, unlike his, was truly miserable. She came from a level of sorrow that breeds empathy. She was particularly empathetic toward men—older men—which really came out of her desire to have her father with her. Indeed she craved his company.

DAVID SHIELDS: Eugene O'Neill's absence was the formative event of Oona O'Neill's life.

A. SCOTT BERG: Oona O'Neill was someone who was clearly attracted to genius, and she knew it when she saw it.

JANE SCOVELL: Between the ages of sixteen and eighteen Oona O'Neill dated [*New Yorker* cartoonist] Peter Arno, Orson Welles, and then J. D. Salinger. It's interesting to think of a sixteen-year-old girl holding such fascination for such an illustrious group of men. But remember, we're talking about a young woman who was intellectually astute, beautiful, shy, loving. Quite an extraordinary young woman with a lot of things to offer these particular men.

GERALDINE McGOWAN: Salinger seems to be attracted to damaged women. He had a sixth sense for them. Oona O'Neill was damaged. I believe he loved her, as much as he could love any woman, but his image of what women are impedes him from truly knowing them. He so strongly has this sense that women don't break. I think that's why he chooses damaged women, even if he doesn't recognize it.

JANE SCOVELL: After school Oona would do her homework and then she'd go to the Stork Club. The Stork Club was very clever to use this beautiful, intelligent, and well-known young woman as a symbol of their club. It was a very good advertising ploy to show everybody that this is where the daughter of our only Nobel Prize–winning playwright was hanging out. So much so that the headmistress of the Brearley School wrote a note to one of her teachers, saying, "Why is Miss O'Neill in the Stork Club? She's sixteen!" They always photographed her with a glass of milk because, of course, she was underage. Still, "teenager" is a funny word to use for somebody like Oona, because she's one of those people who was an old soul. She was very voluptuous as a young girl; I think she began to develop at around thirteen.

LEILA HADLEY LUCE: The Stork Club was the place to be seen in New York City. You couldn't walk in that club without seeing movie stars, politicians, even royals from Europe. It was at the Stork Club that Prince Rainier courted Grace Kelly. You always got to see who was there each night because their pictures were in the papers the next day.

The Stork Club, New York City.

You had people like Oona, Gloria [Vanderbilt], and Carol Marcus. They were wealthy. You have to give them a little credit, though. A lot of them had brains. These girls' escapades were in the headlines: "Just look what Gloria Vanderbilt's doing today! And, oh my! Look at Oona O'Neill!" We like to put them down and say, "Ah, dopey!" but they had brains.

STORK CLUB REGULAR: The show consists of common people looking at the celebrities and the celebrities looking in the mirrors, and they all sit popeyed in admiration.

JOHN LEGGETT: The three of them—Carol Marcus, Gloria Vanderbilt, and Oona O'Neill—were highly sophisticated girls about town. Although they were teenagers, they really knew how to deal with men, and all of them were focused on meeting and marrying someone rich and famous.

ARAM SAROYAN: Carol, Gloria, and Oona were the prettiest, most dazzling girls of their generation in the New York debutante scene. In their various ways, all three were orphans. They huddled together and became co-conspirators in making their lives together. That's the nice thing about it: each of these young women was looking for a father or guardian to usher them into their adult lives. They weren't necessarily looking for contemporaries, for life partners, as other young women might have been. It was a crazy generation of these injured, beautiful, and not quite actualized ladies—kind of a sad story underneath all the glitz.

Here she was, the famous Oona O'Neill of the Stork Club. Jerry Salinger, this young writer she knew, would give her a big song-and-dance about how tacky and insincere the Stork Club was, how they were only trying to boost their attendance at her expense. This only confirmed his worst fears of her superficiality. She wasn't ready to cherish his sacred love. Well, she knew what he was interested in, and it was pretty much the same thing every other boy and man she knew was interested in. That being the case, she might as well marry someone rich and famous. She could see Jerry getting upset by such thoughts. His idea was she was supposed to be madly in love with the fact that he was a writer. Well, her daddy was a writer, too. And most writers made terrible husbands as well as terrible fathers, according to her most intimately detailed information.

JANE SCOVELL: Sometimes Salinger would get a little irritated with Oona, probably because she wasn't giving him as much attention as he wanted.

J. D. SALINGER (*The Catcher in the Rye*):

> Last year I made a rule that I was going to quit horsing around with girls that, deep down, gave me a pain in the ass. I broke it, though, the same week I made it—the same night, as a matter of fact.

SHANE SALERNO: In the fall of 1941, writing to Elizabeth Murray, Salinger called Oona "Bright, pretty and spoiled"; one month later, she is

Oona O'Neill at a nightclub in New York.

"cute as hell." Then "Little Oona's hopelessly in love with little Oona and as we all know and shout from convenient housetops, I've been carrying a torch for myself these twenty-odd years—Ah, two beautiful romances."

ARAM SAROYAN: She was beautiful and Salinger loved her, adored her. Thought she was terrific and superficial. And was very annoyed at her superficiality! Typical writer, I guess.

J. D. SALINGER (*The Catcher in the Rye*):

> Girls. Jesus Christ. They can drive you crazy. They really can.

—

SHANE SALERNO: Salinger had the agent Jacques Chambrun submit one story before he switched to F. Scott Fitzgerald's agency, Harold Ober, where Salinger became a client of Dorothy Olding; they would work together for the next fifty years. *Esquire* turned down "Go See Eddie," praising its "competent handling"; to Burnett, Salinger wrote that this "was like saying, 'She's a beautiful girl, except for her face.'"

PAUL ALEXANDER: Through his agent, Salinger had been submitting stories to the *New Yorker* for some time, all to no avail. On March 17, 1941, he submitted his story "The Fishermen" to John Mosher at the magazine. On Salinger's cover letter, someone at the magazine had written in large block letters the word "NO," then circled it.

PAUL ALEXANDER: The *New Yorker* rejected the next several stories: "Lunch for Three" (Mosher: "There is certainly something quite brisk and bright about this piece"), "Monologue for a Watery Highball," "I Went to School with Adolph Hitler," "Paula," and "The Lovely Dead Girl at Table Six."

DAVID SHIELDS: Salinger asked Dorothy Olding to send "Slight Rebellion Off Madison" to the *New Yorker*, which accepted it in November 1941 and probably planned to run it very soon, as it was a Christmas story. Salinger had fulfilled a dream, breaking into the *New Yorker* at just twenty-two. He wrote to William Maxwell, who would be editing the

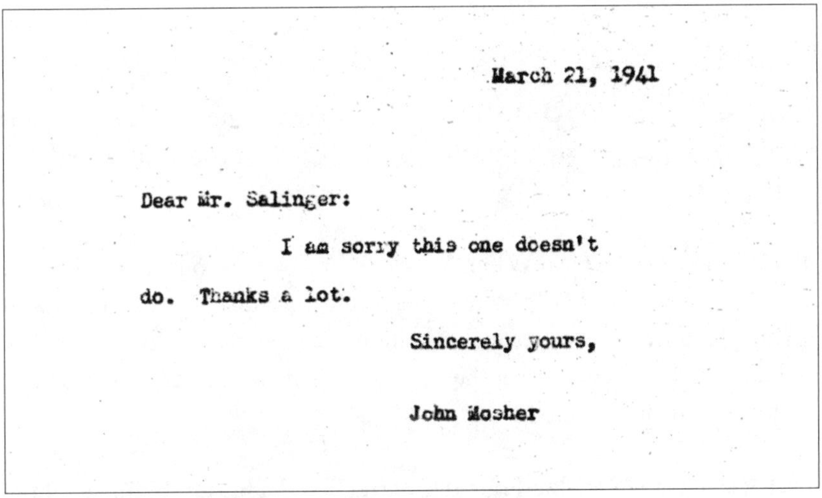

March 21, 1941

Dear Mr. Salinger:

I am sorry this one doesn't do. Thanks a lot.

Sincerely yours,

John Mosher

The *New Yorker*'s rejection of Salinger's story "The Fisherman."

story, and told him he'd written another story about Holden but wasn't going to send it in just yet.

PAUL ALEXANDER: For Salinger, to be in the *New Yorker* was to be accepted by the part of the literary community he cared about: people who worried about good writing, who wanted to make the writing as good as it could be. For Salinger, it meant that as a writer he had arrived.

SHANE SALERNO: On November 18, 1941, Salinger wrote to a young woman in Toronto, Marjorie Sheard, to inform her that he had a new piece coming soon in the *New Yorker*. He described the story as being about "a prep school kid on his Christmas vacation." He indicated that his editor wanted an entire series on the character but that he wasn't sure whether he wanted to go in this direction.

J. D. SALINGER, excerpt from letter to Marjorie Sheard, November 18, 1941:

I'll try a couple more, anyway . . . and if I begin to miss my mark I'll quit.

SHANE SALERNO: Salinger concluded the letter by asking for Marjorie's reaction to "the first Holden story."

—

FRANKLIN D. ROOSEVELT: The United States of America was suddenly and deliberately attacked by naval and air forces of the empire of Japan.

THOMAS KUNKEL: When World War II broke out, the editors at the *New Yorker* felt that "Slight Rebellion Off Madison," this story about a young man and his personal rebellion, seemed trivial and beside the point. It didn't seem appropriate to publish it in the magazine, so the editors put it on the shelf.

EBERHARD ALSEN: Four days after Pearl Harbor, Salinger wrote a letter to his literary mentor Whit Burnett and referred to "the sneaky bombing last Sunday." He also mentioned that he immediately went to enlist in the army, but because of a slight heart ailment, he was "classified I-B with all the other cripples and faggets." In the same letter, he says that "money is a far greater distraction for an artist than hunger," and—after the *New Yorker* had decided, following Pearl Harbor, not to publish "Slight Rebellion"—complains that "somebody's going around hollowing out all my little victories."

DAVID SHIELDS: The I-B classification was given to those fit for only limited military service. "Cripples and faggets" is enormously telling of Salinger's self-assessment, because the "slight heart condition" was almost certainly a convenient fiction to disguise the existence of a congenital deformity. While researching Salinger's second meeting with Hemingway, which would take place in 1944 in the Hürtgen Forest, we discovered an unreported detail about Salinger's physical condition. Werner Kleeman, who served with Salinger, told members of the Queens College WWII Alumni Veterans Project of the City University of New York that he heard Salinger tell Hemingway "that he didn't think the army would take him . . . [because] he had only one testicle." According to Kleeman, Hemingway told Salinger, "Those doctors were such fool[s]. With a touch of the finger, they could have put your other testicle down." Kleeman said, "Salinger must have been all his life with one testicle."

Pearl Harbor, December 7, 1941, "a date that will live in infamy."

New Yorkers responding to the news of the attack on Pearl Harbor.

We were initially skeptical of this claim, but two women independently confirmed that Salinger had this physical deformity, about which, one of them said, he was "incredibly embarrassed and frustrated. [At the time] I knew nothing about men's bodies, but it was a big deal to him. It wasn't an injury. It was an undescended testicle."

JOHN McMANUS: Before Pearl Harbor, and in the early stages of World War II, army doctors were quite selective with new recruits and draftees. When the doctors examined new men, they routinely rejected them for even the slightest physical or emotional problem. Many were turned away for heart murmurs, dental problems, hernias, and the like. In this kind of environment, a missing testicle would definitely have been grounds for immediate rejection. Later in the war, army standards were lowered. At that point, the service needed warm bodies and plenty of them. A missing testicle would not have mattered much anymore.

PAUL ALEXANDER: He was so upset [about his I-B classification] that he wrote a letter to Colonel Milton Baker, the headmaster of the Valley Forge Military Academy, asking his advice on what to do. Baker suggested he join up as a volunteer.

SHANE SALERNO: Instead, on February 15, 1941, Salinger and his Valley Forge friend Herbert Kauffman sailed to the West Indies on a nineteen-day cruise as members of the social staff for the *Kungsholm*, organizing games and dancing with the single women.

PAUL ALEXANDER: Whether or not they were actually involved in the entertainment aspect of the cruise is not known. Even though it was a brief sojourn, the experience would stay with Salinger for years because it was the closest he ever came to the world of entertainment.

J. D. SALINGER ("A Young Girl in 1941 with No Waist at All," *Mademoiselle*, May 1947):

> The young man—his name was Ray Kinsella, and he was a member of the ship's Junior Entertainment Committee—waited for Barbara at the railing on the portside of the promenade deck. Nearly all the passengers were ashore and, in the stillness and

moonlight, it was a powerful place to be. The only sound in the night came from the Havana harbor water slucking gently against the sides of the ship. Through the moon mist the *Kungsholm* could be seen, anchored sleepy and rich, just a few hundred feet aft.

—

ARAM SAROYAN: Oona continued to date Salinger. On March 9, 1942, Eugene O'Neill wrote a postcard to his daughter, telling her he had been sick and thanking her for a picture of herself she had sent him. There were certainly plenty of pictures Oona had to pick from, since she was frequently in the papers. More than likely, this was not a press shot, as O'Neill hated what he regarded as the shallow, society-driven publicity his daughter was getting—a sentiment Salinger shared. These men in her life must have really become upset when, as had been expected, in the spring of 1942, on April 13, Oona was named Debutante of the Year. It would have been impossible for Salinger and O'Neill to miss the news. Stories of her selection, as well as photographs, were splashed across papers nationwide.

BETTMAN ARCHIVES, photograph caption, 1942: Oona O'Neill, No. 1 deb of the year, wears luminous silver jewelry on this black-and-crêpe and velvet dress—a striking contrast for blackout purposes. The heart-shaped pins are handwrought sterling silver by Mary Gage and Marjorie Ralston.

ASSOCIATED PRESS, photograph caption, 1942: Not "Glamour Girl No. 1," but—in deference to the serious times hurting the Stork Club and other hideouts of the elite and near-elite—just plain "Debutante No. 1" is brunette Oona O'Neill, 17, daughter of playwright Eugene O'Neill, elected as the 1942 successor to Brenda Frazier and Betty Cordon in the Stork Club's annual ceremony. Five feet four and 125 pounds, Miss O'Neill is a student at the Brearley School, hoping to study drama.

DAVID YAFFE: J. D. Salinger would have been more comfortable listening to old records than interacting with people. He didn't want to be part of a scene.

Oona O'Neill, Debutante of the Year, 1942.

J. D. SALINGER (*The Catcher in the Rye*):

> There isn't any night club in the world you can sit in for a long time unless you can at least buy some liquor and get drunk. Or unless you're with some girl that really knocks you out.

DAVID SHIELDS: While Salinger was spending nights at the Stork Club with Oona, he was continuing to develop *The Catcher in the Rye*, in which his alter ego, Holden Caulfield, wearing his "people shooting hat," would take dead aim at WASP society.

LEILA HADLEY LUCE: Salinger was a loner. He was not gregarious, but he wanted to be with Oona and he made concessions. It was a remarkable union, really, this classically beautiful young debutante dating this wisecracking, intellectual young man who was so above it all he had not even bothered to take college seriously.

J. D. SALINGER ("The Long Debut of Lois Taggett," *Story*, September–October 1942):

> That winter Lois did her best to swish around Manhattan with the most photogenic of the young men who drank scotch-and-sodas in the God-and-Walter Winchell section of the Stork Club. She didn't do badly. She had a good figure, dressed expensively and in good taste, and was considered Intelligent. That was the first season when Intelligent was the thing to be.

—

DAVID SHIELDS: By the spring of 1942, World War II had overwhelmed most other societal concerns, and Jerry Salinger was reassessed by the military. He was inducted—permanently, it seems.

Oona O'Neill in her dressing room.

SHANE SALERNO: The Oona O'Neill–J. D. Salinger love affair was interrupted by his going into the army.

DAVID SHIELDS: Salinger and Oona sent letters back and forth while he was in basic training, and his love for her deepened. Letters have a way of doing this to letter writers, especially to writers, especially to Salinger. He bragged to his army buddies, "This is my girlfriend," and showed them modeling pictures of her.

HARVEY JASON: Salinger wrote to Oona O'Neill on a daily basis. Ten-page letters, sometimes even longer. Now that's pretty extreme. I can only think he must've been out of his mind with adoration of this woman. It speaks of such an obsessive personality.

LEILA HADLEY LUCE: Now that they were separated, Jerry realized how thoroughly in love with Oona he was.

J. D. SALINGER: I would marry Oona tomorrow if she would have me.

DEBORAH DASH MOORE: For Jews, the war was about what was going on in the European theater. It was the war against Nazi Germany. They really wanted to fight Hitler. This was the motivation for many of the Jewish soldiers who volunteered. Someone like Salinger, who might have been given an opportunity to stay stateside and train other people, for example, would have wanted to go overseas. The choice to stay stateside would have meant that he couldn't fulfill his desire to fight Hitler.

J. D. SALINGER ("Last Day of the Last Furlough," *Saturday Evening Post*, July 15, 1944):

> I want to kill so badly I can't sit still. Isn't that funny? I'm notoriously yellow. All my life I've even avoided fist fights, always getting out of them by talking fast. Now I want to shoot it out with people.

ALEX KERSHAW: Reclassified and drafted, Salinger reported to Fort

Dix on April 27, 1942. He was twenty-three. More than likely, his serial number bore the classification of "H."

DEBORAH DASH MOORE: When they were inducted, American soldiers were given a choice of what religious affiliation they wanted. They could take a "P" for Protestant, which would be marked on their dog tag. Or they could take a "C" for Catholic. If you were a Jew, they didn't give you a "J"; they offered you an "H," which stood for "Hebrew." Now, "Hebrew" was a classification that had been used in immigration to identify Jews from many different countries. It was used during World War II as well, even though a "J" might have made more sense. In many ways, "Hebrew" represented an older, "nicer" way of talking about Jews. To put the "H" on the dog tag was a very significant decision; some guys regularly took it off. Later, during the fighting in Europe, some never flew with their dog tags. In other cases, guys always kept it on because they wanted the Germans to know, if they were captured, that it was Jews up there dropping the bombs.

PAUL ALEXANDER: Salinger decided he wanted to go to Officer Candidate School. To make such a step, which many recruits could not do, he needed letters of reference, and solicited Colonel Baker and Whit Burnett to write these letters.

COLONEL MILTON G. BAKER:

> *I am of the opinion that [Salinger] possesses all of the traits and character which will qualify him as an outstanding officer in the army. Private Salinger has a very attractive personality, is mentally keen, has above-average athletic ability, is a diligent worker, and thoroughly loyal and dependable. . . . I believe he would be a genuine credit to the country.*

WHIT BURNETT:

> *I have known Jerry Salinger, who has taken work under me at Columbia University, for three years, and he is a person of imagination, intelligence, and capable of quick and decisive action. He is a responsible individual and it seems he would be a credit to an officer's rank if he sets his mind in that direction.*

J. D. SALINGER ("The Hang of It," *Collier's*, July 12, 1941):

> The sarge almost had an attack of apoplexy. "Pettit," he said, "you got no place in this man's army. *You got six feet. You got six hands. Everybody else only got two!*"
>
> "I'll get the hang of it," said Pettit.
>
> "Don't *say* that to me again. Or I'll kill ya. I'll akchally kill ya, Pettit. Because I hatecha, Pettit. *You hear me? I hatecha!*"
>
> "Gee," said Pettit. "No kidding?"
>
> "No kidding, brother," said the sarge.
>
> "Wait'll I get the hang of it," said Pettit. "You'll see. No kidding. Boy, I like the Army. Some day I'll be a colonel or something. No kidding."

DAVID SHIELDS: The army turned down Salinger's application for Officer Candidate School early in the summer of 1942.

SHANE SALERNO: When "The Long Debut of Lois Taggett" is published in the September 1942 issue of *Story*, Salinger writes, in his author's note, "I'm in the Officers, First Sergeants and Instructors Prep School of the Signal Corps, determined to get that ole message through. . . . The men in my tent—though a nice damn bunch—are always eating oranges or listening to quiz programs, and I haven't written a line since my re-classification and induction."

ALEX KERSHAW: He was instead sent to Army Air Force basic flying school in Bainbridge, Georgia, where he taught English. In 1943 he was transferred to a base near Nashville, Tennessee, and promoted to staff sergeant, but he was still rankled by his failure to become a commissioned officer. He was re-stationed to Patterson Field in Fairfield, Ohio, and then to Fort Holabird, Maryland, where he became a special agent in the Counter Intelligence Corps.

EBERHARD ALSEN: Around this time, Salinger wrote to Whit Burnett, "These people don't understand that I'm not one of them, that I'm really just a neat infestation of pus. They've got me tagged as a Quiet, Intelligent Guy with one of them dry sense of humors." In a later letter to Burnett, he would say, "My mind is never really with these people. I've been a short story writer since I was seventeen."

ALEX KERSHAW: Salinger's writing during this time, now that his life was consumed by the army, was largely about his military experience, including the short stories "Both Parties Concerned," "Soft-Boiled Ser-

Salinger, Air Corps photo, 1943.

geant," "This Sandwich Has No Mayonnaise," and "Last Day of the Last Furlough"—all of which would be published in the coming months in *Esquire* and the *Saturday Evening Post.*

DAVID SHIELDS: One story that wasn't published anywhere is "The Last and Best of the Peter Pans," which Salinger withdrew from *Story* magazine without explanation, was never published anywhere, and is now housed at Princeton University's Firestone Library (where it's one of the few items of Salingeriana that can't even be photographed), and per his instructions it can't be published until fifty years after his death.

Prefiguring the extended bathroom colloquy in "Zooey," the story is built around a lengthy conversation between Vincent Caulfield and his mother, an actress named Mary Moriarty. She hides a questionnaire the draft board has sent him; he erupts when he finds it, although, as the conversation continues, it becomes increasingly apparent that she was simply trying to prevent from happening to him what has already happened to her other son, Kenneth, who was killed in action. A third brother, Holden, is alluded to but remains offstage. Vincent's younger sister, Phoebe, wears a coat that he finds adorable. So, too, Vincent mentions his baseball mitt, which is covered in poetry, foreshadowing Allie's glove in *The Catcher in the Rye*. Even more striking is the story's ending, in which Vincent realizes how sorry he feels for academicians locked away from life, for unkempt soldiers, for everyone who falls short of excellence, for himself for excoriating his mother when all she was trying to do was lock him away from the entrance to hell.

Under the circumstances, it's impossible to read the story as anything other than Salinger's ferocious love letter to his mother, who worries so much, particularly over kids who are about to fall off a cliff.

J. D. SALINGER ("This Sandwich Has No Mayonnaise," *Esquire*, October 1945):

> I am inside the truck, too, sitting on the protection strap, trying to keep out of the crazy Georgia rain, waiting for the lieutenant from Special Services, waiting to get tough. I'm scheduled to get tough any minute now. There are thirty-four men in this here vee-hickle, and only thirty are supposed to go to the dance. Four must go. I plan to knife the first four men on my right, simultaneously singing *Off We Go Into the Wild Blue Yonder* at the top of

my voice, to drown out their silly cries. Then I'll assign a detail of two men (preferably college graduates) to push them off this here vee-hickle into the good wet Georgia red clay. It might be worth forgetting that I'm one of the Ten Toughest Men who ever sat on this protection strap. I could lick my weight in Bobbsey Twins.

LEILA HADLEY LUCE: Oona loved hearing from Jerry; she loved his letters. They were seductive, delicious, enchanting letters. They were so wonderful that Oona even lent them to Carol Marcus so that Carol could copy them and send them to Bill [Saroyan] to try to seduce Bill and to impress Bill with how well she wrote.

JOHN LEGGETT: When Bill [Saroyan] got drafted in the army and sent to basic training in Sacramento, Oona and Carol and Bill's cousin went off on a gypsy trip down the [Baja] California peninsula that involved nude swimming and other shenanigans. Bill took an immediate dislike to Oona. He felt she was less than ladylike. He felt she had too much control over Carol; he wanted to control Carol. Bill also thought Oona was a bad influence on Carol. Bill knew she was O'Neill's daughter, but he was critical of her. He thought she didn't keep herself clean.

ARAM SAROYAN: Carol, who'd been to Dalton [an exclusive private school in Manhattan] and was very articulate and funny, was still a little daunted by the idea of having to write letters to this famous writer [Saroyan]. At the time, Bill was at the height of his career, as famous as Fitzgerald had been in the 1920s.

Carol cribbed all these witty lines from Salinger's letters to Oona. The only line that I actually remember my mother [Carol] quoting from one of these letters from Salinger was, "I just sent my typewriter to the laundry." I can imagine my dad reading these letters in basic training and saying, "Jesus, I thought she was just a sweet kid. She's one of these 'clever' literary women. I don't want anything to do with that." He finally got the day off, she visited him, and he was strangely subdued. Carol didn't know what was going on.

JOHN LEGGETT: Bill finally figured out that a girl as simple as Carol couldn't have written such elaborate prose. She confessed she had borrowed the endearments from Jerry's letters to Oona.

—

DAVID SHIELDS: Combat and carnage were still a year away. Salinger had been writing since 1940, and many of his stories were published in popular magazines, but if according to Kafka (who would become a crucial writer to Salinger), "A book should be an axe to break the frozen sea within us," Salinger didn't even know yet that his sea was frozen. His mind was still stocked "with some black neckties." He was contemptuous of the superficial society that surrounded him at the same time that he yearned to be exalted as one of its paragons.

There is no knowledge without pain; in his precombat stories, there is "no fire" yet "between the words" (as Salinger would later say to his writer-friend A. E. Hotchner about his stories). Still, Salinger is *trying* to get there. In the 1940 story "Go See Eddie," he repeats in order to dismantle the word "grand," a technique Holden will take to a postwar extreme: "You and your grand persons. You know more god damn grand persons." Salinger thinks he understands that human self-destruction is at the center of the world ("The Hang of It," 1941: "Every fuse has two ends; the one that's lighted and the one that's clubby with the T.N.T."), but he hasn't a clue; the story, written to jibe with the rising patriotism underlying the country's imminent involvement in World War II, was reprinted in *The Kitbook for Soldiers, Sailors, and Marines*.

He's trying to buy distance from the commercial culture to which he was an avid contributor. "The Heart of a Broken Story" not only mocks the formulaic boy-meets-girl stories that appeared with regularity in the "slicks" but is also an early warning of what would become, later on, his increasing reluctance to manipulate his characters; in June '42, he wrote to Burnett, "I'm tired—my God, *so* tired—of leaving them all broken on the page with just 'The End' written underneath." Salinger doesn't love his own psychosis yet, so, in "The Long Debut of Lois Taggett," neither can Lois; she dismisses her husband when he says he's seeing a psychoanalyst. The war has begun and Salinger was initially turned down; Lois's adorable baby boy suffers crib death, which is Salinger's response to the war: he wants you to think he already knows that grief is the only true emotion that unites humanity.

Salinger now has been inducted but has yet to see action; in "Personal Notes of an Infantryman," he expresses his desire for war and oblivion. He's pseudo-war-ravaged before he's war-ravaged: "'All wives are anxious to see their husbands go to war,' Lawlor said, smiling peculiarly." Desperate to serve overseas, he's more desperate still for other people to be beatified by his art; in "The Varioni Brothers," the commercial brother acknowledges about his more artistic brother, "Because I hear the music for the first time in my life when I read his book." Salinger is seeking the purity of art even as he's cranking out product for the slicks. This is a major trope for Salinger; all convenience is mediocre. In the 1944 story "Both Parties Concerned," Billy's wife, Ruthie, mocks him for loving their baby only when "it's convenient for you or something. When it's having its bath or when it plays with your necktie." We're back to Salinger and neckties.

In "Soft-Boiled Sergeant"—published before Salinger had seen combat—a soldier says, "I met more good guys in the Army than I ever knowed when I was a civilian." Salinger came to believe this; his lifelong friendships were with his fellow soldiers. In "Last Day of the Last Furlough," published after but written before D-Day, "It's no good being with civilians any more. They don't know what we know and we're no longer used to what they know. It doesn't work out so hot." Salinger has already divided the world up into us versus them, but he hasn't figured out yet how to stage or frame the conflict. "'I never really knew anything about friendship before I was in the Army. Did you, Vince?'" "'Not a thing. It's the best thing there is. Just about.'" The army has saved him, Salinger thinks, and he loves it, he thinks. The army will save him, transform him, transform his art, destroy him, but all that is to come. For now he is gesturing with increasing eloquence and vehemence toward existential despair, but it's all still a slick magazine writer's guess as to what such despair would actually feel like.

The advent of America's involvement in World War II had caused "Slight Rebellion Off Madison" not to be published in the *New Yorker*—undermining the fulfillment of his childhood dream. Salinger wasn't just trying to survive; while bombs were falling, he was writing stories and seeing them published in well-paying slicks, though not, alas, in the *New Yorker*. He wasn't interested in guns for guns' sake. He was interested in guns for art's sake.

In a March 1944 letter, Salinger writes, "There's a great man in every thousand idiots in the army and perhaps actually, and perhaps only in my mind. But I'm getting him on paper—either as he is, or as he is in my imagination. Anyway, I'm writing real stories." In another letter, written the same month, Salinger writes, "I'm miserable in the Army, but I'm writing better than I ever did and that's all that counts. . . . I'm working with nostalgia chiefly because that's all there seems to be any more."

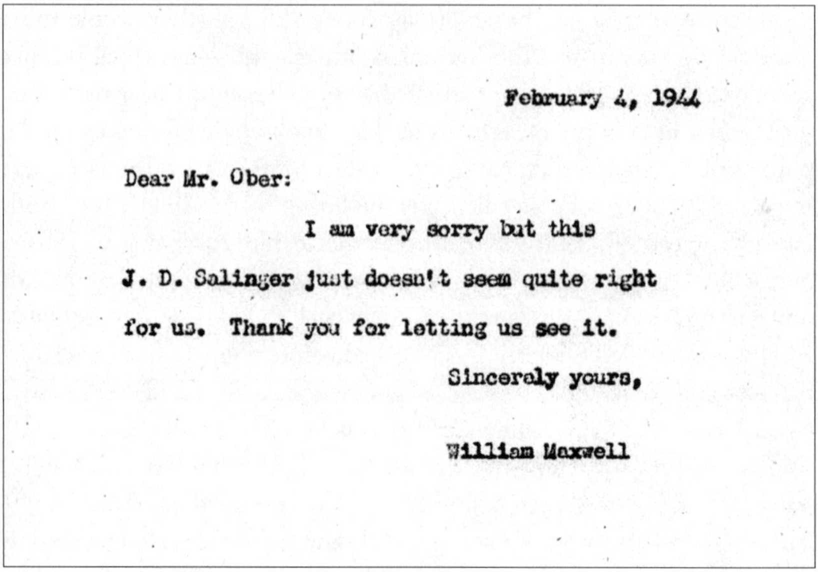

February 4, 1944

Dear Mr. Ober:

I am very sorry but this J. D. Salinger just doesn't seem quite right for us. Thank you for letting us see it.

Sincerely yours,

William Maxwell

Rejection letter from the *New Yorker.*

—

JOHN LEGGETT: In 1942, Oona's mother, Agnes Boulton, was determined to make her daughter a movie star, so she sent her to acting school in Hollywood.

JANE SCOVELL: Oona went to Hollywood and was taken up as a client by Minna Wallis, who was the sister of Hal Wallace, a very important producer of the day. In letters to Carol Matthau, Oona mentioned meeting a lot of men, most of whom wanted to take her out. "They want to sleep with me," she wrote. "It makes me nervous." Nervous or not, Oona was in demand. Her reputation as New York's number one debutante and the well-bred daughter of a Nobel laureate had preceded her. One of her escorts was Hollywood's resident genius, twenty-six-year-old Orson Welles. Welles went for her in a big way and escorted Oona to a nightclub on their first date and volunteered to read her palm. He took her upturned hand in his, gazed at it intently, then raised his head and, looking deeply into her eyes, declared that he saw a love line which led directly to another, older man. Welles even named the man and said Oona would marry him. The man was Charlie Chaplin.

LILLIAN ROSS: Charlie Chaplin was the first international movie star. He was also the first movie figure to be regarded as a genius. Through all the decades since Chaplin's arrival in Hollywood . . . through all the changes and developments that have taken place in the industry with the advent of sound, color, new cameras, new dollies, the wide screen, stereophonic sound, big studios, little studios . . . the tie-ins with books, the tie-ins with records; through the rise of the director, and . . . the rise of movie-theory jargon, through everything, Charlie Chaplin has persisted as a gigantic, incomparable figure. His pictures have by now been seen by billions of people all over the world.

JANE SCOVELL: Oona did a screen test for a movie called *The Girl from Leningrad.* They put a scarf over her head and tied it up to make her look like a little babushka girl. This was not a Russian girl. She still looked like Colleen from County Cork. Minna Wallis heard Charlie Chaplin was making a film that called for a very young girl. She called him up and said, "I think I've got the girl for you. She's terrific. Would you like to meet her?" Chaplin later wrote in his autobiography that when he went to Wallis's he wasn't expecting much, but he said he walked into a room

Oona O'Neill and Charlie Chaplin.

and there was Oona sitting on the floor by the fireplace: the light was playing on her, she looked up, and he just fell in love.

CHARLIE CHAPLIN: I arrived early and on entering the sitting room discovered a young lady seated alone by the fire. While waiting for Miss Wallis, I introduced myself, saying I presumed she was Miss O'Neill. She smiled. Contrary to my preconceived impression, I became aware of a luminous beauty with a sequestered charm and a gentleness that was most appealing.

OONA O'NEILL: Just met Charlie Chaplin. What blue eyes he has!

SHANE SALERNO: Oona stopped answering Salinger's letters, but he didn't know why.

PAUL ALEXANDER: Salinger wrote to Whit Burnett that if he kept making money as a writer he planned on getting married. Salinger did

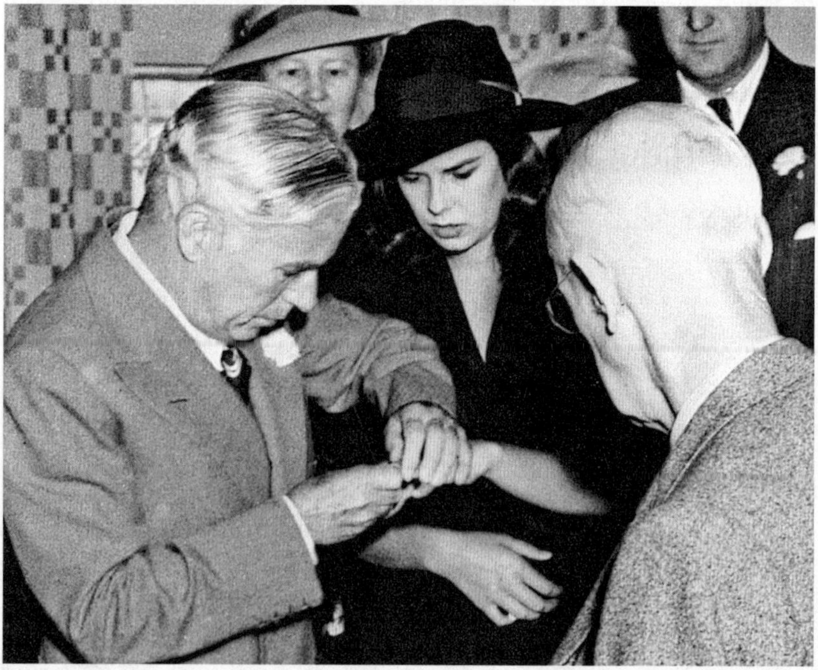

Chaplin puts a ring on Oona's finger on their wedding day.

not say he wanted to marry Oona O'Neill, but instead a girl he had dated before he entered the army, who attended Finch Junior College [a finishing school for upper-class women in Manhattan]. Perhaps Salinger was merely trying to save face with Burnett . . . because by then, the early months of 1943, it was widely known that Oona was having an affair with Charlie Chaplin, the legendary Hollywood actor and director, who was fifty-four years old when he first met Oona.

JANE SCOVELL: Here was Oona, whom Salinger was writing fourteen-page letters to; probably in the back of his mind he thought when the war was over they would get together. And now, it was over.

The minute she turned eighteen, Oona married Chaplin. The news made headlines all over the world.

SHANE SALERNO: Salinger was left to read about the Chaplin-O'Neill wedding in the newspapers, just like everyone else. He couldn't escape the humiliation for months because in many prominent magazines Oona

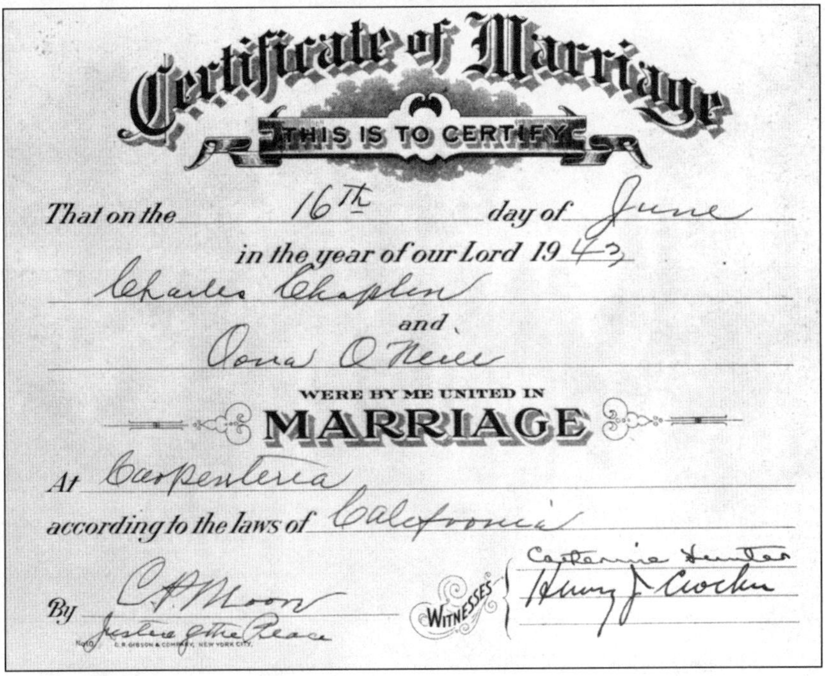

Certificate of Marriage

THIS IS TO CERTIFY

That on the 16th day of June in the year of our Lord 1943

Charles Chaplin

and

Oona O'Neill

WERE BY ME UNITED IN

MARRIAGE

At Carpenteria

according to the laws of California

By C. A. Moore
Justice of the Peace

WITNESSES Catherine Hunter
Henry J. Crocker

Oona and Chaplin's marriage certificate.

78 LADIES' HOME JOURNAL April, 1943

Be a Beauty to your Soldier Boy
Here's how Deb does it!

The magic of a Woodbury Facial Cocktail (simple skin-care with Woodbury Soap) keeps Oona O'Neill's complexion fair and fresh

LIFE for lovely Oona O'Neill, New York's No. 1 deb, is keyed to quick tempo—what with pressing war work and "doing the town." Yet Oona says: "Cross my heart—a Woodbury Facial Cocktail is my only beauty care. You see, Woodbury Soap does such a swell job of cleansing and clearing my skin." What's so "special" about Woodbury Facial Soap? It's 100% *skin* soap. Its purpose—to cleanse the skin, *gently*. A costly ingredient in Woodbury's famous formula makes this soap milder.

1. Who cares if "doggy" cars are out for the duration? Oona borrows a 1907 model of gasolineless "electric" for jaunts with her soldier escort. "Most of the lads," says Oona, "don't even notice your clothes. But what a rush a girl gets if she's reasonably pretty and has a clear, smooth skin!

2. "My glamour technique?" Says Oona: "Even if I had time to waste, I'd still take Woodbury Soap in preference to fancy beauty aids. Woodbury puts sparkle in my skin quickly.

3. "First—a cream-mousse lather of Woodbury Soap to loosen all soil. Second—a rinse like warm spring rain. Then a dash of cold water. Like my complexion? I admit that Woodbury Soap takes the prize for clearing and smoothing my skin.

4. "And do I revel in a luxurious Woodbury Soap bath! It leaves my skin feeling so soft and dainty. Woodbury's lather is mild as milk. The clean fragrance is lovely, too. And the way a firm cake of Woodbury lasts! I'm being super-thrifty when I use Woodbury Soap for *all* my skin."

5. Oona's complexion is really smooth! By cleansing the skin gently, thoroughly, Woodbury Soap helps prevent clogged, stifled pores, and the ill effects to beauty which dirt may cause.

6. Question: Why is Woodbury known as the soap for *"The Skin You Love to Touch"*? Answer: Because it has helped millions of women to win clear, smooth complexions. Just 10¢ for the firm, hard-milled cake. Get Woodbury Facial Soap today.

★ BACK UP YOUR FIGHTING MAN . . . BUY WAR BONDS AND STAMPS ★

Soap ad featuring Oona O'Neill, *Ladies' Home Journal*, April 1943.

O'Neill was featured as the model in a series of cosmetics advertisements: "Be a Beauty to your Soldier Boy[.] Here's how Deb [1942 debutante of the year Oona O'Neill] does it."

PAUL ALEXANDER: Imagine you're J. D. Salinger: you're in the army; you're getting ready to fight in the Great War in Europe; you've professed your complete love to this woman; and then off she goes and marries, on her eighteenth birthday, the most famous movie star in the world.

LEILA HADLEY LUCE: He was very upset about this. You could feel this anger. You could feel this terrible anger.

JOHN LEGGETT: Jerry thought Chaplin, who was fifty-four years old at the time, was far too old for Oona. She was still a teenager when he married her. Jerry thought that was really corrupt.

CHARLIE CHAPLIN: At first I was afraid of the discrepancy in our ages. But Oona was resolute as though she had come upon a truth.

CAROL MATTHAU: It was a great, great love-affair, not only because of the intensity but because of the lasting intensity.

MARK HOWLAND: When I went to the University of Texas Library in Austin to look at the Salinger collection there, I read a number of letters. I have to say that I felt like a voyeur, reading Salinger's letters. A number of them were about Oona O'Neill. Some of them were about Oona O'Neill and Charlie Chaplin. And there were some distasteful bits.

JANE SCOVELL: It was fairly well known that Chaplin got monkey glands, which were the Viagra of the day. Salinger wrote this letter, and then he drew this terrible cartoon. It was this old man, running around waving his—how can I say this nicely?—but waving his—and Oona is somewhere off giggling. And this he mailed to her.

OONA O'NEILL: Salinger said terrible things about my being with Charlie. The things he thought up that we did. It made me glad I was with Charlie and not with Salinger.

Salinger, second from left, shipping off to England to enter the war.

Oona O'Neill and Charlie Chaplin on their wedding day, June 16, 1943.

J. D. SALINGER ("Soft-Boiled Sergeant," *Saturday Evening Post*, April 15, 1944):

> Burke, he didn't stay for the whole show. About halfways through the Chaplin pitcher he says to me, "Stay and see it, Mac. I'll be outside."
>
> When I come outside after the show I says to Burke, "What's the matter, Mr. Burke? Don't you like Charlie Chaplin none?" My sides was hurting from laughing at Charlie.
>
> Burke says, "He's all right. Only I don't like no funny-looking little guys always get chased by big guys. Never getting no girl, like. For keeps like."

ARAM SAROYAN: The crucial distinction for Oona between Salinger, when she knew him, and Chaplin, when she met him, was that Salinger was at the very beginning of his career. He was publishing, but he had not published his important work yet. Chaplin was up there with Albert Einstein and George Bernard Shaw and, yes, her father, Eugene O'Neill. Between Salinger and Chaplin there was no competition. She was not looking for a contemporary to have an adventurous life with. She was looking for someone to be her shelter from the storm, and she was beautiful enough to get it.

JANE SCOVELL: A lot of what happened to Oona later in life had to do with the fact that her father abandoned her. She spent her life looking for a replacement, and she found one in Charlie Chaplin. Charlie just took her and brought her into another world. True to form, when Eugene O'Neill heard about her marrying Charlie Chaplin, he completely and utterly disowned her. He never, ever saw her again, wouldn't allow her to be spoken about in his presence. She wouldn't accept that. She still tried, even when he was dying. She sent a letter to him with pictures and a friend delivered them to O'Neill in the hospital. And O'Neill took the envelope, never opened it, and stuck it under his pillow. And that was that.

LEILA HADLEY LUCE: Oona had lived a life of privilege as a young girl. She was very used to life in New York and Hollywood among the celebrated and famous. She wanted to be with Charlie, who was famous.

She loved the idea of his success. She certainly wouldn't have been happy in Cornish, New Hampshire.

Charlie was much more people-involved than Salinger was. Even when you met Chaplin for the first time, he would make you feel like you were the only person in the world he was talking with. And he would tell these wonderful stories. Offscreen, he was infinitely more amusing, I always felt, than he was on.

JANE SCOVELL: Oona wrote a letter to a friend, saying, "Charlie bought me a mink coat. And you know what? He put it on first and wore it all around. Then he let me wear it." This is not what she was going to get from Salinger. Chaplin offered her so many things and one thing that can never be overlooked: Chaplin made her laugh. She just loved to laugh and this was a man who made the whole world laugh. And now he was making her laugh. Salinger never made her laugh.

OONA O'NEILL: Laughter is one of Charlie's greatest gifts to me. I hadn't known it before. My childhood was not very happy. We met when I was sixteen, a mere child at the time, and I have been in love with him ever since. He is my world.

LEILA HADLEY LUCE: She was just totally devoted to Charlie, and he to her. I think this is why she preferred Charlie to Jerry. Charlie was emotionally so expressive—so caring, so devoted, so extravagantly emotional and expressive. Also, Chaplin wanted to have children. He wanted very much to prove himself as a man, as a father. Jerry, I don't think, really cared about children all that much, or wanted to have children. Oona wanted Charlie Chaplin to be the father she'd never had in Eugene O'Neill. She was looking for somebody who could make up for all the things that her own father hadn't been. I don't think that Jerry was somebody who would give any woman the feeling that he was looking after them.

JANE SCOVELL: I think that must have killed Salinger, the idea that he could be spurned. He had to vent his feelings by calling Oona a gold digger, which I truly don't think she was. I think she did want security, and security is sometimes spelled m-o-n-e-y.

PAUL ALEXANDER: For the rest of his life, Salinger was haunted by this love affair that didn't happen. Salinger tried to forget about Oona by looking forward to the *Saturday Evening Post* publishing "The Varioni Brothers." He anticipated this story's release because he hoped a Hollywood studio might buy it, possibly as a Henry Fonda vehicle. He wanted more than ever the money he would earn by such a sale, but he hoped as well to make a splash in the community that had just accepted Oona.

—

ARAM SAROYAN: Everyone said they would never make it, but ultimately Oona and Charlie proved everybody wrong. They had a beautiful life together, mostly living in Europe. For forty years. Eight children.

OONA O'NEILL CHAPLIN: [Charlie] made me mature, and I keep him young.

A. SCOTT BERG: Certainly the greatest difference between Chaplin and Salinger is that Chaplin was a man who spent his life courting fame, pleasing people, making them laugh and cry, at the same time, if possible. From what we know, Salinger spent most of his life fleeing fame. It's hard to imagine two people more different in that regard.

JOYCE MAYNARD: As late as 1972, Jerry Salinger spoke of Oona O'Neill, and he spoke with surprising bitterness of Charlie Chaplin. The irony was that when Salinger first wrote to me and invited me to move in with him, I was the same age Oona was when she married Chaplin, and Jerry was just a year younger than Chaplin was when he first met Oona.

LEILA HADLEY LUCE: Oona adored Charlie, and she went totally to pieces when he died.

JANE SCOVELL: Once he was gone, she was gone.

ARAM SAROYAN: I was interviewing Oona once. The interview was winding down and it was the last thing I had in my notes, so I said, "You

Oona, Chaplin, and six of their eight children.

knew J. D. Salinger, right?" She looked at me and said, "I'm not going to talk about that."

JANE SCOVELL: At the end of her life she became an alcoholic, that curse of the O'Neills which they speak about. Her brother committed suicide. Her half-brother committed suicide.

PAUL ALEXANDER: The Oona O'Neill–J. D. Salinger relationship would never, ever have worked. Because of who she was, the family she came from, and who she wanted to be in her future life, she would have never stayed in New Hampshire while Salinger was locked up in a bunker in the woods, writing away. So this tragedy in Salinger's life, the loss of the "love of his life," the one woman whom he probably loved more than any other, is to a large degree a fantasy on his part. Salinger never recovered.

DAVID SHIELDS: It's significant and revealing that he carried a lifelong torch for a relationship that apparently was never consummated. He would replicate this relationship with a series of very young women. The girls that followed Oona were time-travel machines. His lifelong obsession with late adolescent girlhood was at least in part an attempt to regain pre-Fall Oona. She formatted him forever.

Conversation with Salinger #1

J. D. SALINGER (*The Catcher in the Rye*):

> What really knocks me out is a book that, when you're all done reading it, you wish the author that wrote it was a terrific friend of yours and you could call him up on the phone whenever you felt like.

Michael Clarkson with his boys and Santa.

MICHAEL CLARKSON: "A man is in Cornish. Amateur, perhaps, but sentimentally connected. The saddest—a tragic figure without a background. Needing a future as much as your past. Let me." That was the note I wrote to J. D. Salinger. It took me two months to write it.

In 1978 J. D. Salinger was, to me, someone worth driving 450 miles to see. He was a missing father figure in my life, a soul mate, someone I wanted to go to Fenway Park with. I had to drive that 450 miles because there was someone in the world who felt the same pain that I did. My own father may have felt that pain, but he never talked to me. I had an emotional hole. I had no one to talk to. J. D. Salinger the writer and his fictional character Holden Caulfield thought like I did.

It was what he called, later, "a very cynical note." However, it obviously worked because the next day, when we met, he mentioned the note.

PAUL ALEXANDER: There have been countless fans now for decades who have done this: they leave notes for him; they go up to his house unannounced; they knock on his front door.

MICHAEL CLARKSON: I wanted to meet that guy and pick his brain and sit down and say, "Do you know something? I had those problems when I was a teenager, and you're the only guy who seems to understand." Like Salinger and Holden, I went to private school. As I understood it, Salinger had a cold, distant relationship with his father. My father was an old Brit and shared nothing with me; if anything, he just put me down. Children are to be seen and not heard. I wanted to tell Salinger, "But you listen to me. You listened to me when I was a teenager. You listen to what children had to say." My father didn't listen to what I had to say. I didn't cry when my father died. I had no one to pour out my feelings to. J. D. Salinger and Holden Caulfield thought like I did. By going to see Salinger, I felt he could help me. I didn't necessarily want him to save me, to catch me at the bottom of the cliff. I was somewhat depressed, but I don't think I was that delusional. I had two young children and I wanted to ask him, "Where do I go from here? What's the next step?" I thought he could make some of the pain go away. At the same time, I had an emotional-spiritual crush on this writer.

During the 1950s and into the 1960s, Salinger spoke against the adult world. This voice coming out of the wilderness, challenging the adult world, was new to me. It was refreshing, and I was attracted to Holden Caulfield as a friend and pied piper. Salinger was the catcher in the rye. He was standing below the cliff and the children were falling off the cliff into the field of rye. That really struck a chord with me because the people I knew were failing as adults, becoming phonies, changing, not in a good way. They were giving up their love and their kindness for money and power. Salinger and Holden were the ones standing below that cliff. They were going to catch these kids and help them make that transition in a noble way, without having to compromise themselves too much.

I read a story about Salinger being a recluse; it made me even more attracted to him and his work. I felt I had to try to seek him out. I wanted to sit down and have a coffee with him. One day I said to my wife, "I've got to try it. I've got to go." I kissed her goodbye, got in my car, and drove from Ontario to Windsor, Vermont, and tried to find Salinger, which was not easy, because the neighborhood people protected him. He'd lived there for some time, and they wouldn't exactly tell me where he lived. I knew he was up on this mountain in a cabin somewhere at the end of a long driveway.

My plan was to pass a note to him through the clerk of a store where I knew Salinger picked up his newspapers every morning in Windsor, so I did. I had written this note, kind of a dramatic note, which I thought only he could react to. I needed to get his attention. The clerk in the store said, "I'll pass it to him. He's a nice man. He let me use his name as a reference for a job interview."

I went to the Windsor Motel that night and hoped and prayed Salinger would pick up the note and come to the bottom of the driveway where I thought he lived and meet me the next morning. All night I was filled with apprehension, thinking if he didn't show up I'd have to drive all the way back with nothing to show for it. The following morning, I went to the store, and, sure enough, he had accepted my note. Then I went to the area near the driveway—I wasn't 100 percent sure I had the right place, but I thought I did—and waited in my car, hoping he would come. I was below this long, winding, gravel driveway. The house was at the top of the hill. I knew that he lived on top of a mountain—this wise man living in a cabin in the White Mountains.

I was waiting for probably thirty minutes, hoping that he would come out and speak to me, when I saw two cars coming down the driveway toward me. Matt Salinger, his teenage son, drove one car. Salinger drove the other, a BMW. His son drove on and Salinger's BMW parked about ten yards away from mine. It may sound dramatic, but when he got out of that BMW in the middle of the forest, to me it was as if he stepped out of a dream. I'd had this dream for so long, an audience with J. D. Salinger. Unfortunately, that dream lasted maybe ten or fifteen more seconds, the time it took him to get from his car to my car.

Salinger had a regimented, military-style walk. He was elongated, with a quite distinguished look about him. He wore a sports jacket, and with his well-combed hair he seemed very Ivy League.

"Are you J. D. Salinger?" I said, because I didn't recognize him from the photographs.

"Yes," he said. "What can I do for you?"

I said to him very dramatically, "I was hoping you could tell me."

He said, "Oh, come on, don't start that kind of thing. Are you under psychiatric care?"

I told him I had left my job and driven all the way from Canada to see him. I told him I was not under psychiatric care and what I really needed was to be published. "You're someone I could sit down and have a coffee with. It's hard finding people I feel comfortable with. You think like I do."

"How do you know I think like you do?"

"Because of your writing."

I was calling him "Jerry" because he was so friendly. I was expecting a dramatic figure like Humphrey Bogart, and here was my Uncle Jarred. He was concerned about why I had come all this way. He was very friendly, but only to a point. Once he found out I was there because I thought he thought like I did and I wanted to talk to him about deep things, he got very frustrated. That really sparked something in him; his tone changed. He stepped back from my car and seemed to grow six inches; his face took on this long, drawn look.

"I'm a fiction writer!" he said. "It's all fiction. There's absolutely no autobiography in my stories. I can't help these people. If I'd have known this was going to happen, I don't think I would have started writing." He stopped. "Do you have any other income besides your writing?"

I told him I was a reporter on the police beat, and at that point he got a little afraid I was going to do a story for the next day's paper. "I've made my stand clear," he said. "I'm a private person. Why can't my life be my own? I never asked for this and I have done absolutely nothing to deserve it. I've had twenty-five years of this. I'm sick of it." For the first time in my life I felt really hated and feared.

His delivery, timing, and flair superbly fit the message. It was like he was acting. He got in his car and dramatically left in a hail of pebbles and surprised me again—by elevating his gangling arm up through the open roof in a friendly wave.

As I sat there I felt that I'd blown it—my chance to talk intimately with J. D. Salinger. I sat in my car for probably another fifteen minutes, writing him another note. I was really sort of angry. It was almost like, "How dare you turn your back on us? We're your fans. We've paid money for your books. You've gotten inside our heads."

The second note I wrote to Salinger read, "Jerry: I'm sorry. It was probably a mistake coming to Cornish. You're not as deep, as sentimental, as I had hoped. If someone had left his family and job and driven twelve hours to see me, I'd surely have given him more than five minutes. If I were after a story, do you think I would have told you I was a reporter? You say that you're a fiction writer, but there's more to it than that; you touch other people's souls. The person who wrote those books I love." I signed it. Then I added, "P.S. I'll be staying at the Windsor Motel until morning."

In the meantime Salinger returned in his car and came back up to me. "Haven't you left yet?" he said. Then he threatened to have the authorities remove me from the premises.

"I was just going to actually pin this note up by your door," I said.

"Well, come over here and give it to me."

I got out of my car, walked over to his BMW, and gave him the note. He took a pair of reading glasses out of a case. He read the note. His face became long and drawn.

That seemed to defuse his frustration from earlier. "Well, I understand," he said, "but I'm becoming embittered. I've gone through this scenario so many times in the last twenty-five years, I'm sick of it. Do you know how many times I've heard this story over and over again? People come from all over the place—from Canada, from Sacramento, from Europe. There was a woman from, I think, Switzerland who wanted to marry me. There was a guy in an elevator I had to run away from. There's nothing I can tell these people to help them with their problems."

He stopped. "Nothing one man can say can help another. Each must make his own way. For all you know, I'm just a father who has a son. You saw my son go down the road. I'm not here to help people like you with your problems. I'm not a teacher or a seer. I'm not a counselor. I, perhaps, pose questions about life in my stories, but I don't pretend to know the answers. If you want to ask me a little bit about writing, I can say something. But I'm not a counselor; I'm a fiction writer."

He went on: "I can't give you a magic quarter that you can put under your pillow, and when you wake up in the morning, you'll be a successful writer. Trying to teach somebody how to write is like the blind leading the blind. If you feel lonely, there are some therapeutic benefits in writing your way out of it. I would suggest reading a lot of other people. Don't write facts. Blend in your own experiences. Plan your stories care-

J. D. Salinger in 1979.

fully. Don't make rash decisions, and don't get too hung up on the critics and all that psychoanalytic madness."

We left amicably. I drove home to Canada. I didn't want to do a story about my trip. I felt this was a very personal experience I had had.

—

MICHAEL CLARKSON: I started thinking, Salinger has never said the things he said to me publicly, and he's never said these things to his fans, all these people who have come to see him like I did. He's never given them, really, two cents. So the following year, 1979, I decided to do a story and went back to see him again. I wanted to ask him if he'd come out for a drink with me one night and we'd talk about the possibility of a story.

This time I went right up to his house. I stopped my car at the driveway where I'd seen him before, walked up the steep driveway, and what

I found was almost a fortress. There was a garage I couldn't get through, with dogs outside, and a cement tunnel that seemed to lead up to the house, so I went up there to the porch. There were glass doors; I looked inside for Salinger and thought, This is like a place Holden Caulfield would have built. It was a ranch-style house, a beautiful, Tyrolean structure, and yet inside, when I looked inside in the glass, it was quite a different world. It seemed like I was going back in time. It was depressing in a way: all these old photographs and hardwood floors, which seemed to be much older than the house, old *National Geographic*s, and old movie reels. It seemed like he was trying to create an old-fashioned atmosphere.

There was a big screen on the wall. Obviously, he'd been watching old films, and there was Salinger himself, sitting on a chair; he seemed to be watching a portable TV and making notes to himself. I felt self-conscious, looking into his little world this way, but when I saw the photographs of his family all over the house, it almost made me feel better about him.

I was knocking on the glass. Salinger turned around and saw me. He looked kind of grumpy at me, like, "Who are you?" He came to the door with a German shepherd, then kicked out a two-by-four so he could release the glass door. He slid the door open and seemed a little puzzled. For one thing, I had a perm—I looked a little different than I did when I saw him the year before—but then he recognized me.

"I remember you," he said. "You look quite a bit better than you did last time."

"Yeah," I said, "I'm feeling better." I thanked him for helping me get into a better frame of mind than I had been in before.

"Are you still reporting?" he said.

"Yes."

"You know," he said, "I think the last time, in a way, you tried to bully me a little bit. I thought you tried to use me for the betterment of your career. Really, the only advice I can give you about writing is, Be yourself. Don't make rash decisions. Plan your work carefully. Don't listen to the critics and all that madness. At the end of the day, you're in your own stew."

I felt good about that and said, "Jerry, I wouldn't have bothered you—I wouldn't have barged in like this—if you'd answered my letters."

"Oh," he said, "maybe they were in with all the other stuff. I don't know. I don't remember seeing a letter from you. If so, I'm sorry." He repeated what he had said a year before: he was just a fiction writer; he wasn't there to help people like me; he was just a father who had a son.

On this second visit, Salinger looked a little older. There was more worry etched in his face. He wore jeans and a T-shirt and seemed quite frail, but his demeanor was about the same. He reiterated his advice: Just be yourself and don't worry too much about the critics.

"Don't you feel you have some obligation to your fans?" I said. "I'd like to do a story down the road, maybe give your side of it. You've never really spoken to your fans."

He went into a bit of a rant, just like he did the first time I saw him. "I can't be held responsible," he said. "There are no legal obligations. I have nothing to answer for. I have no obligations beyond my writing. You're just another guy who comes up here like all the rest and wants answers and I have no answers."

"You've hidden from your fans and stopped publishing."

"Being a public writer interferes with my right to a private life. I write for myself."

"Don't you want to share your feelings on paper with people?" I said.

"No," he said. I remember him pointing his finger at me like a gun. "That's where writers get in trouble." He said he had regrets about his writing career. He called writing "the insanest profession." He thought critics overanalyzed his work.

I asked him if he wanted to go out and have a drink.

He got agitated and said, "Thanks, but no. I'm busy these days."

At that I left him—walked off, climbed down the hill, got into my car, and drove back to Canada.

I wrote a four-thousand-word piece about my two encounters with J. D. Salinger for the *New York Times* syndicate, which distributed it to media outlets throughout North America. I felt I had some sort of obligation to people like me, the fans who had come and had the door slammed in their faces. The article came out about a year and a half after I first met Salinger in 1978. Later on, *People* magazine did a story about my visits with Salinger. I think they tried to interview him about me, but I never did hear back directly.

I saw him outside the Windsor post office once, and he looked very fragile. He looked like he had only enough air to get back to Cornish, back to his house; he started to stumble to his car and was very wary of people on the street. I think he got a lot of mail, which he did not respond to, and in that way, I think, the Windsor post office was a dead letter office.

3

SIX-FEET-TWO OF MUSCLE AND TYPEWRITER RIBBON IN A FOXHOLE

COUNTERINTELLIGENCE, PARIS, AUGUST 1944

Along with the three other members of his unit of the Counter Intelligence Corps—Jack Altaras, John Keenan, and Paul Fitzgerald, the self-dubbed "Four Musketeers"—Salinger interrogates Nazis and civilians. Amid the bloodshed of the war, Salinger, whose job is to imagine what the enemy is doing and thinking, is furiously writing fiction. He undertakes his own private mission in liberated Paris: to find Hemingway, who also believes in producing copy under emotional and physical danger.

ALEX KERSHAW: Salinger played a very important role; anybody who had anything to do with intelligence in the Second World War played an important role. GIs, young guys in squads being asked to attack a village 150 yards away, wanted to know every single thing they could possibly know about that village: where machine-gun nests were, where the alleyways were, where the avenues of fire were. The job of men like Salinger was to provide information that would keep more of those guys alive.

The most important principle of combat is to know your enemy's weaknesses and strengths. Unless you know that, you don't know what you're facing. Salinger's job was to uncover information that would keep

Salinger and two of the other "Four Musketeers": John Keenan and Jack Altaras.

American soldiers alive by letting them know where they were going to be fighting and what they were up against.

LEILA HADLEY LUCE: The few photos I have seen of Jerry over the years are always clandestine-type photos. He is hidden somehow. These photos offer a glimpse at how private Jerry was. He was extremely private about his past and what he did. More than private: secretive. And I gathered that this was because of the war. Because he was in counterintelligence.

JOHN McMANUS: Counterintelligence units tended to be fairly shadowy at the division level. You'd have small teams operating out of either divisional or regimental battalion groups. They had quite a bit of freedom to move around an area of operations. Some concentrated on interrogating German prisoners to gain intelligence; others focused on the local civilian populations. Salinger did both. They operated at the cutting edge, working closely with rifle companies. They had interesting personalities, such as guys who were German-born speakers, emigrants to the United States because of the Nazi takeover of their country, and now they were back interrogating their countrymen. There were also French majors, people with linguistic skills that were useful in Europe. They melded together with what I call the I & R types, the intelligence and reconnaissance guys who're trained to gather intelligence and observe. They were almost always enlisted soldiers doing the field intelligence work. It gets glossed over, but it was some of the most important work of World War II. They were trained to not be prominent; they were supposed to be in the shadows, which is where they remain in history. The U.S. Army tended to underemphasize intelligence. Intelligence officers were thought less of than, say, field engineers or operations types. This led to abysmal intelligence failures such as the Battle of the Bulge, which American command had no clue was on their doorstep.

Counterintelligence required strong interrogation skills. It could mean the bad cop, a heavy-handed, German-speaking GI telling a prisoner, "I've got guys who want to shoot you. Heck, I may shoot you myself if you don't tell me where your unit is." It wasn't so much physical interrogation as mind games. It was the threat of shooting a POW out back. Sometimes it could be the light approach, the good cop, sitting down and establishing a rapport with the prisoner, giving him some food, talking about where his family's from, and here's a cigarette, leading into "Tell me what you know." Counterintelligence officers like Salinger were trained to identify the weak link, the guy most likely to talk in a group of prisoners, and then break them.

IB MELCHIOR: As was standard operating procedure, immediately upon occupying the town, we ordered the population to turn in all cameras and binoculars. This was to prevent the locals from taking pictures of our equipment, buildings occupied by U.S. forces, signposts showing different units, and other subjects that might be helpful to the enemy. . . . These items were collected in large bins, often bathtubs from bombed-out houses; gasoline was poured over them, and they were destroyed.

Our standard procedure in locating suitable accommodations for the team's use was to select an undamaged house that was still occupied by the Germans. We would order the occupants to get out within fifteen minutes, taking nothing but essential belongings, and leaving everything in the house—every door, every drawer, every cupboard—unlocked. As soon as the Germans were out, we'd move in. There was an excellent reason for doing it that way. . . . If you moved into a house, or any building, that was empty, it was liable to be booby-trapped. Favorite spots to place these devious, deadly devices were the bed, the toilet seat, an empty chair, the stove, or a picture of Adolf Hitler on the wall—in that order. Many a GI had blown himself up by flinging himself on a bed or plopping into an easy chair, by using a comfortable toilet seat rather than a slit trench in the cold outside, by trying to get warm at a friendly-looking stove, or by showing his contempt for the Führer by knocking his picture off the wall.

Usually Germans would comply with our order, however sullenly and resentfully. But not always. Some would weep and plead; others seemed too frightened to move on and had to be prodded on their way. . . . One of the teams in our detachment heard two shots when they came to take over a residential house. They immediately took cover, but when no other activity was heard, they entered the house to find a man and his wife had committed joint suicide rather than submit to American demands.

How do you get a man who is unwilling to talk to give you information of a nature obviously destructive to his own side? . . . If the prisoner persisted in his refusal to talk, [intelligence officer Leo] Handel would appear increasingly angry and sharp with his subject. If the man still refused to talk, step two would go into effect. Handel would order his sergeant to grab the prisoner and follow him. He would lead [him] out behind the house or a nearby shed. Here he would grimly draw a rectangle in the dirt the size of a man laid out, six feet by two feet. He'd throw a spade at the PW [prisoner of war] and order him to start digging. A few minutes of working on this cheerful excavation, and contemplating its probable use, as often as not made the PW quite talkative.

Should . . . the trench take shape with no signs of the PW caving in . . . Handel would turn to his sergeant in disgust and say in German, "All right, he's almost finished. I'll get the leader of that band of partisans who's been begging us for a Kraut. They'll take over. I'll be in the interrogation room. You know I can't stomach to watch." And he then turned on his heel to walk away. Death might hold no terrors for the PW, but the prospect of death at the hands of a vengeful band of partisans was usually too much to face. . . . The PW would talk.

JOHN FITZGERALD: There was a bond between my father [Paul Fitzgerald], Jack Altaras, John Keenan, and J. D. Salinger. They served in the CIC together, and my father was the best man at Salinger's first wedding. My father and Salinger stayed in close contact after the war and corresponded for nearly sixty-five years. My dad used to comment that during the war Altaras and Keenan would say, "There was really no time for us to do anything because we always had to stop for Salinger to sit by the roadside, working on short stories or his novel."

J. D. SALINGER, excerpt from letter to Paul Fitzgerald, February 10, 1979:

> *You may be "baldheaded and slightly paunched"—that is, I'll take your word for it—but who's to say that image of you is any less real*

The only photo taken during World War II of Salinger writing *The Catcher in the Rye.*

than the permanent one in my mind's eye in which we're all 1944 types, young guys in our early twenties. I saw John Keenan recently, yes, and spent a long, nice evening with him and Sally and their two grown daughters, and though he was gray and lined, too, and had put on a little weight, the 1944–'45 image of him is the fixed one in my mind, the permanent one. Will always see you with your helmet on, straps dangling. Altaras the same.

SHANE SALERNO: Over the past nine years, while working on this project, we have seen a lot of World War II material, but few items are as evocative as the diary Salinger's fellow CIC agent and friend Paul Fitzgerald kept. The paper was so brittle that I had to take extra care when turning the pages so as not to pull them from the book. Fitzgerald wrote down the names of Germans he and Salinger arrested and the extent of their involvement in the Nazi Party: "Party man since 1933," "Party cashier," "Political leader," "Rabid Nazi," "Very rabid Nazi." Buried in Fitzgerald's diary among other addresses is the following entry:

Jerome D. Salinger
1133 Park Avenue
NYC, NY
Sacramento 2-7544

EBERHARD ALSEN: Even though a girl the narrator had fallen in love with in "A Girl I Knew" and her whole family were murdered by the Nazis, the narrator never expresses outrage against the Germans, nor does he make any statements to the effect that the war was a fight against pure evil. Salinger goes remarkably easy on German soldiers who appear in the story. He would later tell his daughter, Margaret, that anybody—for instance, the clerk at the post office—could turn out to be a Nazi. He implied that if you go looking for evil it is readily found, though probably disguised.

—

ALEX KERSHAW: Salinger witnessed the most beautiful day in history, according to many: the liberation of Paris, August 25, 1944.

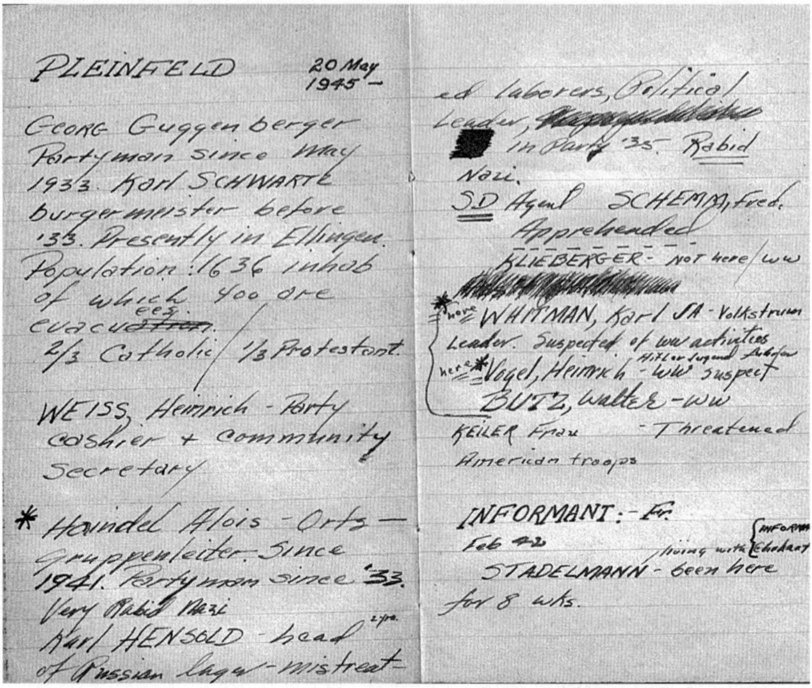
PLEINFELD 20 May 1945 —

George Guggenberger Partyman since May 1933. Karl SCHWARTZ burgermeister before '33. Presently in Ellingen. Population: 1636 inhab of which 400 are evacuees. 2/3 Catholic / 1/3 Protestant.

WEISS, Heinrich - Party cashier + community secretary

* Haindel Alois - Ortsgruppenleiter. Since 1941. Partyman since '33. Very Rabid Nazi

Karl HENSOLD - head of Russian lager - mistreat-

ed laborers, Political Leader, in Party '35. Rabid Nazi.

SD Agent SCHEMM, Fred. Apprehended

KLIEBERGER - Not here / ww

* here WHITMAN, Karl SA - Volkstrum Leader. Suspected of ww activities

here * Vogel, Heinrich - Hitler Jugend Führer - ww suspect

BUTZ, Walter - ww

KEILER Frau - Threatened American troops

INFORMANT: - Fr. Feb '42 STADELMANN - been here for 8 wks. living with Ehrhardt (informant)

Page from World War II diary of Salinger's fellow counterintelligence agent Paul Fitzgerald.

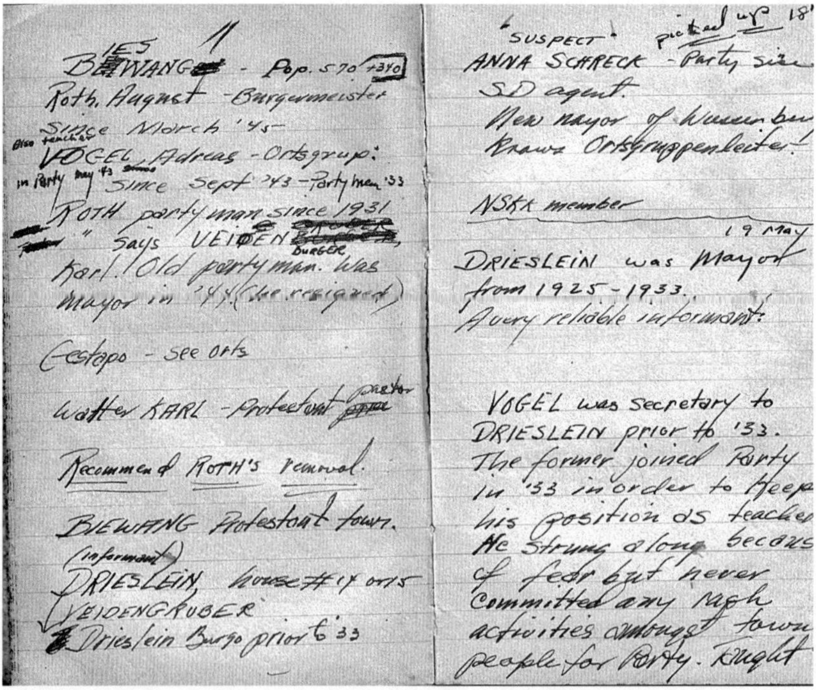
BIEWANG - Pop. 570 +340

Roth, August - Burgermeister since March '45

Also teacher VOGEL, Andreas - Ortsgrup: in Party May '43 since Sept '43 - Partyman '33

ROTH partyman since 1931 " says VEIDENBURGER Karl. Old partyman. Was mayor in '44 (he resigned)

Gestapo - see Orts

Walter KARL - Protestant pastor

Recommend ROTH's removal.

BIEWANG Protestant town.

(informant) DRIESLEIN, house #17 or 15

VEIDENGRUBER

Drieslein Burgo prior to '33

"SUSPECT" picked up 18'

ANNA SCHRECK - Party since SD agent. New mayor of Wassen... Knows Ortsgruppenleiter!

NSKK member

19 May

DRIESLEIN was Mayor from 1925-1933. A very reliable informant.

VOGEL was secretary to DRIESLEIN prior to '33. The former joined Party in '33 in order to keep his position as teacher. He strung along because of fear but never committed any rash activities amongst town people for Party. Taught

Page from Paul Fitzgerald's World War II diary.

Salinger in his jeep after the liberation of Paris.

MARK HOWLAND: I took five students to Princeton. They wanted to see what they could find, what they could discover of Salinger at the Princeton library. After we got into the reading room, we turned the last page of something and came across a three-by-five-inch light green page from a spiral notebook. And it was handwritten by Salinger, about the Allies coming into Paris. He talked about driving in the jeeps into Paris and Parisians holding their babies up for the Americans to kiss. He said that you could stand on the hood of your jeep and take a leak on it and it wouldn't matter; it would be okay. He said anything you did would be fine.

SERGEANT RALPH G. MARTIN: As long as I live I don't guess I'll ever see a parade like that. Most of us slept in pup tents in Bois de Boulogne the night before, and it rained like hell and we were pretty dirty, so they picked out the cleanest guys to stand up in front and on the outside. I had a bright new shiny patch, so they put me on the outside. It was a good place to be too, because every guy marching on the outside had at least one girl on his arm kissing him and hugging him.

We were marching twenty-four abreast right down Champs-Elysées and we had a helluva time trying to march, because the whole street was jammed with people laughing and yelling and crying and singing. They were throwing flowers at us and bringing us big bottles of wine.

The first regiment never did get through. The crowd just gobbled them up. They just broke in and grabbed the guys and lifted some of them on their shoulders and carried them into cafés and bars and their homes and wouldn't let them go. I hear it was a helluva job trying to round them all up later.

JOHN WORTHMAN: The people cheered and laughed and cried and wanted to embrace us, give us a drink, feed us newly ripe tomatoes . . . and just try to believe that we were really there and the Germans gone. I kissed babies, children, young women, old women, and women in between.

DAVID RODERICK: We rode into Paris in two-and-a-half-ton trucks. The reception we received has been a lifelong memory. People crowded in the streets, clapping and yelling, shaking our hands, passing out wine.

SHANE SALERNO: Amid the celebration, Salinger and John Keenan arrested a suspected collaborator, but the crowd beat him to death before the two CIC agents could take him in.

JOHN C. UNRUE: One of the great stories of literary history is the meeting of Ernest Hemingway and J. D. Salinger in Paris.

SEÁN HEMINGWAY: My grandfather was staying at the Ritz and receiving all kinds of visitors.

CARLOS BAKER: Another of Ernest's visitors at this time was a young, dark-haired sergeant in a CIC outfit. His name was Jerome D. Salinger and he was much impressed with his first sight of Hemingway. Salinger was a writer of short stories, twenty years Ernest's junior. At twenty-five he had already sold some of his work to *Story* magazine and the *Saturday Evening Post*.

LEILA HADLEY LUCE: Hemingway was Salinger's icon; he loved the way Hemingway wrote. At the hotel, he went up to Hemingway and told him of his admiration for his work.

CARLOS BAKER: He found Hemingway both friendly and generous, not at all impressed by his own eminence, and "soft"—as opposed to the hardness and toughness which some of his writing suggested. They got on very well, and Ernest volunteered to look at some of his work.

LEILA HADLEY LUCE: Jerry asked Hemingway to look at a manuscript, which took a great deal of derring-do on his part, really. And Jerry was not somebody who would easily go up to someone and ask him to do anything for him.

SEÁN HEMINGWAY: Salinger had with him a copy of the *Saturday Evening Post* that contained a short story he had written, "Last Day of the Last Furlough," which was about World War II. My grandfather was impressed with Salinger as a young soldier, and he was equally impressed with his writing. Upon meeting him, my grandfather told Salinger he had heard of him before, had read the story, and was delighted with it.

J. D. SALINGER ("Last Day of the Last Furlough," *Saturday Evening Post*, July 15, 1944):

> Vincent smiled. "It's good to see you, Babe. Thanks for asking me. GIs—especially GIs who are friends—belong together these days. It's no good being with civilians any more. They don't know what we know and we're no longer used to what they know. It doesn't work out so hot."

SEÁN HEMINGWAY: My grandfather was very much in tune with the price that infantry pay in battle. And I think that would have been kind of a romantic vision on my grandfather's part—for my grandfather to see in Salinger, a talented young writer, fighting in the infantry, during World War II.

EBERHARD ALSEN: It's reported that Hemingway said to someone, "Jesus, he has a helluva talent." I'm sure it got around to Salinger, and that must have pleased him very much.

JOHN C. UNRUE: To Salinger, it was a meaningful endorsement that Hemingway would actually say Salinger had a "helluva talent."

CARLOS BAKER: Salinger returned to his unit in a state of mild exaltation.

BRADLEY R. McDUFFIE: In her memoir *Running with the Bulls*, Valerie Hemingway, who worked as Hemingway's secretary and later became his posthumous daughter-in-law, writes, "The contemporary American authors Hemingway most admired were J. D. Salinger, Carson McCullers and Truman Capote." Hemingway also bought Valerie a copy of *The Catcher in the Rye* shortly after they first met in Spain in 1959. And a copy of the novel rests in Hemingway's library at his home outside Havana, Cuba, a volume that is rumored to be autographed.

PAUL ALEXANDER: For his part, after meeting Hemingway, Salinger wrote in a letter to a friend that the "*Farewell to Arms* man" was "modest" and "not big shotty," which, Salinger said, made him appealing.

LEILA HADLEY LUCE: They stayed in touch, and Hemingway told Jerry how much he liked his writing. Jerry was thrilled. He told me about this incident, how much it had meant to him, because he thought that Hemingway was the greatest writer.

LILLIAN ROSS: He shared with me a copy of the "Dear Jerry" letter Hemingway wrote to him when they were both serving in the second world war—a handwritten letter commenting on unpublished stories Salinger, who was then an unknown young beginner, sent him. "First you have a marvelous ear and you write tenderly and lovingly without getting wet," Hemingway wrote. He added that he hoped he "didn't sound like an easy praiser" and "how happy it makes me to read the stories and what a god damned fine writer I think you are."

SEÁN HEMINGWAY: My grandfather thought of himself very much as a member of the 4th Division. He was assigned to the 22nd Regiment; Salinger was in the 12th. The 4th Division was known as the Ivy Leaf. My grandfather liked to refer to it as the Four-Leaf Clover; he believed a great deal in luck—whether you had it or you didn't.

A. E. HOTCHNER: Hemingway was regarded as Tolstoy was in Russia, as a chronicler of war, a writer, soldier, adventurer, and as somebody who was bulletproof. He was immortal. He was going to live through the wars and through all the hard times. The most glamorous women in the world—Marlene Dietrich, Ingrid Bergman, Ava Gardner—surrounded him. A confluence of all these factors fed the imagination of the American public.

Hemingway's personality aided and abetted his reputation as a writer. He had invested his writing with the style of his actual living. There's no doubt his experience in the Spanish Civil War contributed mightily to *For Whom the Bell Tolls*, which was published in 1940 and was a tremendous bestseller, then a huge success as a movie. Not only did Hemingway receive publicity from where he went and what he wrote, but everything he did was exaggerated. The gossip columns in New York, when he visited there, would have him doing things he didn't really do.

J. D. SALINGER: All writers—no matter how many lions they shoot, no matter how many rebellions they actively support—go to their graves half–Oliver Twist and half–Mary, Mary Quite Contrary.

SEÁN HEMINGWAY: Later, my grandfather is reported to have visited Salinger's regiment. He got into a conversation with Salinger about firearms and which was better, the German Luger or the U.S. Colt .45. My grandfather, according to later accounts, said he believed the Luger was much better, and to make his point, drew the Luger and shot the head off a nearby chicken. Salinger was taken aback.

EBERHARD ALSEN: Now I tend to believe the story because in "For Esmé—with Love and Squalor," Corporal Clay, the protagonist's driver, shoots a cat. Sergeant X, the protagonist, is disgusted with him. I imagine Salinger was probably just as disgusted with Hemingway for shooting the head off that chicken.

J. D. SALINGER ("For Esmé—with Love and Squalor," *The New Yorker*, April 8, 1950):

> X threaded his fingers, once, through his dirty hair, then shielded his eyes against the light again. "You weren't insane. You were simply doing your duty. You killed that pussycat in as manly a way as anybody could've, under the circumstances."

Clay looked at him suspiciously. "What the hell are you talkin' about?"

"That cat was a spy. You *had* to take a pot shot at it. It was a very clever German midget dressed up in a cheap fur coat. So there was absolutely nothing brutal, or cruel, or dirty, or even—"

"God damn it!" Clay said, his lips thinned. "Can't you ever be *sincere*?"

SEÁN HEMINGWAY: I have to say the story sounds apocryphal to me. It plays up a sensitive image of Salinger and a macho image of my grandfather. Shooting the head off a chicken is a lot more difficult than it sounds. In the midst of the horrors that were around them in the war, it seems almost absurd.

BRADLEY R. McDUFFIE: In the years that followed, almost every Salinger critic has reported some version of this story. Unfortunately, the myth has led scholars to ignore the fact that meeting Hemingway during World War II is the most overlooked event in Salinger's formation as a writer. Considering the meeting involves two of the most influential writers of the twentieth century, the oversight is difficult to comprehend.

A. SCOTT BERG: Hemingway had a huge influence on Salinger, and I'm thinking mostly of the style of writing here. Hemingway prided himself on writing according to what he called the iceberg theory. In this theory, as Hemingway first explained in *Death in the Afternoon,* and then in several other interviews and books, he says that if a writer knows enough about what he's writing about, he can omit certain things in the story, and in fact, every time he omits something he strengthens the story. He likened that to the iceberg in which seven-eighths of it is underwater and all you see is the tip. Every time you leave something out, he said, it strengthens the iceberg from below and it affords the reader an even greater reading experience, because [the reader] is basically running the story, doing the film in his own imagination.

There was a corollary as well. Hemingway said if a writer does omit something because he hasn't thought it through, the reader will instantly pick up on that and there will be a huge hole in the story.

Salinger is one of the prime exemplars of the iceberg theory of writing. He did it extremely well. His stories have a spare quality, and every word feels hand-selected.

GORE VIDAL: Hemingway was very good at graphic descriptions of violence and hunting. He was very good at showing how things happen: how you load your gun, how you sight it against the arc the bird is taking, how you fire. He was just very good at that. And there are people, the same people who read *Popular Mechanics*, who love that kind of writing.

A. SCOTT BERG: Hemingway, it has long been thought, had a greater influence on American writing of the twentieth century than anyone else because he introduced a new style, a new sound people read first in the short stories, but especially in *The Sun Also Rises*. This new kind of hard-hammered writing really took hold. Hemingway has had more imitators, more bad imitators, than any other writer of the twentieth century. I'm not suggesting that Salinger imitated him exactly, but I think Salinger got from him a rhythm and certain techniques.

DAVID HUDDLE: Salinger admired Hemingway's front-line productivity, the ability to generate pages daily under any circumstance: it justified the term "professional." Salinger wrote interior prose, quite different from Papa's plain-spoken machismo style. Salinger wasn't famous yet, but he could already match Hemingway in his discipline, pounding away on the typewriter even while Nazis attacked.

J. D. SALINGER (contributor's note to *Story*, November–December 1944):

> I'm twenty-five, was born in New York, am now in Germany with the Army. I used to go pretty steady with the big city, but I find that my memory is slipping since I've been in the Army. Have forgotten bars and streets and buses and faces; am more inclined, in retrospect, to get my New York out of the American Indian Room of the Museum of Natural History, where I used to drop my marbles all over the floor. . . . Am still writing whenever I can find the time and an unoccupied foxhole.

JOHN C. UNRUE: Salinger is reported to have continued writing, not with indifference to the casualties, but with a very great focus on his art—gotten under a table to write during times of attacks because he was intent on finishing something, or perhaps starting something.

DAVID SHIELDS: Salinger took his typewriter on his jeep and would sit in a foxhole and just pound away. Werner Kleeman would watch Salinger write his stories and voraciously read the magazines his mother mailed to him. The two men, both in their mid-twenties, would walk up the hill to the mess hall together. The duo went out on the same boat for training maneuvers and were frequently in "tough spots" surrounded by German artillery fire, Kleeman later told a journalist.

WERNER KLEEMAN: In those days, he was very normal, except that he would never let anybody read his letters home and always forged the signature of a censoring officer.

J. D. SALINGER, excerpt from letter to Elizabeth Murray, August 1944:

> *I can't remember very acutely what happened in the early weeks. I can remember lying in ditches, face in the dirt, trying to get the maximum protection out of me hat. Stuff like that. But I can't remember the intensity of the early frights and panics. And that's nice.*

J. D. SALINGER, excerpt from letter to Frances Glassmoyer, August 9, 1944:

> *I met and have had a couple of long talks with Ernest Hemingway. He's extremely nice and completely unpatriotic. Sitting in my jeep as I write this. Chickens and pigs are walking around in an unbelievably uninteresting manner.*
>
> *I dig my fox-holes down to a cowardly depth. Am scared stiff constantly and can't remember ever having been a civilian.*

J. D. SALINGER, excerpt from letter to Whit Burnett:

> *You never saw six-feet-two of muscle and typewriter ribbon get out*

of a jeep and into a ditch as fast as this baby can. And I don't get out until they start bulldozing an airfield over me.

SHANE SALERNO: Diving out of a jeep under sniper fire, Salinger broke his nose and never got it fixed.

—

DAVID SHIELDS: Salinger needed war, the experience of war, to become a better writer, and he was becoming a more substantial and more serious writer, almost literally story by story. It was all one big bloody mess in his mind and psyche—the war and the writing and the surviving and the survivor's guilt and the artist's guilt and the ecstasy of artistic creation. He was a twenty-five-year-old ghost, looking for rebirth, placing stamps on envelopes sent stateside. Writing about the war was the only way for Salinger to survive the war. He was seeking oblivion, but he was also seeking fame.

Everything changes after D-Day; what Salinger pretended to know before he now knows viscerally and conveys with increasing emotional power. He's learning to aim the gun at himself.

In late 1944, his OCS rejection still stings. In "Once a Week Won't Kill You," a soldier's wife says to him, "I wish you'd phone that man with the thing on his face. The Colonel. In Intelligence and all. I mean you speak French and German and all. He certainly could get you at least a commission. I mean you know how miserable you'll be just being a private or something. I mean you hate to talk to people and everything."

"A Boy in France," which was published in March 1945, is no longer merely entertainment; this is writing. After a "long, rotten afternoon" of combat, Babe Gladwaller finds a blood-soaked foxhole and tries to go to sleep but is close to shell shock: "I'll open the window, I'll let in a nice, quiet girl—not Frances, not anyone I've ever known—and I'll bolt the door. I'll ask her to walk a little bit in the room by herself, and I'll look at her American ankles, and I'll bolt the door. I'll ask her to read some Emily Dickinson to me—that one about being chartless—and I'll ask her to read some William Blake to me—that one about the little lamb that made thee—and I'll bolt the door. She'll have an American voice, and she won't ask me if I have any chewing gum or bonbons, and I'll bolt the door." When U.S. soldiers in Vietnam saw death in its starkest form, they would often say, "There it is." For Salinger, there it is.

Regarding "Elaine," which was published just after "A Boy in France," Salinger wrote to Burnett that it was about "the beginning of the end of beauty; and that's where the war starts, I guess." The prewar, Stork Club, wise-guy Salinger is now MIA. In "This Sandwich Has No Mayonnaise," Salinger's and Holden's bodies are missing, breaking down, going silent: "Drenched to the bone, the bone of loneliness, the bone of silence, we plod back to the truck. Where are you Holden? Never mind the missing stuff. Stop playing around. Show up. Show up somewhere. Hear me? It's simply because I remember everything. I can't forget anything that's good, that's why."

Which is the precise pivot to the postwar art lesson Salinger will spend his life trying to teach himself and the world. In "The Stranger," published in December 1945, "With her feet together she made the little jump from the curb to the street surface, then back again. Why was it such a beautiful thing to see? . . . A fat apartment-house doorman, cupping a cigarette in his hand, was walking a wire-haired along the curb between Park and Madison. Babe figured that during the whole time of the Bulge, the guy had walked that dog on this street every day. He couldn't believe it. He could believe it, but it was still impossible. He felt Mattie put her hand in his. She was talking a blue streak." Only the child can touch the despair burned into the postwar veteran's flesh and mind without hurting him. "His mind began to hear the old Blakewell Howard's rough, fine horn playing. Then he began to hear the music of the unrecoverable years; the little unhistorical, pretty good years when all the dead boys in the 12th Regiment had been living and cutting in on other dead boys on lost dance floors; the years when no one who could dance worth a damn had ever heard of Cherbourg or Saint Lô; or Hürtgen Forest or Luxembourg." Salinger's 12th Regiment was being decimated by the war: because of such pain, he will thereafter seek unity in all things.

Conversation with Salinger #2

The road to Salinger's house and his mailbox, photographed by Ted Russell for *Life* magazine in 1961.

MICHAEL McDERMOTT: Very few photographs have been taken of Salinger. In 1960 *Newsweek* was the first magazine to really look deeply into him. They hired a local photographer, who tried to get a photograph of him. The photographer parked his car near Salinger's house and was ready to ambush him; lo and behold, Salinger and his daughter—I think she was about four years old at the time—were walking down the road.

The photographer walked up to Salinger, introduced himself instead of just grabbing the shot, and melted in his presence. The photographer said Salinger was so polite that he felt ashamed telling him he was in Cornish to take a picture of him for *Newsweek*. Salinger thanked the photographer for not trying to sneak a picture of him and then said, "My method of work is such that any interruption throws me off. I can't have my picture taken or have an interview until I've completed what I set out to do." That's a remarkable statement, and the photographer left without getting the picture.

MARC WEINGARTEN: There was a bounty on Salinger's head. Everyone wanted a photograph of this guy, and no one could get it. *Time* tried. *Newsweek* tried repeatedly. Nothing. Finally, a photographer at *Life* magazine named Ted Russell was given the assignment and a deadline of three days to get a photo of Salinger or pack it up and come home.

TED RUSSELL: I was a *Life* photographer and had been assigned by *Life* to shoot at the U.N. the week in the fall of 1961 that Dag Hammarskjöld, the United Nations secretary general, was killed in a plane crash in the Congo. I got a phone call from an editor at *Life* asking me to leave and go up to New Hampshire and shoot J. D. Salinger. I didn't know much about him at that time. I hadn't read *Catcher in the Rye*. It became well known when I was in Korea [during the Korean War]. I wasn't that familiar with him or his books, or of the fact that he was supposedly a famous recluse.

[The editor at *Life*] said that he hadn't been photographed for a decade, and he was very reclusive. She said if you get a picture of him I'll eat my hat, so that was something of a challenge. I went up there and did my best to get a picture of this reclusive man. The editors put a three-day limit on the job. I was being paid by the day, a hundred a day. And they said go up there and hang out; if it's more than three days, forget about it.

The editor gave me some written notes. The *Life* people were very thorough in their research; they gave me very specific directions on how to find him: go over the covered wooden bridge and drive a mile and a half, take the left-hand fork to the dirt road, et cetera, et cetera. They described the house as being hidden away in this wooded area.

I followed those very well-researched directions in the car I rented. I saw the Salinger mailbox they described, with his name on it. I drove past the house and parked a few hundred yards down the road. I tried to be as unobtrusive and discreet as possible. You couldn't exactly walk down that dirt road with six cameras hanging around your neck. I put my camera in a shopping bag. I looked like a regular guy.

I found a spot with underbrush that provided me a hiding place. Fall hadn't set in yet, and there was plenty of underbrush that gave me good cover. The challenge was not to be seen, so I took advantage of the terrain, hiding in the bushes much in the way that one would if one were hunting an animal. Patience is very important.

I stayed in a hotel in Windsor, across the river from Cornish, New Hampshire. I would drive to Cornish in the morning, find my little hiding place in the bushes, and stay there all day, shivering, and come back the next day until I ran out of daylight. I didn't get up there too early in the morning, but I'd stake out pretty much all day. It was very cold and rainy, and I had a horrible cold bordering on the flu. I waited in that spot for two and a half days. It was miserable. On the third day, he came out very briefly to let his dog out and that was just enough time for me to get off a half-dozen frames. One of my favorite pictures was a photo of his dog with his nose stuck beneath the fence. I thought it was funny that *Life* captioned that photograph as "Salinger's dog takes an un-Salinger-like peek under the fence."

I was using a Pentax 300-millimeter lens handheld. It was one of the first single-lens reflex [cameras] to be widely available. I don't know what the distance was, but I was pretty close. You can tell by the size of the image that with a 100-millimeter lens you can't be too far away. It was maybe 150 feet away. I was afraid that I was close enough that he might be able to hear the clicking of the shutter.

I've always felt somewhat bad about intruding on Salinger's privacy. I did it because it was a challenge; it was an assignment that I'd been given. It was my job to do the assignment to the best of my ability, solve the problems, and do it. But I always had pangs of conscience.

A guy goes to that much trouble to stay out of the limelight—I always thought, gee, I should have left the poor guy alone. I had misgivings. I became offended by the paparazzi people chasing Jackie Kennedy and Jackie Kennedy's children and all the paparazzi people today who descend on Britney Spears. Hanging out and stalking celebrities is a sleazy way to make a living. I really never felt that good about having intruded on his privacy in the way that I did. My one comfort was that if Salinger

Salinger outside the fence of his house, where he lived from 1953 to 1967. *Life* magazine photo, September 1961.

knew how cold and miserable I was, suffering the two and a half days to get those damn pictures, he probably wouldn't have minded as much. He could take comfort in knowing I suffered out there for that photo.

MICHAEL McDERMOTT: It is truly a paparazzi photo, but Ted Russell has an intuitive ability to compose apparently anything that's in front of him and make it beautiful. The balance of the photograph is nice. The dark bar is very symbolic of a Salinger mood. Salinger's wearing his characteristic jumpsuit—his uniform for writing and for gardening. When you see it close up, you can actually see the dark circles on Salinger's eyes—this haunted look.

4

INVERTED FOREST

GERMANY-BELGIUM BORDER, NOVEMBER–DECEMBER 1944

The Battle of Hürtgen Forest is an epic disaster for Salinger and the 4th Division; casualties are staggering for the U.S. Army. Salinger's literary tone turns shell-shocked, a muted elegy for the innumerable GIs, including himself, lost in the slaughter.

ALEX KERSHAW: Salinger's 4th Division entered the Hürtgen Forest on November 6, 1944. It was incredibly eerie, almost medieval. Primal fears came out in the Hürtgen Forest.

STEPHEN E. AMBROSE: Just south of Aachen lay the Hürtgen Forest. Roughly fifty square miles, it sat along the German-Belgian border, within a triangle outlined by Aachen, Monschau, and Düren. The Roer River ran along the eastern edge of the Hürtgen. Beyond it was the Rhine. The U.S. First Army wanted to [get close] to the Rhine, which General James Hodges decided required driving the Germans out of the forest.

Generals Omar Bradley and Hodges remained resolute to take the Hürtgen. They put in the 4th Infantry Division. It had led the way onto Utah Beach on June 6 and [gone] through a score of battles since. Not many D-Day veterans were still with the division; most were dead or badly wounded. In the Hürtgen, the division poured out its lifeblood again.

If the Americans ever got down into the river valley, the Germans could have been bypassed to the south, with the dams as the objective. The forest without the dams was worthless; the dams without the forest were priceless. But the generals got it backward and went for the forest.

The Hürtgen Forest, also known as the "killing field."

Thus did the Battle of Hürtgen Forest get started on the basis of a plan that was grossly, even criminally stupid.

EDWARD G. MILLER: The decision to fight originated in the heady days of Allied optimism in the late summer of 1944. The unexpected success of the Normandy breakout led the GIs of the First Army's VII Corps (and the rest of the Allies for that matter) to believe they were fighting a defeated enemy. The Americans were eager to smash through the German border defenses and cross the Rhine. Barring the way to the Rhine, however, was the Roer River. Between the VII Corps and the

Roer was a densely populated, but narrow, terrain corridor and a large forested area south of Aachen.

WERNER KLEEMAN: My opinion was, it was a waste of time to fight in the Hürtgen forest. If you have to get to the area behind it, go around; don't go through it. The Germans knew every road and they had artillery shells that exploded so that the tree branches would come down and kill soldiers. That, to me, was a suicide mission.

LIEUTENANT GEORGE WILSON: The country was obstacle enough in itself, yet the Germans had two additional advantages. They always knew exactly where we were, having just left there themselves, and thus easily called down shelling on us. They also had prepared in advance a series of defensive positions. Their bunkers were made of thick logs with a few feet of dirt on top. The bunkers were almost immune to artillery which had to arc in overhead. Tree bursts bothered them very little, and there was no chance of our tanks getting anywhere near them for direct fire. The infantry had to take them the hard way, going in after them one at a time, sometimes through barbed wire.

ALEX KERSHAW: The Germans used tree bursts, timing the fuses on 88-millimeter artillery shells so the shell would explode in the treetops. The explosion would rain thousands upon thousands of shards of wood and hot metal shrapnel on the men below.

MAJOR GENERAL RAYMOND G. BARTON: Added to the natural obstacles of tall, closely knit woods, steep hillsides and lack of roads were deliberate mine fields, wire entanglements and booby traps planted by the enemy during the weeks of inactivity in this sector. Continuous rain, snow and freezing weather severely hampered our operations, and during the next month the regiment suffered as many casualties from trench foot and exposure as it did from battle.

ALEX KERSHAW: They called it the meat factory, because it ground up so many Americans. Guys were dying, one per yard.

LIEUTENANT COLONEL WILLIAM GAYLE: The companies moved through the same bit of woods, were pinned down in front of the

American troops advancing in the Hürtgen Forest.

enemy wire, cut to pieces by the unremitting and inescapable tree bursts, [and] in the afternoon [they] went back to the holes they had left in the morning . . . to spend another cold night in icy water.

COLONEL GERDEN F. JOHNSON: Higher commanders had regarded the objectives given the 12th Infantry as nothing but local attacks to straighten the line and thought they would be easy. The heavy opposition the 12th had encountered seemed so out of proportion to the limited objectives that there was a feeling in Division and Corps staffs that the reports of losses were being exaggerated.

J. D. SALINGER (*The Catcher in the Rye*, 1951):

> He [D.B., Holden Caulfield's older brother and a soldier during World War II] once told Allie and I that if he'd had to shoot anybody, he wouldn't've known which direction to shoot in. He said the Army was practically as full of bastards as the Nazis were.

JOHN McMANUS: There was a constant parade of new faces [to replace casualties], especially in the rifle companies. It's hard to get to know the new guys; they don't necessarily have identities the guys you trained with back in England did, and a lot of them are gone quick, dead or wounded. You probably resent them a little bit, too, even though it's not their fault, because they're replacing your buddies. You also don't want to witness them getting chewed up and destroyed like everybody else; an emotional distance has to be maintained in order to retain sanity.

The new guys don't know what they're doing. That makes them dangerous. If you're the vet in a foxhole with a newbie, you're afraid to trust him to stay awake on guard duty or not to give away your position by firing a rifle senselessly or making unnecessary noise. So you maintain a constant state of alertness until it wears you down to nervous exhaustion.

EDWARD G. MILLER: Imagine you're J. D. Salinger. Two years before the Hürtgen Forest battle you're living on Park Avenue and suddenly, on a dark, sleety night in late November 1944, you're in the back of an uncovered two-and-a-half-ton truck. You're bouncing along in the truck, pitch black at night, ten, eleven o'clock, and you go to the assembly area and some voice in the darkness tells you, "Okay, jump out." You get off the truck and you still can't see anything. It's wet. You haven't slept in days. You haven't had a hot meal in days. You haven't had anything akin to a shower in weeks. You're tired going into it. You stay tired. You go forward; chances are you're going to come back later that day wounded. You might come back dead. You haven't learned the names of anybody you're with, the people you're bleeding with, you're fighting with, you're going through this sheer hell with; you don't know who they are, and they don't know who you are. The only hope you have is that the new guy is the one killed or wounded, not you. The average age especially for the rifle replacements by late 1944 was eighteen, nineteen years old.

LIEUTENANT ELLIOT JOHNSON: I was a forward observer at Hürtgen Forest. . . . I knew another forward observer. He went out with his crew. White phosphorus was thrown at them. Two of the men burned before his eyes. He came running to where I was in another part of Hürtgen Forest. I went down the road to meet him. He was sobbing and falling into my arms. He kept saying, "No more killing, no more killing, no more killing."

JOHN McMANUS: The rate of personnel turnover in 4th Division companies was mind-boggling, something like 200 percent casualties. [That is, so many replacement soldiers were killed or wounded that its casualty rate surpassed 100 percent.]

LIEUTENANT COLONEL WILLIAM GAYLE: In Hürtgen Forest the 4th Infantry Division was virtually expended for the second time since it landed in Normandy. Seven thousand men were lost in four weeks of this operation, which meant a turnover of 100 percent to 200 percent in rifle companies and battalion staffs. The total gain purchased at such a price was less than ten square miles, falling far short of planned objectives.

EBERHARD ALSEN: Major General Norman "Dutch" Cota, the commander of the 28th Division—to which Salinger's 12th Infantry Regiment was temporarily attached—decided to split up the regiment's three battalions and give each one its own combat mission. The commander of the 12th Regiment, Colonel James S. Luckett, pointed out that the hilly and densely forested terrain might allow the Germans to surround each battalion, something they would not be able to do if the battalions remained in physical contact. His objection was overruled. What Colonel Luckett feared actually happened. Each of the three battalions was surrounded, and they suffered more than five hundred casualties, including the deaths of 120 men, before they could break out and retreat.

COLONEL GERDEN F. JOHNSON: At 1400 hours the battalion commander notified Col. Luckett that he was gaining no ground and that his losses were heavy and increasing. He stated that the fire was so heavy that all attempts to advance were resulting only in more casualties. Col. Luckett informed the commanding general of the 28th Division of this situation and requested further instructions. He was told bluntly to use fire and movement and to continue the attack at all costs. . . . The battered remnants of the once proud regiment never succeeded in taking either of the important enemy positions in its sector and were in fact virtually lost to the division.

JOHN McMANUS: Salinger's regiment was like most of the other American outfits in the Hürtgen: it got destroyed. The thick woods and lousy weather made it hard for commanders to coordinate regimental movements. The intensity of German artillery fire also negated movement. It was not at all unusual for company-size units to get swallowed up, surrounded, cut off, or destroyed amid the brooding fir trees. The firebreaks were the only places where soldiers could advance in any numbers. Naturally, those firebreaks were zeroed in on with a prodigious volume of machine-gun and artillery fire. Any opening in the trees was swept with grazing fire—waist high or even lower. A man could hug the mud for dear life, only to take a bullet in his shoulder, through his head, or in the back of his thighs since these were generally the highest silhouette parts of his body.

The enemy artillery shells—generically called .88s but also including quite a bit of higher-caliber stuff—usually exploded in the treetops. The resulting bursts sent metal and wood fragments downward, ripping through a man's back, his abdomen, or, most frequently, his arms. Shrapnel wounds were so common that medics were simply overwhelmed. Most ran out of bandages, sulfa powder, and morphine. The mud, rain, and cold only added to their problems because soldiers often had pneumonia, trench foot, or just common head colds. If a man didn't have overhead cover, his foxhole was practically useless because tree bursts would shred him. If he was caught in the open in the middle of a barrage, the safest thing to do was to huddle against a tree. Of course, the problem with that was that trees often took direct hits and exploded or toppled over. The sheer volume of shells exploding in such a confined forest created an avalanche of noise and the sense that the explosions would never stop. Men spent so much time huddling desperately for cover that they felt isolated, cut off from the outside world. The darkness of the forest added to that sense.

In my opinion, this isolation led to a greater rate of combat fatigue cases—and certainly this was the case for Salinger. As for the effect of all this, most participants in the Hürtgen were shattered forever by the abject misery, the shelling, the hopelessness of the entire mess. Some could never set foot in woods again. Quite a few were, from that point on, angry and skeptical about the quality of their leadership. The trauma of Hürtgen never left those who were there.

ALEX KERSHAW: Salinger's division was chewed up in the battle for Hürtgen Forest. Hürtgen Forest was called the Green Hell. The 4th was literally bled dry.

J. D. SALINGER ("The Stranger," *Collier's*, December 1, 1945):

> "Uh, he [Vincent Caulfield] died in the morning. He and four other G.I.s and I were standing around a fire we made. In Hürtgen Forest. Some mortar dropped in suddenly—it doesn't whistle or anything—and it hit Vincent and three of the other men. He died in the medics' CP [Command Post] tent about thirty yards away, not more than about three minutes after he was hit." Babe had to sneeze several times at that point. He went on, "I think he had too much pain in too large an area of his body to have realized anything but blackness. I don't think it hurt. I swear I don't. His eyes were open. I think he recognized me and heard me when I spoke to him, but he didn't say anything at all."

—

ELIZABETH FRANK: J. D. Salinger and Louise Bogan first crossed paths when he wrote to her in November 1944. He may have thought she was the poetry editor of the *New Yorker*. She wasn't; she was simply its poetry reviewer. We don't really know what she thought about the poems themselves, but she was deeply touched that he had written to her from overseas and that his life was in danger. And she passed the poems along to her friend at the magazine, William Maxwell, hoping that he would deal with Salinger.

LOUISE BOGAN:

> *I send you another of Sergeant Salinger's letters. Perhaps getting in touch with this here agent, Harold Ober, would stem the tide. This poor young man has been bombarding me with poems for a week or so. I have written him; but in these situations it is better if you write him too. There isn't time to send them back to him; so will you write a note?*
>
> *Love, Louise.*
> *P.S. They came* Air Mail.

ELIZABETH FRANK: There was an element of concern in her letter about him, although she couldn't really do anything further with

The poet and *New Yorker* poetry critic Louise Bogan, to whom Salinger sent poems from the Hürtgen Forest.

New Yorker fiction editor William Maxwell.

the poems. Bogan was not terribly comfortable being bombarded with poems. Salinger was sending her fat envelopes filled with poems he wanted her to read, and she simply didn't know what to do with them.

LOUISE BOGAN:

> *Dear M,*
>
> *I send you another of Sergeant Salinger's letters. It now appears that he is in France, so everything becomes more touching.*

ELIZABETH FRANK: By November Salinger was actually in the Hürtgen Forest. But clearly what she means is that she recognizes that he's in the army, that he's serving overseas and probably in dire straits.

DAVID SHIELDS: Salinger is in hell, surrounded by death, but he must publish something—a story, a poem, anything—in the *New Yorker* before he dies.

WERNER KLEEMAN: On a November night, while we were stationed in Zweifall, Germany, J. D. Salinger, who was fighting alongside us, suddenly received an order from his drunken commanding captain. It was about 9 pm and Salinger was told to go and stay in a foxhole with his regiment for the night. I felt sorry for him, and then remembered the blanket I had pinched from the Hotel Atlantique. I gave it to him, along with a pair of woolen socks that my mother had knitted and sent to me. He thanked me and left. The next day when I met up with him, I asked, "How was the night?" He told me that, contrary to the captain's orders, he found a place to sleep in a house a few blocks away and did not in fact go to the regiment to sleep in the soggy, snow-filled foxhole.

MARGARET SALINGER: Winter brought the conditions of the 12th from unbearable to unspeakable. Their numbers had been increased by 2,228 replacements, bringing its original 3,080 to 3,362. A terrible month of fighting in Hürtgen Forest saw 1,493 battle casualties, and a loss of an additional 1,024 men from nonbattle causes, mainly from freezing to death in foxholes, half full of icy water, dug in the alternately frozen and wet ground, snow and mud, with no winter boots nor warm coats, nor an adequate supply of dry blankets for a bedroll in the foxholes.

—

WERNER KLEEMAN: One dreary evening around 8 pm, when we were both staying in the same house in Zweifall [a house shared by the Signal Corps and the CIC], he suddenly said to me, "Let's go and look up Hemingway." With that we put on our coats, took a flashlight and started walking. After about a mile, we found a small brick house and noticed a marker P.R.O., which meant "Public Relations Office." A few steps up we found a side doorway, which we entered. Inside we found Captain Stevenson, who was in charge of the office, and there was Hemingway, stretched out on a couch. A visor on his forehead, he was busy writing on a yellow pad. The office had its own generator to produce electricity for war reporters who had checked in for the night. The rest of the town lay in blackness. I felt elated to have this chance to visit once again one of the world's giants, the author who had recently finished *For Whom the Bell Tolls.* I had met up with him about two months before in Bleialf, when I was able to inquire about the two beautiful women he loved and admired, Marlene

Dietrich and Ingrid Bergman. And now, here I was, sitting with Giant and the young aspiring author, Salinger, who had already published several stories. While we sipped champagne from aluminum cups, I was fascinated, thinking that I was in the presence of such gifted men and was able to observe them in such a natural setting. And when I received Jerry's letter 17 years later, I thought about how yes, I did remember that evening just as if it were yesterday. Something so unusual and eventful stays in one's mind for a lifetime. There, in the midst of my official duty, was this unique experience.

DAVID SHIELDS: This is the moment at which—amid war, champagne, and male bonding—Salinger revealed his anatomical deformity to Hemingway, according to Kleeman.

NOAH ROSENBERG: To this day, Kleeman still marvels at Salinger's ability to discuss with Hemingway, at length, the characters from one of Hemingway's stories. "He knew all of the people that Hemingway mentioned," Kleeman recalled with wide eyes. "Two hours later, I wouldn't remember names like that!"

DAVID SHIELDS: Salinger came to be embarrassed by his own literary ambition. Between battles, he developed a friendship with Hemingway and relentlessly submitted his work to the *New Yorker* and many other magazines.

J. D. SALINGER, excerpt from letter to Werner Kleeman, 1961:

> *I have the feeling you must have been saddened, too, over the fact and circumstance of Hemingway's death. Remember the little house where we were staying during the Hurtgen Forest business? I remember his kindness, and I'm sure you do too.*

DAVID SHIELDS: Hemingway committed suicide on July 2, 1961.

—

ALEX KERSHAW: Salinger and the American infantry had fought the European war based on terrain. It didn't matter how good your technology was; the infantry had to move across each individual landscape—

beach, hedgerow, swamp, countryside—fight, and clear the enemy off it. The natural obstacles were the ones that ended up being the most deadly because they gave the Germans perfect defensive positions from which to attack and defend. Hürtgen Forest was the perfect example—some of the worst terrain fought over in the Second World War.

Not only did the perpetually dark forest floor hide a network of ingenious booby traps and mines, but the terrain was also a nearly perfect defender's ground, full of German soldiers in a deadly network of bunkers and fortified positions.

The surroundings were completely oppressive. Above you loomed a hundred-foot canopy. You couldn't go more than two or three yards without coming against endless tree stumps. The ground below you was mined.

EDWARD G. MILLER: The 4th Infantry Division, in a ten-day period in October, gained about three miles and lost at least a thousand casualties per mile.

DAVID SHIELDS: One American captain remarked that they took three trees a day, but each tree cost them a hundred men.

DEBORAH DASH MOORE: Soldiers describe that battle as one where they wish they could crawl inside their helmets. Bullets came from all different directions. They ricocheted off of the trees. You didn't know where the enemy was.

ALEX KERSHAW: Guys would literally have their arms blown off. Half a leg missing. And they'd be laughing as they were taken off in a stretcher because they knew they were going home.

EDWARD G. MILLER: Salinger was consumed with what every soldier was: to get close enough to that tree and pray to God that somebody else buys it.

ALEX KERSHAW: Both sides shelled the hell out of this forest. The only way Salinger could have survived an intense shelling would have been to literally hug a tree.

STAFF SERGEANT DAVID RODERICK: I had a young Jewish kid

from New York City in my company, maybe only eighteen, an All-City basketball player with a good future ahead of him. He was a replacement for one of my men. After the artillery barrage was over, I went to check on the guys. I found him lying in a half-ready foxhole, dead, not a mark on him. Killed by the concussion from a shell. We lost a company commander the same way in Hürtgen Forest. How many other people got killed or wounded by tree bursts, I don't know, but they were terrible.

EDWARD G. MILLER: The isolation for Salinger of being in the foxhole all night. The water filling it up. His boots are leaking. He's soaked. He's freezing. He doesn't know if the Germans have sent out combat patrols or not. The fear of the unknown is just eating away at him. The nights are so bad that he prays for daylight, and at daylight he prays for darkness because in the daylight he's going to fight again.

German veterans of the Eastern Front would tell you today that it was the most brutal combat they, too, faced. The forest area was not very large. The worst of the fighting took place in an area that was maybe seventy square miles. If you look at the casualty rates for the Germans and the Americans, there was, simply put, a lot of killing in a very small area.

ALEX KERSHAW: Whole companies of two hundred men would be down to twenty or thirty after four or five hours.

GORE VIDAL: They just threw one wave in after another wave after another wave.

STAFF SERGEANT DAVID RODERICK: Another young Jewish boy from New York City got a direct hit on his foxhole. And he lay there most of the night, yelling for someone to shoot him because he was in so much pain. He would yell out, "Shoot me, shoot me." I could hear him, you know? I was in a foxhole with one of my men and I really started shaking. And I thought it was because I was chilled. At least that's the excuse I made.

COLONEL GERDEN F. JOHNSON: We flushed three Krauts out of a hole right on our path. We started them across a firebreak, a tank fired at us down the firebreak, the prisoners started to run, the patrolmen opened up on them with their tommy guns, and the three Krauts were kaput. Our men went so far as to run over and pump lead into their heads to stop their yelling. It made me a little sick.

EDWARD G. MILLER: Salinger's unit, the 12th Infantry Regiment, had nothing to show but casualties for its efforts.

FIRST LIEUTENANT JOHN B. BEACH: There were dead bodies all over the place.

LIEUTENANT COLONEL FRANKLIN SIBERT: God, it was cold. . . . The supply line was littered with dead. The men that came out with me were so damned tired that they stepped on the bodies. . . . They were too tired to step over them.

—

EDWARD G. MILLER: The Germans used several types of mines in the forest, and not all of them, in fact few of them, could be detected by the American mine detectors. GIs who stepped on mines typically might lose a foot, part of a foot, a leg, part of a leg; they would be blown backward and there would be powder residue on them. If they were lucky, the mine fragments were hot enough that it would sear the wound and they might not bleed to death.

COLONEL GERDEN F. JOHNSON: During the night, and in the daylight hours that followed, men from Co. G made several attempts to reach the wounded man who lay in the [forest] but were driven back each time by German machine-gun fire. The wounded man, whose left leg had been blown off halfway to the knee, was a member of Co. B, and he had been leading a patrol from his company in an attempt to contact Co. F. Lying helpless in the dark and moaning with pain, he fell victim of a fiendish German plot. Enemy soldiers crawled out to him in the dark, removed his helmet and field jacket, and robbed him of his cigarettes and personal possessions and then placed a booby trap under his back so that when our medics finally reached him, they would be blown to bits the minute they moved him.

EDWARD G. MILLER: Ernest Hemingway was a correspondent with and spent a lot of time in the 22nd, because the Regimental Commander, Charles "Buck" Lanham, and he were quite good friends by that point in the war. After the war, one of Hemingway's books, *Across the River and into the Trees*, had a character named Colonel Canfield. Supposedly, Canfield was modeled on Lanham. One of the great lines in that book is Canfield saying, "I always thought that it would have made more sense just to shoot the replacements in the rear areas than to go to all the trouble for them to de-truck, go to the front, where they were going to be killed, anyway, and then transport them to the rear."

ALEX KERSHAW: Cold, wet, depressing, dark, and incredibly dispiriting—trying to maintain any kind of morale in that battle was very difficult for Salinger.

BOB WANDESFORDE: I hadn't washed or shaved for weeks. Everything I wore or carried was mud brown. I had trench foot; my hands and face were black; my fingertips and lips were split and raw. I had eaten almost nothing but K rations and C rations in my filthy black canteen cup . . . and had slept in bombed-out houses or in the snow for over a month. But I didn't look any worse than the rest of my outfit, and I considered myself lucky to be alive.

PAUL FUSSELL: For those in the know, the horror of Hürtgen could be read in the number of self-inflicted wounds and the unprecedented rates of desertion. It was a desperate moment on the Western front when, to halt the increasing desertions, pitiable serial deserter Private Eddie Slovik was formally shot to death as the only execution for desertion in the whole European Theater.

STAFF SERGEANT DAVID RODERICK: I'd taken cover under a tree during another artillery assault, and the force of the explosion and shrapnel landing on me knocked me out. It gave me a concussion and killed my radioman. I didn't know where I was or who I was or what I was doing. Someone got me to an aid station, and I was evacuated from Hürtgen on November 24, 1944. That happened to a lot of soldiers.

When I got to the hospital I was examined, and they called me "combat-exhausted." What they did was give you a pill that put you to sleep for twenty-four hours. Soldiers called it the "Blue 88." They did it three times, so you slept for about three days.

ALEX KERSHAW: It was an epic disaster, the Battle of Hürtgen Forest. The 4th Division sustained an estimated 5,260 battle and nonbattle casualties. There were unimaginable scenes of destruction.

—

EDWARD G. MILLER: When the Battle of Hürtgen Forest was over, privates were platoon leaders. In one company of the 22nd Regiment, the only existing soldier who started that battle on November 16 and was still a member of that company the first week of December was one lieutenant. The 28th Infantry Division and its attachments lost almost six thousand soldiers—killed, wounded, missing, taken prisoner—in about two weeks.

Throughout the war the 4th Division was authorized at about 14,300 soldiers. In the course of the war from D-Day until May 1945, it sustained something like thirty-five thousand casualties—about 250 percent casualties in the division. Ninety-five percent of those casualties were in rifle units.

ALEX KERSHAW: For those who fought it, Hürtgen Forest was the most enraging defeat. Salinger experienced the defeat firsthand. The Germans inflicted well over twenty-four thousand casualties on American forces, in addition to nine thousand casualties due to fatigue, illness, and friendly fire. Salinger saw the futility and horror of that immense loss of life.

MACK MORRISS: Behind them they left their dead, and the forest will stink with deadness long after the last body is removed. The forest will bear the scars of our advance long after our own scars have healed, and the infantry has scars that will never heal.

EDWARD G. MILLER: The amount of artillery fired was so great that even today the German government contracts with a company to do explosive ordnance disposal work in the Hürtgen Forest.

Conversation with Salinger #3

BARBARA GRAUSTARK: Hardly anyone in a roomful of New York City cops recognized J. D. Salinger when he slipped into town by train from his hermitage in Cornish, N.H., to surprise ex–chief of detectives John L. Keenan, a World War II buddy, at a testimonial dinner in Queens. He struck one diner at Antun's Restaurant as "just another gentleman"—tall, graying, slightly stooped at 59, togged in a blue blazer suit. But his mellow battlefront memories of Keenan ("He was a great comfort in the foxholes. . . . In Normandy, he led us all in song") moved the celebrants, and so did his outgoing manner. Said one, of the recluse's return: "His personality has blossomed."

JOHN L. KEENAN: [Salinger is] very normal. He's a kind, sensitive man, a good person to be with, with a good sense of humor. Everything I know about him is good.

HELEN DUDAR: During the Keenan festivities, a friend of mine, a newspaperman who identified himself by name and trade, had a half-hour talk with Salinger. My friend recalls that he was dressed in well-made tweeds and that he was tall, slightly stooped, gaunt, extremely pale, and entirely gray—a time-eroded image of the luminously dark-eyed young man who allowed his photograph to appear on the jacket of *Catcher* for two editions.

Amiable but guarded, Salinger talked mostly about Keenan and the Keenan family, for whom he has great affection. The conversation was quiet, low-key. My friend does not know whether it was something Salinger said or something his manner conveyed; he remembers simply that he came away with the odd impression that he had just talked to a man who is "scared to death of not-nice people."

DAVID SHIELDS: What strikes me about the Keenan dinner is Salinger's singular devotedness to the cadre of soldiers with whom he served and escaped death. His family, his wives, his daughter, boyhood friends, literary friends, editors, fellow townspeople: he'd left them all long ago.

But thirty-four years later he was willing to expose himself to strangers, even journalists, to relive and share the memories of Normandy with his former—and perpetual—comrades. It's a remarkable statement of the deep impact the war had on him.

SHANE SALERNO: Salinger's December 20, 1979, postcard to Paul Fitzgerald is addressed, thirty-five years after the end of the war, to "old veteran."

5

DEAD MEN IN WINTER

LUXEMBOURG-BELGIUM BORDER, 1944–1945

The Battle of the Bulge, 1944.

The surprise German Ardennes counterattack infiltrates Salinger's depleted 12th Infantry Regiment. Many units are cut off and wiped out. Salinger witnesses the massacre of two armies, the Germans now reduced to using child shock troops. He is a prime candidate to join the anonymous war dead.

J. D. SALINGER, excerpt from letter to Paul Fitzgerald, February 3, 1960:

> *There was a film on TV a couple of weeks ago, about the Battle of the Bulge. How the snow and the road and the sign-posts brought everything back to mind.*

MARTHA GELLHORN: They all said it was wonderful Kraut-killing country. What it looked like was scenery for a Christmas card: smooth white snow hills and bands of dark forest and villages that actually nestled. The snow made everything serene, from a distance. At sunrise and sunset the snow was pink and the forests grew smoky and soft. During the day the sky was covered with ski tracks, the vapor trails of planes, and the roads were dangerous iced strips, crowded with all the usual vehicles of war, and the artillery made a great deal of noise, as did the bombs from the Thunderbolts. The nestling villages, upon closer view, were mainly rubble, and there were indeed plenty of dead Krauts. This was during the German counteroffensive which drove through Luxembourg and Belgium and is now driven back. At this time the Germans were being "contained," as the communiqué said. The situation was "fluid"—again the communiqué. You can say the words "death and destruction" and they don't mean anything. But they are awful words when you are looking at what they mean.

STEPHEN E. AMBROSE: Hitler knew Germany would never win the war by defending the Siegfried Line and then the Rhine River [at Germany's western border]. His only chance was to win a lightning victory in the West. It was almost certainly an unattainable objective, but if surprise could be achieved, it might work. Nothing else would.

WILLIAM L. SHIRER: Hitler realized that by remaining on the defensive he was merely postponing the hour of reckoning. In his feverish mind there emerged a bold and imaginative plan to recapture the initiative, strike a blow that would split the U.S. Third and First armies, penetrate to Antwerp and deprive Eisenhower of his main port of supply, and roll up the British and Canadian armies along the Belgian-Dutch border. Such an offensive, he thought, would not only administer a crushing defeat on the Anglo-American armies and thus free the threat to Germany's western border, but would then enable him to turn against the Russians.

ALEX KERSHAW: Salinger's unit faced a fierce, ideologically committed enemy that was fighting basically to save the Third Reich. It came down to ordinary GIs, men like Salinger, fighting from foxholes in the worst winter in living memory.

U.S. ARMY HISTORICAL DIVISION: [The 4th] Division was by all accounts in poor condition for combat. All the rifle companies lost very nearly all of the men and officers with which they started the [previous] battle. Thus the division moved to Luxembourg with almost completely new personnel in the line companies. In addition, it was understrength about 1,600 riflemen, since no replacements were furnished during the last week in Hurtgen; many of the rifle companies were only about half strength.

SERGEANT ED CUNNINGHAM: In the first frantic days of mid-December, the newspapers called it Von Rundstedt's Breakthrough

Soldiers take defensive positions during the Battle of the Bulge.

in the Ardennes. Then, as the American line stiffened and held from Elsenborn to Bastogne, it became known as the Battle of the Bulge. In between that time it was probably the most frightening, unbelievable experiences of the war.

COLONEL GERDEN F. JOHNSON: The enemy's plan was simple and startlingly clear. In order to secure the main road through Echternach, Lauterborn, Scheidgen and Junglinster toward Luxembourg City, 20 kilometers away, all the towns in the 12th's sector facing the Sauer River and the Siegfried Line had to be taken. Because of the average distance of from three to five kilometers between these towns, it was impossible to prevent the enemy penetrations from surrounding them and cutting off the forces which were in them.

ALEX KERSHAW: The Nazi surprise was caused by lousy Allied intelligence; the generals bungled terribly, misreading and disregarding field intelligence reports. It was the Allies' worst intelligence failure of the Second World War. The battle began with the Americans on the run. They were taken completely by surprise on the 16th of December 1944. Over 200,000 Germans attacked them.

ERNEST HEMINGWAY: There's been a complete breakthrough, kid. This thing could cost us the works. Their armor is pouring in. They're taking no prisoners.

COLONEL GERDEN F. JOHNSON: The front ran for nearly thirty-five miles along the west bank of the Sauer River and the Moselle River, and all three regiments were in the line. Because of its large sector and a shortage of equipment, communications were strained. [The 4th Division's] artillery was scattered and shells were scarce. Its attached tank battalion, which had also taken heavy punishment in the Hürtgen Forest, was trying to repair its tanks in spite of an acute shortage of parts. One-fourth of its tanks were stripped for cleaning; many others would not run. The battalion had only twenty-six tanks which could be considered operational. The 4th Division, in other words, was in no position to fight.

ROBERT E. MERRIAM: Roaring cannons along an eighty-mile front served as the alarm clock for thousands of sleeping American troops that murky morning. It electrified men who felt safe in the assurance that theirs was a rest area. Commanders and their staffs tumbled out of bed, to eye with wonder the flashes of the distant artillery and listen, amazed, to reports from their outposts. They didn't wait long; shortly after six o'clock, the first reports were hastily relayed back to the command posts that through the early morning dark could be seen German infantry, moving forward slowly in that characteristic walk. Behind them snorted the tanks, ready to roar through the gaps cleared by the infantry. In at least one instance, the infantry were driving a herd of cattle before them to detonate any mines which might have been planted in the earth by defending troops.

ALEX KERSHAW: Taking advantage of the cold, foggy weather and the total surprise of the Allies, the Germans penetrated deep into Belgium, creating a dent or "bulge" in the Allied lines. The temperature in the Ardennes during 1944–1945 was the coldest on record [below-zero temperatures]. What remained of Salinger's division was resting on what turned out to be a front line for the German attack. The members of Salinger's division were widely dispersed. What emerged out of the fog was hallucinatory.

PAUL FUSSELL: It was dark and it was foggy when the boys, stomachs paralyzed by fear, first saw shapes moving silently toward them, and then, as the shapes advanced, they saw the white snow garments and unique helmets of the German infantry, psyched up to kill them all. In the ghastly weather, you either fought back a bit against the bayonet and the grenade or you took off. If you were wounded outdoors you froze to death within a half hour.

COLONEL RICHARD MARR: The initial German attacks rolled over or around all the outposts on the 12th Infantry's front without any difficulty, which was inevitable in view of the strength of the German forces. The Americans held their fire until the German lines were fully exposed, then opened a concerted surprise fire of machine guns. [The Germans] cut [the American forces] to pieces, while the riflemen in the houses picked off the forward ranks.

DANNY S. PARKER: The experienced German infantry penetrated the 12th Infantry Regiment in the early morning hours on either side of Echternach.

ALEX KERSHAW: During the most intense parts of the battle, guys Salinger knew were too afraid to fall asleep in their foxholes because they'd freeze to death. It was the last great gasp of Nazi Germany, and the American soldier took the brunt of that attack and held.

JOHN TOLAND: The Battle of the Bulge was the greatest pitched battle ever fought by the United States; it's the only major struggle in the dead of winter. It was as great in scale as the Battle of Stalingrad—over a million soldiers and thousands of civilians were actively involved. Unlike any other campaign in World War II, it was conceived in its entirety by Adolf Hitler. It was his last great offensive, his last great gamble.

STEPHEN E. AMBROSE: To provide the will, Hitler counted on the children. The German soldiers of December 1944 were mostly

Soldiers stay low during the Battle of the Bulge.

born between 1925 and 1928. They had been deliberately raised by the Nazis for this moment, and they had that fanatical bravery their Führer counted on.

ALEX KERSHAW: Suddenly and overwhelmingly, detached American units, including Salinger's 12th infantry, were fighting an enemy as young as fifteen, as old as sixty. Hitler threw everything at them—German weapons and munitions were diverted in massive quantities from the Eastern Front to the Ardennes—because it was Hitler's last chance to gain control and end the war in the West on his terms. Salinger and the remainder of the post-Hürtgen 12th regiment were isolated because they had been spread along a thirty-five-mile front. The isolation, coupled with the intensity of the German attack, bred the fear that if they caved in, if this went badly and they were completely overrun, the war could turn against them, the gains of D-Day rolled back. The ghosts of Hürtgen reemerged. A whole division enveloped by the enemy? It was not beyond the realm of possibility during the opening hours of the battle.

DEBORAH DASH MOORE: In the snow, fog, and dire cold, units like Salinger's 12th were suddenly cut off from each other by German advances into and through their lines.

COLONEL GERDEN F. JOHNSON: The Germans had infiltrated to a depth of four kilometers into the lines of 12th Infantry Regiment and had isolated it company for company.

ALEX KERSHAW: All the GIs could do was stand and hold or run. Many small units fought to the bitter end. For an entire month, Salinger's 4th Division fought in one of the fiercest and bloodiest campaigns of the war.

The record cold in the Ardennes created accumulating problems. Trucks had to be run every half hour or the oil in them would freeze. GIs took to urinating on their weapons to thaw them out.

DEBORAH DASH MOORE: One GI described the routine that he would use. He had three pairs of socks, and he would wear one pair on his feet to keep his feet warm; he would wear one in his helmet for his

In the brutal cold, soldiers receive rations.

head, and he would have the third one in a pocket to try to dry his head off. He rotated these socks each day because he was very worried about frostbite, which was, along with trench foot, a huge problem.

MARGARET SALINGER: My father said that no matter what, he will always be grateful to his mother, who knit him socks and sent them to him in the mail, each and every week, throughout the war. He told me it saved his life in the foxholes that winter; he was the only guy he knew with dry feet.

EDWARD G. MILLER: You pray that you're not another one of those anonymous casualties, because the casualty rate was enormous. The U.S. Army almost ran out of infantry replacements in late 1944.

—

PRIVATE BOB CONROY: [A GI named] Gordon got ripped by a machine gun from roughly the left thigh through the right waist. He . . . told me he was hit through the stomach as well. . . . We were in foxholes by ourselves, so we both knew he was going to die. We had no morphine. We couldn't ease [the pain], so I tried to knock him out. I took off his helmet, held his jaw up, and just whacked it hard as I could, because he wanted to be put out. That didn't work, so I hit him up by the head with a helmet and that didn't work. Nothing worked. He slowly froze to death; he bled to death.

WILLIAM MONTGOMERY: The casualties had been hit by shrapnel the night before and were lost in the dark. One man had frozen, poor guy. The other was a real Survivor—with a capital "S." His leg was shattered, but he had made a tourniquet of his belt. He burrowed down into the snow and covered himself with his shelter-half, lit an alcohol cube with his Zippo lighter, and shoved his rifle butt into the small flame. When the fumes got to him, he put out the flame, flapped the shelter-half, and settled down for a while, then started over again. I remember him well because he was such a vivid example of the hell riflemen had to live through every day. Even now, fifty-five years later, I'm still in awe of what guys like him did. My squad and I carried a lot of them off the line—enough to know that it was the infantry who won the war.

DEBORAH DASH MOORE: The successful penetration of the American lines trapped large numbers of American troops, which is why many were captured. They ran out of ammo, there were no reinforcements, and they lost the resources to fight their way out.

COLONEL GERDEN F. JOHNSON: The enemy hoped to break up and isolate the regiment so that his panzers could pass through. The problem for Col. Chance [Salinger's commanding officer] was to make contact with his isolated units and form a line.

STEPHEN E. AMBROSE: The Americans used desperate methods to bolster the defense. Pvt. Kenneth Delaney of the 1st Infantry Division had been in combat from D-Day to November 15, when he was wounded in the Hürtgen. A month later he was recuperating in a hospital in Liège, Belgium. "On December 17th," he recalled, "the hospital staff informed us that if you can walk or crawl, you will have to go back to your Division as soon as possible."

—

GEORGE KNAPP: On Christmas of '44, in a small town close to the river separating Luxembourg and Germany, I conducted a candlelight service in a barn alongside the road leading to the front line. Candelabra and candles came from a bombed-out church in town. Men of all faiths attended. We only had a trio to sing as the other member of an intended quartet had been captured. The next morning, my Christmas Day Services were conducted in a two-lane bowling alley in another town a bit farther away from the front.

—

COLONEL GERDEN F. JOHNSON: On those days [of warmer temperatures], melting snow revealed the bodies of both German and American soldiers upon the ground where they had been frozen into weird shapes after they had fallen in the winter battles. Hundreds of dead cattle littered the fields, and destroyed vehicles lined the roads along with the carcasses of the horses that had been either partially or completely destroyed, and the wreckage lay untouched where it fell. Human excreta was deposited in the corners of rooms where the fighting had been at such close quarters that even leaving the buildings was an invitation to death. This part of Germany, just north of the point where the borders of Germany, France, and Belgium meet, was the filthiest area the 12th had ever fought through.

MARTHA GELLHORN: There were half-tracks and tanks literally wrenched apart, and a gun position directly hit by bombs. All around these lacerated or flattened objects of steel there was the usual riffraff: papers, tin cans, cartridge belts, helmets, an odd shoe, clothing. There were also, ignored and completely inhuman, the hard-frozen corpses of Germans. Then there was a clump of houses, burned and gutted, with only a few walls standing, and around them the enormous bloated bodies of cattle. The road passed through a curtain of pine forest and came out on a flat, rolling snow field. In this field the sprawled or bunched bodies of Germans lay thick, like some dark shapeless vegetable.

At Warnach, on the other side of the main Bastogne road, some soldiers who had taken, lost, and retaken this miserable village were now sightseeing the battlefield. They were also inspecting the blown-out equipment of two German tanks and a German self-propelled gun which had been destroyed here. Warnach smelled of the dead; in subzero weather the smell of death has an acrid burning odor.

Farther down the street a command car dragged a trailer; the bodies of Germans were piled on the trailer like so much ghastly firewood.

HANSON W. BALDWIN: The fundamental reason for the German failure was a lack of military power to match Hitler's imaginative and extraordinary aims. And, as so often happens in totalitarian societies, the Germans underestimated the staying power of their enemies. . . . After the first shock of surprise had been dissipated, U.S. troops, especially the bloodied veteran divisions, rallied, fought, and died. . . . This is probably the major imponderable of warfare—to know just when men will suddenly, and often of their own free will, commit an act of unthinking, desperate bravery.

PAUL FITZGERALD, excerpt from an unpublished poem:

> The Fighting Fourth Division became a seasoned team, through Normandy, through Paris, and Luxembourg. The Siegfried Line deterred our troops, but soon it was asunder.

COLONEL RICHARD MARR: The 12th Infantry held; held in the face of odds so ominous that it would be difficult, even in retrospect, to believe possible had one not seen, during months of continuous combat, the high courage and honor which marks all ranks of the 12th Infantry.

SHANE SALERNO: Salinger's 12th Infantry Regiment was awarded the Distinguished Unit Citation for its defense of Luxembourg.

MARTHA GELLHORN: There were many dead and many wounded, but the survivors contained the fluid situation and slowly turned it into a retreat, and finally, as the communiqué said, the bulge was ironed out. This was not done fast or easily; and it was not done by those anonymous things, armies, divisions, regiments. It was done by men, one by one—your men.

One soldier stands over a frozen soldier.

JOHN TOLAND: The will of the German soldier was broken. No one that survived the retreat believed there was the slightest chance of German victory.

ALEX KERSHAW: The brutal culmination of J. D. Salinger's combat experience in the European theater of operations was the Bulge, fighting in the Ardennes. He was surrounded by a huge volume of human suffering and annihilation. It's impossible to believe that he wasn't fundamentally altered in unrecognizable ways.

—

SHANE SALERNO: The common understanding is that Hemingway and Salinger met only two times, in Paris and in the Hürtgen Forest. However, another meeting took place during the Battle of the Bulge.

On December 16, 1944, the first day of the battle, although Hemingway was in Paris, recovering from pneumonia, his friend General Barton told him "it was a pretty hot show and to come on up." He did.

CHARLES MEYERS: I was in the Counter Intelligence Corps during World War II. During the Battle of the Bulge I was loaned, along with an Atlantan named Ernie Welch, to the 4th Infantry Division CIC team. The 4th Division anchored the southern hinge of the Bulge in Luxembourg. Its CIC team numbered about fourteen men, six of whom were located in pairs at each of the three regimental CPs. One of these pairs included Jerry (J. D.) Salinger.

Our assignment during that January 1945 required Welch and myself to jeep each day between Division Headquarters and the three regimental CPs. It was cold that winter, and we did a lot of warming up at the regimental CIC billets. Jerry was writing at that time and selling a few of the stories he was then writing in the time he could spare (sometimes a lot) from the war.

Hemingway was at that time attached to the 4th. Jerry gave him some of his stories to read, and one day, when Welch and I had dropped by to thaw again, Jerry showed me a note penciled on a piece of brown paper bag which Hemingway had sent him. The note commended Jerry's "ear" and praised the considerable talent and promise of his stories.

LEICESTER HEMINGWAY: [When Hemingway took a hotel room in Luxembourg, he] came out to relax with good pals . . . [including] Jerome Salinger, who was a good man with the CIC.

—

BART HAGERMAN: Every time it snows . . . I'll think about those days during the Bulge. It brings back memories of the friends that I lost and the desperate feeling that we had in those days, and it kind of irks me that, after 50 years, I still think that way. I should forget it and go on about my life, but . . . it'll always be with me, I guess.

ERNIE PYLE: There are many of the living who have had burned into their brains forever the unnatural sight of cold dead men scattered over the hillsides and in the ditches along the high rows of hedge throughout the world. Dead men by mass production—in one country after another—month after month and year after year. Dead men in winter and dead men in summer.

Dead men in such familiar promiscuity that they become monotonous.

Dead men in such monstrous infinity that you come almost to hate them. These are the things that you at home need not even try to understand. To you at home they are columns of figures, or he is a near one who went away and just didn't come back. You didn't see him lying so grotesque and pasty beside the road in France.

We saw him, saw him by the multiple thousands. That's the difference.

MARGARET SALINGER: I remember standing next to my father—I was about seven at the time—for what seemed like an eternity as he stared blankly at the strong backs of our construction crew of local boys, carpenters building the new addition to our house. Their T-shirts were off, their muscles glistening in the summer sun. After a long time, he finally came back to life again and spoke to me, or perhaps just out loud to no one in particular, "All those big strong boys"—he shook his head—"always on the front line, always the first to be killed, wave after wave of them," he said, his hand flat, palm out, pushing arc-like waves away from him.

6

STILL BURNING

KAUFERING LAGER IV, LANDSBURG, GERMANY;
BUCHENWALD, GERMANY, SPRING 1945

Exhausted at war's end, Salinger and the 12th Regiment enter Kaufering IV. In many ways, Salinger never leaves.

DEBORAH DASH MOORE: Salinger would have recognized it from a mile or two down the road. It always amazes me when local civilians

Kaufering IV, subcamp of Dachau.

say they didn't know what was going on in the camps; the smell just pervaded the countryside.

ROBERT ABZUG: The experience of liberating the camps—the horror, really—began even before they got through the gates.

ALEX KERSHAW: J. D. Salinger was one of the first Americans to witness the full evil of the Nazi regime when he went into a concentration camp in Germany in the spring of 1945. He would have seen unimaginable horrors: burning bodies, piles of burning bodies. It's a truism because it's true: words aren't enough to describe it.

ROBERT ABZUG: You walked through a beautiful, manicured German village, and at the end of the road was this camp that looked like hell piled with corpses.

For a soldier like Salinger walking into a camp, there was a stillness to it and a craziness to it. You were caught off guard. You weren't psyched for battle. These weren't liberations in the sense of busting down the gates or anything like that. The war was over; you could let down your guard a little. These soldiers basically walked into these horrific situations. Unguarded and unsuspecting, they were walking into an open place. This was like opening up, and falling into, a graveyard.

EBERHARD ALSEN: Salinger has never described in writing what he witnessed at the Kaufering concentration camp, but it permeates his life and work.

Burned corpses at Kaufering IV.

SHANE SALERNO: He did comment on it to his daughter, Margaret, and to Jean Miller.

MARGARET SALINGER: As a counter-intelligence officer my father was one of the first soldiers to walk into a certain, just liberated, concentration camp. He told me the name, but I no longer remember.

J. D. SALINGER: You never really get the smell of burning flesh out of your nose entirely, no matter how long you live.

JEAN MILLER: He did not talk about the war and his experiences in the war. The only thing he said to me once is that you never forget the smell of burning flesh.

—

EBERHARD ALSEN: Kaufering IV was a catchall camp for the sick prisoners of the other small camps in the area. It was called the *Krankenlager* (camp for the sick), but it was actually an extermination camp, because the sick prisoners were simply allowed to die from their illnesses or from starvation. On the day before American troops occupied the area, the SS guards evacuated some three thousand prisoners via railroad boxcars and killed all those who were too sick or too weak to travel. They shot, clubbed, and hacked to death ninety-two prisoners, and they burned alive eighty-six others by locking them in wooden barracks and setting the barracks on fire. When the Americans arrived, all the SS guards were gone and only a handful of prisoners were still alive. They had escaped extermination by hiding from the SS. In addition to the 360 prisoners whom the SS had killed before pulling out, the GIs found two mass graves containing the bodies of another 4,500 prisoners who had died from sickness or malnutrition.

The SS evacuated people from Camp IV, the one that Salinger came upon, and as the SS was trying to march them to railroad cars, a lot of the inmates tried to escape and the SS butchered them with machine guns. Some bodies were actually cut in half by machine-gun fire. The SS had also slaughtered them with axes. The GIs found bloody axes next to the corpses.

So as Salinger and his driver drove up to the camp—as a counterintelligence officer, Salinger had access to vehicles other soldiers did not—they saw the almost one hundred corpses lying in the area between the camp and the railroad siding. Then, entering the camp, they saw stacks of emaciated corpses. Salinger and his driver continued into the camp and found the source of the terrible smell: there were three barracks buildings, nothing much more than large doghouses, half underground, and these buildings the Nazis had nailed shut with the sick people inside and set on fire. Salinger and his driver saw the burned bodies still smoldering in those ruins.

ALEX KERSHAW: They were behind barbed wire, starved, beaten, tortured, killed.

ROBERT ABZUG: It was the shock of seeing something unexpected. Kaufering was discovered a day or two before the main camp of Dachau. None of these troops had seen anything like it.

Bodies at Kaufering IV.

EBERHARD ALSEN: The German SS realized the Americans were approaching. They tried to evacuate all the able-bodied prisoners in so-called death marches. In the case of the camp that Salinger visited, the Krankenlager, the camp for the sick, a lot of the people there were unable to walk, so these people were killed by the SS.

When American soldiers discovered the abandoned camp on April 27, 1945, they were greeted by the smell of burning bodies, as the SS had set fire to several earth huts full of prisoners and shot all those who tried to escape the flames. As they went into the camp, the U.S. soldiers saw corpses that had been stacked like cordwood, as one soldier said, and as they looked at these bodies, they saw that they were only skin and bones. The estimate is that most of them weighed between fifty and seventy pounds. They had obviously been starved to death.

Most of what the GIs found were bodies.

JACK HALLETT: The first thing I saw was a stack of bodies . . . that appeared to be about 20 feet long and about as high as a man could reach. . . . And which looked like cordwood, stacked up there. The thing I'll never forget was the fact that closer inspection found people whose eyes were still blinking, three or four deep inside the stack.

DEBORAH DASH MOORE: The camp assaulted Salinger, as it did any of the soldiers who entered it, with the smell and also with the sight of naked bodies stacked up in piles—bodies that looked like they were dead people, but sometimes sounds coming from the bodies and soldiers realizing that in fact they were still alive. They discovered people who were so incredibly thin that their cheekbones stuck out almost like horns. Their wrists protruded. The skin was stretched over their bodies like a nylon stocking: you could see through it to the bones. Nothing in their experience—and Salinger was an experienced soldier by this time and had been through terrible battles—nothing in their experience could have prepared them for the sight.

ALEX KERSHAW: As Salinger looked at them, these men would duck their heads in submission. They looked like beaten dogs. They were afraid to look another man in the eye in case they would be shot or killed or beaten. That image—of men who couldn't even look their liberators in the eye—remained with many of those Americans for the rest of their lives.

SHANE SALERNO: Paul Fitzgerald, Salinger's close friend and fellow CIC agent, was next to Salinger when they liberated the camp. A female survivor handed Fitzgerald a stack of photographs she had of the atrocities that had occurred at Kaufering IV. Fitzgerald held onto these photographs and didn't show them to anyone until 1980, at which point he sent them to the Holocaust Library and Research Center of San Francisco, writing, "I have had this album for thirty-five years now. . . . This is my own personal memory of a terrible nightmare." Max R. Garcia, the director of the Center, wrote to Fitzgerald's intermediary, August Carella, "Please convey my thanks to Mr. Paul J. Fitzgerald for allowing me to see the album of the gruesome photographs he brought back from his WWII days. The photographs of the torture devices I have never seen before and they are indeed eye openers. It and the other photographs clearly indicate the brutality of the Nazi regime that reigned at that time."

ROBERT ABZUG: Soldiers like Salinger, any of the GIs coming into these camps, were shocked, but they somehow had to make human sense out of it all. They'd look at bodies and try to find some human feature, some lifeness. The living dead were even worse for them to confront, because they would stagger right into their faces and sometimes try to embrace them.

When American GIs walked into a camp, the shock was so horrendous that they'd just break down in tears. They'd fall on the ground. Some of them had to be immediately treated by doctors. These are the liberators I'm talking about now, not the inmates.

Medieval painters painted visions of hell, but this was the real thing: a graveyard of corpses and half-dead people. Imagine walking into a place where there are skeletal remains and burnt bodies and the smell of flesh. The stench was impossible to deal with. You would see people piled high on bunks, two and three and four deep. Some were dead, some were alive, and it took some time to figure out who was dead and who was alive. All were gaunt. Their eyes bugged out of their faces. They whimpered. There was the smell of urine and feces and rotting flesh.

ROBERT TOWNE: Eisenhower saw Buchenwald and Dachau the minute they were liberated. His reaction to them was instructive. He insisted that cameramen from all over the world get there and photograph these things. He pulled General Patton and other officers in and said,

"You've got to look at this, because there will come a time when people will not believe that this actually happened. It's too appalling." All you can say for sure is that for someone who was there, it would be the existential moment of his life. It would have to have a lifelong effect on you. I can't imagine it otherwise.

ROBERT ABZUG: There is a famous photo of Kaufering Commandant Eichelsdorfer, standing amid the dead bodies, and the odd part about it is, there he is. He has a straight face, as if this were everyday work. That was the way it happened. The numbness the GIs felt from the sensory overload the Germans also felt, not only because they were ardent Nazis but because they came to live with it. It was daily life, whether you were a guard or a commandant. It was a job. It's clear in the photograph that this was the everyday world for Eichelsdorfer.

Johann Baptist Eichelsdorfer, the commandant of Kaufering IV.

—

ALEX KERSHAW: As Nazi Germany fell apart in the spring of 1945, the prime objective of counterintelligence officers like J. D. Salinger was to try to find the criminals, the Nazis who had created the unimaginable. I befriended an intelligence officer who had the same rank and interrogation duties Salinger had in the spring of 1945. On one occasion, the officer entered a camp hospital, searching for Nazis. He discovered a few in the hospital beds pretending to be wounded or concentration camp survivors—Germans who had taken the shredded uniforms of camp inmates to avoid arrest, pretending to be Jewish forced laborers. They looked unnaturally healthy compared to their disguise. The officer told me counterintelligence officers lost patience with German prisoners after they discovered the camps. Uncooperative Nazis received severe interrogations. It was very hard for interrogators to remain patient when they knew the well-fed German in front of them had probably shot and killed countless civilians.

ROBERT ABZUG: Some GIs handed their weapons to the few healthy prisoners and allowed them to tear apart or shoot (or both) captured German camp guards. There was a whole cycle of almost uncontrollable revenge. It got out of hand for a little while. For a soldier like Salinger, who'd been through so much violence, one would have to wonder, what was the final psychic straw in this illogical world turned upside down? At least in battle you had an enemy.

There was something different about the liberations that pushed soldiers like Salinger over the edge. When you're in the military and fighting battles, there is logic to it. When the soldiers came upon these camps, there was no battle to win. They were at an extremely vulnerable moment, because for most of them this was the very last thing that was going to happen to them during the war.

—

EBERHARD ALSEN: The fact that Salinger was half-Jewish must have made his experience of seeing the atrocities that the Germans committed against Jews even more devastating.

ROBERT ABZUG: Here he was, a survivor of horrendously anonymous, mechanized killing on a vast scale, but the pervading horrors of the camps reminded him he was Jewish.

LEILA HADLEY LUCE: I never thought of Jerry as being Jewish. I never thought of any of my friends as being Jewish. They were just friends. He did remind me that he was very concerned about the Holocaust. He was very emotionally distressed by this, and by the concentration camps.

DEBORAH DASH MOORE: Salinger and the Allies discovered what had been done and wondered, Did we actually win the war? Or did we come too late? Mind-eating questions with no appropriate answer. They already knew; they'd seen and fought it. Europe was a graveyard. Suddenly it was a massive Jewish graveyard.

DAVID SHIELDS: While he was not on the front lines of combat, he was certainly on the front lines of the Holocaust, and it stayed with him forever.

RICHARD STAYTON: We have a hard time understanding, because we aren't Salinger; we weren't there. I've known other GIs who liberated camps and weren't Jewish. The experience broke apart their psyches, too. They've never recovered, either.

—

ALEX KERSHAW: Of the 337 days the war lasted for the American soldier in Europe, Salinger was in combat for 299. How damaged he was we don't know. After two hundred days of combat, you are insane. They did the studies. Even the strong guys, after two hundred days, would lose it. After taking another village, they'd be found somewhere on their own, crying silent tears. Salinger's division was in combat longer than any other division in the European theater. He saw the worst fighting you could possibly see, maybe, in the entire Second World War. Anyone who lived through this level of fierce combat this long would have been profoundly affected.

PAUL ALEXANDER: Salinger told [Whit] Burnett he simply could not describe the events of the last three or four weeks [of the war]. What he had witnessed was too horrendous to put into words. Yet even as he was making this gut-wrenching and dramatic revelation, Salinger still felt compelled to discuss, of all things, business. Apparently, Burnett had last written to suggest that Salinger publish his novel before his story collection. In response, Salinger agreed, adding that he could be finished with the novel in six months once he returned to the States. That's how Salinger left it with Burnett before he thanked him for accepting "Elaine," the story the *New Yorker* had rejected. "Elaine," which centers on a mildly retarded girl with few prospects for happiness, was a longish, informal-feeling piece written before Salinger's experiences in late 1944.

J. D. SALINGER ("Elaine," *Story*, March–April 1945):

> But now—the sudden vast, lonely expanse of a deserted public beach at dusk came as a terrible visitation upon her. The beach itself, which before had been only a fair-sized manifestation of tiny handfuls of hot sand which could slip with petty ecstasy through the fingers, was now a great monster sprawled across infinity, prejudiced personally against Elaine, ready to swallow her up—or cast her, with an ogreish laugh, into the sea.

—

ALEX KERSHAW: I talked to liberators of the camps who said the prisoners would go to the wire and hands would be thrust through, hands that you could hardly recognize as a human hand. There was bone and it was begging. For what? Maybe the flesh the GIs were wearing.

ROBERT ABZUG: The scene is not one of battle; the scene is one of the desecration of humanity. One soldier talked about living skeletons' feeble attempts to applaud the liberating GIs. They couldn't even put their hands together properly; it was almost like act without sound.

DEBORAH DASH MOORE: At the beginning of *Nine Stories* Salinger asks the Zen question: What is the sound of one hand clapping? Well, we know the sound of two. One of the Jewish soldiers who entered a camp heard the sound of people trying to clap for the American GIs. Because there was no flesh on their hands, it sounded strangely muted, otherworldly.

ALEX KERSHAW: For Salinger and his generation of Americans who liberated those camps, the legacy of the war hung on that disconnection, those memories, and many other war moments like it, where at the end of all the suffering and dying, you came to a place of irrefutable justification for the preceding slaughter, a hell needing redemption—you came face-to-face with the greatest victims of that war, the Holocaust victims, but the event has destroyed human experience as they all knew and once understood it. In the memory of witnesses like Salinger, there was nothing that could cleanse or salve, resurrect, or make sense of it. Even those rescued were destroyed.

In Salinger's greatest triumph is the worst tragedy. In the last chapter of a war out of proportion to any that had gone before, of good-versus-

Kaufering IV.

evil where good had won, the good, soul-cleansing final chapter was, perhaps, the most soul-destroying and disillusioning.

LESLIE EPSTEIN: We know, as Seymour [a key figure in many of Salinger's stories and novellas] knew, what men are. No more naïveté, no more denial. There isn't one of us who isn't in some way writing about the war—and the Holocaust, too, though we may not fully know it.

—

ALEX KERSHAW: It had been an epic and enormously costly deployment for the 4th Division, an incredible journey. Salinger saw the worst fighting you could possibly see. It's impossible to imagine what Salinger must have experienced as he endured such enormous pain and suffering and damage done to other human beings around him. He had seen the worst that man can do to man. What Salinger experienced was a continual assault on his senses, physically, mentally, spiritually.

EBERHARD ALSEN: Salinger's daughter, Margaret, examined the letters that her father wrote during the spring and summer of 1945 and reports that his "handwriting became something totally unrecognizable."

DAVID SHIELDS: It's hard not to make the case that, in some sense, the war finally caught up to Salinger.

EBERHARD ALSEN: Salinger's nervous breakdown was not due to the stress of combat . . . because he was not an infantryman. Kaufering Lager IV was what broke Salinger.

7

VICTIM AND PERPETRATOR

The war was over; Salinger's war is just beginning. Hospitalized in Nuremberg for "battle fatigue" [Post-traumatic Stress Disorder], he recovers, marries a German woman, and brings home the "most violent kind of happiness."

NBC BROADCAST: The National Broadcasting Company delays the start of all its programs to bring you a special bulletin. It was announced in San Francisco half an hour ago, by a high American official, not identified, that Germany has surrendered unconditionally to the Allies, no strings attached.

ALEX KERSHAW: There would be no more firing, no more death, no more killing, no more destruction. It was over. They could look forward to life. The sacrifices that had been made, the horrors they'd seen, were over. V-E Day meant that they were on their way home. Salinger survived, but he was terribly, terribly damaged.

JOHN McMANUS: Howard Ruppel, a paratrooper in the 517th Parachute Infantry Regiment, wanted nothing to do with anyone or anything about the war. In an effort to forget the war, he refused to join veteran organizations.

HOWARD RUPPEL: I didn't want to rehash, refight . . . re-create images, or relive memories in a social atmosphere. I sought no recognition or special attention. I didn't want to be thought of as a hero. I didn't want my past life to interfere with my future life. I wanted to get on with living, in the manner I chose.

LAWRENCE GROBEL: Salinger went through a psychic breakdown during World War II. I don't have any doubt it had an enormous effect on his sense of humanity. Why do people go to war? Why do they kill each other? How can there be a Dachau or an Auschwitz? He had seen the other side of man.

EBERHARD ALSEN: Salinger's subversive comments about the war in his fiction are tame compared to what he wrote in a letter to Elizabeth Murray on May 13, 1945. He wrote that even though World War II was over, his "own little war over here will go on for some time." He admits that his "most casual thoughts over here are edgy with treason. It's been a mess, Elizabeth. Wonder if you have any idea." He says he's happy to have missed the V-E Day celebrations back home (they "would have been too poignant, too moving for this kid"); instead, he celebrated V-E Day by "wondering what close relatives would think if I fired a .45 slug neatly, but effectively through the palm of my left hand [a notorious way for soldiers to get cashiered out of a war zone], and how long it would take me to learn to type with what was left of my hand." Salinger concludes by saying, "I have three battle stars and am due a fourth, and I intend to have them all grafted onto my nostrils, two on each side." Salinger wound up receiving five battle stars and a Presidential Unit Citation for Valor. "What a tricky, dreary farce, and how many men are dead."

ALEX KERSHAW: In July 1945 he hospitalized himself in Nuremberg and was treated for combat stress reaction, battle fatigue.

SHANE SALERNO: It wasn't one event that put Salinger in the hospital in Nuremberg. It was a culmination of events: going through eleven months of war, being forced to witness atrocities beyond human imagination. He submerged his feelings—fear, anguish, pain—about losing his brothers-in-arms. Submerging that pain has a cost. At the end of the war, Salinger finally had time to think about what he had just endured over the past year. All of those memories, all of those feelings finally erupted, to devastating effect. And he became so profoundly despondent—he used the word "despondent" himself—that he could no longer function. And he admitted himself to the hospital for psychiatric evaluation.

—

EBERHARD ALSEN: It was extraordinary to visit the hospital where Salinger was treated for two weeks for his nervous breakdown, particularly since the layout of the place hasn't changed very much. For instance, a couple of the windows still had steel bars over them.

LEILA HADLEY LUCE: I felt he'd been seriously distressed by the war. He didn't exactly say that he'd had a nervous breakdown, but you felt—I felt—that was what had happened to him, because he'd been hospitalized in Nuremberg.

EBERHARD ALSEN: It is from there that he wrote to Hemingway in July 1945. In the letter, Salinger reports that he has checked himself into "a General Hospital in Nurnberg" because he has been in "an almost constant state of despondency." He tries to downplay his mental collapse by making fun of the psychiatrists asking him about his childhood and his sex life, but he also makes it clear why he checked himself into a civilian and not a military hospital.

The letter is not dated, but Salinger's reference to the 4th Division having already returned to the United States shows that it must have been written after June 25, 1945. This means that Salinger's nervous breakdown occurred probably just weeks after the end of the war. We know that he committed himself to a civilian hospital in order to avoid a psychiatric discharge from the army, and that his stay at the Municipal Hospital in Nuremberg was for only two weeks. He wrote Hemingway about his breakdown because he knew Hemingway had seen combat firsthand, not just during World War II, when he was an honorary war correspondent, but during World War I, when he was severely wounded. Salinger probably felt Hemingway would understand what he was going through.

J. D. SALINGER, excerpt from letter to Ernest Hemingway, undated:

> *Dear Poppa,*
>
> *I'm writing from a General Hospital in Nurnberg. There's a notable absence of Catherine Barclay's* [the heroine of *A Farewell*

to Arms], is all I've got to say. . . . There's nothing wrong with me except that I've been in an almost constant state of despondency and I thought it would be good to talk to somebody sane. . . . How is your novel coming? I hope you're working hard on it. Don't sell it to the movies. You're a rich guy. As Chairman of your many fan clubs, I know I speak for all the members when I say Down with Gary Cooper. . . . I'd give my right arm to get out of the Army, but not on a psychiatric, this-man-is-not-fit-for-the-Army life ticket. I have a very sensitive novel in mind, and I won't have the author called a jerk in 1950. I am a jerk, but the wrong people mustn't know it. . . . Removed from the scene, is it much easier to think clearly? I mean with your work. . . . The talks I had with you were the only hopeful minutes of the whole business. . . .

P.S. . . . My book of stories project collapsed. Which is really a good thing, and no sour grapes. I'm still tied up with lies and affectations, and to see my name on a dust jacket would postpone [the letter cuts off here].

SHANE SALERNO: In September 1945, Salinger declines Simon & Schuster's offer to publish his story collection. "They write letters like civilians," he says, calling them a "smart-ass publisher."

DAVID SHIELDS: During the war, Salinger had written, in a letter, "I carry a .45 on my hip these days. Woe to the critic who, on reading my collected stories, might call me 'promising' or 'bears watching' or 'immature.'"

What is most interesting about Salinger's letter to Hemingway is the way it careens from charming performance to anguished confession to craven sycophancy. On the one hand, the letter is uncannily prescient—about the former nurse who would become Salinger's third wife, his push-pull relationship with the movies, the fine line between Holden/Salinger's being sensitive and being a jerk; on the other hand, it's an unintentional portrait of a psyche coming undone; this is Sergeant X, in serious distress.

It's also Kenneth Caulfield, Salinger's alter ego in "An Ocean Full of Bowling Balls," written at this time. "Ocean" was never published; it was sold to the *Women's Home Companion* in 1947 but determined to be too "downbeat." Salinger later bought back the story and, as he did with "The Last and Best of the Peter Pans," donated it to Princeton University's Firestone Library. He left instructions that the story can be read only under supervision and cannot be published until 2060.

In "Ocean," Vincent, a writer, writes a story about a man who tells his wife that he goes bowling every week when in actuality he visits another woman instead. After his death, his widow discovers the affair and throws the bowling ball out the window. When Vincent shows the story to his brother Kenneth, Kenneth says that he doesn't like it; it's too harsh in its treatment of both the husband and the wife. In Kenneth's view, Vincent should write about more positive things. Vincent and Kenneth go to the beach, where Kenneth reads to Vincent their brother Holden's letter from summer camp in which Holden criticizes the hypocrisy of the adults there.

Vincent doesn't want Kenneth, who has a heart condition, to go swimming, but he does, saying the ocean looks like it's full of bowling balls. As Kenneth walks out of the ocean, a swell hits him, and he collapses. Vincent rushes him home and calls a doctor, but Kenneth dies.

Survivor's guilt. Many of the stories Salinger was writing in 1944 and '45—"Last Day of the Last Furlough," "A Boy in France," "This Sandwich Has No Mayonnaise," "The Stranger," and "An Ocean Full of Bowling Balls"—feature members of the Caulfield family or their friends. Phoebe appears again in "Ocean." Kenneth becomes Allie in *Catcher*. Vincent becomes D.B. All of these characters are vectors on a fictional grid of the Caulfield family, which then became the Glass family, alternative populations to counteract the horror show.

—

SHANE SALERNO: Salinger was honorably discharged on November 22, 1945, in Frankfurt but signed a civilian contract with the Defense Department as an intelligence agent stationed at Gunzenhausen. It took significant effort to obtain Salinger's military records; for several years we were told they had been destroyed in a fire and then in a flood.

FIRST LIEUTENANT A. RAYMOND BOUDREAU:

To Whom it May Concern:

Jerome D. Salinger has been an agent in the Counterintelligence corps since 1943, serving both in the Zone of the Interior, the United States, and overseas. As a member of the Fourth Infantry Division CIC

Detachment, Salinger came to Normandy as part of the first waves of troops to invade France on June 6, 1944. Later he was transferred to CIC Detachment 970/63 commanded by Lt. Robert Williams under whose supervision he worked until the undersigned assumed command of the detachment in August 1945. Since that time he has performed his duties continuously under my personal direct supervision.

The duties performed by Salinger have varied but always have required a high degree of skill, judgment and honesty. He has conducted investigations, both alone and in connections with others, detailing with de-Nazification, sabotage, espionage, security to American troops and installations as well as intelligence.

At all times he has conducted himself and dispatched his tasks with a brand of performance that has reflected nothing but honor on himself and the Counterintelligence Corps. Both his character and living habits are exemplary, and the pleasantness of his personality has contributed substantially to an efficient, good relationship with all persons with whom he has come in contact.

The writer has been at a loss to replace Salinger's services and recommends him unqualifiedly as one who has contributed much in loyal and devoted services to the armed Forces of the Nation.

EBERHARD ALSEN: After his honorable discharge, Salinger signed up for a new tour of duty in order to be part of the de-Nazification program.

COUNTER INTELLIGENCE CORPS HISTORY AND MISSION IN WORLD WAR II: By 10 May 1945, the 12th Army Group Counter Intelligence Corps Detachment was activated by orders from Theater Headquarters, and the new phase of operations was launched. The personnel of this detachment were prepared for their assignment, both by experience and instruction.

After the unconditional surrender of the enemy to the Allied Forces, greater emphasis was placed on the de-Nazification of Germany. Divisional areas were divided into sectors with a Counter Intelligence Corps team for each, and those party offices and buildings which were sealed during the advance were reopened and thoroughly examined. Informants in each area were developed and leads were secured which led to the arrest of many persons of high rank and position in the Nazi regime.

Largely through the efforts of informants, many former Gestapo

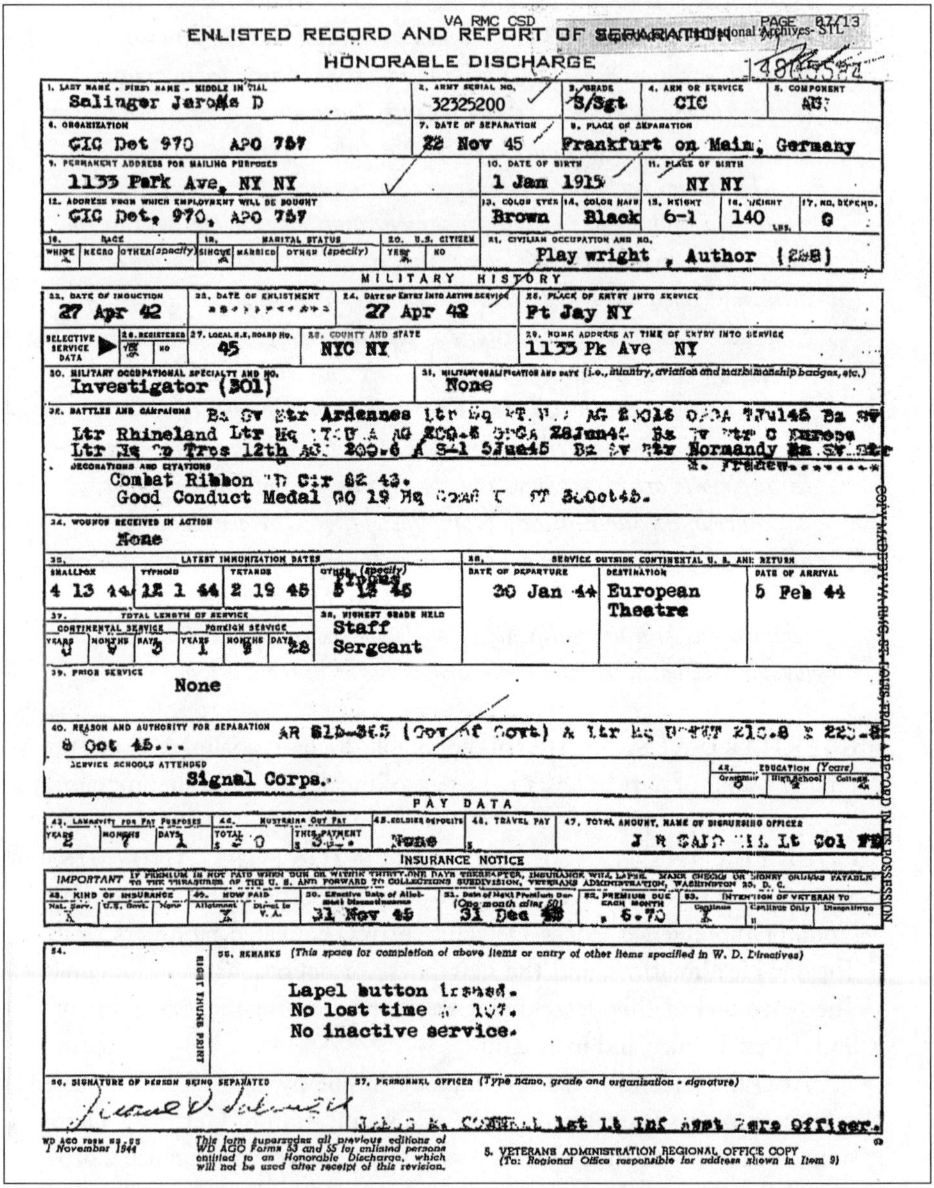

VA RMC CSD PAGE 07/13

National Archives-STL

ENLISTED RECORD AND REPORT OF SEPARATION

HONORABLE DISCHARGE

1. Last name - first name - middle initial	Salinger Jerome D
2. Army serial no.	32325200
3. Grade	S/Sgt
4. Arm or service	CIC
5. Component	AUS
6. Organization	CIC Det 970 APO 757
7. Date of separation	22 Nov 45
8. Place of separation	Frankfurt on Main, Germany
9. Permanent address for mailing purposes	1133 Park Ave, NY NY
10. Date of birth	1 Jan 1919
11. Place of birth	NY NY
12. Address from which employment will be sought	CIC Det, 970, APO 757
13. Color eyes	Brown
14. Color hair	Black
15. Height	6-1
16. Weight	140 lbs.
17. No. depend.	0
18. Race	White X
19. Marital status	Single X
20. U.S. citizen	Yes X
21. Civilian occupation and no.	Play wright, Author (2??)

MILITARY HISTORY

22. Date of induction	27 Apr 42
23. Date of enlistment	**********
24. Date of entry into active service	27 Apr 42
25. Place of entry into service	Ft Jay NY
26. Selective service data: Registered	Yes X
27. Local S.S. board no.	45
28. County and state	NYC NY
29. Home address at time of entry into service	1133 Pk Ave NY
30. Military occupational specialty and no.	Investigator (301)
31. Military qualification and date (i.e., infantry, aviation and marksmanship badges, etc.)	None
32. Battles and campaigns	Bz Sv Str Ardennes Ltr Hq ... AG 200.6 ... Bz Sv Str Rhineland Ltr Hq ... AG 200.6 ... 28Jun45 Bz Sv Str C Europe Ltr Hq ... 12th AG 200.6 A S-1 5Jun45 Bz Sv Str Normandy Bz Sv Str N. France
33. Decorations and citations	Combat Ribbon ... Cir 62 43. Good Conduct Medal GO 19 Hq ... 8Oct45.
34. Wounds received in action	None
35. Latest immunization dates	Smallpox 4 13 44; Typhoid 12 1 44; Tetanus 2 19 45; Other (specify) Typhus 5 12 45
36. Service outside continental U.S. and return	Date of departure 30 Jan 44; Destination European Theatre; Date of arrival 5 Feb 44
37. Total length of service	Continental service: Years 0, Months 9, Days 3; Foreign service: Years 1, Months 9, Days 28
38. Highest grade held	Staff Sergeant
39. Prior service	None
40. Reason and authority for separation	AR 615-365 (Cov of Govt) & Ltr Hq ... 220.8 ... 8 Oct 45...
41. Service schools attended	Signal Corps.
42. Education (Years)	Grammar 8; High School 4; College 2

PAY DATA

43. Longevity for pay purposes	Years 2, Months 7, Days 1
44. Mustering out pay	Total $ 300; This payment $ 300
45. Soldier deposits	None
46. Travel pay	$
47. Total amount, name of disbursing officer	J R SAID ... Lt Col FD

INSURANCE NOTICE

IMPORTANT IF PREMIUM IS NOT PAID WHEN DUE OR WITHIN THIRTY-ONE DAYS THEREAFTER, INSURANCE WILL LAPSE. MAKE CHECKS OR MONEY ORDERS PAYABLE TO THE TREASURER OF THE U. S. AND FORWARD TO COLLECTIONS SUBDIVISION, VETERANS ADMINISTRATION, WASHINGTON 25, D. C.

48. Kind of insurance	Nat. Serv. X
49. How paid	Allotment X
50. Effective date of allotment discontinuance	31 Nov 45
51. Date of next premium due (One month after 50)	31 Dec 45
52. Premium due each month	$ 6.70
53. Intention of veteran to	Continue X

54. RIGHT THUMB PRINT

55. REMARKS (This space for completion of above items or entry of other items specified in W. D. Directives)

Lapel button issued.
No lost time AW 107.
No inactive service.

56. SIGNATURE OF PERSON BEING SEPARATED: [signature]

57. PERSONNEL OFFICER (Type name, grade and organization - signature): J... B. CONNELL 1st Lt Inf Asst Pers Officer.

WD AGO FORM NO. 53
1 November 1944

This form supersedes all previous editions of WD AGO Forms 53 and 55 for enlisted persons entitled to an Honorable Discharge, which will not be used after receipt of this revision.

5. VETERANS ADMINISTRATION REGIONAL OFFICE COPY
(To: Regional Office responsible for address shown in Item 9)

COPY MADE BY VA RMC, ST. LOUIS, FROM A RECORD IN ITS POSSESSION

Salinger's Enlisted Record and Report of Separation, Honorable Discharge.

agents were apprehended, who otherwise might have escaped the notice of the Counter Intelligence Corps. In the crowded cities of Germany, it was almost impossible to ferret these people out without the aid of the native informant who worked undercover.

In general, the mission of the Counter Intelligence Corps was to secure our forces from espionage, sabotage, and subversion and to destroy all enemy intelligence services.

Generally, it had been found that of all the persons included in the Supreme Headquarters Allied Expeditionary Force directives as automatic arrestees, only the lower echelon remained in place, while the higher Nazi Party members moved on. Many of those remaining, often older men, appeared to be shoved into office with the expectation that they would be arrested instead of the more fanatical officials.

The Counter Intelligence Corps in France and Germany did its job well. The security which the Corps afforded to the armed forces was one contributing factor toward the eventual victory of the Allies.

ALEX KERSHAW: Salinger got to be a detective. A detective in uniform. His basic job was to chase down the bad guys, whether they be Nazis that were pretending to be civilians, collaborators, or black-market operators. He actually got to look into the dark heart of Nazi Germany and interrogate the people who committed the greatest crimes in human history. And bring them to justice.

EBERHARD ALSEN: There has been a rumor for many years that one of the people Salinger interviewed and arrested was a woman by the name of Sylvia.

Sylvia's father was Ernst Friedrich Welter. He was born in Paris on March 31, 1890. He had a dual citizenship, French and German, and was a prosperous merchant. Sylvia's mother, born on November 18, 1890, was Luise Berta Depireux. Despite her French surname, she was a German citizen. Sylvia was born in Frankfurt on April 19, 1919, and when her parents registered her birth, the Frankfurt Einwohnermeldeamt (the resident registration office) listed her as a citizen of Germany.

Two months after her birth, the Welter family moved to Lugano in the Italian-speaking part of Switzerland. Sylvia's sister, Alice, was born there in 1921. Later that year the family moved back to Germany. They first lived in the Alpine resort of Garmisch and later moved to Nuremberg, where Sylvia received her secondary education. After graduating in 1938, Sylvia briefly attended several European universities, in Erlangen, Munich, Prague, and Königsberg, before enrolling in medical school at the University of Innsbruck in Austria on November 24, 1941. She received her doctorate in medicine in February 1945. On March 10, 1945, she moved to Weissenburg, Bavaria. On her Weissenburg resident registration form, her nationality is listed as "D.R.," which stands for "Deutsches Reich" (German Empire). Her address in Weissenburg was an apartment in the Kehler Weg 10a (now Schillerstrasse 1). She was employed as an intern at the Weissenburg city hospital from March 12 to June 30, 1945. That hospital was on the Krankenhausstrasse 2, now Dr. Dörfler Strasse 2.

Salinger came to Weissenburg on May 13, 1945, when the CIC established a field office there. It was located in a mansion at Nürnbergerstrasse. Salinger and his CIC buddies were quartered in a house on what is now Dr. Dörfler Strasse. In a letter written on May 13, 1945, Salinger says that he doesn't know how long he'll have to stay with his buddies and that he can't wait to get a room of his own.

Salinger first met Sylvia near the end of May 1945, after he met her sister, Alice, who worked at the Nuremberg military hospital on Rothenburger Strasse. Salinger gave Alice a ride to Weissenburg to visit her mother and her sister, who lived right around the corner from Salinger's quarters. That's how Salinger met Sylvia.

In a letter to Elizabeth Murray in late September 1945, he says that he's going to stay in Germany for another year because he's about to get married to Sylvia. In a letter to a friend, he calls Sylvia a "French girl. Very fine, very sensitive."

MARGARET SALINGER: My Aunt [Doris] described Sylvia to me as a tall, thin woman with dark hair, pale skin, and blood-red lips and nails. She had a sharp, incisive way of speaking and was some sort of a doctor. My aunt said, "She was *very* German."

SHANE SALERNO: We hired the literary scholar, Salinger expert, and German native Eberhard Alsen to travel to Germany to conduct an extensive investigation into Salinger's year in the European Theater and postwar experience in Germany.

EBERHARD ALSEN: In the May 1945 operations report of the 4th

One of many never-before-seen photographs of Sylvia and J. D. Salinger on their wedding day, October 18, 1945.

Infantry Division, there is a directive from its commander, General Harold W. Blakely, saying that violations of the nonfraternization law would be severely punished. American soldiers caught with German women could be jailed for six months and lose two-thirds of their pay. Salinger's reluctance to tell his friends and family in the United States that his bride was a native of Germany is understandable. Not just because of the nonfraternization law, but because the Nuremberg war crimes trials were still going on, and the horrific images of the concentration camps were fresh in everyone's mind.

Salinger and Sylvia were married in the small town of Pappenheim, ten miles south of Weissenburg, on October 18, 1945. Salinger gave his address as Dr. Dörfler Strasse 20 in Weissenburg and Sylvia's as Friedrich Strasse 57 in Nuremberg (her parents' house). The witnesses were two CIC buddies, Paul Fitzgerald and John Prinz. The Standesamt (birth and marriage registry) of Pappenheim listed Sylvia's nationality as French. Utilizing his counterintelligence skills, Salinger forged French identification papers for Sylvia in order to circumvent the nonfraternization law.

While Salinger worked for the CIC as a special agent—from November 22, 1945, to April 30, 1946—his job was to hunt down Nazis who were in hiding. During much of that time, he and Sylvia lived in Gunzenhausen, ten miles northeast of Weissenburg, in a mansion called the Villa Schmidt. The address was Wiesen Strasse 12 (now Rot-Kreuz Strasse 12). They employed a cook and a woman to do their laundry.

J. D. and Sylvia Salinger's wedding day, October 18, 1945, Weissenburg, Germany; center: Sylvia; to her left, Salinger, with his arm around his best man, Paul Fitzgerald.

J. D. and Sylvia Salinger, October 1945.

Sometime in February 1946, Salinger and Sylvia moved into two rooms at the back of her parents' large apartment on Friedrich Strasse in Nuremberg. When Sylvia's cousin, Bernhard Horn, visited her in March, her sister, Alice, warned him that the young couple had been fighting a lot.

According to the Berlin Bundesarchiv, Sylvia was not a member of the Nazi Party, the Reichsärztekammer, the Nazi-controlled National Physicians Chamber, or even the Bund Deutscher Mädels, the Nazi-controlled Federation of German Girls, to which most German girls belonged.

However, there are a number of strange facts about Sylvia's life that suggest she might have been a Gestapo informant. First, when she was in Switzerland in 1939, she lost her passport and had the German consulate in Geneva issue her a new one. This information comes from the Gestapo files in the Nuremberg city archive. Why would the Gestapo have a file on a twenty-year-old student?

Second, between 1939 and 1942, Sylvia was enrolled at six different universities: Erlangen, Munich, Prague, Königsberg, Freiburg, and Inns-

J. D. and Sylvia Salinger on their wedding day, October 18, 1945, with her sister and her parents.

bruck. Before World War II, most German students typically switched universities at least once in their career, but it is highly unusual—really unheard of—for anyone to attend six different ones. This is consistent with Gestapo practices of hiring individuals (particularly attractive young women) who were not "officially" aligned with the party to spy on fellow students and possibly even faculty members. The Gestapo was not a well-staffed organization and relied heavily on paid informants. For instance, the six Gestapo officers of the Nuremberg office were responsible for all of northern Bavaria and employed between eighty and one hundred informants. It is possible that the Gestapo used Sylvia as an informant to gather material on the anti-Nazi student movement. Between 1942 and 1943 the Gestapo arrested and executed many of the leaders of this movement. Among them were Hans and Sophie Scholl, who headed the Munich student resistance group called the White Rose.

Salinger has more to say about Sylvia in a letter to Elizabeth Murray that he wrote on December 30, 1945. The dateline of this letter is

J. D. and Sylvia Salinger, with her family, after the wedding.

the small town of Gunzenhausen, forty miles southwest of Nuremberg, where he and Sylvia were living by that time. They were living in the Villa Schmidt—which had been requisitioned by the CIC—had purchased a new automobile, a Škoda; and had adopted a black schnauzer named "Benny," who rides "on the running board, pointing out Nazis for me to arrest." Salinger signed a six-month civilian contract with the War Department, and he expects to go to America after this contract ended.

Later in the letter, he says that he and Sylvia are very happy, although his comments about her are barbed. He says that at Christmastime they had a big turkey, courtesy of the U.S. Army, and on the stroke of midnight they threw rotten eggs at each other. This, he jokes, is a custom of the people in the area.

—

SHANE SALERNO: His de-Nazification job complete, Salinger was in love with a German woman who was the punctuation to a bout of post-traumatic stress. He brought all this baggage home to New York and his family.

Salinger and his mother-in-law and his beloved schnauzer, Benny (the black dog).

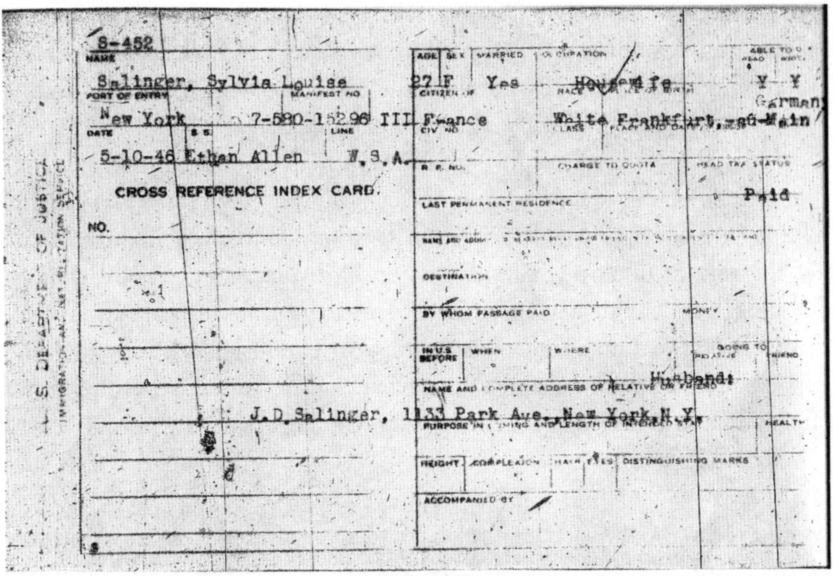
S-452
NAME
Salinger, Sylvia Louise
PORT OF ENTRY
New York 7-580-15296 III
MANIFEST NO
DATE S.S. LINE
5-10-46 Ethan Allen W.S.A.
CROSS REFERENCE INDEX CARD.
NO.
J.D.Salinger, 1133 Park Ave.,New York,N.Y.
AGE SEX MARRIED OCCUPATION
27 F Yes Housewife
ABLE TO READ WRITE Y Y
CITIZEN OF France
RACE
White Frankfurt, a/Main
German
HEAD TAX STATUS Paid
LAST PERMANENT RESIDENCE
DESTINATION
BY WHOM PASSAGE PAID
MONEY
IN U.S. BEFORE WHEN WHERE
NAME AND COMPLETE ADDRESS OF RELATIVE OR FRIEND
Husband:
HEIGHT COMPLEXION HAIR EYES DISTINGUISHING MARKS
ACCOMPANIED BY
HEALTH
U.S. DEPARTMENT OF JUSTICE

Passenger manifest of Sylvia Salinger's arrival in New York Harbor.

EBERHARD ALSEN: I looked at the [Immigration and Naturalization Service] passenger arrival forms for American ships that arrived in America in May and June 1946. The Salingers arrived in New York City on May 10, 1946, on board the ship *Ethan Allen*, which was sailing under the War Shipping Administration. The U.S. Army had leased a large number of vessels to transport GIs back to the United States. Sylvia Salinger gave her middle name as Louise, her age as twenty-seven years, and her nationality as French but her birthplace as Frankfurt am Main in Germany. One question on the form asked for the name of a friend or relative who would vouch for her while she was in the United States. Sylvia wrote, "Husband, J. D. Salinger, 1133 Park Avenue, New York." Salinger and Sylvia decided to withold the information that Sylvia was a doctor. Under profession, she wrote "housewife."

J. D. SALINGER, excerpt from letter to Paul Fitzgerald, May 24, 1946:

> *The trip over was hell, in a small way. Liberty Ship. Twelve passengers. No ballast in the hold. Rough weather all the way. Sylvia was sick the whole way, but Benny and I were old salts. My mother, father and sister were all at the docks.*

EBERHARD ALSEN: On May 10, Sylvia and her husband took up residence in the home of Salinger's parents at 1133 Park Avenue. Sylvia didn't get along with his family. Salinger's daughter, Margaret, claims that Sylvia hated Jews and Salinger hated Germans.

Margaret Salinger reports that her father's family didn't make Sylvia feel welcome when he brought her home to New York. His parents didn't like Sylvia, even though she was apparently a brilliant person, "some sort of doctor." Salinger's sister, Doris, later described Sylvia as looking like Morticia from the TV show *The Addams Family*. Apparently, Sylvia had an abrasive personality to go along with her witchlike appearance. To explain why Salinger had married an anti-Semite in the first place, Margaret quotes her mother, Claire, as saying that Sylvia had "bewitched" him.

ALEX KERSHAW: After the war, Salinger suffered from a classic veteran's syndrome: you come back from a war to the country that you saw so many people give their lives to protect, and all around you people don't have a clue what you did when you were over there.

DEBORAH DASH MOORE: Salinger would've come out of the war with nightmares that would not go away and which he would have been told insistently by society to put behind him. That was the message Americans gave to returning soldiers: "All right, you did a great job. Now put the war behind you and move on." That would've been a very difficult thing to do. Even his family wouldn't necessarily have understood.

STAFF SERGEANT DAVID RODERICK: You think about it daily. You have flashbacks. There was the daily expectation—probability—that you weren't going to make it because you'd be killed or wounded. It kind of wears on you after a period of time, makes it possible for people to snap after a while. There are times now when I'm sitting in my living room and have artillery land in my yard or in my living room. There's a flash, boom, you know it's artillery, and then it passes. I had a lot of times when I was under artillery fire. So you get those kinds of flashbacks. I've never told my wife that. I've never talked to other veterans about that, so I don't know if they're having those kinds of flashbacks or not. Salinger saw the horror I did. I imagine he had the same nightmares.

JOHN C. UNRUE: Sylvia was unhappy in New York. Salinger was unhappy, too, apparently. It was not a good marriage.

EBERHARD ALSEN: Sylvia later told her school friend Hildegard Meyer that her in-laws were very unkind to her and that she never cried as much in her whole life as during her brief stay in America. She was therefore appalled when, one morning, she found an airline ticket to Germany on her breakfast plate. She returned to Europe sometime in June 1946, only a few weeks after she arrived in New York. Salinger wrote a letter to Elizabeth Murray from Daytona Beach, Florida, on June 13, 1946. He reports that he and Sylvia have separated and that his marriage was a failure, or rather the participants were, because they caused each other "the most violent kind of unhappiness."

SHANE SALERNO: Previous biographers have stated that it was Sylvia who filed for divorce, or that she simply left New York to return to Europe. However, we obtained in Germany the official annulment decree, which establishes that Salinger, who hired his father's attorney, Martin A. Fromer, was the plaintiff. The decree states, "Whereas the above lawsuit was initiated by the plaintiff against the defendant in order to obtain an annulment of the marriage between the parties, the reasons being bad intentions and false representation on the part of the defendant." A plausible interpretation of the annulment decree confirms what Miriam and Doris Salinger believed, namely, that Sylvia had some involvement with the Gestapo, that Salinger discovered this, and that this was the primary reason he sought to annul the marriage.

Salinger himself never spoke on the matter. He came closest to an explanation in a letter to his friend Paul Fitzgerald, published here for the first time.

J. D. SALINGER, excerpt from letter to Paul Fitzgerald, November 23, 1946:

> *Sylvia and I separated less than a month after we returned to the States. She's now in Switzerland, practicing medicine. If I gave you all the reasons for the separation, I would have to go straight back to the beginning. As most of the details would probably depress you, I'd*

rather not do that. I'll say briefly that, almost from the beginning, we were desperately unsuited to, and unhappy with, each other. If I gave you one or several reasons, they would undoubtedly sound one-sided. Let's let it go. When we see each other again, and if you're interested in hearing the facts, I'll do my best to give them to you honestly. I just wanted to let you know—straight from the horse—what's happened. I can understand how sorry you must be.

EBERHARD ALSEN: After her return to Germany, Sylvia briefly moved back to Weissenburg, where her mother still lived. In August 1946 she and her mother moved to their old house in Nuremberg. From there Sylvia moved to Geneva, Switzerland, where she was trained as an ophthalmologist.

More than three years later, on January 26, 1949, Sylvia's marriage to J. D. Salinger was officially annulled by the family court of Queens County, New York. Sylvia did not find out about the annulment until August 1950, when she was living in Switzerland, and she had considerable difficulty in getting the Swiss authorities to accept the annulment. She had to write many letters to various officials both in Germany and in France until the French authorities finally accepted the annulment. Sylvia had to sign her name as Dr. Sylvia Salinger-Welter until November 24, 1954.

"Bad intentions" and "misrepresentations": in other words, Salinger was claiming that Sylvia had deliberately deceived him, quite possibly regarding her involvement in the Gestapo. Salinger's family would not have made a distinction between the Nazi Party and the Gestapo, which was, after all, a unit of the Nazi government.

LEILA HADLEY LUCE: Jerry was a very private person. He told me he'd been married, and I said, "What was her name?" He said, "Sylvie." I never knew if it was Sylvia or Sylvie, and I didn't want to ask again. He said he found out some disturbing things about what she did in the war, specifically with the Gestapo. Jerry also told Sid Perelman this. Jerry said she had lied to him and that when he learned what she had really done in the war he could not possibly remain with her.

DAVID SHIELDS: Salinger has done his best to shroud the facts and cover his tracks about her and their relationship; his letter to Fitzgerald—"most of the details would probably depress you"—is his only statement. Nor did Sylvia ever say anything about what happened between herself and Salinger. She maintained her silence for over fifty years and took the answers to her grave.

EBERHARD ALSEN: Sylvia obviously represented something mythic or at least metaphoric concerning Salinger's Nuremberg breakdown and the war and his half-Jewish family.

ALEX KERSHAW: Salinger got to a place intellectually and emotionally—importantly, emotionally—whereby he could identify and sympathize with the so-called victim and the perpetrator so intimately that he would do the opposite of what any so-called decent American would do, which was to go and marry maybe a Nazi, certainly a German, woman.

LEILA HADLEY LUCE: Jerry and Sylvia had total telepathic communication and they met in dreams, which sounded odd to me, but Jerry truly believed that and told me that.

EBERHARD ALSEN: According to Salinger, there were telepathic and trance-state conversations between him and Sylvia. I'd like to know what they discussed.

After they separated, Salinger confessed to friends that he hadn't written during the entire eight months he was married, but that since Sylvia had returned to Europe, he had finished a new story.

From another letter that Salinger wrote to Elizabeth Murray, we learn that "A Perfect Day for Bananafish" was originally entitled "The Male Goodbye" and that it was written in June 1946 in Daytona Beach, immediately after his marriage ended.

J. D. SALINGER ("A Perfect Day for Bananafish," *The New Yorker*, January 31, 1948):

> "Well. In the first place, he said it was a perfect crime the Army released him [Seymour] from the hospital—my word of honor. He very definitely told your father there's a chance—a very great chance, he said—that Seymour may completely lose control of himself. My word of honor."

8

MEASURING UP

NEW YORK CITY; HOLLYWOOD; TARRYTOWN, NEW YORK; STAMFORD, CONNECTICUT, 1946–1950

Back in the social and artistic hubbub of the city he knows so well, Salinger, a twenty-seven-year-old half-Jew divorced from his German wife, a damaged veteran with undiagnosed PTSD, attempts to resurrect his prewar dream—publication in the *New Yorker*, success as a writer—and to reconcile his divided soul, the part of him that remains trapped forever in World War II and the part of him that seeks pragmatically to advance his literary career. What he doesn't realize yet is that he doesn't get to choose what's happening in his head. A compounding irony: only by returning emotionally and imaginatively to the battlefield is he able to advance his art.

MICHAEL SILVERBLATT: Salinger comes back from the war aware that this devastated and shell-shocked tone *is* his tone.

PAUL ALEXANDER: It must have seemed to Salinger as if his life were never going to change. Here he was—one more time—living at home. However, because he had gone to war, because he had seen what he had seen, he *was* different. At night, instead of staying at home and reading or writing as he had done in the past, he started to go out, often ending up in Greenwich Village. Known for its funky bars and jazz clubs, the Village was the kind of place where aspiring writers, singers, and actors would spend the evening hours and meet other young people like themselves.

Thomas Lea's painting of the "two-thousand-yard stare."

A. E. HOTCHNER: It was the year after the war ended, and a lot of us were knocking around New York. We got out of uniform, but it was difficult to get any editorial jobs. The only person I knew who had a job was Don Congdon, who was the fiction editor of *Collier's*. I met him because I had submitted a short story he liked, but he couldn't convince the editor to accept it.

Congdon had an apartment on Charleston Street in Greenwich Village and invited me to his Wednesday-night poker games that included a rotating group of would-be editors and writers. The editors didn't have jobs and the writers hadn't been published but believed they were going to be and nobody understood them yet. We played nickel-and-dime poker. One of the players was a tall, lanky, dark gentleman named Jerry Salinger.

Jerry was a lousy poker player. He refused to bluff and he felt anybody who bluffed was a weenie, as he would say. I said, "But if you don't bluff, you're not going to be a successful poker player." I don't recall Jerry ever winning a round of poker; he was too cautious and suspicious. God knows, Jerry never drew to an inside straight. Afterward Jerry and I would go across to Chumley's, a famous bar in the Village, and nurse a beer and nurse our losings.

Chumley's was a refuge for writers—a small, comforting place where you were never hurried by anybody, waiters or the owner or anybody, to finish your beer. You could sit there for half a day, half an evening, into the wee hours, with a notebook, writing, doing anything you wanted. You'd write and you'd think, "I'm in the tradition of Dylan Thomas and all the

The door to Chumley's bar, where Salinger socialized with A. E. Hotchner and other writers.

other people who have been in Chumley's." It was the equivalent of the Paris café of the 1920s, where you could order a coffee or a glass of wine and sit forever, where Hemingway used to write in his notebooks. That was Chumley's. The bar had this great decor of book jackets. So many writers with book jackets up there began their writing careers in Chumley's.

Jerry mostly liked to listen to his own talk. We'd sit at one of the small tables, and if somebody came in whom he knew and liked, he would join us, but there weren't many people Jerry knew or liked. He was an iconoclast, a loner. I don't know why he decided to spend as much time with me as he did. Maybe it was because I sometimes questioned his literary arrogance; he would put down almost any writer you could talk about. He would carry on about how bad all current writing was—and past writing, too, for that matter. He was beautifully read and had digested what he read. It was amusing to listen to him berate other writers, because it was always wittily done. It was always at a pretty high plane, his criticism of writing, but it was all really posturing: he was insecure about what he was doing.

Dreiser through Hemingway: they were all inferior. The only really worthwhile writer, the only one he accepted, was Melville. Who, conveniently, was long dead. We would get into heated discussions about Hemingway's Nick Adams stories, which I felt were some of the finest writing in the English language. Jerry didn't. He thought they were nothing but diary entries.

DAVID SHIELDS: During the war, Salinger admired Hemingway's work. After the war, after all he had seen, after his own breakdown, he couldn't.

A. E. HOTCHNER: Jerry shared a trait that was, I think, the most predominant of all Hemingway's idiosyncrasies. I'd say to Ernest, "What happened to Bill? He's not here." Hemingway would answer, "He didn't measure up." Now there is no barometer of what that is. Over the years, Hemingway excommunicated friend after friend after friend: they didn't measure up. I don't know how it happened that I escaped that. I didn't toady to him. I don't know why, but for some reason I measured up.

Jerry had his own set of values, his own demands. Whatever it was he imposed on the people he knew, if they didn't measure up to it, they were dismissed. They weren't worthy; they couldn't be trusted. He'd never tell you the requirements, either. They're mysterious, subjective. You can be dismissed at any time. Of course, when you get pathological about it, nobody can measure up. That's maybe what happened to Jerry Salinger. Nobody could measure up to whatever it is he demanded of himself and of you.

Jerry didn't talk much about the war. He talked only about literature. In the period of time when we used to come into Chumley's, Jerry had been writing a couple of stories that were taken by the "slicks"—that is, the general-circulation magazines—but they bore no resemblance at all to what he wrote later on. And at that time I felt he was writing them in order to make the few bucks he needed. It wasn't until later I discovered that he came from a very wealthy family. He lived with them on Park Avenue and money was not a concern of his.

Thinking back on the guys who sat around the poker table, I'd say what distinguished Jerry from the pack was that in his mind there was no doubt he was going to be published, no doubt that he had enormous talent, and no doubt that everybody else at the poker table was inferior to him.

Jerry had written a story called "Holden Caulfield on the Bus," which the *New Yorker* had rejected, but he talked endlessly about how he would rework it and eventually they would realize that it was a new kind of writing and publish it. He had read my stories "Candle in the Poolroom Window" and "An Ocean Full of Bowling Balls," both of which he found amusing—he'd given me his "Bowling Balls" title to use—but he was nevertheless appalled that I would waste my time writing about something that was not connected with my life. "There's no emotion in these stories," he said. "No fire between the words."

DAVID SHIELDS: In mid-November 1946 the *New Yorker* notified Salinger of its plan to finally publish "Slight Rebellion Off Madison" in the coming weeks. After holding the story for five years—so long that Salinger had concluded it was never going to run—the editors had suddenly changed their minds and decided to use it after all. If his boyhood dream had been deferred, it was about to be fulfilled.

BEN YAGODA: In December 1946 the magazine finally published this story about this kid named Holden Caulfield. That seemed to signal a change in Salinger's fortunes.

"Slight Rebellion Off Madison" is an early version of a scene in *The*

Catcher in the Rye. The story follows Holden, who, home from Pencey, goes out with Sally to the movies and then goes skating with her; later that night, he calls drunkenly up to her apartment.

PAUL ALEXANDER: For five agonizing years he had had to wait until his story appeared in the magazine that he respected the most. But once it did, his thinking changed. And after that he wanted to publish only in the *New Yorker*.

—

PHOEBE HOBAN: Salinger loved to go to jazz clubs. He went to hear Billie Holiday.

DAVID YAFFE: When Salinger returned from the war, he would have had the opportunity to witness one of the most extraordinary explosions of jazz in the twentieth century, and it was all happening in New York. You could walk down a single block on Fifty-second Street between Sixth Avenue and Broadway, and Art Tatum would be playing in one club, Charlie Parker in another, and Billie Holiday would be singing right down the street. Salinger regarded the music as pure and uncorrupted and lacking in the phoniness that he saw in so many things. He also liked Blossom Dearie, who was more of a cabaret singer than a jazz singer.

Salinger was a record collector, which is a fascinating species of fetishist. You think of these people who obsessively alphabetize their record collection and have their own private Dewey decimal system. It's a way of ordering experience and having control over it and not dealing with living, breathing human beings.

A. E. HOTCHNER: The best times I had with Jerry were when he would call up and say, "I'm going to the Blue Angel tonight. Want to come along?" We would go to the Blue Angel, which was a nightspot where young talent would try out, hoping to be discovered. I don't think they even got paid. The place itself was pretty grubby. It needed paint; it served booze and a little food. It was not an inviting place, but the talent was inviting, and the man who was the impresario of the

Blue Angel had a good ear: he brought extraordinary young performers to the stage.

Jerry had a wonderful time because he identified with these types who were trying to make their mark in music, just as he was trying to make his mark with his writing. He was charitable, and when once in a while a great talent would show up—a lot of these performers went on to become big stars—Jerry would get word to them and have them come to the table. He loved having them there. It was the most communicative I ever found him. He was a different kind of person when he was enjoying the talent of a singer. These were the best times with Jerry because he was the most natural. He was expressing himself fully to that fellow aspiring artist. At other times he was guarded or angry about writing or about what happened in the news that day.

In all of the times Jerry and I went to nightspots, he never showed any interest in the young women around us. He was consumed with his ambition as a writer. I never heard him say, "Let's have a couple of beers." Jerry was all business. I never saw him pick up anybody at any of these places, so I was rather surprised later on to read about the various alliances he had with much younger women. When I knew him—he must have been twenty-seven, twenty-eight—he didn't have a girlfriend, or at least not one he brought around.

SHANE SALERNO: Salinger met a lot of girls in the drugstore of the Barbizon Hotel for Women on Manhattan's Upper East Side. He would bring them down to Greenwich Village to various clubs and restaurants he frequented. Several of his friends thought he was interested in these girls, at least in part, for the dialogue he could incorporate into his stories. One girl returned to the Barbizon convinced she had just been out on a date with the goalie for the Montreal Canadiens.

He worked out with barbells to build up his skinny body—probably a carryover from the exercise regimen he'd been forced to maintain in the army. He studied Zen Buddhism—quite a departure from the Judaism and Irish Catholicism of his parents. His Zen Buddhism would become a central part of his life. While he studied Zen and hung out in Greenwich Village, he dated a succession of young women. Some of his dates remembered that he was eager to give them reading lists on Zen Buddhism.

PHOEBE HOBAN: Salinger was quite a tall guy. He had an athletic build, even though he was a bookworm, and was pretty suave with the women.

DAVID YAFFE: Salinger was fascinated by the *idea* of Bessie Smith—he idolized and deified her—but if he had been face-to-face with Bessie Smith, I don't think he would have been able to last five minutes with her. She would have represented a very threatening adult female sexuality, precisely the opposite of his obsession: young girls.

—

DAVID SHIELDS: The publication of "Slight Rebellion Off Madison" in the *New Yorker* elevated Salinger's literary status, but the magazine continued to reject many, even most of his stories, so he was forced to continue publishing in the slicks.

A. E. HOTCHNER: His reaction to *New Yorker* rejections was, "They want me to write an O. Henry type of story, but I have to find my own voice, and this is it, and they'll catch up to me." That was Salinger's point of view. "They aren't used to this new voice. They aren't used to my form of short story. But they will come around. I'm not going to compromise on this." And he didn't. He compromised on his stories for the slicks but not on his stories for the *New Yorker*. He was determined that the editors of the *New Yorker* were going to publish more of him.

DAVID SHIELDS: In earlier letters to Whit Burnett, Salinger had complained that the *New Yorker* is interested only in "little Hemingways and little [Katherine] Mansfields," but the "editors really knock me out." He also called Clifton Fadiman, the *New Yorker*'s book reviewer, "smug and patronizing and literarily dishonest." The *New Yorker* had been urging him to write more "simply and naturally," but none of the magazine's editors "really know what a short story is."

SHANE SALERNO: Gus Lobrano had no qualms about turning down Salinger's stories. In fact he turned down many stories that eventually became part of *The Catcher in the Rye*.

BEN YAGODA: In that long period, there was, I think, a mutual dance going back and forth, the *New Yorker* recognizing Salinger's talents but trying to rein him in—"We think Mr. Salinger is a very talented young man and wish to God you could get him to write simply and naturally," William Maxwell once wrote to Olding—and Salinger himself trying to stick to his guns, adapting a little bit but also trying to get the *New Yorker* to stretch and grow.

PAUL ALEXANDER: In January 1947, not long after "Slight Rebellion Off Madison" appeared in print, Salinger decided to leave his parents' apartment once and for all. He moved from Manhattan to Tarrytown, an upper-middle-class community in Westchester County, where he rented a small garage apartment. The living arrangements in Tarrytown were far different from his parents' ritzy Park Avenue apartment, but at least he was on his own and not living under his father's influence.

BEN YAGODA: The very next story that he submitted to [the *New Yorker*] was called "The Bananafish."

WILLIAM MAXWELL, excerpt from January 22, 1947, letter to Salinger's agent Harold Ober:

> *We like parts of The Bananafish by J. D. Salinger very much, but it seems to us to lack any discernible story or point. If Mr. Salinger is around town, perhaps he'd like to come in and talk to us about New Yorker stories.*

BEN YAGODA: The version of this story he had sent to the *New Yorker*, and which later became perhaps his most celebrated story, "A Perfect Day for Bananafish," included only the episode of Seymour at the beach—the somewhat mystifying episode of Seymour Glass on the beach, talking to a little girl—and then killing himself.

What Maxwell was saying, which is understandable, is that there didn't seem to be a reason why Seymour had taken this action. Salinger met with Maxwell, and the result was that another section of the story was added, the opening, in which Seymour's wife is talking on the phone with her mother.

J. D. SALINGER ("A Perfect Day for Bananafish," *The New Yorker*, January 31, 1948):

> "Did he keep calling you that awful—"
>
> "No. He has something new now."
>
> "What?"
>
> "Oh, what's the *dif*ference, Mother?"
>
> "Muriel, I want to *know*. Your father—"
>
> "All right, all right. He calls me Miss Spiritual Tramp of 1948," the girl said, and giggled.
>
> "It isn't funny, Muriel. It isn't funny at all. It's horrible. It's *sad*, actually. When I think how—"
>
> "Mother," the girl interrupted, "listen to me. You remember that book he sent me from Germany? You know—those German poems. What'd I *do* with it? I've been racking my—"
>
> "You have it."
>
> "Are you *sure*?" said the girl.

DAVID HUDDLE: When "A Perfect Day for Bananafish" appeared in the *New Yorker* in 1948, everybody woke up.

JOHN WENKE: "A Perfect Day for Bananafish" is the first demarcation of a new body of material for Salinger.

DAVID SHIELDS: "A Perfect Day for Bananafish" is, quite simply, the announcement of a new sound in American literature.

A. E. HOTCHNER: When Jerry published "A Perfect Day for Bananafish," it caused a great buzz. Everybody was talking about it: "Did you read that story? Isn't it remarkable? That little girl!" He became a name to the intellectual set.

LEILA HADLEY LUCE: We'd call each other on the telephone when the *New Yorker* came out: "Have you read this Salinger story? Have you seen this? And isn't it wonderful?" Everyone was totally captivated by his writing.

GAY TALESE: It really seemed to be the first legitimate young American voice on the printed page that had all the power and song of what would later be in the words of Bobby Dylan, or the Beatles, or the music of Motown. That was later stuff. This one character—that was Salinger. And the word of mouth: I'd be in the city room, and someone would tell me in the cafeteria—we had a coffee break—"Hey, I heard Salinger . . ."

Before Tina Brown thought of buzz, there was this buzz. I'd never heard any word of mouth on an about-to-be-published short story in some magazine. I know the *New Yorker* wasn't just "some magazine," but I don't care. It never happened with Roth or Updike or Don DeLillo or anybody. Half an evening's meal was spent discussing [Salinger's work]. This was very much what was going on. From Chumley's down in the Village; maybe, if you had the money, even Toots Shor's, the old sports bar—you heard about Salinger. He just was a new man on the planet. And he carried us away.

MARC WEINGARTEN: A lot of Salinger's contemporaries were blown away by the piece. Cheever thought it was an absolutely incredible piece of work.

E. L. DOCTOROW: I remember hearing that there was a new Salinger story in the *New Yorker* being passed around school. My wife, who's from North Carolina, remembers being fascinated by those stories because they were about people who lived in apartments and who were very verbal.

TOM WOLFE: I must say, his style was infectious; as a matter of fact, you can see a little bit of it in the first magazine piece I ever wrote, which was "The Kandy-Kolored Tangerine-Flake Streamline Baby." One of the things that made his writing so personal was that he was constantly using expressions such as "If you really want to know the truth, it happened this way," and all sorts of other little touches you use in conversation. Usually they're edited out, but his weren't.

BEN YAGODA: "Bananafish" made a huge splash. He became a sensation in the literary world. Salinger still got rejections—almost nobody got every story accepted by the *New Yorker*—but his acceptance rate became well over 50 percent.

—

DAVID SHIELDS: The month before, in *Cosmopolitan*, Salinger had published "The Inverted Forest," which explores themes that Salinger will pursue the rest of his life: the cost of art, the relation of art to spirituality, and the hunger for spirituality. The story's protagonist, Raymond Ford, writes, "Not wasteland, but a great inverted forest / with all foliage underground"—a pointed rejoinder to T. S. Eliot's *The Waste Land.*

J. D. SALINGER ("The Inverted Forest," *Cosmopolitan*, December 1947):

> "Listen," Corinne said. "You're implying that he's some kind of psychotic. I won't have it, Bobby. In the first place, it isn't true. He's—he's serene. He's kind, he's gentle, he's—"
>
> "Don't be a fool, Corinne. He's the most gigantic psychotic you'll ever know. He *has* to be. Don't be a fool. He's standing up to his eyes in psychosis." . . .
>
> As though it might be best to look immediately for shelter, Corinne had to put the book down. At any moment the apartment building seemed liable to lose its balance and topple across Fifth Avenue into Central Park.

DAVID SHIELDS: In *The Fiction of J. D. Salinger*, the first comprehensive study of his work, Frederick L. Gwynn and Joseph L. Blotner group "The Inverted Forest" with "The Varioni Brothers" as "Destroyed Artist Melodramas" that show "Salinger struggling with a theme he wants to be able to handle but which he really doesn't seem to understand." He does not understand it because he's too close to it.

FREDERICK L. GWYNN and JOSEPH L. BLOTNER: Half a dozen of [Salinger's early stories] introduced sympathetic characters who—under the influence of the same World War II experiences that the writer underwent—develop attitudes and relationships and names that end in the Caulfield and Glass families with whom Salinger is later to feel so much at home.

DAVID SHIELDS: *Good Housekeeping* published "A Girl I Knew" in February 1948. Salinger used his experiences in pre-Anschluss Vienna in 1937 for the story, which he'd originally titled "Wien, Wien." John, the college dropout narrator and Salinger alter ego, says, "My father informed me quietly that my formal education was formally over." His father sends John to Paris and Vienna to learn the family business and pick up "a couple of languages the firm could use." John spends five months in Vienna and falls in love with a young girl named Leah.

EBERHARD ALSEN: Salinger's early efforts to write stage plays are briefly mirrored in this story. A young American reads a play he has written to a Viennese girl, from whom he is taking German lessons.

GLORIA MURRAY: He must have known the girl in the story, although he didn't say if he did. He just said that it was a story he had written very quickly.

DAVID SHIELDS: "A Girl I Knew" is shadowed by the Nazi takeover of Vienna's Jewish quarter in 1938. Margaret Salinger believes that even though her father had left Austria a month before the Nazis annexed the country on March 12, he probably was aware, through the Viennese family he befriended, of the incipient German destruction of the Jewish neighborhood he'd lived in. Salinger was young and in love, and his being Jewish suddenly became a danger that could make the people he loved disappear.

JOHN C. UNRUE: *Good Housekeeping* changed the title of "Wien, Wien" to "A Girl I Knew," and Salinger reacted so strongly that the editor, Herbert Mayes, was puzzled by the extent of his anger.

HERBERT MAYES: I don't know what upset Salinger, but he protested vehemently and ordered his agent, Dorothy Olding, never again to show me any of his manuscripts.

JOHN C. UNRUE: When Salinger was writing for the slicks, he was testing himself constantly. By the time he became what we might call a *New Yorker* author, he had polished his craft. He was able to avoid the formulaic process that he had to employ for the *Saturday Evening Post*, *Collier's*, and even *Esquire*, to some degree.

DAVID SHIELDS: After a decade of innumerable rejections by the *New Yorker*, Salinger had three stories published there in a six-month period. Why? He was finally writing about something real.

BEN YAGODA: Nineteen forty-eight was the turning point for Salinger regarding the *New Yorker*. He published "A Perfect Day for Bananafish," "Uncle Wiggily in Connecticut," and "Just Before the War with the Eskimos." It was really a breakthrough. They were much talked about, and from then on he was known and identified as a *New Yorker* writer.

SHANE SALERNO: The enormous accomplishment and success of "Bananafish" led the *New Yorker* to give him a first-look contract: the magazine paid him an annual retainer in exchange for his giving the *New Yorker* the first chance at publishing his new stories. The magazine would also pay him a higher rate than it had been paying him for the stories it published. Over the years, only the *New Yorker*'s most esteemed writers had received first-look contracts: John O'Hara, Irwin Shaw, John Cheever, S. J. Perelman. Salinger was joining very select company.

J. D. SALINGER, excerpt from letter to Paul Fitzgerald, April 29, 1948:

> *As for me, I signed a year's contract with the* New Yorker. *I like the magazine and I like writing for it. They let me write the kind of stuff I care about—and I don't have to look at a dumb illustration. It's all very straight and satisfactory.*

—

BEN YAGODA: In the beginning, it was just the cognoscenti who had "discovered" this guy, the way people today might discover a singer or a rock band and share it among themselves. A *New Yorker* contributor named Arthur Kober, who was in Hollywood working as a screenwriter, wrote a letter to Harold Ross and said, "Everybody here talks about Salinger. My God, that guy is good! Evenings are spent—and this is on the level—discussing the guy and his work."

DAVID SHIELDS: "Uncle Wiggily in Connecticut" was Salinger's second story about a member of the Glass family—the first being "A Perfect Day for Bananafish"—to be published in the *New Yorker*.

J. D. SALINGER ("Uncle Wiggily in Connecticut," *The New Yorker*, March 28, 1948):

"Stop that," Eloise said. "Mary Jane asked you if you have a beau."

"Yes," said Ramona, busy with her nose.

"Ramona," Eloise said. "Cut that out. But immediately."

Ramona put her hand down.

"Well, I think that's just wonderful," Mary Jane said. "What's his name? Will you tell me his name, Ramona? Or is it a big secret?"

"Jimmy," Ramona said.

"Jimmy? Oh, I love the name Jimmy! Jimmy what, Ramona?"

"Jimmy Jimmereeno," said Ramona.

"Stand still," said Eloise.

"Well! That's quite a name. Where is Jimmy? Will you tell me, Ramona?"

"Here," said Ramona.

Mary Jane looked around, then looked back at Ramona, smiling as provocatively as possible. "Here where, honey?"

"*Here*," said Ramona. "I'm holding his *hand*."

"I don't get it," Mary Jane said to Eloise, who was finishing her drink.

"Don't look at *me*," said Eloise.

Mary Jane looked back at Ramona. "Oh, I see. Jimmy's just a make-believe little boy. Marvellous." Mary Jane leaned forward cordially. "How do you *do*, Jimmy?" she said.

"He won't talk to you," said Eloise.

J. D. SALINGER, excerpt from letter to Paul Fitzgerald, October 19, 1948:

My work goes along pretty much the way I want it to, Paul, since you ask. I don't make barrels of money, but I love what I'm doing. And every once in a while enough dough comes in to let me work on something that has no silver lining. One of my New Yorker stories, called

UNCLE WIGGILY IN CONNECTICUT, sold to Sam Goldwyn and is going to be a picture with Dana Andrews and Teresa Wright. I didn't make a fortune on the sale, but enough to let me go on with my own work for a while without major money worries.

GUS LOBRANO, excerpt from letter to Salinger's agent, Dorothy Olding, December 10, 1948:

Dear Miss Olding,

Here, alas, is Jerry Salinger's latest story ["The Boy in the People Shooting Hat"]. *I'm afraid I'm incapable of expressing adequately and convincingly our* [the *New Yorker*'s] *distress at having to send it back. It has passages that are brilliant and moving and effective, but we feel that on the whole it's pretty shocking for a magazine like ours.*

It would be wonderfully comfortable to rest on the above paragraph, but because we have a real interest in Jerry I have to say further that we feel the story isn't wholly successful. Possibly the development of the theme of this story requires more space. Actually, we feel that we don't know the central character well enough. We can't be quite sure whether his fight with Stradlater was caused by his feelings for June Gallagher or his own inadequacy about his age (which is brought into relief by Stradlater's handsomeness and prowess), or suggestion of homosexuality in Bobby. And it's perhaps our uncertainty about which of these elements is the real one, or the predominant one, that makes it difficult to feel any real compassion for the character, or to feel (except extraneously) that the author has real compassion for him. Our feeling is that, to be quite definite and so sympathetic, Bobby would have to be developed at considerably more length than he is here. . . . I'm convinced that it would have worked out for us if it had been developed as the less complicated theme which Jerry told me about shortly after it had occurred to him, but I imagine that that theme seemed too sparse to Jerry as the character grew in his mind. We are, of course, very grateful to have had the chance to consider the story.

SHANE SALERNO: Not even Salinger was seeing every story accepted by the *New Yorker*, but Samuel Goldwyn bought the film rights for "Uncle Wiggily in Connecticut," assembled a creative team, and spent much of 1949 transforming the brief story into a movie, now called *My Foolish Heart.*

THOMAS F. BRADY: Samuel Goldwyn has borrowed Susan Hayward from [producer] Walter Wanger to play opposite Dana Andrews in *My Foolish Heart*, which will be Goldwyn's next film. . . . Miss Hayward will play the role originally scheduled for Teresa Wright, who parted company with the Goldwyn company after a dispute last December. Mark Robson will direct *My Foolish Heart*, which Julius and Philip Epstein have written from a magazine story "Uncle Wiggily in Connecticut," by J. D. Salinger.

A. SCOTT BERG: Samuel Goldwyn was one of the original Hollywood moguls, one of that group of a half-dozen Jewish immigrants who realized early on that there was not only a lot of money to be made in the movie industry but there was a budding art form there, and a really interesting life could be had making movies. Because of his temper, Goldwyn got kicked out of Paramount Studios, which he helped form, and then he got kicked out of Metro-Goldwyn-Mayer, which he helped form, and ultimately he got kicked out of United Artists, which he supplied most of the movies for. So he started his own company, Samuel Goldwyn Productions.

The Epstein brothers came to Sam Goldwyn with an idea for a movie based on a story they had recently read in the *New Yorker*. The story was "Uncle Wiggily in Connecticut," and the author was a young J. D. Salinger, who was being talked about a great deal. This appealed to Goldwyn on several levels. First of all, the Epstein brothers had worked almost exclusively for Warner Bros. It was a great coup for Goldwyn to nab these great contract writers. Second, they had wonderful credits, so Goldwyn was eager to be working with them. Also, they came up with the idea to do a story that had been in the *New Yorker*, which by the '40s had become one of the most important venues in which to publish serious fiction. That intrigued him a great deal. It's an emblematic Salinger story, written in that spare style. In fact, if you parse it, there's very little plot and very little character development per se.

Frankly, I think that's one of the things that intrigued the Epstein brothers, because they must have thought, "There's so much opportunity for us to fill in what's been left out," and indeed the beauty of the story is how much Salinger left out, and the great delight for the Epsteins was how much they could put in. So when they spun the tale to Goldwyn of what the movie was going to be, it turned from a somewhat bitter, satiric look at a troubled, alcoholic marriage in the Connecticut suburbs into a rather sentimental, talky tearjerker. That's the movie Goldwyn wanted to make and so that's the movie he made. There was inevitably going to be considerable artistic disparity between the original source material and the final product.

LESLIE EPSTEIN: My father and my uncle, the Epstein boys, as they were known, became identified with Warner Bros., even though my father began at RKO. They were a legendary team of screenwriters—certainly, I think, the greatest *team* of screenwriters. My uncle worked on over fifty films. He's the only person I know nominated for an Academy Award every decade from his twenties through his seventies. After they did *Casa-*

Samuel L. Goldwyn.

Screenwriters Julius and Philip Epstein, who wrote the script for *My Foolish Heart*.

blanca together, they were going to be allowed to produce and direct, but my father died soon afterward. He died young, at only forty-two. *My Foolish Heart* was done after *Casablanca*.

PAUL ALEXANDER: Goldwyn's team, composed of some of the top talent in Hollywood, could not have gotten much more than a short film out of Salinger's story. What had to happen was the inevitable: characters, scenes, subplots, and dialogue had to be added. . . . Goldwyn's team added flashbacks . . . [and] created new characters, most notably those of Eloise's mother and father, characters who are not even mentioned in Salinger's story. But what was most egregious was this: manipulating tone and emotional content, Goldwyn's team somehow turned Salinger's bitter indictment of the Connecticut WASP into a picture so unabashedly maudlin that one critic called it a "four-handkerchief" tearjerker.

A. SCOTT BERG: Every time an author sends something to Hollywood, part of him says to himself, "Well, my work is so special that mine won't get changed, and certainly they're not going to rape it." As I think in some ways Hollywood did to "Uncle Wiggily in Connecticut."

LESLIE EPSTEIN: The ads for the film said, "She was a good girl, wasn't she?" In the Salinger story, she says, "I was a nice girl, wasn't I?" In the story, it's not that she's not a good mother; she's not *nice*. The regret she has is about that quality of *niceness*, which is a particular Salinger quality. It's tough for anyone to capture a quality like that outside that particular story and that particular context.

J. D. SALINGER ("Uncle Wiggily in Connecticut," *The New Yorker*, March 28, 1948):

> All of a sudden he [Walt Glass] said my stomach was so beautiful he wished some officer would come up and order him to stick his other hand through the window. He said he wanted to do what was fair.

A. SCOTT BERG: The critical response to the movie was mostly pretty bad, and deservedly so. It's a movie marked by too much sentiment, too much coincidence. There's just too much happening in it. It's got a classic Susan Hayward performance: she pulls her heart out in every scene and was nominated for an Academy Award. It's not a god-awful movie. It's not horrendous. It just bears very little resemblance to Salinger's story.

MARK HOWLAND: I can understand why Salinger was upset with *My Foolish Heart*. As appealing as Susan Hayward and Dana Andrews are, the character of Walt [Dreiser] was not Walt Glass. Not even close.

***MY FOOLISH HEART*, 1949:**

Eloise (to Walt): Is this how it's all going to end? We miss each other very much. We think about each other. I'll be yours; you'll be mine. Is this how you want it to end?

A. SCOTT BERG: Salinger's response to viewing *My Foolish Heart* was extremely violent.

LESLIE EPSTEIN: Salinger hated *My Foolish Heart.*

JEAN MILLER: I remember his spouting off about Hollywood. I think he had just seen *My Foolish Heart* and was fit to be tied. He was furious. And that pretty much took up that evening because he was furious. He didn't understand how intelligent people—of course he'd decided that once you hit the California border there wasn't a brain left—but how anybody could take his story and make such sentimental hash out of it. He felt it had nothing to do with his story, which of course had such a different message. It was trash, and he didn't want anything to do with it.

A. SCOTT BERG: Clearly, the compromise was not worth it to Salinger. He saw the film that was based on something he had written, and I think he was probably embarrassed and humiliated by the movie.

J. D. SALINGER, excerpt from letter to Paul Fitzgerald, August 26, 1949:

> *If you're interested in movies—and I hope you're not—an old story of mine, called UNCLE WIGGILY IN CONNECTICUT is being released pretty soon under the title of MY FOOLISH HEART. Two brothers named Epstein bought the story and wrote a screenplay out of it. I haven't seen it, but from what I've heard they've loused it up nicely. My own fault. Money's the root of you-know-what.*

***MY FOOLISH HEART*, 1949:**

Eloise: The important thing, Lou, is that I'm through hurting people. I'm through doing wrong. I'm paying for what I've done, and now I'm all alone. I don't want others to suffer, too.

JOHN McCARTEN (THE *NEW YORKER*): Full of soap opera clichés . . . hard to believe that it was wrung out of a short story that appeared in this austere magazine a couple of years ago.

JOHN GUARE: I was a kid when I saw *My Foolish Heart*, and I remember laughing at Susan Hayward, but I liked the song "My Foolish Heart."

A. SCOTT BERG: It's got an overdone score and yet the main theme was an Academy Award–nominated song, "My Foolish Heart," which became a big standard in the 1950s and would be covered for years to come. It's a wonderful, slightly schmaltzy melody. It was a marginal movie—not a big hit, not a big loser. It didn't have huge stars. It was not as if he [Samuel Goldwyn] were able to compete against the Clark Gables and the Gary Coopers with this movie. There was no Bette Davis in the film. It did only all right.

MARK HOWLAND: My students love seeing this movie. They get sucked into it; they love the romantic comedy of it. They think the theme song is corny, but otherwise they really like it. At the same time, they immediately recognize that the movie is not the story.

A. SCOTT BERG: It was very glossily done, as almost all of Sam Goldwyn's movies were. The production values were extremely high, perhaps a little too high. Everything in Goldwyn movies was polished just a little too much. The costumes were just a little too perfect. The lighting was just a little too neat. There was never a bit of debris anywhere on any of the Goldwyn sets.

JOYCE MAYNARD: Jerry and I did talk about the movie version of "Uncle Wiggily in Connecticut." The movie was terrible. Jerry said he would never sell his work again. His work was like his children, and his child had been sullied by the movie.

LESLIE EPSTEIN: America and perhaps the world owe my father and my uncle, Philip and Julius Epstein, a great debt—for many things. But perhaps the greatest debt of all, or let's say in a tie with *Casablanca*, is that they spared the world *Catcher in the Rye* being made into a film. That is to say, Salinger so hated their adaptation of "Uncle Wiggily in Connecticut" that he wouldn't allow anyone to touch his work after, and what a blessing that is.

SHANE SALERNO: This is the official version: that *My Foolish Heart* so deeply offended Salinger's sensibility that he never again considered selling his novels and stories to Hollywood. It has been repeated many times, but it's not completely true. As late as 1957 Salinger's agent H. N. Swanson—

who represented F. Scott Fitzgerald, among many other prominent writers and screenwriters—was submitting Salinger's work to Hollywood producers. In a January 25, 1957, letter, one such producer rejected a submission from Swanson on behalf of Salinger.

JERRY WALD, letter to H. N. Swanson, January 25, 1957:

Dear Swanie:

As you know, I am the number one fan of THE J. D. SALINGER FAN CLUB.

Like all of Salinger's work, THE LAUGHING MAN is a touching and delightful story. However, from the point of view of motion pictures, it offers little more than a slender idea upon which to build a comedy. Furthermore, I feel that the particular elements captured in the writing which give the story its special charm and pathos would be difficult to convey when blown up to screen-size reality. Basically, the material is similar to THE SECRET LIFE OF WALTER MITTY, and you may recall what loud criticisms were made about what happened to Thurber's special charm when his story was transferred to the screen by Samuel Goldwyn for Danny Kaye.

I do not doubt that a special and charming comedy could result from this material, but it would pretty much involve starting from the barest essentials of the idea and setting and going on from there. Naturally, this would require a writer in perfect tune with the idea, and this also might be difficult to come by, since Mr. Salinger will not consider working on it himself. My main complaint is that THE LAUGHING MAN gives me too little to work on to make it worth the evident gamble its further development would mean.

Will you please convey to Mr. Salinger that I am still interested in his brilliant CATCHER IN THE RYE, and I wish there was something I could do to convince him that it should be brought to the screen.

I am returning to you herewith the original story of THE LAUGHING MAN.

Warmest regards.

Sincerely,
Jerry Wald

—

EBERHARD ALSEN: When Salinger shows distaste for Hollywood and the movies, it shouldn't be construed as meaning that he hates movies as a form of art; after all, he had an enormous movie collection.

DAVID SHIELDS: In *The Catcher in the Rye*, Holden Caulfield is deeply ambivalent about Hollywood. He has seriously and fascinatingly mixed feelings about his brother D.B.'s working as a screenwriter. He claims he doesn't want to talk about movies, and yet he talks and talks and talks about movies: *39 Steps* and Gary Cooper and Cary Grant. The movies are Holden's idée fixe.

LESLIE EPSTEIN: By many accounts, Salinger's contempt for Hollywood masks a not-so-well-hidden fascination with its star power.

Apparently, and maybe not surprisingly from the creator of *Catcher in the Rye*, he was very intrigued by Marlon Brando.

MONA SIMPSON: Salinger's imagination has always been deeply engaged with fame and popularity; it just has, it's in the books. The Glass family were performers, and there are great strains of that throughout.

EBERHARD ALSEN: When Holden Caulfield says he hates the movies, he's clearly lying because he's constantly acting out scenes from movies. He knows how much he has been influenced by the movies, and he suspects that this makes him to some extent a phony.

J. D. SALINGER (*The Catcher in the Rye*):

> About halfway to the bathroom, I sort of started pretending I had a bullet in my guts.

JOHN SEABROOK: When my college friend Matt invited us to his dad's house, in Cornish, New Hampshire, about half an hour away, to watch an old movie, all parties were relieved. However, as we wound our way along the dirt roads leading up from the Connecticut River, my girlfriend and I became tense all over again, for a different reason. We were both young writers, and we were about to meet J. D. Salinger.

The living room had a dorm-room air about it. We sat down on the uncomfortable, worn furniture and tried to think of something to say to each other. I listened to the popcorn—the first heraldic explosions of the kernels, followed by the dramatic crescendo, and then the dying fall—thinking, J. D. Salinger is in the kitchen making popcorn. After a while, Jerry came out and went to the back of the room, where he kept, on shelves, a collection of old 16-mm. films, the kind where you have to change the reel three or four times in the course of the movie. An old-fashioned projector had been set up behind the sofa. He ran through some titles; we settled on *Sergeant York*. Jerry threaded the film through the projector, and then he turned the lights off and remained behind us, his face illuminated by the flickering projector. The movie was captioned, perhaps because he was going a little deaf. Toward the end, he seemed to get choked up.

—

SHANE SALERNO: Even in this period of his life, the late forties, years before he had the immense cultural and financial cachet that *Catcher in the Rye* brought him, he was adamant about refusing to let anyone alter his work in even the most minor way.

A. E. HOTCHNER: I got a job as an editor of *Cosmopolitan*. In the course of our poker games, Jerry said, "I have a story. I'll submit it to *Cosmopolitan*." I said, "Great." The story was called "Scratchy Needle on a Phonograph Record." He said, "But one thing: tell your editor that not one word can be changed. It's up to you. You've got to watch it, because they like to cut and they like to make it fit a space. If they do that, then it's no go." That was his pride in his writing. So I took it to Arthur Gordon [the editor in chief]. It was an okay story. It was written as a story for a slick magazine.

Jerry was very opinionated about everything, but he had already written a long short story, a novelette, for *Cosmopolitan* called "The Inverted Forest," which Arthur had run. Arthur felt he had great talent. And [Arthur had] announced in the magazine, "This is one of the best pieces of writing of the last twenty years or so." The trouble was, it wasn't very good. And it certainly wasn't fit for *Cosmo*, which was a general-purpose magazine with readers who were used to slick magazine stories. So he got a lot of flack about that from his readers. And Jerry just dismissed it as a fact that the people who read the slicks didn't have any taste.

DAVID YAFFE: "Scratchy Needle on a Phonograph Record," later retitled "Blue Melody," was based on what was then believed to be the story of Bessie Smith's death. It was a story promulgated by John Hammond, the legendary producer at Columbia Records. In the pages of *Downbeat* magazine in 1939, he told the story that Bessie Smith died because she was denied admission to a segregated hospital in Clarksdale, Mississippi. There were plenty of people who said the story wasn't true, and Bessie Smith's biographer finally completely debunked the story, but in 1948 it was still widely believed because it provided a dramatic account of the effects of segregation in the South, a region of the country Salinger knew very little about. Clearly, Salinger had a lot of affection for Bessie Smith, and that comes through. It's a somewhat sentimental story. When one considers that "Blue Melody" was written the same year as "A Perfect Day for Bananafish," the incongruity in quality between the two stories is astonishing.

Even though Salinger begins "Blue Melody" by saying this isn't supposed to be a slam against any part of the country, it's obviously meant to be a slam against the South. To Salinger, Southern music performed in a dive by black musicians is less corny, less phony than something that would be indigenous to New York City—so, yes, he's slamming the South, but there's also an otherness to the South that's appealing to him.

A. E. HOTCHNER: Salinger had been edited, slightly, on previous stories for *Cosmopolitan*, so he even attached a note to the story ["Scratchy Needle on a Phonograph Record"] that said, "Either as-is or not at all." Nevertheless, Arthur wanted to print the story, and I followed through on the galleys. It was fine. However, I forgot to check on the title. Arthur had decided to pander to the taste of his readers and called it "Blue Melody." It never occurred to me he would change the title, and by the time he did, it was in camera-ready copy, which is the prepublication version that comes to you. Even though it says "camera-ready," it can't be altered, because it's already being printed. I thought, "Well, the best thing I can do is meet this head-on." So I called Jerry and said, "Listen, I gotta see you. Can we have a beer at Chumley's tonight?" I met him there and I had the magazine. After I was hemming and hawing, he said, "Hotch, would you get to the point? What's bothering you?" I said, "Jerry, I have

J. D. Salinger.

to explain this to you. I really, very carefully, attended to the prose that you wrote so that nothing was changed, but unbeknownst to me—and I have no control over this because I am not the fiction editor—they put a different title on it."

DAVID YAFFE: Looking at the pseudo–Norman Rockwell artwork in the magazine for "Blue Melody," a drawing of two kids sitting and admiring the music of Black Charles, I think it's obvious the title was chosen for the same reason editors often choose titles: to fit head space. There is room for only two words. Those two words were "Blue Melody." The problem was, that was not the title Salinger gave it. "Scratchy Needle on a Phonograph Record" was Salinger's original title, which does capture a sense of innocence lost Salinger was so clearly obsessed with.

A. E. HOTCHNER: He grabbed the magazine out of my hand and looked at it. His face turned apoplectic red. He blew his stack. He spewed an angry denunciation of me. "What kind of friend are you? How did you let this happen?" I tried to get a word in, saying, "I have no control over what's done in the final edit." He said, "You have to have control. I told you—you were in charge of it and I trusted you with it. I'll never trust you again on anything." He said it was a terrible deceit on my part. I had promised. He was furious about it. And he walked out. That was it. He left me with my beer, sitting at the table. He took the magazine with him. I never saw him again.

Conversation with Salinger #4

SHANE SALERNO: In 1976 Gordon Lish, the fiction editor of *Esquire*, was told by his boss, "We need to publish something that's going to generate a lot of buzz." That night Lish got drunk, typed out a story, and called it "For Rupert—with No Promises." It appeared in the magazine sans byline.

MYLES WEBER: "For Rupert—with No Promises" obviously echoes "For Esmé—with Love and Squalor." Many people thought it might be a new Salinger story. In fact it was a rather brief exercise in mimicking Salinger's style.

PAUL ALEXANDER: The prose style was intended to feel like Salinger might have written it, had it been his first published story in a dozen years.

There was a burst of interest; copies flew off the stands. The magazine literally sold out.

MYLES WEBER: It's astonishing that anyone took it to be a Salinger story because it has none of Salinger's wit and it's not very carefully written.

ANONYMOUS, "For Rupert—with No Promises" (*Esquire*, February 1977):

> If I say more about Rupert in regard of his unearthliness I will not be for long free from confusion. I will—what I want to tell you will—fall victim to the disorder of passion, and I have promised you clarity. I have also promised someone squalor. I now intend, in all scruple and with haste, with reverence and haste, to keep both promises—and to save my brother, and everyone else, in the bargain.

MICHAEL SILVERBLATT: It didn't sound like Salinger, but I figured someone who'd been withholding his fiction for such a long time was not going to sound the same. His sensibility had had a chance to refurbish during this silence. It wasn't going to sound like anything any of us would have expected. I was fooled for a few days, but after a few phone calls it became clear that Gordon Lish, the infamous editor, was behind it. He's interested in literature as infection. He's a Captain Hook type. He likes the down and dirty. He's a profoundly provocative guy.

GORDON LISH: There was an enormous amount of press coverage. The speculation was that either Updike or Cheever had written the story, although many readers believed it may have been Salinger who wrote it. There was colossal interest from TV and radio. *Esquire* sold the magazine out. Two or three months later, I finally told an agent I wrote it because she made me believe I owed her. Within days she was telling people at a cocktail party that I'd written the story. So I came into a great deal of criticism. The story of who the author really was broke on the front page of the *Wall Street Journal.* I heard from Salinger, through that agent, that he thought what I had done was absurd and despicable. That needled me because I didn't think it was either. My feeling was that if Salinger was not going to write stories, someone had to write them for him.

MICHAEL SILVERBLATT: It could only have been done by a scoundrel, and Gordon Lish likes being a scoundrel. Even in the classroom, he tells his students, "You're at the edge of a cliff, and you're going to jump off. Why should anyone be paying attention to you? What can you do with your very first sentence that's going to galvanize attention?" Suggesting the story was by J. D. Salinger was obviously an effective attention-getting device. At the time it came out, it wasn't exactly common knowledge that Salinger was still an object of such adoration that a story purported to be by him would sell out on newsstands across America.

GORDON LISH: I did not see that fiction as a hoax so much as an attractive plausibility.

MARC WEINGARTEN: I believe it remains one of the single best-selling issues of *Esquire* in the magazine's history, but you would have to check that.

9

THE ORIGIN OF ESMÉ

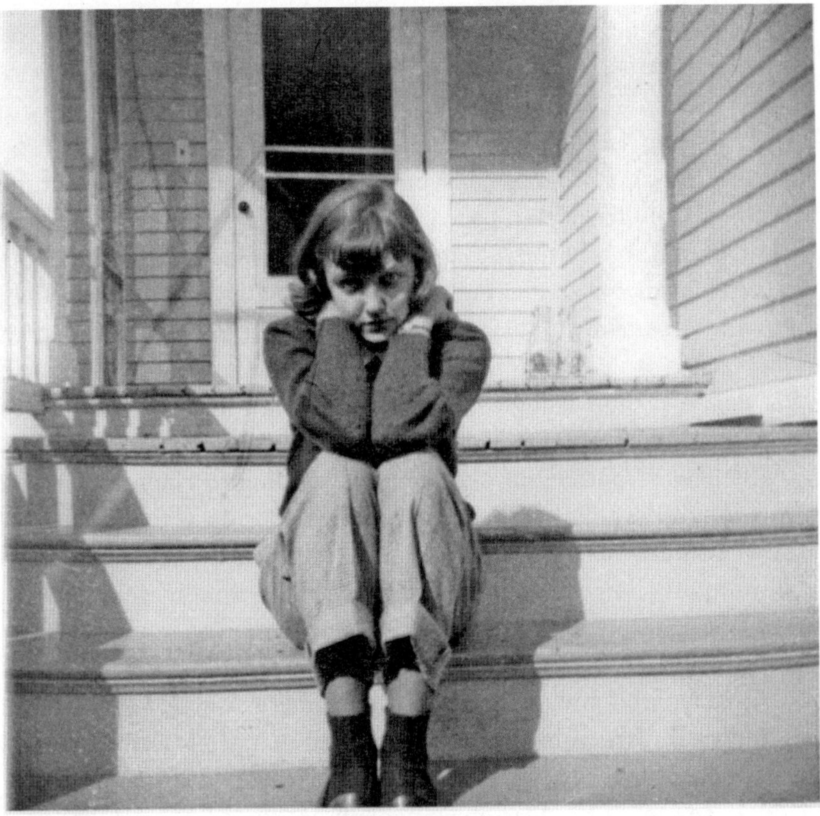

Jean Miller.

Salinger meets a fourteen-year old girl, Jean Miller, and over the next five years corresponds with her, dates her, and seduces her. The same pattern recurs throughout his life: innocence admired, innocence seduced, innocence abandoned. Salinger is obsessed with girls at the edge of their bloom. He wants to help them bloom, then he needs to blame them for blooming.

SHANE SALERNO: When Ian Hamilton was researching his book *In Search of J. D. Salinger*, he visited the archives of *Time* magazine. In the research folders was an item from the West Coast correspondent that was never published. It read, "We have found a lead that may finally open Salinger's closet of little girls." Apparently, Richard Gehman, who had clashed with Salinger when editing his stories at *Cosmopolitan*, had provided *Time* with the tip that Salinger, in his early thirties, had once proposed marriage to a teenage girl. The research speculates that this girl may have been the model for Sybil in "Bananafish."

According to Hamilton, the parents of the teenage girl ended the match, but the friendship lasted "two years." *Time* tracked down the girl's father, who told them that some "ten years earlier," around 1950, "he and his family had met Salinger at a hotel in Daytona Beach, Florida." The father wrote, "He fastened on my daughter, J——— and spent a lot of time with her." J's father speculated that Salinger's standoffish behavior—"he didn't mingle much"—might be attributable to Salinger's being Jewish. "I mean, I thought he might have a chip on his shoulder."

The *Time* reporter's ensuing memo, according to Hamilton, noted: "This establishes that J (the girl) met JDS in Florida. Check pub. dates of Esmé and Bananafish to determine if J, at 16 or 17, could have been the wellspring for either of these fictional girls. Secondly we should redouble our efforts to find a divorce record in vicinity of Daytona"—that is, might J have been the cause of Salinger's divorce?

Time reporter Bill Smith located and interviewed J, now married. He reported, "J tried to be aloof . . . didn't remember where she had met Salinger or what he was like. Well, did she deny that, as a child, she had known him in Florida? She puffed on her cigarette a moment, as if debating over which plea to enter: 'Yes,' she said carefully. 'I think I do deny it.'"

Smith's take on J's response was this: "There is only one reasonable conclusion: that she is lying, presumably to protect Salinger."

The initial "J" is all we had to work on. We did a lot of research and concluded that *Time* came up empty because the magazine not only had the date wrong (it was 1949) but also J's age was wrong (she was fourteen). Finding Jean Miller took years of detective work, and finding her was only the beginning. For sixty years she had kept silent about her relationship with Salinger. It took a number of conversations over many months to convince her to reveal exactly what happened in 1949.

JEAN MILLER: We were in Daytona Beach, and I was sitting at this rather crowded pool at the Sheraton Hotel, by the beach. This was January or February 1949. I was from a little town in upstate New York, and my family always went to Florida for the winter. I went to a little private school there for three or four months, from eight to one, and then I'd spend the afternoons on the beach or by the pool, reading, doing homework.

I was reading *Wuthering Heights*, and a man said to me, "How is Heathcliff? How is Heathcliff?" He said it, I don't know how many times, but I was concentrating, and I finally heard it peripherally. And I turned to him and I said, "Heathcliff is troubled."

Salinger and his sister, Doris, vacationing in Daytona Beach, Florida.

I looked at him. He had a long, wonderful, angular face and deep, brooding, sad-looking eyes. He was in this terry cloth bathrobe, and his legs were very white; he was very pale. He wasn't exactly shivering, but he didn't look like he belonged at this pool.

J. D. SALINGER ("A Perfect Day for Bananafish," *The New Yorker*, January 31, 1948):

> "He won't take his bathrobe off? Why not?"
>
> "*I* don't know. I guess because he's so pale."

JEAN MILLER: He looked old. And he was not going to stop talking, so I put my book aside. We began a conversation, and he was very intense. His mind seem to skitter over various topics. He told me he was a writer and that he had published a few stories in the *New Yorker*, and he felt this was his finest accomplishment.

Jean Miller, age fourteen, on Daytona Beach.

Salinger and Jean Miller would take walks down to this Daytona Beach pier.

We sat there talking for quite a while, and finally he asked me how old I was, and I said fourteen. And I remember very clearly his grimace. He said he was thirty. He made a point of saying that he was thirty on January first so that, in a way, he was just thirty; he had just come out of his twenties. He was funny, sort of a wisecracking sense of humor. We sat there for quite a while. I left, and as I was going away he told me his name was Jerry. I had no idea who he was.

I saw him the next day, and we began these walks. We would walk down to this old rickety pier and find a bench and sit where the wind wasn't blowing, eat popcorn or ice cream, and we'd talk. And we'd feed popcorn to the seagulls. He was having a wonderful time. We walked very slowly down to the pier. It was like he was escorting me. We'd do this every afternoon for about ten days.

He was very deaf in his right ear. I think something to do with the war. He would always have his left shoulder behind me and lean down to hear what I had to say. I would do cartwheels on the beach, and then I would whip off into the ocean, and he would love that. I think he felt it was as close to a perfect, maybe even direct moment that he'd had—maybe ever had. These perfect moments: they got him away from his melancholy, his angst about the war. He seemed to take joy out of my childishness. The frivolity and the pure innocence of fourteen-year-old me, I think, is what he was attracted to.

He was very tall, thin, and I don't know that he was athletic, but he was graceful. He was careful with what he wore; he always looked very neat. He was awfully good-looking. It wasn't his main attraction, but he was very good-looking.

Jerry Salinger listened like you were the most important person in the world. He was the first adult who seemed to be genuinely interested in what I had to say. No grown-up had really listened to me as though I was a person in my own right. Jerry was interested in my opinions; everything about me he was interested in. He wanted to know about my family, about my school, what games I played. He wanted to know who I was reading, what I was studying. He wanted to know whether I believed in God. Did I want to be an actress?

He began talking about the Brontës, the moors, how he loved the Brontës, how everyone—every student, every adult, every old person—should read the Brontës, read them over and over again. He talked most of that day.

He was not pleased at all with all the slick magazines; they would change names or take out sections or rewrite some sections, and never with any permission from the author. [His stories] would just appear in a form that he didn't know was going to happen. He was very down on most every publisher, and of course he hadn't even gone to the book publishing world yet.

He talked about his publishers, what a parasitic group they were. He said publishers were not on the writer's side. The only publishers that he really had any respect for at all, and actually had a great deal of respect for, were the people at the *New Yorker*: Harold Ross, William Shawn, Gus Lobrano, William Maxwell. He would wax on about the *New Yorker* and how it was the only place he wanted to publish. He might publish in *Harper's* or *Atlantic Monthly*, but they didn't pay as well. He very much liked the idea that the *New Yorker* didn't insist upon knowing a great deal about the author. He always felt that what people should know about an author was nothing personal.

He talked about Ring Lardner. He admired Fitzgerald tremendously. He told me what to read, that I should read the classics. Never mind with this modern rubbish. Read Chekhov. Read Turgenev. Read Proust.

He talked about his family, his mother. He adored his mother. His father thought his writing was silly. Self-indulgent.

At night, with the dancing, he was a different person—very gregarious and fun-loving and free. He could be very carefree. He was a very kind, gentle man, very interested in other people. He was not egocentric. He was not a solipsist. He simply was interested in other people.

SHANE SALERNO: Salinger broke up with his first wife, Sylvia, at the Daytona Sheraton in 1946; he began his seduction of fourteen-year-old Jean Miller at the Daytona Sheraton in 1949; he broke up with Joyce Maynard at the Daytona Sheraton in 1972; and he set "Bananafish" more or less at the Daytona Sheraton. He continually returns to the scene of Seymour's suicide.

JEAN MILLER: He talked about his novel quite a bit—how he was working on it and had been working on it. At least one story had been published about Holden. Jerry told me there was a great deal of Holden in him.

J. D. SALINGER, excerpt from letter to Jean Miller, undated:

> *You say you still feel fourteen. I know the feeling. I'm thirty-four and too much of the time I still feel like a sixteen-year-old Holden Caulfield.*

The Daytona Beach Sheraton Hotel.

JEAN MILLER: One of the things that worried him about *The Catcher in the Rye* was that usually books are a hit one year and that's the end of it. You're gonna be constantly under pressure to write another book. I think that made him nervous because he wasn't sure he could write another book, that he had a subject for another book; maybe he wanted to go back to short stories.

According to Jerry, during fallow periods, you may not think you're accomplishing anything, but it's a form of preparation. And it seemed to him the best way to use the fallow years was to really examine your misery—really examine the position you're in. That is the waiting time.

He wasn't worried about his book from an artistic point of view. He wasn't even worried about it from a financial point of view. He was worried about how it was going to be received by people, particularly people he loved: his parents, various friends. He felt nervous about Holden's language. Maybe people would find the language unnecessary. But he wanted people to know, absolutely, that he was trying to write a good book—not just a bestseller, a good book.

I felt very free with him. Lent came, and I said I'm giving up popcorn for Lent. Anybody else I had said that to over the age of thirty would have said, "Fine, fine," but much to my amazement he took it very seriously. He took me very seriously. And because of my age of fourteen, I was very grateful for that. No grown-up had ever really listened to me as though I were a person in my own right.

He talked of Oona O'Neill quite lovingly. Naturalness was a big thing for Jerry. He thought she was unpretentious, almost childlike, and this would very much impress Jerry. Now whether that's true really about Oona O'Neill or whether he just saw that in her, I have no idea. But he obviously loved her very much, even though he no longer saw her. My impression was that he thought she was wonderful. I heard no bitterness in his voice at all. He told me about some of the times he spent with her.

He talked of his first wife a lot. I don't know whether she was French or German, but they married in Europe after the war, and I don't know how they met. He said they kept in touch telepathically.

He did not talk to me about the war.

My mother was taking a dim view of these walks on the beach I was taking with this man. She found out Jerry was J. D. Salinger. She read the *New Yorker*, and she said, "He looks just like Seymour." He did, but I didn't know the story yet. I had no idea who Seymour was. I didn't care.

My mother said, "A man like that is only after one thing, Jean; you better be careful." She knew he had written "A Perfect Day for Bananafish."

Those times at the pier were the most carefree and fun: getting to know each other, enjoying each other. Those two days were probably the most fun we had together. Much later he said, "I wish I could have been able to keep you at that pier." I had never talked to a creative man before. I had never talked to such an erudite man versed in so many subjects. He was very amusing, eyes twinkling and cracking jokes. He saw the humor in things, but it was a very kind humor. If I said something in a gossipy fashion about someone I didn't know, maybe even something mean about someone, he would defend that person. He would say, "That person has something to offer, even if she's an old woman and she's fat. She's not nosy; she has a great curiosity. You should try to look for good in people. Don't see their worst traits all the time."

DAVID SHIELDS: As Zooey tells Franny, "There isn't anyone out there who isn't Seymour's Fat Lady." Salinger repeated this mantra constantly because he was trying to convince himself of the veracity of Zooey's claim. The Fat Lady, Zooey explains to his sister, is Christ himself.

JEAN MILLER: He wanted to know what I was studying. He wanted to know everything about me and tried, I think very subtly, to put some thoughts in my mind of how I might, in the future, center myself and make my life around something that I could work for rather than drifting. He made me start my education. It was the beginning of me thinking, and not necessarily in an intellectual way, although that, too, but to get in touch with my center.

He was after that innocence and purity of childhood, which Zen tries to recapture. Living in the moment, fully, totally in the moment, as children do. A state of grace.

He talked a lot about Judy Garland and child actors, the innocence of actors and the beauty of their purity. He liked the innocence of childhood before pretention set in: the clear, simple way she sang in *The Wizard of Oz*. The direct experience that children had. Learning to walk for the first time. Seeing a camera for the first time. Forming their own opinions. Getting their own experience. That's very close to Zen.

At the end of his stay in Daytona, his very last day, he gave me a little white elephant as a talisman and said, "Even if we never see each other

Jean Miller's mother in front of the Sheraton Plaza Hotel.

again, I wish you all the good." He also said, "I'd like to kiss you goodbye, but you know I can't." It was just a given that we were going to write each other. Before we parted he went up to my mother and said in the lobby of the Sheraton, "I am going to marry your daughter." Well, I can't imagine my mother's reaction to that.

He wrote immediately; a letter arrived right away, mailed to the Princess Issena Hotel, Daytona, where we were staying. He was living in Stamford, Connecticut. The address was on the letterhead, and he asked me to write him, and would it be all right for him to write me, and I wrote back, "Of course it would be okay."

J. D. SALINGER, excerpt from letter to Jean Miller, March 19, 1949:

Dear Jean,

I arrived in New York with my room key from the Sheraton in my pocket.

It's good to think that you're still in Daytona, walking in the sun, sitting in those green canvas chairs by the pool, playing tennis in your red sweater.

Hope you'll write to me at great length, Jean. It's cold and bleak up here. Not a seagull in sight. (The seagull has come to be my favorite bird.)

Yours, Jerry

JEAN MILLER: We began exchanging letters. And later he began sending quite a few Western Union telegrams. He always talked about his work. I wrote him about his story "The Laughing Man." I said I had trouble with the vocabulary, and he wrote back saying that he had trouble with the vocabulary, too. That it was the kind of story that needed big words to hold it together.

J. D. SALINGER, excerpt from letter to Jean Miller, March 28, 1949:

Dear Jean,

Yours is the only letter I've ever had with seagulls in it. Even before I opened the letter, I could hear the flapping of wings inside the envelope. I've set a little pre-summer work deadline for myself, and I may not get much of a chance to write you for a few weeks. But if you have time, you write to me—all right? I miss you and think of you.

Jerry

JEAN MILLER: I remember once getting into a big fight on my village green in Homer, New York, after we returned from Florida, with another girl. We had each other down in the grass, and she gave me a black eye and a bloody nose, and I limped home and I called Jerry. Well, he just thought that was wonderful.

He didn't say, like my mother, "You're too old to be fighting." He was a grown-up on my side. He was always on my side. He didn't judge me. He said, "Well, maybe you should take some karate lessons. Maybe I could get you a Charles Atlas book for young girls. Maybe you've got to do something to build up your muscles." He wasn't even laughing. Of course, I was crying. That's what I mean when I say he took me very seriously.

We used to play softball in our front yard, and he'd want to know how many hits I had, how many times I struck out. He loved people my age. He'd instruct me via letter or via phone on my tennis backhand. He didn't want me to be literary. He wanted to talk about my childhood pursuits.

J. D. SALINGER ("The Laughing Man," *Nine Stories,* 1953):

> Over on third base, Mary Hudson waved to me. I waved back. I couldn't have stopped myself, even if I'd wanted to. Her stick-work aside, she happened to be a girl who knew how to wave to somebody from third base.

JEAN MILLER: I remember early on thinking, "How am I going to write this man?" I could be as chatty as him, but I began worrying about sentence structure at the age of fourteen because of him. And there was really no one to ask. I wasn't going to ask my mother, and no one else knew I knew him. There was nobody who knew. I had no one to ask how to write these letters. There was a lot in me that I did not say to him because I didn't have the nerve to say. I don't know what I thought was going to happen to me if I opened up, but I wasn't taking any chances. I think he sent me about fifty or sixty letters.

SHANE SALERNO: Jean later explained to me that Salinger actually wrote many more than sixty letters to her, but that her mother threw away many of them.

J. D. SALINGER, excerpt from letter to Jean Miller, April 16, 1949:

> *I've been working steadily for weeks, and just finished a very long story. I like it, but the New Yorker doesn't see eye to eye with me on it.*
>
> *People seem so sure that a writer's life is a gay one. No office to go to, no regular hours. All the independence and travel opportunities in the world. And it may be a gay life for some writers. I haven't found it that way.*

JEAN MILLER: He didn't like Stamford, and after a while he moved back in with his family on Park Avenue. That's a very funny letter, because he was in his old childhood room and he lists the things that were there to haunt him: invisible-ink pens and rejection slips and hysterical draft notices and invitations to weddings and tennis rackets and Charles Atlas books falling out of the closet when he opened the door. It was very comical, but he was not pleased to be staying back at his parents' home.

J. D. SALINGER, excerpt from letter to Jean Miller, June 3, 1949:

> *I grew up in this room, and all the unthrilling landmarks still stare at me in the face. If I open a closet door, I'm liable to get hit on the head with an Old Tom Swift book. Or a tennis racket with shriveled strings. My desk drawers are full of stale memories too. You're going to be fifteen soon, aren't you? My best to you, Jean.*
>
> *Jerry*

JEAN MILLER: The next time we met was probably in the spring, when I was in New York City with my family. He came to meet us, and I took a walk with him. I remember exactly what I had on. I had a little tan suit on with little white gloves and a little straw hat. We were walking down the street and the straw hat blew off and I thought, "Oh, how embarrassing." I was very intimidated in New York, anyway. Tall buildings, beautiful hotels. I was a very small-town girl, which probably was part of my appeal to him. He loved the idea of my hat blowing off; he used to refer to it later. He ran like a child to get my hat and stomped on it because the wind would take it away again. And I remember thinking, "He's really having fun."

I was amazed that he would get into this game of chasing my hat. I remember he had very long legs, and he couldn't run very well, and I remember those knees sort of knocking together as he came back and formally gave me my hat, which was a little bit bashed, and put it back on my head. He laughed about it for about fifteen minutes.

My parents were not about to let me out in New York on my own. I just wasn't equipped to do that. He made an arrangement with them. The four of us went out to dinner that night.

He found a cottage to rent in Westport, which he described as being in the woods about a mile from town. He was very pleased at first, but decided that [Westport] was too writer-conscious, so he got his own apartment on East 57th Street. By then it was after *Catcher in the Rye* had been published.

He was getting a lot of attention in New York. After the novel came out, he was very sought after, and he hated that. He hated people's questions. He hated people's praises. He hated people's criticisms. Maybe the criticisms were the worst. People were a distraction. I was having dinner with my parents and Jerry, and a waiter handed Jerry a note from a woman. Jerry went over to her table and spoke to the woman for a couple of minutes and came back. He showed me the note: "Are you J. D. Salinger?" It was all very casual and my only indication of his celebrity.

I always saw boys my own age. At one point I met a boy on a trip to Europe and visited him at Middlebury, where I boasted that I was a friend of J. D. Salinger's. I was more cognizant then that he was famous. The boy I told this to called him up for an interview. He told the boy he didn't do interviews. Jerry reprimanded me gently. He said, "If he was a beau of yours, [I] should have said yes and shot him on the spot." In a distant way he was very tender.

At that point he had moved to Cornish, New Hampshire. He said his friends were concerned about his move to isolation, particularly the ones who liked his fiction. They thought he would lose touch with people and therefore have nothing to write about. It didn't mean he was a hermit. He just didn't want to be with writers. And he certainly didn't want to be the toast of New York. He said there were literary parasites and he didn't want anything to do with them.

J. D. SALINGER, excerpt from letter to Jean Miller, April 30, 1953:

> *I planted some vegetables yesterday. Since then, I've gone out every hour on the hour to see if anything's come up. Have no idea how long it takes for a seed to turn into a carrot.*

JEAN MILLER: I was at a place called Briarcliff Junior College, in Briarcliff Manor, New York, which isn't far from New York City.

J. D. SALINGER, excerpt from letter to Jean Miller, April 30, 1953:

> *You don't think you'll be invited back to Briarcliff next year? Maybe you're exaggerating. If the school has any real sense, it'll take you back. You're probably the only girl with any style there. Lousy grades, maybe, but style.*

Jean Miller, age seventeen.

JEAN MILLER: I remember when I would speak to him about school he was very down on education. "Don't believe everything your professors say," he would tell me. "They're just giving you information. Get your own information on your own terms. Stay detached." This was a theme throughout Jerry's life—professors insisting in a pedantic way on students regurgitating knowledge. No direct experience of learning, of spontaneity, of creating.

I think you can see it in [Salinger's fictional character] Teddy, who says, "I would bring in an elephant, and I wouldn't tell the children that this elephant was an elephant or that it was gray or that is a trunk or this is an ear. I would let them have that direct experience themselves. I wouldn't tell them grass was green. Green is just a color." Jerry quoted Mary Baker Eddy: "Nothing is good or bad; it's what we think that makes it so." His whole life was built on this: trying to reach the state of grace through mysticism. If it hadn't been for Jerry Salinger, I never would have gone through the—gone below the surface at all in my life. A Bhagavad Gita quest. A seriousness in my life: questioning things, learning things, learning things on my own.

Jerry would often send me airline tickets to come visit him.

J. D. SALINGER, excerpt from letter to Jean Miller, October 5, 1953:

> *What a good girl you are, and if things go too roughly this winter—what with parental pressure, etc.—you can arrive up here any time you feel like it, bag and baggage, cigarette holder and all, and I'll share my homely fare with you.*
>
> *It's easy and quick to fly up here. North East Airlines, out of LaGuardia, makes West Lebanon in an hour and forty-five minutes, and that's only ten minutes by car from me. Smith's taxi service, in Windsor, now know where the hell my house is.*

JEAN MILLER: I remember his Cornish home; it was difficult to get there. I was very aware that Jerry Salinger didn't want to be talked about as J. D. Salinger. I might have spoken vaguely about my friend Jerry to my friends, that I was going to New Hampshire some weekend to see him. But I would never say, "I am seeing J. D. Salinger." After that experience with that boy, I was even more careful.

There was never an inkling of anything physical between us until much later. I would go up to Cornish; I'd spend the night with him in the same bed. Me over here, him over there. This happened several times because there was no place else to sleep. We were camping out. It's absolutely the truth. It was a genderless relationship. We were friends. We were buddies. Sex did not come into it.

J. D. SALINGER, excerpt from letter to Jean Miller, undated:

> *I was oddly touched that you'd made the bed before we left the house. It amounts to a beau geste, and I'm duly grateful.*

JEAN MILLER: I remember once, probably pretty early on, we were in a bookstore. I tentatively picked out *Lady Chatterley's Lover*. He looked at me and said, "You don't want to read that." I put it right back. He was very puritanical. He enjoyed being childlike. He didn't like adults particularly. I probably would have fallen into bed with him at about the age of three if he'd asked me, but he didn't. Somehow it never occurred. As long as it didn't occur to him, it didn't occur to me.

DAVID SHIELDS: Salinger's seduction process: adore childhood innocence in a pubescent girl, seduce it and her into (barely) adulthood, reproduce the assignation in his writing, and compare actual physical contact to Esmé or Zen—a comparison no human can survive.

JEAN MILLER: He had a wonderful view of Mount Ascutney. I remember sitting by the fire and dancing with him at night to Lawrence Welk or Liberace or something like that. He liked to dance, Jerry. It was fun. We would look at the people on television dancing and we just would waltz, laughing all the time. He laughed a lot. He seemed filled with joy a great deal of the time. He could be like that when he had guests, too. He was such a big character.

I also remember seeing two beautifully leather-bound books, *The Catcher in the Rye* and *Nine Stories*. And I know from back in Daytona days that he fought being a consumer. He did not want to want things, but leather was a great temptation for him. He just couldn't resist doing that.

He said to me, "I don't belong to you and you don't belong to me, and we just see each other and have this great time." He told me in October 1953 that nothing had changed for him since Dayton Beach.

J. D. SALINGER, excerpt from letter to Jean Miller, October 1953:

> *It still seems completely good and meaningful to see your face and be with you.*
>
> *I simply think you're a beautiful girl in every sense.*

JEAN MILLER: At one point, he asked me to move in with him. That letter doesn't survive. I showed it to a friend of mine, a boy from Amherst. I never, ever would have done it because my parents had too much control over me. But I did think about it. And I thought I could never really survive up there. I had been there. I could see what would be expected of me, which was pretty much drudgery, and I was just too spoiled. I had too much self-interest to really take that invitation seriously.

I began to worship him, which is maybe too strong a word, but I was still young. It had nothing to do with his physical appearance. It was his powerful, brilliant mind. His sheer strength of character. Of the rightness and wrongness of things. The way you should look at things. He was a very persuasive man. He never talked about people.

I'm afraid you do compare other men that come in and out of your life to him. His intensity and his curiosity. His—I was going to say "charm," but I don't know that he necessarily did have charm. His knowledge. Scratch "knowledge." His wisdom. I've known people that have approached it, but not totally. I had a wonderful husband who approached it. But I mean there's no point in looking.

Here was this fascinating man who seemed to like me, and I think in one of the letters he says that we have put each other on pedestals. And if anything is to become of us, we'll have to get rid of those pedestals. We were just sort of dancing on these pedestals, not getting any closer. Both of us would've had to fall off a pedestal. Otherwise I cannot imagine a marriage.

He never told me his real vulnerabilities. We weren't terribly close. I did not feel like a unit with him against the world, as I did with my husband. I was in awe of him. I was tongue-tied. I was gun-shy. He was up there and I was down here. I really didn't know what there could be in me that could affect him.

Jerry Salinger remembered me always on that pier in Daytona Beach, and I was beginning to change. He wrote about my change. He went on to say in another letter how little really he knew about me. There were great parts of me that he didn't know.

I had grown from a little girl to a young woman. My feelings for him developed as I developed. I think he thought I was much brighter than I really was. I'm not saying I'm stupid, but I am saying that I just don't think I was the sensitive person he thought I was. I just knew it in my gut. And there was no point in me trying to be. I was a woman and I was trying to look my best, and when I would meet him, I would do the best I could. We used to meet at the Biltmore under the clock, or he would take me to the Palm Room at the Plaza, where I'd loved to go as a little child. He took me once as a little girl to the Palm to listen to the violins and have tea sandwiches.

Or we'd go to the theater. I remember seeing the Lunts onstage once. I don't remember what play. And that's when he said to me, "Would you like to be an actress? Have you thought of being an actress? I think you should maybe think about being an actress."

He took me to the Stork Club; it was great fun. Other times we'd go to the Blue Angel to hear music. Wonderful atmosphere and greedy-looking people sitting around eating fat steaks and smoking cigars with lots of drinks. You felt as if you were in an important place. I was a woman. He was courting me. We would do things that courting couples do: go to the theater or go to nightclubs.

When he first saw me, he told me, I was talking to an older lady and I yawned, but I stifled the yawn—which is what Esmé does in the story, when she's singing in the choir. He told me he could not have written "Esmé" had he not met me.

But he never told me he was in love with me. He wouldn't always come to New York to see me. He wrote me in one of his letters that he'd made promises to himself. He had to write in Cornish, and he was

Jean Miller, age eighteen.

writing something very autumn, with autumn thoughts, right now, and he couldn't face concrete. In his letter he said what an unromantic man he must seem at that moment, that I'd have every right to tell him to go jump in the lake and to go off with some less neurotic person.

He needed to put himself into a cell-like existence. I don't know that Jerry Salinger necessarily liked the country. I think he probably grew to like the country, but the only thing he wanted to do was write. He went someplace to write that he knew he was going to be comfortable in, and he made it work for himself.

Since deciding to write, he didn't really have a free life. He couldn't take even so much as a drive in the country without having the weight of words on him, pushing him down, whereas a businessman could go for a drive in the country and turn it off. Really he could take his typewriter anywhere. His traveling was not really traveling. It was just taking his typewriter someplace else geographically.

SHARON STEEL: In a letter to Michael Mitchell (the artist who designed the original jacket for *The Catcher in the Rye*) dated May 22, 1951, Salinger writes from London, detailing his experiences sharing drinks with a *Vogue* model he met on the ship. ("No real fun, though.") . . .

Later, he hangs out with Laurence Olivier ("a very nice guy") and his wife, Vivien Leigh, whom he calls "a charmer." Salinger finds himself at a party—where he accidentally snorts gin up his nose—with the Australian ballet dancer Robert Helpmann, described as a "sinister looking pansy," and argues with Enid Starkie about Kafka. He also goes to see a play and compares the theater in New York City to that in London's West End. "The audiences here are just as stupid as they [are] in New York, but the productions are much, much better," he writes to his "Buddyroo," Mitchell.

JEAN MILLER: His work was his karmic duty. His work was what he had. His work was his whole being. He was so focused on his work. I mean he started out as a romantic and ended up pulling back. That's the way I viewed it.

I went to Briarcliff in 1952 and got out in 1954. I was nineteen or twenty. He would come to visit and we would go out to dinner. I remember particularly that he came when I'd had a fencing lesson. Fencing always made me perspire, so my hair looked wonderful. I remember being very pleased about that. He'd be standing at the door, not really wanting to come in, not wanting to be recognized. He'd whisk me away and we'd go up to a restaurant near the Tappan Zee Bridge.

Sometimes he would take me out for an evening in New York. I remember once seeing the George Washington Bridge lit up and thinking how absolutely beautiful—it was insane how beautiful it was. He laughed and said, "Jean, you've got to learn not to say the obvious."

One night he took me for drinks at the Maxwells' [William Maxwell, the writer and *New Yorker* fiction editor, and his wife, Emily], and I remember that particularly because I loved them both. I had a little watch that my grandmother had given me. It was a Tiffany watch and I kept losing it, leaving it in Cornish or leaving it here or there, and Jerry said something about the watch that wasn't true. I don't know what it could have been. But I contradicted him and both the Maxwells said, "Good for you, Jean, good for you." As though I, this little girl, had contradicted Jerry, and Jerry wasn't used to being contradicted.

Only once did I ever hear him speak of being a half-Jew. It was dinner at the Maxwells'. I gathered that his Jewishness was a problem to him. He asked me to sort of back into the ending of "Down at the Dinghy." "Don't be shocked." Or "You may be shocked. I had to write the story. I'm sorry I wrote it, but I had to write the story just once."

I think he was enjoying me as a child all those years. I'm the one who changed it. We were in the backseat of a taxi and I turned and kissed him. It was very natural. I wanted to kiss him, so I kissed him. I suppose I gave him permission—"It's okay now"—but it would never have come from him. Well, probably it would have, but I did it first. My daughter thinks it was important to him to wait for me to reach the age of eighteen before we had sex. I don't think that.

Soon after the cab kiss we went to Montreal for the weekend. I don't remember very much about it, but I do remember sitting in a restaurant and there was a lovely-looking girl who looked very shy and uncomfortable. I remember Jerry commenting on her. There were also two very businessmen-like people talking about mysticism.

We went up to our room and we went to bed. I told him I was a virgin, and he didn't like that. He didn't want the responsibility of that, I guess. The next day, having had my rite of passage, we flew back to Boston; from there, me on to New York and he on to West Lebanon, New Hampshire. Somehow, during the flight to Boston, he got the idea that his connecting plane was canceled. I began laughing because I was delighted that we could spend the afternoon together. I saw this veil come down over his face. I saw the look on his face. It was just a look of horror and hurt. It was terrible and conveyed everything. I knew it was over. I knew I had fallen off that pedestal.

I didn't have a plane until later in the day. He went right to the desk, got the ticket changed, hustled me right onto an earlier plane. There was no questioning, discussion, no ambiguity. I had come between him and his work, and it was over. I got maybe one or two letters from him after that, which don't survive because I was too upset. I suffered, but I also blame myself. After all these years I should have known what he told me. Read the letters. All those letters say, "My work has to come first."

It was extreme, particularly after what had just happened to us the night before, but it had to be. I had no choice but to accept it. I think he all of a sudden realized I was a phony, and that's his word, "phony." That's what I think he thought. Because of being a virgin, which I had never told him. All of a sudden he saw me in an entirely different light.

There was never any question in his mind that he was a writer and that's what he was meant to do: write. It was a Bhagavad Gita duty, as far as he was concerned, although he hated the word "duty." His work was ordained by God. It was his way to enlightenment. He was put on this earth to write. And I became a distraction; it took only two minutes to become a distraction. I was just devastated. I suffered, but I got over it. I had to get over it.

Zen was something that he talked about a lot. In one of his letters, he said, "I'm sorry you couldn't go to the basketball game tonight. There was Zen there." Zen is where you find it. These were perfect moments for him.

In 1955 I was in Daytona again. I was in the Ocean Room, dancing. I looked out a window, and there was Jerry Salinger with this beautiful girl. They sort of looked married to me. Married or not, they were together. They just were a beautiful couple. He was a very good-looking man. She was a lovely-looking woman.

They were walking along. It was above the pool on a walkway, and they looked very comfortable together. They were obviously out for an after-dinner walk. I can't say they looked ecstatically happy. They weren't necessarily arm in arm, but they didn't look unhappy. They looked simpatico.

I was very taken back. I was looking out this window, dancing with somebody, and there he was. I was driving down Main Street the next day and I saw him walking from a bar where I had been with him, where he and my father used to have drinks together, with this woman on his arm who became his second wife, Claire Salinger.

How did I feel? I didn't feel good, but I was powerless to do anything about it. That was the last time I ever saw him. I was shocked when I saw him at that window, but he saw me. I know that. Our eyes met. He saw me. And the next time I looked again, he was gone. They were gone. I had known it ended quite a while before that moment.

He always told me that when you run into somebody, if you get all shy, there's still something there.

When Jerry Salinger was through with somebody, he was through. I knew that he was very definitely out of my life. I adored him and we had a wonderful five years, for which I am very grateful. I am very grateful to have known him. He changed me, but I didn't know it at the time.

He was an avuncular figure in my life. He was my buddy. I never felt—except for the letters—I never felt adored by him. I never felt that he in any way needed me. I felt very close to him, but it seems to me we had parallel lives until the end, and then that turned out to be a disaster. I was damaged by our relationship, in the end. I was. However, that is offset by almost five years of learning, joy, fun, my mind opening up to all sorts of things.

Jerry sent me two books for Christmas: "To Jean, from Jerry, December 1953"—Eugen Herrigel's *Zen in the Art of Archery* and *The Sutra of Hui Neng*. Then he wrote me a long letter explaining to me as best as he could about Zen, which is living in the moment. It's having direct experience, forgetting your ego, losing your ego. People should work against having egos. Childlike, pure, nothing between you and experience: that is the way, according to Jerry Salinger, life should be lived. His great lesson was detachment. All through my life there's a part of me that asked, "Would Jerry Salinger approve of this?" I can go five years without giving him a thought, but if there's a moral dilemma and I'm trying to figure out what the next right step is, Jerry Salinger might pop in my head. I think, "Well, I better not do it that way." Of course, it's difficult if you've been with a man like Jerry Salinger; you do compare other men who come in and out of your life to him. His intensity and his curiosity. His wisdom.

Besides the letters I have from him, there is one thing that will always serve as a memory of that special time long ago, and that is Jerry's wonderful story "For Esmé—with Love and Squalor." He told me he could not have written it if he had not met me.

10

IS THE KID IN THIS BOOK CRAZY?

STAMFORD AND WESTPORT

Written over a decade but based on the first thirty years of his life, Salinger's most popular book, *The Catcher in the Rye*, is published to both loud applause and stinging criticism.

Idiomatic, profane, both antiestablishment and invested *in* the establishment, the novel becomes over the next sixty years a book that tens of millions around the world read and love and see as almost a user's manual for disaffected adolescence. Although the reader is unlikely to know the extent to which Salinger's Post-traumatic Stress Disorder informed *Catcher*, the book is a worldwide phenomenon because he has buried that trauma inside Holden. All of us are broken; everyone, at some point, especially in adolescence, feels irreparably damaged, and we all need healing. *Catcher* provides this healing, but just barely. You don't even know how—there is just enough of an uplift at the end, but you don't feel you've been given a cure-all; you just feel healed on some deep, inarticulable level.

—

SHANE SALERNO: Holden Caulfield was crazy.

That's what Harcourt, Brace & Co. told Salinger about his greatest creation. The *New Yorker* told him they just didn't believe in the character of Holden.

The double blow struck at Salinger's two greatest fears: going insane and, far worse, being a phony.

"My boyhood was very much the same as that of the boy in the book," Salinger said, "and it was a great relief telling people about it."

Well, not at first.

The Catcher in the Rye, the greatest antiestablishment book of all time and one of the biggest bestsellers in history, almost didn't get published. A work that survived the worst horrors of World War II nearly got edited to hell in the jungles of the New York publishing world.

Salinger carried the first six chapters with him on the beaches of Normandy and into the Hürtgen Forest, through the concentration camp, and into the psychiatric ward. Throughout the war he carried the novel in his imagination. It sustained his mind through the unsustainable and bore his heart through the unbearable. It stood between him and the cliff.

The narrative—Salinger's only novel—is told in the first-person voice of Holden Caulfield. That voice *is* Salinger, direct and unfiltered by the artifice of third-person camouflage. It's his life, his thoughts, his feelings, his rage, his big beautiful middle finger to the phonies of the world.

Ten years of agony to get it all down on paper.

> *I'd just be the catcher in the rye and all. I know it's crazy, but that's the only thing I'd really like to be.*

Back in 1940 Salinger had written a note to Whit Burnett, saying that he was working on a "longer, autobiographical piece." He'd already written four short stories about Holden, considered writing a play about him—with child star Margaret O'Brien as Phoebe—and later told Hemingway that he wanted to play Holden himself.

> *I started imitating one of those guys in the movies. In one of those* musicals. *I hate the movies like poison, but I get a bang imitating them. . . . All I need's an audience. I'm an exhibitionist.*

It makes perfect sense: the book is a 214-page soliloquy. In 1944 Salinger told Burnett that he had six Holden Caulfield stories, but he wanted to save them for the novel he was writing, and that he now wanted to take his stories, all written in the third person, and use them as the basis for a novel narrated in the first person. That way, the prose would have a more immediate, personal feel.

While he was still in Europe, Salinger wrote the first short story narrated by Holden himself, the real beginning of *The Catcher in the Rye*, called "I'm Crazy."

> *I stood there—boy, I was freezing to death—and I kept saying goodby to myself, "Goodby, Caulfield. Goodby, you slob." I kept seeing myself throwing a football around, with Buhler and Jackson, just before it got dark on the September evenings, and I knew I'd never throw a football around ever again with the same guys at the same time. It was as though Buhler and Jackson and I had done something that had died and been buried, and only I knew about it, and no one was at the funeral but me.*

"I'm Crazy" is, more or less, an outline for what would become *The Catcher in the Rye*. Holden recounts how he was kicked out of boarding

Salinger's story "I'm Crazy," featuring Holden Caulfield and published in *Collier's*, December 22, 1945, shortly after his release from the Nuremberg mental hospital.

school and offers some brief insights into his own personality. "Only a crazy guy would have stood" on a hilltop in the cold with only a thin jacket on, which is what he's doing at the start of the story. "That's me. Crazy. No kidding. I have a screw loose." From there, he goes home unannounced to his parents' apartment in New York; when he arrives, he wakes his younger sister, Phoebe, from a dead sleep.

> *Old Phoebe didn't even wake up. When the light was on and all, I sort of looked at her for a while. She was laying there asleep, with her face sort of on the side of the pillow. She had her mouth way open. It's funny. You take adults, they look lousy when they're asleep and have their mouths way open, but kids don't. Kids look all right. They can even have spit all over the pillow and they still look all right.*
>
> *I went around the room, very quiet and all, looking at stuff for a while. I felt swell, for a change.*

Salinger had killed off the original Holden Caulfield in some published stories, in which a figure with the same name, who strikingly resembles the protagonist of the novel, is reported missing in action during World War II. The author had no compunction about bringing Holden back from the dead. Salinger was living in his parents' Park Avenue apartment in November 1946 when "Slight Rebellion Off Madison" featuring Holden Morrisey Caulfield, finally appeared in the *New Yorker* on December 21, 1946, and by then he had finished a ninety-page novella called *The Catcher in the Rye*, but he knew he didn't want to publish it in that form; he had more work to do on it.

Salinger needed quiet if he was going to expand the novella. Radio producer Himan Brown had just bought a property in the country, six miles from the center of town near Westport, a place for himself and his family to go and relax on weekends. There was a large studio off the main house. In 1947, a real estate agent came to Brown and said he had somebody who wanted to rent the place for eight or nine months.

A writer.

"And that's how I met a man called J. D. Salinger," Brown told us. "He wanted to be near New York City, I suppose. He had a big, black dog—that was the problem. Some of the people wouldn't rent to him with a dog. I liked the guy; he seemed young, maybe in his late twenties. I didn't know too much about him, but I did know there was a writer called Salinger who wrote for the *New Yorker*, so when he came along, I knew him as the writer of these stories. That's all I knew about him. He looked very presentable; the dog was a lovely, black dog, which I fell in love with, too.

"He said, 'Oh, I love it'—the whole idea of a studio. I think he paid $100 a month or something like that. The room had lots of windows and was thirty by forty feet with maybe a twenty-two-, twenty-four-foot ceiling. It was a perfect place to be creative, I suppose; it had character. There was a staircase going up to the bedroom upstairs, and that's where he wrote. He said to me, 'I'll be writing a book here.' I have six acres in Stamford. There's no traffic: it's a side road, a riverbank road, so he would be completely to himself."

Salinger took the place from September to June 1947, then came back for a full year in 1948.

"He was very quiet," Brown said, "and he told me that all he would be doing was writing—no parties, no visitors. He would walk around, take the dog out. The house was up eighteen or twenty steps on a little hillside. He'd walk down, walk on the roads. It was a very private neighborhood.

Salinger with Benny.

"He was very quiet about what he was doing. I could never really delve into what he was developing. I never really broke into his world of creativity. He always worked well; nothing bothered him about the house. He was in there, and if his typewriter was going, I never really knew what he was writing or what he was doing. He was very private. During the week, he was up there alone, writing, and I was in the city. This was his own world. And I knew enough not to intrude into it."

"I've taken a small place in Westport," Salinger wrote to *New Yorker* editor Gus Lobrano, "and I've started work on the novel about the prep school boy."

Writer Peter De Vries recalled, "During Salinger's brief stay in Westport, we became fast friends. I knew at the time he was writing the book, and I was enormously interested in the idea, without ever dreaming that I was being made privy to the early workings-out of a classic. I remembered saying that it all sounded very wonderful, but couldn't he think up a more catchy title?"

De Vries's son Jon remembered Salinger standing on his head and chugging double martinis. "He'd come over and express doubts about this book he was writing about this kid who said 'goddam' and 'hell' all the time."

Salinger probably wrote most of the book in Westport, but another friend said that he also holed up in a Manhattan hotel room, as well as in Carol Montgomery Newman's office at the *New Yorker*—wherever he could shut himself away to get the book done. Now thirty years old, he had been either contemplating or writing this novel for much of his adult life. It was time to finish it.

"I was eating a sandwich at my desk when our receptionist called," Harcourt, Brace editor Robert Giroux recalled. This was 1949. Giroux had wanted to publish a collection of Salinger's short stories. Salinger had tentatively agreed, but Giroux—who, like Salinger, had been an intelligence officer during the war—hadn't heard anything from the author for quite a while.

"'Mr. Salinger is here,' [my] secretary said, 'and he wants to meet you.'

"I said, 'Salinger? Pierre Salinger?'

"She said, 'Jerome. His name is Jerome.'"

"In he came," Giroux recalled. "He was very tall, dark-haired, had a horse face. He was melancholy looking. It's the truth—the first person I thought of when I saw him was Hamlet. 'Giroux,' he said. I said something like, 'Right. It's nice to meet you, Mr. Salinger.' 'Giroux,' he said again. 'Mr. Shawn [William Shawn, the editor of the *New Yorker*] has recommended you to me. But I want to tell you that to start me out it would be much better to publish my first novel instead of my stories.' I laughed, thinking, You want to be the publisher, you can have my seat. But I said, 'I'm sure you're right about that. . . . I will publish your novel. Tell me about it.' He said, 'Well, I can't show it to you yet. It's about half finished.' I said, 'Well, let me be the publisher.' And he said yes, and we shook hands."

Salinger worked hard on the book through the summer of 1950, and by autumn it was finished. One day Salinger drove from Westport to William Maxwell's home on East 86th Street and read the manuscript to Maxwell in person. He read it in its entirety, finally getting to live out his ambition of performing Holden Caulfield.

Maybe it would have helped if he'd read it aloud to the *New Yorker*. Dorothy Olding, Salinger's literary agent, submitted *Catcher* to the magazine, which promptly rejected it. The editors didn't believe in Holden as a character; they found him too articulate, even precious.

The negative reaction to *Catcher* at the *New Yorker* grew out of the magazine's unwavering bias against what it called "writer-consciousness." This was considered "showy," what the slicks let their writers do.

In a letter dated January 25, 1951, Gus Lobrano wrote:

> Possibly by now you've heard from Miss Olding and know that the vote here went, sadly, against your story.
>
> At least two of us here have read your novel, and to us the notion that in one such family (the Caulfield family) there are four such extraordinary children . . . is not quite tenable.
>
> Another point: we can't help feeling that this story is too ingenious and ingrown. . . . [There is a] prejudice here against what (as you know) we call writer-consciousness.

Lobrano himself felt Salinger was not ready to write the novel; he thought the author seemed "imprisoned" by the novel's mood and scenes. Not only did the *New Yorker* fiction editors reject it, not only did they say that it needed to be completely rewritten, but they said they didn't believe it.

They were telling him that it was phony.

Next it was Harcourt, Brace's turn to commit one of the worst mistakes in publishing history. A messenger came to Giroux's office with a package from Olding. There on the top page was the title: *The Catcher in the Rye*.

Giroux liked the novel and wanted to publish it. Then he gave it to his boss, the Harvard- and Oxford-educated Eugène Reynal, whom Giroux would later call "tactless" and a "terrible snob." Reynal, a member of the New York Social Register, could hardly have represented more exactly everything that Salinger—and Holden—despised.

When two weeks went by without a reply, Giroux went to see Reynal. "He didn't like it," Giroux recalled, "didn't understand it. He asked me, 'Is this kid in the book supposed to be crazy?'" Giroux acknowledged to Reynal that Holden was "disturbed," but asserted that *Catcher* was a great book. "Gene," Giroux said, "I've shaken hands with this author. We have a gentleman's contract at this point. I agreed to publish this book."

"Yes," Reynal answered, "but, Bob, you've got to remember, we have a textbook department."

"The *textbook* department?" Giroux asked.

"Well, it's about a kid in prep school, isn't it? I'm waiting for their reply." So Gene Reynal sent *The Catcher in the Rye* to the textbook people. Not surprisingly, they were unenthusiastic, although some people in the company fought for the book.

Giroux, realizing that Harcourt was not going to publish *The Catcher in the Rye* in its current form, took Salinger to lunch to try to get him to consider rewriting the book. Salinger said nothing during the meal. There was absolutely no way he was going to rewrite *Catcher*.

Back in his office, Giroux repeated to Salinger Reynal's question about Holden: "Is he crazy, this kid?" Salinger didn't answer, and then Giroux realized why—he was weeping. Salinger got up, left the office, went down to the ground floor, and phoned Olding. "Get me out of this publishing house," he said. "They think Holden is crazy." Giroux made up his mind that day to leave Harcourt. Or at least that's the story Giroux told for decades; in actuality, he didn't leave until 1955. The inconsistencies in Giroux's story led me to want to hear directly from someone who knew all the principals involved. In July 2013, I spoke to Gerald Gross, now ninety-two, who worked for fourteen years with Eugène Reynal, first at Reynal & Hitchcock and then at Harcourt, Brace; Gross has never spoken publicly about this matter before. In his job at Harcourt, Brace, Gross handled the manuscript of *The Catcher in the Rye*; it's quite possible he's the last person alive who touched the original manuscript.

Gross explained that when Reynal's partner, Curtice Hitchcock, died, Reynal sold his company to Harcourt, Brace; the merger occurred in 1947. One year later, only three employees from Reynal & Hitchcock were still employed by Harcourt.

According to Gross, Reynal, who was head of the trade division at Harcourt, "couldn't understand" *Catcher* and said, "We should let people in the school division read this." The Harcourt vice president in charge of the school division—the perfectly named Dudley Meek—told Reynal, "If we publish this as written, it will kill our school division business." Gross said, "Back in those days, things were very conservative. The school division was the most lucrative division" at Harcourt, and "Meek was afraid of the language." The official version of the story has a scapegoat (Reynal) and a martyr (Giroux), but it is not the full truth. A business decision was made that, rather than saving Harcourt embarrassment, cost the company tens of millions of dollars, and likely much more.

Gross said, "Bob Giroux instructed me to get the manuscript back from the printer after Meek spoke to Reynal. The word was: we must make some changes." It's now easy to forget what a radical book *Catcher* was for America at that time—how revolutionary it was in everything from its use of "fuck" to its fuck-you attitude toward the status quo.

According to Gross, at that point Salinger made the decision to pull the book and take it to Little, Brown. As Louis Menand pointed out more than fifty years later in, of all places, the *New Yorker*, the editor at Little, Brown, John Woodburn, "was evidently prudent enough not to ask such questions." Little, Brown became the publisher of *The Catcher in the Rye*. (And in an eerie echo, Giroux soon after rejected *On the Road*, when Jack Kerouac refused to revise it. In a brief span, Harcourt passed on two of the most beloved American books of the twentieth century.)

Giroux was furious at Harcourt about *Catcher*, but he didn't quit in protest, as he has claimed and has often been written. That is the story he created years later.

Actor Edward Norton says, "What I like about the story of *Catcher*'s rejections is that it makes you realize that the gatekeepers aren't gatekeepers. They have the gate, but there's no fence around the gate. You know what I mean? They're standing at some door, but the best things just walk around the door."

—

Book-of-the-Month Club News, July 1951.

Under normal circumstances, a prepublication procedure occurs: the publisher packages the book, giving it a jacket design featuring a photograph and a short biography of the author on the back cover. At the same time, advance copies of the book are mailed out to magazines and newspapers for review, and journalists are approached to write about the book and its author.

But this author was J. D. Salinger, and the circumstances weren't going to be normal. First, he demanded that Little, Brown not send out any advance copies of the book, an unheard-of request for a fiction writer to make. Since the copies had already been shipped, Salinger ordered the publisher not to forward him any of the book's reviews. In addition, Salinger decided he wouldn't do any publicity. An author who wrote a book for the public refused to talk to the public except through his book.

I can't explain what I mean. And even if I could, I'm not sure I'd feel like it.

The Book-of-the-Month Club chose *The Catcher in the Rye* as the main selection for its midsummer list, a rare coup for a first novel. The only interview Salinger gave concerning the publication of *The Catcher in the Rye* was to the *BOMC News*, which had commissioned Salinger's editor and friend William Maxwell to write the piece. "It means a great deal to say that a novelist *works* like Flaubert (which Salinger does)," Maxwell wrote, "with infinite labor, infinite patience, and infinite thought for the technical aspects of what he is writing, none of which must show in the final draft. Such writers go straight to heaven when they die, and their books are not forgotten."

"I think writing is a hard life," Salinger says in the interview. "But

Salinger with signature cigarette.

it's brought me enough happiness that I don't think I'd ever deliberately dissuade anybody (if he had talent) from taking it up. The compensations are few, but when they come, if they come, they're very beautiful."

On July 16, 1951, Little, Brown released the hardback edition of *The Catcher in the Rye*.

Priced at three dollars, the book featured a dust jacket with flap copy that Salinger had written himself but that—nevertheless—seemed to be struggling to make sense of the book:

> Anyone who has read J. D. Salinger's *New Yorker* stories—particularly "A Perfect Day for Bananafish," "Uncle Wiggily in Connecticut," "The Laughing Man," and "For Esmé—with Love and Squalor"—will not be surprised by the fact that his first novel is full of children. The hero-narrator of *The Catcher in the Rye* is an ancient child of sixteen, a native New Yorker named Holden Caulfield. Through circumstances that tend to preclude adult, secondhand description, he leaves his prep school in Pennsylvania and goes underground in New York City for three days.
>
> The boy himself is at once too simple and too complex for us to make any final comment about him or his story. Perhaps the safest thing we can say about Holden is that he was born in the world not just strongly attracted to beauty but, almost, hopelessly impaled on it.
>
> There are many voices in this novel: children's voices, adult voices, underground voices—but Holden's voice is the most eloquent of all. Transcending his own vernacular, yet remaining marvelously faithful to it, he issues a perfectly articulated cry of mixed pain and pleasure. However, like most lovers and clowns and poets of the higher order, he keeps most of the pain to, and for, himself. The pleasure he gives away, or sets aside, with all his heart. It is there for the reader who can handle it to keep.

Salinger allowed a brief biography of himself to appear on the dust jacket, but it gave only a bare-bones outline of his life:

> J. D. Salinger was born in New York City in 1919 and attended Manhattan public schools, a military academy in Pennsylva-

nia, and three colleges (no degrees). "A happy tourist's year in Europe," he writes, "when I was eighteen and nineteen. In the Army from '42 to '46, most of the time with the Fourth Division. I've been writing since I was 15 or so. My short stories have appeared in a number of magazines over the last ten years, mostly—and most happily—in *The New Yorker*. I worked on *The Catcher in the Rye*, on and off, for ten years."

"I seldom care to know a writer's birthplace," Salinger says elsewhere, "his children's names, his working schedule, the date of his arrest for smuggling guns (the gallant rogue!) during the Irish Rebellion. The writer who tells you these things is also very likely to have his picture taken wearing an open-collared shirt—and he's sure to be looking three-quarter-profile and tragic. He can also be counted on to refer to his wife as a swell gal or a grand person. I've written biographical notes for a few magazines, and I doubt if I ever said anything honest in them."

I think, even, if I ever die, and they stick me in a cemetery, and I have a tombstone and all, it'll say "Holden Caulfield" on it, and then what year I was born and what year I died, and then right under that it'll say "Fuck you."

Salinger loved the design his Westport friend Michael Mitchell created for the cover of *Catcher*: a raging, red carousel horse. A haunting photograph of Salinger appeared on the jacket photograph of the first and second printings of *The Catcher in the Rye*. By the third printing, Salinger expressly requested that Little, Brown remove his picture from the book.

Salinger was starting to turn inward on himself, trying to shut out the world and separate himself from his book. It was a naïve wish. He'd started a revolution, and the world reacted. And yet the initial response, from reviewers, was mixed. In the *Chicago Daily Tribune* on July 15, 1951, Paul Engle wrote, "Here is a novel about a 16 year old boy which is emotional without being sentimental, dramatic without being melodramatic, and honest without being simply obscene." Then he gave it the backhanded compliment, "It largely succeeds."

The *Los Angeles Times* critic Irene Elwood thought it was "so real it

The famous photo on the back of *Catcher in the Rye* that Salinger had removed.

hurts, and all the muddled adults will read it avidly for their own enjoyment and hide it immediately from their children."

Renowned editor, critic, and radio personality Clifton Fadiman was the chief book critic for the *New Yorker* until 1943. Writing about *Catcher* for the *Book-of-the-Month-Club News*, he spoke of the pleasure of "sponsoring a brilliant, new, young American novelist."

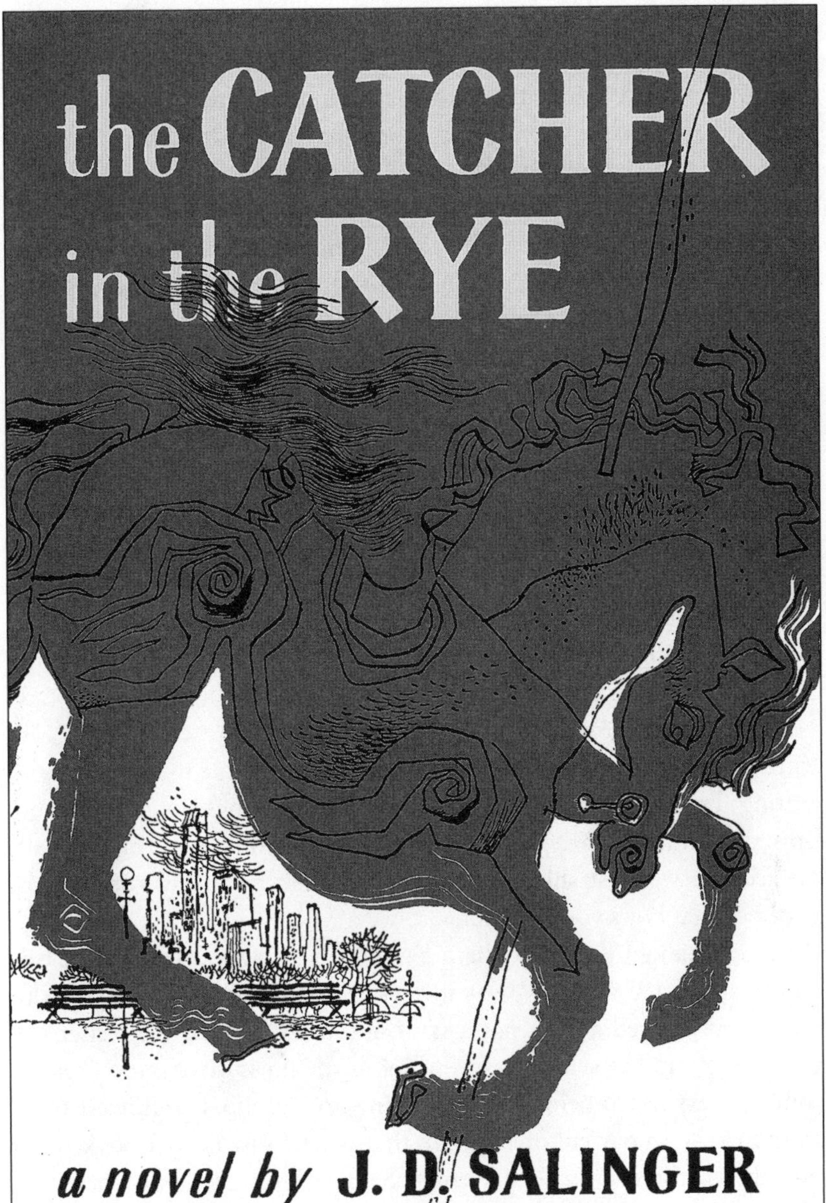

The original hardcover of *The Catcher in the Rye*, published by Little, Brown; cover design by Salinger's friend Michael Mitchell.

The *New York Times* had an almost schizophrenic view of the novel, attacking the book one day in the *Times Book Review*, praising it the next in the daily edition. The *Book Review*'s James Stern complained on July 15 that Salinger was a "short story guy" and that *Catcher* was "too long. Gets kind of monotonous. And he should've cut out a lot about these jerks and all at that crumby school. They depress me. They really do." Stern recovered sufficiently from his ennui to express astonishment that he liked the section about "Mr. Antolini, the only guy Holden ever thought he could trust, who ever took any interest in him, and who turned out queer—that's terrific. I swear it is." On July 16 the daily *Times*'s Nash K. Burger praised "the strange, wonderful language" in "an unusually brilliant first novel" and observed that he wouldn't be surprised if the fictional character Holden "grew up to write a few books (he talks about books quite a lot), books like 'Of Human Bondage,' 'Look Homeward, Angel,' or 'The Catcher in the Rye,'" a wry comment on the novel's autobiographical origins.

In a startling volte-face, the *New Yorker*, whose editors had called the book "writer-conscious" and its main character not believable, now called *Catcher* a "brilliant, funny, moving novel."

"*Catcher in the Rye* caught my attention when it first came out," Gore Vidal recalls. "There was a certain knife's, a razor's edge to what we were writing during the war, since we knew that we might end very soon. Boys do think about dying. Previously, Salinger wasn't getting beneath surfaces; he was just shining surfaces. So when he finally got a bright glitter of that boy's voice, it shone."

No less a figure than William Faulkner, visiting Washington & Lee University in 1958, said, "I was impressed with [*Catcher*]. It seemed to me that it showed a—it's not a fault, it's an evil which the writer has got to—to arm himself against—which is the pressure of our culture to compel everyone to belong to something, to a group. It's difficult to be an individual in our culture. I think that what I saw in that book was a tragedy which, in a way, represented Salinger's own tragedy. There was a young man, intelligent, a little more sensitive than most, who simply wanted to love mankind, and when he tried to break into mankind, to love mankind, man wasn't there. That, to me, was the tragedy of the book." He also called *The Catcher in the Rye* the best novel by a writer of the next generation.

And Samuel Beckett wrote to a friend, "Have you read *The Catcher in the Rye*? . . . I liked it very much indeed, more than anything for a long time."

What really knocks me out is a book that, when you're all done reading it, you wish the author that wrote it was a terrific friend of yours and you could call him up on the phone whenever you felt like it. That doesn't happen much, though.

The business with the photograph was not the only odd behavior Salinger exhibited surrounding the publication of *Catcher*. Once the book came out, he cut off most of the people in his life and dropped a lot of his friends.

People are always ruining things for you.

In the fall of 1952 Salinger briefly dated a fellow writer named Leila Hadley. He "talked about Holden as if he were a real live person," she recalled. "I would ask him about what he was doing at some point in the past and he would say, 'Well, that was when Holden was doing this or that.' It was as if Holden really existed, which I couldn't understand."

What was there not to understand? Holden *did* exist. He was J. D. Salinger.

"I fought alongside him in the war," said his comrade Werner Kleeman. "I knew right away it was his life story."

"So personal," Tom Wolfe calls *Catcher*. "So revealing. It seemed like someone stripping the layers away from his soul."

"I felt he was talking to me," Salinger scholar John Wenke says. "In fact, he was not only talking to me—in a very real sense he was writing me."

Edward Norton says, "Your first experience of *The Catcher in the Rye* is not that you think Holden would be your friend. It's that you think Holden is you. Literally." Hundreds of thousands of readers would have that experience: they would relate to Holden as an alter ego, a secret friend, a co-conspirator against the tyranny of an indifferent world. "I didn't know that a writer could go as deeply into my own life and my consciousness as that book went," Aram Saroyan said. "I stayed up all night reading it and I forgot I was reading. It went deeper than I could go." Screenwriter Robert Towne summed it up when he said, "Like a whole generation, I thought he was writing about me." Asked in December 1951 by the *New York Times* what books he would give as presents, Salinger said, "I may give [*The Catcher in the Rye*] away this Christmas, but not till I'm sure that boys really talk that way."

They do:

Catcher became the literary anthem of a generation. Disaffected young people in the 1950s suddenly found a voice: Holden wasn't interested in getting the good job, the house in the suburbs with the 2.5 kids, the perfect dry martini, the right clothes. He was a rebel for a generation desperately in need of one. This was the Eisenhower '50s. A war-weary country was back at war—a cold war against the Soviets, a hot war in Korea—and what the country wanted was conformity. The House Un-American Activities Committee and Joe McCarthy had stifled dissent, and society suffocated individualism. And here came this novel about a boy who would not conform, by an author who refused to be the Man in the Gray Flannel Suit of the publishing world.

Holden Caulfield was James Dean before James Dean, cool before "cool." He was Marlon Brando and Montgomery Clift. In the words of screenwriter Nicholas Meyer, he was an "icon of restlessness, discontent, rebellion, opposition to the status quo." As critic Geoff Pevere writes, "If the teenager as we know it was a creature that crawled from the shadows of the atom bomb, World War II and the numbing malaise of affluence, Salinger's expelled boarding school brat was one of the first fully-formed figures to emerge from the fallout. By the end of the decade, Caulfield's grip could be felt in every spasm of pop cultural adolescent cage-rattling from Marlon Brando's *Wild One*, James Dean's *Rebel without a Cause*, Elvis, Kerouac, *Blackboard Jungle* and the insolent uptown vulgarity of Lenny Bruce.

"I remember it being the first book that you took with you when you walked around," actor John Cusack recalls. "You just wanted to have it with you." "Carrying *Catcher in the Rye* around was code," says biographer A. Scott Berg. "It suggested you had lost your literary virginity. It suggested you were in the know: there were certain rules in society and it was okay to break them. We really hadn't seen that kind of rebellion yet."

Catcher became a password to a subversive secret club, as society seemed divided into those who knew Holden and those who didn't. For those who did, no explanation was necessary; for those who didn't, no explanation was possible. In 1957, Jack Kerouac's *On the Road* would be hailed for launching the Beat Generation, but Kerouac was six years late—Salinger had already done it; the beatniks who hitchhiked on those long highways to find America did so with *The Catcher in the Rye* tucked in the pockets of their jeans. Salinger was a seminal influence in the creation of the counterculture, his creation Holden not only the original beatnik but also an inspirational figure to the hippie generation.

"[Holden Caulfield is] the Malcolm X of white suburban boys," actor Jake Gyllenhaal says.

—

The writer Andy Rogers has a different theory—that *Catcher*, although published in the 1950s, is a novel of the 1940s: a war novel. In "The Inverted Forest," Salinger writes, "A poet doesn't invent his poetry—he finds it. . . . The place where . . . Alph the sacred river ran—was found out, not invented." Salinger found out Holden on the battlefields of Europe. "Holden Caulfield," Rogers writes, "has more in common with a traumatized soldier than an alienated teenager. His prematurely gray hair serves as fodder for teasing and insecurity, but it also symbolizes something rather obvious: Holden is an old man in a young man's body.

> *It rained on his lousy tombstone, and it rained on the grass on his stomach.*

"This places Holden in an estimable literary lineage of characters who feel that their youth has been lost in the war." Salinger didn't write a book about a soldier at war with the enemy; he wrote a book about an adolescent at war with society and with himself. And like Salinger, Holden could not find the help he needed to heal. "The mental health professionals who are there to help him [Salinger] will not listen to his recounting of the horrors he witnessed and endured," Rogers writes. "Salinger then return[s] home having learned to remain outside of a mental institution and witnesses the pageantry of a society overjoyed to see [him] hide his symptoms.

"The brutality, the stupidity, the cruelty, the horror of war is transmogrified into saccharine and mindless speeches, songs, and movies. And what good would it do to point out the truth about the war when the problem is not that people just don't know better, but that people just don't care."

> *If you sat around there long enough and heard all the phonies applauding and all, you got to hate everybody in the world, I swear you did.*

It's that indifference that fuels Holden's anger: "Salinger's quarrel," says Rogers, "if not his struggle for his very existence, would no longer have been against a set of experiences that permanently damaged him, but against a society of willful naivety that manufactures death and destruction and continues on after 'Victory' in its cannibalism with cheers for those who won't call it what it is, and mental institutions for those who do."

Salinger couldn't write directly about it; he had to "change the context, choose characters and situations who had nothing to do with the war, universalize the sense of alienation to gain the approval of a mass audience; his own experiences and thoughts could then emerge in such a context, safe from the psychiatrists and patriots of the world, and his quarrel with phoniness/bullshit could be presented." And so he invented Holden Caulfield.

Salinger can't summon up the memories of his slaughtered comrades, so Holden remembers the crushed body of James Castle. Salinger can't grieve for them, so Holden misses Ackley and Stradlater. Salinger can't recall his own suicidal despair after Kaufering, so he has Holden contemplate self-destruction. "Salinger will never be the boy who went to prep school again," Rogers writes, "thus Holden is Salinger and the Salinger who will never be again."

> *When I was* really *drunk, I started that stupid business with the bullet in my guts again. I was the only guy at the bar with a bullet in their guts. I kept putting my hand under my jacket, on my stomach and all, to keep the blood from dripping all over the place. I didn't want anybody to know I was even wounded. I was* concealing *the fact that I was a wounded sonuvabitch.*

Holden dances with his kid sister, Phoebe, and "Then, just for the hell of it, I gave her a pinch on the behind. It was sticking way out in the breeze, the way she was laying on her side. She has hardly any behind." Flirtation with the girl-child's body is the beginning of spiritual awakening. "You should've seen her. She was sitting smack in the middle of the bed, outside the covers, with her legs folded like one of those Yogi guys. She was listening to the music. She kills me." The author's sensuality is private trauma. This is how paranoids, mystics, and pedophiles think: "I don't like people that dance with little kids, because most of the time it looks terrible. I mean if you're out at a restaurant somewhere and you see some old guy take his little kid out on the dance floor. Usually they keep yanking the kid's dress up in back by mistake, and the kid can't dance worth a damn *any*way, and it looks terrible, but I don't do it out in public with Phoebe or anything. We just horse around in the house." Kids are potentially the adult dead. They need to be homeschooled by the sage of Hürtgen. Ultimately, Holden's/Salinger's world is MIA; nervous breakdown is spiritual-military progression. There is vacillation on the nerves between a veteran's silence ("Don't ever tell anybody anything. If you do, you start missing everybody."), isolation ("I was the only one left in the tomb then. I sort of liked it, in a way. It was so nice and peaceful."), loss of the body ("I felt better after I passed out."), and the new bullet of obliteration ("Anyway, I'm sort of glad they've got the atomic bomb invented. If there's ever another war, I'm going to sit right the hell on top of it. I'll volunteer for it, I swear to God I will."). *Catcher* is America's endless war in words.

When you think of World War II authors, you generally think of Norman Mailer and James Jones, but is it possible that J. D. Salinger wrote in the same book the last novel of the war *and* the first novel of the counterculture?

The critic Ihab Hassan writes about *Catcher*, "The controlling mood of the novel—and it is so consistent as to be a principle of unity—is one of acute depression always on the point of breaking loose." However, as psychologist Jay Martin says, "One of the processes we see in creativity is that the creative person solves a problem. That is, he's depressed, he's anxious, he's uncertain, he's mourning, he's grieving. He writes, and in the process of writing, he doesn't necessarily cure himself, but he gets some perspective by writing. By putting one sentence down after another, you get a perspective on your own disorder. . . . I would guess that if Salinger was depressed, he found a way to rid himself of his depression by giving it to someone else. It's almost like black magic, in which you put your anger or hatred into a character and discharge it there." After the war, Salinger was profoundly, suicidally depressed, but he found a way to rid himself, temporarily, of his depression by giving it to someone else—to Holden ("I was feeling sort of lousy. Depressed and all. I almost wished I was dead.") and to us, which is why so many people worship the book. He names our sadness for us and converts it into a weird kind of joy. The black magic played out like this:

—

Within two years of publication, *Catcher* was being banned. Pamela Hunt Steinle, the author of *In Cold Fear:* The Catcher in the Rye, *Censorship Controversies, and Postwar American Character,* has pointed out that it is simultaneously the most frequently taught novel in American high schools and the second most frequently censored. Teachers were fired for assigning *The Catcher in the Rye*. In 1963, the American Book Publishers Council noted that *Catcher* had become the most censored book in America's public schools. "I'm aware," Salinger had written in a statement that the publisher omitted from the book's jacket, "that a number of my friends will be saddened and shocked, or shocked-saddened, over some of the chapters of *The Catcher in the Rye.* Some of my best friends are children. In fact, all of my best friends are children. It's almost unbearable to me to realize that my book will be kept on a shelf out of their reach."

It wasn't just the language, although words like "crap" and "fuck"—a few years earlier Norman Mailer's novel *The Naked and the Dead* used "fug"—and endless "goddams" certainly played a part. The chief objection to the book was that it was un-American.

Catcher wasn't the phony America that Madison Avenue was foisting on a public that had just discovered television. It wasn't the insanely paranoid America of the McCarthy hearings or the sanitized America of Disney. It was real. Real thoughts, real feelings, real pain.

> *Among other things, you'll find that you're not the first person who was ever confused and frightened and even sickened by human behavior.*

As Michael Silverblatt, the host of the nationally syndicated radio show *Bookworm*, says, "Here was someone saying, 'I have access to authenticity.'" "Salinger was prescient," the scholar John C. Unrue writes, "He knew where the country was going. *Catcher in the Rye* is as relevant today as it was in 1951. We have the same conditions. We have the same liars, the same frauds, the same hypocrites, speaking daily, not entirely on our behalf." But it wasn't just about rebellion and alienation. Salinger was not just another nihilist; Holden was not just another lost boy. The book and the boy were spiritual. Holden was not just on the run from something; he was seeking transcendence of the materially obsessed culture.

Catcher is a rescue fantasy. As Phoebe points out to Holden, he has the Robert Burns line wrong: it's not "if a body catch a body"; it's "if a body meet a body." Holden doesn't want to love other people—he wants to save other people. Big difference. "Readers tend to romanticize Holden Caulfield's failure to fit in," John Wenke says. "But at a deeper level, there is a spiritual hunger. It's the spiritual hunger that works with people. The spiritual hunger is what leads people to not only see themselves in him but to celebrate the book. Ironically, of course, Salinger became the very kind of absent presence that he wrote about. He was so ambitious and then he rejected the very thing that he most desired: the fame and recognition that *The Catcher in the Rye* brought him."

The film and stage director Elia Kazan, who wanted to turn *Catcher* into a play and bring it to Broadway, found Salinger's house, knocked on the door, and said, "Mr. Salinger, I'm Elia Kazan."

"That's nice," Salinger said.

I can be quite sarcastic when I'm in the mood.

Then Salinger closed the door.

Billy Wilder took a shot at it, too. His agent in New York hounded Salinger for the movie rights. "One day," Wilder said, "a young man came to the office of Leland Hayward, my agent, in New York, and said, 'Please tell Mr. Leland Hayward to lay off. He's very, very insensitive.' And he walked out. That was the entire speech. I never saw him. That was J. D. Salinger and that was *Catcher in the Rye*."

Everyone from Jerry Lewis to Steven Spielberg to Harvey Wein-

Elia Kazan.

stein offered Salinger as much as $10 million for the film rights to the book. Salinger turned them all down.

The goddam movies. They can ruin you. I'm not kidding.

So we don't have a movie image of Holden, and that's probably a good thing. He lives in our imaginations. But, in a sense, he's already been portrayed in *Rebel without a Cause*, *The 400 Blows*, *The Graduate*,

Billy Wilder.

Less than Zero, and a thousand other movies about alienated youth in an emotional wasteland. It's virtually impossible to imagine modern film without the presence of Holden Caulfield.

So, too, Ishmael, Natty Bumppo, Huckleberry Finn, Tom Joad, Holden Caulfield: they're all wanderers, pilgrims, searchers, lost saints. Their journeys have no end; their wanderings are wired into the collective American psyche. "Holden Caulfield is not likely to go away," says literary critic Nancy C. Ralston. "The echo of his voice hovers over the ubiquitous examples of phoniness whenever and wherever they dare to appear. His shadow haunts every display of obscene graffiti scrawled in millions of public places. Holden knows no generation gap. He is the super-adolescent of yesterday, today, and tomorrow."

In 1961, *Catcher* was selling 250,000 copies a year and was being taught at 275 American colleges. By 1981 translations of *Catcher* had appeared in twenty-seven countries; in eleven countries, all four of Salinger's books had been published. *Here's* another number, which will tell you that Holden's not going anywhere: 65 million. *The Catcher in the Rye* has sold more than 65 million copies worldwide. And if 65 million people have bought the book, that means that hundreds of millions are likely to have read it. It's tough to get a hard count on this kind of thing, but it's something like the eleventh bestselling single-volume book of all time. A recent Harris poll has *The Catcher in the Rye*, sixty-two years after its publication, as the tenth-favorite book of all time among American readers.

After the publication of *Catcher* in the fall of 1951, Salinger was an overnight success. He was rich, famous, and sought after: the American dream. And he walked away from it.

People always clap for the wrong things.

When he stayed away, people said he was crazy and phony. He continued to stay away.

I don't care if it's a sad good-by or a bad good-by, but when I leave a place I like to know I'm leaving it.

Did Salinger see a crazy, phony version of himself—propelled by fame and success—running headlong through a field of rye toward a cliff, with only his authentic self to save him? He came to profoundly regret writing and publishing the book, because of the way in which fame framed and warped the last sixty years of his life—the way it enslaved him, "froze him in time," as Phoebe Hoban says, in the public's imagination. But if *Catcher* became Salinger's burden, it also was a gift. "The compensations are few, but when they come, they're very beautiful." He had to know the pride of writing not only a great novel but one that spoke at the most profound level to tens of millions of readers. So, too, without it, he would never have had the worldwide platform to use his next three books to "circulate" (his word) the ideas of the Vedanta religion. But in his lifetime, he never published another novel or another word about Holden. Following the massive public outpouring of adulation for *Catcher*, he pivoted into an increasingly private and obscure realm, both in his work and in his life. He did everything possible not to repeat the success of *Catcher*.

"I suspect," the author Lawrence Grobel says, "Holden Caulfield went up to New Hampshire, found himself a place to live, kept his hunting cap on, found a wife, had kids, and that's it. We never hear from him again. That's what I think happened to Holden Caulfield because that's what happened to J. D. Salinger."

Sleep tight, ya morons!

He went to Cornish.

11

WE CAN STILL RUN AWAY

NEW YORK CITY; CORNISH, NEW HAMPSHIRE, 1952–1953

Salinger's New York life mimics Holden's psychic difficulties and behaviors: flirtation, antisocial overreaction, and, finally, disappearance to a ninety-acre woodland in Cornish, New Hampshire—the embodiment of Holden's seclusion. *Catcher* takes hold not only as a book but as a cult. A cult needs a leader—a role Salinger can't and won't fill.

PAMELA HUNT STEINLE: First published in mid-July 1951 by Little, Brown and Company, *Catcher in the Rye* was simultaneously published as a Book-of-the-Month Club selection. By the end of July, Little, Brown and Company was reprinting the novel for the fifth time, and by late August, *Catcher* had reached fourth place on the *New York Times* best-seller list.

PHOEBE HOBAN: I don't think Salinger was prepared for the instant celebrity of *The Catcher in the Rye.*

A. E. HOTCHNER: Overnight, *Catcher in the Rye* transported Salinger from being a relatively obscure writer who had written a few stories into a major writer and personality.

HARVEY JASON: I think that when an author achieves a tremendous amount of fame at a very early age, it's bound to have repercussions across the board. To somebody like Truman Capote, all it did was increase an already inflated ego. For Harper Lee, it forced her into hiding.

It's intimidating to achieve tremendous fame at an early age, and it could go either way for you, depending upon your psychological makeup.

JOHN WENKE: As the first wave of attention subsided, Salinger breathed a sigh of relief.

EBERHARD ALSEN: In 1952, a year after *The Catcher in the Rye* was published, Salinger said that he found the media attention accompanying his fame to be "professionally and personally demoralizing" and that he was looking forward to the day when he would see his photograph from the dust jacket of *The Catcher in the Rye* "flapping against a lamp-post in a cold, wet Lexington Avenue wind, in company with, say, the editorial page of the *Daily Mirror*."

—

PAUL ALEXANDER: In the fall of 1951, as *The Catcher in the Rye* remained on the *New York Times* bestseller list, Salinger tried to get his life back to normal. In his East Side apartment, he worked on another story, this one a long and unusual piece called "De Daumier-Smith's Blue Period." Wry and whimsical, it was not like the other stories he had been writing. When he was not working, Salinger kept up with the worsening health of Harold Ross. In mid-November, *New Yorker* editor Gus Lobrano wrote to Salinger with disappointing news. The *New Yorker* editors were rejecting "De Daumier-Smith's Blue Period," which Salinger's agent, Dorothy Olding, had recently submitted to them. Deciding not to buy the story had turned into a terrible ordeal for them,

Lobrano said, but ultimately the editors did not feel the piece succeeded. The notion behind the story was too complicated, Lobrano believed; its events were "too compressed." Finally, the piece seemed almost willfully strange, which Lobrano knew wasn't true, but that was how it *seemed*. Salinger was affected by this rejection more than most, not only because he had worked hard on the story, but because he had reached the point where the *New Yorker* accepted almost any story he submitted to them. On November 15, Salinger wrote to Lobrano to tell him he was profoundly disheartened by the rejection.

JOHN LEGGETT: I am aware of a party that took place in New York at this time for Hamish Hamilton, Salinger's British publisher. There were young people present; Salinger was attracted to a girl and proposed an adventure with her—another of those vanishing-to-Cornish adventures, which of course didn't take place. It wound up in typically Salingerian fashion: his resentment of the Harvard boys who were present—anger, shouts in the street. It was a real Jerry Salinger event: the cocktail party that got out of hand. He was attracted to women and felt he was able to persuade them. It may have been a game that he played—mashing, so to speak, on girls, persuading them that they should go off with him tomorrow or the next day. Many of the girls *were* persuaded; this was likely to wind up in bad feelings because of the escorts the girls had come with. He had a lot of girlfriends and a lot of experiences like this. That's what the talk was, anyway.

THE WIFE OF AN EDITOR: I was not prepared for the extraordinary impact of his physical presence. There was a black aura about him. He was dressed in black; he had black hair, dark eyes, and he was of course extremely tall. I was kind of spellbound. But I was married, and I was pregnant. We talked, and we liked each other very much, I thought. Then it was time for us to leave—I had gone to the party with my husband and another couple, two friends of ours—and I went upstairs to where the coats were. I was just getting my coat when Jerry came into the room. He came over to me and said that we ought to run away together. I said, "But I'm pregnant." And he said, "That doesn't matter. We can still run away." He really seemed to mean it. I can't say I wasn't flattered, and even a bit tempted maybe.

DAVID SHIELDS: Salinger is Holden-like in a variety of ways, not least of which is his tendency to wildly overcommit and then disappear, always executing the disappearance with an actor's instinct for the perfect gesture.

J. D. SALINGER (*The Catcher in the Rye*, 1951):

> If you want to know the truth, I don't even know why I started all that stuff with her [Sally]. I mean about going away somewhere, to Massachusetts and Vermont and all. I probably wouldn't've taken her even if she'd wanted to go with me. She wouldn't have been anybody to go with. The terrible part, though, is that I *meant* it when I asked her. That's the terrible part. I swear to God I'm a madman.

JOHN LEGGETT: I was rather surprised to go to a cocktail party, and there he was. It was someplace on the East Side where a lot of young people involved in publishing were gathered. Joe [Fox, an editor at Random House] said, "Salinger's that guy standing over there," and to me this was terribly exciting. Then Joe told me, "He's coming to dinner." It was a time when we would go to cocktail parties, then we'd all go out to French restaurants in that part of Manhattan. We went to this restaurant and they shoved tables together and, sure enough, there was Salinger. He sat down at the table and we were all thrilled to be in his presence. He got up and muttered to somebody that he had to make a phone call, disappeared, and never came back. We all felt this man had eluded us once more. He's off in the night and gone. He didn't want to join up or be a real person with us.

LEILA HADLEY LUCE: I met him a long, long time ago. Way back in '51, '52. And we went out quite a few times. Five or six times, I think. He's seven years older than I am. I had a great friend by the name of S. J. Perelman, who was an extraordinary humorist and writer for the *New Yorker*. He introduced me to Jerry because Jerry had mentioned to him that he was interested in Zen Buddhism. Sid thought that I could talk with Jerry about Buddhism, but I couldn't because he was interested in Zen Buddhism, which is a meditative kind of Buddhism, and I was more interested in Mahayana Buddhism, which is more like

Tibetan Buddhism is now. He said travel was pointless. What mattered was inner travel.

[For our first date] he came and he picked me up at my mother's house, which was on 72nd Street and Park [Avenue]. He came in, and he was very, very tall. Very thin. Elongated and attenuated, like a candlestick, a Giacometti statue, you know, not like a lantern. And he had these wonderful eyes, the color of black coffee. Very intense. You could feel it suddenly, his extremely intense presence. Jerry looked very neat and dapper in a navy blue blazer with three brass buttons. He had on a white shirt and a regimental striped tie, what he later described in one of his stories as "Eastern Seaboard regimentals," with charcoal gray trousers. He looked very spiffy, very clean-shaven; his hair was in place—that lovely dark hair he had. We went to his place, which was on the ground floor of an apartment building on 57th Street, on Second or Third Avenue, about 300 East 57th. His place was very, very neat. Very clean. He wanted to show it to me. In the little kitchenette the cans and all the glasses were arranged in parade formation. There was a picture on the wall of himself in uniform. We talked for a while. He seemed quiet, shy: he didn't speak much at all. He rebuffed all personal questions. He wasn't easy to talk with, really. I was used to people who laughed a lot more and told jokes or who said funny things, but he didn't. He was very serious and quiet. He didn't ask questions or anything. I was the one asking him questions, because Jerry at that point had just written *The Catcher in the Rye*. And he'd also had lots of short stories in the *New Yorker*. I was familiar with his work and I wanted to ask him about it. We had dinner at an Italian place nearby that he liked.

I admired his writings so. I admired talent and was willing to put up with personal idiosyncrasies that might not be adorable, just for the sake of being with somebody whose writing truly interested me. I mean, I loved his writing. No one else has ever done short stories like those. "Perfect Day for Bananafish," "Uncle Wiggily in Connecticut," "For Esmé—with Love and Squalor." He had a new voice, an original voice. You can always tell a Salinger short story.

I'd say, "What are you gonna do?" or "What did you do last week?" And he'd say, "Well, now that was when Holden was doing something or other." He would say, "Well, Holden loved the Metropolitan Museum. We can go there." "Holden would like this" or "He wouldn't like that." Or "Phoebe would like this" or "Phoebe wouldn't like that." He totally identified with Seymour Glass and Franny and Holden. He talked about them as if they were totally real people, and I began to feel they were as real to me as they were to him. He was the only writer I've ever known who talked about his characters in that way.

He talked about [*New Yorker* editors William] Shawn and [Harold] Ross. And then, without any difference at all, he'd talk about his own characters, about Holden Caulfield, about Esmé, about the whole Glass family—Seymour Glass or Bessie Glass or Boo Boo Tannenbaum. I think that's why his stories were so good, because they were completely intense, and the people were really real. They were all fresh. Some people write dialogue with words that are tin-canned. But his words were always very fresh.

Even when he spoke, he was not easy to talk with because if it was raining and I said, "Oh, I don't mind, I like to walk in the rain," he'd say, "Oh my goodness, what a cliché." I didn't realize walking in the rain was a cliché at that point, but he did. Every cliché I used, he would say, "Oh, that's a cliché. How can you say that?" I felt very self-conscious talking with him, because he was, of course, a perfectionist. He was much more concerned with his own life, what he was doing, what he was thinking, than what anybody else was, not just me, but everybody else. He would comment on what I said. For instance, at one point I said, "Oh, I'd love to have a Cranach painting—that would be so wonderful to have." He said, "You want to own a painting? Why do you want to own a painting? You can have it all in your head. You don't need to own anything. You don't need to own any of it." And that was an interesting idea to me—that one could have everything in one's mind rather than in a material way.

Jerry would say, you know, "There are some people who like to please, and there are other people who want people to please them." And Jerry was definitely in that second category. He wanted people to please him. He got very distressed if an editor changed the title of the story or if anybody wanted to change anything in any of his stories; he wanted everything just the way he had it. Only at the *New Yorker* were the editors respectful of writers.

He felt that authors were the ones who should dictate how their work should be presented. I mean, people would think that was very arrogant, but Jerry was self-absorbed. He wanted nothing to come between him and his characters. He moved them about the stage, like God. It's like being omnipotent, to move the characters the way you want them. And you wouldn't want any interference with this. I think he wanted to be alone. He wasn't interested so much in what other people thought—except for his stories, obviously, where he got everything beautifully, marvelously, perfectly done. A few lines of dialogue, and you knew these people. All these stories were so perfect of their kind. But for the people outside of his stories, he wasn't interested.

He didn't come on with any great charismatic push or anything. He just sort of came in quietly. And very dear. Now I was about twenty-five, and he was seven years older. But it was a very Platonic going out. I mean, he didn't try to kiss me or hug me or squeeze me or anything, the way other people did. He was perfectly friendly and nice. But formal, you know. We just talked. Maybe I was too old for him. I think he liked younger girls. I was only seven years younger. I think he preferred them twelve years younger. Well, younger than that.

I think he liked putting me down. There was something sadistic about it. He was very much like Raymond Ford, that character of his in "The Inverted Forest." It wasn't a sexual power; it was a mental power. You felt he had the power to imprison someone mentally. It was as if one's mind were at risk rather than one's virtue.

—

PAUL ALEXANDER: That fall [1951], Salinger began to consider leaving New York. He was tired of living in the city and longed for a quiet solitude he thought he could find in the country. He also so disliked the personal attention he was getting because of *Catcher* that he wanted to isolate himself.

J. D. SALINGER, letter to Harold Ross, October 6, 1951:

> *Dear Mr. Ross,*
> *Just to say that I'm afraid I can't take you up on your kind invitation. . . . I'm much too jumpy these days to do any visiting. . . . I'm in bed with a case of shingles.*

JAMES LUNDQUIST: He escaped some of the publicity following the success of his novel when it was published in 1951, by going to Europe. The next year he visited Mexico.

TONY BILL: I don't think there's anything more difficult than dealing with early fame and success. I would like to think that Salinger figured it out early on, the way Holden figures out who's a phony—that Salinger figured out fame is one of the worst things that can happen to a human being. It's a form of brainwashing—a very, very unpleasant burden to bear. You can't have a life. You're denied a real life when you're famous. I would consider it a huge curse to not be able to walk down the street or walk into a restaurant without being recognized. It's a horrible burden to bear. And it changes people almost as certainly as brainwashing can change them.

JOHN UPDIKE: Celebrity is a mask that eats into the face. As soon as one is aware of being somebody, to be watched and listened to with extra interest, input ceases, and the performer goes blind and deaf in his overanimation. One can either see or be seen.

EDWARD NORTON: Maybe what he did was liberate himself to actually experience the world more truthfully. With some anonymity intact. Because being known is not a liberation. It's a cage.

ALEX KERSHAW: He wrote, at a young age, an instant or near-instant classic. And he was held up as one of the greatest writers of his generation. He then turned around and said, "You know what? Big deal. There's more to life than that."

A. E. HOTCHNER: I think the wash of that undulation of praise drove him, to some extent, out of the city.

SANFORD GOLDSTEIN: This is the Zen way. Don't think of applause. Don't think of ego. Don't think of fame. Don't think of money. Focus on the writing, writing for yourself.

JOHN GUARE: I could imagine a man saying I just want to live my life and write as much as I can and not be buffaloed by overpraise and savage dissection. And just saying, "Let me live my life as a writer in a nice town up in New Hampshire and I'll come down to New York and see my friends when I want to." It obviously gave him no pleasure, the life of a celebrated writer. Salinger had seen what fame did to Hemingway, who because of his adulation and his need to live in that spotlight could produce a book like *Across the River and into the Trees*, which is a self-parody because he was surrounded by people saying "Yes, yes, yes."

ARAM SAROYAN: After going through the war, Salinger went through the huge threshold of fame. He'd already had a nervous breakdown and probably had some level of Post-traumatic Stress Disorder. Salinger became very, very famous, the way Hemingway and Fitzgerald were in their heyday. And maybe, at that point, he just beat a hasty retreat and said, you know, "I need something else. I need peace, I need quiet. I need to get out of this. I've had quite a trip."

PAUL ALEXANDER: When you read *Catcher in the Rye*, you just know that some day, some way, Salinger is going to end up in a spot that he considers his seclusion. And Cornish, New Hampshire, was that for him.

A. SCOTT BERG: When there was this sudden onslaught, he suddenly realized, "I don't really need this and I don't want this," and I think that's the moment he just turned on his heels and disappeared into the mountains of New Hampshire.

EDWARD NORTON: He was wise and true to his beliefs after being confronted with fame in a way that very, very few people are. Some people say he was crazy. He wasn't crazy. The truth of the matter is, it's the opposite: people who pursue fame are crazy. People who pursue fame are way crazier than people who have the wisdom to step away from it. Salinger liberated himself to experience life in a more authentic way than becoming the character J. D. Salinger. He got to walk around in the world and not be defined by some *Time* magazine version of his life.

RICHARD STAYTON: We're all pursing our different versions of the American dream: wealth, fame, glory, career, multiple houses, more real estate, possessions, possessions, possessions. Salinger is perhaps the only successful novelist to turn his back on all that and not only turn his back on it in life but turn his back on it in his fiction. He turned his back on celebrity before celebrity was celebrity.

MARGARET SALINGER: I know he and his sister, when he had a little bit of money in his pocket from the publication of *The Catcher in the Rye*, took a drive out into the country to find someplace where he could work and live in peace. And that dream is *straight* out of *The Catcher*. The house, *our* house in Cornish, when you read what Holden dreams of his little place that is partway in the sunshine where he asks Sally Hayes, I think it is, a girl he does not even like very much, to run away with him and "we'd have children and hide them away and teach them how to read and write ourselves." Again and again I would find my mother stepping into the play he had written for his life; that reality would sort of form out of this stuff of fantasy and there you have it. There we are in Holden's cabin.

—

William Maxwell's wife, Emmy, with Salinger in Cornish, 1953.

PAUL ALEXANDER: [Salinger's] 90-acre tract of land was high on a hill across the Connecticut River in New Hampshire.

DAVID SHIELDS: Salinger bought the land from Carlota Saint-Gaudens, a granddaughter of Augustus Saint-Gaudens, the celebrated Irish-born sculptor who had lived and worked in Cornish from 1885 to 1907. An artists' colony formed around Saint-Gaudens, and Cornish became a popular summer resort for New Yorkers and Bostonians. It was trendy enough to attract Ethel Barrymore and Isadora Duncan, and

Woodrow Wilson established the summer White House in Cornish from 1913 to 1915. The colony faded away after Saint-Gaudens's death in 1907, though, and after World War I the seaside resorts on Cape Cod and the Hamptons began drawing visitors away from Cornish.

SHANE SALERNO: On May 16, 1953, Salinger took official possession of the Cornish property.

PAUL ALEXANDER: Salinger had bought a small, gambrel-roofed cottage that, while attractive, needed both plumbing and a furnace. So what Salinger saw when he moved there in the dead of winter was a place that needed work but a place that was *his*. What's more, it was far enough away from normal civilization that he could live his life in seclusion. As soon as he moved in, Salinger started making arrangements to winterize the cottage, deciding he would do much of the work himself. Until the house was modernized, however, Salinger had to carry water from a nearby stream for cooking and bathing, and cut firewood in the surrounding forest to keep warm.

MARK HOWLAND: For a New York boy—a Park Avenue boy—Cornish is a tremendous change. A life-altering change, daily-routine change. There's a certain self-sufficiency in cutting your own wood that I imagine appealed to him.

JOHN SKOW: That winter [of 1953] he happily carried water from his stream and cut wood with a chain saw. For company he hiked across the river to Windsor, Vermont, and passed the time with teenagers in a juke joint called Nap's Lunch. The kids loved him, but mothers worried that the tall, solemn writer fellow from New York would put their children in a book.

JEAN MILLER: He wanted the peace and quiet to do his work, and this is where he found it. He felt that he couldn't live in an apartment in New York with all the distractions.

ETHEL NELSON: In 1953 Windsor, Vermont, like most towns, was pretty laid-back. Cornish, New Hampshire, is right across the covered bridge, and I guess that's why a lot of people were moving into the area—because they liked the quietness. Most people left other people alone. They didn't try to bring you into their lives, and they didn't want you to try to come into their lives. You met on the street, you said hello, and you went on your way.

PAUL ALEXANDER: Immediately upon arriving in Cornish, I was struck by the bucolic beauty of the place. The wooded hills were a shock of yellows, oranges, greens, and reds. Besides the landscape, the other fact I noticed about Cornish was that, for all intents and purposes, it's a town that doesn't exist. It has no business district—no shops, no restaurants, no offices, no gas stations.

JEAN MILLER: It didn't mean that he was a hermit, you know; he had plenty of social life. Certainly when I knew him he did in Cornish, in Windsor, in Vermont. He didn't want to be with writers and certainly didn't want to be the toast of New York. He felt that would just be ruinous to his writing, to succumb to anybody else's opinion.

The only opinion that mattered to him was his own opinion. And that's it. He often said that to me, "The only opinion that should be important to you is your own opinion."

Cornish was an ideal situation. He wandered all around, looking for ideal situations. He finally found it. It was in a field, but he did have some neighbors.

He wasn't in flight. He was protecting himself. His motives were really very pure. He just wanted to write, and this looked like an isolated enough place where he could get his work done. Plus do a few things like have a little farm and have vegetables and chop wood and take walks, and he would get enough physical exercise.

A. E. HOTCHNER: It may well be he didn't want any of that social interaction and decided he was going to retreat into solitude. A writer writes alone in a room with no distractions. The minute he's distracted he loses the cathedral in which he must perform, which is himself.

—

MICHAEL CLARKSON: His best friends, perhaps his only friends, were kids. He related to them. He talked to them about what it was like to be a teenager.

PHOEBE HOBAN: Salinger himself resented having to grow up and lose that contact you have with innocence before corruption and what Holden would call phoniness creep in.

EBERHARD ALSEN: I think Cornish was a castle to which he retreated; it protected him from the rest of the world.

DAVID SHIELDS: People in New York City, which is one of the most parochial places on the planet, thought of Salinger as having moved to Antarctica. In fact, he was within a few hours' drive of both Boston and New York, and in the coming decades he'd frequently return to Manhattan.

A. E. HOTCHNER: I checked with [fiction editor of *Collier's*] Don Congdon about him. Don said, "We've lost track of him. Jerry has just absolutely deserted all of us and we don't hear from him." And he was a very close friend of Don's.

S. J. PERELMAN, excerpt from letter to Leila Hadley Luce:

> *We have a date to meet Jerry Salinger and have dinner with him up there* [in Vermont], *entailing a 50-mile drive for him from his mountain retreat at Windsor. He has been holed in there all this time presumably foraging verbs and gerundives. Personally I'd go crazy all alone on a crag, and I fully expect him to break into wild laughter during the meal and goose waitresses.*

ETHEL NELSON: I was part of a high school gang Jerry used to take in his jeep to ball games [shortly after he moved to Cornish]. He was just one of the guys. I don't think anybody was awestruck. He had written *Catcher in the Rye*, but we really didn't know about that. We just enjoyed him because he was someone willing to be there and take us to games and he was fun to be around. He was a good guy. You know, back then, who thought about what you did? I was a student at Windsor High School with a girl named Shirlie Blaney. She was a year ahead of me, but we all went to the games together. If it was an away game, Jerry would be there with his jeep, and we'd all climb in and as many as could squeeze in went. The rest had to find another way to go.

It was an old open jeep; it didn't have a hood on it or anything. It was all open and it was fun. All the girls wanted to go. We would go to the game, and then a lot of the girls who were allowed to would continue on by going to the restaurants and having meals with him. I wasn't allowed to. My parents were pretty strict, so I would find a ride home because I lived in Cornish and we were in Windsor. There was a soda fountain in Windsor that most of us gathered at, and Jerry used to come right in and be a part of it. He seemed to like the youth. Jerry was such an energetic person that he put energy out to everyone around him, and it was so contagious. The girls were screaming and laughing and giddy and you could get a headache pretty easy. I guess that's why the guys didn't go along, because there was so much noise. Jerry was a careful driver. You wouldn't think of it to hear all the noise. I can hear it just sitting here, thinking about it. I guess he allowed us to be ourselves, whereas at home with Mom and Dad you were always trying to be the perfect child to do whatever they expected of you. With Jerry around, you could do what you wanted and not think you were going to be reprimanded. It was all laughter. That's how the whole time was—all laughter. It was neat.

Most of the time, the jeep filled up fast. You didn't think of him as an adult. He was, but he was laid-back, fun to be around, very handsome, very smooth-skinned and very thin, and always willing to take you where you wanted to go, like he had all the time in the world. The guys seemed to have the vehicles, but we girls were stranded, and Shirlie Blaney ended up quite friendly with Jerry and they went on several dates.

In all my high school years with Shirlie Blaney, I don't think I ever met her parents. I really didn't know them. Shirlie was like most of us: if we wanted to do something bad enough, Mom and Dad were never going to know about it until it was too late. I have a feeling her parents probably didn't know all that was going on.

While Jerry was picking us up and taking us for rides to different places, he and Shirlie would talk; she was editor of the yearbook. She did a lot of newspaper work during high school, so they did have this connection, this love for writing, and that might have been a big reason why Shirlie and Jerry got drawn together—because they had this writing business that they wanted to talk to each other about and maybe build each other up a bit on.

The people did know that he was a writer. Nobody really gave it

SHIRLIE ALICE BLANEY ***"Shirl"*** **Civic**
Sociable . . . a flare for writing . . . petite . . . chatter box . . . "Milt" . . . photogenic.
Chorus 3, 4; Ensemble 4; Orchestra 3, 4; Majorette 1, 2, 3, Drum Majorette 4; Glee Club 1, 2, 3; Dramatics 1, 2; Dramatics 3, 4; Senior Play; Yearbook 4; Student Council 3; Windsor Highlights 3; Cheerleader 2, 3, 4; Dance Committees 2, 3, 4; All-State Chorus 3, 4; All New England 4.

Shirlie Blaney's yearbook photo.

much thought, least of all us kids. Everyone always asks, "Why did he hang around with the kids?" Well, because we didn't care about what he did. We were friends. Until Shirlie Blaney blew that.

Shirlie started getting serious about Jerry and wanted to be more than a friend. When they started going together, we all teased her a bit. I mean, here was Jerry Salinger the writer, and who did she think she was? She said, "You'd be surprised what I'm going to do with this." She just continued going out with him.

SHIRLIE BLANEY: I knew all about him before I ever met him.

ETHEL NELSON: When Jerry came down to pick us girls up to go to the games, he and Shirlie would be in the front seats, and they would do a lot of talking while we were on our way. She started going to his home. He had a lot of things he wanted to teach her on the writing-type thing. There were four or five of us girls there, and we were all just wide-eyed over him, too. I think if he had given any of us the eye, we probably would have jumped in with both feet and been very proud to have done it.

During the time Shirlie Blaney was going with Jerry—I don't know if I have the right to use the word "dating," but they were getting together, and we would call that a date—she was very popular in school.

She was a beautiful girl; she had beautiful blond hair. The boys in school wanted to get together with her, too.

SHIRLIE BLANEY: He seemed to be delighted. He cried, "Come on in," and started bringing out the Cokes and potato chips. After a while he began playing some records on his hi-fi; he had hundreds of records, classics and show tunes. We were there a long time and I finally told my date, "Come on, let's get out of here; Jerry doesn't want to be bothered with us." But every time we started to leave Jerry would say, "Stick around. I'll play another record." . . . He'd play whatever record we asked for on his hi-fi—my favorite was *Swan Lake*—and when we started to leave he'd always want to play just one more. . . . I couldn't understand why he put up with us, but he didn't seem to want us to go. I never saw anyone fit in the way he did. He was just like one of the gang, except that he never did anything silly the way the rest of us did. He always knew who was going with whom, and if anybody was having trouble at school, and we all looked up to him, especially the renegades. . . . He seemed to love having us around, but I'd sit there and wonder, Why is he doing this?

SUSAN J. BOUTWELL and ALEX HANSON: [Joyce Burrington] Pierce was a 19-year-old Windsor High graduate back in the days when Salinger would drive into town in his little Hillman sports car, his pet schnauzer riding in the back. Salinger would visit with the Windsor teens, watching their high school football games, attending movies with them and inviting them to his house to listen to Billie Holliday records or play with his Ouija board, recalled Pierce.

JOYCE BURRINGTON PIERCE: My father was a bit leery of us spending so much time with him. He'd say, "You girls are going to end up in a book." I read all of his stories looking for me.

SHIRLIE BLANEY: Finally I decided that he was writing another book about teenagers and we were his guinea pigs. I don't mean that he was looking down his nose at us or had us on a pin or anything like that. He was very sincere. There's nothing phony about him. He's a very nice person. Once I told him that I thought I'd like to be a writer, that I was lying awake at night trying to think of ideas. He nodded very sympathetically and said, "That's the best way. Be sure to get up and write them down, so you don't forget them."

—

JOHN C. UNRUE: Salinger has a great need to preserve the innocence in young people—to stop time as much as possible.

JOHN WAIN: [Salinger] seems to understand children as no English-speaking writer has done since Lewis Carroll.

J. D. SALINGER (*The Catcher in the Rye*, 1951):

> The best thing, though, in that museum was that everything always stayed right where it was. Nobody'd move. . . . Nobody'd be different.

DAVID YAFFE: Salinger often conflates sexuality and young girls. There is something weirdly lecherous about Salinger's description of Phoebe sleeping. On the one hand, it's a very pure image. But on the other hand there are gratuitous descriptions of Phoebe drooling on her pillow, and Salinger seems to take great delight in these descriptions—just the way that they're written.

J. D. SALINGER ("A Girl I Knew," *Good Housekeeping*, February 1948):

> Leah's knock on my door was always poetry—high, beautifully wavering, absolutely perpendicular poetry. Her knock started out speaking of her own innocence and beauty, and accidentally ended speaking of the innocence and beauty of all very young girls. I was always half-eaten away by respect and happiness when I opened the door for Leah.

ETHEL NELSON: At that time, we never gave it a thought at all. Later, I know it was questioned as to why Jerry always went to the younger female sex partner. I really think it was because he wanted to stay young. I think he was afraid to grow old.

—

CATHERINE CRAWFORD: [One day he] was having lunch in a café where he always had lunch, and Shirlie Blaney saw him and asked if she could interview him for the high school paper. These were his friends, really, the people he liked to hang out with, and he didn't see any harm in it; it seemed like he just wanted to do a favor for a friend.

SHIRLIE BLANEY: Our page came out once a month—that is, if we were lucky. There wasn't much news in Windsor. We were having our usual trouble filling the page this day, and then I happened to look out the window—we were up on the second floor—and there across the street was Jerry. I told another girl to come along and ran downstairs after him. I had a wonderful idea.

I said "Jerry, I need a story for the paper. Tell me some things I can write about."

He said "What paper?"

"Our high school page in the *Eagle*."

"Sure. Let's go inside."

ETHEL NELSON: He gave her an interview with the promise from her that it was for the school paper—just the school paper. Shirlie wrote the article.

ERNEST HAVEMANN: The Windsor High School [paper] came out the following Monday . . . her interview was not there. That evening Salinger called her at home—a surprising action, it seems to me, for a man who hates publicity—and said, "That story wasn't in the paper. What's going on?"

DAVID SHIELDS: There it is, the characteristic Salinger gesture: his deeply ambivalent, genuinely confused relationship to attention. Go away. Where did you go? Blaney's article appeared not in the high school paper but in the local paper, the *Daily Eagle*.

THE *CLAREMONT DAILY EAGLE*: During the preparation of the recent student edition of the *Daily Eagle*, Miss Shirlie Blaney, of the class of 1954 at Windsor High School, spied Jerome David Salinger, author of the bestseller *Catcher in the Rye* in a Windsor restaurant. Mr. Salinger, who recently bought a home in Cornish, obliged the reporter with the following interview.

An author of many articles and a few stories, including *Catcher in the Rye*, was interviewed and provided us with an interesting life story.

A very good friend of all the high school students, Mr. Salinger has many older friends as well, although he has been coming here only a few years. He keeps very much to himself, wanting only to be left alone to write. He is a tall and foreign looking man of 34, with a pleasing personality.

Jerome David Salinger was born January 1, 1919, in New York. He went to public grammar schools while his high school years were spent at Valley Forge Military Academy in Pennsylvania. During this time he was writing. His college education included New York University, where he studied for two years.

Shirlie Blaney, editor of the high school yearbook, 1953.

With his father, he went to Poland to learn the ham shipping business. He didn't care for this, but he accomplished something by learning the German language. Later he was in Vienna for ten months but came back and went to Ursinus College. Due to lack of interest, he left at midyear and went to Columbia University. All this time he was still writing. Mr. Salinger's first story was published at the age of 21. He wrote for two years for the *Saturday Evening Post*, *Esquire*, *Mademoiselle*, and many more. He later worked on the liner *Kungsholm* in the West Indies, as an entertainer. He was still writing for magazines and college publications. At the age of 23, he was drafted. He spent two years in the Army, which he disliked because he wanted all of his time to write.

He started working on *Catcher in the Rye*, a novel, in 1941 and finished it in the summer of 1951. It was a Book-of-the-Month Club selection and later came out as a pocket book. The book is a study of a troubled adolescent boy. When asked if it was in any way autobiographical, Mr. Salinger said: "Sort of. I was much relieved when I finished it. My boyhood was very much the same as that of the boy in the book, and it was a great relief telling people about it."

About two years ago he decided to come to New England. He came through this section. He liked it so much that he bought his present home in Cornish. His plans for the future include going to Europe and Indonesia. He will go first to London perhaps to make a movie. One of his books, *Uncle Wiggily in Connecticut*, has been made into a movie, *My Foolish Heart*.

About 75 percent of his stories are about people under 21 and 40 per cent of those about youngsters under 12. His second book was a collection of nine stories. They first appeared in the *New Yorker*.

CATHERINE CRAWFORD: The daily newspaper, the *Claremont Daily Eagle*, published Shirlie's story on their front page. This was the ultimate intrusion for Salinger.

ETHEL NELSON: It really went well if it could have just stayed that friendship, but when Shirlie started getting serious—not just a friend but wanted to be more than that—I think that's when Jerry put a stop to it all. He gave her an interview in good faith and she hurt him; she used him. Shirlie found a way to make some fast bucks, I think. He was very, very unhappy about that, and I think I would have been, too. There were a lot of personal things in there that were just for the local people, so he was very hurt by it. Then Jerry didn't trust any of us. He was not our friend anymore.

Jerry didn't want to be approached by anybody, and if you started toward him, he would just put his head down and walk right away, so you knew immediately that wasn't the right thing to do, and it was very hard. After I got married to Wayne in 1954, Wayne knew Jerry even better than I did because he worked for him off and on, cutting his wood, chopping the hay down in the field, and he was really friendly with him. I would go over with him to the house when he would work, but Jerry would never speak—so yeah, it hurt.

DAVID SHIELDS: In *The Catcher in the Rye*, Holden says, "You can't ever find a place that's nice and peaceful, because there isn't any." By the end of 1953, Salinger had come to the same conclusion. Self-contempt was becoming world-contempt.

LAWRENCE GROBEL: Salinger ended up building a wall. Literally, he built this wall around his house and just shut the kids out. He never saw them again. The wall never came down.

Conversation with Salinger #5

Betty Eppes, 1980.

GEORGE PLIMPTON: Betty Eppes is a reporter from the *Baton Rouge Advocate*. In the spring of 1980 she was a Special Assignments Writer for the "Fun" section which appears in both the *Advocate* and the *State Times*, the morning and afternoon papers respectively. That spring she decided to spend her summer vacation trying to interview J. D. Salinger, the author famous for his reclusive behavior.

SHANE SALERNO: Betty Eppes was maligned by certain members of the press after her 1980 interview with Salinger, and George Plimpton distorted some of her story when he reedited and republished it in the *Paris Review* in 1981. Since then she has made no comments about the interview, but I tracked her down in Costa Rica, and after a number of conversations she finally agreed to an interview. She retraced her steps in Cornish, then traveled to New York for a formal interview, where she told the full story.

BETTY EPPES: When I went to do the Salinger story, it followed a period that was very difficult for me. I had hit forty, which no woman wants to do. I had a very serious health issue that I dealt with, not elegantly or with grace, but I dealt with it. I was bored with the newspaper I worked at. I had taken time off and come back. I thought, "Why am I still at this newspaper?" I decided if I could do something significant I could continue. I was talking to a friend who owned a bookstore. I said, "I'm really thinking I'll just go up to New Hampshire and find J. D. Salinger," and he said, "Well, you know, I think you ought to call up NASA and bum a ride on the next space shuttle, too." I wanted to do it on my own. I didn't want to talk to an editor, who would have said no. I thought, I'll have to finance this on my own, so on the trip I'm going to do a series of stories I can sell, regardless of whether I can get to Salinger, because I didn't expect to succeed with him, really.

When I went to rent a car, I said, not thinking, "I don't want to spend a lot of money. I want the cheapest one." So there I was in New Hampshire, driving a sky-blue Pinto that would barely move on those mountains; sometimes I thought it was going to roll back. On the way, I thought I'd find the story that that high school girl had done with Salinger, so I went to the newspaper that had published it. An old wooden building. Down in the basement, the morgue of the newspaper was incredible. Newspapers were just thrown in there, but we actually went back and found that article. And I had looked up what else I could find about Salinger. There was not a great deal of material, but I found what I could.

The minute you go into town and say "J. D. Salinger," everybody becomes your enemy. One lady would not sell me an ice-cream cone after I mentioned his name. I thought, "Whew, not the friendliest place."

I walked into the butcher shop, asked the owner if Salinger was a customer, and he said, "Oh, no. If J. D. Salinger were my customer, I would know that." I described what I thought Salinger might look like. The guy said, "Well, I do make deliveries to someone like that." I said, "Would you call the person's house for me and allow me to speak? I won't ask you for the number." He said, "I always speak to the housekeeper." I said that would be great. He got her on the telephone. Immediately she wanted to know how I knew Salinger shopped at that butcher shop. The shop owner didn't realize it was Salinger because Salinger used an alias.

The housekeeper was very nervous because she was afraid she'd be fired. She said I absolutely could *not* come to Cornish. I said, "No, I want to leave a message." I asked if there was an answering machine and she said no. She asked if I was going to try to come to Salinger's house and I told her I was not. She calmed down and told me to write a note, put his name on the envelope—I didn't need a mailing address—and leave it at the post office in Windsor, where he went three to five times a week. I bought a notebook, went outside, sat on a curb, wrote a note, bought an envelope. I went to the post office and bought a stamp and left it there at about four in the afternoon.

EDWIN McDOWELL: In her letter to Mr. Salinger, Miss Eppes, who arranged her vacation so that she could search for him, said she was a woman who supported herself as a writer. She explained that since she was staying at a motel with no telephones in the rooms, she would wait for him at a designated location in Windsor for 30 minutes beginning at 9:30 the next morning, and that if he did not show up she would wait there again the following morning before returning to Baton Rouge.

BETTY EPPES: What did I write in the note? Well, first of all, it was rather intimidating. I thought, What can I write to this man that might inspire him to respond? I opened the letter, as my grandmother would say, in a mannerly way. I commented on the beauty of the area. It really is remarkably beautiful. I could understand why he would choose to live in such a beautiful place.

PAUL ALEXANDER: Betty Eppes was a character unto herself. Emerald green eyes, a shock of red hair—a knockout. In her soul, she was pure Cajun Creole, all hot-blooded and fiery. But she was also smart and cagey and ambitious.

CATHERINE CRAWFORD: Betty Eppes had been a model and a tennis champion, and now she was a reporter, and she jumped right into it. She decided this was a fascinating story and just went for it.

BETTY EPPES: I told him that I would be sitting in a sky-blue Pinto right by the corner and just up the road from the covered bridge and that I was tall with green eyes and red-gold hair. I said, I will make no further effort to seek you out, not because of guard dogs or fences, but because I do not want to anger you or cause you grief.

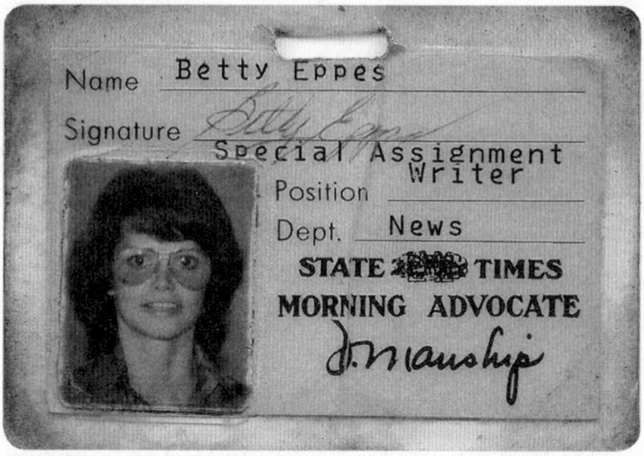

Betty Eppes's press pass.

I was determined not to go to his property. I was determined not to cross that river. I thought if he came in voluntarily to where I was, that no one could ever say with any truth that I had waylaid him or any of those things.

I knew before I went there he was very interested in women. We all knew that, right? I did think I had a better shot because I was a woman; that gave me an edge. He was always very kind to all his female characters. The night before, I was a wreck. I second-guessed myself all the time. I thought about all the questions you can't answer: What on earth am I doing here? Am I insane? Of course, the answers were "I don't know" and "You're insane." It sounds a little bizarre, a little sixth sense, call it what you will, but I knew he was coming to meet me. I really did.

The next day I was sitting on the Windsor side of the Connecticut River covered bridge, on a very public corner, because I was determined no one could ever say I had sabotaged the man. I was perfectly calm. I didn't doubt he was coming; I knew he was coming.

Salinger walked across the bridge, stepped out of the shadows and into the sunlight, and there he was. And I was ready to put my fist in the air and do the "yes" dance and all that stuff. As he started walking toward me, I got out—with my notebook and pencil in hand, of course—stood beside the car, and waited. He was carrying an attaché case. Once he appeared, I was shocked: he was as tall as I thought he would be, but he had snow-white hair. We've all seen that photograph on the back of the book. You expect people to age, but somehow it's not the same as seeing it.

He walked up. "Betty Eppes?"

We shook hands, and I began to try to talk to the man.

He said, "If you're a writer, you need to quit that newspaper." That was the first thing he said.

I said, "Okay. We can talk about that."

He thought newspapers served no purpose, and he thought publishing was the worst thing a person could do. One of the things he talked about was politicians. He said the problem he had with politicians was that they tried to limit our horizons and he tried to expand them. I pushed a few buttons and a few other things—asked for his autograph just to see what would happen. Well, whew, that got a response. I got another lecture. He came to lecture. It made you wonder whether he wasn't a retired professor. The man really wanted to climb on his soapbox.

I continued on, using the notes I had made from the Shirlie Blaney interview. "You told Miss Blaney you were going to London to make a movie. Did you?"

Instead of answering the question, he said, "Where'd you get all this old stuff?" If I mentioned any of the things from Miss Blaney's interview, he'd come back with "old stuff." It was getting very frustrating.

"Did you make or work on a movie?" I said. "Will you in the future?"

"Can we go on to something else?"

"Of course, but just for fun, do you remember the name of the ship you worked on as an entertainer?"

He became furious. I was beginning to realize I was accomplishing nothing, but he did remember the name of the ship. "I do, yes," he said. "The *Kungsholm*." He wouldn't talk about what kind of entertainment he did on board.

"You were in the counterintelligence corps," I said. "How many languages do, or did, you speak?"

"French and German, but not very well. And a few phrases of Polish."

"Given your family background, why writing?"

"I can't say exactly. I don't know if any writer can. It's different for each person. Writing is a highly personal act. It's different for each writer."

"Did you consciously opt for writing as a career or did you just drift into it?"

"I don't know." There was a long pause. "I truly don't. I just don't know."

J. D. SALINGER (contributor's note for "Down at the Dinghy," *Harper's*, April 1949):

> I've been writing seriously for over ten years. Being modest almost to a fault, I won't say I'm a born writer, but I'm certainly a born professional. I don't think I ever *selected* writing as a career. I just started to write when I was eighteen or so and never stopped. (Maybe that isn't quite true. Maybe I *did* select writing as a profession. I don't really remember—I got into it so quickly—and finally.)

BETTY EPPES: I asked him several times whether he was writing. He insisted each time he was. But he would not comment at all about he nature of the projects, whether they were short stories, books, screenplays, movies. He just wouldn't.

I asked questions, and he would always come back with, "Where did you find all of this? Why are you asking me this? Let's talk about writing." He always wanted to talk about writing.

Salinger wouldn't discuss whether he had written more about the Glass family. He insisted he had more important issues to address with his writing. He wouldn't expand on what they were.

J. D. SALINGER: I will state this: it is of far more significance than anything I ever wrote about Holden. I have really serious issues I am trying to tackle with these new writing projects.

BETTY EPPES: I wanted to know what they were. I got zip.

J. D. SALINGER: I'm tired of being collared in elevators, stopped on the street, and of interlopers on my private property. I've made my position clear for 30 years. . . . I want to be left alone, absolutely. Why can't my life be my own?

BETTY EPPES: I asked him whether there would there be a sequel to *Catcher in the Rye*. He was vehement: "No!" He became rather annoyed, agitated. He said creating Holden was a mistake, and if there was anything else I wanted to know about Holden, I should reread *Catcher*. He was adamant that there would be no more Holden.

When we did talk about writing, he became more of a person; he didn't seem defensive. He clearly thought about the value of writing, but he was always guarding the gate of privacy as the domain of the writer. He said he wished he had never published *Catcher in the Rye.* It had had such a terrible impact on his life he wished he had never done it. At those moments, you felt like you were talking to a person. The other moments, no, but those moments you thought you were talking to a person and he was probably answering honestly—telling you what he felt and what he thought. He lost some of his intensity. A couple of times he even uncrossed his arms, but he never lapsed into conversation, never. I'd never encountered such intensity in a person, the way he stared. It was unnerving. He didn't blink as much as I thought he should've. He didn't blink at all. I was very uncomfortable with that.

He insisted that he was working. He said that he was working for himself, and that's what writing should be. Writers write for their own reasons, but it should be for themselves alone, and the only important thing was the writing, according to J. D. Salinger.

Salinger seemed a very argumentative, angry person. I was surprised. I thought I was going to find a grown-up Holden. I thought there would be this pleasant guy; maybe we'd even laugh once or twice. Forget it. You don't laugh in his presence. The guy is so intense. It made you want to take a step back, maybe two. He's one of those people who get in your face because he wants to make his point. He's very tall, and so he looked down deliberately and with great intensity.

When I began, I was stupidly enthusiastic because I thought Salinger was going to talk to me, and we were going to have a conversation. Instead he delivered these little minilectures. I had hoped I would come away with a scoop of some kind, that he would tell me what he was doing, something specific, no general mumbo jumbo. I was very persistent. If he *was* writing, then tell me about it. If it wasn't about Holden, what was it about? If it was not a sequel to *Catcher in the Rye*, was it a continuation of the Glass family? Every time: "No, no, no."

So I finally put the notebook down, put my pen down, looked up at him, and said, "Why did you bother to come here to see me? Why didn't you stay up on your mountain? Why didn't you just ignore my letter?"

"I write, you write," he said. "I came here one writer to another." He wanted to know whether I had written a novel. Goodness me, J. D. Salinger asking Betty Eppes about her work. I told him I had, and he asked me if I intended to publish it. I told him I had a contract and the publisher and I had disagreed, and I, being stubborn as a mule, withdrew the manuscript. He thought that was perfect. If I wanted to write, I should write it all, put it in a drawer, and save it. The only important thing was the writing, according to him.

—

PHOEBE HOBAN: Salinger apparently told Betty Eppes, "I'm tired of people asking me about Holden. It's over. Holden's a moment frozen in time." Perhaps Salinger himself is frozen in time.

PAUL ALEXANDER: He didn't have to go down and meet Eppes at her Pinto. If he really wanted to protect his seclusion, he wouldn't have gone. Obviously he had planned this out in advance. He did it with the introduction both to *Franny and Zooey* and to the last book as well, *Raise High the Roof Beam, Carpenters and Seymour: An Introduction.* In both instances, those little introductions, those tidbits, were clearly calculated to get attention from the public. Here's the bottom line: if he hadn't wanted to talk to Betty Eppes, if he hadn't wanted to talk to Michael Clarkson, or to the other journalist-fans who have wandered up there through the years, he wouldn't have talked to them.

BETTY EPPES: After the interview, I went to Boston, where I had a flight to Baton Rouge. I called my newspaper from Boston, asked for my editor, and got immediately patched through, which was highly unusual. He came on the line and said, "Where the hell are you?" I said, "Well, at this moment, I'm in Boston." He said, "You know, I've already had two phone calls. I know where you've been. Can we talk about this now?" I said, "Well, actually, I have to get going." So he told me that as soon as I got back into Baton Rouge I should call him and come in to the office. He said he would find out the time of my plane and meet me at the paper. And he did.

He kept pressuring me for the story, but I wasn't ready to write it. Finally, I did write it. It caused an incredible commotion. First of all, the newspaper did all kinds of promotions for it. There were interviews with TV stations and radio stations ad infinitum, and it was really rather bizarre. We had the story in our paper first. The *Boston Globe* reprinted it, and then the story went international.

Salinger walking away from the interview with Betty Eppes, June 13, 1980.

There were a lot of calls, a lot of job offers from newspapers and TV stations. I wasn't interested, not in the least. I just wanted the furor to die down. I really hadn't anticipated the commotion that would be caused by the story and the interview. And I wasn't interested in moving to a different part of the country. I was okay in Baton Rouge, so I stayed.

I had told Mr. Salinger that I would send him a copy of the story. And I did. After I'd finished it, I sent it, and a week or ten days later, I received something from Windsor, Vermont. It didn't have his return address on it or anything, but it was some photocopies of orders he had placed. And then, after that, there were, I think, three packages from Windsor that came altogether. In one there was a photostat of part of *The Catcher in the Rye*. It was just a photostat. In another one, there were about four letters that he had written to different firms in New York. Always photostats, never a word, nothing, but always with the postmark of Windsor, Vermont, which was peculiar, to say the least.

12

FOLLOW THE BULLET: *NINE STORIES*

CORNISH, NEW HAMPSHIRE, 1953

So far the novels of this war have had too much of the strength, maturity and craftsmanship critics are looking for, and too little of the glorious imperfections which teeter and fall off the best minds. The men who have been in this war deserve some sort of trembling melody rendered without embarrassment or regret. I'll watch for that book.

J. D. Salinger, 1945

From the dozens of stories Salinger had written by 1953, he selected and arranged nine stories to form the war novel he'd been waiting for. According to Margaret Salinger, her father told a student seeking information that all biographical facts and traumatic events can be found in his work. In *Harper's*, Gilbert Highet wrote that in every story in *Nine Stories* "there is a thin, nervous intelligent being who is on the verge of breakdown: we see him at various stages of his life, as a child, as an adolescent, as an aimless young man in his twenties. . . ." What incarnations does this being take? He is Seymour, of course, in "A Perfect Day for Bananafish" and Sergeant X in "For Esmé—with Love and Squalor," but he is also Eloise in "Uncle Wiggily in Connecticut," Ginnie (and Franklin) in "Just Before the War with the Eskimos," Lionel in "Down at the Dinghy," Arthur in "Pretty Mouth and Green My Eyes," and the title characters in "The Laughing Man," "De Daumier-Smith's Blue Period," and "Teddy." *Nine Stories* is the serial self-portrait of someone committing suicide, or considering it very seriously. Follow the bullet.

DAVID SHIELDS: From war to postwar trauma to suicide to believing children will save you to knowing they can't (because you can't have them) to looking for visionary illumination either through suicide or enlightenment to realizing suicide *is* enlightenment: only in reincarnation will you ever find relief from never-ending anguish, and this belief in reincarnation can come only through Vedanta (for you).

You get off at the fifth floor, walk down the hall, and let yourself into Room 507. The room smells of new calfskin luggage and nail-lacquer remover. You glance at the girl lying asleep on one of the twin beds. Then you go over to one of the pieces of luggage, open it, and from under a pile of shorts and undershirts you take out an Ortgies calibre 7.65 automatic.

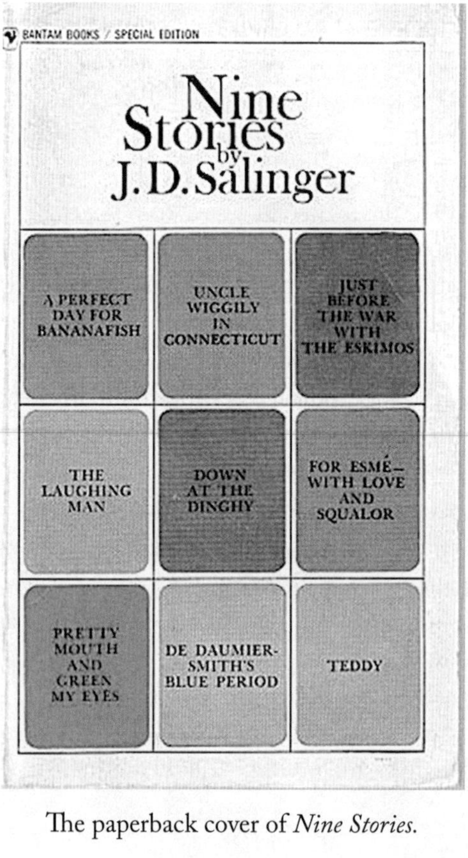

The paperback cover of *Nine Stories*.

You release the magazine, look at it, then reinsert it. You cock the piece. Then you go over and sit down on the unoccupied twin bed, look at the girl, aim the pistol, and fire a bullet through your right temple.

Why do you do this? Why does the room smell of calfskin luggage and nail-lacquer remover? Why do you look first at your wife? Is it, in some sense, Sylvia, the enemy combatant you married, and by marrying, hoped to heal yourself and unify the world, and whom you now want to punish by traumatizing forever?

Why is it a German pistol? For you, the only great poet of the century is Rainer Maria Rilke, who could not be more Germanic.

Is there a chance you'll completely lose control of yourself? Is it a crime that the army released you from the hospital? You're so pale; are you sick or something? You're utterly broken, so all you see everywhere is brokenness; everywhere you go you see more glass. The one person who might cure you (not really—otherwise why would her name be Sybil?—she's an oracle of your own death—and why would you evoke her nemesis, Sharon Lipschutz, by quoting *The Wasteland*?) is a little girl.

Let's go look for "bananafish"—your father's invention. You hate your father, his gross materialism: bananafish swim into a hole in which there are a lot of bananas. They're very ordinary-looking fish when they swim in, but once they get in, they behave like pigs; some bananafish swim into a banana hole and eat as many as seventy-eight bananas. After that, they're so fat they can't get out of the hole again, can't fit through the door, and die. Notice, Seymour, how your critique of your father is also a parable of your own experience in war.

You hate the adult world. You hate the postwar civilian world. You hate adult women dying their hair mink. You slough off your Jewish sister, Sharon Lipschutz. You want Sybil, oblivion in a perfect little girl.

A raving maniac, you undo the belt of your robe. You take off the robe. Your shoulders are white and narrow, and your trunks are royal blue. You fold the robe, first lengthwise, then in thirds. You unroll the towel you had been using over your eyes, spread it out on the sand, and then lay the folded robe on top of it. You bend over, pick up the float, and secure it under your right arm. Then, with your left hand, you take Sybil's hand. Notice how in performing this action you are preparing exactly for your final action; by taking Sybil's hand—the girl you can't have—you're killing yourself.

You take Sybil's ankles in your hands and press down and forward.

The float noses over the top of the wave. The water soaks Sybil's blond hair—crucial, that Germanic/un-Jewish blondness. Her scream is full of pleasure. You call her "my love" for a lot of reasons, not least of which is that she tells you that she has just seen a bananafish. Wait, not just one. Six. She possesses a child's unself-conscious imagination, but when you pick up one of her wet feet and kiss the arch, she protests, so you stop. Why are you fixated on very young girls, especially young girls' feet? Does it have anything to do with using girls as time-travel machines to a period before the war and before you perforce became embarrassed about your own anatomy?

In the elevator, you accuse the woman in the elevator of looking at your feet. Why is it so important that she's wearing zinc salve on her nose? It's rather like nail-lacquer remover, isn't it?—an emblem of adult womanhood, exactly what you don't want, because after the war bodies aren't sexy; they're fatal corpses. You accuse Zinc Salve of being a goddamned sneak about it, because, of course, you were a goddamned sneak about kissing Sybil's feet. You know this, you know this. How could you not?

Then you let yourself into Room 507. You shoot yourself for a variety of reasons—we'll spend the rest of this book and many other books trying to figure out why—one of which, overtly enough, is postwar trauma, but the other main one is that you can't join the adult world of luggage and zinc salve and Muriel/Sylvia (remember, she's a corpse). Postadolescence, post-Oona, postwar, you have nowhere to go. You are a dead man.

Ghosts are more powerful than the living. The idealized potential of a life cut short can never be superseded. Your brother Walt, say, whose regiment was resting someplace. It was between battles or something; a friend of Walt's wrote all this to his college girlfriend, Eloise. Walt and some other boy were putting a little Japanese stove in a package. A colonel wanted to send the stove home. Or they were taking it out of the package to rewrap it; Eloise doesn't know exactly. The stove was full of gasoline and junk and it exploded in their faces; the other boy just lost an eye. When Eloise tells this story, she tears up; she puts her hand around the empty glass on her chest to steady it. Walt's death wasn't an accident; it was the direct result of the colonel wanting a war relic. (Later in the book, your brother in Albany will put in a request for bayonets and swastikas for his kids now that "the g.d. war is over.")

There is always war. There is always trauma. There is always a child. There is always the adult world of sexuality and the child world of innocence—irreconcilable. There is always art. There is always imagination, which becomes a search for transcendence/spirituality/mysticism.

Eloise, never recovering from Walt's loss, has passed on this loss to her daughter, Ramona, who has a make-believe playmate, Jimmy Jimmereeno, who has left his sword outside. Jimmy Jimmereeno is more real to Ramona than anyone human is (Jimmy gets killed, but he quickly gets replaced by Mickey Mickeranno), just as Walt is more real to Eloise than her husband, to whom she says, "Why don't you boys form a platoon and march home? You can say that hut-hope-hoop-hoop business." Eloise's former college classmate's husband was stationed in Germany, where they had their own horse; the groom for the horse used to be Hitler's own private riding master or something. Eloise's drinking companion, Mary Jane, had been married to an air-minded aviation cadet who spent two of the three months she was married to him in jail for stabbing an MP.

Just after Walt had been drafted, he and Eloise were on the train from Trenton to New York. It was cold in the car, and she had her coat over the two of them. Walt sort of had his hand on her stomach—you know. Walt said Eloise was so beautiful he wished some officer would come up and order him to stick his other hand through the window. He said he wanted to do what was fair. This is the stirring of mysticism.

You know what Walt said once? He said he felt he was advancing in the army, but in a different direction from everybody else. He said that when he'd get his first promotion, instead of getting stripes he'd have his sleeves taken away from him. He said that when he'd get to be a general, he'd be stark naked. All he'd be wearing would be a little infantry button in his navel. Don't you think that's funny?

Postwar. Stateside. Nobody gets it: the unbridgeable gulf between civilians and veterans. Ever cut your finger, right down to the bone and all? Selena's brother, Franklin, urges Ginnie to stick around—he's bleedin' to death; he may need a goddam transfusion. Well, not right down to the *bone*, but he has cut himself. He's bleedin' like mad. Ginnie, the ideal nurse, explains that he should stop touching the wound and use iodine rather than Mercurochrome. Selena's sister, Joan, the Queen of the Snobs, who isn't half as good-looking as she thinks she is, is marrying a commander in the navy. Franklin wrote her eight goddamn letters, not one of which she answered. He couldn't serve in the war—bad ticker. He worked for thirty-seven months in a goddamn airplane factory in Ohio during the war. Did he like it? He loved it. He just adores airplanes. They're so *cute*.

Looking down from his apartment at the street, he sees the goddam fools who are all going over to the goddam draft board. We're gonna fight the Eskimos next. Why the Eskimos? How the hell should he know? This time all the old guys are gonna go. Guys around sixty. Nobody can go unless they're around sixty. Just give them shorter hours is all. Big deal. Let the rear-echelon motherfuckers serve up front this time. Ginnie points out that he wouldn't have to serve, anyway, and she also explains that when he holds his finger down it causes it to bleed more. She is the ideal wartime or peacetime nurse, urging him to put a Band-Aid on it or something—doesn't he have a Band-Aid or something?

Eric, Franklin's suitor, who worked with him in the airplane factory, takes the lapel of Ginnie's polo coat between his fingers, declaring it "lovely. It's the first really *good* camel's hair I've seen since the war. May I ask where you got it?"

Transformed by Franklin's wounded gentleness, Ginnie doesn't throw away the sandwich half Franklin gives her; she puts it back in her coat pocket. A few years earlier, it had taken her three days to dispose of the Easter chick she had found dead on the sawdust in the bottom of her wastebasket.

Life has been completely desacramentalized. How can we ever make it a sacrament again? (Hint: we will return to children and wastebaskets and sacraments with Sergeant X.)

There is always storytelling within the story. There is always a girl, all the better if she's unclassifiably beautiful at first sight, her name is Mary Hudson (not Sharon Lipschutz), she goes to Wellesley, she wears a beaver coat, smells of a wonderful perfume, talks a blue streak on the bus, smokes cork-tipped Tareytons, and hits a triple on the first pitch; her stickwork aside, she happens to be a girl who knows how to wave to somebody from third base. She also steals second three times. (Is she pregnant? Never mind.)

You, on the other hand: your head has been placed in a carpenter's vise. You grow into manhood with a hairless, pecan-shaped head and a face that features, instead of a mouth, an enormous oval cavity below the nose. Your nose consists of two flesh-sealed nostrils. When you breathe, the hideous, mirthless gap below your nose dilates and contracts like some sort of monstrous vacuole. Strangers faint dead away at the sight of your horrible face.

You can hang around HQ as long as you keep your face covered with a pale-red gossamer mask made out of poppy petals. The mask not only spares your brothers-in-arms the sight of your face; it also keeps them aware of your whereabouts. Every morning, in your extreme loneliness, you steal off, as graceful on your feet as a cat, to the dense forest surrounding the enemies' hideout. There you befriend dogs, white mice, eagles, lions, boa constrictors, wolves. When you remove your mask and speak to them, softly, melodiously, in their own tongues, they do not think you ugly. (You actually wind up marrying one of them.)

You're one for keeping an ear to the ground: you pick up the enemy's most valuable secrets; you're in the CIC, after all. You don't think much of army SOP, though, so you freelance around the countryside, murdering when absolutely necessary. Soon your ingenious methods, coupled with your singular love of fair play, find a warm place in the nation's heart.

You're obligated to lock up your enemies in a deep but pleasantly decorated mausoleum; although they escape from time to time, you refuse to kill them. There's a compassionate side to your character that just about drives everyone crazy. You cross the border into Paris, where you flaunt your high but modest genius in the face of an internationally famous detective, Marcel Dufarge, and his daughter, who become two of your worst enemies. You toy with them, leaving no even faintly credible indication of your escape method.

You amass the largest personal fortune in the world—most of it contributed anonymously to the monks of a local monastery—humble ascetics who dedicate their lives to raising German police dogs. Your personal wants are few. You subsist exclusively on rice and eagle's blood, in a tiny cottage with an underground gymnasium and shooting range, on the stormy coast of Tibet. Four blindly loyal confederates live with you: a glib timber wolf named Black Wing, a lovable dwarf named Omba, a giant Mongolian named Hong (whose tongue was burned out by white men), and a gorgeous Eurasian girl who, out of unrequited love and deep concern for your personal safety (she, too: the perfect nursemaid), sometimes has a pretty sticky attitude toward crime. You issue your orders to the crew through a black silk screen. Not even Omba, the lovable dwarf, is permitted to see your face.

But love, after the war, is impossible. The human body is wrecked.

No baby carriages for you and Mary Hudson. At all costs, you have to stifle your natural hideous laughter. Follow the bullet:

Your best friend, your timber wolf, Black Wing, falls into a trap set by the Dufarges, those Vichy collaborators, who—aware of your fierce loyalty—offer his freedom for your own. You agree. You meet the Dufarges at midnight in a section of the dense forest surrounding Paris, where they plan to double-cross you with a stand-in, but they haven't counted on your sentimentality and command of timber-wolf language. After Mlle. Dufarge ties you with barbed wire to a tree, you raise your beautiful, melodious voice—true—in a few words of farewell to your supposed old friend. The stand-in, impressed by your command of his language, informs you that he's not Black Wing, but that he'll never go with you to another country. You, infuriated, remove your mask and reveal your naked face in the moonlight. Dufarge passes out; Mlle. Dufarge lies supine on the moonlight ground.

When Dufarge comes to, he puts two and two together (what have you done—molested his daughter, killed her?) and fires at you four bullets, which you regurgitate. The Dufarges drop dead at your feet, decomposing. You're close to death, bleeding profusely. In a hoarse but eloquent voice, you appeal for help from the forest animals, who summon Omba, the lovable dwarf, but by the time he arrives—with a medical kit and supply of eagle's blood—you're in a coma. Omba's first act of mercy is to retrieve your mask, which he places respectfully over your hideous features. Then he (another ideal wartime nurse) dresses your wounds.

But you don't drink from the vial of eagle's blood. Instead, you weakly pronounce your beloved Black Wing's name. Omba bows his own slightly distorted head and reveals to you that the French have killed Black Wing. You crush the vial of eagle's blood in your hand. You again remove your mask. Because you failed to save your beloved, you don't deserve to live. You commit suicide (again).

Remember: it will always be postwar. There is always trauma, and how do we get through trauma? There is always the gorgeousness of children and/but the illicit appeal of adult-child contact. This time it's a boy, and this time, just once, we acknowledge the six million. Your mother, Boo Boo, is, in terms of permanently memorable, immoderately perceptive, small-area faces, a stunning and final girl. You are so traumatized that when your friend Naomi tells you she has a worm in her thermos, you seek refuge under a sink in the basement. Your mother peels down her cigarette army style. When you run away to sit in the stern of your father's dinghy—why have you run away?—she declares herself vice admiral, come to inspect the "stermaphors." You're wearing khaki-colored shorts. Just because she doesn't shoot off her mouth about it, people don't realize Boo Boo is an admiral; she almost never attempts to discuss her rank with people—she'd be drummed out of the bloomin' service. Sounding a bugle call, a peculiar amalgamation of "Taps" and "Reveille," she salutes the opposite shoreline. If you tell her why you've run away, she'll issue secret bugle calls that only admirals are allowed to hear. (She commands a fleet, after all.) You have goggles that once belonged to your dead uncle, a suicide. Sailors never cry, except when their ships go down or they're shipwrecked, on rafts and all. You have run away because somebody called your daddy a big sloppy kike. Informed that a kike is one of those things that go up in the air, with string you hold, you—since you are four years old—are able to join that kite in the air. Your mother loves your adorable, precious, time-dependent innocence so much that she can't help but kiss your neck and then put a wild hand inside the seat of your trousers, startling you considerably, although she almost immediately withdraws her hand and decorously tucks in your shirt for you. In your innocence, you have intuited that in this family there is a secret, that something is wrong, and that this has to do with the war, Jewishness, the Holocaust. Can you redeem us? No, because I will cross the line into adult-child eroticism, which I must do—after the war, all other bodies are dead to me. And so now we come to it: the war itself. Your trigger finger is itching imperceptibly, if at all. Flashes of lightning either have your number on them or they don't. The only people who can ever save you are children, who, luckily enough, are singing in a church at 3:15 p.m. Unfortunately, you can't marry any of them—not Sibyl or Ramona or Lionel or Esmé—so you'll commit suicide or come this close.

Listening to the children's chorus, you would experience levitation if you were a more denominational man. That is, you're seeking religious salvation, and you'll find it in Esmé, whose voice leads the way. You leave the church before the chorus director's speaking voice can entirely break the spell. The adult world ruins the child world for you. You can't exist in the former (your mother-in-law asks you to send her cashmere yarn first chance you get away from "camp") and you don't belong in the latter (you can't marry a twelve-year-old and, anyway, she will turn into a woman soon enough).

Proof of this: she's wearing a military-looking wristwatch that is marking that very passage into adulthood. Are you deeply in love with your wife? No, because she's an adult. War damage is everywhere: Esmé's father was killed in North Africa; her mother (in all likelihood) in the Blitz. The book begins with a Zen koan: "What is the sound of one hand clapping?" Here is another one: "What did one wall say to the other wall?" The only way past a koan is to progress beyond rationality; the only way past the damage is a leap into the mystical, which is almost always accessed through the unself-consciousness of a child, who—in this case, Esmé—is asking you to write a story, which is, of course, the very story we are reading and you are writing. You notice that, after the rainstorm, a lot of the wave in Esmé's hair is coming back; also, quite a bit more to the point, when she crosses her feet, she aligns the toes of her shoes, she's wearing white socks, and her ankles and feet are lovely. Wanting to kiss her, you kiss her brother, Charles—give him a loud, wet smacker—but you hate that both Charles and Esmé are headed toward a less sentimental way of life, that is, they will grow up and become self-conscious, lose their gorgeous access to their own feelings.

As for you, you're getting better acquainted with squalor all the time. You haven't come through the war with all your faculties intact. You've had a nervous breakdown, spending two weeks in a military mental hospital. You look like a goddam corpse. You had been triple-reading paragraphs; now you're triple-reading sentences. You've been chain-smoking for weeks. Your gums are bleeding. The goddam side of your face is jumping all over the place. You press your hands against your temples (in an earlier incarnation, you shot yourself to death in the right temple). To you, life is hell, and hell is the incapacity to love, and your incapacity to love is because Esmé etc. Temporary expiation: you grab the wastebasket and vomit. You're truly saved when Esmé sends you a broken watch, temporarily arresting time and temporarily joining her life to yours. The age difference disappears: you can live, in your imagination, through her imagination, forever.

After the war, you return home. Home sweet home. Christ. You're losing your goddam mind. You're thinking you may go back in the army—with your little helmet and big, fat desk and nice, big mosquito net. At least it's oblivion. Your wife has fled you to be with an untraumatized man. You're too weak for her. You're weak—that's the whole thing in a nutshell. Every night you have to keep yourself from opening every goddam closet door in the apartment, expecting to find a bunch of bastards hiding all over the place. (You'll never not be in the CIC.) She's an animal. You're not a goddam animal. You must be bigger/better than that. To you, the body is the site of all woe. You want an adult woman to save you and she can't, even if she holds a flashlight while you change a tire, buys you a suit that fits, or quotes a romantic poem. You're not savable, salvageable. No real woman can be equal to the mythic wilderness of your mind/imagination. No real woman or family can coexist with your postwar rage and sentimental pioneering in Cornish/Hürtgen.

What, then, is the way out? Is there any alternative to suicide the nth? Will you always be at best a visitor in a garden of enamel urinals and bedpans, with a sightless, wooden dummy-deity standing by in a marked-down rupture truss? The thought wouldn't be endurable for more than a few seconds. But here it comes: a transcendent experience, a case of genuine mysticism: a hefty woman is changing the truss on a wooden dummy in a shop window. She is, of course, the Fat Lady. She is Jesus Christ Himself, Buddy. When she sees you, she falls down (being thirty and hefty, she's beside the point), but the sun speeds toward the bridge of your nose at the rate of ninety-three million miles a second. Blinded and frightened, you put your hand on the window glass to keep your balance. The Transcendent Experience lasts no more than a few seconds, but when you get your sight back, the woman has left the window, leaving behind a shimmering field of exquisite, twice-blessed, enamel flowers.

What has happened? Have you levitated or been obliterated? Both, of course, and a child will again solve that particular koan:

Although, in this incarnation, you are only ten years old, you remind yourself to find your father's dog tags and wear them whenever possible—"it won't kill you and he will like it." In your opinion, life is a gift horse. You wonder why people think it's so important to be emotional. Your mother and father don't think a person is human unless he thinks a lot of things are very sad or annoying or unjust. Your father thinks you're inhuman. If you have emotions, you don't remember when you ever used them; you don't see what they are good for. You love God, but not sentimentally. You love your parents, but only in the sense that you have a strong affinity for them. In an earlier incarnation, you were a man from India making very nice spiritual progress. Your father thinks you're freakish because you meditate. Your mother worries that thinking about God is bad for your health. You think it's silly to be afraid of dying; all you do is get the heck out of your body when you die. My gosh, everybody's done it thousands and thousands of times. You know that you have a swimming lesson in about five minutes, and you know that your sister, Booper, is going to push you in and you will fracture your skull and die.

PTSD—with its endless embodied flashbacks—is a form of reincarnation, is it not? The little girl is no longer a figure of redemption; Booper pushes you to the death you eagerly embrace because you have found, in Vedanta, the source of solace: a reincarnation myth. Better luck next time. No pain—one can hope—the next go-round. Just as you forced your first wife to watch your first suicide, you are now traumatizing Booper, punishing her for being human; she will relive her participation in your death the rest of her life. Your genius/heroic/suicides/near-suicides throughout your various incarnations are a pacific/hostile action against the world's war. Walking *into* the wound is more important to you than the world that caused the wound. Suicide *is* enlightenment. You are in this world but not of it. You are now free to be with those you love, whether they are religions or historical figures, personal friends or fictional characters.

Conversation with Salinger #6

PAT YORK: In 1966 I was invited to photograph the actors Marlon Brando and Robert Forster in the film version of Carson McCullers's novel *Reflections in a Golden Eye*. It was a night shoot starting at dusk and continuing until daybreak, with the location at the Mitchel Military Base on Long Island. . . .

As usual on a film set, there was time spent waiting for scenes to be set up. During one of those breaks a handsome mature man approached me and started a conversation. He kept telling me he loved my voice and also asked many questions about my views on certain topics, my likes and dislikes. There was no opportunity to ask him about himself, as he was questioning me without a break and kept telling me how much he liked my voice. I thanked him but could not understand his obsession with my vocal cords.

Finally he mentioned that he could not believe I had no trace of an accent and inquired what part of Italy I was from. I told him I was an American who had been born in Jamaica and attended a French school in England and had also been tutored in Germany, with the rest of my education in the States.

He looked stunned. He told me that he had been asking various people who I was and had been told by at least three that I was Italian. We both laughed, and I introduced myself and he then gave me his name: J. D. Salinger. . . .

I knew that Salinger had become a recluse, and I couldn't equate this fact with the man I was speaking with so freely. I told him how much I loved "The Catcher in the Rye" and that my young son, Rick, had just read the book and could talk about nothing else. Its author said he would like to be in touch with Rick and asked for his name and address. . . .

J. D. Salinger did have a correspondence with my son. A few years later, Rick was studying in Paris. We met for dinner one evening and he was desolate. His apartment had been ransacked and, among other items, the suitcase where he kept all Salinger's letters had been taken. He didn't care about losing many other possessions, but he couldn't accept that his idol's correspondence had been stolen.

PART II

GARHASTHYA

HOUSEHOLDER DUTIES

13

HIS LONG DARK NIGHT

CORNISH, NEW HAMPSHIRE; NEW YORK CITY, 1953–1960

From the late 1940s onward, Salinger becomes increasingly committed to Eastern philosophy and religion, especially Vedanta. Visiting the Ramakrishna-Vivekananda Center of New York, going on retreats in upstate New York, and reading sacred Hindu texts, he bases virtually every decision of his life on Vedanta's tenets. Vedanta's prescription for the second stage of a man's life: become a householder—marry and create and support a family. Salinger marries Claire Douglas, the model for his story "Franny," and is a member of three families: his own; the fictional Glass family; and a third, the *New Yorker* of editor William Shawn, enabler of Salinger's obsessions, especially purity and silence and (ultimately) the purity of silence. Salinger writes, obsessively, in a bunker separated from the main house. Salinger talks as if his fictional characters exist in the world outside the page. He exists in a no-man's-land among his fictional families, the Glass and Caulfield clans, the pre- and postwar worlds, and the lives of young women he tries to seduce into his imagination and life. As paterfamilias, he is juggling these multiple families. He is trying to save postwar, childhood innocence from his own postwar trauma. The implicit tension is bound to cause destruction.

PAUL ALEXANDER: Following the episode with Shirlie Blaney, Salinger decided to go out and reconnect with people in his community. He was looking to become friendly with older people, going around to various parties he was invited to.

SHANE SALERNO: In fall 1950, Salinger, who was thirty-one, met Claire Douglas, who was sixteen—a senior at Shipley, a girls' boarding school in Bryn Mawr, Pennsylvania—at a party given by Bee Stein, an artist, and her husband, Francis Steegmuller, a translator and writer for the *New Yorker*. Claire's parents lived in the same apartment building as Steegmuller and Stein, on East 66th Street.

MARGARET SALINGER: She arrived at the party looking strikingly beautiful, with the wide-eyed, vulnerable, on-the-brink look of Audrey Hepburn in *Breakfast at Tiffany's* or Leslie Caron in *Gigi* . . . Claire wore her chestnut hair smoothed back from her lovely forehead. . . . The night my parents met . . . she was wearing a mid-blue linen dress with a darker blue velvet collar, simple and elegant as a wild iris.

CLAIRE DOUGLAS: *God*, I loved that dress. . . . It matched my eyes perfectly. I've never worn anything more beautiful in my life.

SHANE SALERNO: At the party Jerry and Claire couldn't talk much, because they came with other people, but the next day Salinger called to thank Bee Stein and ask for Claire's address at Shipley. The next week she received a letter from him. He phoned and wrote to her throughout the 1950–51 school year.

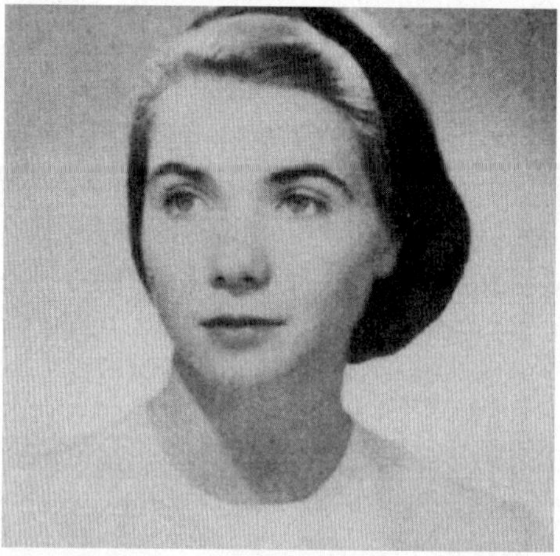

Claire Douglas as a Radcliffe student.

PAUL ALEXANDER: The moment Salinger saw her he was infatuated with her. She was attractive and very personable. She was pretty in a charming sort of way, and she had a softness and a delicateness to her that Salinger found very appealing. . . . As Salinger grew older, he was consistently attracted to women in their late teens. There was the young woman in Vienna, then Oona O'Neill, and now there was Claire.

Salinger discovered that her father was Robert Langdon Douglas, the well-known British art critic. Interestingly enough, she had been a product of a marriage in which her father was significantly older than her mother, so it wasn't unusual for her to be attracted to Salinger.

DAVID SHIELDS: Claire came from an illustrious family: her much older half-brother, William Sholto Douglas, served in the British Royal Air Force for most of the 1914–47 period, including both world wars. He commanded postwar British occupation forces in Germany for a year before becoming the chairman of British European Airways. He also became a member of the peerage and the House of Lords. Her father, who enlisted in World War I at age fifty, was an expert in Sienese art. He died in Florence in 1951. Claire was used to being around older men who'd fought in the world wars. Like Salinger, she was also half-Irish.

MARGARET SALINGER: Her childhood was not one that set her up with any kind of foundation. She was sent off to convent boarding school at age five, in and out of eight different foster homes, off to another boarding school.

DAVID SHIELDS: Salinger is interested in very, very young women—girls, really—but so are a lot of men. What's revealing about Salinger's fixation on girls is that he views them, essentially, as escapes to a time when no one "had ever heard of Cherbourg or Saint Lô, or Hürtgen Forest or Luxembourg." (Salinger, "The Stranger," *Collier's*, December 1, 1945.)

GERALDINE McGOWAN: Salinger was an extraordinarily attractive person, with tons of charisma, and from what we know he bombarded everybody with affection at the beginning of the relationship. They were the best, they were the loveliest, they were the smartest, they were gifted. And then he gets them and it ends.

DAVID SHIELDS: The summer after her freshman year at Radcliffe, Claire returned to New York City to model for Lord & Taylor.

SHANE SALERNO: Claire would visit Jerry's apartment on East 57th Street, where she'd spend the night on his black sheets, but they wouldn't have sex. Salinger was already under the influence of *The Gospel of Sri Ramakrishna*: "avoid woman and gold."

CLAIRE DOUGLAS: The black sheets and the black bookshelves, black coffee table, and so on matched his depression. He really had black holes where he could hardly move, barely talk.

SHANE SALERNO: Claire hid certain facts in the early stages of her relationship with Salinger. She hid her Lord & Taylor modeling job from him because she knew his response would be negative.

In 1953, after Salinger had moved to New Hampshire, he visited Claire at Radcliffe, where he wooed her with long conversations and riverside strolls. But in between the visits, he remained distant, and Claire would feel abandoned. When Salinger surprised her by asking her to drop out of school and move in with him in Cornish, she refused. Hurt, he disappeared. Claire was distraught and drove up to Cornish to speak to him, but he was nowhere to be found.

PAUL ALEXANDER: Salinger disappeared when Claire first hedged about moving into his house.

DAVID SHIELDS: Salinger left to spend several months in Europe.

SHANE SALERNO: During this time, he also continued to be in touch with Jean Miller.

J. D. SALINGER, excerpt from letter to Jean Miller, 1953:

> *I've never loved anyone enough, it seems to me, to go up and break the glass walls I've put the person inside. It makes it very hard on everybody concerned. Maybe one day I'll change. I honestly don't know. I've never really felt integrated enough to love anyone freely. I've never felt enough like just one man, instead of twenty men.*

PAUL ALEXANDER: Claire collapsed physically and mentally. She endured mononucleosis and an appendectomy, landing her in the hospital for quite a period of time. A Harvard Business School grad named Coleman Mockler who was infatuated with her repeatedly visited her in the hospital.

DAVID SHIELDS: Claire was an echo of eighteen-year-old Oona O'Neill a decade earlier and a pre-echo of Yale freshman Joyce Maynard two decades later. Salinger's sexual and romantic imagination circled obsessively around the same, usually dark-haired, boyishly built, gamine figure, from Miriam to Doris, Sylvia, Jean Miller, and onward. He was also repeating the Oona-Chaplin-Salinger triangle.

Claire was already entwined with Mockler, who was newly and deeply involved with fundamentalist Christianity. She and Mocker spent the summer together in Europe. When she returned in mid-September, Salinger wouldn't take her calls.

SHANE SALERNO: In an undated 1953 letter he informs Jean Miller that his recently published collection of stories, *Nine Stories*, is "selling very well, but I won't get any of the money till September." (The book reached the top spot on the *New York Times* bestseller list and was on the list for fifteen weeks.) In subsequent letters to her, he begins to discuss Eastern philosophy.

J. D. SALINGER, excerpt from letter to Jean Miller, 1953:

> *The word is Ko-an, or just Koan. And a Koan is an intellectually insoluble problem given to Zen monks by their masters. I was just telling you a few of them as they came to my mind.*

J. D. SALINGER, excerpt from letter to Jean Miller, April 30, 1953:

> *I've had two invitations for dinner this weekend from local people. I've lied and said I'm going to Boston. I suppose I'll have to go now. Damn people.*

J. D. SALINGER, excerpt from letter to Jean Miller, 1954:

> *About those two books I sent you. The little archery book isn't an orthodox Zen text or anything like that, but it's nice—the Zen is pure.*

And besides the beauty of Zen is constantly absorbed in the fact that Zen is where you find it.

J. D. SALINGER, excerpt from letter to Jean Miller, 1954:

I know it's worrying some of my friends, especially the ones who like my fiction. I think some of them guess that I may turn into a really monastic type sooner or later, give up my fiction, never marry, etc. Nothing is further from my mind at this point. What a low and specious thing "religion" would be if it were to lead me to negate art, love.

DAVID SHIELDS: Following Mockler's many visits to Claire at the hospital, he proposed marriage to her and—in the wake of Salinger's silence—she accepted, but in the summer of 1954 Salinger visited her; she was reading *The Way of a Pilgrim*. Salinger drew her away from Mockler and his Christian fundamentalism via Vedanta, the Hindu philosophy that was overtaking Salinger's life. Claire soon divorced Mockler. Four months shy of graduation from Radcliffe, she was forced by Salinger to choose between him and a college degree.

SHANE SALERNO: Claire's feeling for Salinger remained strong, and after breaking off the marriage to Mockler, Claire moved in with Salinger. They married on February 17, 1955, in Barnard, Vermont. Salinger and Claire drove through sleet on a bleak February day to get married by a justice of the peace. On the marriage certificate Salinger said this was his first marriage, completely removing any legal trace of his first wife, Sylvia Welter.

JOHN SKOW: Uncharacteristically, Salinger threw a party to celebrate his marriage. It was attended by his mother, his sister (about whom little is known except that she is a dress buyer at Bloomingdale's and has been divorced twice). Claire's first husband was also present. A little later, at the Cornish town meeting, pranksters elected Salinger Town Hargreave—an honorary office unseriously given to the most recently married man; he is supposed to round up pigs whenever they get loose. Salinger was unamused.

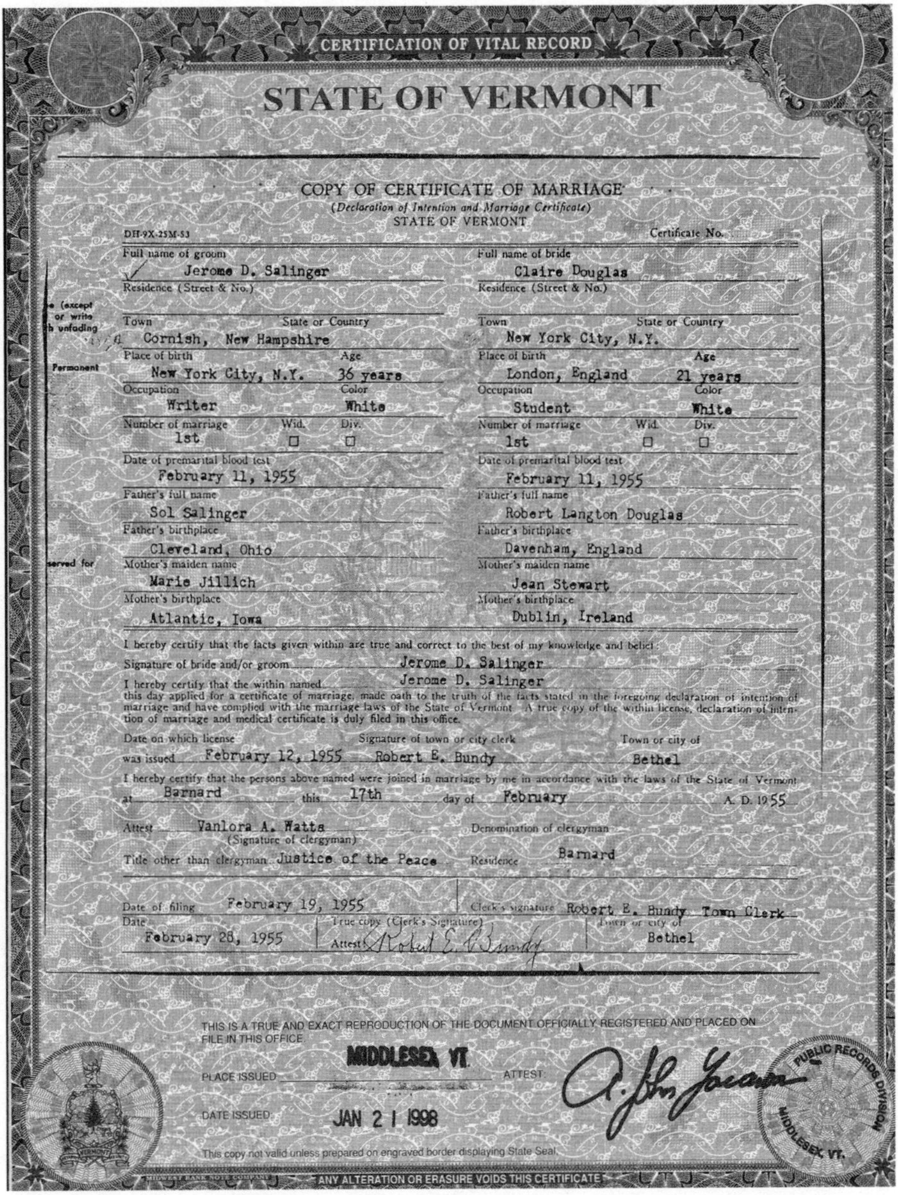

CERTIFICATION OF VITAL RECORD

STATE OF VERMONT

COPY OF CERTIFICATE OF MARRIAGE
(Declaration of Intention and Marriage Certificate)
STATE OF VERMONT

DH-9X-25M-53 — Certificate No.

Full name of groom	Jerome D. Salinger	Full name of bride	Claire Douglas
Residence (Street & No.)		Residence (Street & No.)	
Town, State or Country	Cornish, New Hampshire	Town, State or Country	New York City, N.Y.
Place of birth	New York City, N.Y.	Place of birth	London, England
Age	36 years	Age	21 years
Occupation	Writer	Occupation	Student
Color	White	Color	White
Number of marriage	1st	Number of marriage	1st
Date of premarital blood test	February 11, 1955	Date of premarital blood test	February 11, 1955
Father's full name	Sol Salinger	Father's full name	Robert Langton Douglas
Father's birthplace	Cleveland, Ohio	Father's birthplace	Davenham, England
Mother's maiden name	Marie Jillich	Mother's maiden name	Jean Stewart
Mother's birthplace	Atlantic, Iowa	Mother's birthplace	Dublin, Ireland

I hereby certify that the facts given within are true and correct to the best of my knowledge and belief.
Signature of bride and/or groom Jerome D. Salinger
I hereby certify that the within named Jerome D. Salinger
this day applied for a certificate of marriage, made oath to the truth of the facts stated in the foregoing declaration of intention of marriage and have complied with the marriage laws of the State of Vermont. A true copy of the within license, declaration of intention of marriage and medical certificate is duly filed in this office.

Date on which license was issued February 12, 1955 — Signature of town or city clerk Robert E. Bundy — Town or city of Bethel

I hereby certify that the persons above named were joined in marriage by me in accordance with the laws of the State of Vermont at Barnard this 17th day of February A. D. 1955

Attest Vanlora A. Watts (Signature of clergyman) — Denomination of clergyman
Title other than clergyman Justice of the Peace — Residence Barnard

Date of filing February 19, 1955 — Clerk's signature Robert E. Bundy Town Clerk
Date February 28, 1955 — True copy (Clerk's Signature) Attest: Robert E. Bundy — Town or city of Bethel

THIS IS A TRUE AND EXACT REPRODUCTION OF THE DOCUMENT OFFICIALLY REGISTERED AND PLACED ON FILE IN THIS OFFICE.
PLACE ISSUED MIDDLESEX, VT. ATTEST:
DATE ISSUED JAN 21 1998
This copy not valid unless prepared on engraved border displaying State Seal.
PUBLIC RECORDS DIVISION MIDDLESEX, VT.
ANY ALTERATION OR ERASURE VOIDS THIS CERTIFICATE

Jerome D. Salinger and Claire Douglas's marriage certificate.

PAUL ALEXANDER: Salinger's wedding present to Claire was the manuscript of "Franny"; Franny appears to be based on Claire, and it's not difficult to see Salinger's portrait of Franny's painfully conventional boyfriend, Lane Coutell, as being none-too-subtle mockery of Mockler.

—

BEN YAGODA: Salinger's long story "Franny," published in 1955, created a sensation. People were talking about it all across the country—the characters, the situations, and especially what had happened to make the main character Franny faint. Was it an existential crisis, or was she pregnant?

JOHN WENKE: When he wrote "Franny" I think Salinger really still wanted to be a popular writer. On the one hand, it was very chic at that time to be a falling-apart rich girl who is having a religious crisis, and I think that became a culturally revolutionary act in the mid-fifties, particularly with the more sanitized Eisenhower administration modality.

J. D. SALINGER, excerpt from letter to Gus Lobrano, *New Yorker* editor, December 20, 1955:

> *I've been putting this off and putting this off. Mostly because of the Nineteenth Floor criticism that Franny might be pregnant—it seemed to me such a deadly idea, if it was the main one that the reader came away with.*

DAVID SHIELDS: Many *New Yorker* readers thought Franny was pregnant. "She held that tense, almost fetal position for a suspensory moment—then broke down." If pregnancy is not the main idea here, what is? That Franny, a mythological female, is suffering a postwar nervous breakdown? The mystic's confused searching for meaning is fulfilled through the use of young girls' bodies. The womb is the reincarnated war wound. Franny is prayerful witness to the necessity of her creator's war survival.

MAXWELL GEISMAR: As in any good Scott Fitzgerald tale, it is the weekend of the Yale game. . . . In his Burberry raincoat, Lane Coutell is reading Franny's passionate love letter. . . . Franny, listening to him "with a special semblance of absorption," is overcome by her distaste for his vanity, his complacency. It is not only him, it is his whole life of habits, values, standards that she cannot bear. She ends up not only with an indictment of upper-class American society, but almost all of Western culture itself.

J. D. SALINGER ("Franny," *The New Yorker*, January 29, 1955):

> Lane had sampled his [martini], then sat back and briefly looked around the room with an almost palpable sense of well-being at finding himself (he must have been sure no one could dispute) in the right place with an unimpeachably right-looking girl—a girl who was not only extraordinarily pretty but, so much the better, not too categorically cashmere sweater and flannel skirt.

PAUL LEVINE: Alienated from her Ivy League boyfriend and everything he represents, she turns inward, with the help of a mystical book about a Russian peasant who found God [in tune] with his heart beat when he repeated the "Christ prayer" over and over. Suffering from psychosomatic cramps induced by an environment she can no longer stomach, Franny rejects the comfort of a public restaurant for the awkward privacy of a lavatory, where, in a curiously fetal position, she can pray.

PAUL ALEXANDER: "Franny" is an indictment (as is, of course, *Catcher in the Rye*). What Salinger is attacking is not specific, but general, even societal. Franny hates insincere people and phonies, yet she is forced to deal with them at college. Even worse, she's dating one, and for that she has no one to blame but herself, maybe, although in the course of the story she never accepts responsibility for her failure to break up with him. Instead, "Franny" seems to imply that because the world is full of phonies, all one can do is retreat from it into some form of religion. In Franny's case, she seeks solace in the Jesus Prayer. Ultimately, however, even religion is not enough. As she tries to cope with her life by clinging to religion, she slips deeper into mental distress, until she is barely able to hold on to her sanity. In *Catcher in the Rye*, Holden ends up in a mental institution. Franny ends up in an unfamiliar room, babbling a prayer to herself, unsure of where she is and where she is going next.

JAMES LUNDQUIST: *The Way of a Pilgrim* and the Jesus Prayer are by no means being put forth as answers to anything by Salinger. . . . A major idea in Zen . . . is that people who are too critical of others, who are too concerned with the analysis of particulars, fail to reach an understanding of the oneness of all things, and eventually disintegrate themselves.

THE WAY OF A PILGRIM: We must pray unceasingly, always and in all places . . . not only when we are awake, but even while we are asleep.

JOHN WENKE: It's a hunger that Franny, for example, feels and responds to with the Jesus Prayer. It's not so much the prayer; it's the desire for something that will fill that hole. And Salinger's characters are people who have holes that can't be filled.

THE JESUS PRAYER: Lord Jesus Christ, have mercy on me.

SHANE SALERNO: There was so much goodwill built up for Salinger after *Catcher* and *Nine Stories* that he was once again seen to be leading the culture, years ahead of the Beats and early Zen adopters. He had once again caught the moment before the moment arrived, but he was in deeper trouble than he realized. At the time, he didn't think he was undergoing a crisis, but he was—a marital crisis and an artistic crisis and a religious crisis. Years later Salinger would thank his spiritual guide Swami Vivekananda for getting him through this "long dark night."

—

HENRY GRUNWALD: Stories about his wife [Claire] are even rarer and equally cherished as collector's items. There is, for instance, the occasion when Salinger was meeting an English publisher at the Stork Club, and Claire and a friend sat at a nearby table, pretending to be tarts. Or the time, after "Franny" was published, when friends would come upon Salinger and Claire, their lips moving silently. It was a private charade—an acting out of the near-final lines in the story: "Her lips began to move, forming soundless words."

SHANE SALERNO: Salinger and Claire set about building a life for themselves in step with the purity of their religious beliefs and independent of the conventional 1950s obsession with status and appearance. It was a life of simplicity, with an emphasis on nature and spirituality.

The couple vowed to respect all living things and, according to Gavin Douglas, Claire's brother, refused to kill even the tiniest of insects. Their afternoons were filled with meditation and yoga; at night, they snuggled together and read *The Gospel of Sri Ramakrishna* and Paramahansa Yogananda's *Autobiography of a Yogi.* From the beginning of their marriage, Salinger worried that Claire would be unable to adapt to the solitude and simplicity of life in Cornish.

ARTHUR J. PAIS: Claire Salinger was attracted to Yogananda's thinking, too, and got into Kriya yoga. A greater hero for the couple was Lahiri Mahasaya, Yogananda's guru, who was a married man, proving that yogic attainments could be open to family men and women.

PARAMAHANSA YOGANANDA: You have been chosen to bring spiritual solace through Kriya Yoga to numerous earnest seekers. The millions who are encumbered by family ties and heavy worldly duties will take new heart from you, a householder like themselves. You should guide them to understand that the highest yogic achievements are not barred to the family man. . . .

No necessity compels you to leave this world, for inwardly you have already sundered its every karmic tie. Not of this world, you must yet be in it.

"My son," Babaji said, embracing me, "your role in this incarnation must be played before the gaze of the multitude. Prenatally blessed by many lives of lonely meditation, you must now mingle in the world of men."

DAVID SHIELDS: Margaret Salinger credited Lahiri Mahasaya's advice for giving her father and mother the approval needed to go ahead not only with the marriage but the birth of their daughter.

CLAIRE DOUGLAS: On the train home to Cornish that evening [after seeing a yogi in Washington, D.C., in early 1955], Jerry and I made love in our sleeper car. . . . I'm certain I became pregnant with [Margaret] that night.

PAUL ALEXANDER: On December 10, 1955, J. D. Salinger became a father. His daughter, Margaret, was born. It was obviously an ecstatic

Drawing of Claire, pregnant.

event for Salinger, the birth of his first child. But, ironically, the way he viewed Claire changed after that. Before that, she had been very much the image of the late teens, early twenties woman he was initially fascinated by. Now she was a mature woman. She was the mother of his child. And so, while he was still attracted to her, because she had given him this great gift, his view of her changed, and the birth of the child had a permanent effect on their relationship.

Claire was a smart, attractive, and—one would assume—energetic woman who had come from a proper family in England. She had attended Radcliffe. She was a woman who was connected to the world. And because of the routine of Salinger's writing life, that ended.

THE GOSPEL OF SRI RAMAKRISHNA: A man may live in a mountain cave, smear his body with ashes, observe fasts, and practice austere discipline, but if his mind dwells on worldly objects, on "woman and gold," I say, "Shame on him!" But I say that a man is blessed indeed who eats, drinks, and roams about, but who keeps his mind from "woman and gold."

[In response to a disciple who was still having sex with his wife,] Ramakrishna says, "Aren't you ashamed of yourself? You have children, and still you enjoy intercourse with your wife. Don't you hate yourself for thus leading an animal life? Don't you hate yourself for dallying with a body which contains only blood, phlegm, filth, and excreta?"

CLAIRE DOUGLAS: We did not make love very often. The body was evil.

J. D. SALINGER, excerpt from letter to Swami Nikhilananda, 1972:

> *Between extreme indifference to the body and the most extreme and zealous attention to it (Hatha Yoga), there seems to be no useful middle ground whatever, and that seems to me one more unnecessary sadness in Maya.*

SHANE SALERNO: During this time, the mid-1950s, Salinger met and developed a close relationship with one of his neighbors, Judge Learned Hand, who was Margaret Salinger's godfather and whom the *New York Times* has said "belongs with John Marshall, Oliver Wendell Holmes, Louis Brandeis and Benjamin Cardozo: among the eminences of the American judiciary." Often called the "tenth justice of the Supreme Court," he was viewed by Salinger as a "true Karma Yogi." Salinger's description here conveys how deeply involved he now was with the language and vision of Vedanta. In a letter to Hand, Salinger wonders "whether I'm still [plying] my trade as a short story writer or whether I've gone over to propagandizing for the loin-cloth group."

To make matters worse for Claire, Salinger was absorbed by his work throughout the first year of their marriage. He frequently took trips to New York City, where he would hole up in the *New Yorker* offices and work. S. J. Perelman, the *New Yorker* humorist who'd gotten to know Salinger as a colleague at the magazine, visited him often in Cornish.

LEILA HADLEY LUCE: Sid [S. J. Perelman] said, "It's very strange: he's got this concrete bunker where he works, but he's got a great big statue of Buddha in the garden, and he's got a lot of these Buddhist priests around him." Sid thought [Claire] was just a collegiate type of girl.

J. D. SALINGER, excerpt from letter to Jean Miller, 1954:

> *The house was very still when I got here, and I sat down and thought for hours. In the end, it seemed to me that if I'm to get my work done, if I'm to do my "duty" (a word I hate) properly—that is, more or less in the Bhagavad Gita sense of the word—I ought to and must stay away from the city.*

—

SHANE SALERNO: Claire must have dreamed about a life with Salinger and a family in the quiet woods of New Hampshire, but she quickly learned that he already had a family: the Glasses.

SANFORD GOLDSTEIN: You've got this very, very bright family, the Glass family. It's a very concentrated picture of troubled humanity and we want to know them. We want them to get beyond their problems; we want to learn from them.

GERALDINE McGOWAN: One of the odd things about comparing real children to the Glass children is nobody would want their children to be the Glass children. They're all suffering terribly. They're all in a lot of pain most of the time. Salinger's real children may have thought their father preferred the Glass children. That is part of the dysfunctional quality associated with Salinger, because if you loved your children, why would you ever wish upon them that life?

J. D. SALINGER, excerpt from letter to Paul Fitzgerald, February 3, 1960:

> *We have a second child due very shortly, and I've been working overtime to beat the clock. You must have a pretty good idea by now how little peace there is around the house when a new baby is around. And I agree with you about old friendships. Especially war ones.*

ETHEL NELSON: When I started taking care of his kids, it was through Wayne, my husband, because he was already working for Jerry down there. Claire was due to have Matthew and they had a little girl, Margaret. They needed help keeping Margaret busy so that Claire could do what she had to do. Jerry knew me from back when he hung out with me and my friends in the Windsor High School days, so the hiring process was pretty simple.

My job was to take care of Margaret, who we called Peggy. She was about four or five years old at the time and a sweet girl, very sweet. And Jerry, I knew he was around, but I never saw him because he was down [the hill], working on his books, and just didn't come up around the house at all. I really don't know if the children got to know him very much in the early years. I've seen some pictures where he carried Peggy around, but how many times did that happen?

The house was a cute house, kind of like a dollhouse, right near the road and with a big fence for protection. I think there were a few flowers out front. Claire attempted to make a garden and have everything look nice, but it was not friendly soil. It hadn't been worked up or fed for years and years. The land was very rustic, with lots of woods around and fields. Behind the house you had a deep incline, which is where Jerry built the other building so he could write down there.

It wasn't a house; it was just a small building. I would think of it like a dynamite house. That's where he would go down, anytime, day or night, go in and shut the door, and you wouldn't see him for a week or longer, because he got into a writing mode and had to be left totally alone. I don't think it was much more than a room, room and a half, his writing building.

Wayne cleared brush, cut down trees that were bothersome, mowed the lawns, did gardener types of things. Wayne would go down and work around the woods and kept the path cleared between the house and the writing building.

I never went down there. Wayne did one day; he was out there working, and Jerry went to the door and asked him if he wanted something cold to drink. Wayne sat down and chatted with Jerry, which I know today is a very rare thing. They just got to talking, and Jerry asked Wayne if he'd like an autographed copy of *The Catcher in the Rye*. And Wayne said, "No, that's all right, Jerry, but thank you. I don't read all that much." My husband was just a farm boy; he didn't think too much about it.

I guess that signed copy would be worth quite a bit of money today. Wayne told me there was quite a mess of papers down there. I guess all authors have a mess of papers, but I don't know any other authors.

When I was working for Claire, I very seldom ever saw Jerry. I would go in and straighten up the kitchen and talk with Margaret, and Matthew being the baby, I didn't have to do too much with him. That's where Claire was busy. I never fixed a meal. Claire was great at that sort of thing. She was a good cook. I just cleaned up, played with Margaret, and went home.

I'd get there at eight-thirty. If there were dishes around, I'd do them up. Usually Peggy was still with Mom and in the other room, and then she would come out and I'd have the housework part done. We went out for walks, not too far. Jerry wouldn't allow you to go too far, so we'd go out on the side of the house and we'd pick flowers and bring them into Mom, or Margaret would get up on a stool and help me with the dishes. Or we would get things out for her to color. We spent a lot of time just chatting together. Peggy was a neat kid. I could keep her busier by being outside, walking and looking at flowers and talking about things outside that way. But you know, three- or four-year-olds, you can't talk a whole lot to them about stuff.

She was happy; Margaret was always very happy. Always had that big smile. I don't recall anyone having to speak to her more than once, so she was being brought up well to listen when things were said. I think she really needed a friend young in life. You always picture those kinds of kids as being brought up happy. I just hate to think of children growing up so lonely, so alone. I don't think they ever really knew a home life, and I feel sorry for that. Every child needs a home life.

At the time I was there, I don't think Peggy was affected that much with [the solitude]. She was only three and four years old. I think as she got to be eight, nine, and ten, it affected her a lot. By that time, Jerry had also put that apartment over the garage, and that's where he sat and wrote "Raise High the Roof Beam." If he was in either of those places, the kids weren't allowed to get near him. Neither was his wife. You kind of fantasize that if people have money, they have happiness. It's not so.

Claire impressed me greatly for putting up with so destitute of a husband. He was just never there, and she's just the kind of a lady you imagine with a long dress and a neat hairdo and a glass of wine in her hand, talking with lots of New York people. Well, that's how she always appeared to me. Her role just didn't seem right.

GERALDINE McGOWAN: Claire was very young, but Salinger always treated women like they were unbreakable. He has this idea that little girls especially can be leaned on by adult males. It's a bizarre, bizarre thing to think. But he does, and in the fiction it's almost like he's writing an urban Heidi or an urban Pollyanna. These little girls, who come in and save the world, don't need any help from anybody, no matter what they've suffered. It's a fairy tale, of sorts. Women have a fairy-tale quality in his work.

Esmé has lost both her parents, but she helps Sergeant X. Zooey says some of the nastiest things in the world to his mother, Bessie; she never blinks, just worries about Franny. Women don't break, in [Salinger's] view; they're always just there to support these very sensitive men. I don't think he thought much about Claire. I think this image of women was so strong within him, he didn't think there was any reason for him to worry about Claire, whereas, of course, any woman alone—with a baby at the age of twenty, no family, no friends—would need help. That did not seem to occur to him.

—

BEN YAGODA: In that period, 1955, Salinger was clearly concentrating on this family he had invented, the Glass family. "Franny" was quickly followed by "Raise High the Roof Beam, Carpenters," a wonderful novella about members of that same family.

BRUCE MUELLER and WILL HOCHMAN: The importance of "Raise High the Roof Beam, Carpenters" within Salinger's body of work cannot be overstated. This 1955 story assembles and introduces the Glass family in its entirety and may be considered a watershed event in Salinger's publication history.

DAVID SHIELDS: It's as if he is pulling an immense blanket over himself: from now on he will keep himself warm by the heat of this impossibly idealized, suicidal, genius, alternative family. This will become his mission: to disappear into the Glasses.

JAMES LUNDQUIST: ["Raise High the Roof Beam, Carpenters"] centers on sacrament and celebration, although ironically at first. It deals with Seymour's wedding to Muriel, but Seymour does not appear, and Buddy, the only member of the Glass family who is able to be present for the ceremony, is forced into a car with four other wedding guests to be driven to the apartment of the bride's parents for what has turned out to be a non-wedding reception. The situation Salinger utilizes to build his story around is a classic one in vaudeville and burlesque humor.

JOHN UPDIKE: [It is the] best of the Glass pieces: a magic and hilarious prose-poem with an enchanting end effect of mysterious clarity.

EBERHARD ALSEN: Seymour is presented as both highly educated and mentally unstable. The story is told by Seymour's brother Buddy, and Seymour's character emerges from Buddy's conflict with the irate wedding guests and from his attempts to understand Seymour's unstable behavior. These attempts include lengthy quotations from Seymour's diary, which contains many references to Eastern religions, chiefly classical Taoism and Vedanta Hinduism.

J. D. SALINGER, excerpt from letter to Swami Adiswarananda, 1975:

> *I read a bit from the [Bhagavad] Gita every morning before I get out of bed.*

LESLIE EPSTEIN: What a triumph "Raise High the Roof Beam, Carpenters" is. It's a magnificent story and a perfect counterweight to "Bananafish."

SHANE SALERNO: In "Franny" and "Raise High," both published in 1955, Salinger still had the balance about right: 80 percent story and character, 20 percent religion and lecture.

J. D. SALINGER ("Raise High the Roof Beam, Carpenters," *The New Yorker*, November 19, 1955):

> "We were up at the Lake. Seymour had written to Charlotte, inviting her to come up and visit us, and her mother finally let her. What happened was, she sat down in the middle of our driveway one morning to pet Boo Boo's cat, and Seymour threw a

stone at her. He was twelve. That's all there was to it. He threw it at her because she looked so beautiful sitting there in the middle of the driveway with Boo Boo's cat. Everybody knew that, for God's sake—me, Charlotte, Boo Boo, Waker, Walt, the whole family." I stared at the pewter ashtray on the coffee table. "Charlotte never said a word to him about it. Not a word." I looked up at my guest, rather expecting him to dispute me, to call me a liar. I am a liar, of course. Charlotte never did understand why Seymour threw that stone at her.

DAVID SHIELDS: In her book, Margaret Salinger says she doesn't understand why Seymour throws the rock at Charlotte, but it's clearly meant as a parable: the young, beautiful Charlotte was too beautiful to remain undamaged in this world. Margaret, having lived with Salinger, doesn't believe in damage as revelation. This, though, is Salinger's major chord. Seymour never appears in the story except when Buddy reads his diary or characters describe his actions, all of which occur off the page as ritualized funeral ablutions, washing the body in preparation for its spiritualized reincarnation in thousands of future dead GIs and Jews. Seymour writes that he told his fiancée, Muriel, that a Zen Buddhist master answered the question "What is the most valuable thing in the world?" with the answer "a dead cat was, because no one could put a price on it." Seymour tells Muriel's mother that the war seems likely to go on forever, but if he is ever released from the army he would like to return to civilian life as a dead cat.

IHAB HASSAN: In the story of his wedding and the record of his buried life Salinger has exercised his powers of spiritual severity and formal resourcefulness to their limit, and it is indicative of Salinger's recent predicament that in the story the powers of spirit overreach the resources of form. He is seeking, beyond poetry, beyond all speech, the *act* which makes communion possible. As action may turn to silence, so may satire turn to praise.

SUBHASH CHANDRA: Salinger kills Seymour—his chief protagonist of several works—in one of the early stories ["A Perfect Day for Bananafish"]. In the later works, the novelist proceeds with dexterous artistry to re-create and rebuild all those circumstances and reasons responsible for his hero's tragic end. This enables the novelist to construct a corpus of investigation on which he slowly but surely goes to delineate his concept of man. In doing so, a visibly perceptive change comes in the form and the structure of the later works when it becomes clear that the thematic interest triumphs over the fictional interest.

PHILIP ROTH: He has learned to live in this world—but how? By not living in it. By kissing the soles of little girls' feet and throwing rocks at the head of his sweetheart. He is a saint, clearly. But since madness is undesirable and sainthood, for most of us, out of the question, the problem of how to live *in* this world is by no means answered; unless the answer is that one cannot.

—

DAVID SHIELDS: There was the Salinger family and the Glass family, but there was also a third family: the *New Yorker*, with William Shawn as patriarch. In contemporary parlance, he was Salinger's enabler: he encouraged Salinger's best tendencies (his devotion to literary art) but also his worst tendencies (toward recusal, toward retreat, toward isolation, renunciation, purity, inscape, even silence). Salinger found an artistic, neurotic soul mate in Shawn; while he reaped the artistic benefits that resulted, Claire and their children were left to fend for themselves in the hermetic Cornish paradise Salinger had built for himself, not for others.

ROGER ANGELL: When he first came to the [*New Yorker*], Salinger worked with Gus Lobrano [and William Maxwell], but William Shawn took over [after Lobrano's death]. . . . When I came to the fiction department, none of the editors in the department dealt with Salinger—only Shawn.

BEN YAGODA: What elevated Shawn professionally was World War II. Shawn used the war to transform the magazine from a sophisticated humor magazine into a magazine that published serious journalism, culminating in the publication of John Hershey's "Hiroshima," which occupied one entire issue. It was shepherded by Shawn. He was the one who germinated the idea with Hershey, argued it should take up the entire issue, edited it, and brought it into print. That elevated Shawn in the halls of the *New Yorker* and in the literary world.

William Shawn, editor of the *New Yorker* and Salinger's editor, loyal defender, and close friend.

THOMAS KUNKEL: Shawn always wanted to be a writer, and because of that, he just understood the writer's psyche in a way that few people ever have. He understood what they were trying to do and how hard it is, but also knew how it could be put into print.

A. SCOTT BERG: Shawn didn't want to be seen or known about, wanted to print his authors rather selflessly, and knew that often the time that an author needs an editor most is not when the book is all done but while he's actually writing it. Shawn was the presence on Salinger's shoulder.

VED MEHTA: Shawn got involved in every little thing at the *New Yorker*. J. D. Salinger wrote about this family of geniuses. In a way, the atmosphere at the *New Yorker* was that of an extended Salinger family. Mr. Shawn really didn't want to be a wise father; he was like a wise brother on the nineteenth floor. You consulted him on anything and everything. If you needed a psychoanalyst, you would ask Shawn.

Shawn never gossiped. If you said something to him, it was like shouting it in a tomb. There was never this worry, "Oh God, people will know that a third of my piece had to be cut because it was badly written." It was all so secret. After all, he was the most private man I've known, except maybe for J. D. Salinger.

LAWRENCE WESCHLER: Imagine the most phobic man in the world. He lives in a city surrounded on all sides by water, and he is afraid of everything—bridges, tunnels, buses, limousines, helicopters, planes, ferries. He cannot bring himself to get off that island, but he is also the most curious man in the world. He wants to know about everything and everyone and every place. And now imagine that by some fluke this man has come into what amounts to limitless wealth: he can take people and train them as his surrogates and then send them forth. "Go," he tells them. "Go—take however long you need, but then write me back what it is like there, what the people are saying and feeling, how they spend their lives, what they worry about—write me all that, make it complete, and make it vivid, as vivid as if I'd been able to go there myself." And each week he puts together a folio of their letters, of their reports, and he produces a little private magazine, just for himself. And everybody else gets to read over his shoulder (he doesn't mind, but he hardly notices). That's what it's like to work for William Shawn. He really is the *New Yorker*.

ROBERT BOYNTON: Beyond what he accomplished as an actual editor, Shawn was important because of the cult of personality that arose around him.

THOMAS KUNKEL: Shawn was a person of very set routines. He edited only with certain kinds of pencils. He did have a lot of idiosyncrasies, but that was part and parcel of the person, and I think one of the reasons that writers responded to him so well was that the insecurities and phobias actually humanized him a little bit.

PAUL ALEXANDER: Shawn would go to lunch every day at the Algonquin and order Corn Flakes.

BEN YAGODA: In the summer, Shawn wore wool suits and sweaters and overcoats. He left the state of New York only once in the last fifty years of his life, to visit his family in Chicago. He was introverted and never gave interviews. His whole life was wrapped up in the *New Yorker* and his writers until the end of his life. Two employees were outside his office to prevent people from walking in unexpectedly.

TOM WOLFE: Shawn went to work at the *New Yorker* building on Forty-third Street with an attaché case. As soon as he entered the building, an elevator operator would put a hand across the elevator entrance so nobody else could get in. They'd ride Shawn up to his office. Inside the attaché case was a hatchet. In case he got stuck between floors he would be able to chop his way out. Good way to get killed. That was Shawn's personality.

THOMAS KUNKEL: It was very much the *New Yorker*'s editing style to be obsessive in a lot of different ways. The editors—Shawn principally among them—were equally passionate about where the commas should go and whether this warrants a dash or not. A writer would get to the point where he was answering countless questions; there were iterations and iterations and iterations of galleys.

A final proofreader found a spot that he felt needed a comma. He went to Maxwell, who looked at it and said, "Well, it looks like it needs a comma to me." They couldn't find Salinger, so they went ahead and put the comma in. When the story came out, Maxwell said Salinger was melancholy about that comma and never forgot it. Maxwell said, "I never again introduced another piece of punctuation into a Salinger story without talking to him."

BEN YAGODA: It's hard to know much about the precise nature of the collaboration between Salinger and Shawn because, let's face it, we're dealing with two of the most private men in the history of literature, if not the world. But we do know that when Salinger submitted "Zooey," the sequel to "Franny," to the *New Yorker* in 1957, the fiction editors unanimously agreed to reject the story.

When I interviewed William Maxwell, who was one of the editors, he said the reason was that the *New Yorker* didn't publish sequels, but they had before. I think he was being tactful. I think they just didn't like the story.

DAVID SHIELDS: The *New Yorker* was trying to tell Salinger not to throw over art for religion, but he didn't listen. Why should he? The *New Yorker* had rejected *Catcher.* So, too, on November 18,'57, *Time* said, "The one new American author who has something approaching universal appeal is J. D. Salinger."

BEN YAGODA: Shawn intervened. He was the editor in chief, and he decreed that the magazine would publish the story; he edited the story and worked with Salinger on it.

In a 1959 letter, William Maxwell wrote to Katherine White [fiction editor], who had retired, alluding to the earlier Salinger incident. Maxwell wrote, "I do feel that Salinger has to be handled specially and fast, and think that the only practical way of doing this is as I supposed Shawn did do it: by himself. Given the length of the stories, I mean, and the Zen Buddhist nature of them, and what happened with 'Zooey.'"

—

DAVID SHIELDS: "Zooey," a 50,000 word sequel to "Franny," takes place two days after Franny has returned from her date with Lane. While she's in the living room in the Glass family apartment in New York, having a breakdown, her brother Zooey is taking a long bath and reading a long letter from their brother Buddy; his mother, Bessie, barges in, wanting to talk with him about Franny. A large percentage of the story occurs in that bathroom while Zooey and Bessie talk and smoke.

JOHN WENKE: The action of "Zooey" picks up two days after Franny has fainted at Sickler's restaurant. It is Monday morning at the Glass family's Manhattan apartment. Franny's breakdown continues, and Mrs. Glass does not know what to do. . . . Zooey seems, in Bessie's view, to be the only one available who might be capable of helping Franny get beyond her exasperating and frightening behavior. . . . [The story] resembles a one-act play of three scenes in which the players transact their business almost solely through dialogue.

MAXWELL GEISMAR: "Zooey" is an interminable, appallingly bad story. Like the latter part of "Franny," it lends itself so easily to burlesque that one wonders what the *New Yorker* wits were thinking of when they published it with such fanfare.

MICHAEL SILVERBLATT: I was looking at "Zooey," and there we are in that bathroom, right? Forty pages of someone in a bathroom being bothered by his mom. We want to get out of this bathroom. Why can't we get out of this bathroom? Why won't Salinger let us out? It's so imprisoning, so claustrophobic. It's not Kafka-claustrophobic or Beckett-claustrophobic. It's boring-claustrophobic. Bathroom claustrophobic. I'm thinking, "Let's get out, face the world, get to business." I think that [claustrophobia] is the state a writer is in at his desk. He is asking you to experience being in that bathroom, unable to leave, the way a writer experiences being at the desk, unable to leave.

DAVID SHIELDS: "Raise High the Roof Beam, Carpenters" comes close to structural perfection, whereas the problem with "Zooey," and why it took Salinger so long to write it, is that he is blatantly pontificating about religion, which he was criticized for having done in previous stories. Increasingly, he is determined to present his religious beliefs through his stories.

PHOEBE HOBAN: It's interesting that Salinger uses letters so much in his books. One of the reasons he does that is that, for Salinger, writing is the most perfect form of communication; almost all of his stories have a pivotal letter in them. He begins "Zooey" with a four-year-old letter from Buddy that Zooey's reading in the bathtub and gaining wisdom from so that he can then tell Franny how to get through her breakdown.

DONALD COSTELLO: "Franny" and "Zooey" speak to one another: they're separate yet nicely joined. Franny's sick of ego. "Ego, ego, ego!" she says. She finds a mystical connection with the Jesus Prayer. It's also very Buddhist, of course, in its philosophy of withdrawal. Zooey, on the other hand, argues, as Mr. Antolini does, and as Holden allows Phoebe to do at the end [of *Catcher in the Rye*], for engagement.

ERNEST HAVEMANN: Near the end of the new book, Zooey tells his sister [Franny] about the time that Seymour urged him to shine his shoes before appearing on the [radio quiz program *It's a Wise Child*]. Zooey objected that nobody could see his shoes, but Seymour insisted: "He said to shine them for the Fat Lady. . . . He never did tell me who the Fat Lady was, but I shined my shoes for the Fat Lady every time I ever went on the air again. . . . This terribly clear, clear picture of the Fat Lady formed in my mind. I had her sitting on this porch all day, swatting flies. . . . I figured the heat was terrible, and she probably had cancer. . . ." Then Zooey goes on to say, "There isn't anyone anywhere that isn't Seymour's Fat Lady. . . . And don't you know—listen to me, now—don't you know who that Fat Lady really is? . . . It's Christ Himself, Christ Himself. . . ." And upon hearing these words, Franny, who has been having the symptoms of a nervous breakdown in connection with her religious strivings, relaxes and falls into a deep and soul-satisfying sleep, and the story is over.

ALFRED KAZIN: In each story ["Franny" and "Zooey"], the climax bears a burden of meaning that it would not have to bear in a novel; besides being stagey, the stories are exalted in a way that connects both of them into a single chronicle. . . . Both Franny and Zooey Glass are, indeed, pilgrims seeking their way in a society typified by the Fat Lady. Not only does the entertaining surface of *Franny and Zooey* depend on the conscious appealingness and youthfulness and generosity and sensitivity of Seymour's brother and sister, but Salinger himself, in describing these two, so obviously feels such boundless affection for them that you finally get the sense of all these child prodigies and child entertainers being tied round and round with the veils of self-love in a culture which they—and Salinger—just despise.

S. J. ROWLAND: The cumulative effect is bright and tender rather than powerful, and poignant rather than deep: these are the strengths and limitations of Salinger as a writer. These granted, he has an almost Pauline understanding of the necessity, nature, and redemptive quality of love.

VED MEHTA: Salinger was the first one, at least in my consciousness, to put his finger on the fakery; to be an enlightened person, to be a good person, you had to avoid phoniness. You had to avoid all this fakery even if that made you become very solitary and cut off. At the same time—I'll never forget—there is the wonderful scene about loving a fat lady, which was, in a way, the unconscious *New Yorker* principle: you didn't reject people because they were fat or they were ugly; each human being had to be prized as him- or herself. I think it was very much the *New Yorker* ethos, a Shawn ethos, and I have no idea, actually, whether Salinger got that from Shawn or Shawn got that from Salinger.

STEPHEN GUIRGIS: When I started writing my play *Jesus Hopped the A Train*, I wrestled with the idea of God. I was stuck, and I read *Franny and Zooey*. It just blew me away. I'm still writing about religion, still trying to figure out how to get by in this life. Salinger's explanation at the end of that book is as good as any I have to go on.

—

PAUL ALEXANDER: During 1958, Salinger had begun work on "Seymour: An Introduction," yet another novella about the Glass family, and the densest thing he had ever written. As a result, he found work on "Seymour" to be unusually difficult, much more so than anything he had written up until then. Throughout the fall of 1958, his work in Cornish was hampered by minor illnesses and the unavoidable distractions caused by Claire and the baby. Finally, in the spring of 1959, Salinger realized that if he were going to finish the novella, which the *New Yorker* was pressuring him to do, he needed to have a stretch of time during which he could focus only on his work. So he went to New York to work in the *New Yorker* offices, something writers did when they needed to devote large blocks of intense, uninterrupted work to a piece of prose. He had tried writing several days in an Atlantic City hotel room, but he had not been able to accomplish what he had hoped to.

PHOEBE HOBAN: In letters, he reported that his work habits were hard on Claire—and on himself. He worked so feverishly on one story that he got shingles. Working on the Glasses, he wrote, put him in a constant "trance."

***NEW YORKER* INTERN:** He was in New York, working on "Seymour." He'd come up to the office at night and there'd be just the two of us in this big dark building. He was working seven days a week and it was the hardest work I've ever seen anyone do.

PAUL ALEXANDER: Eventually, Salinger worked so hard he made himself sick. Returning to Cornish, he stayed there long enough to get well; then he went back to New York for another several-days-long editing session in the *New Yorker* offices to finish the piece.

BEN YAGODA: The turning point with Salinger and the *New Yorker* and the Glass family came in 1957, with the publication of "Zooey," which wasn't as immediately accessible as the previous works. "Seymour: An Introduction" intensified this sense that he was getting more remote from readers. It added to the sense that Salinger was growing more wrapped up in his own world. Not that he didn't still have ardent fans. There were still many people who snapped it up as soon as it came out.

WILLIAM WIEGAND: In "Seymour," Buddy takes up one at a time the pertinent characteristics and activities of his brother. . . . If I pull myself together, Buddy says, Seymour who has killed himself may yet be reconstructed—his eyes, his nose, his ears may rematerialize, even his words may be heard without the echo of the tomb. . . . Buddy becomes almost indistinguishable from Seymour. Buddy himself notices this. The object-observed has become the observer. All the air has been pumped out of the bell jar. . . . Consequently the description of the relationship is so great an effort that Buddy breaks into a cold sweat or sinks to the floor. . . . He [Seymour] is ephemeral, and no matter how many homely anecdotes are told about him, he has grown too diffuse to look at in the daytime; his talents have become supernatural.

JAMES LUNDQUIST: It is the idea of compromise that Buddy is mulling over at the age of forty when "Seymour: An Introduction" begins. He is speculating about his own career as a writer, a career that at first does seem like a considerable compromise when contrasted to that of Seymour. Buddy is a writer of fiction who must worry about communicating with the "general reader." . . . The quotations from Kafka and Kierkegaard along with the corresponding implications of Zen art do suggest one thing—that the entire story is a fictional treatise on the artistic process.

GRANVILLE HICKS: Self-consciousness gives the story its peculiar quality, and although the tone is beautifully sustained, as always in Salinger's later work, the self is exceedingly obtrusive.

JOHN WENKE: At the very outset Buddy Glass confronts the necessary (and intrinsically self-defeating) paradox of his condition. The only way to introduce the late Seymour is to use language; the use of language by nature is doomed to fail.

J. D. SALINGER ("Seymour: An Introduction," *The New Yorker*, June 6, 1959):

> There are one or two more fragmentary physical-type remarks I'd like to make, but I feel too strongly that my time is *up*. Also, it's twenty to seven, and I have a nine-o'clock class. There's just enough time for a half-hour nap, a shave, and maybe a cool, refreshing blood bath. I have an impulse—more of an old urban reflex than an impulse, thank God—to say something mildly caustic about the twenty-four young ladies, just back from big weekends at Cambridge or Hanover or New Haven, who will be waiting for me in Room 307, but I can't finish writing a description of Seymour—even a bad description, even one where my ego, my perpetual lust to share top billing with him, is all over the place—without being conscious of the good, the real. This is too grand to be said (so I'm just the man to say it), but I can't be my brother's brother for nothing, and I know—not always, but I *know*—there is no single thing I do that is more important than going into that awful Room 307. There isn't one girl in there, including the Terrible Miss Zabel, who is not as much my sister as Boo Boo or Franny. They may shine with the misinformation of the ages, but they shine. This thought manages to stun me: There's no place I'd really rather go right now than into Room 307. Seymour once said that all we do our whole lives is go from one little piece of Holy Ground to the next. Is he *never* wrong?

MICHAEL WALZER: [Since *The Catcher in the Rye*] Salinger has written almost entirely of the Glass family, a clan of seven precocious children, of Irish-Jewish stock and distinctly Buddhist tendencies. The main theme of these stories has been love. . . . The family here is a mythical gang, truly fraternal, truly affectionate; it is as if, remembering Holden's loneliness, Salinger is determined never again to permit one of his characters to be alone.

—

EBERHARD ALSEN: Salinger's withdrawal from those who should be closest to him took its first toll in early 1957, while he was finishing "Zooey." On a trip to New York City, his wife, Claire, suddenly packed up their baby daughter, Margaret, and left him. Supported by her stepfather, Claire and her baby lived in New York City for four months until she gave in to Salinger's pleading and returned to Cornish.

JOHN C. UNRUE: Early every morning Salinger went to that bunker with his lunch and wrote until late in the evening, giving strict orders that he was not to be disturbed for anything unless the house was burning down. I think Salinger built a bunker because he associated it with impenetrability. He regarded it as a safe place, a good place to write. Whether there were bombs falling, whether there were animals attacking, whatever, it was the place nobody could enter. It was the sacred place for him. It was important for Salinger to have a completely private space and a space that was uniquely his. It was almost a holy spot that no one else should ever come in.

STEPHEN GUIRGIS: I think he's a guy who went into that bunker and wrote every day. He wrestled with himself and wrestled with demons and wrestled with the muse and tried to make good work. I can't even imagine the degree of introspection, gut-wrenching, soul-searching discipline, commitment, self-abuse it must have taken to produce some of the work that he produced.

DAVID SHIELDS: It's hard not to think of the bunker as a way to return to the war, World War II. The bunker would remind Salinger that he should be writing about the most serious matters of existence. The bunker also functions as a fence between yourself and the world. God forbid you might hear a radio from a car passing by or a bird flying overhead. As a writer, you want to be driven by your own aesthetic impulses, but the world has to come in to you, lest you disappear down your own alimentary canal. You have to have the world come in, and then you want to send messages out. It's supposed to be a two-way communication system.

J. D. SALINGER ("Seymour: An Introduction," *The New Yorker*, June 6, 1959):

> Yet when I first read that young-widower-and-white-cat verse, back in 1948—or, rather, sat listening to it—I found it very hard to believe that Seymour hadn't buried at least one wife that nobody in our family knew about. He hadn't, of course. Not (and first blushes here, if any, will be the reader's, not mine)—not in this incarnation, at any rate. . . . And while it's possible that, at odd moments, tormenting or exhilarating, every married man—Seymour, just conceivably, though almost entirely for the sake of argument, not excluded—reflects on how life would be with the little woman out of the picture . . .

PAUL ALEXANDER: Claire and the domestic life she represented were always secondary to his almost maniacal drive to write, to write every day, to write all day long.

There was another problem that developed in the marriage. Salinger became obsessed with eating organic foods prepared only with certain cooking oils. Now you might think that that's a minor development in one's life, but when someone is exerting that level of control, controlling what his spouse is allowed to eat, it's got to have an obvious and profound effect on the relationship.

Eventually, Claire simply couldn't take it anymore: the isolation, the weird eating habits, the emotional abuse as a result of this isolation. She went to see a doctor in nearby Claremont and complained of restlessness, inability to sleep, loss of weight, all the classic signs of someone who was depressed.

THE GOSPEL OF SRI RAMAKRISHNA: It is "woman and gold" that binds man and robs him of his freedom. It is woman that creates the need for gold. For woman one man becomes the slave of another, and so loses his freedom. Then he cannot act as he likes.

PAUL ALEXANDER: There would be long stretches of time when he wouldn't come out of the bunker at all. He would stay down there. He put an army cot in there. He put a phone in. It was designed so that he literally never had to leave the bunker. He could stay down there and write, day and night, for days and days and days, eventually weeks on end. And you think about the life [the children's babysitter Ethel Nelson] saw. Salinger's family—they were up in one house, living their lives, and here he was, only a few yards away. Secluded, holed up in a bunker. Writing and writing and writing and writing, with clear instructions to Ethel and to Claire and the children not to be disturbed, ever, under any circumstances. What a bizarre existence this was.

DAVID SHIELDS: In 1961, when Margaret was five, she would sometimes walk through the woods to bring her father lunch in his bunker. In his bunker were a cot, a fireplace, and a manual typewriter. Claire and Margaret had reality to contend with, whereas the Glass family could be what his imagination needed them to be, wanted them to be. It was almost inevitable that when there was a competition between the two families that Salinger created, the Glass family would win out in the end.

—

SHANE SALERNO: As director of linguistic studies at Behavioral Research Laboratories in Menlo Park, California, Gordon Lish asked Salinger, among many others, to write an essay for the Job Corps "Why Work" program.

GORDON LISH: In February 1962 the telephone operator at the Behavioral Research Lab said she had a Mr. Salinger on the phone for me, and because of the nature of the laboratory I thought that she was talking about Pierre Salinger, the press secretary to President Kennedy. So I was surprised to discover that it was J. D. Salinger. He started by saying, "You know who I am and you know I don't reply to telephone calls and mail, and I'm only doing this because you seem to be hysterical or in some sort of difficulty." That struck me as amazing since the telegram had gone out in the fall sometime and here it was winter. But that was the pretext of his phone call—he said I was in some kind of problem. Then he said, "You only want me to participate in this because I'm famous." And I said, "No, no, no, it's because you know how to speak to children." He said, "No, I can't. I can't even speak to my own children."

I said it was easy to speak to children if you open up your heart to them. After this, we talked for about twenty minutes, chiefly about children. His voice was very deep. Haggard-sounding, weary-sounding. He didn't sound at all like I expected Salinger to sound. He didn't sound verbal. He possessed none of the adroitness I would have anticipated. Anyway, he did tell me he never wrote anything if it was not about the Glasses and the Caulfields, adding that he had shelves and shelves filled with the stuff. So I said, "Well, gee, that will be fine. Just give me some of that." Soon the phone call ended, and, of course, he didn't agree to provide me with a piece on why he loved his work.

A. E. HOTCHNER: He retreated more and more into a cement bunkhouse and God knows what else, rejecting marriage and other things.

14

A TERRIBLE, TERRIBLE FALL

CORNISH, NEW HAMPSHIRE, 1959–1965

I have a feeling that you're riding for some kind of a terrible, terrible fall.

J. D. Salinger, *The Catcher in the Rye*, 1951

Newsweek, *Time*, and *Life* write major investigative stories on Salinger; he refuses participation in the fame-making machinery, which, of course, does nothing but deepen the mythology that surrounds him. Literary critics attack his work, and Salinger retreats deeper into the bunker, producing in response the novella "Hapworth 16, 1924," whose main impulse, manifested as stylistic indulgence, is to protect his death-dealing soul.

MEL ELFIN: Ever since Jerome David Salinger's one novel *The Catcher in the Rye* became a best seller nine years ago, readers have been asking questions and getting no answers about the most mysterious of modern writers. For example, in New York last week, telephone calls to Salinger's literary agent, his publisher, *The New Yorker* (which prints his short stories), and even to that great stone storehouse of information the New York Public Library, produced monotonously discouraging replies: "Salinger? I'm sorry, there's not much we can tell you." . . .

Salinger has built an iron curtain of secrecy which extends not only to his family, but to the characters of his fiction as well. Not long ago stage director Elia Kazan was supposed to have cornered Salinger and pleaded for permission to stage *The Catcher* on Broadway. After listening to Kazan's sales talk, Salinger, a tall, handsome man with a melan-

Salinger residence, 1961.

choly air, replied: "I cannot give my permission. I fear Holden wouldn't like it."

SHANE SALERNO: *Newsweek* was the first publication to reveal the existence of Salinger's bunker.

MEL ELFIN: For Salinger, writing is an extremely difficult business. It means, for one thing, getting up at 5 or 6 a.m. and walking down the hill to his studio—a tiny concrete shelter with a translucent plastic roof. Salinger, who chain-smokes while he works, will often put in as many as fifteen or sixteen hours a day at his typewriter.

BERTRAND YEATON: Jerry works like a dog. He's a meticulous craftsman who constantly revises, polishes, and rewrites. On the wall of the studio, Jerry has a series of cup hooks to which he clips sheafs of notes. They must deal with various characters and situations, because when an idea occurs to him he takes down the clips, makes the appropriate notation, and places it back on the proper hook. He also has a ledger in which he has pasted sheets of typewritten manuscript on one page and on the opposite one has arrows, memos, and other notes for revisions.

ETHEL NELSON: The only ones I ever saw were Claire and the two children, never saw Jerry. He more or less lived down in that bunker. When he was writing a book, you did not bother him. Claire was not allowed to bother him. You couldn't call him; you couldn't go down, knock on the door; you left him alone until he came out. So I only saw Claire, and I would do light housework and play with the children, keep them busy. But you'd think she was a single parent as far as seeing Jerry around. I just never saw him.

MARC WEINGARTEN: *Newsweek* had a big coup with the bunker reveal, and they also provided some telling insights into Salinger's private life, such as the fact that Salinger, as a registered Republican, would have been a Nixon man in 1960. And that he liked Japanese poetry and detective novels.

The second magazine to weigh in on Salinger was *Time*. When the

Life magazine photo of Salinger's dog peeking out from under the fence.

magazine's subscribers checked their mailboxes the week of September 15, 1961, and found forty-one-year-old Salinger on the cover, it was a very, very big deal.

ROBERT BOYNTON: The cover of *Time* magazine in 1961 was reserved for statesmen and Nobel laureates.

MARC WEINGARTEN: Nikita Khrushchev was on the cover the week before. It instantly vaulted Salinger onto another plateau of fame.

STEVEN WHITFIELD: The image of Salinger on the cover of *Time* wasn't a photograph; it was a drawing. It's an imaginary portrait of Salinger with a cliff behind him. It conveys the sense that the author has enough integrity not to be part of the publicity machine.

PHOEBE HOBAN: My father, Russell Hoban, illustrated the 1961 *Time* magazine Salinger cover story when *Franny and Zooey* was published, and he had a vision of those characters as looking like haunted spirits in bedlam.

JOHN SKOW: It is sunny at the edge of the woods, but the tall man's face is drawn and white. When he came to Cornish, N.H., nine years ago, he was friendly and talkative; now when he jeeps to town, he speaks only the few words necessary to buy food or newspapers. Outsiders trying to reach him are, in fact, reduced to passing notes or letters, to which there is usually no reply. Only a small group of friends has ever been inside his hilltop house. Not long ago, when he and his family were away, a couple of neighbors could stand it no longer, put on dungarees and climbed over the 6½-ft. fence to take a look around.

What they saw behind a cluster of birches was a simple, one-story New England house painted barnred, a modest vegetable garden, and—100 yards and across a stream from the house—a little concrete cell with a skylight. The cell contains a fireplace, a long table with a typewriter, books and a filing cabinet. Here the pale man usually sits, sometimes writing quickly, other times throwing logs into the fire for hours and making long lists of words until he finds the right one. The writer is Jerome David Salinger, and almost all his fictional characters seem more real, more plausible, than he.

September 15, 1961, cover of *Time* magazine.

The appearance this week of his new book, *Franny and Zooey*, actually two long, related stories that originally ran in *The New Yorker*, is not just a literary event but, to countless fans, an epiphany. Weeks before the official publication date, Salinger's followers queued up, and bookstores sold out their first supplies. To a large extent, the excitement is fueled by memories of Salinger's most famous work. For all of the characters set to paper by American authors since the war, only Holden Caulfield, the gallant scatologer of *The Catcher in the Rye*, has taken flesh permanently, as George F. Babbitt, Jay Gatsby, Lieut. Henry, and Eugene Gant took flesh in the '20s and '30s. . . . As nearly as possible in an age in which all relations are public, J. D. Salinger lives the life of a recluse. He says that he needs the isolation to keep his creativity intact, that he must not be interrupted "during working years." But the effort of evading the world must by now be almost more tiring than a certain amount of normal sociability would be. One critic and fellow novelist, Harvey Swados, has in fact suggested, pettishly, that Salinger's reputation is in part a consequence of his "tantalizing physical inaccessibility." . . . He will turn and run if addressed on the street by a stranger, and his picture has not appeared on a dust jacket since the first two printings of *Catcher* (it was yanked off the third edition at his request). He has refused offers from at least three book clubs for *Franny and Zooey.*

JEAN MILLER: A friend who was at a cocktail party met a *Time* magazine reporter who said, "We're working on a story about J. D. Salinger," and my friend said, "Well, I went to school with a girl who knew him very well." And they tracked me down.

I was married and living in Maryland in a farmhouse, pretty much away from anywhere. All of a sudden this very tall man appeared in the doorway. He was from *Time*, and he said he understood that I knew Jerry Salinger, and I said, "Only slightly." We sat in the living room and stared at each other for about fifteen minutes. I can remember it as though it were yesterday. He said, "Why is it that people who knew him won't talk about him?" I said it's because Jerry doesn't want the people who knew him to talk about him. And he finally left. The magazine article said I wouldn't talk because I was recently married. I don't know why they said that. It had nothing to do with it.

MARC WEINGARTEN: *Time* magazine went so far as to track down Salinger's sister, Doris, who was a buyer at Bloomingdale's, and these are

Salinger residence, 1961.

the reporter's notes from that moment: "Doris, tall, handsome woman in late 40s, hair medium brown, well groomed. She acted put upon. 'I wouldn't do anything in the world my brother didn't approve of. I don't want to be rude, but you put me in a very difficult position. Why don't you just leave us alone?'"

Life's feature on Salinger, which was the last of the three major pieces to run, arguably had the greatest impact. For one thing, it was a huge spread: nine pages. But the main event was the fact that one of the magazine's photographers had snapped a picture of the great man. This was like getting a picture of Bigfoot. Salinger is wearing a one-piece jumpsuit, leaning on a cane. His face is gaunt; he wears a downcast expression. In short, he looks terribly unhappy. That one picture would crystallize the Salinger legend for decades to come.

ERNEST HAVEMANN: At one side of the road, on a brief clearing which serves as an outdoor garage, stood Salinger's two cars: his old beat-up Jeep, a new gray Borgward. On the other side was that forbidding fence. I parked next to the Jeep and walked to the gate. It was solid like the rest of the fence, and was locked. I called hello. It was a rather tremulous hello; I confess it. I was intimidated by that fence.

On the other side a baby began to cry. A screen door quickly slammed. A woman's voice quietly comforted the child. And then the gate opened—not wide, a tentative slit. A young woman with blondish hair, barefoot, and without makeup, stood there, holding her startled baby in her arms. Behind her was a little girl who had a friendly and expectant look as if she hoped I had brought a playmate. I was meeting the author's 27-year-old wife, British-born, Radcliffe-educated Claire Douglas Salinger, his 5-year-old daughter, Peggy, and his 18-month-old son Matthew. When I announced myself as a journalist, Mrs. Salinger's eyes said unmistakably, "Oh, Lord, not another one!" She sighed and told me that she has a set piece for visitors who want to meet her husband, the gist of it being absolutely no. There was no point in making her recite it.

GLENN GORDON CARON: I remember reading in *Life* magazine about this man Salinger who lived in an isolated country house, didn't want visitors, didn't want to discuss himself. I was puzzled, because I suddenly realized there were famous people, who have extraordinary lives, and then there were the rest of us—but here was a man who had an opportunity to have, at a young age, what you thought was an extraordinary life, and he was saying, "I'd rather not, please go away."

MARC WEINGARTEN: *Newsweek* and *Life* pointed out that Salinger had this charmingly dilapidated mailbox on the country road with his name imprinted on it. Both magazines ran pictures of this mailbox, as if it were a major "get." Now, I ask you, if Salinger truly wanted to be left alone, why the hell would be put his name—in block letters, no less—on that mailbox? You don't necessarily *need* to have your name on a mailbox. It's because he wanted people, reporters especially, to lean in and crane their necks, but only just a little. He was teasing people with his reticence.

ROBERT BOYNTON: The magazines were just trying to understand what the pathology is of this guy who has fame at his fingertips and hasn't used it, hasn't partaken of it in any way. And then there's this crazed paparazzi, investigative-reporter approach: people peeking over the wall, invading his property. It's all about the spectacle of trying to figure out this enigma. He doesn't go to parties. He doesn't have a house in the Hamptons. He just focuses on this one thing: writing. Talking to him would be like interviewing a monk and asking him about his prayers and his daily routine. I'd ask Salinger: "What exactly is it you do every day?"

GEORGE STEINER: He has adopted a T. E. Lawrence technique of partial concealment. He does not sign books at Brentano's nor teach creative writing at Black Mountain. "I was with the Fourth Division during the war. I almost always write about very young people." That's about all he wants us to know.

MARC WEINGARTEN: Photographers hiding in bushes for days in the rain just to get a photograph of Salinger! Fans are coming from miles away and camping out in Cornish—literally making pilgrimages, as if on a religious quest. All for this man, who wrote one novel and a handful of stories in a decade. It's madness, really.

What does Salinger make of all this? It had been nearly a decade since *Catcher* was released; he has published only a handful of stories in the interim. Then *Franny and Zooey* comes out and, boom, the incandescent light of the media shines on him. He was being besieged by the worst possible enemy of his post-*Catcher* existence: reporters with large readerships. It is really the first time in American literary history that a prominent writer actually ran away from attention.

—

J. D. SALINGER (dedication to *Franny and Zooey*, 1961):

> As nearly as possible in the spirit of Matthew Salinger, age one, urging a luncheon companion to accept a cool lima bean, I urge my editor, mentor, and (heaven help him) closest friend, William Shawn, *genius domus* of *The New Yorker*, lover of the long shot, protector of the unprolific, defender of the hopelessly flamboyant, most unreasonably modest of born great artist-editors, to accept this pretty skimpy-looking book.

PAUL ALEXANDER: The admission that Shawn was his best friend because Shawn loved long shots, protected unprolific writers, and defended flamboyant people—all of these, of course, were references to the way Salinger must have viewed himself. The "heaven help him" comment was Salinger's clue to let his readers know he understood that by naming Shawn as his best friend he was unleashing a stream of ardent fans onto Shawn, who would harass him in hopes of finding out more about Salinger—a fate Shawn could not have cherished.

SHANE SALERNO: Both Salinger and Shawn are supposed to be deeply private, even reclusive men, and yet the gesture of this dedication could not be more exhibitionistic. Would a true "recluse" do that?

J. D. SALINGER (*Franny and Zooey* flap copy, 1961):

> "Franny" came out in *The New Yorker* in 1955 and was swiftly followed, in 1957, by "Zooey." Both stories are early, critical entries in a narrative series I am doing about a family of settlers in twentieth-century New York, the Glasses. It is a long-term project, patently an ambitious one, and there is a real enough danger, I suppose, that sooner or later I'll bog down, perhaps disappear entirely, in my own methods, locutions, and mannerisms. On the whole, though, I am very hopeful. I love working on these Glass stories, I've been waiting for them most of my life, and I think I have fairly decent, monomaniacal plans to finish them with due care and all-available skill.
>
> A couple of stories in the series besides "Franny" and "Zooey" have already been published in *The New Yorker*, and some new material is scheduled to appear there soon or Soon. I have a great deal of thoroughly unscheduled material on paper, too, but I expect to be fussing with it, to use a popular trade term, for some time to come. ("Polishing" is another dandy word that comes to mind.) I work like greased lightning, myself, but my alter-ego and collaborator, Buddy Glass, is insufferably slow.
>
> It is my rather subversive opinion that a writer's feelings of anonymity-obscurity are the second-most valuable property on loan to him during his working years. My wife has asked me to add, however, in a single explosion of candor, that I live in Westport with my dog.

SHANE SALERNO: When Salinger wrote in *Catcher*, "What really knocks me out is a book that, when you're all done reading it, you wish the author that wrote it was a terrific friend of yours and you could call him up on the phone whenever you felt like it," that simple line had the effect of sending a signal to a certain type of reader and drew seekers to his driveway for decades. In the same way, the flap copy for *Franny and Zooey*—describing his working methods, his fictional alter ego, his grand plan for future Glass stories, and especially the secrecy and mystery of it all—significantly heightened interest in him and made him a fascinating subject for press attention.

MARC WEINGARTEN: Salinger was really the first celebrity recluse; Howard Hughes hadn't really gone around the bend quite yet, and even Garbo wasn't as monastic as Salinger. Well, who doesn't want to know more about a recluse? Salinger had transcended mere literary fame; he was now a public figure whose renown functioned independently of what he had accomplished as a writer. Salinger was a source of intrigue because he was so tantalizingly inscrutable and mysterious.

Of course, the residual effect of all this intrigue was that it was great for sales. *Franny and Zooey* sold 125,000 copies the first two weeks, reached the top spot of the *New York Times* bestseller list, and stayed number one for 26 weeks, selling 938,000 copies in its first year.

GRANVILLE HICKS: There are, I am convinced, millions of young Americans who feel closer to Salinger than to any other writer.

JOYCE MAYNARD: He despises literary prizes, reviews, New York intellectuals. He hates artiness in writing and writerliness and writers who seem to court an image with as much calculation as movie stars—tweedy types sucking on cigars on their book jackets or exquisitely sensitive-looking women in black turtlenecks. Jerry knows all their names and follows what they've been up to more closely than I would have supposed, and possesses little but contempt for what he sees of the literary world.

SHANE SALERNO: Donald Fiene was a former high school English teacher who had been fired for recommending *The Catcher in the Rye* to his students. He first wrote to Salinger in 1960, and Salinger wrote him back a long and sincere letter, ending with this: "I suppose the sad truth is that you've come down with a case of personal principles, and I don't honestly wish you a cure."

Perhaps believing that they had established a relationship with this exchange, Fiene wrote to Salinger again in 1961, this time requesting Salinger's cooperation and assistance in the preparation of the first complete bibliography of Salinger's work and translations. Salinger, not surprisingly, declined and cited as a reason the grief that recent press attention had caused his friends, his family, and, most important, his work.

J. D. SALINGER, excerpt from letter to Donald Fiene, July 30, 1961:

> *I'm a living, working writer, and I'm trying rather desperately to hang on to what little undocumented peace and privacy I have left.*
>
> *I don't think you have any idea how hellish the summer has been for my family and me. My close friends, my family in New York have been bothered.*

ERNEST HAVEMANN: Salinger has suffered; anybody can tell that just from reading his stories. . . . It is the suffering that makes *Catcher* so agonizingly identifiable and irresistible to young people of all ages. He suffered in the war, and his war stories are great because every sensitive person suffered in the war, or expects to suffer in the next one.

—

PHILIP ROTH: The response of college students to the works of J. D. Salinger should indicate to us that perhaps he, more than anyone else, has not turned his back on the times, but instead, has managed to put his finger on what is most significant in the struggle going on between the self (all selves, not just the writer's) and the culture.

JOHN ROMANO: Reading *Franny and Zooey*, girls found a way of sounding like the interesting people they wanted to be. And I use the word "girls" advisedly. These are eighteen-year-olds. There's always a risk for the writer that he'll become part of our nostalgia for previous versions of ourselves, and in Salinger's case, his writing participated very much in our creating of ourselves.

JOHN SKOW: The characters of Salinger's most astonishing legend belong to a gaudy and eccentric family named Glass. The chronicle of the clan's fortunes is far from finished (the Glasses have so far made their appearance only in "Franny," "Zooey," and five other stories), but it is already one of the indelible family sagas to appear in the U.S. The elder Glasses are Irish-Jewish vaudevillians now retired to a life of comfortable reminiscence. Les Glass and Bessie Gallagher, professionally known as Gallagher & Glass, achieved "more than just passing notability on the old Pantages and Orpheum circuits." They are descended from "an astonishingly long and motley double-file of professional entertainers"; Les' grandfather, for instance, was "a quite famous Polish-Jewish carnival clown named Zozo, who had a penchant—right up to the end, one necessarily gathers—for diving from immense heights into small containers of water." The seven children, too, have been professionals; they were all prodigies, and they all appeared, at one time or another, on a radio kiddy-quiz show called, slyly enough, *It's a Wise Child.*

Any author who promises board and room to seven fictional child prodigies would seem to be diving into a container of water that is very small indeed. The Glass children, moreover, are brave, clean, reverent, and overwhelmingly lovable. Yet they never become the seven deadly siblings (at least they are never all deadly at the same time). The Irish strain makes them formidably talkative and occasionally fey. The Jewish strain lends the family warmth as well as a talent for Talmudic brooding. The vaudeville heritage provides theatricality.

Despite the meagerness of his output, Salinger, at 42, has spoken with more magic, particularly to the young, than any other U.S. writer since World War II. . . . Some readers . . . object to the book's italicized talkiness. But the talk, like the book itself, is dazzling, joyous, and satisfying. Above all, by sheer force of eye and ear—rather than by psychologizing, which he detests—Salinger has given them, like Holden, an astonishing degree of life, a stunning and detailed air of presence.

CHARLES POORE: *Franny and Zooey* is better than anything Mr. Salinger has done before. It doesn't lean on a familiar plot structure (adventures of a runaway boy, as in *The Catcher in the Rye*); it has, instead, a fading sort of timeliness in that it presents retired electronic quiz demons. As children, Zooey and his sister Franny were public freaks. . . . Now, launched on their twenties, they are still freaks—and aware of that with a fearful, rueful sense of perpetual exasperation.

BLAKE BAILEY: Salinger, it bears repeating, was a sore point [for fellow *New Yorker* writer John Cheever]. *Franny and Zooey* had been published that September and had dominated the best-seller lists ever since, at a time when Cheever was struggling to get on with another novel while supporting himself, as ever, with inventive—but relatively less acclaimed (and now maimed)—short fiction for the *New Yorker*. Reading the [1961] *Life* tribute, Cheever went into a "slow burn" and began drinking heavily, until finally he phoned [William] Maxwell in a rage; he recounted his rant thus: "You cut that short story . . . and I'll never write another story for you or anybody else. You can get that Godamned sixth-rate Salinger to write your Godamned short stories, but don't expect anything more from me. If you want to slam a door on somebody's genitals, find yourself another victim. Etc."

GERALDINE McGOWAN: *Catcher in the Rye* was an enormous success in 1951. *Nine Stories* was published to serious acclaim in 1953. When *Franny and Zooey* was published in 1961 to even greater fanfare, the literary knives came out. In 1961 and '62 Salinger got the harshest criticism of his entire publishing life. Joan Didion, John Updike, Lionel Trilling, Alfred Kazin, Mary McCarthy—it seemed like there was a cabal against him, except you couldn't even say that they were friends. You can't even say that one knew what the other was doing.

DAVID SHIELDS: Updike's review was brilliantly conceived, seemingly delivered more in sorrow than in anger, but containing within it the seeds of his competitor's destruction.

JOHN UPDIKE: Not the least dismaying development of the Glass stories is the vehement editorializing on the obvious—television scripts are not generally good, not all section men are geniuses. Of course, the Glasses condemn the world only to condescend to it, to forgive it, in the end. Yet the pettishness of the condemnation diminishes the gallantry of the condescension.

In "Raise High the Roof Beam, Carpenters," Seymour defines sentimentality as giving "to a thing more tenderness than God gives to it." This seems to me the nub of the trouble: Salinger loves the Glasses more than God loves them. He loves them too exclusively. Their invention has become a hermitage for him. He loves them to the detriment of artistic moderation.

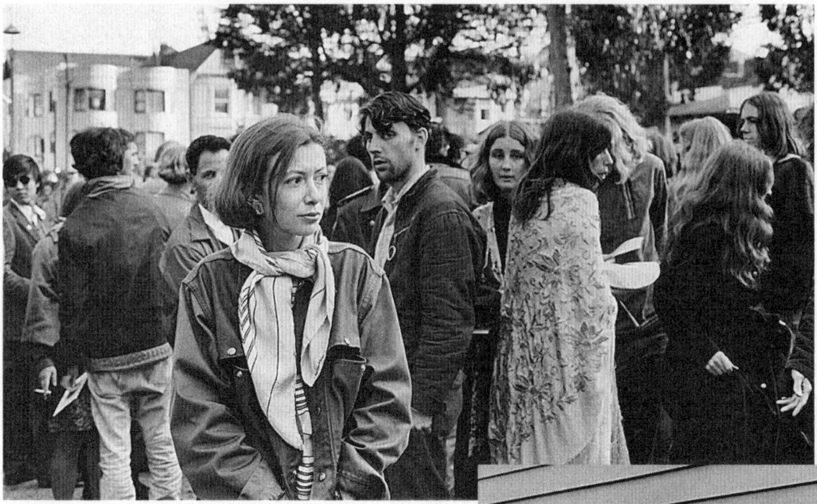

Joan Didion.

John Updike.

Alfred Kazin.

Lionel Trilling.

JOAN DIDION: What gives [*Franny and Zooey*] its extremely potent appeal is precisely that it is self-help copy: it emerges finally as *Positive Thinking* for the upper middle classes, as *Double Your Energy and Live Without Fatigue* for Sarah Lawrence girls.

ALFRED KAZIN: I am sorry to have to use the word "cute" in respect to Salinger, but there is absolutely no other word that for me so accurately typifies the self-conscious charm and prankishness of his own writing and his extraordinary cherishing of his favorite Glass characters.

SEYMOUR KRIM: [Salinger's] stories read like slow-motion close-up movies instead of conventional fiction because the flair of theater is in his bones. . . . But stop and think. If it weren't for his shimmering nightclub performance in prose, would you read him with such fascination? Hardly.

ISA KAPP: In spite of the intellectual sponginess of our time, it is still strange to see the optimistic American reader gobbling up J. D. Salinger's stories of defeatism, self-deprecation, and nervous breakdown. . . . Salinger himself persists in a low opinion of mankind. If one of his characters happens to find a friend, the chosen person is usually between ten and fourteen years old, or dear because departed.

GERALDINE McGOWAN: Gore Vidal said Mary McCarthy was one of our greatest critics, because she was uncorrupted by compassion. She couldn't abide writers, including Hemingway, who showed any signs of elitism; it didn't matter how beautiful their writing was. She simply took a stand against that. McCarthy took offense to the way Salinger's work changed, beginning with *Nine Stories*. People talk about how he got clobbered by the critics in 1961 and 1962 and that there was a lot of literary envy at the bottom of it. But what's not so often said is with that huge success something happened to him: it didn't go to his head, but it changed his writing. He went to a place that people didn't expect him to go.

MARY McCARTHY: In Hemingway's work there was never anybody but Hemingway in a series of disguises, but at least there was only one Papa per book. To be confronted with these seven faces of Salinger, all wise and loveable and simple, is to gaze into a terrifying narcissus pool.

Salinger's world contains nothing but Salinger, his teachers, and his tolerantly cherished audience—humanity; outside are the phonies, vainly signaling to be let in, like the kids' Irish mother, Bessie, a home version of the Fat Lady, who keeps invading the bathroom while her handsome son Zooey is in the tub shaving. . . .

Yet below this self-loving barbershop harmony a chord of terror is struck from time to time, like a judgment. Seymour's suicide suggests that Salinger guesses intermittently or fears intermittently that there may be something wrong somewhere. Why did he kill himself? Because he had married a phony, whom he worshipped for her "simplicity, her terrible honesty"? Or because he was so happy and the Fat Lady's world was so wonderful? Or because he had been lying, his author had been lying, and it was all terrible, and he was a fake?

DAVID SHIELDS: In a June 16, 1962, letter to William Maxwell, McCarthy acknowledged that part of the motivation for her attack on Salinger was her anger at the *New Yorker* for canceling its first-look contract with her.

Mary McCarthy.

GORE VIDAL: This ghastly, self-observant family, going on and on and on about everything of importance to them, which they assume is important to all the world.

ANNE MARPLE: This "prose home movie" ["Zooey"] is unwieldy as a short story. . . . The frequent inclusion of diaries and letters in the Glass Saga indicates that Salinger is having additional mechanical difficulties with his embarrassing wealth of Glassiana.

HOWARD M. HARPER: Salinger's skillful use of concrete details creates a certain reality in the Glass stories, but it is a surface reality. Beneath it is an essentially misanthropic view of life, in which the Glasses hold a monopoly on goodness, sensitivity, intelligence, and so on.

—

SHANE SALERNO: Donald Fiene resurfaced in 1962. Despite Salinger's refusing to cooperate with his book, Fiene had stubbornly pressed forward and contacted Salinger's friends, including one of the "Four Musketeers," Jack Altaras, who was a successful lawyer in Cleburne, Texas. When Salinger learned of this intrusion, he wrote Fiene an angry letter urging him to stop his plan to publish a book on his work.

J. D. SALINGER, excerpt from letter to Donald Fiene, September 10, 1962:

> *Part of my mind is simply unable to believe that you plan to go ahead with this book about me despite our exchanges on the subject.*
>
> *I find it almost impossible to believe that you've gone right on writing letters to friends and acquaintances of mine.*
>
> *I beg you leave off.*

—

DAVID SHIELDS: "Raise High the Roof Beam, Carpenters" and "Seymour: An Introduction" were published in the *New Yorker* in 1955 and 1959, respectively, and they had been discussed in reviews in the years immediately following, but they weren't published together as a book until 1963. It was number one on the *New York Times* bestseller list for ten weeks; the reviews were merciless.

ORVILLE PRESCOTT: "Seymour: An Introduction" is only a story by the most generous definition of the word. . . . [A] turgid and static discourse . . . it lacks the charm, humor, and surface brilliance which distinguish most of Mr. Salinger's stories. . . . [Buddy] rambles, digresses, pontificates, and fails completely to make Seymour Glass seem a believable human being.

IRVING HOWE: Both of these stories ["Raise High the Roof Beam, Carpenters" and "Seymour: An Introduction"] are marred by the self-indulgence of a writer flirting with depths of wisdom, yet coy and embarrassed in his advances. . . . And as the world of Salinger comes more fully into view, it seems increasingly open to critical attack. It is hard to believe in Seymour's saintliness, hard even to credit him as a fictional character, for we are barely able to see him at all behind the palpitations of Buddy's memory. The Salinger world is coated with the sentimentalism of a "love" that, in refusing to distinguish among objects and qualities, ends by obliterating their distinctive life.

JOSE de M. PLATANOPEZ: I have just finished reading "Raise High the Roof Beam, Carpenters" and "Seymour: An Introduction" and should be interested in any evidence your [the *New York Times Book Review*] readers can provide that J. D. Salinger is still alive and writing.

NORMAN MAILER: It is necessary to say that the four stories about the Glass family by J. D. Salinger, published in two books called *Franny and Zooey* and *Raise High the Roof Beam, Carpenters*, seem to have been written for high-school girls. The second piece in the second book, called *Seymour an Introduction*, must be the most slovenly portion of prose ever put out by an important American writer. It is not even professional Salinger. Salinger at his customary worst, as here in the other three stories of the two books, is never bad—he is just disappointing. He stays too long on the light ice of his gift, writes exquisite dialogue and creates minor moods with sweetness and humor, and never gives the fish its hook. He disappoints because he is always practicing. But when he dips into Seymour—the Glass brother who committed suicide, when the cult comes to silence before the appearance of the star—the principal, to everyone's horror, has nausea on the stage. Salinger for the first time is engaged in run-off writing, free suffragette prose; his inhibitions (which once helped by their restraint to create his style) now stripped. He is giving you himself as he is. No concealment. It feels like taking a bath in a grease trap.

. . . But it's a rare man who can live like a hermit and produce a major performance unless he has critics who are near to him and hard on him. No friend who worried about Salinger's future should have let him publish Seymour an Introduction in *The New Yorker* without daring to lose his friendship first by telling him how awful it was. Yet there was too much depending on Salinger's interregnum—he was *so inoffensive*, finally. So a suspension of the critical faculty must have gone on in the institutional wheels of *The New Yorker*, which was close to psychotic in its evasions.

SHANE SALERNO: Salinger made no public response to the criticism. Quite to the contrary, he pushed his work even further away from the style that had made him a household name. And he seemed happy not to be the popular writer everybody loved. In fact, in the spring of 1963, Jacqueline Kennedy personally telephoned Salinger, urging him to attend a White House celebration of writers and artists. In Margaret's view, one of the main reasons he declined was Claire's eagerness to attend. "Woman and gold."

The only time Margaret ever saw her father cry was several months later—while watching JFK's funeral on television.

—

MARC WEINGARTEN: Salinger was a big movie buff; he understood as well as anyone how myths were constructed. But he also knew how to do it in a way that wasn't so transparent. It was myth-building by subtraction.

SHANE SALERNO: One of the enduring Salinger myths is that he was so disgusted by his story "Uncle Wiggily in Connecticut" being transformed into *My Foolish Heart* that he swore off Hollywood forever. In actuality, while Salinger seemingly was working to keep the world away, he was eagerly engaged in a secret film collaboration with television writer and producer Peter Tewksbury. This story has never been told.

CIELLE TEWKSBURY: My husband, Peter Tewksbury, was a most amazing man. He was my father's best friend, and they started a community theater in a very small town in California. From there, he landed a job directing the television show *Life with Father*, and one of the things he did brilliantly was to work with children and young people. From there, he went to *My Three Sons*, again with young children. And then he landed the one thing that was kind of the pièce de résistance of his work in television: a series called *It's a Man's World* that only had thirteen episodes. He was able to produce and direct and edit and write the entire series—that was the way he wanted to work because he had full control of what was happening. It was a wonderful series about young people.

He wasn't an easy man to work with, but he was brilliant. He was extraordinarily demanding and then could turn around and be beautifully kind, but he really made you work as a performer. The sponsors were a little nervous about the message of really interesting, passionate young people. They were not really comfortable with that. It wasn't the cliché version of what young people were like in the '60s. It was quite a different avenue.

He had a way of grabbing onto something and never letting go. He had a concentration and a dedication and a very strong sense of ethics, which is why, in the late '60s, we left Los Angeles. He said, "I don't want the rest of my life to be in this world. I want a different life." I kid you not, he went up in the closet, pulled out the two Emmys he had won, walked straight in the backyard, threw them in the trash can, we packed up and moved to Vermont, and that was the end of his film career.

Peter adored Salinger's work because the way the young children verbalized their world was so perfect. We were sitting at the kitchen table, very much like this one—in fact, it may have been this one—and we were reading the short stories. We'd just finished "For Esmé." He picked up the book, looked at it, turned it over, put it down on the table, and said, "My God, this would make such an extraordinary film." Of course, he knew Salinger's reputation for being a recluse and, of course, he was kind of a recluse himself. I just watched that look on his face—real, real yearning.

Apparently what he did, unbeknownst to me, was to pull out two copies of what he felt were the best episodes of *It's a Man's World*, packed them up, and sent them to Salinger. He said in a letter, "This series would never have occurred had I not been so influenced by your work." Time went on. Nothing. Peter said, "Okay, I haven't heard from him. I am just going to have to go meet the man." I said, "I don't think he accepts visitors." He said, "I have to meet him. I have to find out if there's any way to do this film." So we got in the car in the dead of winter. It was snowing and we drove to Cornish, New Hampshire. We got totally lost, wandering around in this little village. Finally, we stopped at a small gas station and asked for directions to Salinger's home. The man in the store said, "Well, you're on the right road, but those folks, they don't much care for visitors." Which we well knew, but on we went because that is the way Peter was. He really wanted to do that film. We found the house, took one look at it, and went, "Oh boy," because there was an eight-foot-tall fence surrounding the house. There was a gate in the fence. Peter got out of the car and said, "Come on." I got out of the car, we walked to the gate, we went up to the door, Peter knocked, and a very tall, lean man with incredibly penetrating eyes was standing in the doorway. Peter said, "My name is Peter Tewksbury. I sent you some films and I want to talk to you about 'Esmé.'"

Salinger said, "Yeah, I got the films. I liked them. They were interesting. Come in." It was very much like this place—unpretentious. There was a round table, a fireplace, wood floors, old sturdy rugs on the floor. He says, "I want you to meet my wife. This is Claire, and this is my son. Now we are going in the kitchen to talk." She was charming. She served us coffee and obviously was kind of the foil for the rather tensile quality that Salinger had. She was the softener. I'm sure she was probably very tired of intrusions like ours, but she was very gracious. She backed off. She didn't sit down and listen to the conversations. She didn't participate in any of what was happening. She was with her young child, with the little boy, and they were conversing in the living room while we were sitting in the kitchen. She had a lovely, nice quality, but there was a reserve. Like, "I have been through this a lot, and it is not easy to be with someone of that notoriety. It colors my relationship and it colors my life, and I wonder where my place is in this."

I remember sitting there, looking at these two incredibly intense individuals, both of them going back and forth in conversation. He did spend quite a bit of time, Salinger did, querying Peter about the *Man's World* series and why it was canceled and what he thought about it and how he saw the characters. I gather he was quite a film buff himself.

Then they got around to "Esmé." Peter tried to explain why he thought it could be such a perfect film. He said, "You could practically lift it off the pages just the way it's written. So filmic." Salinger said, "Well, what do you think about Esmé?"—the character of Esmé. Peter said, "She's right on the edge between the innocent wise child and the woman. And the whole story rests on that moment. It is like an in-breath the moment before it is an out-breath, or a minor chord that builds up to that peak moment before it becomes a major; that's where she is." Salinger said, "Yes."

They talked a little bit more and then Salinger said, "I'll let you do this under one condition: that I cast the role of Esmé." When you say that to a director, that's a hard one, especially because Peter had a wonderful way of drawing out young performers. I was watching his face and I thought, "Oh boy," but he said, "All right, I'll agree to that." We said goodbye and went back to our farm in Vermont.

Peter started working on the script. The first thing he did was outline it according to the sequence of the scenes, not changing a lot. He made a few little changes and sent it off to Salinger. And it came back, very quickly—about three days later. Every single change that Peter had suggested had been put back into the exact same order it was written in the book. Peter said, "All right, let's see what happens with the scenes when we are dealing with dialogue." He began to break down the scenes—a couple of the early scenes with Esmé and her brother. He changed a sentence or two, moved around the order slightly here and there. He sent the first two scenes off to Salinger; we waited, and this time it was maybe a week and a half before they came back. Once again, almost every single change Peter had made had been carefully returned to the original order that you find in the story. This went on, oh, maybe three months—back and forth: corrections and changes that were then changed back. Finally, at one point, I remember Peter sitting at his desk and saying, "Okay, we will just film this exactly as he wrote it, because if we don't, we won't be doing this."

Now it was time to meet the young woman that Salinger wished to cast in the role of Esmé. The young woman was the daughter of Salinger's good friend Peter De Vries, and her name was Jan, an aspiring young actress, probably around twelve, thirteen maybe. We went to meet her. Salinger was not there. It was just De Vries and his daughter. In about half an hour, Peter came back and I knew that it hadn't gone well. He sat down and said, "She's too old. She is past that delicate moment that makes the miracle of Esmé. And if I cast this young woman in the role, I would be destroying the beauty of Salinger's work, and I won't do that." He called Salinger and said, "I really wish that I didn't have to say this, but I do: she is too old. So there will be no film."

I have often thought it would have been a very beautiful film, because the parallels between Salinger and Peter were quite unbelievable. Their experiences in the Second World War were almost parallel. Peter was in the army with a group that had to go onto the islands of Japan and ferret out the remaining Japanese forces hiding in caves. He went in with thirty-five men; he came out with four. All our married life, I could never walk up behind him and surprise him. There were deep scars for all of them. It was all held within. Both of my children said, "You never want to make him angry." You see that in "Esmé." It is right there in the story of the sergeant. That is the other part that Peter really understood: he knew what that was. And he knew he could film it well. The reclusiveness, the experiences in the war, and the infinite understanding of young people were the three things that they really walked the same path on.

—

BEN YAGODA: In the early '60s in New York, strange and new things were happening in writing. The *New Yorker* had been on the top of the heap for many years in fiction, journalism, and as a magazine of New York. But there was a whole other group of people who later became known as the New Journalists who were stirring up a lot of trouble writing for the *Herald Tribune*, *New York* magazine, and *Esquire*. They—especially Tom Wolfe, but also writers like Norman Mailer and Gay Talese—represented everything the *New Yorker* didn't. The *New Yorker* was quiet and subdued. The New Journalists were loud. The *New Yorker* was respectful. The New Journalists were loud.

MARC WEINGARTEN: In 1965 Tom Wolfe was thirty-four, a general assignment reporter for the *New York Herald Tribune*, a struggling newspaper. He was a writer desperately in need of making a name for himself. If you were a no-longer-quite-so-young writer trying to make a name for yourself in New York, it was not necessarily a great career move to attack the *New Yorker*. It was counterintuitive on Wolfe's part, but he was canny enough to realize, "Look at my work. I use six exclamation points in a row. I use semicolons with impunity. I'm never going to get published in the *New Yorker*, anyway. William Shawn would never give me the time of day."

TOM WOLFE: Shawn, it's my contention—and I got into a lot of trouble over this—was, in effect, an embalmer. He was going to keep the *New Yorker* exactly the way it was under [founding editor Harold] Ross, but he didn't have Ross's temperament. Ross was starstruck with New York; that awe and vitality showed through. And he never would publish something called a "short story." They were all called "casuals." The idea was, "We're not going to strain your brain with these short stories—this is not English Literature; this is the *New Yorker*. We're sophisticated and we don't get carried away."

The *New Yorker* by the mid-'60s was this revered corpse. They had a snoozy nepotism. It's amazing the things they would print if you were kin to somebody already in the magazine. John Updike's mother worked and wrote under another name there. I can't remember what her pen name was. That's how Updike came into the picture. It had gotten pretty dreary.

MARC WEINGARTEN: The *New Yorker* writers all shared a certain sense of propriety. They didn't like to get themselves mired in the muck of this strange new youth culture that they probably felt was metastasizing

Tom Wolfe.

out of control—certainly out of their control. They approached it from a certain discreet remove. There were exceptions to this rule in the magazine's history, like John Hershey's "Hiroshima" and Lillian Ross's pieces, but there was a general sense of, "We're not equipped to really get our hands dirty in this new insurgent thing that's happening in the country."

BEN YAGODA: As Wolfe later recounted, the piece originated one day when he and Clay Felker, the editor of the *Herald Tribune* Sunday magazine section, *New York*, were sitting around and remarking that all the tributes to the *New Yorker* that were marking the magazine's fortieth anniversary neglected to mention one thing: the *New Yorker* had for some years been, as he called it, unbearably dull. Wolfe decided he would try "having a little fun with the magazine," in the style of Wolcott Gibbs's celebrated 1936 *New Yorker* takedown of Henry Luce: write a profile of Shawn in a style that mocked the *New Yorker*'s own.

Shawn informed Wolfe that he would not grant an interview or answer questions in writing, nor verify facts presented to him before publication, all of which made the prospect of doing a profile rather daunting. Wolfe decided he would write what he called an antiparody.

MARC WEINGARTEN: The first part, which appeared on April 11, 1965, was called "Tiny Mummies," and its subhead was "The True Story of the Ruler of Forty-third Street's Land of the Walking Dead." The piece gunned down the establishment of the *New Yorker* and everything it stood for. It portrayed Shawn as a passive-aggressive enabler of soporific culture who put out the magazine with his horsehair-stuffing shabby gentility. It showed him as a dunderhead who shuffled around the office in his slippers and used Coke bottles for ashtrays. He was undynamic and the magazine relied on old-time lifers who were there forever, producing sludgy, gray prose. Wolfe's was a frontal attack on an almost untouchable cultural institution. No one else had dared.

TOM WOLFE ("Tiny Mummies! The True Story of the Ruler of 43rd Street's Land of the Walking Dead," *New York* magazine, April 11, 1965):

> They have boys over there on the nineteenth and twentieth floors, the editorial offices, practically caroming off each other—

> bonk old bison heads!—at the blind turns in the hallways because of the fantastic traffic in memos. They just *call* them boys. "Boy, will you take this, please . . ." Actually, a lot of them are old men with starched white collars with the points curling up a little, "big lunch" ties, button-up sweaters, and black basket-weave sack socks, and they are all over the place transporting these thousands of messages with their kindly old elder bison shuffles.

BEN YAGODA: Shawn made probably one of the dumbest moves of his career, which was to try to use his influence with the publisher of the *Herald Tribune* to prevent the second half of the article from being published.

WILLIAM SHAWN:

> *To be technical for a moment, I think that Tom Wolfe's article on the* New Yorker *is false and libelous. But I'd rather not be technical. . . .*
>
> *I cannot believe that, as a man of known integrity and responsibility, you will allow it to reach your readers. . . . The question is whether you will stop the distribution of that issue of* New York. *I urge you to do so, for the sake of the* New Yorker *and for the sake of the* Herald Tribune. *In fact, I am convinced that the publication of that article will hurt you more than it will hurt me.*

JIM BELLOWS: I sent over Shawn's letter [to *Time* and *Newsweek*]. I let them know that the *New Yorker*'s lawyers were seeking an order of prior restraint to keep us from publishing [the second part of] Tom's article. If that wasn't a story, I didn't know what was. . . .When Jimmy Breslin learned that Shawn was desperately trying to keep the *Tribune* from publishing Tom's series, he called Shawn on the telephone and said he had a method by which this could be accomplished if Shawn would meet him at Toots Shor's bar. He never dreamed that Shawn would show up. Jimmy was at the bar, talking to friends, when he noticed a little man crawling up behind him. Jimmy took him over in the corner and said: "I can stop the publication. It's very simple—we just blow up the building!" Shawn left in a hurry.

TOM WOLFE: We began to hear from people like E. B. White. Joseph Alsop, who wrote for my own newspaper, protested. Walter Lippmann, the dean of all the national and international political pundits, wrote a letter in the *Village Voice* saying this man, Wolfe, is an ass. It doesn't get much better than that, really.

Lyndon Johnson's number one speechwriter, Richard Goodwin, called up Clay Felker. I happened to be in the office at the time. With the receiver at Clay's ear, you could practically hear [Goodwin]. He said, "This is Richard Goodwin. I'm calling from the White House." He used this phrase "I'm calling from the White House" about ten times. "I just want you to know we have never seen anything more despicable than this piece by Tom Wolfe. We're convinced it cannot continue; that's our feeling here at the White House." My God, by this time, we didn't know what they would do to us. There was the little gunboat incident in a creek off of Vietnam. They sent 500,000 soldiers over there. What were we? Clay was great. He said, "Well, Mr. Goodwin, if you will put what you just said in written form, I assure you, it will get very prominent play in the *Herald Tribune*." Of course, that was the end of that.

The pièce de résistance, however, was that for the first time in I don't know how many years, the world heard from J. D. Salinger, and people couldn't believe it. He sent a letter to Whitney. It was the most lucid and comprehensible thing he had written in a decade. It was a telegram, so he didn't want to get too wordy. It was very clear what he wrote, assuring Whitney he was gonna go to hell and there was gonna be fire down there.

J. D. SALINGER, telegram to the *Herald Tribune*, spring 1965:

> With the printing of that inaccurate and sub-collegiate and gleeful and unrelievedly poisonous article on William Shawn, the name of the *Herald Tribune*, and certainly your own will very likely never again stand for anything either respect-worthy or honorable.

GORE VIDAL: What do you make of someone like Salinger, who comes to the defense of the editor of the *New Yorker*, as though he were an important figure? The editor of the *New Yorker* is of no importance in the scheme of things, except to a writer who writes for the *New Yorker*. He makes Shawn into a master of American literature; he was just another editor.

TOM WOLFE: At first, when we heard from these people, and also from the occasional big-time outsiders like Walter Lippmann, Clay

Felker and I thought the sky was falling. I figured, well, I'm through in this town. The only thing that happened was that about ten days later Clay and I began to get invitations to parties from people we'd never met in our lives. Because in New York, a party is not a thing you invite friends to; you invite people that you think you should know. Pretty soon it was obvious that Clay and I had become, in the perversity of New York society, hot stuff.

MARC WEINGARTEN: At the *New Yorker*, the Wolfe attack really stung. If the *New Yorker* writers hadn't felt personally offended and hadn't felt there was some truth to what Wolfe was saying, they wouldn't have risen up the way they did in defense of the magazine. They felt, deep in their bones, that their time was up, that they were perhaps becoming obsolete, writing for an older audience. There was an elegiac sense of one era passing and another one beginning.

TOM WOLFE ("Lost in the Whichy Thickets," *New York* magazine, April 18, 1965):

> *The New Yorker* comes out once a week, it has overwhelming cultural prestige, it pays top prices to writers—and for forty years it has maintained a strikingly low level of literary achievement. *Esquire* comes out only once a month, yet it has completely outclassed *The New Yorker* in literary contribution even during its cheesecake days.

LAWRENCE GROBEL: Salinger got angry, a little humiliated: "Why the hell are all these people attacking me and my magazine? I'm giving and they're not taking." He receded and then, two months after "Lost in the Witchy Thickets" [the second part of Wolfe's attack on the *New Yorker*] was published, "Hapworth" appeared.

—

JANET MALCOLM: When J. D. Salinger's "Hapworth 16, 1924"—a very long and very strange story in the form of a letter from camp written by Seymour Glass when he was seven—appeared in the *New Yorker* in June 1965, it was greeted with unhappy, even embarrassed silence.

It seemed to confirm the growing critical consensus that Salinger was going to hell in a handbasket.

JOHN WENKE: That issue of the *New Yorker* [June 19, 1965] was mainly "Hapworth" and advertising; everything else was stripped out. "Hapworth" is a completely unreadable work in which an unbelievably precocious seven-year-old child offers a thirty-thousand-word reading list.

J. D. SALINGER ("Hapworth 16, 1924," *The New Yorker*, June 19, 1965):

> It was suddenly borne in upon me, utterly beyond dispute, that I love Sir Arthur Conan Doyle but do not love the great Goethe! As I darted idly through the water, it became crystal clear that it is far from an established fact that I am even demonstrably fond of the great Goethe, in my heart, while my love for Sir Arthur Conan Doyle, via his contributions, is an absolute certainty! I have rarely ever had a more revealing incident in any body of water. I daresay I shall never get any closer to drowning in sheer gratitude for a passing portion of truth. Think for a stunning moment what this means! It means that every man, woman, and child over the age, let us say, of twenty-one or thirty, at the very outside, should never do anything extremely important or crucial in their life without first consulting a list of persons in the world, living or dead, whom he loves.

JONATHAN SCHWARTZ: A seven-year-old boy at summer camp writing in an adult voice, asking for the most abstruse books to be sent to him from his parents—once you do that, you can't go back to the conventions of realistic fiction again. You've crossed a line. It's simply out of the question. In my opinion, if he's written anything since, he's moved "Hapworth" forward. To me, that's thrilling. We've had our *Franny and Zooey* and we've had our other stories, but after "Hapworth," how are you going to go back again?

BEN YAGODA: "Hapworth," published in the *New Yorker* only because of William Shawn's position and regard for Salinger, was Seymour writing from camp, and it was just too much: impossible to believe and created to be unpalatable to the public and critics.

DAVID SHIELDS: In a June 26, 1965, letter, *New Yorker* poetry editor Louise Bogan wrote, "The Salinger is a disaster. Maxwell came to call, and rather deplored its total cessation of talent."

MARC WEINGARTEN: "Hapworth" was the final manifestation of Salinger's hermetic worldview. He had retreated so far into the bunker of his mind that he was writing for an audience of one.

PAUL ALEXANDER: "Hapworth" is an indication that maybe Salinger had finally lost it.

SHANE SALERNO: The isolation of that bunker and his complete immersion in Vedanta destroyed his art. He lost the ability to create characters who are believable and not mouthpieces.

DAVID SHIELDS: Art is either quick or it's dead. Most of Salinger is quick, but "Hapworth" just seemed dead on arrival—deliberately, angrily, fascinatingly so. It's the barely sublimated anger that interests me most. After the cascade of criticism of his own work, the attack on the *New Yorker*, the relentless parade of seekers and reporters to his door, he has had enough. He finally fires back, phrasing fury as blithe indifference. He wants to maim or kill all his critics, but to admit he reads his press clippings would be anathema to the persona of spiritual seeker he has created in his fiction. "Hapworth" careens wildly between murderous rage and a desire for peace. Telling critics they can't hurt him, he's claiming to be disassociated from pain. This psychic pressure is itself a flashback to war.

CHRIS KUBICA: "Hapworth 16, 1924" wasn't received well by anybody. The questions were not literary but personal: What's happened to Salinger? Is he a crackpot?

***TIME*:** After six years of painful, reclusive silence, Author J. D. Salinger, 46, has produced another story. It's no *Catcher in the Rye* or *Franny and Zooey*—just one more refraction through his magic Glasses in the form of a fictional family's letter that Seymour Glass, the presiding guru and ghost, wrote home from Camp Hapworth, Maine, at the tender age of seven. Published in *The New Yorker*, the note is introduced briefly by Family Historian Buddy Glass, who for years has been garrulously obsessed by the memory of his suicide brother. By the letter, Childe Seymour seems to have been, practically from birth, a perfervid scholar, linguist, spiritual genius and altogether verbose little man who finds everything in life "heart-rending," or "damnable." "My emotions are too damnably raw today, I fear," he starts, and in 28,000 words plunges forth to speculate on God, reincarnation, Proust, Balzac, baseball and the charms of the camp director's wife ("quite perfect legs, ankles, saucy bosoms, very fresh, cute hind quarters"), while insistently querying his parents about "what imaginary-sensual acts gave lively, unmentionable entertainment to your minds."

DAVID HUDDLE: Think about how clean, precise, exact, and devastating "A Perfect Day for Bananafish" is. Place that beside the garrulous, chatty, tedious voice in "Hapworth 16, 1924." It's almost as if the mental acuity of Salinger is diminishing right in front of you.

JOHN WENKE: Salinger may have laughed or been disgusted at "Hapworth" 's reception. He made an artistic choice to valorize the involuted ramblings of his alter ego, Buddy Glass. The creation of Seymour is Salinger bowing out, creating a character he knew would be unpopular. It is artistic contempt coupled with an aesthetic of silence. The creation of "Hapworth" was his goodbye song to this world.

GERALDINE McGOWAN: "Hapworth" turned a lot of people away, and that suited Salinger perfectly. All the complaints that it was too cumbersome to read gave him the idea that now he was writing real art again.

LESLIE EPSTEIN: Why does that story upset people so much? "Hapworth" has a purity and integrity to it: the boldness of a boy looking us in the eye and telling us things that he makes us believe, even though he's predicting the future, predicting his own death. ("I'll live about as long as a good telephone pole, about thirty years.") He shot himself at thirty-one. People thought it was a trick. It wasn't a trick. I think it was the culmination of this struggle in Salinger to come to terms with the bullet that went through Seymour's brain. I think he succeeded in doing it in "Hapworth."

IAN HAMILTON: Nobody writes about suicide as much as Salinger without actively considering it himself. And ["Hapworth"] looks like an act of literary suicide for Salinger as well as a character suicide for Seymour. I believe Salinger keeps delaying publication because he's not quite ready to die.

DAVID SHIELDS: On the flap copy of *Raise High the Roof Beam, Carpenters and Seymour: An Introduction*, Salinger had made clear that he had more Glass stories in the works and that they would see publication soon. Nonetheless, there is little question that Salinger was driving toward no longer publishing his work, as he needed to do this to fulfill his Vedantic beliefs: withdraw from society, renounce the world. The 1965 attack on the *New Yorker* and Shawn and the baffled silence that greeted "Hapworth" must have accelerated that decision to go silent, even as Vladimir Nabokov was calling Salinger and Updike "by far the two finest artists in recent years."

—

ETHEL NELSON: I don't think Claire thought that was going to be her life with Jerry—left to do all the things for the children and make all the decisions for weeks, weeks at a time. She was alone.

SHANE SALERNO: In the summer of 1966, Claire and Jerry Salinger told their children that they were getting divorced. On September 9, 1966, Claire filed for divorce.

DAVID SHIELDS: According to Salinger's sister, Doris, Salinger should never have married.

DR. GERARD L. GAUDRAULT: Mrs. Claire Salinger has been treated by me professionally on occasions since the summer of 1966. She complained of nervous tension, sleeplessness, and loss of weight, and gave me a history of marital problems with her husband which allegedly caused her condition. My examination indicated that the condition I found would naturally follow from the complaints of marital discord given to me. I gave treatment to her for the conditions I found, and in my most recent examination of her, on September 21, 1967, I found some improvement in her condition, but the continuance of her marriage appears to prevent a complete recovery. It is my opinion that her health has been seriously injured as a result of this marital condition, and that a continuance of the marriage would seriously injure her health and cause continued physical and mental upset.

MARGARET SALINGER: No one said, "Don't talk about this. Don't think that." I mean, you don't have to to a kid. Kids pick up what the elephants are in the room that the family is not talking about.

CLAIRE DOUGLAS: The libelee, wholly regardless of his marriage covenants and duties has so treated the libelant as to injure her health and endanger her reason in that for a long period of time libelee has treated libellant with indifference, has for long periods of time refused to communicate with her, has declared that he does not love her and has no desire to have their marriage continue, by reason of which conduct the libelant has had her sleep disturbed, her nerves upset and has been subjected to nervous and mental strain, and has had to seek medical assistance to effect a cure of her condition, and a continuation of the marriage would seriously injure her health and endanger her reason.

PAUL ALEXANDER: When you read the divorce papers, it's clear that Claire was going to become the primary custodian of the children and

THE STATE OF NEW HAMPSHIRE

SULLIVAN, SS. SUPERIOR COURT September Term 1966
October Return Day

Claire Salinger

v.

Jerome D. Salinger

LIBEL FOR DIVORCE

Claire Salinger of Cornish, in the County of Sullivan and State of New Hampshire, whose mail address is R. F. D., Windsor, Vermont, complains against Jerome D. Salinger of said Cornish, his address also being R. F. D., Windsor, Vermont, and says:

he was going to provide them with support and pay for their education. Claire may have planned out where they were going to go to school and how they were going to go to school, and Salinger was going to pay for it, but interestingly enough, Salinger, who had failed in prep school, didn't mind at all sending his children to prep school. There is some inherent contradiction in that, but Salinger's life is full of inherent contradictions.

GERALDINE McGOWAN: When I read the divorce papers, it occurred to me that it nearly matches what happens in one of the short stories ["For Esmé—with Love and Squalor"]: "'What is hell? I maintain that is the suffering of being unable to love.'"

***TIME*:** Divorced: J. D. Salinger, 48, solitary author, whose Glass family chronicles have been produced painfully and slowly (only one story in the *New Yorker* in the past eight years); by Claire Salinger, 33, his second wife; after twelve years of marriage, two children; in Newport, N.H. She charged treatment "to injure health and endanger reason" based on his indifference and refusal to communicate. He did not contest.

SHANE SALERNO: At the same time that Salinger was retreating from the New York publishing world and isolating himself from Claire, his sister, Doris, a fashion coordinator for Bloomingdale's, was repeatedly quoted about the latest fashions in the *New York Times* style pages. Claire had been scared that her modeling job would turn Salinger off, but if he truly hated the frivolity of fashion and materialism, why didn't he repudiate Doris?

When Salinger and Claire divorced, she was granted, with no contest, custody of the children. She was also granted the original ninety acres that Salinger had purchased in Cornish as well as the cottage. Salinger never fought that award. He must have known that had Claire not been awarded the cottage, the land, and a considerable amount of money, she would have left Cornish. She would have taken the children with her. He allowed the divorce agreement to stand in the hope that Claire would remain in Cornish and therefore he would have his children across the road. He wound up building another home for himself, within walking distance.

After the divorce, Salinger stopped going to the bunker. He started writing in a room above the garage in the new house but would never publish again. His decision is best explained by how seriously he took the following passage from the Bhagavad Gita, II, 47–49: "You have the right to work, but for the work's sake only. You have no right to the fruits of work. Desire for the fruits of work must never be your motive in working."

ETHEL NELSON: I had a family to bring up. We moved to Connecticut. I was out of the area for a while, and when I came back and heard that Jerry and Claire had gotten divorced, I was crushed, because I hate divorce. And then I thought of Claire and what I'd seen her go through. Her children were about all grown at the time I came back to Cornish, so I thought, "She's free. Claire's free. Now she can go and become her own person." The original house is just down the road from where he is now. I think [Margaret] hit the nail on the head somewhat when she said [in her 2000 book, *Dream Catcher*] that if you weren't perfect, Dad didn't want anything to do with you. He wanted perfection. If you let him down in any way, you were no longer to be associated with him. He would not be your friend. He would not speak to you.

My mom and dad brought us kids up in a loving home. Claire did the same. Claire was a lady, and she deserved to be treated like one. Jerry didn't treat her like one. So I was glad to hear that she was free. Sorry. I'm sorry. That was hard. I just didn't like seeing anyone go through that.

I just had no idea. I'm glad I was a poor man's daughter, I really am.

SHARON STEEL: In a letter to Michael Mitchell dated October 16, 1966, Salinger [writes that] Peggy and Matthew are in New York City for a visit and a trip to the dentist. They stay at the Sherry-Netherland Hotel, in the same suite that the Beatles stayed in the last time they played New York. Peggy loves this, and Salinger loves her and Matthew—he reads in bed while they sleep in the same room, and considers them both "pretty hot stuff." The next day, he takes them to a bookstore and lunch at Reuben's, followed by "a walk on a darkened Fifth Avenue." In the meantime, Salinger stopped by the *New Yorker* offices. He tells Mitchell that he misses him quite a lot, and hopes that he's found love again since his divorce [from his ex-wife Bet].

EDWARD JACKSON BENNETT: I had moved to Cornish to live alone for a year. I was going through a divorce, and after attending to the responsibilities as publisher of the *Claremont (N.H.) Daily Eagle*, my remote cottage in Cornish was a place to retire alone to read, write, take

Salinger with his neighbors at the Cornish Fair.

long walks on remote country roads, and to generally lick my wounds and reassess life. As the harsh winter of 1968 gave way to long days of March sunshine, I would often make up a small pitcher of martinis on Sundays and sit outside in the sunshine.

On such a Sunday, J. D. Salinger sauntered by. We waved our usual silent exchange; then on the spur of the moment I said, "Come up and have a martini."

Salinger paused. Then he made his move, striding up to me with a hand extended. We made no introductions, nor were names exchanged. Instead we chatted about the hard winter, the birds, and whether or not we'd be planting peas this May in the upland country.

Salinger thanked me for the libation, but before he left I said, "I see by Friday's *Eagle* that we do have something in common besides being silent neighbors."

I pointed out to him a clipping which listed divorces granted at the January term of court. The name "Salinger" appeared next to "Bennett." Our divorce decrees had been granted, quite coincidentally, at the same time. A trace of what might be called a smile creased Salinger's somber countenance.

"You have a point there," he said, "and perhaps we share other similarities, too. Thanks for the drink."

SHANE SALERNO: Salinger never published again after "Hapworth 16, 1924." Claire Douglas became a clinical psychologist, writer, and Jungian analyst. She trained at the New York Association for Analytical Psychology and has successfully reinvented herself; in fact, as of 2013 she has published more books than her ex-husband has. She lectures and writes books and articles on Jung and women's psychology. Everything she's done has been independent of the fact that she was once married to J. D. Salinger. She has never spoken on the record about him. A 2013 biographical note about Douglas ends with this: "She is deeply grateful to live and still practice in a house on a bluff looking out over the Pacific Ocean."

J. D. SALINGER (*The Catcher in the Rye*, 1951):

> "This fall I think you're riding for—it's a special kind of fall, a horrible kind. The man falling isn't permitted to feel or hear himself hit bottom. He just keeps falling and falling. The whole

arrangement's designed for men who, at some time or other in their lives, were looking for something their own environment couldn't supply them with. Or they thought their own environment couldn't supply them with. So they gave up looking. They gave it up before they ever really even got started."

SHARON STEEL: On December 27, 1966, Salinger writes another letter to Michael Mitchell. This letter finds Salinger purging his hatred for New York City, a place that makes him feel lost. All the haunts he once enjoyed are gone—with the exception of the Museum of Natural History. A lifetime before the hipsterfication of Kings County, however, Salinger wishes he could explore Brooklyn. He has a faint hope of meeting an old Hasid "from the eighteenth century" who will invite him to his house for some soup or tea. Salinger goes on to discuss how difficult it is to find love after you've lost it. "You can't erase a person," he tells Mitchell, "anymore than they can erase you."

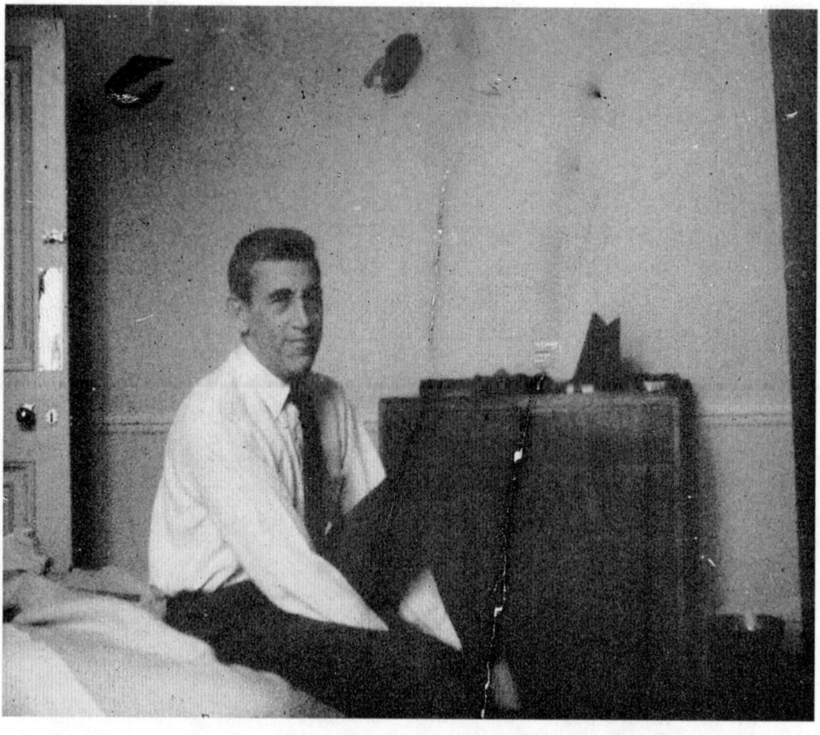

Salinger at home, in his bedroom, postdivorce, April 1968.

Conversation with Salinger #7

TOM WOLFE: Charlie Portis wrote *True Grit* and *The Dog of the South*. Before all that, he was a reporter on the *New York Herald Tribune*. We worked [there] at the same time [the early-1960s], and I remember Charlie telling me he was sent up to New Hampshire, to Concord, on some political story. He was heading back to New York on one of these little commuter flights. This was a propeller plane, and two men sitting right in front of him, one on one side of the aisle on the outside seat, one on the outside seat of the other side of the aisle, realized they know each other. They had to shout almost, because of the noise of the airplane. The one on one side said, "Well, I'll be damned. Jerry! I haven't seen you in so long! What the hell have you been up to?"

It dawned on Charlie Portis that this was J. D. Salinger. He was filling in almost the last ten years of his life for his friend, and Charlie, like any good newspaperman, is taking this down, a mile a minute.

When they landed, he went up to Salinger partly just to make absolutely dead sure this was J. D. Salinger. He said, "Mr. Salinger," and this guy turned around. Charlie said, "Hi, my name is Charles Portis. I'm from the *New York Herald Tribune*. I just happened to be sitting behind you." He said he got no further than that when Salinger turned white.

Salinger said, "You wouldn't. You wouldn't."

Charlie said to me, "You know? I wouldn't. That guy looked so awful."

Conversation with Salinger # 8

ETHEL NELSON: With Jerry's withdrawal, the part that hurt the very most for me is when my mom and I went to his new house. He had the first house where his kids grew up, and then he moved to this other house across the road. His new house had a big porch on it and a driveway, so he could could step on the porch and look down at the driveway; he hollered at us to go away and don't come up. I said, "Jerry, we're here for the Red Cross drive. You always give to it." He said, "You take any more steps toward me and I'm going to shoot at the ground right in front of you." He had his gun in his hand. He did not want people trespassing on his land. He said, "You wait a minute. I'll go in and write a check and I'll throw it down to you." That's how distrusting of people he had become. And that hurt, because we'd always been friends.

PART III

VANAPRASTHYA

WITHDRAWAL FROM SOCIETY

15

SEYMOUR'S SECOND SUICIDE

CORNISH, NEW HAMPSHIRE, 1953–2010

The one constant in Salinger's life, from the early 1950s until his death in 2010, was Advaita Vedanta Hinduism, which transformed him from a writer of fiction into a disseminator of mysticism, destroying his work and, over time, causing him to turn silent in order to fulfill the final stages of his religious doctrine. As a writer, when he was lost, he was found, and when he was found, he was lost: at his height, Salinger was writing to save his own soul; by the end, to the degree he was writing at all, he was writing to inform you how you could save your soul.

—

DAVID SHIELDS and SHANE SALERNO: Salinger's mother was born into a Catholic family and converted to Judaism; his father was Jewish. Salinger could follow neither faith. He explored Scientology, Hinduism, Ayurveda, Christian Science, and Zen Buddhism; as drawn as he was to Buddhism, he recoiled from its atheism. He also explored bodily therapies, such as Kriya yoga, homeopathy, acupuncture, and macrobiotics.

In 1988, Ian Hamilton wrote, "For some years, Salinger has needed to set his gaze on some high purpose, and his dedication to his craft has often had a monkish tinge. Up until 1952, the order he aimed to belong to was an order based on 'talent' as if it were the same thing as 'enlightenment' and [now he] will seek in the curricula of holy men as a way of dissolving what has all along been for him an irritating, hard to manage separation between art and life, that is to say, his art, his life."

In our research we have discovered that as early as 1946 Salinger learned about Vedanta Hinduism from Somerset Maugham's novel *The Razor's Edge*, which explains the most important ideas of Advaita Vedanta. The book's epigraph—"The sharp edge of a razor is difficult to pass over; / thus the wise say the path to Salvation is hard"—is from *Katha Upanishad*, a holy text of Hinduism, and the novel consists of Laurence "Larry" Durrell's search for spiritual meaning after his best friend dies in World War I while saving Larry's life. According to Margaret, even before *Catcher* was published in 1951, Salinger had become friends with the Zen adept D. T. Suzuki, had meditated at a "Zen center"—actually, the retreat of the Ramakrishna-Vivekananda Center—in the Thousand Islands region of northern New York, and was thinking seriously of becoming a monk.

After *Catcher*, Salinger became increasingly devoted to and influenced by Advaita Vedanta Hinduism, the religious and philosophical teachings that Swami Vivekananda brought to the West in 1893. Salinger's discovery of *The Gospel of Sri Ramakrishna* (translated by Swami Nikhilananda and Joseph Campbell and published by the Ramakrishna-Vivekananda Center of New York) was a major event in his life, second only to the war. The damage the war wrought compelled him to seek not only transcendence but erasure.

—

From his introduction to Vedanta until his death in 2010, Salinger's life strictly followed the four stages of life, or *asramas*, as explained by Salinger's spiritual teacher Swami Nikhilananda:

1. *Brahmacharya*: the stage of study, apprenticeship. The apprentice should be celibate, injure no living thing, honor his parents and teachers, and study the scriptures. During this phase of his life, Salinger attended classes, wrote for the slicks, and went to war. Though he did not become a disciple until the early 1950s, when he was in his early thirties, he never consummated his relationship with Oona O'Neill, Jean Miller had to throw herself at him to get him to respond, and Leila Hadley Luce describes her dates with Salinger as Platonic. In

"Teddy," the protagonist says, "I never saw such a bunch of apple-eaters."

According to a proponent of Vedanta and Buddhism, Donald Simons, in 1952, while reading *The Gospel of Sri Ramakrishna*, Salinger "experienced a transformation. . . . [He told his friends about] a profound change in his life"; according to the Center, it was a "life-altering" experience for Salinger. Drawn toward Vedanta's ideas about detachment, celibacy, karma, and reincarnation, Salinger attempted, also in 1952, to get his British publisher, Hamish Hamilton, to issue a complete edition of what Salinger called "the religious book of the century."

2. *Garhasthya*: the householder stage, when one should marry, create and support a family, and contribute to the welfare of the community. To restate briefly: Now this previously somewhat monastic and nomadic man bought a house in Cornish, married, and fathered two children. *The Gospel of Sri Ramakrishna* advises, "A man may live in a mountain cave, smear his body with ashes, observe fasts, and practice austere discipline, but if his mind dwells on worldly objects, on 'woman and gold,' I say, 'Shame on him!' 'Woman and gold' are the most fearsome enemies of the enlightened way, and woman rather more than gold, since it is woman that creates the need for gold. For woman one man becomes the slave of another, and so loses his freedom. Then he can not act as he likes." Ramakrishna admonishes a husband who enjoys making love with his wife, "Aren't you ashamed of yourself? You have children and still you enjoy intercourse with your wife? Don't you hate yourself for thus leading an animal life? Don't you hate yourself for dallying with a body which contains only blood, phlegm, filth, and excreta?" In 1954, Salinger and Claire found a new guru, Paramahansa Yogananda, who believed that women could be holy and marriage sacred. Margaret believes that her father would never have married and raised children without Yogananda's guidance.

According to Margaret, both Salinger and Claire read Yogananda's *Autobiography of a Yogi* and asked the Self-Realization Fellowship to recommend a teacher-guru; the nearest disciple was Swami Premananda, in Washington, D.C., who in 1955 agreed to initiate them as householder devotees. "They were instructed to abstain from eating breakfast on the day of their arrival and to bring offerings of fresh fruit, flowers, and a little money." According to Simons, Salinger and Claire were initiated into "Kriya yoga in a Hindu temple in Washington, D.C., whereupon they received a mantra and practiced pranayama (breathing exercises) twice a day."

Claire told her daughter, "On the train home to Cornish that evening, Jerry and I made love in our sleeper car. It was so nice to. We did not make love very often . . . [since] the body was evil. . . . I'm certain I became pregnant with you that night."

Why, in 1959, did Salinger break his silence to write a letter to the *New York Post* in which he argued against mandatory life sentences for mass murderers? Was he newly empathetic to the incarcerated of Sing Sing? It's difficult not to see his letter as an extraordinarily apposite trope for the life sentence in which he found himself: wanting desperately to break out of the maximum security prison of his own (war-shadowed) ego.

He was so damaged from the war that not only was he using religion to make the most important decisions about his life—marriage, children, work—but he needed to yield control of his life to another authority. In effect, he was no longer a free agent.

Also in 1959, James Thurber published *The Years with Ross*, which was highly critical of Harold Ross; Salinger composed a twenty-five to thirty-page defense of Ross, which the *Saturday Review* turned down owing to its "length and unusual style." Salinger's interest in mentors, gurus, and swamis led him into bombast here and elsewhere.

3. *Vanaprasthya*: when the householder's children have left home and he is too old to be of much practical use to his community, he should withdraw from society and retire into the forest, where his responsibility is to continue his religious studies. For Salinger, this stage appears to have begun when he was forty-six. In 1965 he stopped publishing, preparing himself for the final stage of Vedanta (renunciation).

In 1967 he wrote to Swami Nikhilananda, "I, too, have been reading about Stalin's daughter, and I can well understand your inclination to offer her those three books, simply as a gift." Salinger is being used here, awkwardly, as a liaison, but both he and Swami Nikhilananda must insist on the otherworldliness of the mission. "It seems to me that the *Life of Swami Vivekananda* might appeal to her especially at this period of her life. I'm thinking, of course, of the chapters telling about Swami Vivekananda's life in America. The people, the lectures, the press, the kindnesses, the prejudices, the generosities, the good and not-so-good of it, the bitter and sweet of it."

In *The Influence of Eastern Thoughts on "Teddy" and the Seymour Glass Stories of J. D. Salinger*, Sumitra Paniker notes that "Brahmadrari Buddha Chaitanya . . . who works with the Ramakrishna Vivekananda Centre in London, in a letter dated July 18, '69 wrote: 'Salinger presented the Swami [Nikhilananda] with a copy of *Franny and Zooey* when it was first published, and I saw the inscription by the author, but the exact wording escapes me now. Something about Salinger's being able to circulate the ideas of Vedanta only through the medium of such stories as these, and expressing appreciation for his contacts with the Swami.'" Salinger did indeed keep writing, though not publishing, and the work is focused heavily on Vedantic ideas.

In 1972 Salinger wrote to Swami Nikhilananda:

> *I'm so sorry about your need of the wheel chair and the chair-lift. I sometimes wish that the East had deigned to concentrate some small part of its immeasurable genius to the petty art or science of keeping the body well and fit. Between extreme indifference to the body and the most extreme and zealous attention to it (Hatha Yoga), there seems to be no useful middle ground whatever, and that seems to me one more unnecessary sadness in Maya. . . . I've forgotten many worthy and important things in my life, but I have never forgotten the way you used to read from, and interpret, the Upanishads, up at Thousand Island Park. . . .*
>
> *With great affection and respect, always,*
> *Sincerely, J. D. Salinger*

Later in 1972, Salinger wrote to Swami Nikhilananda to express his gratitude to the man who had guided him out of his "long dark night." At this point, healing the wound had become immeasurably more important to Salinger than transforming the wound, as becomes clear in a letter he wrote in 1973 to Swami Adiswarananda: "Part XVI of 'Vital Steps Toward Meditation' is beautifully saturated with *Vivekachucamani*. That marvelous and incomparable book. It was one of the first books Swami Nikhilananda recommended to me, many years ago. Almost every sloka speaks volumes. 'In the forest-tract of sense pleasures there prowls a huge tiger called the mind. Let good people who have a longing for Liberation never go there.' I suspect that nothing is truer than that, and yet I allow myself to be mauled by that old tiger almost every wakeful minute of my life." There it is: Salinger's life story and spiritual autobiography in nine words: *forest-tract*; *sense pleasures*; *tiger*; *mind*; *liberation*; *mauled*; *wakeful.* If the mind must be renounced, writing is over.

In 1975 Salinger wrote again to Swami Adiswarananda, "I read a bit from the [Bhagavad] Gita every morning before I get out of bed, Swami Nikhilananda's annotated version. (It seems such a reasonable pleasure to imagine that [the eighth-century mystic] Shankara would have approved unreservedly of Swami's inspired intelligence, devotion, and authority. How could he not?)" It's striking how verbally and syntactically simple Salinger's letters to the swamis are; perhaps they were written this way to ensure that they could be understood by correspondents for whom English was not their first language. Even so, Salinger seems to be teaching himself how to write and think in as plain and flat a manner as possible.

4. *Sannyasa*: the stage in which one renounces the world, becomes a wandering monk, and is honored as a spiritual leader of society. By giving up the world, one becomes a *sannyasin*, a holy man. It's impossible to write in such a state, let alone publish. According to the announcement of his death, Salinger "had remarked that he was in this world but not of it."

For the last five decades of his life, Salinger had an enduring relationship with the Ramakrishna-Vivekananda Center and its founder, Swami Nikhilananda. He accepted the swami as a spiritual teacher, attending services and classes at the Center, located at 17 East Ninety-fourth Street in Manhattan (just three blocks north of his parents' apartment), and also at the Vivekananda Cottage retreat in Thousand Island Park.

On April 12, 2013, "To preserve the legacy of J. D. Salinger's association with the Ramakrishna-Vivekananda Center and the significance of Vedanta in his life, and to commemorate the 150th birthday of Swami Vivekananda," at New York's Morgan Library and Museum, the Ramakrishna-Vivekananda Center of New York presented a gift to the Morgan: a collection of more than twenty letters (and related papers) written by Salinger to Swami Nikhilananda, to his successor Swami Adiswarananda, and to the Center.

—

Ramakrishna died in 1886. His student, Vivekananda, popularized Vedanta in the West in the late nineteenth century. Tolstoy called Vivekananda "the most brilliant wise man. It is doubtful in this age that another man has ever risen above this selfless, spiritual meditation." Other adherents of Vedanta were Jung, Gandhi, Santayana, Henry Miller (a lifelong devotee), Aldous Huxley (who called Vedanta "the most profound and subtle utterances about the nature of Ultimate Reality"), and George Harrison, according to whom Vedanta has one goal: "the realization of God." Harrison also said, "If there is a God, we must see him. And if there is a soul, we must perceive it." The author A. L. Bardach summarizes Vedanta's conception of the mind as a drunken monkey stung by a scorpion and then consumed by a demon. In Vedanta, "the same mind, when subdued and controlled, becomes a most trusted friend and helper, guaranteeing peace and happiness." Salinger's work from 1952 to 1965 is an increasingly explicit attempt to perform these actions: to realize God, see God, perceive the soul, and subdue and control his own and the reader's demons, guaranteeing peace and happiness.

The teachings of Vedanta are rooted in the Vedas, ancient Sanskrit texts from India that underlie Buddhism and Hinduism.

Vedanta: "God is everywhere." Teddy: "All she was doing was pouring God into God."

Vedanta: "Each soul is potentially divine." Zooey: "There isn't anyone *any*where that isn't Seymour's Fat Lady. Don't you know that? Don't you know that goddam secret yet? And don't you know—*listen* to me, now—*don't you know who that Fat Lady really is?* . . . Ah, buddy. Ah, buddy. It's Christ Himself. Christ Himself, buddy."

Vedanta: "The goal is to manifest that divinity within by controlling nature, external and internal." Zooey: "Detachment, buddy, and only detachment."

Vedanta: "As soon as I think of myself as a little body, I want to preserve it, protect it, to keep it nice, at the expense of other bodies. Then you and I become separate." Buddy: "An unknown boy ('some shnook he never saw before in his *life*') had come up to Waker and asked him for his bicycle, and Waker had handed it over. Neither Les nor Bessie, of course, was unmindful of Waker's 'very nice, generous intentions,' but both of them also saw the details of the transaction with an implacable logic of their own. What, substantially, they felt that Waker should have done—and Les now repeated this opinion, with great vehemence, for Seymour's benefit—was to give the boy a nice, long ride on the bicycle. Here Waker broke in, sobbing. The boy didn't *want* a nice, long ride, he wanted the *bicycle*. He'd never *had* one, the boy; he'd always *wanted* one. I looked at Seymour. He was getting excited."

—

From *Catcher* onward, Salinger's work became more and more one of "translation" and popularization—taking the metaphysical and religious ideas with which he was consumed and finding ways of disseminating these ideas by making them vivid, funny, and attractive to his (largely secular or at least non-Hindu) readership. As his audience grew, his concerns became increasingly abstruse, and he had trouble bridging that gap.

Surely, one of the main reasons he stopped publishing was the difficulty of being the servant of two masters, art and religion. His intolerance of civilian life in New York. His flight into isolation. His love of uniformity. His experience of critical attacks as a revisitation of the shelling. His hatred of intellectual dissection. His need for very young girls, healers, nursemaids, innocents to rewind the clock. His homeopathy as battle triage. His need for control—titles, commas, everything else. His short temper. His hatred of being touched by strangers. His taste in movies. His driving his Jeep "like a nutcase." His silence, above all his literary silence as an acknowledgment that there is no way to ever redeem the dead. By his own admission, Salinger was "a condition, not a man." That condition, from 1945 until his death in 2010, was PTSD.

Many commentators have claimed that Salinger made art his religion; instead, suffering from PTSD and searching for meaning and God, he made religion his art. Salinger's work became increasingly informed by and then inundated by references and odes to Christ, St. Francis, Buddha, Sri Ramakrishna, Vivekananda, Shankaracharya, Lao-tzu, Chuang-tzu, and Hui-neng—all of whom are, to a greater or lesser extent, antihierarchical religious prophets. Remember grunts' contempt for REMFs: rear-echelon motherfuckers. Just as he gave over command of his life to religion, he now gave over his work.

Story by story, from "Teddy" forward, Salinger's work moves from religion as a factor or even a crutch in his characters' lives to religion as the only thing in their lives that matters to the work's entire purpose being to cryptically convey religious dogma. As the author A. L. Bardach says and as we have noted earlier, Salinger "confided to Nikhilananda that he intentionally left a trail of Vedantic clues throughout his work from *Franny and Zooey* onward, hoping to entice readers into deeper study."

"Teddy" appeared in the *New Yorker* on January 31, 1953, to much acclaim, angst, and controversy. Readers debated who died, who killed whom—ten-year-old Teddy walks into his own death, allowing his sister, Booper, to push him into the empty pool—and were uncomfortable with the willful death of a child, which goes to the very core of the story. "The trouble is most people don't want to see things the way they are," Teddy informs Bob Nicholson, with his wonderfully ordinary name. "They don't even want to stop getting born and dying all the time. They just want new bodies all the time, instead of stopping and staying with God, where it's really nice." Many of Teddy's observations throughout the story are explicitly Vedantic ("I met a lady, and I sort of stopped meditating"), but the story is under exquisite formal control. Religion is still, just barely, serving art.

The same is true for "Franny." Throughout the novella, which was published in the *New Yorker* on January 29, 1955, Franny is taking the Salingerian/Vedantic line:

> I'm sick to death of just liking people. I wish to God I could meet somebody I could respect.
>
> I am just sick of ego, ego, ego.
>
> I mean all these really advanced and unbogus religious persons that keep telling you if you repeat the name of God incessantly, something *happens*. Even in India. In India, they tell you to meditate on the "Om," which means the same thing, really, and the exact same result is supposed to happen.

The reader is meant to sympathize and fall in love with Franny, but we still read at least partway *through* her, past her, into her psyche. We're not meant to view her, quite yet, as a godhead.

"Raise High the Roof Beam, Carpenters," which appeared in the November 19, 1955, *New Yorker*, is a crucial transition for Salinger's work, since for its first three-quarters it's an elaborately and brilliantly rendered account of a wedding day "flatting," and then Seymour's diaries take over the proceedings. From here on we will get tighter and more glamorous close-ups of Swami Seymour, an enlightened being who is trying to teach certain key concepts to his younger siblings (who are trapped performing such lower-level activities as acting, writing, and teaching) before he kills himself. Salinger's answers, delivered almost always through Seymour, are invariably taken directly from Vedanta. Seymour: "I've been reading a miscellany of Vedanta all day."

Which is pretty much what happens, or doesn't happen, in "Zooey" (*The New Yorker*, May 4, 1957). Not that anything has to "happen" in a work of fiction. It's not the stasis of "Zooey" that kills the pleasure of the text for many critics; it's the syrupy certainty of the solution. Zooey tells Franny, "One thing I *know*. And don't get upset. It isn't anything bad. But if it's the religious life you want, you ought to know right now that you're missing out on every single goddam religious action that's going on around this house. You don't even have enough sense to *drink* when somebody brings you a cup of consecrated chicken soup—which is the only kind of chicken soup Bessie ever brings to anybody around this madhouse." Think how far we've come from Teddy's pouring God into God. We were with Teddy; we're being *enlightened* by Zooey. Certainty has won out. In "Seymour: An Introduction," appearing in the June 6, 1959, *New Yorker*, Buddy Glass says, "I tend to regard myself, if at all by anything as sweet as an Eastern name, as a fourth-class Karma Yogin, with perhaps a little Jnana Yoga thrown in to spice up the pot." Buddy is referring to two related Vedantic concepts, that of the four *yogas* or paths to salvation, and that of the four *asramas* or stages of life. Salinger saw his own spiritual progress in precisely the same terms. By now, form and content have come completely apart: "Seymour" feels like outtakes from *The Gospel of Sri Ramakrishna*, and Bardach sees *Franny and Zooey*, when published together, as an "emotional, humorous, and easily understood version of *The Bhagavad Gita*," with its preaching of selfless action.

For most readers, if "Seymour" comes right up to the precipice of legibility, logic, and sense, "Hapworth 16, 1924" (*The New Yorker*, June 19, 1965) falls into the crevice. Wisdom delivery system overrules realistic representation: seven-year-old Seymour delivering arias on philosophy and religion. Buddy types up Seymour's impossibly rococo letter for us, adding an extra layer of discipleship between us and the godhead, in a way that's exactly reminiscent of the layers of discipleship in *The Gospel of Sri Ramakrishna*, a quotation from which appears on Seymour and Buddy's beaverboard. Seymour says, "*Raja-Yoga* and *Bhaki-Yoga*, two heartrending, handy, quite tiny volumes, perfect for the pockets of any average, mobile boys our age, by Vivekananda of India. He is one of the most exciting, original and best equipped giants of this century I have ever run into; my personal sympathy for him will never be outgrown or exhausted as long as I live, mark my words; I would easily give ten years of my life, possibly more, if I could have shaken his hand or at least said a brisk, respectful hello to him on some busy street in Calcutta or elsewhere." This is literal hagiography.

After *Catcher*, Salinger was no longer a novelist per se, and in a sense it's possible to see him as no longer especially devoted to fiction writing, at least as conventionally understood. He was seeking to write, and indeed was writing "wisdom literature"—metaphysical uplift—adapting Eastern satori for Western consumption. As Som P. Ranchan writes in

An Adventure in Vedanta: J. D. Salinger's The Glass Family:

> One of the visions of the great Vedantist Vivekananda was to bring the message of Vadanta from the cloisters and the forest where it was first discovered and propounded by the sages and the disciples into the mainstream of daily existence. It is a tribute to the creative genius of Salinger that he has done it. He has brought it into the routine of teaching, acting. He has brought it into a New York apartment, into its living room, bedroom. He has brought the Ganges from the head of Siva into the tub where Zooey splashes like a porpoise while reading his [brother's] letter replete with Zen satories and Vedantin affirmations. He has broadcast it coast to coast through a quiz program and that too from the voices of children. He makes us smoke it through cigarettes and cigars. While we inhale the acrid smoke from the freshly-lit cigars of Zooey, as we travel in taxis with crooked taximeters, while rummaging through loaded ashtrays, he makes Vedanta real—something that Raja Rao the self-confessed Vedantist could not do. Vedanta thus ceases to be the sacred preserve of the monks. . . . In a word, the vision of Ramakrishna is made real with such fun, mischief, metaphysical seriousness and profound, symbolic gravity. Finally, it must be said that Salinger has profound grasp of the methods of action exemplified in Franny and Zooey, of worship leading to gnosis exemplified in Buddy, and of gnosis and love exemplified in Seymour, and in the beginning and the end and behind them all, exemplars of various approaches stands the dynamic Mother Bessie who is the crazy, cosmic vibration of Prema, and love.

In "'The Holy Refusal': A Vedantic Interpretation of J. D. Salinger's Silence," Dipti Pattanaik writes, "Thus the conventional quest theme of *Catcher* gradually gives way to stories which deal more and more with mysticism. From the busiest places in the world Salinger moves in his later stories to narcissistic autonomous families and cocooned individuals. Like the shift of themes there is predictable shrinking of language. From Holden's slang, signifying a language of mass consumption, there is movement towards a solipsistic voice—a voice that is often a monologue (Buddy's), confiding secrets ([Seymour's] letter), offering an advice (Zooey's advice to Franny), or speaking to and about itself (Buddy as an artist talking about the intricacies of writing a fiction)—almost a voice of the monastery."

Indeed, Salinger's late novellas—"Zooey," "Seymour," "Hapworth," with their loose form, overlapping tales, diary entries, letters, Socratic dialogues, dueling swami-wisdom jousting tournaments—resemble nothing so much as *The Gospel of Sri Ramakrishna*. The man and writer who had once been opposed to all established authorities and guidelines had succumbed to the rules of a religion and, in so doing, had absolutely nowhere to go but deeper into the forest of his own silence.

Three key Vedantic tenets, as summarized by Bardach: "You are not your body"; "You are not your mind"; "Renounce name and fame." Relief from Salinger's anatomy; relief from postwar psychic trauma; the last forty-five years of his life. His commitment to Vedanta was, by far, the most serious and long-lasting commitment of his life. His religious devotion exists in direct relation to his postwar trauma—it's a heartbreaking attempt to retire it—but it wound up being his second suicide mission. War killed him the first time; Vedanta, the second.

Conversation with Salinger #9

A. SCOTT BERG: I never met Salinger, but I came close. In the early 1970s, when I was researching my book on Max Perkins [the legendary editor of Hemingway, Fitzgerald, and Thomas Wolfe], I spent a lot of time with all the Perkins relatives. Some of them lived up in the ancestral home of the Everetts and the Perkinses, which is in Windsor, Vermont. Right across the longest covered bridge in the United States, which crosses the Connecticut River, is Cornish, New Hampshire.

I went up to visit Max Perkins's sister, a woman named Fanny Cox—Mrs. Archibald Cox Sr., the mother of the Watergate prosecutor, Archibald Cox. She invited me to dinner. As we were sitting at dinner, I said, "Gosh, you know, as I was driving up, it occurred to me that across the covered bridge is Cornish, New Hampshire. J. D. Salinger lives over there. Have you ever seen him?" She said, "Well, why do you want to know?" I said, "I was just curious." She said, "As a matter of fact, he sat in that chair you're sitting in just last night. I served him dinner, just the way I'm serving you dinner." I said, "You're—you're kidding." She said, "No. He comes over here regularly because he comes over to pick up his mail and do some shopping on this side of the river."

Fanny Cox was then in her eighties. She looked like this great American pioneer woman, something between Jane Darwell in *The Grapes of Wrath* and Beulah Bondi [a character actress who specialized in maternal roles; she played Mrs. Bailey in *It's a Wonderful Life*]. She *was* the United States of America. We chatted about Max Perkins and this and that. Then I said, "Listen, J. D. Salinger was here? He was here just last night?" She said, "Oh, are you a great fan of J. D. Salinger?" I said, "Actually, I'm not really, but he's J. D. Salinger. Shouldn't I want to go to Cornish to see him?" She said, "Well, do you have anything to say to him?" I said, "Not really." She said, "If I had J. D. Salinger to dinner, what would you want to know?" I said, "I'd want to know if he's still writing." She said, "Yes, he's still writing." I said, "Okay." She said, "Is there anything else you'd want to know?" I said, "No, just that he's okay." She said, "He's fine. So there is no reason for you ever to see him, is there?" Dinner was over. That was that. It's the closest I got to J. D. Salinger.

16

DEAR MISS MAYNARD

CORNISH, NEW HAMPSHIRE, 1972–1973

Joyce Maynard is a world-weary eighteen-year-old Yale freshman who becomes famous when, on April 23, 1972, she publishes a *New York Times Magazine* cover story, "An 18-Year-Old Looks Back on Life," about what it's like to be a world-weary eighteen-year-old Yale freshman: "We inherited a previous generation's hand-me-downs and took in the seams, turned up the hems, to make our new fashions. We took drugs from the college kids and made them a high-school commonplace. We got the Beatles, but not those lovable look-alikes in matching suits with barber cuts and songs that made you want to cry. They came to us like a bad joke—aged, bearded, discordant. And we inherited the Vietnam War just after the crest of the wave—too late to burn draft cards and too early not to be drafted. The boys of 1953—my year—will be the last to go."

Salinger, fifty-three, who doesn't believe in author photographs, is captivated by Maynard's cover photograph and dying-swan syntax. During their nine-month relationship he will wind up telling Maynard, "I couldn't have created a character as perfect as you." Maynard will later say, "In his letters he appears to be talking about me. Reading what he has to say now, I see something else. His letters are about himself." Here, in excerpts from these letters—which were later sold and removed from the public record, but which we have now obtained—is the only self-portrait available of a man who had removed himself from the public eye decades before.

Dear Miss Maynard,

A few unsolicited words in strictest privacy, if you can bear it, from a countryman, of sorts, one who is not only an equally half-and-half and right-handed New Hampshire resident but, even more rare and exciting, perhaps the last active Mousketeer east of the White House. . . . My guess is that you'll be receiving a pretty interesting-peculiar assortment of letters as a result of this past Sunday's Times Magazine. In my probably over-earnest way, I ask you to be almost inhumanly cautious about accepting any offers or invitations that come in from anybody and everybody—publishers, editors, *Mademoiselle* staff people, television talk-show hosts, movie people, etc.

Do, please, watch over your own talent with some realistic (or duly cynical or bitter) awareness that no one else is really fit to do it. I know a little bit about the risks and rather doubtful attractions of early publication.

I think you're sounder of mind, limb, and psyche than I ever was at eighteen. Better wired. . . . You're twice the writer and observer at eighteen that I was—ten times, if not more. I was immature, melodramatic, full of self-protective lies, ruses. I wrote and wrote, but badly, really badly. . . . I needn't have suggested so glumly that you let things build rather slowly. "Fame and success." No great worry for you because you're both clever and intelligent, I think. One good mouthful of it and the taste for it alters, drastically or Subtly. Surely "fame" for a practicing writer is mostly comprised of assorted forms of conspicuousness, and nearly all of them, while they last, interruptive and more.

Be determinedly wise.

I feel a need to make it pretty clear to you, first, that I'm not wise, at all, and it would shake me more than a little if you thought I might be. I'm mainly just middleaged, suspicious, untrusting, solipsist—a "dirty Capricornian" some new and valued friend called me at dinner in N.Y. last week, in the same awful boat with Howard Hughes and Richard Nixon.

I've spent a great part of my life in grave and increasingly sad doubt about almost every value I've ever had a good, long look at. My little conclusions about this and that sometimes almost sound wise to *me*, even, but I'm not really taken in, because I really and truly haven't the character, the strength of character, to be wise.

I'd like to clear the way for us to be friends without any hitchy illusions. I think we almost certainly are friends. *Landsmen*, if you know that old intelligent Central European word.

I'm not surprised that you see already that the written word from strangers holds frightening power. . . . More formidable still, strangers use that power with such maddening insensitivity, lack of responsibility. . . . Half the time, one isn't even written to—one's written at. In my heaviest publishing years, the whole damn setup very nearly undid me. I must say I handled the whole thing, all those years, with something horribly close to masterly incompetence. I did just about everything wrong, responded to everything in the most uncool way imaginable. A few letters, over the years—a very few—were on the wonderful side. . . . The odd, rare letter from a sort of kinsman or kinswoman or kinschild. But those were very rare, and I can tell you without fake modesty (because it has nothing to do with modesty) that maybe no fiction writer living has had more bagfuls of public mail than I have.

Friends, relatives—they're hell on the practising writer, too. *My* relatives, at least—the ones I begrudgingly and gracelessly and forcibly acknowledge as relatives—I grew to loathe during my years of most conspicuous success. Every relative of mine took unto herself or himself an emotional piece of action. Or worse. . . . You've seen a little of that in the last couple of weeks, haven't you. The new life in the dining hall at Yale. Envy, resentment, fawning.

I think I'm as sure as I am of anything that you are a natural writer, if there is such a thing. . . . So, please, let neither yourself nor any maddening friends or relatives or lovers or critics give you any great or lasting doubts about that. . . . Do your work, do the kind of writing you like to do, and try very hard to be cool about the rest, to allow nobody in newsstandland to push your private buttons. Let nobody out there make you either grieve or worry inordinately—or, just as important, maybe more, let nobody's opinion or two-cents about your output make you inordinately *happy*.

I'm sort of a fifty-three-year-old pantywaist and indoors country type.

I love to shoot pool, or used to.

If you'd like to go on Mr.-Salingering me, please do—whatever suits you—but nearly everybody calls me Jerry except myself.

It's hard to be real, but landsmen stand as good a chance of simply talking together by mail as anybody else.

One of my time-eating interests, passions, is Medicine, anything that concerns healing, repairing, or just generally offsetting disintegration. . . . Both kids are tremendously experienced in recounting symptoms to me—a detailed, really careful recital of symptoms. It's terribly touching, or at least is when I'm detached enough to think of it that way. In the end, it may be the one thing of any use that I may be able to give them.

You may wonder what's a Fiction Writer doing getting himself all wound up for years and years with medical philosophy, therapy. I've done more or less the same thing with some aspects of religious philosophy, mysticism, and a few other things. Sometimes I get sidetracked from my own fictions for long months at a time, even a year or two a time, and it's sort of a worry to me, but not always. Somebody could glibly say that all interruption of work routines is probably "karmic," and God knows I've used and abused and even wallowed in that brilliant and really perilous word in my life, but the word hasn't been coming to my mind lately, and I'm glad and relieved about it—I seem to get along best when I let my mind steer clear of *all* attractive Far-Eastern glossary words, marvelous and sui-generis as those words can be.

I loved all your letter, and the way your mind goes, works, and one of the reasons I couldn't get a mailable letter out to you all weekend was that I caught myself writing to you as though we were of an age, alumni of the same years, wars, marriages, books, etc., and what you really are is an eighteen-year-old girl, though not like any other.

I think there is no limit to what you can do in your lifetime if you want to, Joyce.

This last thing, the Measure for Measure production, must have been a big strain. That whole production couldn't sound more 1972, more With It. Almost every public step taken, in the arts or anywhere, seems to be in a nether direction, downward, maggotward. . . . I don't know anything for sure about sex—I would swear no writer does or he wouldn't have bothered all that much to be a writer in the first place—but I think the Masters and Johnson report was one of the worst things that could have happened to girls and boys, males and females, in our time. A good friend and counsellor of mine is a Reichian psychiatrist . . . and I asked him if he didn't think the whole Masters and Johnson study was fallacious because it was made in our time and our culture, at a time when all true and real orgasmic normalcy is withheld or partially withheld, and he jumped up, in real excitement, and said *yes*.

I watch a terrible amount of television. . . . I'm a natural watcher. I can watch the worst of anything on television if the set's on. . . . I do know the show Let's Make a Deal—all those afternoon souls who have been directed to squeal incontinently when they win the stereo-broiler-exercycle combinations, the same way those couples on The Newlyweds have been instructed to kiss or bump heads when their answers tally. . . . I've seen some of the early Andy Griffith–Mayberry half-hours, with Opie, Barney (who was once marvelously and incessantly called Bernie by some out-of-town trollops).

Oh, actors! I was one myself once. . . . I don't really like theater as *theater*. I don't like Curtains, I don't like entrances, exits, movement on stage, larger-than-life readings of lines. I don't like "beautiful" sets, I don't like bare sets. Directors, producers, programs—there's magic in it all, no doubt, but it acts on my system like small amounts of poison.

I love, really love, writing for the printed page. . . . What I *love*, what intrigues me, is the little theater inside the private reader's head. Maybe, in fact surely, not *all* private readers' heads. . . . I don't read much fiction anymore.

I myself have never had Sheer Guts. I've chickened out of many things, but many. . . . I don't think not having some courage necessarily disqualifies anyone from certain kinds of bravery. I myself have been peculiarly brave, unnoticeably brave, a few times in my life, and I have never felt like a "coward" for not having much natural or ready courage. . . .

The very few people I have known whom I've considered to be out-and-out cowards were in most popular respects fearless insensitives. I once shared a foxhole for part of an afternoon with a nearly fearless lout, and it was a revelation.

You're surely not lacking *anything* important, Joyce. That piece you did for the Times Magazine Section was written by a girl who has everything.

I really don't understand these exchanges between us, this kind of talking we do. I can tell you I'm not accustomed to any of it. . . . If it's sometimes hard to write back and forth, maybe it could be because we are, or have the makings of, close friends, but on short acquaintance. Hurray for us for managing anyway!

I haven't shaved in a week. . . . I look like a black-hat type in a Monogram Western.

Just in case of anything at all, my phone number here is 603-675-5244.

Next Saturday . . . I'll be driving down to Boston to collect Peggy and her stuff—end of term. I thought of asking you what you might think of [a] handshake between us, on the way, but I think while you have work going, work-about-to-be-finished, that's probably not such a hot idea. Still it would be so very nice, from my point of view, to meet you before too very long.

If you'd left four-foot margins in the last letter, I think I'd be replying, responding, to every word in it. . . . I want to answer or answer back to little tiny worries and things in your letter. . . . I think I tend to form lasting attachments to anything personal you say in my direction. Miss Maynard.

You really have to let me defend myself against the accusation that I overestimate you. . . . You also said, in this last letter, that I make you feel much more special than you really are. . . . Something in or around it all, your writing, lets me have peace, satisfaction, arouses affection in me, makes me feel all right. . . . Your mind happens to put me in a nondescript state of armistice. Your words suit me. When you call yourself Good-sense-ish, the word calms me, works on me just right—I'm both happy and not surprised that you consciously or unconsciously discarded Sensible for this much better, righter word. . . . For me, you write and think the way you look.

About the world being full of people with whom I'd feel equally close if they, not you, came to visit. . . . It's utterly unlike me . . . to walk into a news store in Windsor on a Sunday morning with a Guest. . . . It seemed natural to appear there with you.

I, too, have never had a friendship like this. At no time. It makes me cheerful, even outwardly, on the whole. For instance, I smile (I think) at your tendency to look ahead and worry that we'll make each other miserable. It's exactly the kind of grey reflection that usually goes through *my* head. . . . I don't picture us making each other miserable, and what I don't picture I don't tend to believe. Do you picture us making each other miserable? (I said do you, not can you.)

I can see that I might sometimes hover, watch you anxiously. Partly my age, partly not my age, at all—there is a yin, a pretty feminine side to my nature that crops out; I'm as maternal with kids, for instance, my own or not necessarily just my own, as I am paternal. . . . Medicines, food, hatha yoga, publishing—all a form of hovering, of unsolicited watchmanship. . . . On the other hand, I'm usually so self-centered or so self-absorbed, like any inveterate writer and narcissist, that I scarcely notice what people are doing or wearing or eating.

Every time we publish something, produce something, air something, we're about to be re-judged, weighed, tagged, squeezed, bagged all over again. I think we have it coming to us, for a lot of reasons. . . . But something else you said does make me sort of lean my mouth and chin into the palm of my hand pretty gravely, maybe too solemnly. The word "embarrassment" as you used it—underlined—embarrassment. I know that kind of embarrassment. . . . We don't have to feel that kind of embarrassment, and I say we shouldn't, that it's bad for us, a little too damaging. . . . Please determine and succeed in being wise about this one little matter. Please try to see the readership, the publishing-time attention of close and dear relatives, friends, all really ardent well-wishers with as much pure detachment as you can. Maybe it's sort of cruel to deliberately cast an occasional highly-detached eye—a cold eye, to spit it out—on the best and closest we've got, but it can be done pretty privately, with no pain for *them*, only a little guilt for *us*. . . .

I don't understand what I'm talking about, yet I go on talking.

I've missed you all day.

It makes me uneasy to realize that I may sooner or later be at least one kind of annoyance to you.

So many thoughts of you.

Shall we think about our plays and our sumptuous suite at the Waldorf or the Claridge? The answer to that could well be an emphatic yes rising out of me, but right now, today, at this pasty midnight hour, I don't feel up to thinking about matters so concrete and explicit.

I miss you pretty sorely.

Never thought of it, but we should have had a go at reading "A. and Cleopatra" out loud, just for fun.

A whole week we had, nearly. A great portion of fairness in my life. We didn't do, so much; we were.

I miss you very uncomfortably, and I can't say that I have

anything particularly contributive to add to your grave ruminations about common sense and your age (or mine) and moving in and (spear through the stomach) moving out. If Movings In inevitably lead to Movings Out, I emphatically tend to be in favor of separate quarters, be they ever so bleak or humble or dessicating. Maybe that's going too far, but it's very plain to me that I'm not responding to any of your goings, leavetakings, Standby Flights with anything that could pass for genuine Cool. . . . What the hell is Cool, anyway? Freedom from, or severance from, attachment. I've been examining the matter, off and on, for a lot of years, and I remain the same lightweight outsider-onlooker that I was at seventeen.

Your beautiful letter. Oh, yes—beautiful.

I was very conscious . . . of Peggy's not knowing or understanding or loving anything about Jews and Jewishness—Torah Jews, shtetl Jews, displaced Jews—and probably the only ones she will ever know are a few private-school boys cut off from all that, and glad of it, in most cases. Beards without Jews. One of the Hasidic Rebbes casually, sadly, alluded to a man in his congregation who had fallen seriously from grace as "a beard without a Jew."

I miss you, love you, love your two letters, and I have no idea, by the way, how Holden got so much into one night. I could ask Joyce Brothers. Boy, is she smart.

I feel your not-here-ness countless times a day, and I don't know what's wise to do about it, or even if there is anything wise to be done about it, and so, because I know nothing, I write and mail jaunty-sounding letters.

I've been around jazz enthusiasts a lot of my life, having known a few jazz people, and certainly I've listened to quite a lot of it, and I don't think I listen to it like an out-and-out dummy—at least, my foot keeps time and I may occasionally tap out the beat with my finger on my water glass. I like a lot of it, in short, and I know about the fun they have, the improvisers. Why shouldn't they? They mostly do what they do in groups of two or more, and they feed each other pre-stylised musical patterns, musical idioms, almost always identifiably based on past sets, other sittings, performances, pieces. Even the jazz musician working alone, the soloist, rarely does anything distinctly new, anything never-done, anything mouth-shuttingly firsthand. Even when the jazz improviser is in top form, hottest, what he's mostly doing is relying (with almost perfect confidence) on a composite or combination of . . . effects that are already developed within himself and that he knows will almost absolutely surely rearrange themselves in "new" kaleidoscopic (sp.?) patterns if he applies himself to his instrument assiduously, affectionately, in the mood with the others or just with the occasion, and provided he isn't too drunk or stoned. I've seen it happen again and again, and it never fails to under-impress me, even when I'm listening with real pleasure.

It just seems to me a perfect unwonder that writing's almost never terrific fun. If it's not the hardest of the arts—I think it is—it's surely the most unnatural, and therefore the most wearying. So unreliable, so uncertain. Our instrument is a blank sheet of paper—no strings, no frets, no keys, no reed, mouthpiece, nothing to do with the body whatever—God, the unnaturalness of it. Always waiting for birth, every time we sit down to work.

I love your life, and I love writing that's real writing.

When your days at the Times are over this week—Thursday? Friday?—do you think you might be able or willing to take a plane up here, stay here . . . till Sunday or Monday or Tuesday, and then fly or drive to New York with me? . . . Does that sound any good or possible?

I have only movies, no Films, including, I'm afraid, "Lost Horizon." I'm really a terrible lightweight.

When you're in New Haven next year, I thought I might rent a place in Westport or Stamford, kind of halfway between New Haven and New York. Does that seem to you a fairly thoughtful idea? I don't think I could take stewing in my own juices up here all winter, almost totally out of sight of you. And though there's no good reason why I couldn't see you in New Haven, occasionally spend the night, say, on your chiffonier, it would be a bad idea, I think, if I were to move into New Haven on any more staying-on basis—you'd have no easy or "normal" campus life, college life, with me around, and I comport myself lousily around campuses anyway, but really lousily. . . . What I learned, if anything, while you were in Miami is that I am not able to be bleedingly alone and cut off while you're away. I take to it badly, really badly. . . .

My mind is complicated, and I have to take measures, always, to live as I'd advise myself to live if I were my own mentor.

What a relief, pleasure it is to love your mind, really love it.

The Prom piece is so good. Even when you're busy just reporting, it always comes out real writing, and all your own. I think I would know your writing anywhere.

You *play the bugle well,* as the man said, and I read you with an old and passionate love for writing that I seldom feel any more or, for that matter, miss. . . .

When I pulled up at the Post Office yesterday afternoon, Peggy and Matthew pulled up behind me. A lot of grinning, happy looks exchanged in a flash. God, it's good to love a few people in the world.

I miss you and gave myself a rotten short haircut. On your head be it.

I think very, and only, lovingly of you. I love lastingness, permanence, and I wish us nothing less. Permanence, not petrifaction. There must be a difference.

About five hours later. Guests have come and gone. It was strenuous talking, question-and-answer talking, and one of the reasons why I moved up here in the first place. I'm full of my own wine and beer at this point. How I dislike drinking on social occasions—that is, pure social occasions, not connected with contentment or some sort of celebration. . . . I wish I felt closer to them all. They act as though they feel close to *me*, and that makes me feel guilty and irritated at once. It was pretty, up on the hill, though, and I really like them all; I just like smaller doses. . . . Even when I was being drawn, as though forcibly, into the worst and deadliest kind of literary talk, I recovered some balance simply by thinking of you and my love for you.

I feel restive and very edgy. I always was a poor yogi. It sometimes seemed to me all my real yoga was in knowing that.

Love,
Jerry

17

DEAR MR. SALINGER

CORNISH, NEW HAMPSHIRE; DAYTONA BEACH, FLORIDA, 1972–1973

I spend a long time composing my response to J. D. Salinger's letter on my yellow legal pad. When I'm done I type it carefully. Like my mother, I place a piece of carbon paper and second sheet underneath: "Dear Mister Salinger, I will remember your advice every day of my life. I read your letter over and over, and carried it in my pocket all day. I no longer need to read it. I know it by heart. Not just the words, but the sentiments expressed.

Joyce Maynard

JOYCE MAYNARD: My first experience of Holden Caulfield was not in *The Catcher in the Rye*. It was in the letters of J. D. Salinger. It was that voice; if the letter writer had been someone I'd never heard of, I would still have responded to that voice. It's exactly the response that generations of readers of *Catcher in the Rye* have experienced—the sense, finally, that there was somebody who knew me, recognized me, and understood me as I felt nobody ever had. I fell in love with the voice in his letters.

Within three days, there was a second letter and then a third and a fourth. I just told him about my life, told him college stories. It may have been part of his attraction to me because he was living a very isolated life, high on a hill in New Hampshire, cut off from many things. I brought news of the world from a young person out there in it. I told him about all the girls jumping on and off scales, weighing themselves; I was one myself. I told him that I liked to ride my bicycle into the countryside outside New Haven. I told him that I didn't have many friends there, that I made dollhouse furniture, that I listened to music, that I drew. I

Joyce Maynard.

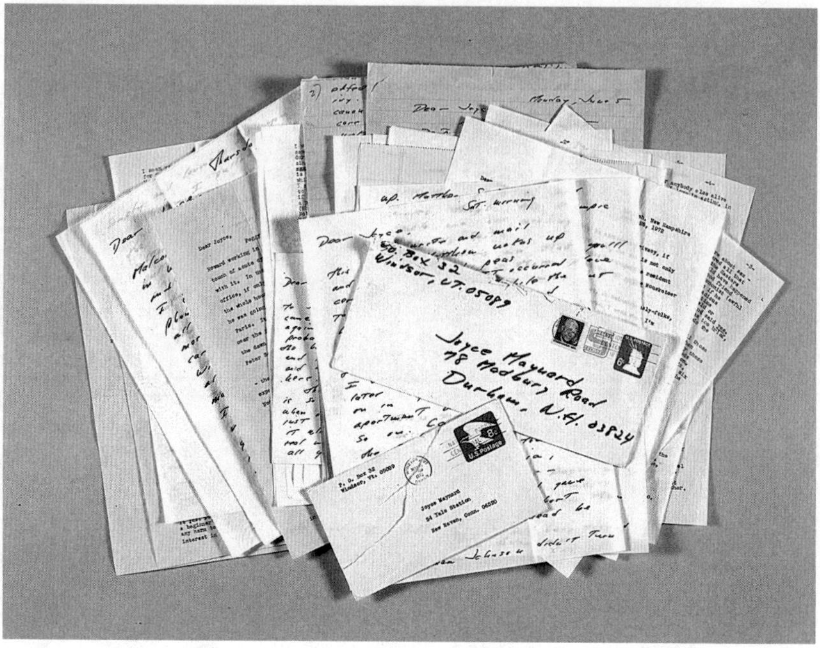

Letters Maynard received from Salinger.

told him about the three girls who were my roommates; I was the only one who didn't have a boyfriend, so I left for a "psychological single."

Both of my parents were brilliant, gifted artists. My father for thirty-some years was an assistant professor of English at the University of New Hampshire, never promoted. His true passion was art. He painted in total obscurity for almost all of his life. He never made any money. My mother had a Ph.D. from Harvard and couldn't get a job at the University of New Hampshire because she was a woman married to a man who had one. I felt a huge obligation to deliver at my parents' feet the success and acknowledgment that had eluded them.

I would tell my father stories; I loved to entertain him, which had been my role in my family. He described Scheherazade to me, how she keeps on telling stories so she won't be killed, and I always felt a little bit like Scheherazade, not because my life was in danger, but my place in the world was ensured by my storytelling. I didn't know who I would be if I didn't entertain and charm and delight.

And now I was entertaining and charming and delighting Salinger. I knew that I had won the approval of this great man, and I knew that

Fredelle Maynard, Joyce's mother.

Joyce's father, Max Maynard, a painter, in his studio.

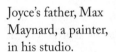

A young Joyce Maynard with her parents.

it would make my parents very happy. For my mother, it was as if J. D. Salinger had recognized her, since I was her product. My mother was a little unclear of boundaries—where she left off and I began.

I was not a relaxed and comfortable college student. I was anxious and tormented in a lot of ways. If I were a person who was having a happy life at college, I probably would have responded very differently to this voice than I did, but I was living alone in a top-floor dormitory room, and I poured out my heart to him. More and more, the energies that other people might have been putting into friendships, classes, and Yale went into those letters.

I sensed from the beginning he had an idealized vision of me. I was perfect. I didn't want to do anything to disappoint him.

One of the very early pieces that I published ran in *Newsweek*, in the "My Turn" column, and was called "Searching for Sages." I was looking for a sage and the meaning to life. I found it with Salinger. I was raised in a family with huge respect for language and art. Some people could be seduced by a Jimi Hendrix guitar riff; I could by words. Words were the religion of my family, as were intelligence, excellence, and humor—all of which I found in Salinger's voice. Before I could physically write, I gave dictation. My mother typed up my work. We would sit around the living room, reading our manuscripts. The moments of purest joy and perfection in that relationship with Jerry lay in the weeks before I ever met him when we communicated on the page, and on the page it was perfect.

There's only one other time in my life when I experienced the phenomenon of letters having an equivalent power of seduction, seduction by words. It was a man serving life in prison for double murder. He had only words to pull in a woman, and he did it very well. Salinger was a master at that. Getting a letter from J. D. Salinger was like getting a letter from Holden Caulfield, but written just to me—Holden Caulfield telling me how wonderful, perfect, lovable, and brilliant I was. It was a pretty strong drug. It was the only drug I took in college.

He had suggested that I call, collect.

"Is this Jerry?" I began, when he picked up the phone that first night. "This is Joyce Maynard calling."

"What do you know? That's terrific," he said. He was a little out of breath. "I was just down at the garden, putting in the last of my tomato plants. Black flies are murder this year. What have I been telling you? Everybody's after your blood."

Once we started exchanging letters, I always knew we would meet. There was never any question that we would meet. There was never any discussion; it was just understood. On the one hand, I couldn't wait to meet him. On the other, I was afraid that I might disappoint him and that the meeting couldn't live up to what the correspondence had been. Of course, it turned out I was right, although our first meeting, after I got the courage to go up there, was wonderful. School got out in early June and that's when I went to meet Jerry. I had been raised to believe that I was going to do big, important things, and this was a sign that I was going to.

My favorite English teacher from high school, from Phillips Exeter, was driving up to Hanover, so he drove me. He was an early encourager of my work, a real friend. Many people, I know, look back on it all now and wonder, "My God, what was going on there?"

This part makes me sad—because I really loved my mother, and I know her to have been a wonderful woman, but she offered me up to Jerry Salinger in a way. She sewed me a dress for our meeting. The fabric was meant to be curtain fabric for a child's room. It was the A-B-C's. I was very skinny; it didn't take a whole lot of fabric.

It was a basically an A-line dress, very short, with two very large

Joyce Maynard's mother, sewing.

buttons at the shoulder. You just unbuttoned them and the whole dress would fall off. There were two very large pockets onto which she had appliquéd letters: an A on one pocket, and a Z on the other. Very bright primary colors. A very short dress. It looked a lot like the dress I wore to first grade. And that's the dress that I was wearing the day I met him.

He raised his hand and was waving as if he were somebody coming

Joyce Maynard, 1973.

in off a boat. He actually jumped over the banister; there was something very boyish about him and very graceful. He was like a soft-shoe artist, and we just started right in. Finally I was here. I threw my arms around him. I hugged him. He hugged me back. The very first thing Salinger said was, "You're wearing the watch." It was a very large watch, a man's watch. Clearly he'd really studied my photograph in the *New York Times*.

"We are *landsmen*, all right," he said.

My heart lifted. I had spent less than an hour in the company of Jerry Salinger, but I was feeling something I'd never experienced before.

"I've waited a long time for you," he said. "If I didn't know better, I'd say you belong here."

I jumped in the front seat of his little BMW. I'd never known anybody who had a standard-shift BMW. I felt like I was in a French film. He drove fast and skillfully, but now and then he looked over at me sitting on the passenger side and smiled. We drove very fast along New Hampshire and Vermont roads, under covered bridges, winding up the hill to his house. It was hard to know where to begin. On the other hand, there seemed no need to say anything. For the first time in as long as I can remember, I felt no need for speech.

There was nothing particularly fancy about the house. Books stacked everywhere. Movies stacked everywhere. In Peggy's room there were just stacks and stacks of movie reels. The living room had soft velvet couches and piles and piles of *New Yorker* magazines. Deck in the front looking out at Mt. Ascutney. There were no personal items, photograph albums, photographs, letters. And then there was another wing of the house, which was his bedroom and his writing room, but I didn't see that until later.

Nothing seemed strange to me; it was as if this were the most natural thing in the world. It confirmed what I had been raised to believe: I was going to do important things, and I was going to spend time with this wonderful man. I was going to learn many things.

He made a bowl of popcorn, threaded a film through the projector, turned out the lights, and it was movie time. That first night, we watched *The 39 Steps*; that was one of his absolute favorites. Afterward we talked and I went to bed.

I slept in Peggy's bedroom. She was out, playing basketball, and then off with her boyfriend; she was going to be gone very late. And Matthew was also spending the night. So I did meet Matthew, who was a very lovable, happy, funny, charming twelve-year-old boy.

Salinger's house, where he lived from 1967 to 2010.

Peggy came in in the middle of the night, very late. I recognized on that first visit he was very critical of her in ways that he wasn't of his son, but she was strong and tough. Not too many people challenged J. D. Salinger, and she did. I don't think Margaret was more rebellious than any other sixteen-year-old. She was just doing her job, which amazed me, because I hadn't done my job.

I don't remember feeling embarrassed that I was here, visiting their father. Everything was unusual. J. D. Salinger was unusual. What was normal life? This was J. D. Salinger's life.

There was no question that I was going to see him again. Ten days after I'd begun my summer job as an editorial intern with the *New York Times*, Jerry drove five hours to pick me up. I was house-sitting a Manhattan brownstone for the summer; when he pulled up in front of the brownstone on West 73rd Street, I came running into his arms. He stroked my hair. "God, I've been waiting forever for this," he said.

We bought a bag of bagels and lox on the Upper West Side. Then he turned right around and we drove, very fast, the full five hours straight back to New Hampshire.

Over the course of that summer, I probably visited Jerry two or three times, for the weekend. I still had my job in New York, and he'd come down to see me; he stayed at the house on West 73rd once. But by July I missed him too much. I wanted to be with him all the time. I'll put it a little differently: I felt I needed to be with him all the time. I began to feel what the relationship required was for me to be with him all the time. I don't suppose that I was really listening to my own feelings as much as what I felt were the requirements for me—and that had been my story all my life. So I turned in my notice at the *New York Times*. In fact it was no notice at all. I said, "I'm leaving," then I called up the family who had given me responsibility for their house on West 73rd and said, "You're going to need to find another house sitter." And within a couple of days, I was gone. I published, I think, two editorials; two editorials written by me were published in the *New York Times*—without my name attached, of course—that summer. And then I moved into Jerry's house, but still with the belief that I was going back to Yale in the fall.

In the article that inspired him to write to me, I had mentioned that I was a virgin. I talked of the sexually open climate at Yale my freshman year and how uncomfortable it was to be a virgin there. One of the many offers that had come my way, as a result of that article, was an invitation from *Mademoiselle* to write an article, which was published that summer, called "The Embarrassment of Virginity," with a photograph of me sitting in my dormitory room being a virgin.

The next time I came up from New York for the weekend, it was different, and I guess I knew that it was going to be, although I didn't have a clue how it would happen because I had kissed two boys in my life and no men. Nothing was discussed. He took me into his room, and I didn't ask any questions when he took my clothes off. I had no frame of reference, didn't know how else it could be, but it wasn't a particularly tender romantic scene. We got into the bed and he kissed me and then he began to—I'm very careful when I use the phrase "make love," because it gets thrown around a lot, and this actually was not really making love—an attempt was made to have intercourse. There was no discussion of birth control, although I was eighteen years old, but it was not possible, anyway. I couldn't do it. It didn't happen. The muscles of my vagina simply

Joyce Maynard, meditating.

clamped shut and would not release. After a few minutes we stopped.

It was excruciatingly painful and I almost instantly developed a headache the likes of which I had never experienced. My whole head was exploding. I felt very embarrassed; that was my chief emotion. We didn't discuss it, and over the course of the weekend it was attempted on numerous other occasions and the same thing happened. At the time, I was mortified and felt like an absolute failure and a freak. He said gently, "Tomorrow I'll look up your symptoms in the *Materia Medica*," an ancient Chinese homeopathic text. Jerry spent a great deal of time researching homeopathic remedies for me to assist my condition.

Nothing that took place with Jerry Salinger had remotely the aspect of a boyfriend-girlfriend, dating relationship. I was his sidekick, his partner, his protégée, his student. I was his student of writing, I was his student of life, and I was (and I was certainly a failure here) his Zen acolyte. I studied, through him, health principles and homeopathy, but I was *not* his girlfriend.

He assigned to me some of the responsibilities of a sexual partner. I'd follow him into the bedroom. We'd stand together at the sink, brushing our teeth. I'd take off my contact lenses, go into the bedroom, take off my jeans and underwear, and put on my long flannel nightgown. Jerry would come into the room. He'd undress, put on his nightshirt, and climb onto his side of the bed. I'd get onto mine. His hand would reach for my shoulders. He'd stroke my hair, then take hold of my head with surprising firmness, and guide me under the covers. Under the covers, with their smell of laundry detergent, I'd close my eyes. Tears would be streaming down my cheeks. Still, I wouldn't stop. So long as I kept doing this, I knew he would love me.

He certainly said he loved me, always, almost from the beginning. I certainly told him every day that I was with him that I loved him, but it was its own category.

We had a very set routine—the things that we did and the foods that we ate and the times that we did these things. We were very early risers. The first thing we did was have a bowl of Birds Eye frozen Tiny Tender Peas, not cooked, but with warm water poured over them so they'd defrost a little bit, so they were just cool. There was a book whose principles he subscribed to called *Food Is Your Best Medicine*. He was a believer in raw food; he was actually way ahead of his time in many ways. Then we'd

Cover of *Food Is Your Best Medicine.*

Salinger in his jumpsuit.

meditate, or at least he would meditate and I would try to meditate. Jerry tried to make me into a student of Zen to leave worldly things behind, but my mind kept on wandering to things of the world, which was a big problem.

He would meditate for a long time and I would get restless and then we would get to work writing. He would put on a one-piece canvas jumpsuit with snaps up the front and he'd put it on like a uniform. It was kind of like he was a soldier or something, only he was going off to wage his war at the typewriter. He sat on a high chair at his high desk in his writing room and worked on his typewriter, a very old typewriter that clicked. I heard typing every day. I saw two thick manuscripts. I've written nine books now. I know what the size of a book manuscript looks like, and these were thick. I never read anything. He did show me one thing, although it wasn't like I got to sit down and read it, and that was an archive of the Glass family; it was almost a genealogy. He was as protective of those characters as if they were his children. I never laid eyes on a page that he was writing. Never. And there was one other space that was off the bedroom and I believe that was his safe. We met at lunch to discuss life, and I would show him my pages. I had signed up to write an expansion of the *New York Times* piece into a book.

I knew, without asking, the nature of Jerry's view of publishers. "Give me two hours in the dentist chair before I'll spend another minute in a publisher's office," he said. "All those insufferable literary types, thoroughly pleased with themselves, who haven't read a line of Tolstoy since college. All feverishly courting bestsellerdom. Not that the absence of any true original gift or insight keeps them from demanding all manner of pointless alterations to a writer's work, for the sole purpose of proving their own irreplaceable talents. They've got to offer up all these bright ideas. Unable to produce a single original line themselves, they're bound and determined to put their stamp squarely on *your* work. It happened to me plenty of times. Polite suggestions that I change this or that, put in more romance, take out more of that annoying ambiguity . . . slap some terribly clever illustration on the cover. . . . The minute you publish a book, you'd better understand, it's out of your hands. In come the reviewers, aiming to make a name for themselves by destroying your own. And they will. Make no mistake about it. It's a goddamn embarrassment, publishing. The poor boob who lets himself in for it might as well walk down Madison Avenue with his pants down."

Every afternoon we drove down the hill and bought the *New York Times*. And many of those afternoons, as we came down the hill and passed the mailbox, there would be some seeker standing at the foot of the driveway. In all of the time that I was there, nobody ever knocked at the door. It was an unwritten rule of the religion perhaps. Then we'd come back and watch TV. He loved *Mary Tyler Moore*, *Andy Griffith*—Ron Howard with his fishing pole over his shoulder. We used to watch the *Lawrence Welk Show*. It was partly sort of a kitsch thing that we did, but it was also about watching America. He officially cut himself off from a great deal of the world but maintained a huge interest in observing it. We'd watch the show and we would dance. I was, you know, a girl of the '60s and '70s. I didn't know couples dancing. And he was a very good dancer, so we would dance in the living room to Lawrence Welk while all of my contemporaries were off in New Haven, doing drugs and listening to Led Zeppelin. Sometimes we'd go to the

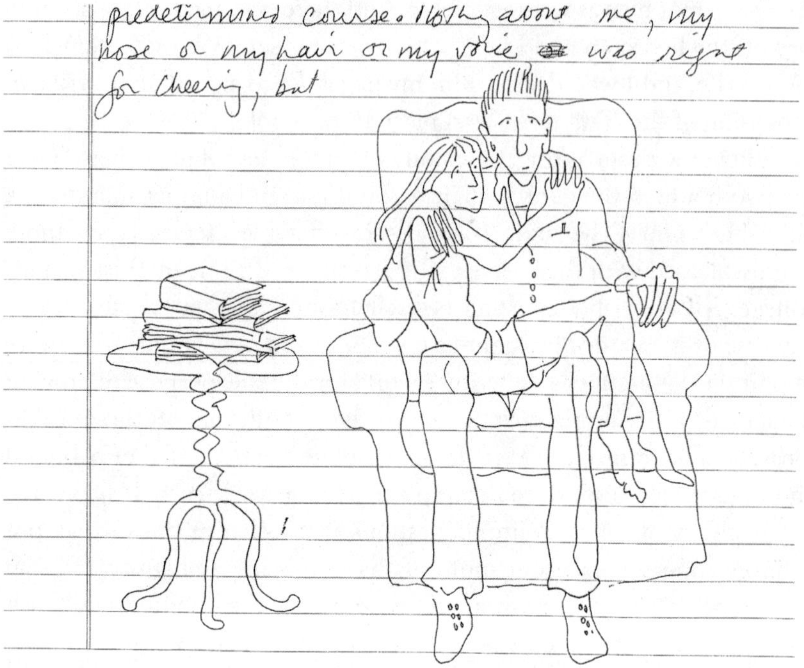
predetermined course. Nothing about me, my
nose or my hair or my voice was right
for cheering, but

Joyce Maynard's drawing of herself sitting on Salinger's lap.

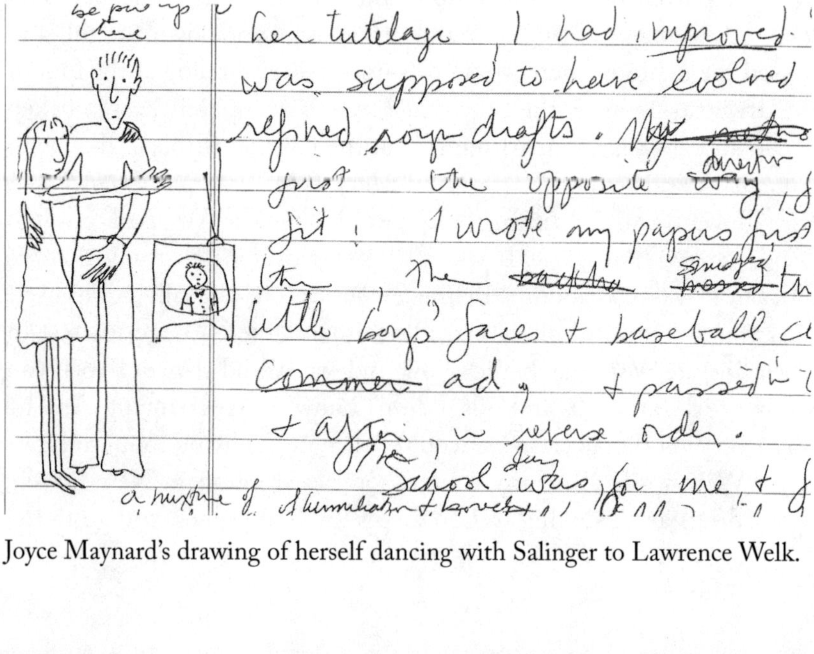

Joyce Maynard's drawing of herself dancing with Salinger to Lawrence Welk.

movies—not very much—because mostly we watched old movies in Jerry's living room.

He loved *Maltese Falcon*, *Casablanca*, *The Lady Vanishes*, W. C. Fields. He loved *Lost Horizon*. He had a deep interest in Marlon Brando. Jerry's first love had been acting, and he was a wonderful performer. Very funny. And he had a beautiful voice. He said that the only person who could ever play Holden Caulfield was himself. But even he acknowledged he was too old for that, although, in some ways, he was playing Holden Caulfield forever. He had been pursued, of course, for years for the movie rights to *Catcher in the Rye*, but the one who was determined to play Holden Caulfield was Jerry Lewis. He said Jerry Lewis always called him, but he said he would never let Hollywood make any movie of his again.

It's a long list of institutions that Jerry had contempt for: Western medicine, mainstream Hollywood (although I think he was secretly semi-dazzled by it), psychiatry, Ivy League education, families (there was another institution). I remember listening to very old recordings of the Andrews Sisters and Glenn Miller and an obscure German singer whose name I don't remember but who was a singer from World War II. And then we'd go to bed.

I moved into Jerry's house that summer, still believing that I was going back to Yale in the fall. I had rented an apartment, using part of the book advance from my book that I was due to deliver within a few months and that I'd been working on. I had gone out and bought furniture. I bought plants. I got dishes. I unpacked my bags. I registered for classes. Jerry made a joke about how I'd probably meet some Joe College, and then I'd forget all about him.

I never attended a single class of my sophomore year. I withdrew from Yale two days later, forfeiting that fall's tuition, plus my scholarship. I remember the movie that Jerry brought to screen when he came to get me. He brought the projector and everything to my apartment on George Street in New Haven, he set up the projector, and we watched *A Night to Remember*, the real *Titanic* movie. I piled my clothes in the back of his car. He'd brought the BMW, not the Blazer, so I left most of my possessions in the apartment.

For most of that year, I lived with him, believing that despite the thirty-five years separating us, we would be together always. I didn't think I'd ever leave again after that.

When he was loving, he was extraordinarily tender and certainly funny. I found myself in a relationship with him that reminded me, with the exception of the drinking, of my relationship with my father. I was entertaining him, trying to make him happy, and not very successfully. The moment I moved in, I could do very little right. He said to me the day I moved in, "You're behaving like a teenager," which I was.

I didn't swim that summer, or ride my bike, or drive anywhere without Jerry, except one time, when I got to take the Blazer (never the BMW) to a Singer sewing machine store. I spent $400 on a Singer Golden Touch and Sew machine. "This baby would have come in handy in a foxhole," he said as he lifted it out of the back of the car and carried the machine up the stairs for me. "Put one of these on your head and you wouldn't have to worry about shrapnel fire." I should have been buying an electric typewriter. I had to write a book in the next three months.

My birthday in November passed as just an ordinary day. Three days later, Nixon was reelected. Neither of us voted.

Only one time did I meet friends of his, and that was this memorable

Lillian Ross and William Shawn.

and disastrous lunch; I don't have a clue what he was thinking. We drove into New York in the BMW, very fast, as always—a trip that took probably about five, six hours. We went to the Algonquin, and there was this tiny little man who I realize now was probably only in his late fifties, but he seemed very old to me at the time: William Shawn. I had heard about him for as long as I'd known Jerry. And with Shawn was Lillian Ross, whose work I knew; I'd read it and studied it and admired it. This was years before her book in which she disclosed this information, but I knew from Jerry that Lillian Ross and William Shawn had been lovers for years. It was a known thing in certain circles, but never referred to, even with Jerry.

We took our places around this table at the Algonquin. I remember being really excited that I was meeting the editor of the *New Yorker* and this writer whose work I'd read and thought was so wonderful. She asked me what sorts of things I'd written, and, well, my main publication had been in *Seventeen* magazine. So I began talking to her about writing for *Seventeen*, judging the Miss Teenage America pageant, and interviewing Julie Nixon Eisenhower. I realize now that she was rather baiting me, while I thought I

Lillian Ross, a writer at the *New Yorker.*

was being amusing and entertaining. Ross shot Shawn a look. The same eye that I had so admired on the page looking critically and highly perceptively at other people's foibles was suddenly turned to me. I can imagine the cruel "Talk of the Town" piece she could've written about me.

When lunch was over, Jerry put me into a taxi, and we went directly to Bonwit Teller, rode the elevator up to whatever floor it was that sold the most elegant, most sophisticated coats of a sort worn most particularly by middle-aged, professional women in New York City. He bought me a very expensive, black, cashmere coat of the sort that Lillian Ross might've worn, which was not at all like what the rest of my wardrobe resembled. I'm sure I was wearing a miniskirt that day. I'm sure Jerry was ashamed of me; that's why he wanted to put me in an expensive coat.

I was writing *Looking Back* and it was going to be published in a few months. Every day I worked on the book, I showed him my manuscript pages; I read every page out loud to Jerry over the course of the months I spent writing it, much in the way I used to read my work out loud to my father and mother. Certain sections Jerry typed for me. He made handwritten comments in the margins on yellow legal pads. After he completed reading over my manuscript one morning, he said to me, "Plants and animals are the telling omissions in your recollections. Too many passing fads here. Too little that is lasting."

I drove down to New York with Jerry to have my photograph taken for the book. I posed in Central Park with him standing just off to the side, watching. I met editors to discuss promotion of the book. We never discussed how on earth Jerry was going to maintain his privacy—I won't even call it privacy; the secrecy of our relationship—with a major publisher's publicity campaign well under way to promote the book. I don't really believe that Jerry felt we had a future anymore. He just didn't tell me. I can even feel some sympathy for him: I suspect he didn't know how on earth he was to get out of this mess.

One day I heard the telephone ring and wasn't supposed to answer it, ever, so I listened to Jerry answer the phone and there was a very brief conversation, then a click. He emerged from his office with a kind of anger on his face I had never seen anywhere. He said, "*Time* magazine has got my number; you have ruined my life." The call had been a reporter from *Time* and it became, a week later, an item in *Time*'s gossipy "Newsmakers" column: "Former Yale coed, Joyce Maynard, is living with J. D. Salinger."

Worried about Jerry, I decided not to promote the book. I would just let it be put out there without my presence. My editor at Doubleday, Elsa van Bergen, wrote me a letter expressing her concern and dismay about my decision not to participate in the publicity. What Elsa said in her letter made sense to me, and for a moment, reading it, I felt a small surge of hopefulness. Maybe I didn't have to close myself off from the world altogether. Perhaps my continued interest in things like bookstore appearances and interviews was not unforgivable. I brought the letter to Jerry, who read it only partway through, then folded it neatly and handed it back to me with a sigh. "Perhaps you're like the rest of them after all," he said.

I felt like a fraud. In the name of protecting Salinger, I had betrayed myself. There was no way to write the story of myself without explaining the story of Salinger.

During all this period, although it became increasingly dark, I never thought of leaving. I never imagined that the relationship would end. I continued to envision and actively discuss a future, although the dream of a romantic sexual relationship was over before it began. The dream of parenthood replaced it; what I wanted most was a family. I pictured having a child with Jerry, and it was always very specific: I pictured a little girl. How this child was to be conceived I can't imagine because nothing was happening that would have made that possible, although we actually had a name for this child.

It was a name that Jerry came up with in a dream: "Bint." The little girl was always referred to as "Bint."

Only much later, after I published *At Home in the World*, did I get a letter from a British scholar who said, "Do you know what the word 'Bint' actually means? It's a word that means 'whore,' worse than 'wench'; it's a very ugly word for a woman." I didn't know that at the time. We were going to have Bint because one of the things you do if the present isn't so great is think about the future.

Apart from our trips to New York City, we'd never actually been anywhere together. Jerry announced we were going to take a trip to Florida in March, during Matthew and Peggy's school vacation. Truthfully, I would have loved to have taken a trip that was just the two of us, but I was not about to argue about anything in that relationship. I was happy to be going to Florida because it was very cold, dark, and snowy that winter, like most winters in New Hampshire, but it was particularly cold and dark in my memory of it. Jerry was a serious follower and student of homeopathic medicine. He located a homeopathic practitioner in Daytona Beach whom he wanted to consult about my inability to have sex. This was not, of course, described to Matthew and Peggy, who thought we were just going to Florida for a vacation.

On day two [of the Florida vacation], Jerry left Matthew and Peggy at the hotel pool and we went off to see the doctor. He didn't identify himself as J. D. Salinger, of course; he called himself John Boletus ("boletus" is a type of mushroom), and I was his friend whom he was assisting with her problem. Jerry didn't identify himself as my sexual partner. I was silent throughout this entire meeting, but Jerry explained the nature of the problem in very clinical terms and then stepped out of the room so she could examine me. I'd never been examined that way by a doctor before. She invited him back into the room and discussed, mostly with Mr. Boletus, various homeopathic remedies that might be used on me. We paid and left.

Matthew wanted to, I think, fly a kite, or he wanted to play in the water, or he wanted to do something that a twelve-year-old boy would, understandably, want to do with his dad on a vacation. After Jerry played with Matthew in the water for a while, he came back to the towel where I was sitting. He looked very tired—not just tired; he looked weary—and he said to me, "I can't do this anymore. I'm finished with all of this. I'll never have any more children." I said, "Then I can't stay." And he said, "You'd better leave now then."

I think I knew I had to leave right then: I picked up my towel off the sand and I started walking back toward the hotel. Staggering is probably more like it. And I know I believed that he would come after me. But he didn't. He stayed on the beach with the children. And I went back into the hotel room. And I didn't have any money, I didn't have a charge card, I really didn't have anything, I was just there in Daytona Beach with my towel. I called my mother, and I said I have to come home now. And then she said, well, I'll try to find you a flight. But there was no flight until the next day. So I had to spend one more night there.

We carried on in a kind of a way and we went out to dinner. Then we did what we usually did: we saw a movie. We went back to the room and I should say that we had two hotel rooms, one of which was Matthew and Jerry; the other was Peggy and me. We shared a room. Peggy and I were never friends. Peggy didn't really talk to me and I was afraid of Peggy, but Peggy and I were in a room together. So I knew that I still couldn't make a sound. I lay in the bed just kind of trembling, and I couldn't stand it anymore, I had to see Jerry, so when it was very late and I thought that Peggy was asleep and Matthew was asleep, I went in and I got Jerry.

We went into the only place where we could be alone, which was the bathroom. And I said please. I can't leave you. Please. Let me stay. I don't have to have any children. It was the last piece I think of me that I relinquished at that moment. And he said no, you need to go. And the next morning I packed my bathing suit and my flip-flops in my bag, and I rode the elevator down to the lobby with him. He called for a taxi and he leaned over and said to the driver, This girl needs to go to the airport now, and gave me, put two $50 bills in my hand.

And I drove away

I don't remember how I got back to New Hampshire. I know snow covered the steps to his house when I climbed them. The heat was off; it was very cold. I packed up all my things and called my mother to come and pick me up. The last thing I did, rather melodramatically, before I left the house, was to write, in the ice on the window, BINT. I went home.

Three weeks later, my memoir *Looking Back* was published—a 160-page book ostensibly about my life as an eighteen-year-old, in which I never mentioned that my father was an alcoholic or that I, the anointed youth spokesperson of 1973, had dropped out of her Ivy League college and moved in with a fifty-three-year-old man who happened to be J. D. Salinger. None of it appeared in the book, although it was written in his house.

After he was gone from my life, I called him. It's embarrassing to think how long and how pitifully I pursued him. Calling him and begging him to come and see me, talk to me, take me back. I felt as if I was in exile. The same voice that had spoken to me with such exquisite tenderness and concern was almost unrecognizably cold. And I knew his heart had left the room. I continued to send him letters. I called him for way too long—trying to get back to that place I had known, that little patch of sunlight I felt I had briefly inhabited with him. I lived a very solitary life. I was on my own at this point. When I called Jerry, it was clear that my calls were excruciating to him. He just wanted me gone. He wanted me off the phone. I don't think he ever quite hung up on me, but in essence he didn't have to. His response was so dismissive and withering. I couldn't bear it. He finally said, "Go away. Stop calling me." He said, "I have nothing to say to you." I would say, "I don't know what to do, I don't know where to go."

Cover of the book Joyce Maynard wrote while living with Salinger, who was five feet away when this picture was taken.

I bought a house in Hillsboro, New Hampshire, and I was living there and really trying to create a life Salinger would think was a good one. It was never enough just to have the good life. It had to be a life that he thought was a good one. I bought books. I made a little writing space for myself, which I kept asking him to come and visit and see. Finally, I think just to get me off his back, he agreed that he would drive by, and I was extraordinarily excited and anxious. I remember preparing for days for his visit—cooking a meal by the specifications that I knew would meet his standard. He arrived about ten minutes late with Matthew and left about fifteen minutes later. That was the last time I saw him for over twenty years.

Once, when he and I were still together, in the car on the way back to Jerry's house, he made a comment that took my sister by surprise. "I suppose you always looked up to Joyce, as younger sisters do," he said.

That was odd. Rona was not only four years older but married, with a baby. I had even told Jerry the story of my sister's sense of displacement at my birth. And I had just recently turned nineteen.

"Joyce is four years younger than I am, actually," she told him quietly. "I'm twenty-three."

"Oh well," Jerry said, taking the BMW into fifth gear. "You're both little girls to me."

A thought entered my head: *What if I'm getting too old for him?*

One day at around this time, my mother said to me, "Your face certainly is getting round. I guess we don't need to worry anymore about that concentration camp look of yours."

The house Joyce Maynard bought in New Hampshire after her relationship with Salinger ended.

Conversation with Salinger #10

PAUL ALEXANDER: In early November 1974, *New York Times* reporter Lacey Fosburgh took a phone call. Who was on the other end? J. D. Salinger. She had called his agent earlier in the day and asked for an interview. A variety of men, all using the name John Greenberg, had been traveling around the country, selling pirated copies of his uncollected short stories. Salinger had filed a lawsuit against the bookstores that were selling the books, and she had been following up on the story.

SHANE SALERNO: David Victor Harris is Lacey Fosburgh's widower.

DAVID VICTOR HARRIS: Lacey had just moved [to the Bay Area], and she was now on the National desk working out of the San Francisco Bureau of the *Times*. She had had this throwaway assignment covering this standard lawsuit, and suddenly it became a groundbreaker.

New York Times reporter Lacey Fosburgh on assignment.

Lacey and I were sitting in the kitchen, looking out at the backyard of my house in Menlo Park. The phone rang. I answered it, and a male voice asked, "Is Lacey Fosburgh there?" I got her and she picked up the phone. The first thing he said to her was, "This is a man called Salinger."

She goes [whispers to Harris], "Salinger, Salinger. Give me some paper, give me some paper." So I was scurrying around, grabbing some paper, and she was furiously writing notes on anything that was around.

Salinger had met his match with Lacey. He was playing against a pro. She was certainly capable of taking his charm and running with it, and I'm sure part of what kept him on the phone was this lovely female voice that sounded as good as she looked. He had no idea what she looked like, of course, but I'm sure that didn't keep him from flirting on the phone and wanting to connect with this woman. She led him right down that path. She let him talk about himself and make his connection with her. Obviously, he was upset about this pirated publication. These were stories he did not want in circulation—stories from his early writing period he did not feel were mature work; he wanted them just to die

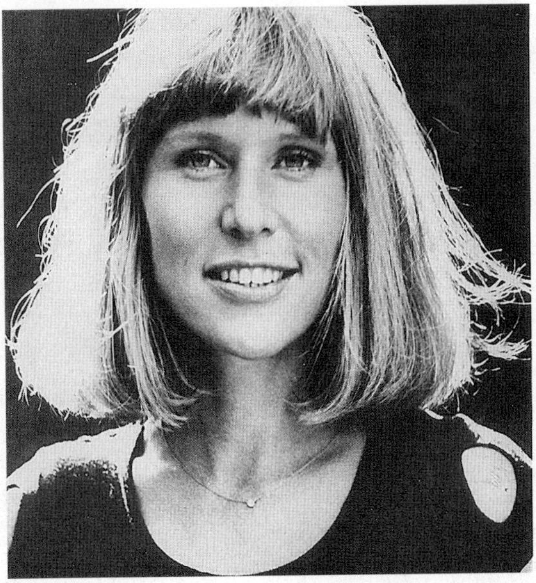

Lacey Fosburgh.

in old magazine pages at the library. That was his motivation for making the phone call. The rest was up to Lacey, who had this incredible capacity to get people to talk. When she turned her charm on you (and I don't mean some sleazy kind of charm; it was a far more genuine article than that: she was gracious, she was open, she was caring), she had a way of eliciting stuff from you that you would never say otherwise.

This was a little legal story, which seemed destined to be buried on page 18. Lacey had been working on it for more than a day. She had checked out the guy who was being charged in the suit and she had talked to some lawyers and put in the obligatory call to Salinger's lawyer and agent, saying she wanted to talk to Salinger, but she had no expectation that Salinger would call back. Nobody, least of all Lacey, expected anybody was going to talk to J. D. Salinger. When it did happen, it caught her totally by surprise.

She got Salinger to comment on the short stories in the pirated editions. She got him to tell her how he felt about the ordeal. I could see Lacey was keeping him going. Every time Salinger stopped talking, she was trying to roll it over and get him to answer more questions. She was a very good interviewer. She obviously had hooked him and was furiously scribbling these notes.

After Salinger hung up, Lacey immediately got on the phone with the National desk of the *New York Times* to say, "Hey, I just talked to Salinger." Everything began roaring along, and suddenly she was over on the typewriter jamming out this piece. They were treating it big and she knew it was big, so she was cranking out the piece the rest of the day. She had to drive up to the San Francisco Bureau to actually transmit it on the computer system that was up there, but the next day [Sunday] there it was—front page. Which was extraordinary. This was before the *Times* format had changed, so running soft news on the front page was a big deal.

LACEY FOSBURGH: What prompted Mr. Salinger to speak . . . was what he regards as the latest and most severe of all invasions of his private world: the publication of *The Complete Uncollected Short Stories of J. D. Salinger, Vols. 1 and 2*. During the last two months, about 25,000 copies of these books, priced at $3 to $5 for each volume, have been sold—first here in San Francisco, then in New York, Chicago, and elsewhere, according to Mr. Salinger, his lawyers and book dealers around the country.

"All the News That's Fit to Print"

The New York Times

LATE CITY EDITION
Weather: Chance of showers today, tonight. Partly cloudy tomorrow. Temperature range: today 47-57. Saturday 63-73. Details on Page 87.

SECTION ONE

VOL. CXXIV..No. 42,652 © 1974 The New York Times Company NEW YORK, SUNDAY, NOVEMBER 3, 1974 60 CENTS

CAREY IS FAVORED TO UNSEAT WILSON IN TUESDAY'S VOTE

6 Million Expected at Polls—Candidates Press Drives on the Final Weekend

JAVITS IN HEATED RACE

Statewide Offices at Issue—Legislators and Judges Also Up for Election

By FRANK LYNN

Representative Hugh L. Carey is the heavy favorite, according to politicians and pollsters alike, to defeat Governor Wilson Tuesday and end 16 years of Republican rule in New York State.

The campaign began 10 months ago with both men as relatively obscure political figures. When he made his first upstate swing in the January cold, Mr. Carey was known mostly to his Brooklyn constituents and his fellow Congressmen; Mr. Wilson was just beginning to emerge from the large shadow of his predecessor and political benefactor, Nelson A. Rockefeller.

Extensive Election

Both candidates campaigned in the metropolitan areas yesterday, imploring crowds of supporters to get out the vote. Election officials expect about six million New Yorkers from 18 years up—75 per cent of those registered—to vote for national, state and local officials, the most extensive election in the four-year-election cycle.

The polls will be open throughout the state from 6 A.M. to 9 P.M.

In addition to a Governor, voters will also elect a Lieutenant Governor, Attorney General, Controller, two Court of Appeals judges, a United States Senator, 39 members of ... House of Representatives ... State Senators, 150 Assemblymen, District Attorneys in ... areas including Manhattan ... Nassau, Suffolk, We... and Rockland Counties ... York City Council ... Supreme Court judges ... out the state, Civil C... in New York City ... in New York City ... and district judges ... cials throughout the state.

Javits Chall...

In the United St... campaign, a heated ... developed as Senator Javits, a Republ... serving his third ... been seeking to ho... challenges from Rams... the Democrat, and ... Keating, the Conservative ...

However, the election ... Governor is clearly the ... significant for state resid... A Carey victory would ... the 55-year-old Brooklyn...

Continued on Page 72, Column 1

Democrats Likely to Make Larger Than Usual Gain

The Party's Candidates Are Favored in Contests Tuesday for Senate, House and Governors' Posts

By CHRISTOPHER LYDON

Special to The New York Times

WASHINGTON, Nov. 2—Two years after a sweeping Presidential victory, the Republican party is braced for another harsh dose of Watergate medicine in the elections Tuesday. At stake are all 435 House seats, 34 Senate seats and 35 governorships.

In each of these categories, Democrats are now favored to win somewhat more than the normal midterm gains for the party out of the White House. The prospect is all the more unusual because, in each category, the Democrats would be broadening big majorities that survived President Nixon's landslide re-election of 1972.

Senate Gain Forecast

In the House, the last round of polls and professional estimates point to a Democratic gain in excess of the average off-year increment for opposition parties, which has been 30 seats since 1946. Building on a 248-member majority at the close of the 93d Congress, the Democrats appear to have an outside chance of gaining the 42 seats that would give them a two-thirds majority in the 435-member House.

State-by-state reports on Senate contests forecast a net gain of five or more seats on the Democrats' current 58-to-42 majority, with important new inroads in normally Republican Middle Western and Rocky Mountain states. The average modern loss for the President's party in an off-year election is four Senate seats.

Small Turnout Expected

In state races, Democrats are reported likely to add seven or more governorships to their current base of 32, exceeding the average gain of six governorships for the opposition party and at least matching their own peak total of 39 governorships in the late nineteen-thirties.

More important, perhaps, the likelihood of capturing Republican Governors' offices in Massachusetts, New York and California, and a close race in Michigan, give the Democrats a chance of "governing" all the 10 largest states and, in all, more than 85 per cent of the American people.

Democratic candidates, often adapting to conservative trends on specific issues, have broadly benefited from resentment about inflation, the recession

Continued on Page 74, Column 1

The Shah of Iran greeting Secretary of State Kissinger on his arrival Friday for talks in Teheran

Associated Press

Nixon Still Remains Under Critical Care; Begins Eating Again

By LAWRENCE K. ALTMAN

Special to The New York Times

... BEACH, Calif., Nov. 2 ... medical bulletin ... independent

Continued on Page 7, Column 1

MINE TALKS REACH A CRUCIAL STAGE

Pessimism Rises as Time Needed to Prevent a Coal Strike Is Running Out

By BEN A. FRANKLIN

Special to The New York Times

...TON, Nov. 2—In ... of gathering pessimism ... for the coal ... miners union ...

Continued on Page 7, Column 1

Shah and Kissinger Hint At Bid to Hold Oil Prices

No Hope for Reduction Offered—Iranian Tells West to Lower Costs of Exports

By JAMES F. CLARITY

Special to The New York Times

TEHERAN, Iran, Nov. 2—Shah Mohammed Riza Pahlevi and Secretary of State Kissinger agreed today that the oil-producing countries and the industrialized consumer nations must cooperate to prevent world disorder stemming from inflation.

The Shah and Mr. Kissinger discussed the oil-price crisis for more than four hours last night. They hinted that Iran would seek to keep prices from rising again next month when the Organization of Petroleum Exporting Countries meets in Vienna to review its price policies.

But except for brief mention of one of the plans the Shah has long advocated publicly, neither Mr. Kissinger nor the Shah indicated how oil prices could be held at present levels, which have quadrupled in less than a year.

Stable Prices' First

... the Iranian ruler not... Secretary, in separate news conferences, offered any hope that prices would be reduced for consumer nations in the foreseeable future. "Before you can have lower prices, you have to have stable prices," Mr. Kissinger said.

The Shah said that in Vienna he would press his plan to set a single OPEC price system for oil that would close loopholes that permit oil companies to hide their profits. Under questioning by newsmen, however, he conceded that this plan, already under consideration by

Continued on Page 7, Column 1

78 KILLED IN FIRE IN HEART OF SEOUL

Blaze Cuts Through Hotel and Crowded Club

SEOUL, South Korea, Sunday, Nov. 3 (UPI)—A fire swept through the crowded upper floors of a seven-story office-building complex in downtown Seoul early today, killing scores of persons. Some leaped to their deaths in panic.

The police said that at least 78 persons had been killed and 40 others injured in the three-hour blaze at the Daewang Building. The fire broke out about 2:50 A.M.

Rescue workers first announced a death toll of only 16. Later, however, they found other bodies on the sixth floor, where a "go-go" club and a hotel were situated.

Mostly Young People

Some of the victims were killed instantly when they leaped from upper stories, but many others died of inhalation of toxic gas, firemen said.

Witnesses said the fire had broken out in a room of the Brown Hotel on the sixth floor

Continued on Page 7, Column 1

PALESTINIAN SAYS ARABS MUST GIRD FOR ANOTHER WAR

Official of Guerrilla Group Asserts 'Wounded Wolves' of Israel Plan Attack

U.S. DIPLOMACY SCORNED

Leaders at Rabat Meeting Are Said to Have Rebuffed Proposals by Kissinger

By JUAN de ONIS

Special to The New York Times

BEIRUT, Lebanon, Nov. 2—The information chief of the Palestine Liberation Organization said today that the "primary duty" of the Arab countries was to ready themselves militarily and economically to face a new war that he said Israel was preparing.

Yasir Abed Rabbo, a member of the Executive Committee of the Palestine Liberation Organization, the main grouping of guerrillas, said there was no hope for a peaceful settlement of the Arab-Israeli conflict so long as Israel and the United States refused to include the Palestinian national movement in negotiations.

Mr. Rabbo said that the Arab chiefs of state, at the recent conference in Morocco, had rejected an approach to peace proposed by Secretary of State Kissinger.

Four-Point Plan Described

The Palestinian spokesman, speaking at a news conference, said that the Arab leaders, "including those leaning toward the United States," had rejected what he described as a four-point proposal by Mr. Kissinger to move toward an Arab-Israeli agreement.

The proposal, as described by Mr. Rabbo, called for the following steps:

¶A limited withdrawal of Israeli forces in the Sinai Peninsula in exchange for a declaration of nonbelligerance by Egypt that "would end the state of war permanently between the two countries."

¶A final settlement with Jordan that would give King Hussein administrative control of the principal towns in the West Bank of the Jordan River "except Jerusalem," while Israel maintained military control of the countryside in the West Bank territory.

¶A minor withdrawal by Israel on the Golan Heights in the vicinity of El Quneitra that ... continuing Israeli occupation of

Continued on Page 10, Column 3

Associated Press

Yasir Abed Rabbo speaking in Beirut yesterday.

Jersey Casino V... Law Enfo...

J. D. Salinger Speaks About His Silence

By LACEY FOSBURGH

Special to The New York Times

SAN FRANCISCO, Nov. 2—Goaded by publication of unauthorized editions of his early, previously uncollected works, the reclusive author J. D. Salinger broke a public silence of more than 20 years last week, issuing a denunciation and revealing he is hard at work on writings that may never be published in his lifetime.

Speaking by telephone from Cornish, N. H., where he makes his home, the 55-year-old author whose most recent published work, "Raise High the Roof Beam, Carpenters" and "Seymour, an Introduction," appeared in 1962, said:

"There is a marvelous peace in not publishing. It's peaceful. Still. Publishing is a terrible invasion of my privacy. I like to write. I love to write. But I write just for myself and my own pleasure."

For nearly half an hour after saying he intended to talk "only for a minute," the author, who achieved literary fame and cultish devotion enhanced by his inaccessibility following publication of "The Catcher in the Rye" in 1951, spoke of his work, his obsession with privacy and his uncertain thoughts about publication.

The interview with Mr. Salinger, who was at times warm and charming, at times wary and skittish, is believed to be his first since 1953, when he granted one to a 16-year-old representative of the high school newspaper in Cornish.

What prompted Mr. Salinger to speak now on what he said was a cold, rainy, windswept night in Cornish was what he regards as the latest and most severe of all invasions of his private world: the publication of "The Complete Uncollected Short Stories of J. D. Salinger, Vols. 1 and 2."

During the last two months, about 25,000 copies of these books, priced at $3 to $5 for each volume, have been sold—first here in San Francisco, then in New York, Chicago and elsewhere, according to Mr. Salinger, his lawyers and book dealers around the country.

"Some stories, my property, have been stolen," Mr. Salinger said. "Someone's appropriated them. It's an illicit act. It's unfair. Suppose you had a coat you liked and somebody went into your closet and stole it."

Continued on Page 69, Column 3

Pictorial Parade

J. D. Salinger in 1951, before he withdrew from the public eye. For more than 20 years he refused to be photographed.

This is another in a series of articles on the world food situation.

to the Secretary General of the United Nations.

In a late draft of his speech, obtained by The New York Times, Mr. Kissinger recommends limiting the council's authority primarily to overseeing the activities of four groups of technical experts who would deal, respectively, with food aid, trade, production and reserves.

Administration officials are divided over whether Mr. Kissinger's speech will generate action to help assure survival and whether it will stress sufficiently the idea that scarce

Aaron to Milwaukee

Henry Aaron, baseball's career home run champion, was traded yesterday by the Atlanta Braves to the Milwaukee Brewers. Details, Section 5.

Associated Press

2-7-0-0 . . . HIKE! President Ford snapping football to Ambrose Cronin, a Portland businessman, during auction in that city Friday night. Mr. Cronin had just paid $2,700 for the ball, autographed by Mr. Ford and players of the Portland Storm, a W.F.L. team. Mr. Ford knows football well: he was the University of Michigan's star center and was named the Wolverines' most valuable player in 1934. Yesterday, he flew to Utah, Colorado and Kansas to bolster G.O.P. candidates. Details, Page 23.

Pictorial Parade

Today's Sections

Index to Subjects

SAN FRANCISCO BOOK DEALER: They're selling like hotcakes. Everybody wants one.

LACEY FOSBURGH: Since last April, copies of *The Complete Uncollected Short Stories of J. D. Salinger, Vols. 1 and 2*, have reportedly been peddled in person to bookstores . . . by men who always call themselves John Greenberg and say they come from Berkeley, California. Their descriptions have varied from city to city.

PAUL ALEXANDER: For Salinger fans, the most important thing Salinger told Fosburgh was that he continued to write on a daily basis. I think that was the whole point of the phone call. He was annoyed and angry with the pirated editions, but a lawsuit was taking care of that. He wanted the public to know that he was still writing and what he was not doing was publishing. In 1970 J. D. Salinger paid back—with interest—Little, Brown the $75,000 advance it had given him for his next book. Salinger was willing to draw that distinction between writing and publishing; he had been drawing that distinction since 1965. This was the first interview that Salinger had granted since 1953. He painted a self-portrait of someone who was still completely devoted to his craft.

J. D. SALINGER (quoted in the *New York Times*, November 3, 1974):

> I'm not trying to hide the gaucheries of my youth. I just don't think they're worthy of publication. I wrote them a long time ago and I never had any intention of publishing them [in a book]. I wanted them to die a perfectly natural death. Some stories, my property, have been stolen. It's an illicit act. Suppose you had a coat you liked and somebody went into your closet and stole it—that's how I feel. It's amazing some law-and-order agency can't do something about this. I'm just trying to protect what privacy I have left.
>
> There is a marvelous peace in not publishing. Publishing is a terrible invasion of my privacy. I love to write. But I write just for myself and my own pleasure. I pay for this kind of attitude. I'm known as a strange, aloof kind of man. But all I'm doing is trying to protect myself and my work. I've survived a lot of things and I'll probably survive this.

PAUL ALEXANDER: Salinger had made a habit of telling the world that he was a recluse. But if he were really a recluse, he wouldn't have picked up the phone and called a reporter from the *New York Times.* He'd say he was a recluse, but his actions were those of someone who was very clearly manipulating the subject of his reclusiveness. He'd sold millions and millions of books. He was an extremely sophisticated man. He knew exactly what he was doing.

—

RICHARD STAYTON: In the early '70s, I was living in San Francisco and heard there was a new work by J. D. Salinger out. You could always find books at the secondhand bookstores in Berkeley, so I went over to Berkeley and on Telegraph Avenue found these two volumes, two slim paperbacks. I didn't have a lot of money in those days, so I just bought volume one. I took it home and was very excited to find all these early Salinger stories, including ones with Holden Caulfield, pre–*Catcher in the Rye.* When I went back to buy the second volume, not only were both volumes gone, but the store owners declined to admit they'd ever sold the first volume, which was absolutely baffling to me. I went to several secondhand bookstores: nobody had ever heard of the book. I'd lost my mind, evidently. I found an article in the *San Francisco Chronicle* that explained why I'd never be able to buy volume two of *The Complete Uncollected Short Stories of J. D. Salinger*: "A collection of early short stories by J. D. Salinger, author of *The Catcher in the Rye*, was once widely available in San Francisco, but has largely disappeared, local bookstore proprietors said today." I didn't want to violate J. D. Salinger's beliefs, but I certainly wanted volume two, and I've never found it.

MARK HOWLAND: In the 1970s I walked into a bookstore in Worcester, Massachusetts, called Ephram's. It's a great place, about three stories, lots of cobwebs, dust, catacombs, floor-to-ceiling stacks—some new books but mostly used. I remember walking down from the street level to the basement. There were books stacked right along the stairwell and I saw three copies of the two-volume *Complete Uncollected Short Stories of J. D. Salinger.* Immediately I knew what they were and couldn't believe I was standing in front of a gold mine. I went to the owner of the store and said, "Where did you get these?" He said, "I was in a café in Paris and a traveling book salesman with a briefcase came by, sat down at the table, and pulled these out." He told me he bought them for a dollar apiece, and I bought them for three dollars apiece from him. One of the big regrets of my life is that I didn't get all three. I got just one of each.

Conversation with Salinger #11

MICHAEL McDERMOTT: In 1979 I received an assignment from *Newsweek* to photograph J. D. Salinger. I'd photographed other people for *Newsweek* before, so I just asked the editor for the telephone number and address; I thought it was a regular assignment, but it wasn't. "It's not that easy, Mike," he told me. "We don't have personal information. He doesn't like to be photographed, we don't have an address to send you to or a telephone number to give you, but we do know he picks up mail in Windsor, Vermont."

I went to the public library, did a little research on Salinger, and found the photograph Lotte Jacobi took of him in 1951 for the book jacket of *The Catcher in the Rye*. *Life* magazine ran a photo in '61. Those weren't too much help. I started to realize this was a very reclusive person I was supposed to photograph, but I wasn't worried. I was a brash twenty-year-old, you know?

So, first day, after sitting there for four hours in my 1978 light metallic-green Volkswagen diesel Rabbit, drinking Pepsi and eating Cheetos, making myself sick, I didn't have him. I decided, it's five-thirty, the post office is closed, nobody's going to come and get their mail that day.

Then I just walked the streets late at night. I started to wonder if somebody tipped him off.

I never felt like I was chasing him or stalking him. It wasn't really a paparazzi shot. It was a very private photograph that I took from across the street. He never even knew I took his picture. He was probably really surprised when he saw it in *Newsweek*. He never saw me, and just as I got the first few shots off and thought I was going to get a better shot at him coming to his car, a couple of teenagers came up and stopped him and began to talk to him. He was friendly—chatted for a couple of minutes—then he said goodbye to them and I pulled the camera back around and I snapped off a couple more frames as he walked to his car. I knew I had it. He was even smiling a little. It was a beautiful photograph, perhaps the only candid photograph of J. D. Salinger that was ever taken, and I had it. On the drive back to Brattleboro, I was so happy, but I needed to make sure that the license plate number from the car he got into came back as Jerome David Salinger, and it did.

UNITED STATES
POST OFFICE
UNITED STATES
POST OFFICE

There were stories in newspapers; the AP ran it on the wire. There was a television story about me getting that photograph. Over the years I've thought about that picture quite a bit. It was a big deal.

SHARON STEEL: In a letter to Michael Mitchell dated August 31, 1979, Salinger starts updating Mitchell on Matthew, who is a sophomore in college, and Peggy, who is married and living in Boston. He had to deal with "two shitty literary kids" who took a photo of his face outside of the post office, which ran in a "news magazine." "Piss on 'em all," Salinger gripes.

Conversation with Salinger #12

SHANE SALERNO: On October 31, 1983, *People* magazine published an article about Salinger's son, Matthew Salinger.

PAUL CORKERY: "I love acting, it's great fun, but I don't want to be a celebrity or a superstar, don't want attention. I don't feel comfortable with it." That may seem a contrary opinion coming from a youth in a field where public recognition is practically the coin of the realm, but it's a lot less surprising given the genes involved. The speaker is Matt Salin-

Salinger's son, Matthew, an actor, in a CBS movie of the week.

ger, 23, the only son of one of the world's most notable recluses, author J. D. (*The Catcher in the Rye*) Salinger.

The elder Salinger hasn't appeared in print since 1965, when the *New Yorker* published his short story "Hapworth 16, 1924," and hasn't made a public appearance in almost as long, despite being steadily sought—and sometimes stalked—by nosy interviewers. Matt has inherited that same distaste—only now he's about to step onstage as a Studio 54 doorman, of all things. The play is *One Night at Studio*, written by his Princeton classmate Jordan Katz. The drama will run in a small theater in L.A. Even Matt acknowledges the play needs all the attention it can get. "It seems so selfish not to do interviews if people are curious about me because of my name and that will help the play," he says gamely. But before you can ask the first question, he lays down the ground rules: "I won't let people try to get at my father—find out about his life—through me. I know how much he does not want public attention. He is a wonderful father and I respect him, so I won't talk about him."

All right, let's talk about Matt. He and his sister, Margaret, 28, who is studying labor relations in England, were born and raised in Cornish, N.H., where J.D. still resides. His father and his mother, Claire Douglas, a Jungian psychologist now living in San Francisco, divorced when Matt was 6. But they lived near each other, and the children divided their time between them. "I was not the child of split parents," says Matt. "I was lucky, I thought. I liked the change of pace, and I got to know my parents as individuals. They became friends to me."

After two years as a boarder at a ski-oriented private school and four more at Andover, Matt found himself at Princeton, where he was as uncomfortable as Holden Caulfield in prep school. "At Princeton they were still stamping out Southern gentlemen for life in high corporate echelons, and that was just a little stifling," he recalls. "People knew all about everyone else. I didn't want that. I resent any sort of categorization." So he crossed the Hudson and joined the class of 1982 at Columbia. "It was wonderful," he says. "It was completely anonymous. One day I was walking across from building to building and found myself smiling. It was because I didn't know anyone, and no one knew me."

After trying his hand at several seasons of summer stock and getting his degree in art history, Matt worked briefly at Sotheby's auction house, appraising paintings and wondering if acting was for him. He lives in an Upper West Side Manhattan walk-up and dates Betsy Becker, 27, who

Matthew Salinger, second from left, top row, Phillips Andover athletic team.

was a coworker at Sotheby's. He has had roles on the soap operas *Ryan's Hope* and *One Life to Live*. Surely the name helps a little? "Up until now I've gotten every acting job I've had without anyone knowing who I am," Matt says. "I feel very good about that. In fact, only two people have ever recognized me on the street. One was a guy who tried to sell me a nickel bag on Columbus Circle in New York. He asked me, 'Wasn't you messin' with Cassie [in *One Life to Live*] on the stories?'"

The current role of Pete the doorman is Matt's first big part, and he relishes the challenge. "It's fun playing a bastard," he says. "I fill up pages and pages of a journal about Pete—how he'd behave in cold weather, what he has for breakfast. It's nice thinking and writing about those things. It's fun." Wait, did he say writing? "Well, yes," he admits sheepishly. "Right now I'm writing a screenplay with a fellow actor." But that's all he'll say. Anyway, he has been contemplating a more urgent challenge: opening night, Oct. 25, when he must face the critics as well as his mother. "She'll be coming down to the opening," he says with a small smile, "but I don't think my father will be coming here."

DAVID SHIELDS: Then, on December 28, 1984, the *Washington Post* published "Matt Salinger, Into the Spotlight," which was written by David Remnick, who would later succeed Tina Brown as the editor of the *New Yorker*. The interesting thing for me about the article is how thoroughly it plays out as a scene from "Franny": Matthew keeps trying to figure out if he's Lane Coutell or Lane Coutell's creator. Just slightly offstage are Dudley Moore and J. D. Salinger as opposing models: Moore, ex-Oxford satirist turned into one-note Hollywood shtick, vs. his father—encased in his art on a hill in New Hampshire. Even Remnick's tone is perfectly pitched between purr and scratch. Fame is what is being debated in every syllable: between and among Remnick, Moore, Matthew, and his father, and everyone in the room—including a couple putting on their coats—is completely confused about it. With every attempt to separate himself from his father, Matthew is hugging him ever more tightly.

DAVID REMNICK: Just a few years before he stopped publishing and went into seclusion, J. D. Salinger urged his friend and editor at *The New Yorker*, William Shawn, to accept the dedication of "Franny and Zooey" "as nearly as possible in the spirit of Matthew Salinger, age one, urging a luncheon companion to accept a cool lima bean."

Matthew Salinger is 24 now, tall and rangy like his father, handsome like his mother Claire, an actor like his father's creation Zooey. He has appeared as a hyperlibidinous lacrosse coach in the soap opera *One Life to Live*, as a crusher of slide-rule-bearing pipsqueaks in the movie *Revenge of the Nerds*. And he is now the star of Bill C. Davis's *Dancing in the End Zone*, which opens Jan. 3 at Broadway's Ritz Theatre. He plays a college football star tormented by the demands of his mother, his coach and his tutor.

"This is it for me," Matt Salinger says as he urges a luncheon companion to take a seat. "You don't get a chance on Broadway every day of the week."

Salinger is sitting now in an Upper East Side bistro that serves 300 varieties of omelet. "I don't know about fame," he continues. "I want to be successful as an actor, and if fame is a byproduct of that, well, then it's a necessary evil. It's not something I aspire to."

Dudley Moore is sitting over in the corner. An excruciatingly casual couple enters the restaurant. They notice Moore and start fumbling with their coats a little longer than absolutely necessary so they can stare at the movie star (but not forever, of course, this being just about the center of the sophisticated universe).

Salinger is the first to notice this little drama: "Fame is . . . well, you look over in the corner there at Dudley Moore. Everyone's staring at him. It's a loss of privacy."

Fame has been a constant and nagging companion to the Salinger family. *Catcher in the Rye*, published 34 years ago, was precisely the sort of intimate book that (in the words of Holden Caulfield), "when you're all done reading it, you wish the author that wrote it was a terrific friend of yours and you could call him up on the phone whenever you felt like it."

J. D. Salinger is about the last author in the world you could call up on the phone. It's unfair to speculate on what he felt or why, but something made him stop publishing and keep his distance from the public world. . . .

Salinger shuns interviews and makes it clear to his family and friends that he would rather not be talked about in public. He gave a brief interview to a girl from a local school in 1953 and to Betty Eppes of the "Fun" section of *The Baton Rouge Advocate* 27 years later. . . .

Matt [Salinger says,] "Obnoxious people would show up at the house and start demanding things. There were reporters, photographers, aspiring writers. He was as polite as they were. I just sort of accepted it all like you would a surrealist drama.

"I see red now when I hear about people bothering him. My father does not want a public life. That's been clear for many years now. He wants to write for the page and he wants his characters to be on the page and in the readers' minds. He doesn't want people to make him into something he's not. He thinks it's bad for him and his work to have a public life."

Happily not everyone joined in on the crush. "I read my father's books at the usual age, junior high and after. I love his writing. But my teachers were always sensitive enough not to teach them in the classes I was in, even though they normally would have. That was wonderful that they were so thoughtful."

Salinger began his acting career as Mouse Soldier No. 17 in a production of *The Nutcracker* at Norwich Elementary School in Norwich,

Vermont, just across the river from Cornish. At Andover, Salinger had the lead role in *Charley's Aunt*, which, he says, "was about the biggest thing I've done in theater until now."

Dancing in the End Zone is a drama marked by rather preachy writing and a set of conspicuous parallels and symbols. But the acting is strong and Salinger is a boyish, affecting presence on stage. At the opening preview last week, he fumbled his first line slightly, but as the play developed he looked comfortable and his performance was effective. Two highly experienced Broadway actors, Pat Carroll and Laurence Luckinbill, have been sage supports.

"Matt's doing great," Luckinbill says. "He sweats the details. He takes notes on what everyone says. He's not really that inexperienced. And if he's young, well, the kid in the play is supposed to be young in feeling. If he's not, he's not right."

Says producer Morton Gottlieb: "We auditioned about 100 guys for the part and we loved Matt. He's a wonderful actor and he looks like a football player. When we auditioned him, we didn't even know if he was related to the writer. It really doesn't matter. It may get us an extra mention or two in print, but I don't think anyone goes and buys a ticket because one of the actors is related to J. D. Salinger."

In *Revenge of the Nerds*, Salinger paid a multitude of Hollywood dues. As an apish football player, he somehow managed to ride a tricycle, dress as a woman and join in a group mooning session all within a couple of hours. "Great scenes in cinematic history," he calls them. Salinger turned down two movie roles to appear in *Dancing in the End Zone*. For sizable sums he could have beaten hell out of Rob Lowe in *St. Elmo's Fire* and polished a Ferrari in *Summer Jobs*.

Salinger is more than willing to work in the movies as well as on stage. "I'm getting married to jewelry designer Betsy Becker pretty soon and I do have to think about earning a living," he says. But Salinger's stint in Hollywood was not always pleasant.

"You're always having meetings with people you have little or no respect for. I've had people try to offer me things in exchange for doing something having to do with my father's work. You know, buy the rights to his work. You want to spit at people like that.

"When I first started acting I tried to make sure that as few people as possible knew who my father was. I was very self-conscious. My first agent didn't know and the agent that I've got now, her partner didn't even know until he saw a little squib in *Time* magazine. But I've finally realized that there's too much money at stake for someone to hire me if I didn't have any talent.

"Two years ago when I was first starting out, I never would have done an interview like this because it would have been all about my father. There would have been no purpose. Now there's a play. Maybe I can help the play.

"I love my father. I'm not rebellious against him at all. He's made a decision about how he wants to live. Why would I ever want to violate that in any way? It's me who's chosen a more public life. That's acting. That's the way it is."

DAVID SHIELDS: What's heartbreaking about these two profiles is the secret father-son compact: *People will pretend to be interested in the insignificant play or film in which you, my son, have a minor role, when what they want to hear about is me (which, you suspect, is the reason you got the role in the first place). You, Matthew, will dispense as much information as you need to in order to obtain the publicity, while maintaining a lofty distance toward any such calculation. And woe unto you if you prove to be less pure than I (who sat for a glam-photo shoot and then was shocked to find the photos in wide circulation).* It has to be soul-killing. The problem lies in the beginning: Salinger is having it both ways, the way most people do, being contradictory and even hypocritical, the way most people are, but insisting always that he—the author, the creator, the progenitor, the father—is the lone representative of clean hands, of saving spirituality. The Oedipal nature of it all is pretty explicit: Salinger supposedly hating Hollywood but not so secretly loving it, even being obsessed with it; his son seeking to become a successful actor, often playing the preppy monsters his father ridiculed.

SHARON STEEL: In a letter from Salinger to Michael Mitchell dated December 16, 1992, Salinger wishes Matthew had chosen a profession that didn't beat him down quite so much and wonders if he'd be happier doing something less "chancey" than "the acting business."

18

ASSASSINS

LAUREL, MARYLAND, 1972; NEW YORK CITY, 1980; WASHINGTON, D.C., 1981; BRENTWOOD, NEW YORK, 1983; HOLLYWOOD, 1989

The Catcher in the Rye reemerges in the 1980s, misinterpreted as an assassination manual.

DAVID SHIELDS: There's a huge amount of psychic violence in the book; Holden's voice is full of hellacious fury. If you read the book out of neediness or desperation, you will read Holden's antipathy to the culture as a license to kill. In the "wrong" hands, read the "wrong" way, the book's emotional rage can become an endorsement to express your hatred toward "phonies" through violence.

Is *Catcher* a dangerous book? When interviewed by us, John Guare, the author of *Six Degrees of Separation*, said, "If one person used something I had written as the justification for killing somebody, I'd say, 'God, people are crazy,' but if three people used something I had written as justification, I would really be very, very troubled by it. It's not the one; it's the series of three." The complicating factor in Salinger's case—the deepening factor—is the extraordinary intimacy he creates between narrator and reader, and this intimacy is mixed with sublimated violence. He's so good at creating a voice that seems to be practically caressing your inner ear.

It's as if the assassins and would-be assassins who read *The Catcher in the Rye* are reading the book too literally. Everywhere Holden goes—Pencey, Manhattan, his parents' apartment—he's an utterly powerless individual. What the book shows you is how Holden comes to accept and even embrace the weakness—the brokenness—within himself, within Phoebe, within everybody. If you're reading the book through an especially distorted lens, you feel so acutely Holden's powerlessness that you say, "Yeah, I feel powerless, too," and you don't make the crucial leap that Holden finally does and Salinger always does at the end of every book and what the imaginative reader is asked to do—which is to come to see the Fat Lady as Jesus Christ himself, buddy.

—

SHANE SALERNO: In John Guare's play *Six Degrees of Separation*, the protagonist, Paul, talks at length about *Catcher*.

JOHN GUARE: PAUL: A substitute teacher out on Long Island was dropped from his job for fighting with a student. A few weeks later, the teacher returned to the classroom, shot the student unsuccessfully, held the class hostage and then shot himself. Successfully. This fact caught my

Mark David Chapman.

eye: last sentence. *Times.* A neighbor described him as a nice boy. Always reading *Catcher in the Rye.*

The nitwit—Chapman—who shot John Lennon said he did it because he wanted to draw the attention of the world to *The Catcher in the Rye* and the reading of that book would be his defense. And young Hinckley, the whiz kid who shot Reagan and his press secretary, said if you want my defense all you have to do is read *Catcher in the Rye.* It seemed to be time to read it again. . . .

I borrowed a copy from a young friend of mine because I wanted to see what she had underlined and I read this book to find out why this touching, beautiful, sensitive story published in July of 1951 had turned into this manifesto of hate. I started reading. It's exactly as I remembered. Everybody's a phony. Page two: "My brother's in Hollywood being a prostitute." Page three: "What a phony slob his father was." Page nine: "People never notice anything."

Then on page twenty-two my hair stood up. Remember Holden Caulfield—the definitive sensitive youth—wearing his red hunter's cap. "A deer hunter hat? Like hell it is. I sort of closed one eye like I was taking aim at it. This is a people-shooting hat. I shoot people in this hat."

Hmmmm, I said. This book is preparing people for bigger moments in their lives than I ever dreamed of. Then on page eight-nine: "I'd rather push a guy out of the window or chop his head off with an ax than sock him in the jaw. I hate fist fights . . . what scares me most is the other guy's face. . . ."

I finished the book. It's a touching story, comic because the boy wants to do so much and can't do anything. Hates all phoniness and only lies to others. Wants everyone to like him, is only hateful, and is completely self-involved. In other words, a pretty accurate picture of a male adolescent.

And what alarms me about the book—not the book so much as the aura about it—is this: The book is primarily about paralysis. The boy can't function. And at the end, before he can run away and start a new life, it starts to rain and he folds.

Now there's nothing wrong in writing about emotional and intellectual paralysis. It may indeed, thanks to Chekhov and Samuel Beckett, be the great modern theme. The extraordinary last lines of *Waiting for Godot*—"Let's go." "Yes, let's go." Stage directions: They do not move.

But the aura around this book of Salinger's—which perhaps should be read by everyone *but* young men—is this: It mirrors like a fun-house mirror and amplifies like a distorted speaker one of the great tragedies of our times—the death of the imagination.

—

JAMES YUENGER: Chapman was graduated from high school in 1973. His yearbook photo shows an apple-cheeked young man with dark hair combed over his forehead in [a] Beatle cut. For some time he had been a YMCA counselor and was well-liked. He was especially effective with young people with drug habits. He stayed on at the "Y" while he attended classes for 18 months at the local DeKalb County Junior College.

TONY ADAMS: [I remember] a guy down on one knee, helping out a little kid, or with kids just hanging around his neck and following him everywhere he went. I've never seen anybody who was as conscientious about his job and as close to children as he was. The kids always called him Captain Nemo. That's what he wanted everybody to call him.

JAMES YUENGER: Too unsettled to continue in college—he was twenty and itching to wander—Chapman enlisted Adams's help in getting a job with a YMCA student work program in Beirut, Lebanon. That, too, did not work out.

"Once he got there, he stepped into the middle of a civil war," Adams said. "He had to stay in a shelter and he was just never able to do what he wanted to do there—work with kids."

JACK JONES: Chapman and another young volunteer spent their days huddled under furniture while bombs, rockets, and gunfire erupted in the streets outside. The YMCA volunteers were among the first evacuated from the country. Frightened and disappointed, he returned home to Decatur where his friends recall that he spoke fearfully of the experience and played cassette tapes he had recorded of gunfire and bombs exploding in the streets outside his hotel.

JAMES YUENGER: Chapman returned from Lebanon so depressed that YMCA officials arranged for him to work in a resettlement program for Vietnamese refugees at Fort Chaffee, Arkansas.

MARK DAVID CHAPMAN: I had come off the important experience of a trip to Lebanon—the first foreign trip I'd had—and surviving in a war zone, to the success of Fort Chaffee. Then, all of a sudden, there I was at Covenant College [a Presbyterian college in Tennessee], studying hard, not knowing what on earth hit me and not knowing until this day, this morning, why I was depressed. The true reason was that I felt like a nobody. . . . I wasn't in charge of anything. I wasn't in a foreign country taping bomb sounds down on the avenue. . . . I was just like everybody else—a nobody.

PAUL L. MONTGOMERY: Paul Tharp, community relations director of Castle Memorial Hospital on Oahu [Hawaii], said the young man had worked at the hospital's print shop from August 1977 to November 1979. . . . He said Mr. Chapman had left to seek work as a security guard.

Gloria H. Abe . . . was married to Mr. Chapman on June 2, 1979. . . . She worked in a travel agency in Honolulu. Mr. Chapman's mother also lives in Hawaii and was said to have lent him money for his New York trips.

JON WIENER: Mark David Chapman was going downhill. He had a job as a security guard [in Hawaii] where he'd been seen putting Lennon's name on a piece of tape over his own name on his uniform. He was becoming obsessed with John Lennon.

PAUL L. MONTGOMERY: On Oct. 27, Mr. Chapman paid $169 in cash for a five-shot Charter Arms revolver with a two-inch barrel at J&S Enterprises-Guns, Honolulu. The revolver is of a style that is easily concealed.

JON WIENER: He wrote to a friend, saying, "I'm going nuts." He was clearly aware that something bad was happening to him. He quit his job and decided to let his wife support him. That didn't make him feel any better. He was a guy who was increasingly having delusions, hearing voices, being troubled, and disturbed by the whole world around him.

J. REID MELOY: In the case of Mark David Chapman, we have an individual who had a variety of psychiatric and mental disorders. This was an individual who had a blighted life, whose father abused his mother, whose mother had a highly eroticized relationship with her son. Chapman himself did not have any whole, healthy sense of who he was.

JON WIENER: Then, in November 1980, he read Laurence Shames's article in *Esquire* about John Lennon, who had been one of his heroes. As the plane lifted from the ground and banked north toward New York City, Chapman was absorbed in the magazine's cover story, a critical and scathing commentary on the opulent life-style of sixties peacenik John Lennon.

LAURENCE SHAMES: On February 3, the *Los Angeles Times* let out that [Lennon] forked over $700,000 for a beachfront home in Palm Beach, Florida. In May, the *New York Daily News* reported that Lennon had picked up a sixty-three-foot sailboat and was mooring it on Long Island, where he also happened to own a home—this one a $450,000 gabled job in Cold Spring Harbor.

JON WIENER: Lennon was a man who represented all the hopes and dreams and utopias of the sixties. He had said, "Imagine no possessions; it isn't hard to do." The *Esquire* article was an exposé of Lennon as an over-the-hill capitalist, a rich person who had abandoned his ideals and who owned four mansions, a yacht, swimming pools, and many real estate holdings. He had tax lawyers finding loopholes for him. The theme of the article was: John Lennon is a sellout. He is a phony. This had special meaning to Chapman because he was one of the tens of millions who had read *The Catcher in the Rye*, and one of the things that meant the most to him in the novel was the idea of the phony, the person who isn't what he pretends to be. That was the source of the problems in the world, as Mark David Chapman came to see it.

Part of Chapman's mental illness was that he was very preoccupied with the evil forces in the world that were fighting the good forces. He heard voices he thought were the voices of the devil's minions. He said he heard them inside himself—the classic paranoid schizophrenic delusion. He had tried to kill himself several years earlier. Now he read the *Esquire* article and conceived a new mission. Lennon was a phony, and he decided he was going to do something about it.

JAY MARTIN: Having failed to kill himself, Chapman's identification with Lennon became more and more sinister. He projected his own suicidal wishes onto the object of his identification. Then, to kill the bad things in himself, he had to kill his double, Lennon. Once he had come to consider Lennon a phony, a betrayer of his generation's ideals, an impostor, he decided that to kill him would be to kill his own bad side. Apparently, Chapman came to see his task as a purification of his fictions. If he could kill the phony, bad Lennon, a forty-year-old businessman who watched a lot of television and who had $150 million, a son whom he doted on, and a wife who intercepted his phone calls—that's a description from Chapman himself—then Satan's demons would be defeated, and as a result the world and Chapman himself would be cleansed. One last time, he called his cabinet [the delusional steering committee over which he presided] of his internal world into session and submitted to [these] little people the proposal that he kill the John Lennon impostor.

JON WIENER: John Lennon kind of withdrew from the world for four years. I see this as a time of recovery and healing from all of the turmoil and misery of this two- or three-year immigration battle. He wanted to raise his young son, Sean. And then in 1980 he went back to making music, which was something his fans had missed for a long time. The last Lennon record had come out in 1975, so it had been five years of no music. In December 1980 Lennon was back in the studio. He was recording. He released a single, "Starting Over," that was going to be part of an album. After a period of withdrawal, Lennon was coming back.

The theme of the *Esquire* article was John Lennon is a sellout. John Lennon is a phony.

LAWRENCE GROBEL: And look at this guy, you know, he's a big rock star and he comes in a limousine. Phony stuff, Chapman says.

MARK DAVID CHAPMAN: Well, he, he's a phony.

J. REID MELOY: The word "phony" is used over thirty times in *The Catcher in the Rye*. . . . The word "kill" is used a lot in the book.

LAWRENCE GROBEL: You want me to teach you what reality is. . . . BANG!

—

JACK JONES: Returning to Reeves's apartment [childhood friend Dana Reeves, a sheriff's deputy in Henry County, Georgia], Chapman confided that he had brought a gun with him from Honolulu to New York City. He brought the gun for personal protection, he said, because he was carrying a large amount of cash and he feared being attacked and robbed on the violent sidewalks of New York. He told Reeves he had brought no ammunition from Hawaii, and explained that he had been unable to get bullets in New York. He asked Dana if he could spare a few extra shells for the gun that was still in a suitcase under the bed at his hotel . . .

Chapman refused to accept the standard, round-nosed, jacketed shells that Reeves initially offered him. He wanted something "with real stopping power," he said, "just in case." He selected five hollow-point Smith & Wesson Plus P cartridges designed to explode with the deadly effect of tiny hand grenades inside the soft tissue of anticipated human targets . . . just in case.

STEPHAN LYNN: Hollow-point bullets are made to explode and expand [after impact]. Chapman knew that. He knew what these bullets could do.

JON WIENER: In the future, Chapman would say he had wanted to be Holden Caulfield. That was a healthy wish. Caulfield was lonely and troubled, but he was wonderfully sane. Chapman had a moment like that when he returned to New York from going to Atlanta at the end of November. He called his wife and told her, "I've won a great victory. I'm coming home." He made an appointment at the Honolulu Mental Health Clinic for November 26. He was right: that decision was a great victory, a victory of sanity over the internal forces that tormented him. But it was only temporary. He never went back to the clinic, and a week later he started hanging around in the front of the Dakota. Mark David Chapman had lost his struggle.

Chapman was staying in a place not far from the Dakota. He was reading *The Catcher in the Rye*. In early December 1980 he acted out the key scenes in *Catcher.* On the morning of December 8, he joined a group of fans waiting outside the Dakota for autographs. Everybody knew where John Lennon lived in New York City. It was known he was recording now, so it wasn't unusual for there to be a half dozen fans waiting for him.

MARK DAVID CHAPMAN: On December 8, 1980, Mark David Chapman was a very confused person. He was literally living inside of a paperback novel, J. D. Salinger's *The Catcher in the Rye.* He was vacillating between suicide, between catching the first taxi home, back to Hawaii, between killing, as you [Larry King] said, an icon. . . . Mark David Chapman at that point was a walking shell who didn't ever learn how to let out his feelings of anger, of rage, of disappointment. Mark David Chapman was a failure in his own mind. He wanted to become somebody important, Larry. He didn't know how to handle being a nobody. He tried to be a somebody through his years, but as he progressively got worse—and I believe I was schizophrenic at the time, nobody can tell me I wasn't, although I was responsible—Mark David Chapman struck out at something he perceived to be phony, something he was angry at, to become something he wasn't, to become somebody.

J. REID MELOY: For Chapman, *The Catcher in the Rye* became the instrument of the murder he would carry out. *The Catcher in the Rye* is a sweet book. Holden's fantasy is to save those children. It's not a dark fantasy; it's not a killing fantasy. The perversion in cases [like Chapman's] is that you pull out passages to use to give you a rationale to carry out murder. It's important to recognize that with any narrative, if you are intent on homicide you can extract from the pages the rationale that allows you to go and kill.

Chapman traveled to New York City. He engaged in behaviors like Holden did in the book. He hired a prostitute. He met with that prostitute. But then the aggression came into play and he began to plan and carry out the act that brought him to New York City in the first place. He coveted what John Lennon had. He wanted to take that from him.

PAUL ALEXANDER: In the late morning [of December 8], Chapman greeted Lennon's housekeeper when she took Sean for a walk, even going so far as to pat the five-year-old on the head. *Double Fantasy,* Lennon's new album on which he had collaborated with Yoko Ono, had been released three weeks earlier by Geffen Records.

MARK DAVID CHAPMAN: The adult and the child got up that morning and laid out all the important things to the child: The Bible. The photo with the Vietnamese kids. The music [*The Ballad of Todd Rundgren*, an album by Lennon rival Todd Rundgren]. The pictures of *The Wizard of Oz*. The passport and the letters of commendation for my work with the Vietnamese kids. This was the child's message, the tableau that said: This is what I was. These are the things that I was. I'm about to go into another dimension.

PAUL L. MONTGOMERY: About 5 p.m. . . . Mr. Lennon and Miss Ono left the Dakota for a recording studio. Mr. Chapman approached Mr. Lennon for an autograph . . . and he scribbled on the cover of his new album, *Double Fantasy*, recorded with Miss Ono and released two weeks ago.

MARK DAVID CHAPMAN: I left the hotel room, bought a copy of *The Catcher in the Rye*, signed it to Holden Caulfield from Holden Caulfield, and wrote underneath that "This is my statement," underlining the word "this," the emphasis on the word *this*. I had planned not to say anything after the shooting. Walked briskly up Central Park West to 72nd Street and began milling around there with fans that were there, Jude and Jerry, and later a photographer that came there. . . .

[Lennon] was doing an RKO radio special, and he came out of the building and the photographer . . . Paul Gores, he kind of pushed me forward and said, here's your chance. You know, you've been waiting all day. You've come from Hawaii to have him sign your album. Go, go.

And I was very nervous and I was right in front of John Lennon instantly and I had a black, Bic pen and I said, John, would you sign my album. And he said sure. Yoko went and got into the car, and he pushed the button on the pen and started to get to it write. It was a little hard to get it to write at first. Then he wrote his name, John Lennon, and underneath that, 1980.

And he looked at me . . . he said, is that all? Do you want anything else? And I felt then and now that he knew subconsciously that he was looking into the eyes of the person that was gonna kill him.

PAUL L. MONTGOMERY: A newspaper reproduction of a picture [of the encounter] taken by a freelance photographer [Gores] shows Mr.

Mark David Chapman.

Chapman with tousled hair and wire-rim glasses, wearing a dark raincoat and a scarf.

JAY MARTIN: Chapman urged the photographer to remain on the scene until Lennon returned. "You never know," he said. "Something might happen." The photographer left, but Chapman stayed.

PAUL ALEXANDER: At one point, Chapman returned to his hotel room, where he had left his autographed copy of *Double Fantasy*. He then returned to the Dakota.

JON WIENER: Eventually, Lennon's car came back with John and Yoko in it. Chapman was waiting outside.

PAUL L. MONTGOMERY: The Lennons returned to the Dakota at about 10:50 p.m., alighting from their limousine on the 72nd Street curb although the car could have driven through the entrance and into the courtyard. . . . Three witnesses—a doorman at the entrance, an elevator operator and a cab driver who had just dropped off a passenger—saw Mr. Chapman standing in the shadows just inside the arch. . . .

MARK DAVID CHAPMAN: John came out, and he looked at me, and I think he recognized, here's the fellow that I signed the album earlier, and he walked past me. I took five steps toward the street, turned, withdrew my Charter Arms .38, and fired five shots into his back. . . . Before, everything was like dead calm. And I was ready for this to happen. I even heard a voice, my own, inside me say, do it, do it, do it. You know, here we go.

PAUL L. MONTGOMERY: As the couple walked by, Chief Sullivan said Mr. Chapman called, "Mr. Lennon." Then, he said, the assailant dropped into "a combat stance" and emptied his pistol at the singer.

Mr. Lennon staggered up six steps to the room at the end of the entrance used by the concierge, said "I'm shot," then fell face down.

MARK DAVID CHAPMAN: Afterwards, it was like the film strip broke. I fell in upon myself. I like went into a state of shock. I stood there with the gun hanging limply down at my right side and José the doorman came over and he's crying, and he's grabbing and he's shaking my arm and he shook the gun right out of my hand, which was a very brave thing to do to an armed person. And he kicked the gun across the pavement, had somebody take it away and I was just—I was stunned.

JAY MARTIN: Immediately following the shooting, Chapman calmly removed his coat and sweater—apparently so the police, when they arrived, would see that he was unarmed and intended no further harm—and took his copy of *The Catcher in the Rye* and read with intense concentration. . . . To have the book with him—he was right there with J. D. Salinger, right there with Holden.

—

STEPHEN SPIRO: I was a police officer in the Twentieth Precinct. I was in a radio car at approximately 10 minutes till 11 on the evening of December 8 when my partner, Peter Cullen, and I pulled up to the

Dakota. There was a man standing out in the street, pointing into the archway, saying, "That's the man doing the shooting!" I got out of the car, drew my gun, and proceeded to walk up against the side of the building until I saw a man standing there with his hands up. It was very dimly lit, but because he had his hands up and the shirt he was wearing was white, I saw right away he didn't have a gun. I proceeded, trying to size up what was happening. I walked in, grabbed the man around the shoulders, and switched them around so his back was to me and I had my arm around his neck, because I thought maybe there were more shooters; maybe they were robbing somebody in the Dakota.

At that point I turned to my right and saw a gentleman who I knew as the doorman, José. José said, "He's the only one." I looked at the guy I had and threw him up against the wall. Just as I was doing this, José yelled out, "He shot John Lennon! He shot John Lennon!" I said, "Oh, my God."

I said to the guy, "You did what?" He said, "I acted alone." I thought, "That's the strangest statement I've ever heard." I pushed him against the wall and handcuffed him as my partner came in behind me.

There were other police officers responding to the scene and they had run into the vestibule, where they found John Lennon bleeding to death. They picked him up—two of them, Herbie Frownberger and Tony Palmer, who were both weightlifters. When I turned around, I saw them carrying John Lennon at shoulder height. His eyes were closed and blood trickled out of the side of his mouth. Right away, when somebody is face up and blood is coming out of his mouth, you know his lungs are filled up with blood. It was obviously a serious wound. I knew they must have decided they could get him to Roosevelt Hospital faster than an ambulance could. Maybe they could save his life that way.

DAVID SHIELDS: Lennon was carried into the squad car of officers Bill Gamble and James Moran and driven to Roosevelt Hospital about a mile away.

PAUL L. MONTGOMERY: Officer Moran said they stretched Mr. Lennon out on the back seat and that the singer was "moaning." [Officer Moran] said he had asked, "Are you John Lennon?" and Mr. Lennon had moaned, "Yeah."

STEPHEN SPIRO: I stood at the Dakota in amazement. I had the guy against the wall—later I'd find out his name was Mark David Chapman—and he was saying, "Don't hurt me!"

I said, "Nobody's going to hurt you. We're going to take you down to the stationhouse." I looked on the ground and said, "Are these your clothes?" He had taken off his outer garments to make sure it was noticeable he was wearing white. He was only 500 feet from a subway station. He could've run away and been gone in a matter of seconds. It was clear he wanted to stay there.

"Are these your clothes?" I said. He said, "Yes, and the book is mine, too." The book was *The Catcher in the Rye*. I picked it up. I told him we would take it along with his clothes.

When we got him to the stationhouse, we took him to a detention cell, where we did a strip search to make sure he had no more weapons

Mark David Chapman being arrested; on his right, NYPD officer Stephen Spiro.

on him. At that time, we found out he was from Hawaii and he was wearing thermal underwear when it was 50 degrees outside. When I looked inside the book, he had written, "This is my statement." I didn't understand what that meant at the time.

—

STEPHAN LYNN: I arrived at the emergency room before the patient. The chief surgical resident was standing there when the patient rolled in. He didn't come in by ambulance; the police actually carried the patient into the room.

We rushed into the trauma room. We took off his clothes. There were three wounds in the left upper chest and one through the left arm. There was no blood pressure, no pulse, no vital signs, no response. We knew exactly what we had to do: IVs, blood transfusions, surgical procedure in the emergency department. We opened the chest to look for the source of the bleeding. In the process, the nurses took the wallet out of the pocket of the patient. They said, "This can't be John Lennon." We realized it was when Yoko Ono came into the emergency room.

When we opened the chest, we saw there was a tremendous amount of blood. Those three bullets destroyed the vessels leading out of the heart, cut them to bits. We tried. We gave him blood. We pushed on the vessels that were broken. I literally held his heart in my hand. We massaged his heart, but it was empty. There was no blood in it. We tried to get the heart started again. There was nothing we could do. After about 20 minutes, we declared John Lennon dead. When we were done, the nurses, I, everybody in the emergency room, stopped for a second to realize what had happened and where we had been.

My next task was to speak to Yoko Ono. David Geffen was with her. I said, "I have bad news for you. He's dead, in spite of all of our efforts." Yoko refused to believe it. She said, "No! It's a lie! It can't be. You're lying to me. It can't be true. Tell me he's not dead." But after about five minutes, she understood. The first thing she said after that was, "Doctor, please don't make the announcement for 20 minutes so I can go home and see Sean and tell him what's going on."

—

Yoko Ono escorted by police to John Lennon's memorial.

RICHARD STAYTON: I was in a restaurant, having a steak, watching *Monday Night Football.* I remember Howard Cosell interrupting the game by saying, "Sometimes events change the way you see your life, and why are we watching this game? The game doesn't matter. John Lennon has been murdered." Frank Gifford said, "John Lennon?" Everybody where I was sitting said, "John Lennon? You got to be kidding." It was the blow I felt when I heard Robert Kennedy was shot and murdered, but I felt closer to John Lennon than I felt when RFK or JFK was killed.

MARK DAVID CHAPMAN: I never wanted to hurt anybody, my friends will tell you that. I have two parts in me. The big part is very kind. The children I work with will tell you that. I have the small part in me that cannot be understood. . . . I did not want to kill anybody and I really don't know why I did. I fought against the small part for a long time. But for a few seconds the small part won. I asked God to help me but we are responsible for our own actions. I have nothing against John Lennon or anything he has done in the way of music or personal beliefs. I came to New York about five weeks ago from Hawaii and the big part of me did not want to shoot John. I went back to Hawaii and tried to get rid of my small part but I couldn't. I then returned to New York [on December 6, 1980, after leaving Honolulu] on Friday, December 5, 1980. I checked into the YMCA on 62nd Street. I stayed one night. Then I went to the Sheraton Centre 7th Ave. Then this morning I went to the bookstore and bought *The Catcher in the Rye*.

I'm sure the large part of me is Holden Caulfield who is the main person in the book. The small part of me must be the Devil. I went to the building; it's called the Dakota. I stayed there until he came out and asked him to sign my album.

At that point my big part won and I wanted to get back to the hotel, but I couldn't. I waited until he came back. He came in a car. Yoko walked past me first and I said hello. I didn't want to hurt her. Then John came, looked at me and printed me. I took the gun from my coat pocket and fired at him. I can't believe I could do that. I just stood there clutching the book. I didn't want to run away. I don't know what happened to the gun, I just remember José kicking it away. José was crying and telling me to please leave. I felt so sorry for José. Then the police came and told me to put my hands on the wall and cuffed me.

STEPHEN SPIRO: What confuses me is these people follow this book like it's the bible for achieving something in life, when this kid was a mixed-up adolescent visiting New York City and fantasizing about certain things. I don't think J. D. Salinger ever meant for anybody to hurt somebody with his thoughts. Mark David Chapman portrays himself as the catcher in the rye to stop children from jumping over the cliff after they run through the field of rye and he's going to stop them and be their savior. Well, I don't see how that equates to him killing people.

DAVID SHIELDS: After being charged with second-degree murder, Chapman decided in January 1981 to use his trial to broadcast his interpretation of *The Catcher in the Rye*. Chapman told his attorney, Jonathan Marks, that God told him to plead guilty. Two weeks later, on June 22, Judge Dennis Edwards questioned Chapman at the start of the trial and found him to be of sound mind. Edwards accepted the guilty plea and sentenced Chapman to twenty years to life on August 24.

Courtroom sketch of Mark David Chapman, who stated that his defense can be found in *The Catcher in the Rye.*

STEPHEN SPIRO: Mark David Chapman wrote me a letter that I should read *Catcher in the Rye* to understand why he committed this murder.

MARK DAVID CHAPMAN, excerpt from letter to Stephen Spiro, January 28, 1983:

> *The reason I wanted to write you was that from the time of my arrest I have felt close to you. It is something that would happen to Holden Caulfield. If you are familiar with him and* The Catcher in the Rye, *please reread the book. It will explain a lot of what happened on the night of December 8th. To answer your question of what was meant by "This is my statement," the only way I can explain it is this way. Do you remember the young woman in Saigon during the Vietnam War who immolated herself? I believe her name was Nhat Chi Mai. She believed so strongly in the purpose that she*

chose to end her life rather than continue living in the phony world. The damn war did this to her. What a noble lady. Poems were found on her and around her concerning her beliefs. This was her statement to leave to the world. Catcher in the Rye *is my statement. The book is incredible.*

JAY MARTIN: A dramatic moment occurred in the court when the judge, before sentencing, asked Chapman if he had anything of his own he wanted to tell the court that might influence the sentencing. Perhaps it would explain why he did what he did. Chapman said, "Yes." He was going to have a vow of silence, but first he would speak and speak from his heart. God allowed him to become Holden Caulfield and to speak Holden's words. He had killed phoniness. He had murdered evil. He had rid the world of death. He was the catcher in the rye.

So when Chapman spoke, his words came directly from *The Catcher in the Rye*, only he recited them as if they were his own words and as if they expressed the precise position at which he personally had arrived. "I kept picturing all these little kids playing some game in this big field of rye and all. Thousands of little kids. And nobody's around, nobody big, I mean, except me. And I'm standing at the edge of some crazy cliff. What I have to do, I have to catch everybody if they start to go over the cliff. I mean, if they're running and they don't look where they're going, I have to come out from somewhere and catch them. That's all I'd do all day. I'd just be the catcher in the rye and all. I know it's crazy, but that's the only thing I'd really like to do." That's the only thing Chapman wanted to do—to become Holden Caulfield. He acted the passage out as if he were Holden Caulfield because he believed he was. Those were his last words in the court.

Chapman's final testimony amounted to this: He himself had ceased to exist. In a letter to his wife, he stated that this was so. He no longer existed in his own being. He had found his true being in Salinger's novel.

Chapman took from Holden the opposite of freedom. He identified so extremely that the identification became self-sustaining, because it gave him a self that he didn't possess before. He had to do what Salinger didn't do and what Holden himself didn't do: go with it fully. *Catcher in the Rye* is not meant to be a dangerous book. It's meant to be a curative book.

MARK DAVID CHAPMAN, excerpt from letter to Stephen Spiro, January 15, 1983:

> *Have you read* The Catcher in the Rye*? I know this will help you to further understand, to answer your questions.* The Catcher in the Rye *is the statement. I probably forgot to tell you that I underlined the word "This," so it read "*This *is my statement," meaning the book itself. Did you ever see what I sent to the* New York Times *on February 9, 1981?* [The newspaper published a letter written by Chapman.] *This further explains what happened on the night of December 8, 1980. I will let you decide whether Mr. Lennon was a phony or not. His own words shot his life purpose full of holes. If you dig deep and not idolize, it is all there. Yes, Lennon was a phony to the highest degree and there were others who could and would have served the same purpose.*

J. REID MELOY: Holden Caulfield was not an assassin. Yet with his psychopathology, Mark David Chapman was able to twist that book and extract from it a narrative he could identify with that led him somehow to assassinate John Lennon. Chapman came to believe that he was the Holden Caulfield of his generation and that he could save his generation. That is pure grandiosity—what is referred to as pathological narcissism, where you become a legend in your own mind. There was an aggression tied to that narcissism that gave him the drive and the means and the motivation to kill.

JAY MARTIN: Salinger certainly had no intention with *Catcher* of anything other than writing a good book—a book that, he said, needed to be written. The effect of what Salinger did in placing his own distress into a character was to make that character available to millions of people. Of those many millions, maybe a few will take it more seriously, more dramatically, than a normal reader, who will simply say, "That's an interesting book."

—

MARK DAVID CHAPMAN: So it didn't end with the death of John Lennon and that's, you know—you keep paying for this over and over

John Hinckley, who, under the influence of *The Catcher in the Rye*, attempted to assassinate President Ronald Reagan.

when you hear of the death of a celebrity and maybe they've got *The Catcher in the Rye*, as John Hinckley did.

JOHN GUARE: Yes, *The Catcher in the Rye* is a wonderful book for adults to read about a certain time of life. But it also gives validity to fifteen-year-olds to say, "I am the only thing on this planet and you are all worthy of annihilation because you're all phony." I use it in *Six Degrees of Separation* because the play asks the question: Is this young man [Paul] authentic or false? And *Catcher in the Rye* embodies the conflict between what is true and what is false.

DINTY MOORE: Across from the Dakota that evening [of Lennon's murder], thousands of mourners began immediately to congregate. Among them was John Hinckley Jr. Hinckley had seen the movie *Taxi*

Driver—fifteen times—and had begun to imitate Travis Bickle's preference for fatigue jackets, army boots, and peach brandy. He also developed an obsession with Jodie Foster, the child-prostitute in the film, and began to stalk her.

JACK JONES: The list of ingredients on Hinckley's murder recipe, like Chapman's and [Robert] Bardo's [who later killed the actress Rebecca Schaeffer], included a .38 caliber Charter Arms Special and a copy of *The Catcher in the Rye.*

JAY MARTIN: Chapman's in the papers. He's being shown on TV. He's a character as much as Holden. And so you copycat him. So you go ahead and look at *Catcher in the Rye* and you say, "That's how I'll become John Hinckley, by becoming Mark David Chapman and by becoming Holden Caulfield, and eventually it might be by reading J. D. Salinger."

DINTY MOORE: Hinckley settled on assassination as his best strategy to win Foster's heart, and on March 30, 1981, fired six times at President Ronald Reagan outside of the Hilton Hotel in Washington, DC. In Hinckley's hotel room, police found a John Lennon calendar and a paperback copy of *The Catcher in the Rye.*

CYRUS NOWRASTEH: When Reagan left the luncheon, he walked out of the hotel. There was a very small group of people waiting to see him, cordoned off by some tape, and John Hinckley was waiting in the group. In fact, he had been there when the president arrived and had wandered around outside the hotel; he had gone inside and come back out. He may have been debating with himself whether he was really going to go through with it.

Something within Hinckley clicked when Reagan emerged from the luncheon, and he pulled the trigger.

J. REID MELOY: John Hinckley talked about how he wanted to be linked forever with Jodie Foster—which, through this act of attempting to assassinate Ronald Reagan, he has. In the minds of many people, he's linked with her, and it's unlikely she'll ever forget the name "John Hinckley."

CYRUS NOWRASTEH: Why repeat the same story? With Hinckley, you've got a much sexier cast: it's Jodie Foster, *Taxi Driver*, De Niro, Scorsese, people the media can hound and show clips of, and that's much more immediate than this book, which they'd already covered as the foundation to events.

—

ROBERT D. McFADDEN: A teacher's aide dismissed recently after a fight with a student returned to a Long Island school yesterday, wearing military fatigues and carrying a rifle, shot the youth and the principal, and took 18 students hostage.

Nine hours later, after releasing 17 hostages unharmed in groups and singly through the day and the evening, the gunman, 24-year-old Robert O. Wickes, fatally shot himself in the right temple.

JAMES BARRON: Mr. Wickes was calm, never pointed the gun at the hostages and tried to soothe them when they became nervous. He freed the students who were most uneasy and kept the calmest ones with him the longest. He even consulted some of the students before firing shots.

"He asked me if it was O.K. if he shot a few rounds at the map," Bryant [a student] said. "He was very polite. I said, 'Please, no, I get too nervous at guns.'"

Inside the second-floor social studies classroom, with a garbage can atop the teacher's desk to hide behind and shoot if the police stormed the room, Mr. Wickes told the students over and over that he trusted no one and that his dog, Goalie, was his only friend.

Nancy DeSousa, Mr. Gonzalez's daughter, noted Mr. Wickes's recent interest in Judaism and said he had been studying Hebrew. He talked of going to Israel, she said. "Bobby was very interested in everything, everything," she said. "He just was very intelligent."

Mrs. DeSousa spoke of his love for J. D. Salinger. "Bobby always carried around *Catcher in the Rye*—it was like his Bible," she said. "He was more thoughtful than the average boy his age. There's a deep story here. It's not just a mad killer with a gun."

—

MARCIA CLARK: During 1989 Robert Bardo had been communicating with Rebecca Schaeffer, sending postcards and letters for quite some time. Initially he wrote to her that she was someone he admired, someone who was not the usual Hollywood starlet type. She responded only twice, with postcards that were very neutral, very nice—thank-you-for-your-support kind of thing—and nothing more. There was nothing personal, nothing that seemed inappropriate at all.

J. REID MELOY: What Schaeffer didn't know was that Bardo had actually come to Los Angeles on a couple of occasions to look for her, driving around the Hollywood Hills because he had read in an article in *TV Guide* that she lived in the Hollywood Hills and he thought that by just driving around on the streets he would find her. He had come to the Warner Bros. ranch where she was shooting [the television show] *My Sister Sam* and made contact with the security guard there. Bardo had

Robert Bardo, who, under the influence of *The Catcher in the Rye*, killed the actress Rebecca Schaeffer.

chocolates and a big teddy bear for her, but the security guard told him, "You're not going to get to see her and you really ought to go home." The guard tried to counsel him and actually drove him back to the bus station because he thought he was harmless, a lonely kid who was in love with a star but who would never be seen or heard from again.

On July 18, after he had paid a private investigator in Tucson $250 for Schaeffer's address, Bardo came to her neighborhood with what could be termed his assassination kit: a CD, a gun, a bag, and a copy of *The Catcher in the Rye*.

STEPHEN BRAUN and CHARISSE JONES: From his parents' house in a treeless, sun-parched subdivision in Tucson, Robert John Bardo wrote letter after letter to actress Rebecca Schaeffer, missives to another world.

Scrawled shakily in pen, the letters were Bardo's way of reaching out from the boredom and insignificance of his young life. At 19, a janitor at a succession of hamburger stands, he was on the cusp of manhood, but going nowhere.

Bardo detailed his chaste devotion to the fresh-faced young woman who appeared to him only when his television set glowed. He quoted John Lennon lyrics. He told her he was "a sensitive guy." In one passage, he explained: "I'm harmless. You could hurt me."

Just before his journey to Los Angeles, he wrote his sister in Knoxville, Tenn., saying: "I have an obsession with the unattainable and I have to eliminate (something) that I cannot attain."

ASSOCIATED PRESS: The star of the television series "My Sister Sam" was shot to death outside her apartment here Tuesday, and a man described as "an obsessive fan" was being held today in Arizona in the shooting.

California authorities filed a felony arrest warrant today for the man, Robert John Bardo, 19, of Tucson, Ariz., a former fast-food restaurant worker who was arrested by Tucson police earlier today for running in front of cars.

STEPHEN BRAUN and CHARISSE JONES: Later, acting on information supplied by Bardo, police would find a gun holster in the alley just south of and parallel to Beverly Boulevard. A yellow shirt was found on the roof of a cleaners. And on the roof of a rehabilitation center came a final piece of evidence—a red paperback copy of the novel *The Catcher in the Rye.*

—

J. REID MELOY: It's important to remember that these three males—Chapman, Hinckley, and Bardo—were all in their early to mid-twenties when they did what they did. It takes a young male's aggression to carry out an act of assassination. These individuals are not just pursuing a celebrity figure; they are intent on killing the celebrity figure. We know murder is an act of young men.

If you are driven by homicidal urges, if you have a desire to kill certain figures, the book becomes a rationale for your killing and for the planning of that assassination. Holden Caulfield feels emotionally impotent. Chapman, Hinckley, and Bardo felt emotionally impotent. The gun became the equalizer. The gun brought potency to these young men, for a moment, through their assassinations.

MICHAEL SILVERBLATT: Let's examine the record: The diary purported to be by [Arthur] Bremer, who shot George Wallace [a copy of *The Catcher in the Rye* was found in Bremer's Milwaukee apartment after the shooting], contains references to Dostoevsky, especially to Raskolnikov [the main character and murderer in Dostoevsky's *Crime and Punishment*]. Dostoevsky is thought to be a big inspirer of assassins and bomb throwers—who knows why I find it easier for people to think of Dostoevsky than J. D. Salinger as a terrorist tutor? You're talking about a very particular kind of assassin, someone who feels neglected and lost, and I do think that Salinger is a great romantic about loneliness, about not being loved or wanted, about not being able to figure out how to move on.

What could be more beautiful? Who didn't want a masked avenger to protect you if you were the pimply guy whom no one wanted to talk to or who wasn't let into the room when the clique was meeting? In Salinger's very last published work ["Hapworth 16, 1924"], Seymour Glass is telling his family that they have superpowers. Buddy can read and memorize an entire novel in twenty minutes. They're a family of superheroes, and they're warned not to tell the librarians and teachers about their ability. These characters clearly are on earth to rescue the rest of us.

HENRY GRUNWALD: The discussion can easily become obsessive and excessive. Perhaps we should all observe a moratorium on Salinger talk. But we won't, and [the literary critic] John Wain has explained why not. Wain dislikes "Seymour" for all the usual reasons, and in fact suggests rather plaintively that Salinger brutally maltreats his readers in that story. But, he admits, "We won't leave. We stay, rooted to the spot. [We're] not in a position to go elsewhere. Because no one else is offering quite what Mr. Salinger is offering."

MARK DAVID CHAPMAN: I'm not blaming a book. I blame myself for crawling inside of the book and I certainly want to say J. D. Salinger and *The Catcher in the Rye* didn't cause me to kill John Lennon. In fact, I wrote to J. D. Salinger, I got his box number from someone, and I apologized to him for this. I feel badly about that. It's my fault. I crawled in, found my pseudo-self within these pages . . . and played out the whole thing. Holden wasn't violent, but he had a violent thought of shooting someone, of emptying a revolver into this fellow's stomach, someone that had done him wrong. He was basically a very sensitive person and he probably would not have killed anybody, as I did. But that's fiction, and reality was standing in front of the Dakota.

John Lennon wasn't the only person to die because of this. . . . Robert Bardo wrote me three letters. I don't have them anymore. I tore them up. They were very deranged letters. . . . I got frightened.

DAVID SHIELDS: During a period of four months, a world-famous musician/political activist was killed and the president of the United States was nearly killed, winning admiration for uttering the movie-like line, "I should have ducked." Both John Hinckley and especially Mark David Chapman cited *The Catcher in the Rye* as an influence. Salinger drove into Windsor, Vermont, every day to pick up the *New York Times,* which his letters indicate he read carefully. A large satellite dish was attached to his house; he watched quite a lot of television, including the news. In late 1980 and early 1981 he must have been inundated with information about the role his iconic novel played in these two traumatic events, about which he never made a public comment. Maybe he felt found out. Maybe he thought Chapman and Hinckley had gotten the blood-soaked violence buried within the pages of his beautiful book. Reportedly, in 1979 he pulled back a story—already in galleys—from the

New Yorker at the last minute. He never published another story or book, never even came very close, and it's difficult to believe Chapman and Hinckley weren't forever standing guard at the gates of his imagination.

ETHEL NELSON: I remember seeing Jerry a week or so after John Lennon was murdered. Jerry was walking the streets alone, head down. I said hi to him and he walked by without even saying hi. And I knew him since 1953.

PART IV

SANNYASA

RENUNCIATION OF THE WORLD

19

A PRIVATE CITIZEN

CORNISH, NEW HAMPSHIRE, 1981–2010

For the past two decades [1966–86] I have elected, for personal reasons, to leave the public spotlight entirely. I have shunned all publicity for over twenty years and I have not published any material during that time. I have become, in every sense of the word, a private citizen.

J. D. Salinger

DAVID SHIELDS: Salinger spent 1950–80 crafting a myth. He will spend 1980–2010 fighting to control, protect, and defend that myth. He's in a defensive crouch—battling his daughter, his former lover, his would-be biographer. He loves to hate them, to see in them only ego. He's partly right: the world provides minute-by-minute proof of human corruption. But in Salinger's flexible moral compass, his nonabsolute absolutism, one can see ego as well. This contradiction doesn't sit well with the Salinger purity narrative, and so he moves to quash rumors of his human foibles, anxiously managing his image while pretending to be above any such base considerations. Salinger is a man hungrily alive to the sound of his own righteousness. His message to Ian Hamilton, Joyce Maynard, and Margaret Salinger: "I don't know who you are," which for him is the definition of oblivion. Complicating irony: in his zeal to save himself, he destroys himself—his reputation, his writing life, his relationships with friends, loved ones, family members.

—

S. J. PERELMAN: [After a visit to Martha's Vineyard] I ended up spending a night with Jerry Salinger, up on the Vermont border, in his aerie. We hadn't seen each other for six years, and I'm glad to report that he looks fine, feels fine, and is working hard, so you can dispel all those rumors, manufactured in Hollywood by the people to whom he won't sell *Catcher in the Rye*, to the effect that he has taken leave of his senses.

ANDREAS BROWN: Through the years, Salinger would come into the store five or six times a year, usually with his son. He normally made a beeline for the philosophy/religion alcove, and if Mrs. Steloff, who founded our store, was in, he'd sit and talk with her for a considerable length of time. His demeanor in our store was this: If he needed something, he would talk to the staff. We treated him offhandedly, as if he was nobody, because that's the way he wanted to be treated. We would help him, quote books for him we thought he might be interested in, and search for books for him on occasion. But if a fan came up to him and wanted to strike up a conversation or wanted him to sign something or talk to him, he would excuse himself and almost always leave the store. People would always want him to explain why Holden Caulfield did something in chapter seven—that sort of thing. Or they'd ask him what he meant by something in *Franny and Zooey*. They'd be playing college sophomore. Then again, more than one generation has grown up with Salinger.

The first time he brought in Matt, I thought to myself, "That's Holden Caulfield, he's stepping right off the paperback," because Matt had his baseball cap sideways or backwards at a time when kids didn't wear baseball caps that way. This little kid came into the store looking just like that, and he'd be completely disinterested in what his father was doing. He'd find the cartoon books. He could sit on the floor for hours looking at Charles Addams.

CATHERINE CRAWFORD: One example of the lengths that fans will go to get Salinger's attention was when a number of high school kids devised this elaborate plan, and they actually threw one of their friends out of a car. They drove by his house, and they had covered the kid in ketchup to make him look bloody and he landed on the ground outside of Salinger's house, moaning, rolling around. Salinger came to the window, took one look and knew it was fake, so he shut the blinds and went back to work.

—

DAVID SHIELDS: In 1981 Elaine Joyce, one of the stars of *Mr. Merlin*, a sitcom, received a fan letter from Salinger—the same M.O. he followed with countless other young, talented, beautiful women. A correspondence ensued.

PAUL ALEXANDER: As he had with Maynard, Salinger eventually arranged for [himself and Elaine Joyce] to meet. Subsequently a relationship developed. They spent a lot of time in New York. "We were very, very private," she says, "but you do what you do when you date—you shop, you go to dinner, you go to the theater. It was just as he wanted it." In May 1982, when the press reported Salinger showing up for an opening night at a dinner theater in Jacksonville, Florida, where Joyce was appearing in the play *6 Rms Riv Vu*, to conceal their affair she denied knowing him. "We were involved for a few years through the middle eighties," Joyce says. "You could say there was romance." Eventually the romance ended and, ironically enough, she moved on to marry the playwright Neil Simon.

SHANE SALERNO: After his brief relationship with Elaine Joyce, Salinger dated Janet Eagleson, who was much closer to Salinger's age than most of the women he dated.

J. D. SALINGER, excerpt from letter to Janet Eagleson, August 9, 1982:

> *The more I age, senesce, the more convinced I am that our chances of getting through to any intact sets of reasons for the way things go are nil. Oh, we're allowed any number of comically solemn assessments—the burning of "Rosebud" the adored sled, or, no less signally, the burning of the new governess's backside—but all real clues to our preferences, stopgaps, arrivals, departures, etc., remain endlessly hidden. The only valid datum, anywhere, I suspect, is the one the few gnanis adamantly put forward: that we're not who or what we thing* [sic] *we are, not persons at all, but susceptible to myriad penalties for thinking we're persons and minds. . . .*

I'm o.k., I think, and so is Matthew, thanks for asking. He's in California, at the moment. Talking to actors' agents, etc. My other kid, Peggy, is off to Oxford for two years, on some sort of academic scholarship. She and her mother are looking rather exalted about it. Exemplary achievers, both of them, mother and daughter.

MYLES WEBER: In 1982 an aspiring writer named Steven Kunes submitted an interview with J. D. Salinger to *People*. The magazine prepared to publish it. Salinger caught wind of the hoax, brought suit against Kunes, and stopped publication of the interview.

J. D. SALINGER, excerpt from letter to Janet Eagleson, August 9, 1982:

I'm in the middle of some legal action, irritating and wearying, and probably hopeless. Meaning that no sooner is one opportunist and parasite dealt with than the next guy turns up. Some prick took out a whole page ad in the Sunday Times Book Section pretending it was me or my doing. It, too, shall pass, no doubt, as Louis B. Mayer once said, but it would be nice to know when.

***THE NEW YORK TIMES*:** According to the suit, Mr. Kunes "offered for sale to *People* magazine a completely fictitious 'interview' with J. D. Salinger" and misrepresented it as "a transcript of an actual interview." "The fraudulent interview," the suit adds, "grossly distorts and demeans the plaintiff's character, it misrepresents the plaintiff's opinion, and it falsely imitates his style."

JOHN DEAN: My immediate reaction was: this is another scam like the Howard Hughes book, when Clifford Irving pretended to have Howard Hughes's permission. Salinger put it to sleep very quickly when he filed a lawsuit and prohibited *People* from using the interview.

ASSOCIATED PRESS: A settlement has been reached in a suit filed by J. D. Salinger against a New Yorker he accused of impersonating him and passing off his writings as those of the novelist and short-story writer.

Judge David N. Edelstein of the United States District Court approved the settlement in which the defendant, Steven Kunes of Manhattan, agreed to be permanently enjoined from representing by any means that he is associated with or ever met Salinger.

The agreement also barred Mr. Kunes from exhibiting, transmitting or distributing documents, writing or statements attributed to Mr. Salinger. Mr. Kunes is also required to collect and turn over any such documents or writing for destruction. Mr. Salinger, in turn, agreed to withdraw his claims for monetary damages and legal costs.

—

MARC WEINGARTEN: Ian Hamilton was a very respected British biographer. He had written a biography of Robert Lowell that was quite well received. Hamilton was known for heavily leaning on letters in his biographies. He decided that he was going to tackle the biographer's dream project: a book about Salinger. His big mistake was obtaining a cache of Salinger's letters and using them as the narrative spine of the book.

IAN HAMILTON: Four years ago [in 1983], I wrote to the novelist J. D. Salinger, telling him that I proposed to write a study of his "life and work." Would he be prepared to answer a few questions? . . . I assured him that I was a serious "critic and biographer," not at all to be confused with the fans and magazine reporters who had been plaguing him for thirty years. . . . All this was, of course, entirely disingenuous.

J. D. SALINGER, excerpt from letter to Ian Hamilton, undated:

Dear Sir:

You say you've been commissioned by Random House to write a book about me and my work (you put it, perhaps undeliberately, in just that order), and I have no good reason to doubt your word, I'm exceedingly sorry to say. . . . I've despaired long ago of finding any justice in the common practice. Let alone any goodness or decency.

Speaking (as you may have gathered) from rather unspeakably bitter experience, I suppose I can't put you or Random House off, if the lot of you are determined to have your way, but I do feel I must tell you, for what very little it may be worth, that I think I have borne all the exploitation and loss of privacy I can possibly bear in a single lifetime.

SHANE SALERNO: There had been dozens and dozens of books and articles about Salinger's work; this threatened to be the first book to examine his *life*, which is what unnerved him.

PHOEBE HOBAN: Salinger's letter to Hamilton brought up a good point: apart from a criminal, nobody comes under as much scrutiny as the subject of a biography.

Jason Epstein [Hamilton's editor at Random House] wrote back to Salinger, saying that he was indeed a worthy and suitable subject for a biography, that he was a public figure, and that a biographer had a right to explore his life and work.

Ian Hamilton, the author of *In Search of J. D. Salinger.*

SHARON STEEL: [In a letter to Michael Mitchell,] Salinger has "murder in my heart" because a "sore English prick," otherwise known as Ian Hamilton, has been digging around for material for a biography of the author's life, commissioned by Random House. . . .

[In a December 25, 1984, note to Mitchell written on the back of a Christmas card,] Salinger seems particularly depressed and detached, and hell-bent on hiding it. He writes of visiting London to see Peggy over the holiday, who, by some miscommunication, went to Boston. So Salinger decided to knock around the city alone. "I feel closed off from all general or personal conversation, these years, and consort with almost no one but one or two local drunks or distant madwomen." He'd rather not do anything unless it involves the writing he's working on. Salinger wishes Mitchell "intactness and sanity" for 1985.

—

JOHN DEAN: The U.S. law for letters is not unlike England's common law: a letter has really two aspects. One is the physical aspect of the letter and the other is the content of the letter. The person who receives the letter owns the physical possession of the letter but not the content of the letter by the author. The author retains the copyright. Only the physical letter can be sold. Salinger's lawyers notified Hamilton of their client's displeasure with his use of Salinger's letters in the galleys of Hamilton's biography. They argued that Hamilton's use of the Salinger letters would prevent Salinger from using them for his own commercial use at some future point. They demanded that Hamilton take the letters out of the book. Hamilton tried to appease Salinger by paraphrasing from the letters. But Salinger wasn't happy with the paraphrasing, sued, and was issued a temporary restraining order on the book by a New York district court.

PHOBE HOBAN: [Hamilton] just used his thesaurus to come up with synonyms. Instead of having Salinger's beauty and elegance of language and original cadence, he came up with these heavy-handed, awkward, clumsy, hideous parodies of Salinger's sentences that anybody would've been injured and insulted by.

JOHN DEAN: Salinger said, "No. This is not acceptable. I'm not happy with your modification, and we're going forward with this [lawsuit]."

There's nothing private about a lawsuit. It's probably the most exposed way you can go, because discovery is open, and [Salinger] knew he'd have to come forward [to testify]. He knew he could lose, but he was willing to take that gamble and try to control his writings and his letters.

DAVID SHIELDS: Why was he willing to take such a gamble? According to several of Salinger's ex-girlfriends we spoke with, one of Salinger's primary motivations was to prevent the exposure of his many epistolary relationships with very young girls—his pursuit, over many decades, of girls as young as fourteen.

PHOEBE HOBAN: The irony was overwhelming: the most famously private writer had to testify in court in Manhattan and make his very private personal letters public by filing them at the Library of Congress. As a result of the litigation, Salinger not only testified but also had to register all seventy-nine disputed letters at the Copyright Office, where any person willing to pay $10 can peruse them.

It's remarkable to have a window into Salinger's life through his actual postcards and letters, which were written in his actual hand. It really is like reading one of his characters' diaries or something like that—a way to have the most intimate possible contact with this impossibly reclusive person.

LILLIAN ROSS: That terrible ordeal they put him through. . . . I had to go to court with him and hold his hand. He was so upset. He would come over to my place and wait until we'd have to go and I'd go with him. Literally, sometimes I'd have to hold his hands he'd be shaking so badly. Afterwards I'd make him chicken soup at the end of the day. He was such a sensitive and fragile person, so vulnerable to the world. He was such a sweet man.

J. D. SALINGER (October 7, 1986):

Q **[ROBERT CALLAGY, ATTORNEY FOR RANDOM HOUSE]:** "At any time during the past 20 years have you written any fiction which has not been published?"

A **[SALINGER]:** "Yes."

Q: "Could you describe for me what works of fiction you have written which have not been published?"

A: "It would be very difficult to do."

Q: "Have you written any full-length works of fiction during the past twenty years which have not been published?"

A: "Could you frame that a different way? What do you mean by full-length work? You mean ready for publication?"

Q: "As opposed to a short story or a fictional piece or a magazine submission."

A: "It's very difficult to answer. I don't write that way. I just start writing fiction and see what happens to it."

Q: "Maybe an easier way to approach this is, would you tell me what your literary efforts have been in the field of fiction within the last twenty years?"

A: "Could I tell you or would I tell you? . . . Just a work of fiction. That's all. That's the only description I can really give it. . . . It's almost impossible to define. I work with characters, and as they develop, I just go on from there."

ROBERT CALLAGY: My thought is that he was not the J. D. Salinger who had been the vibrant novelist back in the 1950s, but he was definitely angry or disturbed or upset about something. Something must have happened [long ago] because when I asked him about letters written around that time, I'd say, "What did you mean?" And he'd say, "The young boy meant . . ." I thought it was odd that he'd describe himself in the third person. In all of the depositions that I've done, no one has ever referred to himself in the third person.

DAVID SHIELDS: He was trying to tell himself that he was no longer that young boy.

IAN HAMILTON: There is an overexcited, wound-up tone to those letters. He obviously did see some terrible things [during the war], and in some way I think he may have cracked up.

MORDECAI RICHLER: The letters are also, as Mr. Salinger noted with hindsight in court, occasionally gauche or effusive. "It's very difficult," he said. "I wish . . . you could read letters you wrote forty-six years ago. It's very painful reading."

ROBERT CALLAGY: At one point there was a sad episode that occurred when during one of the breaks he asked me for a Manhattan telephone book. I got it and gave it to him. He was clearly having trouble finding the number he wanted, so I said, "Can I look up the number for you?" And he said, "I'm trying to find my son's phone number. He lives over by the Roosevelt Hotel." And then he said he couldn't find the number in the book, so he was not going to be able to contact him, which I thought was very sad.

MARK HOWLAND: [My high school students and I] read the actual deposition, which was some forty pages long, complete with instructions to Salinger's lawyer not to interrupt Hamilton's lawyer [Callagy]. It's about as close as we felt we were ever going to get to the man, to hearing his words, even though they were just transcribed on a paper. Just when things started to get interesting, when the lawyer started asking about what he was working on now, how often he wrote, did he plan to publish, we turned the bottom of the last page and—blank. There was nothing else. Don't know what happened to whatever was left of the transcription, but it wasn't there.

PETER DE VRIES: If there are gaps in your story, they're Salinger wants in the story.

JOHN WENKE: There's a part of him that enjoys the power game that went on when the Ian Hamilton biography was making its way through the courts. He wanted to be able to assert ownership of the letters that somebody else owns. An actual recluse or mystic wouldn't care.

JOHN DEAN: I thought how little Salinger really needed to do [to make his case], other than he had to appear [for the deposition]; he had no choice because otherwise he could have been defaulted out of the litigation. He had to establish that he still was writing, that he was confident in his ability to write, and especially, that he had some use he could make of these letters, not that he couldn't have maybe made the same claim to pass them on to his estate. I think it was stronger in the eyes of the court if he could make the point: Indeed I am still writing actively, and what I'm writing is none of your business; however, in that context, these letters are of interest to me.

PHOEBE HOBAN: Salinger said, "You're chiseling away at my property at the same time as you're saying you're not stealing it."

JUDGE PIERRE N. LEVAL: It is my view that the defendants have made a sufficiently powerful showing to overcome plaintiff's claims for an injunction. The reasons that support this finding are: Hamilton's use of Salinger's copyrighted material is minimal and insubstantial; it does not exploit or appropriate the literary value of Salinger's letters for future publication. . . . The biographical purpose of Hamilton's book and of the adopted passages are quite distinct from the interests protected by Salinger's copyright. . . . Although [Salinger's] desire for privacy is surely entitled to respect, as a legal matter it does not override a lawful undertaking to write about him using legally available resources.

JOHN DEAN: [Leval] ruled against Salinger, finding that Hamilton had made fair use of Salinger's letters. This was a very good district judge. He was a very fair and objective judge, and you couldn't ask for a better trial judge. Salinger's legal team appealed the case to the U.S. Second Circuit Court of Appeals.

—

JUDGE JON O. NEWMAN: In July 1983 Hamilton had informed Salinger that he was undertaking a biography of Salinger to be published by Random House and sought the author's cooperation. Salinger refused, informing Hamilton that he preferred not to have his biography written during his lifetime. Hamilton nevertheless proceeded and spent the next three years preparing a biography titled *J. D. Salinger: A Writing Life*. An important source of material was several unpublished letters Salinger wrote between 1939 and 1961. Most were written to Whit Burnett, Salinger's friend, teacher, and editor at *Story* magazine, and Elizabeth Murray, Salinger's friend. A few were written to Judge Learned Hand, Salinger's friend and neighbor in New Hampshire, Hamish Hamilton and Roger Machell, Salinger's British publishers, and other individuals, including Ernest Hemingway.

Ian Hamilton located most, if not all, of the letters in the libraries of Harvard, Princeton, and the University of Texas, to which they had been donated by the recipients or their representatives. Prior to examining the letters at the university libraries, Hamilton signed form agreements furnished by the libraries, restricting the use he could make of the letters without permission of the library and the owner of the literary property rights.

In response to Salinger's objections, Hamilton and Random House revised the May [1987] galleys. In the current version of the biography (the "October galleys"), much of the material previously quoted from the Salinger letters has been replaced by close paraphrasing. Somewhat more than two hundred words remain quoted. Salinger has identified fifty-nine instances where the October galleys contain passages that either quote from or closely paraphrase portions of his unpublished letters. These passages draw upon forty-four of the copyrighted letters, twenty to Burnett, ten to Murray, nine to Hamish Hamilton, three to Judge Hand, one to Machell, and one to Hemingway.

A few examples should suffice. Salinger, complaining of an editor who has rejected one of his stories—though calling it "[c]ompetent handling"—writes [that it was] "like saying, She's a beautiful girl, except for her face." Hamilton paraphrases: "How would a girl feel if you told her she was stunning to look at but that facially there was something not quite right about her?"

Salinger writes, "I suspect that money is a far greater distraction for the artist than hunger." Hamilton paraphrases, "Money, on the other hand, is a serious obstacle to creativity."

Salinger, conveying the adulation of Parisians toward Americans at the liberation of Paris, writes that they would have said, "What a charming custom!" if "we had stood on top of the jeep and taken a leak." Hamilton paraphrases, ". . . if the conquerors had chosen to urinate from the roofs of their vehicles."

The breach of contract claim was based on the form agreements that Hamilton signed with Harvard, Princeton, and University of Texas libraries. Salinger alleged that he was a third-party beneficiary of those agreements.

As to the standard, we start, as did Judge Leval, by recognizing that what is relevant is the amount and substantiality of the copyrighted *expression* that has been used, not the *factual content* of the material in the copyrighted works. However, that protected expression has been "used" whether it has been quoted verbatim or only paraphrased.

The "ordinary" phrase may enjoy no protection as such, but its use in a sequence of expressive words does not cause the entire passage to lose protection. And though the "ordinary" phrase may be quoted without fear of infringement, a copier may not quote or paraphrase the sequence of creative expression that includes such a phrase.

In almost all of those instances where the quoted or paraphrased passages from Salinger's letters contain an "ordinary" phrase, the passage as a whole displays a sufficient degree of creativity as to sequence of thoughts, choice of words, emphasis, and arrangement to satisfy the minimal threshold of required creativity. And in all of the instances where that minimum threshold is met, the Hamilton paraphrasing tracks the original so closely as to constitute infringement.

IAN HAMILTON: Public awareness of the "expressive content" of Salinger's letters was instantly extended the day after this judgment was released. The *New York Times* felt itself free to quote substantially not from my paraphrases but from the Salinger originals that I had so painstakingly, and—it now seemed—needlessly attempted not to steal.

ARNOLD H. LUBASCH: A biography of J. D. Salinger was blocked yesterday by a Federal appeals court in Manhattan that said the book unfairly used Mr. Salinger's unpublished letters.

Reversing a lower court decision, the appeals court ruled in favor of Mr. Salinger, who filed suit to prohibit the biography from using all material from the letters, which he wrote many years ago.

"The biography," the appeals court said, "copies virtually all of the most interesting passages of the letters, including several highly expressive insights about writing and literary criticism."

In a footnote, the appeals court's decision cited a letter . . . [in which Salinger] criticized Wendell Willkie, the 1940 President candidate, saying, "He looks to me like a guy who makes his wife keep a scrapbook for him."

The decision included another footnote referring to a 1943 letter in which "Salinger, distressed that Oona O'Neill, whom he had dated, had married Charlie Chaplin, expressed his disapproval of the marriage in this satirical invention of his imagination: 'I can see them at home evenings. Chaplin squatting grey and nude, atop his chiffonier, swinging his thyroid around his head by his bamboo cane, like a dead rat. Oona in an aquamarine gown, applauding madly from the bathroom. . . . I'm facetious, but I'm sorry. Sorry for anyone with a profile as young and lovely as Oona's.'"

ROBERT CALLAGY: If you take this opinion to an extreme, what it says is that you can't quote anything that has not been published before, and if you attempt to paraphrase, you're at serious peril. Copyright law was created to protect an author in a property right, not to permit an author to obliterate the past.

JOHN DEAN: To be reversed by the Court of Appeals was a little bit of a reach. In a sense, Salinger got lucky on this one.

LEILA HADLEY LUCE: I was appalled to hear that Hamilton couldn't even abstract or write about Jerry's letters to Oona. Psychologically, that makes sense because they talk about the litigiousness of the paranoid. I suppose that's what Jerry is: he's paranoid. He always thinks people are going to encroach on his privacy.

ELEANOR BLAU: The Supreme Court yesterday let stand a lower-court ruling blocking publication of an unauthorized biography of J. D. Salinger.

Without comment or dissent, the justices declined to act on the decision last January by the United States Court of Appeals for the Second Circuit in New York City that the biographer, Ian Hamilton, had unfairly used unpublished letters written by Mr. Salinger.

Random House, Inc., the publisher of *J. D. Salinger: A Writing Life*, said the company and Mr. Hamilton would decide in the next few weeks which of two steps to take.

PAUL ALEXANDER: In a sense Salinger *had* killed Hamilton's book, period.

PHOEBE HOBAN: If, in fact, unpublished letters are copyrightable, then biographers and journalists are highly constrained. It was a precedent-setting case. . . . Ian Hamilton was not allowed to publish his original biography.

JOHN DEAN: For any of us who've ever wondered about Salinger's reclusiveness, there were some answers that came as a result of his lawsuit. This is not something somebody does who is afraid of a little publicity, because there's nothing private about a lawsuit. Which shows the adamancy with which he believes in his privacy and the extent to which he is willing to go, which was obviously a painful route for him.

To continue to protect that privacy, in a broader sense, there are some controls he could ask for in the court; he could ask the judge, who knew he was reclusive and very private, to keep this as private as possible. But the fact that it went as far as it did, went through the process the way it did, shows that he was determined to prevail in the case. A deposition is more fun to take than to give. I've been on both sides, and believe me—it's easier to ask the questions than answer them. To do it for any length of time is always difficult.

When an author writes a book and becomes successful, in a sense he's saying, "Look at what I'm writing." He's thrusting himself out there. But I have a tremendous empathy for those who would like to retain their privacy. It is very difficult to do once you become a public figure. Salinger's effort to do so by stopping all public appearances is about as extreme as possible. Now is he a public figure? Yes, he is.

—

DAVID SHIELDS: In January 1987, at the same time Salinger was under siege on the legal front, not only was William Shawn eased out at the *New Yorker*, but the owner of the magazine, S. I. Newhouse, chose as his replacement Robert Gottlieb, the editor in chief of the book publisher Knopf, rather than Charles McGrath, the magazine's deputy editor and presumed successor. Salinger signed a three-paragraph petition that 153 other writers, editors, cartoonists, and *New Yorker* staff members also signed, urging Gottlieb to turn down the position, to no avail. Salinger's last and best defender, who had overruled the other editors' unanimous rejection of "Zooey" and had served as Salinger's only editor until 1965, was out. So too, in a sense, was Salinger.

—

PAUL ALEXANDER: In 1987 Salinger created an enormous amount of buzz throughout the entertainment business. While he was embroiled in the lawsuit with Ian Hamilton, Salinger fell in love with another television actress, Catherine Oxenberg, who was appearing on *Dynasty*. She was young, beautiful, and vivacious, and she and the show attracted a huge following. According to Ian Hamilton, Salinger fell in love with Oxenberg the moment he saw her on television. Salinger had an M.O.

for television actresses. He would call them up on the phone and say, "I'm J. D. Salinger and I wrote *The Catcher in the Rye*." Talk about a pickup line! According to Hamilton, Salinger traveled to the West Coast to pursue Oxenberg. Press reports at the time said Salinger showed up at the studio unannounced and had to be escorted away from the studio. When these newspaper reports appeared, Salinger had his attorneys find Oxenberg's agent and threaten a lawsuit, but no lawsuit was ever filed.

JEAN MILLER: The trip to Hollywood to see Catherine Oxenberg—I just didn't want that to be true, but I knew how he felt about child actresses. It was just acting, so it was just as phony as anything else. It's just as phony as a rock musician playing the same thing over and over again and getting the audience all riled up, and then stalking off the stage filled with ego.

DAVID SHIELDS: He wants to be a pure dharma being, but he falls head over heels for Catherine Oxenberg. Nearly every Salinger story traces the same circular movement: a character wants to escape the world, wants to graduate beyond desire and ego and other people, but by the end, the protagonist always comes back to the ordinary human drudge, to just living. Salinger's life is a failed Salinger novel: he never truly re-embraces existence.

—

PHOEBE HOBAN: Ian Hamilton took a postmodern gambit and wrote a really crummy book about his search for Salinger and how he wasn't allowed to write about Salinger.

MYLES WEBER: Hamilton asserted that Salinger became more famous by trying not to be famous; that he sold more books by not publishing any more books; that, in fact, it was his deliberate design.

MORDECAI RICHLER: Mr. Hamilton's biography is tainted by a nastiness born of frustration, perhaps, but hardly excused by it. Mr. Salinger is never given the benefit of the doubt. He is described as a "callow self-advancer." Aged twenty-two, we are told, "the Salinger we were on the track of was surely getting less and less lovably Holden-ish each day. So far, our eavesdropping had yielded almost nothing in the way of human frailty and warmth." This vengeful book is also marred by Mr. Hamilton's coy, tiresome device of splitting himself in two, as it were, referring to Mr. Salinger's biographer in the third person.

—

DAVID REMNICK: In the spring of 1988, the editors of the *New York Post* sent a pair of photographers to New Hampshire with instructions to find J. D. Salinger and take his picture. If the phrase "take his picture" had any sense of violence or, at least, violation left in it at all, if it still retained the undertone of certain people who are convinced that a photographer threatens them with the theft of their souls, then it applied here. There is no mystery why the *Post* pursued its prey. . . . His withdrawal became for journalists a story demanding resolution, intervention, and exposure. Inevitably the *Post* got its man. The paper ran a photograph on the cover of a gaunt sixty-nine-year-old man recoiling, as if anticipating catastrophe. In that instant, the look in Salinger's eyes was one of such terror that it is a wonder he survived it.

PAUL ALEXANDER: One day in April 1988—under the banner headline "GOTCHA CATCHER!"—the *New York Post* ran a full-page photograph of Salinger on its front cover. Obviously agitated in the picture, Salinger has one fist pulled back as if he is about to punch the camera. Paul Adao and Steve Connelly, both freelance paparazzi, had gone to New Hampshire, as had become the custom of so many fans and journalists through the years, and stalked Salinger for several days until they saw him coming out of the post office in Windsor. Clicking away, they photographed him as he walked up and spoke to them. "Listen," he said sternly, "I don't want to be interviewed. I don't want any part of this."

MYLES WEBER: An editor of the *New York Post* defended the work of his journalists by saying that, in fact, it was Salinger who was interfering with his journalists doing their job.

PAUL ALEXANDER: [Adao and Connelly] left, but three days later they returned and talked to people about Salinger again until they spotted him leaving the Purity Supreme supermarket in West Lebanon, New Hampshire.

Adao blocked Salinger's car into its parking space, and after Connelly got out of their car, both of them began taking pictures of him. Furious, Salinger came at them, smashing his grocery cart into Connelly and hitting Adao, still in the car's driver's seat, with his fist. It was one of the times Salinger was drawing his fist back to swing at Adao that the photographer caught the gesture on film. Soon, giving up, Salinger covered his face with his hands and tried to open the door to his jeep, but the photographers kept snapping shots. Several shoppers stopped to gather around what had turned into a minor mêlée. "What are you doing to him?" one finally shouted out at the photographers. "He's a convicted murderer!" Adao yelled back, a comment Adao later said he regretted. Finally, Salinger got into his jeep and, when Adao saw that Salinger was about to back into his car, he moved the car and Salinger drove away.

DAVID SHIELDS: Margaret says, "He still drives his Jeep like a nutcase, or a sane person being shelled, same regulation haircut, only gray now."

After the picture appeared on the front page of the *Post*, a controversy ensued, with many readers disapproving of the way the paparazzi had stalked Salinger. Later, Don DeLillo said that photograph inspired him to write *Mao II*.

DON DeLILLO: The withheld work of art is the only eloquence that's left.

—

JOHN DEAN: Clearly Salinger has not withdrawn from society. He is very aware of what's happening as it is related to him. He's probably got counsel keeping an eye on things and alerting him to misuses of his name.

DAVID SHIELDS: While he hadn't fully withdrawn from society, he was clearly retreating. In 1990, Dorothy Olding, Salinger's agent for fifty years, had a stroke. Her assistant, Phyllis Westberg, became his agent. Two years later, his editor, champion, and friend William Shawn died.

—

WILLIAM H. HONAN: Mr. Salinger's modest house, surrounded by three plain garage-like structures, including the author's writing studio, is positioned for privacy. To reach it, one crosses an old covered bridge high above a roaring brook and grinds for several miles up a steeply winding, hard-packed dirt road. The last 100 yards are an extremely steep grade, and the Salinger house, nearly invisible from the road, seems almost an eagle's nest with a panoramic view of Mount Ascutney across the Connecticut River in Vermont. An immense white satellite dish behind the house suggests that Mr. Salinger is still in touch with the outside world, at least through television.

DAVID SHIELDS: In Cornish, Salinger surrounded himself with the dense, tall evergreens, the cold, dark winters, and the isolating terrain of Hürtgen, but now from a commanding position: he could easily detect approaching dangers—not artillery, of course, just literary tourists who wanted to invade his hilltop perch. He needs life to feel difficult.

LILLIAN ROSS: He liked living in New Hampshire, but he often found fun and relief by coming down to New York to have supper with me and Bill Shawn. In a note he sent after the three of us got together for the last time, he wrote, "It will set me up for months. I was at peace."

—

SHANE SALERNO: Paul Fitzgerald was one of the "Four Musketeers" who served alongside Salinger during the war in the counterintelligence section of the 4th Division. From D-Day to Kaufering IV, Salinger and Fitzgerald were always together. The two men maintained a strong and warm relationship until Salinger's death in 2010, writing each other frequently. The excerpts from Salinger's letters to Fitzgerald that appear throughout this book have never been published before.

J. D. SALINGER, excerpt from letter to Paul Fitzgerald (July 27, 1990):

> *I'm impressed, mightily, at the easy way you reel off the names of just about the whole CIC detachment people, victims, whatever it was we were. . . . Am very glad you're well and happy, Paul. Stay that way. It takes some doing, at times, but do it anyway.*

SHANE SALERNO: In September 1991, on a cross-country car trip, Fitzgerald surprised Salinger at his home in Cornish, New Hampshire.

PAUL FITZGERALD, diary entry, September 26, 1991:

> Windsor, Vermont/Cornish, New Hampshire: Just across the Delaware River is a town called Cornish. The directions proved correct. Way on top of a wooded rolling hill sat Salinger's abode. When he came to the door he looked inquisitive. Looking into the face of a baldheaded person changed by 46 years. I recognize him, tho he appeared much less vital—the eyes mellowed by age and serenity in the paradise. He was emotionally warm and welcoming. Entertaining his son and daughter-in-law. Invited in. They were having dinner.

Salinger and Paul Fitzgerald in Cornish, September 26, 1991.

PAUL FITZGERALD, diary entry, September 27, 1991:

> Called on Salinger "way up the hill" at 3:15. Talked about old times. He's a very warm person. Denise [Fitzgerald's wife] liked him very much. His view is magnificent. He has 300 acres up here. Took off for parts unknown at 5.

—

ASSOCIATED PRESS: J. D. Salinger's home was heavily damaged in a fire early today. No one was injured. Mr. Salinger's wife, Colleen O'Neill, reported the blaze, Fire Chief Mike Monette said. He would not say if the reclusive writer was home at the time. The cause of the fire and damage estimates have not been determined.

DAVID SHIELDS: This was the first time—in 1992—that the public learned of Salinger's third wife, forty years his junior. Colleen, a nursing student who worked as an au pair for someone else and married in the early 1980s, met Salinger, corresponded with him, and left her husband for the author.

PAUL ALEXANDER: Colleen directed the annual Cornish town fair.

BURNACE FITCH JOHNSON: Jerry used to come and walk around the fairgrounds with her. Colleen would have to repeat things to him when people spoke to him, because he's quite deaf.

WILLIAM H. HONAN: Not even a fire that consumed at least half his home on Tuesday could smoke out the reclusive J. D. Salinger, author of the classic novel of adolescent rebellion, *The Catcher in the Rye*. Mr. Salinger is almost equally famous for having elevated privacy to an art form.

His fastidiously preserved seclusion was threatened on Tuesday when his third wife, Colleen, reported a fire in their home to the volunteer fire department. Within minutes, the blazing house was surrounded by fire trucks and emergency vehicles from Cornish, the New Hampshire towns of Plainfield, Meriden, and Claremont, and two small towns in Vermont, Windsor and West Windsor.

Mike Monette, Cornish's fire chief, said the fire was brought under control in about an hour. No injuries were reported, he said, but "damage to the house was extensive." Neither he nor anyone else was able to say whether any of the author's unpublished manuscripts were destroyed.

On Thursday afternoon, Mr. Salinger, now 73 years old, cavorted around his property playing hide-and-seek with a reporter and a photographer who had come to learn how he was bearing up.

When first spied, Mr. Salinger, lanky and with snow-white hair, was outside his house talking to his wife and a local building contractor. As strangers approached, Mr. Salinger, like the fleet chipmunks that dash across his driveway, scurried into his charred retreat. The contractor barred the way of the pursuing reporter and pleaded, "You've got to understand, this is a man who is really *serious* about his privacy."

Meanwhile, Mr. Salinger's wife, who is considerably younger than her husband, strode vigorously toward a blue Mazda pickup truck in the driveway.

"I have things to do!" she announced, brushing aside all questions and glaring as she leaped into the vehicle and roared away. . . .

Mr. Salinger has kept aloof from his neighbors in Cornish as well as from prying journalists and the public. For example, Clara Perry, who was Mr. Salinger's next-door neighbor for 20 years, ran a kindergarten attended by both of Mr. Salinger's children, Matt, an actor, and Margaret Ann, now both grown. Mrs. Perry refers to him affectionately as Jerry but says that neither she nor her husband [was] ever invited into Mr. Salinger's house. . . .

Mrs. Perry said that she and her six children had never cracked one of Mr. Salinger's books because *The Catcher in the Rye* was banned at the Windsor public school they attended.

After the book became accepted, she said, the Windsor school used to send groups of students to visit with him. "But pretty soon he stopped that," Mrs. Perry said. "It got to be too much for him."

J. D. SALINGER, excerpt from postcard to Paul Fitzgerald, December 1993:

Thanks, too, for your concern about the fire and the house, old friend. . . . The house has been pretty much re-built, and we're now in it, at long last. . . . All kinds of D-Day commemorative stuff is slated to take place next June, or so I hear. In America, France, Germany. Speeches, no doubt. Lots of old guys standing around in Hawaiian shirts and little overseas caps. Still, there'll be some long thoughts, here and there, surely. Myself, I think mostly of how young we all were.

SHARON STEEL: A fire ravaged Salinger's home, and destroyed everything except a piece of his bedroom and, [as Salinger said,] "providentially," his workroom, where he kept his papers and manuscripts.

—

JOYCE MAYNARD: There was this one woman overseas who had well over a hundred pages of letters from Salinger. He decided to come and visit her. He flew to London to meet her, and the excitement must have been extraordinary, I can imagine, because I know the excitement I felt when I pulled up to the Hanover Inn after just eight weeks of correspondence, and these two had been corresponding for much longer. She was a young woman, but it turned out she was not a particularly pretty woman. She was very tall and big-boned and kind of awkward.

DAVID SHIELDS: On this trip—to Edinburgh, actually—Salinger took his daughter with him. He said he said they were going to tour the Scottish settings for *39 Steps*, the Hitchcock movie he especially loved.

PAUL ALEXANDER: Salinger had planned a meeting with a young pen pal amour at the Edinburgh airport. Upon meeting her there, Salinger expressed his embarrassment and guilt to Margaret. The young girl had simply turned out to be ugly.

JOYCE MAYNARD: Salinger evidently saw her and left. He told her he would see her again, and he asked her to send back the letters so that he could keep them for her when she came over to visit him. She mailed all of the letters back to Salinger and never heard from him again.

MARGARET SALINGER: His search for landsmen led him increasingly to relations in two dimensions: with his fictional Glass family, or with living "pen pals" he met in letters, which lasted until meeting in person when the three-dimensional, flesh-and-blood presence of them would, with the inevitability of watching a classic tragedy unfold, invariably sow the seeds of the relationship's undoing.

JOYCE MAYNARD: There was another story about Jerry, and this one I heard not from the woman herself, because I don't think that she was in a state to report it, but somebody else told me, a man who knew Jerry in town. Jerry corresponded with a young woman and had invited her to come and see him. She had actually moved to the town of Hanover to be near him, and she had come to see him, but he had very swiftly tired of her.

Jerry told a neighbor that he didn't know how to get rid of the woman; she kept coming round and he reported her to the police, filing a complaint against her. I'm not going to ascribe total blame for this next event to Salinger, but I do understand the power of his dismissals and how crushing it could be. The woman had a total breakdown and was hospitalized in Concord, New Hampshire.

MICHAEL SILVERBLATT: Salinger's books are in some crazy sense love letters to people he'd be reluctant to meet. In particular, they're love letters to the lost—all versions of the fat lady who's so normal she loves to laugh at the television set, and you're doing it for the fat lady; he's doing it for his fat lady readers.

—

JOYCE MAYNARD: I had a good friend named Joe, who was a Vietnam vet—100 percent disability for Post-traumatic Stress Disorder. We were sitting in my kitchen one day, the year that Audrey [Maynard's daughter] turned eighteen, and I was talking to him about the strange and unexplainable anxiety I was feeling about her going away from home. I'd always been a pretty relaxed and comfortable parent. He listened to me speak for a while and finally said, "So tell me, Joyce, what happened to you when you were eighteen?" I'd never mentioned Jerry Salinger to him, but I knew right away what the answer to that question was.

Joe suffered a Post-traumatic Stress Disorder breakdown when his oldest son reached the age Joe was when he went off to Vietnam. I remember waiting until my children went off to their father's house that weekend; by this time, I was divorced for a number of years. I went to the back of my closet, where there was a shoebox, didn't even know right away where that box was. I hadn't looked at the letters from Jerry Salinger in twenty-some years.

I took them out, laid them out on my bed, and began to read them. They were letters I'd known very well. I could have recited some of them, I'd read them so carefully when I was young. I was reading them now as a forty-three-year-old woman, and the voice that moved me and melted my heart when I was eighteen struck me in a very different way at forty-three.

As hard as I had worked as a writer, and as much work as I had been doing over those twenty years, a crucial piece that I hadn't addressed made it almost impossible for me to be honest and authentic about anything else.

In the winter of 1984 I was living in New Hampshire, married to my husband, Steve, and pregnant with our third child, our son, Willy. We had made a very rare trip to New York City to attend the publication party for a book in which I had an essay. It was a collection of essays by women writers who had published "Hers" columns in the *New York Times*, so there was a roomful of women writers. I was feeling a little unglamorous and unsophisticated and un–New Yorkish at that party, eight months pregnant, surrounded by slim, sophisticated New York writers. One came up to me and said—this happened periodically, somebody would refer to Salinger, and it was always an awkward moment when they did, because I didn't speak of him and I never knew what to say—but this was a particularly awkward moment because I was at this party and couldn't just walk away. She was a well-known writer, also in the collection. She came up to me and, apropos of nothing, said, "You know, I had an au pair girl who got letters from J. D. Salinger."

I didn't quite go into early labor, but it was that intense of a response. I felt my whole body shift. Up until that moment I knew that I had lost the love and high regard of Salinger, but I believed I occupied an absolute place in his heart and mind. I alone had experienced this, to me, intimate, sacred correspondence. Suddenly this woman I'd never met was telling me that her au pair had a packet of letters from Salinger. I was stunned, but I said nothing.

Quite a few years later I contacted her again and asked her to tell me more about the au pair girl and the letters. She explained the story:

Joyce Maynard with her first husband, Steve Bethel.

there had been a young woman named Colleen who had been a nursing student and then a nurse in Maryland. Colleen lived with her for a time, helping her take care of her children. At one point Colleen went up to Hanover to visit a boyfriend, got off a bus, and Salinger had given her a ride into town. They'd struck up a conversation and then had a correspondence. Colleen continued to see her boyfriend; she didn't picture her correspondence with Salinger as a romantic situation. The writer went on to say that her au pair, Colleen, had married her boyfriend, and she had attended the wedding. She said, "I'll send you a photograph from the wedding." So a week or so passed and in an envelope came this photograph of a very pretty, smiling young woman wearing a taffeta dress, with her arm around a nice-looking young man.

—

MARK HOWLAND: In 1997 there was a lot of publicity about "Hapworth" coming out as a book. The word was that Salinger had to have absolute control over everything, including typeface and font size.

JONATHAN SCHWARTZ: There were rumors that Salinger was talking to a Virginia publisher about publishing "Hapworth." Apparently they met several times.

IAN SHAPIRO: In 1988, Roger Lathbury, an English professor at George Mason University and owner of a small literary publishing outfit based in his house in Alexandria [Virginia], decided on a lark to write to J. D. Salinger, asking if he could publish "Hapworth 16, 1924," Salinger's last published work, which appeared as a story in the *New Yorker* in 1965 and never made it into book form. Amazingly, Salinger wrote back promptly, saying, essentially, "I'll think about it." Then, nothing. For eight years. Until July 26, 1996, when Lathbury, just having completed teaching his morning classes, picked up the phone in his home office.

ROGER LATHBURY: Here was the voice: "I would like to speak to Mr. Lathbury." People don't know how small the operation is here. His voice had a New York accent . . . and sounded like the recording of Walt Whitman that's available. He identified who he was—I don't remember if he said, "This is J. D. Salinger" or "This is Salinger"—and I said, "Well, um . . . I am delighted that you called."

DAVID SHIELDS: Lathbury and Salinger arranged a meeting in Washington, D.C., at the cafeteria of the National Gallery of Art.

ROGER LATHBURY: I was a bit nervous. . . . His back was by the wall. He was waiting patiently. I shook hands with him and apologized for being late. . . . He was trying to make me feel at ease, but he was probably nervous, too.

IAN SHAPIRO: Salinger insisted on having no dust jacket, only a bare cover with cloth of great durability—buckram. They talked pica lengths, fonts, and space between lines. They were going to do a press run somewhere in the low thousands. No advertising whatsoever. But for how much? Lathbury remembers that Salinger did not ask for an advance and that any money to be made would come from sales.

DAVID SHIELDS: Lathbury filed a Library of Congress cataloging record for the book, a necessary first step toward publication. A very small magazine in Virginia heard that Lathbury had filed this information and called him to find out more.

ROGER LATHBURY: I foolishly gave an interview, but I thought nobody would see the article.

DAVID SHIELDS: A reporter for the *Washington Post* saw Lathbury's interview and broke the news. Ego. Ego.

DAVID STREITFELD: J. D. Salinger, whose life has been one long campaign to erase himself from the public eye, is reversing himself somewhat at the age of 78. Next month will see the publication of *Hapworth 16, 1924*, the first new Salinger book in 34 years. Salinger is one of the most enduring and influential postwar American writers, and any New York publisher would have paid a bundle for the rights to the story, which appeared in the *New Yorker* in 1965. But in the literary coup of the decade, the book will be issued by Orchises Press, a small press in Alexandria run by George Mason University English professor Roger Lathbury.

MYLES WEBER: The book was listed for publication through Amazon and on the publishing company's website.

SHANE SALERNO: In early February 1997, *Hapworth 16, 1924* was—via prepublication orders—the #3 bestselling book on Amazon.

ROGER LATHBURY: This is a book meant for readers, not for collectors. Part of the reason for not revealing a press run is to discourage investing. I want people to read the story.

JONATHAN SCHWARTZ: When word got out [that the book was going to be published], Michiko Kakutani, the lead book critic at the *New York Times*, excoriated this story that had not been in print since 1965.

MICHIKO KAKUTANI: Seymour was the one who said that "all we do our whole lives is go from one little piece of Holy Ground to the next." Seymour was supposed to be the one who saw more. It is something of a shock, then, to meet the Seymour presented in "Hapworth," an obnoxious child given to angry outbursts. "No single day passes," this Seymour writes, "that I do not listen to the heartless indifferences and stupidities passing from the [camp] counselors' lips without secretly wishing I could improve matters quite substantially by bashing a few culprits over the head with an excellent shovel or stout club!" . . . In fact, with "Hapworth," Mr. Salinger seems to be giving critics a send-up of what he contends they want. Accused of writing only youthful characters, he has given us a 7-year-old narrator who talks like a peevish old man. Accused of never addressing the question of sexual love, he has given us a young boy who speaks like a lewd adult. Accused of loving his characters too much, he has given us a hero who's deeply distasteful. And accused of being too superficially charming, he has given us a nearly impenetrable narrative, filled with digressions, narcissistic asides and ridiculous shaggy-dog circumlocutions.

DAVID SHIELDS: According to Lathbury, Salinger broke off contact with him due to Lathbury's unintentional betrayal of confidence, but isn't it plausible to think that this was only Salinger's cover story for his bruised feelings about Kakutani's critique? Perhaps Salinger was testing the water for the possible publication of future Glass stories, and when the "newspaper of record" weighed in so heavily against, he retreated.

ROGER LATHBURY: My general feeling is anguish. I am very sorry. Those stories by Salinger provide release and delight for millions of people, and I could have helped to do that. I never reached back out. I thought about writing some letters [to Salinger], but it wouldn't have done any good.

MYLES WEBER: It was reportedly withdrawn due to Salinger's distaste for all that publicity, which really wasn't much publicity at all by most publishers' and writers' standards. That's one of the largest pieces of ammunition that scholars have to accuse Salinger of constructing an author persona, of having a deliberate agenda.

DAVID SHIELDS: In 2004 Lathbury revealed that he had lost the rights to publish "Hapworth" but refused to say how or why; in 2009 he showed up in a *Washington Post* profile, still refusing to talk about exactly what had happened.

JOHN WENKE: The aborted publication of "Hapworth 16, 1924" as a book is a perfect case study. The mystique really drives the obsession: people just want something else by Salinger.

There's no aesthetic reason that I can think of for why Salinger would want "Hapworth" to be in print. The very fact that he'd had a deal with a small press in Virginia indicates that he was perfectly aware of the kinds of things likely to happen. I got phone calls from half a dozen newspapers about the publication of that book. I even got a call from [Australian Broadcasting Company] Radio in Sydney. I had to tell people that it's not a new book; it's something that he published in 1965 and anybody can walk to the library and pull down the issue of the *New Yorker* it's in and read it. But he engineered that, and he did it very consciously, knowing there would be this stir.

RON ROSENBAUM: ["Hapworth" is] like the Dead Sea Scrolls of the Salinger cult. The real fascination is that somewhere buried in it you might find the key to Salinger's mysterious silence ever since.

LESLIE EPSTEIN: "Hapworth" is a triumph; that's the voice more than any other that reaches me. Why does that story upset people so much? There's something about the purity of it, the integrity of it: the boldness of a boy looking us in the eye and telling us things that he makes us believe, even though he's predicting his own death.

Cover of June 1997 *Esquire.*

—

SHANE SALERNO: Having written two hundred pages of her memoir *At Home in the World*, Joyce Maynard went to Cornish on her forty-fourth birthday, November 5, drove to Salinger's house, walked up to the front porch, and anxiously knocked on the door, believing this confrontation would provide closure.

DAVID SHIELDS: Writers know how vampiric other writers are. The only reason Maynard went to Cornish was to get a dramatic ending for her book.

JOYCE MAYNARD: I borrowed a truck and made my way to Cornish. I found to my surprise that I knew just how to get to Salinger's house. I drove up the hill and parked the truck; the house looked surprisingly the same, although there was a satellite dish on the roof now. The garden had been cut back for winter. I walked up the steps to the door and thought, "This is the kind of moment when I should be really scared."

But I wasn't scared. I felt very calm. I knocked on the door. I heard a commotion in the kitchen and a woman called out to me, "What do you want?" I said to her, "I've come to see Jerry. Would you tell him Joyce Maynard's here?" She turned and looked at me through the window and smiled. I recognized Colleen: the face of the au pair girl in the blue taffeta dress in the wedding picture sent to me years before, a little older now but still a lot younger than me. I stood there and waited. I didn't want to have it said I ambushed him, that I had caught him unaware. Jerry was warned I was there and he had his own choice to make—to come to the door or not.

I waited a long time (I'm guessing ten minutes at least) but I knew that he would come to the door, and he did. The door opened and he stood there, wearing a bathrobe, very tall still, though a little more hunched over. He still had all his hair, but it was white. His face was much more lined. It was a face familiar to me, but the expression on that face was of great rage, something more than rage—hatred—more than I have ever experienced.

He shook his fist at me and said, "What are you doing here? Why didn't you write me a letter?" I said, "Jerry, I've written you many letters; you've never answered them." He asked again, "What are you doing here? Why have you come here?"

"I've come to ask you a question, Jerry. What was my purpose in your life?" When I asked him, his face, already filled with contempt, was transformed into this mask. "You don't deserve an answer to that question," he said. I said, "Yes, I believe I do."

He exploded with a torrent of putrid language—the ugliest I'd ever heard—from this man who'd written some of the most beautiful words that had ever been written to me. He told me that I had led a shallow and meaningless existence, I was a worthless human being, and I'm actually grateful that he said those things to me because I knew those things weren't true. Although he'd still written the same great books, was still the same wonderful, original, funny writer, he was no sage to me. He was no spiritual guide and the position that he occupied on the planet was the same as the rest of us: a flawed human being.

"I've heard you're writing something," he said. This was very like him: my book hadn't even been written, yet word had leaked out in the press that I was going to be writing this memoir, and Jerry always watched what was going on and what was said about him in particular. He said it as if it were an obscene act to be writing a book. "Yes, I am writing a book; I'm a writer," I told him. It's odd. For all the years I'd been a writer, and all the books I'd written, I had never said "I'm a writer." I always said "I write."

I realized this was the breakthrough that allowed me to write my book: I had nothing to be ashamed of. Other people may say differently. I told the story that I had lived.

"The problem with you, Joyce," he said, "is you love the world."

DAVID SHIELDS: Salinger is expressing the core principle of Vedanta's fourth stage: renunciation of the world. Writing, publishing, Joyce Maynard in all her ambition—they are the exact opposite.

JOYCE MAYNARD: When he said it, I felt as if he had just released me. Because to me that isn't a problem at all. I said, "Yes, I do love the world and I have raised three children who love the world and I'm glad of that." He replied, "I always knew this is what you'd amount to—nothing." This was the man who had written me, who had told me to never forget that I was a real writer and to let nobody ever tell me differently. "And now you mean to exploit me." I said to him—one of those rare moments when you actually do say the thing, you don't just think of it later—I said, "Jerry, there may be somebody standing on this doorstep who exploited somebody else standing on this doorstep, but I leave it to you to determine which one is which." I said goodbye. I am quite sure that is the last time in my life that I will ever see J. D. Salinger.

PAUL ALEXANDER: As she was walking away, Salinger shouted after her, "I don't even know who you are!"

JOYCE MAYNARD: [I felt] different stages of distress from the moment of his initial rejection of me. I expected to be with him forever. I really did. I felt the reverberations of his disdain and contempt for years. After almost everything else was gone, I held on to this idea that I once was special and deeply loved by him. I had lived for his approval and it was a very painful thing to lose it and then to discover that I hadn't in fact been this single and precious person. I had been one of a series of who knows how many.

DAVID SHIELDS: The damage inflicted feels intentional. It's punishment on Salinger's part—punishment for being alive.

JEAN MILLER: That poor girl—he was so casual and cold to her. She was very courageous in breaking the code that we all had, not verbally but emotionally, signed onto: don't talk. I thought her parents were similar to mine. I also think, when you compare a picture of me and her picture on the back of her book, we look very much alike.

GORE VIDAL: Since Maynard was the victim, she has the right to complain first. She was the victim of an old man's lust and whatever happened between them. Who knows? Who cares? I think the defense always has the right to come forward with their case first. So she did. So she did.

JOYCE MAYNARD: For twenty-five years, I did not write or speak of what happened. The [critical] attacks, not only on my book but on my character, were brutal, intensely personal, and relentless, and even now—several years later—hardly a week goes by in which someone or other

doesn't remark to me, "Oh, you're the one who wrote the book about Salinger." I'm never angry when they say that. Of course that was said in the press about the book. My response is: I didn't write a book about J. D. Salinger. I wrote a book about myself, and J. D. Salinger chose to be a part of my life and I chose to no longer exclude that fact of my life.

I did, however, receive affirmation of the work I'd written. I received letters from women and men well acquainted with shame and secret-keeping in their own lives, thanking me for my willingness to speak openly of experiences they had supposed were theirs alone or simply too painful to speak of. . . . Not wholly surprising to me were the letters I received from three other women telling me they had engaged in correspondences with J. D. Salinger eerily like my own, one within weeks of his dismissal of me. I have no doubt these women's stories were true. They quoted lines from Salinger's letters to them nearly identical to ones in his letters to me, whose contents had never been made public. Like me, these women had been approached by Salinger when they were eighteen years old. Like me, they once believed him to be the wisest man, their soul mate, their destiny. Like me, they had eventually experienced his complete and devastating rejection. Also like me, they had maintained for years the belief that they were obligated to keep the secret out of fear of the very form of condemnation I was now receiving for having refused to do so. My book's not really a story about J. D. Salinger; it's a story about shame and a young girl giving over her power to a much more powerful older man, and that's a rather universal story, or at least a common one.

Joyce Maynard with her three children.

—

JOYCE MAYNARD: Evidently it appeared to many of my critics that the sole significance of my life had been sleeping with a great man.

DAVID SHIELDS: It's not as if Maynard isn't highly exploitative in her own right, but it's a bit of a daisy chain, because so much is at stake—the myth of the isolated male genius artist—and everyone is invested in it: newspapers, magazines, publishers, Salinger himself. The mystery surrounding the sphinx gets maintained.

LARISSA MacFARQUHAR: In the 25 intervening years, Maynard bought a house, nearly had a nervous breakdown, lost her virginity to the soundtrack of *Pippin*, met Mary Tyler Moore and Muhammad Ali, was raped, got married, appeared on TV, had three children, emptied her breast milk into the Atlantic, planted a garden, went broke, had an abortion, clawed through a heap of garbage looking for a lost retainer, wrote three novels, watched her parents get divorced and die, got divorced herself, bought another house, got breast implants and took them out, took tennis lessons, sold most of her possessions and moved from New Hampshire to California. Over the years, Maynard has related many of these events in her syndicated newspaper column and in articles for women's magazines.

ELIZABETH GLEICK: Flatly written, with detail piling upon detail like so much slag on a heap, Maynard's memoir returns repeatedly to the idea of emotional and literary honesty. "Some day, Joyce, there will be a story you want to tell for no better reason than because it matters to you more than any other," Salinger [once told] her. "You'll simply write what's real and true." Maybe this is it. But where Salinger, or many a better writer, would have fictionalized his truths, opening up new universes for the reader, Maynard sheds no light on anything beyond the little spotlight she is standing in. She had a complicated childhood, a shattering love affair, a complicated adulthood. Join the club, kiddo, as Salinger himself might say.

CYNTHIA OZICK: What we have is two celebrities, one who was once upon a time a real writer of substance and an artist, and one who has never been an artist and has no real substance and has attached herself to the real artist in order to suck out his celebrity. It's really such a Jamesian story, isn't it?

JONATHAN YARDLEY: [*At Home in the World* is] smarmy, whiny, smirky, and, above all, almost indescribably stupid.

JOYCE MAYNARD: I wonder, why you are so quick to see exploitation in the actions of a woman—sought out at eighteen by a man thirty-five years her senior who promised to love her forever and asked her to forswear all else to come and live with him, who waited twenty-five years to write her story (HER story, I repeat. Not his). And yet you cannot see exploitation in the man who did this. I wonder what you would think of the story if it were your daughter. Would you still tell her to keep her mouth shut, out of respect for this man's privacy?

JULIET WATERS: The intensity of the literary catfight sparked by Maynard's *At Home in the World* is a bit disturbing. There was a lacerating review in the *New Yorker* that casually dismissed the emotional and sexual abuse Maynard suffered at the hands of her parents with the claim that this paled compared to the sin of having "led their daughter to believe that she, and everything she says or writes, is of supreme interest."

MICHIKO KAKUTANI: Although many readers will doubtless find the Salinger chapters the most compelling—and unsettling—part of this book, "At Home in the World" is not a sleazy tell-all memoir about the author's affair with a famous (and famously reclusive) man. It's actually an earnest, if at times self-serving, autobiography that, in the course of tracing the author's coming of age, delineates her first serious love affair, one that happened to be with the author of "Catcher in the Rye."

LISA SCHWARZBAUM: Defiant, taunting, score settling, and exhibitionistic as this memoir is, at least it isn't as exasperatingly self-satisfied as most of Maynard's other personal journalism; in its twisted way, and with a long, long way to go in the self-awareness department for the memoirist, it may be the most honest autobiographical work she's done.

KATHA POLLITT: It's easy to make fun of Joyce Maynard. As if her relentless self-marketing and theatricality weren't enough, the very fact that she presents herself as vulnerable, a victim in recovery, leaves her open to mockery. In our heard-it-all-before sophistication, we shouldn't lose sight of the fact that while still very young Maynard was on the receiving end of quite a bit of damage from adults. If she doesn't always seem to understand her own story—if she seems like a 44-year-old woman who is still 18—maybe that goes to show how deep the damage went.

JOYCE MAYNARD: Anybody who had a correspondence of any length with Salinger probably knows two things about him. One is how funny and lovable and tender and utterly winning he could be. The other is how cruel. If you've experienced the cruelty, if you've been burned by that flame, you might not be very quick to go anywhere near it again. I heard quite a few stories from women after I published *At Home in the World*.

DAVID SHIELDS: One of the most powerful contradictions in Salinger consists of how little contradiction this completely contradictory, even hypocritical, man can countenance in others.

JOYCE MAYNARD: Based on what was so often said about me for breaking my own silence, the fears of these women to speak of their experiences appear justified. Even now, it seems, there are many who would say it remains a woman's obligation to protect the secrets of a man for the simple reason that he demands it. More than that, it appears to be a matter of some dispute whether a woman has the right to tell the truth about her life—and if she does, whether the story of a woman's life is viewed as significant or valuable.

I was giving a speech one time, and the woman who introduced me said, "Well, she used to be J. D. Salinger's girlfriend." I thought, "God, is that all I've been?" I didn't want to be reduced to that.

A MAN MAYNARD DATED: Fifteen minutes into our first date [in the 1990s], Joyce kept referring to this guy named Jerry. She was talking about "Jerry this" and "Jerry that." It was as though they still knew each other. It took me a few minutes to figure out that the Jerry she was talking about was J. D. Salinger.

—

J. D. SALINGER, excerpt from card to Paul Fitzgerald, December 1998:

> *Paul, old friend, No real news, and little cheer this year, but winter, snow on the ground, is so reminiscent of places and Times half a century old. Not bad at all that we survived them. . . . A book I like very much, and you might, too Berlin Diaries, 1940–1945, by Maria Vassiltchikov.*

—

CATHLEEN McGUIGAN: Now, 27 years later, "Miss Maynard," as he addressed her, is putting up that letter and 13 others for public auction next month at Sotheby's in New York. . . . So rare are Salinger letters—and so notorious is their romance—that Sotheby's estimates they will sell (as a group) for $60,000 to $80,000. . . .

Selling the letters, she says, is practical. "I'm a single mother of three children," explains Maynard, 45, from her home in California. "I don't feel any embarrassment at the financial reality of being a writer who's not J. D. Salinger." . . .

The new letters are hardly lurid or full of secrets—Maynard already described them in her memoir. Yet actually reading them . . . is a treat. . . . "[There are] wonderful things in those letters," notes Maynard. "But there's also an enormous amount of bitterness and disdain for the world." . . .

Salinger is seductive in his praise of Maynard's writing, her mind, his suggestion that they are soul mates. He signs off, "Love, Jerry." What bright but naive 18-year-old with literary ambitions wouldn't fall for this from a brilliant, sensitive, famous writer?

Writer Joyce Carol Oates says she has "mixed feelings" about the sale of the letters but notes that the press has treated Salinger "like he's sacrosanct. . . . How old was he then? He must have known at the time that this was reckless behavior." And Maynard apparently wasn't the only woman to whom Salinger, now 80 and remarried, wrote. Oates says she has a close woman friend who had an affair with Salinger and has letters from him. Maynard herself has heard of others. "It was a painful discovery that there had been other girls," she says. "But it began to set me free from the worship of this man who had presided over my life for so long." When his letters go on the block in June, Maynard will be there to hear the gavel fall.

JOYCE CAROL OATES: What of the letter-writer's complicity in his "betrayal"? No one forced J. D. Salinger in the spring of 1972 to initiate an epistolary relationship with an 18-year-old college freshman; no one forced the 53-year-old writer, at the height of his perhaps sufflated fame, to seduce her through words, and to invite her to live with him in rural New Hampshire.

Though Joyce Maynard has been the object of much incensed, self-righteous criticism, primarily from admirers of the reclusive Salinger, her decision to sell his letters is her own business, like her decision to write about her own life. Why is one "life" more sacrosanct than another? In fact, we might be sympathetic to J. D. Salinger's increasingly futile efforts to safeguard his precious privacy, as we might be sympathetic to anyone's efforts, but that he happens to be a writer with a reputation is irrelevant.

JOHN DEAN: When Maynard decided she was going to sell Salinger's letters, she was smart enough, I'm sure, to know, because of Salinger's lawsuit against Random House, she could not sell the content of the letters: all she could do is sell her right to own the physical letters themselves. She turned them over to Sotheby's to sell; all they sold was the physical paper.

MAUREEN DOWD: I went to Sotheby's . . . to have a gander at the notorious letters. The exercise was fascinating and a little creepy. The 53-year-old author kept warning his 18-year-old friend about the ways that celebrity and conspicuousness can warp talent. Now those warnings against exploitation are being exploited. His counsel for privacy and subtlety are being publicly and unsubtly sold to the highest bidder.

PHOEBE HOBAN: The only reason those [letters] are not in some private person's hands now, but back in Salinger's possession, is that Peter Norton, the software developer, thought it was such a terrible act of disloyalty that he bought the letters and returned them to Salinger. I thought it was one of the noble acts of the twentieth century.

JOHN DEAN: The buyer of the letters, Mr. Norton, returned them to Salinger: all he was doing was returning the physical possession of the letters because Salinger already owned the content of the letters. This kept them out of public circulation.

MARC PEYSER: Peter Norton, a software millionaire and art collector, forked over $156,000 last week to buy Salinger's letters from navel-gazing writer Joyce Maynard, who lived with the reclusive author in the 1970s. Norton doesn't criticize Maynard; he just wants to keep the letters from ruining Salinger's privacy.

PETER NORTON: My intention is to do whatever he wants done with them. He may want them returned. He may want me to destroy them. He may not care at all.

—

DAVID SHIELDS: Shortly after Salinger survived the attack from Maynard, he needed to gear up to do battle with another young woman about the same age as Maynard—his daughter, Margaret.

DOREEN CARVAJAL: The daughter of the obsessively private author J. D. Salinger is preparing to publish a memoir of her childhood and relationship with her father. The book by Margaret (Peggy) Salinger, 43, is tentatively titled "The Dream Catcher" and is scheduled to be published by Simon & Schuster's Pocket Books in the fall of 2000. Ms. Salinger received an advance from Pocket Books of more than $250,000.

DAVID SHIELDS: In 2000 Salinger's daughter, Margaret—who had graduated Phi Beta Kappa from Brandeis, received a master's degree from Oxford, and attended Harvard Divinity School—published a book about her life with her father, *Dream Catcher*, which portrays Salinger pursuing cult-like Eastern religions, using herbal medicines, sitting in an orgone box in an attempt to gain certain benefits and cures, and drinking his own urine. Margaret says that her father wasn't a catcher for her and suggests that he shouldn't be a catcher for readers, either. Evoking many unhappy moments between herself and her father, she bears down particularly hard on what she considers his indifference toward her.

MARGARET SALINGER: It turned out that I had a classic case of a "new" or newly discovered disease first called Epstein-Barr virus, or CFS—chronic fatigue syndrome—or in England, myalgic encephalomyelitis. When I could no longer safely hold a teacup in my hand without dropping it, fibromyalgia was added to the pot. . . . I received notice that my disability payments were to be terminated. . . . I called and told my father the grave news that my disability payments had been cut off.

A week or two later, something arrived in the mail. He had taken out a three-year subscription, in my name, to a monthly booklet of testimo-

Margaret Salinger.

nials to miraculous healing put out by the Christian Science Church. . . . I would get well when I stopped believing in the illusion of my sickness. What began to crack was my belief in the illusion of my father.

DINITIA SMITH: The Plaza [Hotel in New York] is a place of happy memories, where she used to stay with her father when they visited her godfather, William Shawn, the editor of the *New Yorker*. She is looking at photographs in her book about her handsome young father, beaming as she learns to walk, as she sits on his shoulders, plays the piano. "He loves me," said Ms. Salinger, as if surprised. "Isn't he sexy! How funny he was."

Her father loved her, but he was also pathologically self-centered, Ms. Salinger says. Nothing could interrupt his work, which he likened to a quest for enlightenment. He was also abusive toward her mother, Claire Douglas, Ms. Salinger says, keeping her a virtual prisoner in his house in Cornish, N.H., refusing to allow her to see friends and family. There is one moment that stands out above all, she said. "It is so horrible, it's so powerful." When she was pregnant and sick, instead of offering help, her father "said I had no right to bring a child into this lousy world," she writes, "and he hoped I was considering an abortion."

JOYCE MAYNARD: I read Peggy's book. I think of her as Peggy because I knew her as Peggy when she was young. I feel great compassion and sympathy for her: she was treated terribly by her father; a father shouldn't extract unconditional loyalty and silence. A child deserves support and loyalty, which she didn't receive. She was abandoned by her father. . . .

I recognized on that first visit [to Salinger's house] that he did not think everything about his daughter was great. I could really respect her, because I'd always been a pleaser. I'd been a good girl, I was somebody who wanted approval, who wanted to be loved, and she was more of a "Fuck you" kind of person than I had ever dared to be. It took me decades to get to be somebody like that. But she was strong, and she was tough, and she was a little bad.

She sometimes said no to her father. Not too many people challenged J. D. Salinger, and she did, even then. She challenged him just with the choices she'd made for her life. She wasn't a literary, academic type. She was a girl with a passion for basketball. She had a Native American boyfriend. The two of them hung out on the couch, drinking soda and watching TV. And I thought, "How can she do this?" She was being her own person.

MARGARET SALINGER: Certainly, in my family, [writing] was what Daddy did. I didn't take English classes. I didn't do creative writing. It was trespassing on his turf. I did everything else *but*. . . . So, in a sense, becoming a writer was really, as one journalist said, "Could we look at it as a declaration of independence?" That is, I think, overly dramatic but, in a sense, it's true. We were supposed to be anything but writers. He was tremendously relieved when I went into business years ago. . . .

I don't think [*Dream Catcher*] is a tell-all. I was speaking with Susan Stamberg from NPR the other day, and she said someone asked her if my book was a "Daddy Dearest," which is what you think of with a tell-all. She said she thought it was a "Daddy, Why?" It's an ask-all rather than tell-all, asking questions.

One of the things I wrestled with in writing this book was knowing that if I disobeyed him in this kind of way, there was a good chance he would cut me off like he cut off everybody else who committed a misdemeanor in his eyes. And this was not going to be any misdemeanor. I also realized pretty early on that this was the death of a wish, not a reality. I'm never going to have the mommy and daddy I wished for. What I really had to lose wasn't a whole lot. Even on good terms with him, I never saw my father much. I miss him, but—and I don't mean this in a cute way at all—I miss my daddy, not my father.

RON ROSENBAUM: She says she wrote it for her own sake, as therapy, as deprogramming for her cultic upbringing. . . . In both his life and his work J. D. Salinger brought the war home, brought it home in the form of a desperate search for peace that torments his characters and seems to have tormented his own character. Holed up in his hilltop retreat in New Hampshire, Salinger waged the war for peace with one spiritual weapon after another. As his daughter chronicles it, it was "Zen Buddhism, Vedanta Hinduism, 1950's on and off; Kriya yoga, 1954–55; Christian Science, 1955 off and on to the present; Scientology, called Dianetics at the time, 1950's; something having to do with the work of Edgar Cayce; homeopathy and acupuncture, 1960's to present; macrobiotics, 1966. . . ."

What these disciplines all have in common, of course, is the promise of relief from, or transcendence of, the sufferings of the flesh. The problem for Margaret Salinger was that her father often extended those experiments to his family.

Margaret reports that almost from birth she served as a guinea pig for her father's spiritual enthusiasms. When she fell ill as a baby, she says, she wasn't taken to the doctor. Salinger "had suddenly embraced Christian Science, and now, in addition to being forbidden any friends or visitors, doctors were out."

She says she wrote the memoir for the sake of her young son, so that he will understand the family history and the chain of suffering will be broken. Very noble, but there's something a bit disingenuous about this piety: if the account is really just meant as therapy, what need was there to publish it? . . . Or if it was somehow necessary to publish it, what need was there to rush it into print when her father, now eighty-one, was still alive to be hurt by it? Unless the hurt was part of the therapy. . . . Still,

Salinger has the right to tell her own story as she sees it. . . . And whatever her other motives, she clearly believes that it is we too who need to be disillusioned as she was; that it is important to destroy the illusion that the authors we love are perfect gurus and saints as well.

DAVID SHIELDS: The book is replete with photos of Margaret and her father in loving embrace, but these pictures stop well before the end of adolescence. Here, too, Salinger stopped loving a girl once she became a woman. She was now dirty.

THOMAS CHILDERS: One woman, responding to a website devoted to the children of World War II veterans, wrote of her POW father, "My father's undiagnosed and untreated PTSD kept my family from living full and normal lives, lives others take for granted. . . . I was never 'Daddy's little girl,' but I certainly was his POW."

—

LINDSAY CROUSE: When Margaret wrote this book exposing the intolerance in her father, the rigidity in her father, the serious damage he had done to her, people didn't want to hear that.

GERALDINE McGOWAN: I felt sorry for his daughter. She didn't have a chance. When you're up against such a celebrity, when people find your artistic value much lower than someone else's, you almost don't count.

BENJAMIN ANASTAS: Of all the private documents that have lately found their way into print under the abused publishing category known as "memoir," only one, Margaret Salinger's *Dream Catcher*, is so unequivocally removed from the realm of literature—so inward-looking, so ungenerous, so artless—that it achieves a perfect state of irrelevance, the nadir, if you will, of the autobiographical practice, revealing falsehood where it seeks to expose the "truth," and truth where it reveals the hollows of the secret-teller's damaged little heart.

One would have thought that Margaret Salinger, of all the writers' children in the world, would have a better grasp on the numberless value of what remains unspoken; that she would have found a way, somehow, to avoid indulging in the kind of confessional writing that her father, in a more comic vein, once described as taking on "precisely the informality of underwear." As it is, the secrets are out, the dirty laundry has been aired, and nothing is changed, really, but for another dream of "wellness" written, bound, and cast atop the discounted pile in the memoir section. And at what cost? Another dream, just as foolish, coveted by Seymour Glass and shared by kindred spirits everywhere—the peace, the quiet, the respite, the *relief* of an unexamined life.

SVEN BIRKERTS: It seems to me that these [parent-child] relationships are private not merely in popular designation, but in their ontological essence as well. Which is to say that they constitute, emotionally and psychologically, worlds of their own. They are profoundly contextual. Wrest them into the public glare and they often collapse into near unrecognizability or become caricature. This does not mean that personal memoirs of this sort ought not to be written, simply that they should be viewed by readers as intrinsically suspect. Only where a writer is skillful enough to recreate the complex atmosphere of interactions is there a chance that the figures will live. Ms. Salinger is not a writer of this caliber.

Second, I would invoke—or propose—the worthiness law: that the memoirist ought to be, in some core perceptual way, the equal of her subject. It seems evident that the lesser cannot comprehend the greater.

JONATHAN YARDLEY: *Dream Catcher* is indeed in almost all respects an unattractive and unwelcome book. Had its author been anyone except the only daughter of this country's most famously reclusive novelist—yes, even more famous than if not quite so reclusive as Thomas Pynchon—it certainly would not have been published. It is too long by at least two hundred pages, it is almost indescribably self-indulgent, and it invades the author's father's cherished privacy to the point of disloyalty and exploitation. . . . It may seem a bold gesture for Peggy Salinger to say that she meant "to defy his cult of secrecy by writing this book," but it remains that her father is entitled to his secrecy, or privacy, and that this book is a willful violation of it. That being the case, *Dream Catcher* must be seen not as an attempt at self-exploration and self-understanding but as an act of revenge and betrayal: a blow beneath the belt.

VED MEHTA: J. D. Salinger was someone who wanted to be private, which was so heroic in this publicity- and advertising-driven society; he didn't want to be part of this climate. Then this daughter went and wrote about all kinds of quirks he has. I was appalled at that book. I think *Dream Catcher* is a very good argument for not having children.

JUDITH SHULEVITZ: Ladies and gentlemen, the jury has filed back into the room, and a verdict has been announced. J. D. Salinger is the victim of a literary crime. His daughter, Margaret Salinger, is the guilty party. (This time, that is. Last time it was his ex-lover, Joyce Maynard.) *Dream Catcher*, Margaret's memoir of her life as the problematic daughter of the most misanthropic author in America, strikes "a blow beneath the belt," critic Jonathan Yardley says. Another, Sven Birkerts, charges that Margaret Salinger has broken two laws of nature. The first of these is the father-child bond, whose "ontological essence" she violates by exposing its intimate details to public scrutiny. . . . The second dictates the proper place of the unskilled writer, which is at a respectful distance from the more accomplished one. "It seems evident that the lesser cannot comprehend the greater," Birkerts writes. Actually, what seems evident is that if writers adhered to Birkerts' exacting code of conduct, literature as we know it could no longer be produced. . . .

Margaret Salinger understands the world's attachment to the myths she's out to dispel. She grew up in their shadow. By that she means, at first, that Salinger couldn't tolerate the disruptions to work caused by the birth of his first child. Before long, she developed a full-fledged rivalry with her father's imaginary children. Note that J. D. Salinger could be a sweet father as well as one who was impossible to please. He was by turns an uncondescending playmate, a wiseacre older-brother type, and a lively travel companion. But Peggy's all-too-human needs proved too much for him, as they did for her mother, and when the daughter reached eighth grade, the parents (now divorced) parked her at boarding school.

PAUL ALEXANDER: Just the idea of Margaret writing a book about her father, the last private man in America—regardless of the revelations in it, some of which were startling—was enough to offend many Salinger loyalists. Readers and commentators alike were shocked by the book's revelations, such as Salinger's practice of drinking his own urine.

MARGARET SALINGER: Gosh, I wish I hadn't put in everything about drinking urine, because that's all I'm reading [in reviews]. It speaks to my odd upbringing that I didn't find this particularly peculiar. I never expected to see that as sort of a "shockeroo" headline. It's quite a common practice of yogis, having to do with self-purification. Not being a practitioner myself, I don't know anything about it, but I was certainly surprised at the attention drawn to that.

I tried to be careful in my book of not having sexy, quotable quotes that can be taken out of context. My real desire with this book was to put things in context and to de-sensationalize and make human.

LINDSAY CROUSE: The public wants to take Salinger in its arms and hold him out of gratitude. Here comes little Margaret, writing her book; she's a detractor and she's throwing water on all that. She's speaking to other kinds of universal truths. It's difficult and it's disquieting and it's upsetting that you've got J. D. Salinger in your arms and you'd just like to write him a love letter. But he needs privacy. Writers need privacy. You're bringing something to birth and it's not for everybody to look at while you're doing that.

She couldn't get into his room, so how did she get in? Through the same medium her father used: she wrote. She went down that road herself, alone. And her purpose wasn't fame and fortune and reaching the masses. Her purpose was, for one moment, for one damn moment, to find her father, to find her real father. I think she accomplished it. It's palpable. You feel it.

ETHEL NELSON: I was sorry after I read some of her book that I didn't stay in touch and didn't get to know her more just because I think she really needed a friend. I sat and cried reading that book. I haven't read it all. I couldn't go back to it. It's too sad. You always picture those kinds of kids as being brought up happy. I don't know how much of her book is really true and how much isn't, but I think it's the saddest thing I ever read.

LINDSAY CROUSE: There is a moment in *Dream Catcher* where Salinger says to his daughter, Christ, you're sounding just like every other woman in my life, my sister, my ex-wives. They all accuse me of neglecting them. . . . I can be accused of a certain detachment, that's all. Never neglect.

DAVID SHIELDS: It's difficult to discern the difference between parental detachment and parental neglect. Is Salinger aware of the dubiousness of the distinction? This is absence reframed as a philosophical position.

MARGARET SALINGER: I really would like to have the image put forth which is the same thing I try to convey to my son, that you don't have to be perfect to be lovable, that you may not like some of the things someone does, but that doesn't mean you have to dismiss the person. And in my father's world, you're either perfect or you are an anathema. And I don't feel that way. I don't love him less for understanding him more.

Ian Hamilton thought my dad would be so proud of him and sent him the galleys. I know better. I have not been in contact with him since it hit the press that the book was coming out. Call me chicken. There hasn't been any formal, "Oh, we're not talking to each other." I want to wait until his anger subsides some, and he's had a chance to read the book, and then we'll see what happens.

In many ways, the historical research I did took the man off the pedestal of this sort of myth that he sprang from nowhere, that he is a recluse not attached to any family or community or background, and put him squarely in the realm of human beings, which is not a bad place to be. I think you dehumanize someone when they are on a pedestal, and they become a projection of one's wishes, rather than who they really are. . . .

I think it's lovely to have a book mean something to you. And I don't think anything in my book should take away from [a reader's] cherished memory of reading his books, or new readers coming to them, fresh.

What I do attack is the idolatry, the notion that the person who wrote these wonderful books will be your "catcher," the kind of people who troop to his house expecting him to be the one to understand them, to be their "catcher in the rye," and that's fair enough. I think the things expected of him as the writer of the book are not appropriate.

LINDSAY CROUSE: As you move toward the end of the book, you feel her starting to mature and to extricate herself from this poison, this toxicity that she grew up with. You feel her rise almost to a spiritual plane and begin to develop compassion for her father. And when she comes to it, it's stunning.

JEAN MILLER: I read it with great interest. Jerry said to his young daughter, "You never forget the smell of burning flesh." He had said that to me, and it rocked me. It was something he carried with him. Also, Margaret mentions that he got a letter from his first wife, with whom he had corresponded telepathically; he told me he got a letter from her, and he didn't even open it up. He was like that. Margaret said when he was through with somebody, he was through. And I thought that is so true. When it's over, it's over.

DAVID SHIELDS: In the early 1970s, Salinger received a letter from Sylvia but tore it up and threw it away without reading it.

ETHEL NELSON: Margaret wrote her book to let her dad know her feelings, to communicate with him, because there was no other way she could. I have no idea if he ever read it or not, but I know he gets quite angry when his kids do things he doesn't understand.

LINDSAY CROUSE: If she wrote it only for herself, you wouldn't be so moved in reading it. She gouged it out of a hillside, grubbed it out of the ground, that book. She wrote it in order for life to come up through hard concrete. Her purposes were to dig through the mine to her dad. It was an act of generosity; although the world might not perceive it that way, it was an act of generosity on her part. Drama is based on love; otherwise, everybody would just leave the room. She could have just said, "To hell with you," and stayed in a shrink's office. But she didn't. It's not my reading of *Dream Catcher* that J. D. Salinger is a monster. It is my reading of her experience, her early experience with him, that there wasn't any margin for her.

Margaret is as extraordinary as her father, and I think he is extraordinary. One of the only places we can put love, frankly, is in art; it can be very afflicted in other arenas. She put it in her life.

I found *Dream Catcher* gripping. I was astounded by the clarity of Margaret's memory, by her ability to go back and reconstruct just what happened, and it made me feel there had to have been a reason for that. When I go back and think of what happened to me in third grade or sixth grade, it's pretty much a wash. I'd have to concentrate very hard to try to call something up specifically; she had reams of memory at her fingertips, it seems. Which indicates that there was a good reason to remember: there was a vigilance.

—

DAVID SHIELDS: The king chose not to defend the realm himself; he sent out his loyal foot soldier, Matthew, who many years earlier had tried to fulfill his father's other ambition: acting.

MATTHEW SALINGER: I love my father very much and I wouldn't want him to be different. Just wish I'd see him more. The public image of my father has been filtered through the lens of people who are angry, whether it be a daughter or an ex-lover, or journalists who can't get interviews.

I'm not in contact with my sister now, nor will I ever be. But Dad has been remarkably untouched by the book; I was more upset by it than he was. He's a very kind man who was a terrific father; I had a wonderful childhood.

MARGARET SALINGER: I would prefer not to speak about someone else's relation with another person from my perspective. My brother and father have their own relationship, and I'm not comfortable speculating on that, other than to say that siblings can have extremely different experiences of growing up, and both are telling the truth.

MATTHEW SALINGER: Of course, I can't say with any authority that she is consciously making anything up. I just know that I grew up in a very different house, with two very different parents from those my sister describes. I do not remember even one instance of my mother hitting either my sister or me. Not one. Nor do I remember any instance of my father "abusing" my mother in any way whatsoever. The only sometimes frightening presence I remember in the house, in fact, was my sister (the same person who in her book self-servingly casts herself as my benign protector)! She remembers a father who couldn't "tie his own shoe-laces" and I remember a man who helped me learn how to tie mine, and even—specifically—how to close off the end of a lace again once the plastic had worn away.

20

A MILLION MILES AWAY IN HIS TOWER

Completely devoted to the fourth stage of Vedanta—renunciation of the world—Salinger spends the last two decades of his life in isolation in Cornish, readying himself for the next world and his work for posthumous publication.

ETHEL NELSON: The woman he's with now [Colleen O'Neill] I've met, and she's delightful. From what I understand, their marriage came to be so that she could take care of him, because at this time he's pretty feeble and he really needs someone there with him. He couldn't be alone and he couldn't very well have a nurse or a person taking care of him in there and not be married. A relative would be fine, but a single person—out.

JULIE McDERMOTT: I have no idea when she came to Cornish, or where Jerry met her, or any of the basics of their relationship. I only know that when I started working at the co-op [in Hanover], they were together. She never said, "I'm married to him." She never said, "This is my husband." I just assumed that they were a couple and that they were together. You found out bits of information, that they were husband and wife. At one point, someone said something to him about his daughter, and he said, "That's not my daughter; that's my wife!" He was quite adamant that people knew exactly who Colleen was.

As a couple, Colleen and Jerry were not what I would have pictured. I would have thought that maybe he would be with someone older, but I had heard that wasn't his preference. I think that she loves him as a person and for who he is. She doesn't want to expose him to the public eye. One time, Colleen and I were carrying on a conversation and I found out that she was a nurse. She also owns her own quilting business.

She's a wonderful person. I really could be fond of her if I got to know her more. I saw her once at a department store and we talked quite extensively. I had just gotten my hair cut and she was telling me that it looked nice. She was buying undergarments for Jerry. They were never really an affectionate couple that I could tell. Every once in a while, Colleen would put her arm on Jerry's shoulder, but to hug or show affection of any sort—they didn't do that. Jerry would look around and be really anxious to try to find out where Colleen was, if she was down at the meat counter instead of at the deli section. He was always pushing the cart really fast so that she would have to hurry along. I could tell sometimes that Mr. Salinger was agitated and that he really wanted to be quick about what he was doing in the store.

Colleen keeps her personal life really quiet; having been with him throughout the years, she doesn't want people to know any more about her life than Jerry does his. Maybe he's impressed that upon her. The more people know, the more they can use it against you. I heard one time J. D. Salinger was on a cruise. He signed a credit slip. Someone picked it up off the table and sold it on eBay. I believe he took legal action against that person.

SHANE SALERNO: Salinger once wrote to Hemingway that he was going to attempt to find a girl like Catherine Barkley, the nurse heroine of *A Farewell to Arms*: British, regal, beautiful. Apparently, he found her in Colleen O'Neill.

DAVID SHIELDS: Because it's such an extreme lab experiment—Salinger's isolation—it matters to a lot of people what Salinger wrote the last forty-five years of his life. Among contemporary American writers, there are many more or less isolated writers: Cormac McCarthy, Thomas Pynchon, Philip Roth, Don DeLillo. Is it a phenomenon exclusive to male writers of that approximate generation? In any case, very few writers have ever isolated themselves as thoroughly as Salinger has, or have refrained from publishing for half a century. Salinger dodged Betty Eppes's question regarding whether he's continued to write about the Glass family. In the deposition he gave to Hamilton's lawyer, he refused to say what genre the work falls into. Well, "unclassifiable" can mean genius, but it can also mean inchoate. Very, very few writers produce memorable work after, say, age seventy-five, but Salinger stopped publishing at age forty-six.

LAWRENCE GROBEL: When I interviewed Truman Capote in 1980, we talked about Salinger. Capote said that he knew on good authority that Salinger was writing, or had already written, five or six novellas, and that the *New Yorker* had rejected all of them. So I said to Capote, "Do you really believe the *New Yorker* at this stage would reject J. D. Salinger's work?" "Oh, of course they would," he said. "They're not artists."

PAUL ALEXANDER: I talked to Roger Angell, who's been a fiction editor at the *New Yorker* for years and years. He told me, definitively, that if any Salinger story had come in, from 1965 on, they would have found a way to publish it, if for no other reason than its historical value. It's hard to imagine Capote would know something that Angell, a fiction editor at the magazine, didn't know.

PHOEBE HOBAN: Yes, it's credible that Salinger sent stories to the *New Yorker* over the last three or four decades that were turned down. I've heard that Shawn turned down at least one manuscript when he was still editor. Salinger had trust in Shawn, who was very protective of him. Think about it this way: Salinger took himself out of the world forty years ago. It's very possible Salinger is completely out of touch with reality and there's no way he can reflect that reality in a meaningful way in literature anymore. It's very possible that the stories he sent in suffered from that and that people who loved him and his work didn't want those works to be published because of it.

I think he still wrote about the Glasses, but the Glasses can't grow up. Where can they go? You can't keep writing indefinitely about this family of whimsical child geniuses who never grow up. If they grow up, they're no longer the Glasses. I just can't believe he left the Glasses. I think they were his family and he continued to write about them.

RENATA ADLER: Salinger had invited me for a short visit to his house in the country. He said that the reason he chose not to publish the material he had been working on was to spare Mr. Shawn the burden of having to read, and to decide whether to publish, Salinger writing about sex. This went too far. The writer who originated, and was the most extreme example of, a recoil from publication and publicity had become something of a prisoner of his sympathy for the editor who had become, yet again, a source of disinclination to publish. A doctrinal circle of pure inhibition seemed to have closed.

JOYCE MAYNARD: Jerry loved the Glass family. Jerry did not love his real family. I'm not speaking of his children—he loved his children—but the Glass family were the ones he talked about as if they were his family. In my memory there was actually a book; he'd made a book of the background of all the members of the Glass family. I just had a general sense there was this book, almost a genealogy of the Glass family. Not that I ever saw it. Jerry loved and was protective of those characters, as if they were his children.

LAWRENCE GROBEL: Unless he was a totally crazy man who went off into his studio and sat there and stared out the window, we have to believe what Joyce Maynard saw when she was with him, what the *Time* researchers saw when they jumped over his fence to steal a look at what he was doing.

WALTER SCOTT: Salinger has been seen in the Dartmouth College library hard at work on a novel, purportedly based on his World War II experiences. He is expected to finish the book sometime this year.

RICHARD HAITCH: "He's just working, working and working—that's all," says his literary agent in New York, Dorothy Olding. Is he writing for publication? "I just don't know," Miss Olding says.

RICHARD BROOKS: Another friend, Jonathan Schwartz, tells how his girlfriend, Susan, spent the night at Salinger's house after pretending that her car had broken down. After eating a meal of his staple diet, nuts and peas, she too saw the safe and the books. . . .

Phyllis Westbery, Salinger's agent at Harold Ober Associates in

New York, would not comment on whether there were any unpublished books. However, Westbery did say that she spoke to Salinger on a "very regular basis" about what he was doing.

To those who have seen him, Salinger comes across as a person who has for most of his adult life been emotionally stuck in his late teens. . . . Salinger, who is eighty, does not seem to have had an obviously unhappy childhood. He is described by friends who knew him at the time as "confident and even swaggering." But when he was twenty-five he seems to have had a nervous breakdown while serving in the U.S. army at the end of the second world war in Europe. . . . He walks about in a blue mechanic's uniform and, when he does go to local restaurants, eats in the kitchen to avoid people.

MATTHEW SALINGER: My sister and I used to tell people when they asked about my father that he wasn't a writer; he was a plumber.

LILLIAN ROSS: At one point during the more than half century of our friendship, J. D. Salinger told me he had an idea that someday, when "all the fiction had run out," he might try to do something straight, "really factual, formally distinguishing myself from the Glass boys and Holden Caulfield and the other first-person narrators I've used." It might be readable, maybe funny, he said, and "not just smell like a regular autobiography." The main thing was that he would use straight facts and "thereby put off or stymie one or two vultures—freelancers or English-department scavengers—who might come around and bother the children and the family before the body is even cold."

—

HILLEL ITALIE: Salinger's place in Cornish history is mostly that he lived here. He was not the town sage, the town drunk, or even, reputation aside, the town eccentric. He was simply the tall, dark-eyed man who liked to watch the horses at the county fair, buy lettuce at the market or invite children inside for hot cocoa.

KATIE ZEZIMA: Mr. Salinger was a regular at the $12 roast beef dinners at First Congregational Church in Hartland, Vermont. He would arrive about an hour and a half early and pass the time by writing in a small, spiral-bound notebook, said Jeannie Frazer, a church member. Mr. Salinger usually dressed in corduroys and a sweater, she said, and would not speak. He sat at the head of the table, near where the pies were placed.

ETHEL NELSON: We went to many suppers and Jerry was always there as Jerry. He wasn't made up in a disguise at all. You still couldn't go up and say hi. Colleen will not allow you to approach him. It's still going on. It's never going to end. If you approach him at these suppers, she will step between you and him. When we go to these suppers, Jerry and Colleen are always the first ones there: they'd get the very first seats and they would go up toward the front so they couldn't be seen readily. At one point I wanted to go up and speak to him, because I hadn't seen him in quite a few years, but I was promptly told by one of the people I was sitting with, "Don't, because she won't let you near him." Colleen is a giving person and I think she saw a need there and she fulfilled it. She could take care of him. She could make his elderly life a little more comfortable.

DAVID SHIELDS: They went to the suppers, but Salinger kept himself closed off at them. Approach. Avoid. Attract attention. Spurn it.

In 2009 Margaret Tewksbury, a fellow organic gardener, also in her nineties, who lived in Windsor, related that although he still visited her, Salinger's health had declined. "He's so deaf you have to yell."

JOHN CURRAN: Salinger would occasionally take in a basketball game at Dartmouth, in Hanover.

Martha Beattie, fifty-five, of Boston, who coached his son, Matt Salinger, on the crew team at Phillips Academy-Andover in Andover, Mass., and met him once in the 1970s, saw him at games in Hanover twice in the past month—once at a women's game, once at a men's game.

Both times he was alone, sitting in the same spot, wearing big, round, tortoise-shell eyeglasses and a scarf, reading the program, she said. Each time, she said hello.

"He looked like a writer," she said. "He was a little hunched over, but he didn't look like ninety-one."

KATIE ZEZIMA: He would, until recent years, vote in elections and attend town meetings at the Cornish Elementary School, and he went to the Plainfield General Store each day before it closed. He was often spotted at the Price Chopper supermarket in Windsor, separated from Cornish by a covered bridge and the now ice-jammed river, and he ate lunch alone at the Windsor Diner.

ASHLEY BLUM: Gwen Tetirick, one of Salinger's neighbors, said that several times reporters or other visitors knocked on her family's door asking for directions to Salinger's home, but they would just pretend to not know who he was.

GWEN TETIRICK: We would just say "J. D. Salinger who?" They think we are a bunch of stupid hicks who don't know who Salinger is.

ANABELLE CONE: In order to be accepted by the town you have to follow the code. One of the codes of Cornish is you don't run your mouth about Salinger.

MIKE ACKERMAN: [Salinger] was like the Batman icon. Everyone knew Batman existed, and everyone knows there's a Batcave, but no one will tell you where it is.

TOM LEONARD: Locals concur that Salinger is seen out far more infrequently than in the past. Apart from the supermarket, he and his wife occasionally go to a local café in Windsor, the nearest town, for coffee and a sandwich ("he likes the spinach and mushroom wraps," said the manager), and a restaurant there.

ASHLEY BLUM: During the last two years of his life, when he could no longer go to the [church] dinners himself, he would have an attendee pick up dinner for him.

SUSAN J. BOUTWELL and ALEX HANSON: His wife stopped by the last two Saturdays to purchase roast beef, mashed potatoes, and cole slaw to bring home to Cornish, said Larry Frazer, one of the meal's organizers.

—

Salinger and Colleen O'Neill, smiling, 2008.

CHARLES McGRATH: J. D. Salinger, who was thought at one time to be the most important American writer to emerge since World War II but who then turned his back on success and adulation, becoming the Garbo of letters, famous for not wanting to be famous, died on Wednesday at his home in Cornish, New Hampshire, where he had lived in seclusion for more than fifty years. He was ninety-one.

Salinger's literary representative, Harold Ober Associates, announced the death, saying it was of natural causes. "Despite having broken his hip in May," the agency said, "his health had been excellent until a rather sudden decline after the new year. He was not in any pain before or at the time of his death."

HAROLD OBER ASSOCIATES: In keeping with his lifelong, uncompromising desire to protect and defend his privacy, there will be no service, and the family asks that people's respect for him, his work, and his privacy be extended to them, individually and collectively, during this time. Salinger had remarked that he was in this world but not of it. His body is gone, but the family hopes that he is still with those he loves, whether they are religious or historical figures, personal friends, or fictional characters.

COLLEEN O'NEILL: Cornish is a truly remarkable place. This beautiful spot afforded my husband a place of awayness from the world. The people of this town protected him and his right to his privacy for many years. I hope, and believe, they will do the same for me.

DOUG HACKETT: Obviously, we're prepared for whatever happens, but we're hoping people allow the family to grieve in peace, and honor him the way he lived, which is quietly.

LILLIAN ROSS: No one else could make me laugh—genuinely laugh aloud—as he could. His positives are familiar to Colleen O'Neill, his wife of the last several decades, to his son, Matthew, and to whatever other sacred and private relationships he had.

JOHN CURRAN: Matt Salinger answered the doorbell at the home Thursday by rolling open a kitchen window and speaking through it.

"My father was a great father," was all he said.

—

JENNIFER SCHUESSLER: J. D. Salinger, who died last month at 91, had a perfect best-seller record, sending all four of his books onto the list. "The Catcher in the Rye" spent 29 weeks on the list, peaking at No. 4. "Nine Stories" made it to No. 9. "Franny and Zooey" and "Raise High the Roof Beam, Carpenters," collections of previously published stories released after Salinger had retreated to self-imposed literary silence in rural New Hampshire, both reached No. 1.

ADAM GOPNIK: There are lots of good writers. There are lots of hugely skilled writers. There's lots of us who write about many subjects with curiosity and diligence. But there are very few writers in this century who find or forge the key that enables them to unlock the hearts of their readers and of their fellow people. And Salinger did that. He did it repeatedly. And whether he was silent for forty years or miserably grumpy for half a century, I don't care. He did that. And he alone did that.

RICK MOODY: Ernest Hemingway famously said of Mark Twain's legacy that "we all of us came out from under Huck Finn's skirts." The same can be said, for contemporary writers, of Holden Caulfield, the narrator of J. D. Salinger's *The Catcher in the Rye*. It's impossible to be an American writer now and not feel the influence of Holden and of Salinger generally. The most perceptible way that we feel this is in Salinger's understanding of voice, the loose, colloquial, humane voice of Holden Caulfield, that very personal first-person, which became the template for so much American literature that came after. You can hear him in *Bright Lights, Big City*; you can hear him in *Less Than Zero*; you can hear him even in a television program like *My So-Called Life*.

The second part of Salinger's outsized legacy has to do with his commitment to the theme of family. I'm thinking especially of the four novellas that make up the last works he published in his lifetime, *Franny and Zooey* and then the two works titled "Raise High the Roof Beam, Carpenters" and "Seymour: An Introduction." Over the course of these novellas, Salinger's commitment to the Glass family, the protagonists of these works, deepened to an almost obsessive level, and while the Glass family was anything but functional, since it was noteworthy for suicide, religious obsession, and game show appearances, Salinger was never less than devoted to them, and to the complexity of their interactions. A whole literature of the so-called dysfunctional family, including at least one work, *The Ice Storm*, by this writer, was spawned by these Glass chronicles.

DAVID SHIELDS: Jean-Marie Gustave Le Clézio, the 2008 winner of the Nobel Prize in Literature, said Salinger had influenced him more than any other writer.

MICHIKO KAKUTANI: Some critics dismissed the easy surface charm of Mr. Salinger's work, accusing him of cuteness and sentimentality, but works like "Catcher," "Franny and Zooey," and his best-known short stories would influence successive generations of writers. . . . Like Holden Caulfield, the Glass children—Franny, Zooey, Buddy, Seymour, Boo Boo, Walt, Waker—would emerge as avatars of adolescent angst and

Mr. Salinger's own alienated stance toward the world. Bright, charming and gregarious, they are blessed with their creator's ability to entertain, and they appeal to the reader to identify with their braininess, their sensitivity, their febrile specialness. And yet as details of their lives unfurl in a series of stories, it becomes clear that there is a darker side to their estrangement as well: a tendency to condescend to the vulgar masses, an almost incestuous familial self-involvement and a difficulty relating to other people that will result in emotional crises and in Seymour's case, suicide.

—

STEPHEN METCALF: Lost along the way, much as it had been lost when Holden was taken up as a hero of the counterculture, was the precise nature of Salinger's genius. He was the great poet of post-traumatic stress, of mental dislocation brought upon by warfare. Salinger himself broke down under the strain of Utah Beach, and all of his best, most affecting work gives us a character whose sensitivities have been driven by the war to the point of nervous collapse. That very balance—between the edge of sanity, and a heightened perception of being—is echoed formally in Salinger's best writing, his short stories. In these, Salinger brought together a most distinctly unprophetic form—the classic *New Yorker* story, in which tight WASP propinquities are displayed neatly upon a small canvas—with at least the possibility of prophecy. I find (and am ready to stand corrected) very little assertion by Salinger on behalf of his characters' holiness—their status as special creatures vis-à-vis another world—though much is made of their piety, their tendency to, their thirst for, belief. For Salinger, this was an after-effect of the war. His characters look at the world, at the implacable surface of post-war affluence, and cannot believe nobody else sees the cracks veining slowly through it. What will pierce the surface of things? Jesus? The Bodhisattva? Psychosis? He never said.

JOHN ROMANO: It was always there in Seymour: he had to commit suicide. I refuse to describe it as a cause for mourning; I think that was the internal momentum of a voice. The prediction was in the writing. It's not entirely unreasonable that the voice should have in some way confounded itself, and caught itself up, and finally come to silence.

LESLIE EPSTEIN: I think what happened is that when Salinger wrote about Seymour's suicide the equivalent had to take place for him, and the equivalent was to withdraw, to become a recluse, to become a hermit, to leave life the same way that Seymour left life. The character became the author, rather than the other way around. I think there was something inevitable about what's happened with Salinger. Something endemic in his work forced him into being a recluse.

MICHAEL TANNENBAUM: I have never been bothered by Salinger's withdrawal from public view, because in following his own heart he reiterated that becoming an icon is not an inherently virtuous achievement. Sometimes you have to kill what others make of you.

ANABELLE CONE: Everyone is trying to keep this fable going. It's kind of funny, this legend. The media, they want to maintain an aura about this mysterious hermit.

CHARLES McGRATH: Depending on one's point of view, he was either a crackpot or the American Tolstoy, who had turned silence itself into his most eloquent work of art.

MYLES WEBER: One of Salinger's lawyers maintained that we have the right to free expression, but that he had a First Amendment right not to speak. He had a First Amendment right not to be an author, and I'd say he wasn't an author. In a fair universe he wasn't an author, but in our universe it turns out he was an author. Everyone insists upon him being an author. They insist that he was—I don't even know what to call it, not publishing—but he created this major fifth text of his. He had four books published, but it seems like he had this fifth text that just keeps growing and growing and growing, and that was his silence.

—

A. SCOTT BERG: There's a high artistic price to be paid if you seclude yourself. For all we know, everything he's writing is no good. Maybe it has all the air sucked out of it. Maybe he's become tone-deaf. We saw this in another medium with Stanley Kubrick in the last twenty years of his life. His films were just out of sync in a way. They didn't fit in with reality. Perhaps that has happened to Salinger. I presume he has a television. I presume he keeps reading. It's not as if one is completely shut off from the world. I'm presuming that he knows what's going on in the world, that there are a handful of people he communicates with. But perhaps he is cut off and perhaps his fiction reflects that.

ROBERT BOYNTON: There are essentially three possibilities. One is that the safe is entirely empty and the last forty-plus years of silence have been a charade. The second possibility is that the safe in which he kept his work is stocked full of great manuscripts and Salinger's promise will be redeemed and all of his fans will be delighted. The third, and I think most likely, possibility is that there is some work in there. Some of it is brilliant, and most of it probably isn't all that great, because that's the way it is for most writers.

DAVE EGGERS: My own pet theory is that he dabbled with stories for many years, maybe finished a handful, but as the distance from his last published work grew longer, it became more difficult to imagine any one work being the follow-up; the pressure on any story or novel would be too great. And thus the dabbling might have continued, but the likelihood of his finishing something, particularly a novel, became more remote. And so I think we might find fragments of things, much in the way [Nabokov's] *The Original of Laura* was found. But there's something about the prospect of actually publishing one's work that brings that work into focus. That pressure is needed, just like it's needed to make diamonds from raw carbon.

Of course, the possibility most intriguing—and fictional-sounding—would have Salinger having continued to write for fifty years, finishing hundreds of stories and a handful of novels, all of which are polished and up to his standards and ready to go, and all of which he imagined would be found and published after his death. That, in fact, he intended all along for these works to be read, but that he just couldn't bear to send them into the world while he lived.

DEAN SIMONTON: It may be the case that J. D. Salinger didn't want criticism. He wanted to speak his mind, but he didn't want anybody to say, "This is terrible." He wanted to get the last word and the best way of getting the last word is to do exactly what he did: write these things and lock them up in the vault for posterity.

HILLEL ITALIE: Jay McInerney said he has an old girlfriend who met Salinger and was told that the author was mostly writing about health and nutrition.

DAVID SHIELDS: The writer Richard Elman got to know Salinger in the early 1980s, when both of them had children at a private school in Lake Placid. He said Salinger told him that it's "really nice not to have to publish anything until the work is completed."

MICHAEL SILVERBLATT: The myth doesn't interest me. Can somebody just sneak me the writing?

MICHAEL McDERMOTT: Why wasn't he more generous with those words? Sharing them with us? I know other artists who create work just for themselves. I understand that he liked to write for himself. I just don't understand why he didn't want to share the work with all of the huge, loving, adoring fans.

LESLIE EPSTEIN: You son of a bitch, why won't you give us more? Why won't you give us the rest of it?

GORE VIDAL: How can someone write eighteen hours a day and then not publish for forty years? Well, thank God he didn't, is all I can say.

DAVID SHIELDS: The problem with the vault is that it's directed toward the next world, whereas we're living in this world. The impulse not to publish seems to be, above all, a futile attempt to transcend the ego. Most of Salinger's work—certainly everything from *Nine Stories* onward—is about the Glasses striving to get past the prison of the ego.

JOHN WENKE: I believe Salinger was writing. I think he was writing for an audience of one. That one might have been himself; it might have been an image of God. I think he wrote for that person; it had to do with a belief that a public silence is a work of art, or a form of art. I think he moved closer to what we normally think of as a mystic.

JOHN C. UNRUE: Salinger's decision to stop publishing was heavily influenced by his Vedanta Buddhism. He was very eager to bring as little attention to himself as possible, to give up his ego. He was also eager not to continue to make himself a target of critics who were often ruthless in their attacks on him. He moved more and more toward silence.

JOHN LEGGETT: It's a lovely idea that there's a vault in his mysterious stockade in Cornish and that it holds two or three Salinger masterpieces and it's quite credible from what I know of Salinger that there is such a book or books waiting for us all. But from what I know of Salinger it's not necessarily the truth. It is just as likely that there will be nothing there but an old box of Saltines. My money would be on the Saltines.

JONATHAN SCHWARTZ: There's no question he's written. On that Fourth of July weekend in 1971, my friend Susan saw the vault, so I know that it exists. I strongly believe that writing exists—writing of an important nature that will touch people, get under our skin in so many different ways, in that voice that communicates so intimately and so dramatically. I would just have to say, if there is nothing there, how sad.

A. SCOTT BERG: Only Salinger and those who came and went in his house know whether he was still a writer. He will always be an important figure in midcentury America literature. I'm hard-pressed to name another writer with as big a reputation based on so small a published output.

It would now be very difficult for him to publish anything, just because there's no way it could live up to the expectations. The morning line would be, "We've waited fifty years; is there fifty years' worth of greatness in this novel or this short story?" It just seems impossible for anything to live up to that.

If his heirs discover there are manuscripts to be published, and they decide to publish them, it will be a huge publishing event, whether the material is good or bad. I think there will be nearly endless curiosity in seeing all of it, no matter what the quality. We are going to want to know, if nothing else, what it is we all fell in love with back in 1951. Was it just of a moment, or is there something that speaks to us for decades and maybe centuries thereafter?

A. E. HOTCHNER: Joe Gould was a character in [Greenwich Village] who allegedly was writing an oral history of the world. For years, he would go around and interview people. He'd move his cache of writing from one place to another. He'd put it in somebody's barn or in somebody's cellar. Then Joe Gould died. All these boxes. He hadn't written anything.

It occurs to me: What if after all these years when Jerry's been in his block house and allegedly writing all this stuff that's too good for people to see because they're going to distort it; what if when Jerry dies and they go into his vault and they open up his alleged treasure trove, what if there's nothing there? What if Jerry's written his last thing and maybe this was a defense against the fact that he's been blocked and there's nothing written? It's a speculation that tickles my fancy. Maybe he hit a wall and didn't want to have to face that. Who knows? It may be just one of the great hoaxes. Not that he perpetrated it for his advantage. He received nothing in this hoax. But it would be a divine ploy, wouldn't it?

I've never known a more private person than Salinger. It's as if he lived in a vault and all of his emotions were in that vault and he would dribble out a little bit of interest in somebody, a little bit of affection, but mostly it was in the vault.

SHANE SALERNO: A week after Germany surrendered on May 7, 1945, Salinger wrote to Elizabeth Murray, "Most of what I have written over here will not be published for several generations." Salinger told Margaret that for him writing and enlightenment were synonymous; he was spending his life writing a single great work.

DAVID SHIELDS: Salinger's best work isn't good. It's not very good. It's not great. It's perfect. "Perfect," though, isn't necessarily the highest praise. "Bananafish," "Esmé," *Catcher*, "Franny," "Raise High"—they're airless; they're claustrophobic; they leave the reader no room to breathe. The work was perfect because it had to be: Salinger was in such agony that he needed to build an exquisitely beautiful place in which to bury himself.

MARGARET SALINGER: My father on many occasions told me the same thing, that the only people he really respects are all dead.

J. D. SALINGER (*The Catcher in the Rye*, 1951):

> Boy, when you're dead, they really fix you up. I hope to hell when I do die somebody has sense enough to just dump me in the

> river or something. Anything except sticking me in the goddam cemetery. People coming and putting a bunch of flowers on your stomach on Sunday, and all that crap. Who wants flowers when you're dead? Nobody.

SHANE SALERNO: As quoted in the statement released by Harold Ober Associates, Salinger's final words are an explicit fulfillment of the central idea of the fourth and final stage of his Vedantic beliefs: renunciation of the world.

J. D. SALINGER: I am in this world but not of it.

21

JEROME DAVID SALINGER: A CONCLUSION

NEW YORK CITY, 1919–CORNISH, NEW HAMPSHIRE, 2010

DAVID SHIELDS and SHANE SALERNO: As death approached, Salinger looked forward to "meeting up with those he loves, whether they are religious or historical figures, personal friends or fictional characters." He had long ago given up on the physical world, which had failed him. His first and second marriages had quickly collapsed. His third marriage was a caretaking operation. Even before he entered the war he was scarred, and after the war he was scarred more deeply and forever, so he sought to exit the world into a purely metaphysical realm. But this didn't succeed, it can never succeed, because we are flesh-and-blood beings. Salinger didn't understand or didn't allow himself to understand this.

He was born with a congenital deformity. He lost Oona O'Neill to Charlie Chaplin and for the rest of his life mythologized this relationship; for the rest of his life he was obsessed with girls on the cusp of adulthood, both as a way to revisit this lost romance and as a way to revisit the moment before the dawn of adolescent self-consciousness about his own body. He served in five bloody battles of World War II and for a brief time transformed his accumulated pain into imperishable art. These body blows not only generated his art but made him an artist who demanded of himself perfection. But each time he tried to enter the adult world of conversation and commerce, he was viewed as (he

The last known photograph of J. D. Salinger alive, 2008.

always viewed himself as) broken. Then endlessly reliving and revisiting his wounds became far more important to him than the world that had caused the wounds, so he retreated to Cornish, retreated to the bunker, never to engage meaningfully again with the world. Through Vedanta the world vanished, and with it, his art.

His life was a slow-motion suicide mission; the aim was to disappear. In one letter he wrote, "I'm a condition, not a man." The conditions were many:

CONDITION 1: ANATOMY

Salinger was born with only one testicle. His mother babied him; Salinger joked that she walked him to school until he was twenty-six, as all mothers do. For no apparent reason, Holden pays the prostitute Sunny but refuses to have sex with her. In "Franny," Lane finds Flaubert (one of Salinger's favorite writers) wanting because he lacks "testicularity"—perhaps an inside joke to Claire, to whom the story was presented as a wedding gift. As Howard M. Harper, the author of *Desperate Faith: A Study of Bellow, Salinger, Mailer, Baldwin, and Updike*, points out, in "Zooey" all of the ridiculed academics have double-entendre names: Manlius, Fallon, Tupper, Sheeter. Adult sexuality is inevitably associated, for Salinger, with stupidity and vulgarity. In story after story, men are fixated on girls' feet: nongenital sexuality in which performance is beside the point.

Throughout Salinger's life, he was drawn to very young, sexually inexperienced girls whom he knew he was unlikely to become intimate with, or if they did become sexual partners, they were unlikely to have enough experience with male anatomy to judge him. He almost always backed away from his lover immediately after the consummation of the relationship, thereby avoiding rejection. One of his lovers told us that he was "incredibly embarrassed and frustrated" by his undescended testicle. Surely one of the many reasons he stayed out of the media glare was to reduce the likelihood that this information about his anatomy would emerge. He embraced Eastern religions that endorsed chastity: "avoid woman and gold." His second wife became a psychologist, and his third wife was a nurse.

The war was one wound, but his body was the other. It was the combination of these wounds that made Salinger; together they produced a man "in this world but not of it," a man who needed to create flawless art.

CONDITION 2: OONA

Salinger mocked Oona O'Neill for being superficial ("little Oona is in love with little Oona"), but what he loved about her was her stunning beauty, and of course he was at least as narcissistic himself (as he acknowledged). It's significant and revealing that he carried a lifelong torch for a relationship that apparently was never consummated. Endlessly revisiting pre-Fall Oona, he would replicate this break time and time and time again with Jean Miller, Claire Douglas, Joyce Maynard, and many other young women; with Maynard, Salinger was nearly the same age as Chaplin when he met Oona, and Maynard was exactly the same age as Oona when she met Chaplin. The eighteen-year-old girl, the mirror self, the triangulated relationship, the love-hate investment in Hollywood, innocence over experience, chastity: Oona was the movie always in his mind.

CONDITION 3: WAR

What if he had never gone to war and instead spent 1942–46 on the Upper East Side? We probably would not have heard of J. D. Salinger. He would certainly not have become an icon. The war, destroying him, created him.

In 1944 the *New Yorker* editor William Maxwell, rejecting yet another Salinger story, judged the author to be "just not right for us." Salinger got right for the *New Yorker* by getting wrong in the head, by getting his soul ripped to pieces. War gave him the emotional ammunition to fulfill his Valley Forge dream: he not only published in the *New Yorker*; he became the magazine's marquee attraction.

For several magnificent years—from the publication of "Bananafish" in 1948 to "Esmé" in 1950, *Catcher* in 1951, *Nine Stories* in 1953, and "Franny" in 1955—Salinger converted his war wounds into the bow of timeless art. "Writing as an art is an experience magnified," he advised A. E. Hotchner; here was experience not only magnified but distilled into essence, crystallized, caught forever in exquisitely, almost painfully perfect art. The success of *Catcher* has to do in part with its encapsulation of adolescent rebellion; it's also a dissection of damage, and a slightly hidden reason that so many people connect with the book is that we are all damaged. (In adolescence we tend to be most self-conscious about this damage, want to wallow in it.)

In *The Veteran Who Is, the Boy Who Is No More,* Andy Rogers says about *Catcher*, "Holden's voice is Salinger's, but it is also his silence, and his silence about the war renders his voice as the most appropriate literary voice after World War II. Resurrecting Holden was exactly what Salinger had to do to not only avoid writing about the war, but more importantly, to write about the war." And *Nine Stories*, as we have argued, is the war novel Salinger said he was looking for: full of the "glorious imperfections which teeter and fall off the best minds. The men who have been in this war deserve some sort of trembling melody rendered without embarrassment or regret."

In a note written when he was nearly eighty, Salinger was still trying to convince himself and Paul Fitzgerald that it was good that they had survived the onslaught. The final sixty-five years of Salinger's life were a series of increasingly futile attempts to wipe the slate clean.

And yet Salinger's war damage carried deep into his later life, into the end of the twentieth century. The bullet that entered Seymour's brain in 1949 kept traveling through American history, all the way to John Lennon, Ronald Reagan, and beyond. *Catcher* is so saturated with war damage that sociopaths can see it, as if with X-ray glasses; the mayhem continued. The assassinations and attempted assassinations are not a coincidence; they constitute frighteningly clairvoyant readings of *Catcher*—the assassins intuiting the underlying postwar anger and violence in the book.

CONDITION 4: VEDANTA

Remember the statement released by Salinger's family upon his death, which is an explicit articulation of Salinger's renunciation of the world, the fourth and final step of the Vedantic way. He had already quite purposefully fulfilled the other three stages: apprenticeship, family life, and withdrawal.

Until his bar mitzvah, Salinger thought both of his parents were Jewish. From childhood onward, he was confused about his religious identity; he knew only that he was not truly Jewish or Catholic. After the war, his life became above all a search for religious healing and religious identity; he was a broken man seeking glue. It's impossible to fathom Salinger without understanding how central religion was to every aspect of his life from 1948 onward.

Tunneling deeper into his wounds, further away from the taint of the real, he disappeared into the solace of Vedantic philosophy, entering a more and more completely abstract realm. Salinger's work tracks exactly along this physical-metaphysical axis. *Catcher* could not be more embodied in the world. *Nine Stories* is underpinned by the war, even as it gestures, in later stories, toward increasingly religious epiphanies. In "Teddy," many of Teddy's observations are explicitly Vedantic. *Franny and Zooey* is the precise pivot point; "Franny" is located in the world, but it yields, through *The Way of a Pilgrim*, to the spiritual teaching of "Zooey." Similarly, the meticulously rendered 1942 in "Raise High the Roof Beam, Carpenters" gives way to Seymour's rather pious diary entries, resulting in the religiomysticism of "Seymour: An Introduction." In "Hapworth 16, 1924," Seymour describes Ramakrishna's disciple Vivekananda as "one of the most exciting, original and best equipped giants of this century."

There are two critical demarcations in Salinger's life: pre- and postwar, and pre- and postreligion. The war broke him as a man and made him a great artist; religion offered him postwar spiritual solace and killed his art.

CONDITION 5: CORNISH

After experiencing the nightmare of the war, Salinger gamely tried to reenter the world, impersonating Hail-Fellow-Well-Met in New York City, but such a performance had no chance of succeeding: such a person, if he had ever existed, had been killed on the battlefield. After the war, Salinger's mind was now full of those "glorious imperfections," "trembling," "teetering." The secular, materialistic life of postwar Manhattan seemed to him grotesque. Having written Holden's dream of leaving New York for rural isolation—running away with Sally Hayes—and after semiseriously asking a woman at a book party to run away with him to bucolic splendor, he went about the business of fulfilling the dream, moving in 1952 to Cornish, which bears shocking topographical similarity to the Hürtgen Forest.

These were, he knew, his "working years" (fewer than hoped for). This cutoff, disembodied existence was exactly what he, as someone who was now a celebrity, needed and exactly what he, as an artist, didn't need. An inward-turning man turned ever more inward. The signal from the world got considerably fainter; the signal going out to the world got increasingly faint. It was as if, by his late thirties, he already wanted to cease existing as an actual person. In a later letter, he wrote, "We're not . . . persons at all, but susceptible to myriad penalties for thinking we're persons and minds."

CONDITION 6: WIVES

Salinger wasn't temperamentally inclined to become a husband or father, but Vedanta's second stage is to create a family, which he dutifully went about doing. He loved his fictional characters, Holden Caulfield and the Glass family, in exactly the way he wanted to but couldn't love humanity—especially his own family. How could his wife and children possibly compete with the Glasses, in all their doomed, fictional, idealized perfection?

Again, "avoid woman and gold": Salinger avoided sex with Claire except for procreation, and once she'd become pregnant, he found her repellent. One of Claire's grounds for divorce was that her husband refused to communicate with her. In his loyalty to abstract principles, he ignored Claire, as if she didn't exist. In "Raise High," we're informed that "marriage partners are to serve each other. Elevate, help, teach, strengthen each other, but above all, *serve*." Salinger found it difficult to embody these verbs in real life. He hated people who were "not-nice," which was pretty much everyone, including, especially, himself. He didn't admire anyone except dead people, which also included, crucially, himself. The bunker was a tomb in which to bury himself so as not to have to walk around in the daylight world of flesh and blood.

CONDITION 7: CHILDREN

In "Raise High," Salinger wrote, "[Marriage partners are to] raise their children honorably, lovingly and with detachment. A child is a guest in the house, to be loved and respected—never possessed, since he belongs to God. How wonderful, how sane, how beautifully difficult, and therefore true. The joy of responsibility for the first time in my life." And yet when Margaret was acutely sick as a young woman, her father sent her a letter containing not money but a Christian Science pamphlet. When she was pregnant, he urged her to have an abortion; she had, he informed her, no right to bring a child into the world.

He could hardly have invented two more perfect embodiments of two parts of himself than Matthew and Margaret. Matthew was compliant, reverential, caretaking, appreciative; he is now the executor of the Salinger estate. Margaret was the iconoclast, bringing home a Native American boyfriend, playing basketball, questioning the great man, writing a book that deeply undermined the myth and caused her to be estranged from her father for the rest of his life. Matthew was the part of him that was dutiful, Ivy League, respectful, "preppy," "Eastern Seaboard regimental"—he and his father attended Dartmouth College football games together; his father, registered as a Republican in 1960, was snobbish, misogynistic. Margaret was an equally alive part of Salinger that was in full flight from that, mad with fury, antiestablishment, existentially lost.

Margaret demonstrated the spunk that Salinger venerated in, say, Franny. Matthew behaved as Salinger himself behaved in real life. And we know Salinger's scathing assessment of himself. As an adult, Matthew said that he wished he saw his father more often and that they could see a few more Red Sox games together; for him, paternal detachment worked. Margaret was so desperate to connect with her father she wrote not a letter but a 450-page, heartbroken love song. Didn't matter. He was a million miles away in his tower.

CONDITION 8: GIRLS

Take a look at photos of Miriam, Doris, Sylvia, Oona, Jean, and Joyce when each of them is eighteen years old. It's impossible to miss how stunningly similar all these young women are. They are, for all intents and purposes, to Salinger's imagination, the same woman, the same girl, the same healing mother, the same ministering sister-angel, the same second self, the same ideal and idealized childhood playmate (until, of course, they mature). Why was Salinger obsessed, in his work and in his life, with girls on the cusp of their sexuality? Why, in his work, do so many of his male protagonists express their ardor toward girls by worshipping and cradling their feet? Salinger's was a prejudgment physicality, a pre-Fall sexuality, pre-Oona, prewar (after which he could never view the human body as anything except ravaged). The girls were self-torture racks, through which he endlessly revisited that time before his body could be viewed as wanting, before Oona, before the war turned all bodies into corpses for him.

Throughout Salinger's life, he repeated this pattern over and over and over again with girls-on-the-verge-of-becoming-women. He was forever replaying the Oona-Chaplin-Jerry triangulation, repeating it between himself and his second wife, Claire, and her then-husband, Coleman Mockler, and Maynard and the world he said she loved and he didn't. Many of the girl-women are Jewish or half-Jewish or "Jewish-looking" innocents on the edge of uninnocence; upon consummating his relationships with them, they are not only immediately undesirable to him but also immediately repellent and just as immediately eliminated from his life.

When Peter Tewksbury said to Salinger that Esmé is poised at the exact moment between an intake and an outtake of breath, Salinger—who almost never agreed with anyone, especially an artistic man from his own generation—said, emphatically (that Salinger word), "Yes." Salinger came tantalizingly close to making a film of "Esmé" with Tewksbury, but the project came to naught when the girl whom Salinger wanted to play Esmé edged ever so slightly into adolescence. Throughout his life he was fixed upon this pivot point between childhood and adulthood. He called his local market, Purity Supreme, "Puberty Supreme." At age ninety he was a regular attendee of Dartmouth College women's basketball games.

Salinger convinced Joyce Maynard to drop out of Yale and leave a promising writing career in New York City for an isolated life with him in Cornish. What was he trying to save her from? *Experience.* He was obsessed with innocence; in many ways, it was his deepest or at least most persistent subject. Maynard wore an oversized men's watch in her photo for the cover of the *New York Times Magazine.* He loved childhood, wanted to canonize it, couldn't or wouldn't or didn't want to enter what the French writer Michel Leiris called "the fierce order of virility"; one of Salinger's early "lost" stories is called "Men Without Hemingway." He was wedded to ceremonies of innocence and yet also wanted to drown these ceremonies, was devoted to sullying innocence. If he never got to be innocent, no one else would, either.

It was a Holdenesque impulse to invite Maynard to Cornish, because only one Jesus child is allowed per family. Two solipsists can't occupy the same writing desk. It couldn't work and didn't work for very long. He seems to have been hoping, somehow, to deprofessionalize her writing—make her forever a journal-keeper, a diarist, a Franny-poet, a person without a life before her life had really even begun. He didn't want to implant his seed into Maynard; he wanted to pour Salinger—see his five-thousand-word letters to her on the most abstruse of subjects.

One of the crucial ways Maynard and Salinger connected was their love of old-timey TV shows: *I Love Lucy*, *Andy of Mayberry*, *The Dick Van Dyke Show*. One of his favorite movies, *Lost Horizon*, offered the same salvation that he sought in time travel back to prewar folly and innocence, although in truth he was too broken down for any such deliverance. Salinger's love of movies and television shows, his love of actors and acting, his addiction to the fairy-tale world of the midcentury *New Yorker* and its infantilization of its writers, his unpersuasive insistence upon the absolute separation between his life and his art—all of this, everything in his life and work, *everything* bespeaks damage, survivor's guilt, wished-for and never achieved oblivion.

CONDITION 9: SECLUSION

Salinger sent out, through *Catcher*, an SOS, and when the world answered the distress call with swooning love, he immediately put up a DO NOT DISTURB sign. Salinger didn't love the world—he loathed himself, which he reframed as hatred of the world—and he needed the world to prove that it was unworthy of his love. And the world managed to fulfill that role very nicely for him on a daily basis.

Outside the compound were critics, *Catcher*-reading assassins, and, in a way worst of all, would-be acolytes, who meant nothing to him because he knew he had nothing to give them.

He was thought to be indifferent to publicity, but he ferociously monitored every blip on the radar screen and cared hugely about his reputation—for instance, seeking out all the reviews of *Catcher* after telling Little, Brown he didn't want the publisher to send him the reviews. He refused to talk to the press, but whenever the press had forgotten about him for too long, he interacted with journalists, especially when they were extremely beautiful women—talking on the phone to the *New York*

Times's Lacey Fosburgh for half an hour and not only wanting to see what red-haired, green-eyed Betty Eppes looked like but answering her questions and even, at one point—although we weren't able to include this detail in Conversation #5—inviting her to dinner.

Salinger detested dealing with the avalanche of mail he received, but he bemoaned that there was no mail delivery on Sunday.

Presenting himself as a hermit, he was certainly more secluded than most people, even than most writers, but in fact he maintained lifelong friendships through extensive travel in the United States and abroad, and through letters, phone calls, and frequently hosting visitors to his house. He controlled the communication, the narrative. He wasn't opposed to investigations; he just wanted to be the one conducting them. There's no member of the CIC like a former member of the CIC.

As Paul Alexander says, Salinger was a recluse who liked to flirt with the public to remind them that he was a recluse. Complete withdrawal from society is not only the fourth step in Vedanta but also, quite conveniently, the perfect publicity strategy: by being invisible to the public, he could be everywhere in the public imagination.

CONDITION 10: DETACHMENT

Zooey: "You can say the Jesus Prayer from now till doomsday, but if you don't realize that the only thing that counts in the religious life is de*tach*ment, I don't see how you'll ever even move an *inch*. Detachment, buddy, and only detachment."

In real life, the religious life played out like this:

Salinger's sister, Doris, said, "I hate to say it, but he's a bastard. What can I say? I was all alone when I had my heart attack and he's been useless to me. Visited two, maybe three times. Hardly a phone call. When I had my heart attack, I was sick and alone. That's a terrible thing to be, sick and alone. But anything that interferes with his work is dismissed."

His daughter, Margaret, wrote, "He is detached about *your* pain, but God knows he takes his own pain more seriously than cancer. . . . There is nothing remotely detached about my father's behavior toward his own pain, in his hemorrhages about anything personal being known about him. . . . It finally dawned on me that my father, for all his protestations and lectures and writing about detachment, is a very, very needy man. . . ."

Salinger spent his life trying to maneuver himself out from under his body, but the cure never took, because he was the disease. The wound was so deep and so multiple that he wanted the reader to concentrate entirely on his art. The only way the art was going to rescue him was if it couldn't be tied back to war wounds and the body-wound. The wounds made him; for nearly a decade, he transformed the wounds into agony-fueled art, and then—because he could not abide his own body, himself, his own war-ruined mind, the attention, the criticism, the love—he came to revile the world, so he disappeared into Vedanta. The pain was severe and profound, and he couldn't fully face it or alleviate it. Desperate for cures, he destroyed himself: withdrawal, silence, inward collapse. The wounds undid him, and he went under.

22

SECRETS

CORNISH, NEW HAMPSHIRE, 1965–2010

SHANE SALERNO: While the Salinger estate has refused to acknowledge that Salinger's legendary secret manuscripts even exist, there is a clear record of their existence from eyewitnesses dating back decades.

On the 1961 dust jacket of *Franny and Zooey*, Salinger states that he is at work on a "narrative series . . . about a family of settlers in twentieth-century New York, the Glasses." He calls it "a long-term project" and confesses, "I love working on these Glass stories, I've been waiting for them most of my life, and I think I have fairly decent, monomaniacal plans to finish them."

On the 1963 dust jacket for *Raise High the Roof Beam, Carpenters and Seymour: An Introduction* Salinger writes, "The two long pieces in this book originally came out in *The New Yorker*. Whatever their differences in mood or effect, they are both very much concerned with Seymour Glass, who is the main character in my still-uncompleted series about the Glass family." He then adds, "There is only my word for it, granted, but I have several new Glass stories coming along—waxing, dilating—each in its own way." He concludes, "Oddly, the joys and satisfactions of working on the Glass family peculiarly increase and deepen for me with the years."

Salinger's own words are revealing: "long-term project" and "several new Glass stories coming along." We know two things for certain. First, Salinger published only one more story, and that was "Hapworth 16, 1924." Second, Salinger continued to write. He simply chose not to publish.

Numerous eyewitnesses report that Salinger was writing every day, had a vault in which he stored completed manuscripts, and had a detailed, color-coded filing system for the condition of each story.

On October 16, 1966, Salinger wrote a letter to his friend Michael Mitchell. As reported by Sharon Steel: "The letter closes with a description of Salinger's new manuscripts, which he's hidden for a decade and doesn't feel up to showing anybody. Salinger writes, 'I have ten, twelve years of work piled around. . . . I have two particular scripts—books, really—that I've been hoarding and picking at for years, and these two I think that you would love.'"

In 1972 Joyce Maynard heard "typing every day," reported seeing "two full manuscripts," and was shown a "genealogy of the Glass family." She also confirmed the location of a "safe" just off Salinger's bedroom. In *At Home in the World* she writes, "He has compiled stacks of notes and notebooks concerning the habits and backgrounds of the Glasses—music they like, places they go, episodes in their history. Even the parts of their lives that he may not write about, he needs to know. He fills in the facts as diligently as a parent, keeping up to date with the scrapbooks." Maynard confirmed and expanded these statements when I interviewed her for eighteen hours over two days in 2008.

Scottish poet Alastair Reid—a longtime friend of Salinger's dating back to Sarah Lawrence College, where Reid was teaching and where Salinger was dating a student—visited him in Cornish. "There are more books," Reid told the *Sunday Herald* of Scotland. "I know that they exist. He showed me them, handled two of them in front of my eyes. And he said to me once, "You know, the Glass family have been growing old just as you and I have."

In November 1974 Salinger told *New York Times* reporter Lacey Fosburgh, "I like to write, I love to write"; he was "writing, long hours, every day." He added, "I don't necessarily intend to publish posthumously."

In the summer of 1980 Betty Eppes interviewed Salinger and asked him what he was writing about. "I will state this," Salinger told her. "It is of far more significance than anything I ever wrote about Holden. I have really serious issues I am trying to tackle with these new writing projects."

In 1992 William Maxwell, Salinger's former *New Yorker* editor, told John Blades of the *Chicago Tribune* that he and Salinger "talk once a year, every two years, or letters go back and forth. To the best of my knowledge, he's never stopped writing. It must be quite a pile by now."

In March of 1999 and again in 2010, Jerry Burt of Plainfield, New Hampshire, a former neighbor who was friendly with Salinger, told the Associated Press that Salinger told him "he was keeping a stack of manuscripts in a safe."

On September 13, 2000, Margaret Salinger told NPR's Diane Rehm, "I do know he's been working all these years because, probably the second time I'd ever been allowed in his study, he very proudly showed me a set of files, where a red dot meant this is ready to go upon my death, a green dot meant this needs editing, but it's okay. It just needs some editing."

There is no question that the manuscripts exist. The question is, What are they?

In 2008 J. D. Salinger created the J. D. Salinger Literary Trust, of which he was sole trustee during his lifetime. On July 24, 2008, Salinger assigned copyright "in *The Catcher in the Rye,* along with other works authored by him, to the Trust and duly recorded that assignment." Salinger signed this document on October 15, 2008, in Hanover, New Hampshire. Betsy H. Bowse was the notary. Upon his death, his wife, Colleen M. Salinger, and his son, Matthew R. Salinger, became the coexecutors of the J. D. Salinger Literary Trust and were bound by the trust and Salinger's express wishes, which included never allowing a film of *The Catcher in the Rye* to be sold or produced and, most important, authorizing a specific timetable for the release of more than forty-five years of work after his death.

—

Based on private interviews conducted over nine years, we have learned that J. D. Salinger approved works for publication.

We were able to obtain information about a number of those books and stories.

The following information was provided, documented, and verified by two independent and separate sources.

The first book is titled *The Family Glass*; it collects all the existing stories about the Glass family together with five new stories that significantly extend the world of Salinger's fictional family. The five new stories are about Seymour Glass; the first four explore the thirty years leading up to Seymour's suicide and his lifelong quest for God. In the first new story, Seymour and Buddy are recruited at a party in 1926 for the children's quiz show *It's a Wise*

Child. The last story deals with Seymour's life after death. The stories are narrated by Buddy Glass and are saturated in the teachings of the Vedantic religion. The book opens with a detailed genealogy of the Glass family.

Salinger has also written a "manual" of Vedanta—with short stories, almost fables, woven into the text; this is precisely the form of *The Gospel of Sri Ramakrishna*, which Salinger called, in 1952, "the religious book of the century." Salinger's "manual" is the explicit fulfillment of his stated desire to "circulate," through his writing, the ideas of Vedanta. Further evidence of Salinger's devotion over more than half a century to Vedanta is that he donated a substantial and continuing portion of his estate to the Ramakrishna-Vivekananda Center of New York and to other organizations that share similar religious beliefs.

In addition, there is one novel, a World War II love story based on Salinger's complex relationship with his first wife, Sylvia Welter. The two main characters—Sergeant X from "Esmé," recovering from a nervous breakdown, and Sylvia's fictional counterpart—meet in post–World War II Germany and begin a passionate love affair. As did Salinger and Sylvia, the two characters share telepathic communication.

Salinger has also written a novella that takes the form of a counterintelligence agent's diary entries during World War II, culminating in the Holocaust. The diary entries take place in many different towns and cities and involve his interactions with civilians and soldiers struggling with the day-to-day horror of war.

Separate from the new Glass stories, the Vedanta manual, and Salinger's new war fiction is a complete retooling of Salinger's unpublished twelve-page 1942 story "The Last and Best of the Peter Pans." The original version can be found at Princeton University's Firestone Library and is one of the earliest of the Caulfield stories, in which a very young child nears the edge of a cliff. This reimagined version of the story will be collected with the other six Caulfield stories as well as new stories and *The Catcher in the Rye*, creating a complete history of the Caulfield family.

Salinger's chronicles of two extraordinary families, the Glasses and the Caulfields—written from 1941 to 2008, when he conveyed his body of work to the J. D. Salinger Literary Trust—will be the masterworks for which he is forever known.

These works will begin to be published in irregular installments starting between 2015 and 2020.

FICTION IN CHRONOLOGICAL ORDER OF PUBLICATION

1940

"The Young Folks." *Story*, March–April, 26–30.

"Go See Eddie." *University of Kansas City Review* 7 (December 1940): 121–24.

1941

"The Hang of It." *Collier's*, July 12, 1941, 22.

"The Heart of a Broken Story." *Esquire*, September 1941, 32, 131–33.

1942

"The Long Debut of Lois Taggett." *Story*, September–October 1942, 28–34.

"Personal Notes on an Infantryman." *Collier's*, December 12, 1942, 96.

1943

"The Varioni Brothers." *Saturday Evening Post*, July 17, 1943, 12–13, 76–77.

1944

"Both Parties Concerned." *Saturday Evening Post*, February 26, 1944, 14, 47–48.

"Soft-Boiled Sergeant." *Saturday Evening Post*, April 15, 1944, 18, 82, 84–85.

"Last Day of the Last Furlough." *Saturday Evening Post*, July 15, 1944, 26–27, 61–62, 64.

"Once a Week Won't Kill You." *Story*, November–December 1944, 23–27.

1945

"Elaine." *Story*, March–April 1945, 38–47.

"A Boy in France." *Saturday Evening Post*, March 31, 1945, 21, 92.

"This Sandwich Has No Mayonnaise." *Esquire*, October 1945, 54–56, 147–49.

"The Stranger." *Collier's*, December 1, 1945, 18, 77.

"I'm Crazy." *Collier's*, December 22, 1945, 36, 48, 51. Incorporated into *The Catcher in the Rye*.

1946

"Slight Rebellion Off Madison." *The New Yorker*, December 21, 1946, 82–86. Incorporated into *The Catcher in the Rye*.

1947

"A Young Girl in 1941 with No Waist at All." *Mademoiselle*, May 1947, 222–23, 292–302.

"The Inverted Forest." *Cosmopolitan*, December 1947, 73–80, 85–86, 88, 90, 92, 95–96, 98, 100, 102, 107, 109.

1948

"A Perfect Day for Bananafish." *The New Yorker*, January 31, 1948, 21–25.

"A Girl I Knew." *Good Housekeeping*, February 1948, 36–37, 186, 188, 191–96.

"Uncle Wiggily in Connecticut." *The New Yorker*, March 20, 1948, 30–36.

"Just Before the War with the Eskimos." *The New Yorker*, June 5, 1948, 37–40, 42, 44, 46.

"Blue Melody." *Cosmopolitan*, September 1948, 50–51, 112–19.

1949

"The Laughing Man." *The New Yorker*, March 19, 1949, 27–32.

"Down at the Dinghy." *Harper's*, April 1949, 87–91.

1950

"For Esmé—with Love and Squalor." *The New Yorker*, April 8, 1950, 28–36.

1951

"Pretty Mouth and Green My Eyes." *The New Yorker*, July 14, 1951, 20–24.

The Catcher in the Rye. Boston: Little, Brown, July 16, 1951.

1952

"De Daumier-Smith's Blue Period." *World Review*, no. 39, May 1952, 33–48.

1953

"Teddy." *The New Yorker*, January 31, 1953, 26–34, 36, 38, 40–41, 44–45.

Nine Stories. Boston: Little, Brown, April 6, 1953.

1955

"Franny." *The New Yorker*, January 29, 1955, 24–32, 35–43.

"Raise High the Roof Beam, Carpenters." *The New Yorker*, November 19, 1955, 51–116.

1957

"Zooey." *The New Yorker*, May 4, 1957, 32–139.

1959

"Seymour: An Introduction." *The New Yorker*, June 6, 1959, 42–119.

1961

Franny and Zooey. Boston: Little, Brown, September 14, 1961.

1963

Raise High the Roof Beam, Carpenters and Seymour: An Introduction. Boston: Little, Brown, January 28, 1963.

1965

"Hapworth 16, 1924." *The New Yorker*, June 19, 1965, 32–113.

LOST STORIES, UNCOLLECTED STORIES, AND PUBLISHED LETTERS

"The Survivors," 1940. Bibliographer Jack R. Sublette indicates that Salinger refers to this story in a 1940 letter to Whit Burnett. The story was never published and cannot be found anywhere now.

"The Lovely Dead Girl at Table Six," 1941. Biographer Ian Hamilton says that Salinger wrote this story in August 1941. The story was never published and cannot be found anywhere now.

"Lunch for Three," 1941. Ben Yagoda, author of *About Town: The New Yorker and the World It Made*, writes that in 1941 the *New Yorker* considered this story, which was never published and cannot be found anywhere now.

"I Went to School with Adolf Hitler," 1941. Yagoda says that in 1941 the *New Yorker* turned down this story, which cannot be found anywhere now.

"Monologue for a Watery Highball," 1941. Yagoda indicates that in 1941 the *New Yorker* turned down this story, which was never published and cannot be found anywhere now.

"Mrs. Hincher," 1941. In an October 31, 1941, letter to Elizabeth Murray, Salinger refers to this story as being nearly completed. The story, whose protagonist is Paula Hincher and which was later titled "Paula," was never published and cannot be found anywhere now.

"The Kissless Life of Reilly," 1942. Sublette says that, in a 1942 letter to Burnett, Salinger refers to this story, which cannot be found anywhere now.

"Men Without Hemingway," 1942. Hamilton says that, in a 1942 letter to Murray, Salinger refers to this story, which the *New Yorker* turned down. It was never published and cannot be found anywhere now.

"Over the Seas Let's Go, Twentieth Century Fox," 1942. Hamilton writes that, in a 1942 letter to Murray, Salinger refers to this story, which the *New Yorker* turned down. It was never published and cannot be found anywhere now.

"Paula," 1942. Salinger's first bibliographer, Donald M. Fiene, indicates that this story, formerly called "Mrs. Hincher," was bought by *Stag* magazine in 1942, but the story was never published. The magazine no longer has the story, which cannot be found anywhere now.

"Paris," 1943. In a 1943 letter to Elizabeth Murray, Salinger refers to this story, which was never published and cannot be found anywhere.

"Rex Passard on the Planet Mars," 1943. Sublette indicates that, in a 1943 letter to Burnett, Salinger refers to this story, which was never published and cannot be found anywhere now.

"Two Lonely Men," 1943. Sublette writes that the story is set "at a United States Army base in the South [and] tells the story of a developing friendship between Master Sergeant Charles Maydee and Captain Huggins," but "Maydee apparently begins having an affair" with Huggins's wife. The story—listed in the table of contents for Salinger's book *The Young Folks*, which Story Press planned to publish but never did—can now be found, and read only on location, in the Whit Burnett–*Story* magazine archive in the Firestone Library at Princeton University.

"The Broken Children," 1943. Sublette says that, in a 1943 letter to Burnett, Salinger refers to this story, which was never published and cannot be found anywhere now.

"Bitsey," 1943. Sublette indicates that, in a 1943 letter to Burnett, Salinger refers to this story, which was included in the table of contents for *The Young Folks*. "Bitsey"—or "Bitsy"—cannot be found anywhere now.

"The Children's Echelon," 1944. Sublette writes that the story's narrator is Bernice Herndon, an eighteen-year-old diarist, one of whose entries refers to children riding a carousel. "The Children's Echelon" was listed in the table of contents for *The Young Folks* and can now be found, and read only on location, in the Burnett-*Story* archive in Princeton' s Firestone Library.

"Boy Standing in Tennessee," 1944. Sublette states that, in a 1944 letter to Burnett, Salinger refers to this story, which was listed in the table of contents for *The Young Folks* and cannot be found anywhere now.

"Total War Diary," 1944. Sublette says that, in a 1944 letter to Burnett, Salinger refers to this story, which was probably rewritten and retitled "The Children's Echelon."

"What Babe Saw, or Ooh-La-La!" 1944. Sublette says that, in a September 9, 1944, letter to Burnett, Salinger refers to this story, which was revised and/or retitled, then published in the March 31, 1945, issue of the *Saturday Evening Post* as "A Boy in France." The original manuscript of "What Babe Saw, or Ooh-La-La!" cannot be found anywhere now.

"What Got into Curtis in the Woodshed," 1945. This story was included in a list compiled in 1945 by Salinger's literary agency, Harold Ober Associates, and was also included in the table of contents for *The Young Folks*. The story cannot be found anywhere now.

"The Ocean Full of Bowling Balls," 1945. Sublette states that in this story, "Vincent Caulfield writes of his relationship with one of his younger brothers, Kenneth, and of Kenneth's death" after swimming in rough Cape Cod waters. A younger sister, Phoebe Caulfield, is mentioned; Holden Caulfield writes a letter from summer camp. "The Ocean Full of Bowling Balls" was listed in the table of contents for *The Young Folks*, and the eighteen-page manuscript (typed) can now be found, and read only on location, in the Burnett-*Story* archive in Princeton's Firestone Library.

"Birthday Boy," 1946. "Birthday Boy" concerns Ethel's visit to the hospital to see her alcoholic boyfriend, Ray. Never published, a nine-page, typed manuscript of "Birthday Boy" can be read, only on location, in the Harry Ransom Center at the University of Texas, Austin.

"The Male Goodbye," 1946. Hamilton writes that, in a 1946 letter to Murray, Salinger refers to "The Male Goodbye," which is the first story he wrote following his separation from his first wife, Sylvia. The story cannot be found anywhere now.

"The Boy in the People Shooting Hat," 1948. In *About Town*, Yagoda reproduces a photocopy of the *New Yorker* editor Gus Lobrano's rejection letter, which indicates that in this story Bobby and Stradlater fight over June Gallagher. Holden, who also fights with Stradlater over June, says that his red hunting hat is "a people shooting hat." The story cannot be found anywhere now.

"A Summer Accident," 1949. Yagoda states that Salinger returned his focus to *The Catcher in the Rye* after the *New Yorker* turned down this story. The story cannot be found anywhere now.

"Requiem for the Phantom of the Opera," 1951. In a 1951 letter to Lobrano, Salinger refers to this story, which was turned down by the *New Yorker* in January and cannot be found anywhere now.

"The Daughter of the Late, Great Man," 1959. Sublette indicates that, in a 1959 letter to Burnett, Salinger attempted to buy the story, which he had submitted many years before and which Burnett, preparing to revive the magazine, had found in the *Story* magazine files. Burnett compared "The Daughter of the Late, Great Man" to his earlier stories that Burnett had published: "The Long Debut of Lois Taggett" and "Elaine." However, Burnett returned the story (which is listed in the table of contents for *The Young Folks*) to Salinger when he declined permission to publish it. A reasonable conjecture is that this 1959 story can be located among the papers in Salinger's literary estate.

"A Young Man in a Stuffed Shirt," 1959. Sublette states that, in a 1959 letter to Burnett, Salinger attempted to buy this story as well, which Burnett had also found in the *Story* files. Again, Burnett returned the story (which is listed in the table of contents for *The Young Folks*) to Salinger when he declined permission to publish it. A reasonable conjecture is that this 1959 story can be located among the papers in Salinger's literary estate.

"Man-Forsaken Men," December 9, 1959. Salinger's letter to the editor of the *New York Post Magazine*, in which he argues against prisoners being sentenced to life without the possibility of parole: "The New York State lifer is one of the most crossed-off, man-forsaken men on earth." The magazine chose the headline. The full letter—which some scholars believe Salinger's friend Judge Learned Hand may have encouraged him to write—is printed in Fiene's "A Bibliographical Study of J. D. Salinger: Life, Work and Reputation."

Manuscript about Harold Ross, William Shawn, and the *New Yorker*. In 1959 James Thurber published a memoir, *The Years with Ross*, which was highly critical of Ross, the magazine's founding editor. In defense, Salinger wrote an approximately twenty-five-to-thirty-page letter about Ross, which he sent to the *Saturday Review*. Fiene states that, in an October 8, 1962, letter, Hallowell Bowser, the general editor of the *Saturday Review*, said that Salinger's letter was "rejected because of its length and unusual style"; that is, as James Bryan indicates in "Salinger and His Short Fiction" (1968), "the piece must have been, as I heard, embarrassingly fulsome." A reasonable conjecture is that this long letter can be located among the papers in Salinger's literary estate.

THE GLASS FAMILY

Les Glass: The family's patriarch, Les is a Jewish vaudeville performer on the Pantages circuit. From 1921 to 1923 he and his wife, Bessie—along with their five oldest children—tour Australia. In Manhattan they live first in the Hotel Almanac, on Riverside Drive and 110th Street, in the Morningside Heights neighborhood, and later in an apartment in the East Seventies. In 1925, at his retirement party, he meets a man who signs up Seymour and Buddy to perform as regulars on a new national radio quiz show called *It's a Wise Child.* All of the Glass children take turns appearing on the show—their parents teach all of them how to dance and juggle—and their combined earnings send all of them through college. Later, Les works as a talent scout in Los Angeles for a movie company. In "Seymour: An Introduction," after losing badly in a pinochle game, he visits the apartment that the adult Seymour and Buddy share on Seventy-ninth Street near Madison Avenue. Keeping his overcoat on the whole time and scowling, he checks Buddy's hands for nicotine stains, asks Seymour how many cigarettes a day he smokes, and becomes even more agitated upon discovering a fly in his highball. His mood lifts when he looks up and sees a photo on the wall of Bessie and himself, because it reminds him of the family's vaudeville tour through Australia.

Bessie (Gallagher) Glass: Born in Dublin to Roman Catholic parents, Bessie was once a "widely acknowledged public beauty, a vaudevillian, a dancer, a very light dancer," but by 1957 she has become a "medium stout dancer" whose age is "fiercely indeterminate." In "Zooey" she wears a hairnet and an old Japanese kimono to which she has added "two oversize hip pockets which contained two or three packs of cigarettes, several match folders, a screwdriver, a claw-end hammer, a Boy Scout knife that had once belonged to one of her sons, and an enamel faucet handle or two, plus an assortment of screws, nails, hinges, and ball bearing casters—all of which tended to make Mrs. Glass chink faintly as she moved about in her large apartment." As adults, all of her children worship her as the embodiment of common sense and straightforward love.

Seymour Glass: Worshipped by his six siblings as genius and saint, by age six Seymour has read everything he can find in the local library about God. At seven his Hindu meditation exercises allow him to glimpse his previous and future incarnations. Between ten and fifteen he's the star of *It's a Wise Child.* He attends Columbia University at fifteen; at eighteen he receives his Ph.D. and becomes a professor. Nearing a full professorship at twenty-one, he speaks German and French fluently and reads Chinese and Japanese. In 1941 he's drafted into the army; on leave in 1942, he marries Muriel Fedder, whose earnest simplicity he hopes will balance his otherworldliness. At twenty-five Seymour is going bald; he's five-foot-ten-and-a-half, with a receding chin, large nose, large ears, and teeth stained yellow from nicotine and wears ill-fitting clothes. During World War II he serves in Europe and has a nervous breakdown. After the end of the war, before being sent home, he spends three weeks in the psychiatric wards of army hospitals. Two weeks after his arrival in the United States, on a second honeymoon with Muriel, he commits suicide. His siblings try to live by his teachings, which combine wisdom from the Old and New Testaments, Taoism, and Advaita Vedanta.

Webb Gallagher (Buddy) Glass: Born in 1919 (the year in which Salinger is born), the second oldest Glass sibling, an author, and, as such, Salinger's self-acknowledged alter ego, Buddy narrates "Raise High the Roof Beam, Carpenters," "Zooey," and "Seymour: An Introduction." Transcriber of the letter that Seymour, at seven, writes home from summer camp ("Hapworth 16, 1924"), he also claims authorship of *The Catcher in the Rye* and the stories "A Perfect Day for Bananafish" and "Teddy." He teaches creative writing at a girls' junior college in upstate New York, but he considers his purpose in life to be Seymour's disciple and chronicler. Buddy is proud of his physical resemblance to Seymour, with whom he shares a receding chin and large nose. However, he believes he has always been a snappier dresser than Seymour.

Beatrice (Boo Boo) Tannenbaum: Born in 1920, the third oldest of the Glass children, Boo Boo works as a secretary for an admiral in the navy during World War II. In "Down at the Dinghy," she, her husband, and her three children live in Tuckahoe, an affluent town in Westchester. Boo Boo is a "small, almost hipless girl of twenty five," and "her joke of a name aside, her general unprettiness aside, she was—in terms of permanently memorable, immoderately perceptive, small-area faces—a stunning and final girl." When she asks her son, Lionel, why he is so upset and wants to run away from home, he tells her that he overheard their maid call his father a "big—sloppy—kike." Lionel, four, doesn't understand, and Boo Boo doesn't endeavor to explain, anti-Semitism. Instead, she consoles him by telling him that what the maid said "isn't the *worst* that could happen."

Walter F. Glass: Walt was born in 1921, twelve minutes ahead of his twin, Waker. In "Uncle Wiggily in Connecticut," the central character, Eloise Wengler, says that Walt, her college boyfriend, is the sweetest and funniest person she has ever known. When Walt is drafted into the army, he tells Eloise that he's advancing in the service in a different direction from everyone else: "He said that when he'd get his first promotion, instead of getting stripes he'd have his sleeves taken away from him. He said when he'd get to be a general, he'd be stark naked. All he'd be wearing would be a little infantry button in his navel." In the fall of 1945, while serving with Occupation forces in Japan, Walt is killed in a freak explosion.

Waker Glass: Both Waker and his twin brother, Walter, are infants during the Glass family's tour of Australia. As do the other Glass children, the twins receive wide-ranging religious instruction from their older brothers, Seymour and Buddy. At nine, Waker gives away his well-over-budget birthday present, a brand-new bicycle, to an unknown boy in Central Park. When his parents say he should have just given the boy a nice long ride on his bike, Waker says, "The boy didn't *want* a nice, long ride, he wanted the *bicycle*. He'd never *had* one, the boy; he'd always *wanted* one." Later, Waker converts to Catholicism, spends World War II in a conscientious objectors' camp, and after the war becomes a Carthusian monk.

Zachary (Zooey) Glass: Zooey is born in 1930, the second-youngest of the Glasses, nine years after the twins, Walker and Waker, and five years before Franny. Next to Seymour, Zooey is the audience's favorite on *It's a Wise Child*. He understands Seymour better than Buddy does; in "Zooey," he's able to use Seymour's teachings to pull his sister Franny out of her spiritual crisis: for instance, that you should work not for reward but for the sake of doing it as well as you can. An actor, Zooey is a leading man in television movies. Although he is slight of build and one of his ears protrudes more than the other, "Zooey's face was close to being a wholly beautiful face," because there is "an authentic *esprit*" superimposed across it.

Frances (Franny) Glass: Born in 1935, Franny is the youngest of the Glass children—eighteen years younger than her oldest brother, Seymour. When Franny is a ten-month-old baby, crying, Seymour reads her a Taoist tale in order to calm her down. Later, Franny swears she remembers the event. In "Franny," she's a twenty-year-old college student who is obsessed with *The Way of a Pilgrim*, a book of Russian spirituality. Her Ivy League boyfriend, Lane Coutell, doesn't share her admiration for the book, but he considers Franny "an unimpeachably right-looking girl—a girl who was not only extraordinarily pretty but, so much the better, not too categorically cashmere sweater and flannel skirt." In the course of the novella, Franny has a nervous breakdown. Her older brothers Seymour and Buddy have been nurturing her mysticism since her infancy and, as a result, she has trouble interacting with the ordinary—in herself and everyone around her.

BIOGRAPHICAL NOTES

Robert Abzug, an adviser to this book, is the Audre and Bernard Rapoport Regents Chair of Jewish Studies at the University of Texas, Austin, and the author of *Inside the Vicious Heart: Americans and the Liberation of Nazi Concentration Camps* and *America Views the Holocaust 1933–1945*.

Mike Ackerman was a neighbor of J. D. Salinger.

Tony Adams was the executive director of the Atlanta-area YMCA at which Mark David Chapman worked as a counselor in the 1970s.

Renata Adler is the author of the novels *Speedboat* and *Pitch Dark* and the memoir *Gone*.

Paul Alexander, an adviser to this book, is the author of biographies of J. D. Salinger, Sylvia Plath, James Dean, and Andy Warhol.

Eberhard Alsen, who undertook extensive research throughout Europe and America as a consultant to this book, is a professor of English at State University of New York, Cortland, and the author of *A Reader's Guide to J. D. Salinger* and *Salinger's Glass Stories as Composite Novel*.

Stephen E. Ambrose, the author of several best-selling books about World War II, died in 2002.

Benjamin Anastas is the author of the memoir *Too Good to Be True* and the novels *An Underachiever's Diary* and *The Faithful Narrative of a Pastor's Disappearance*.

Roger Angell, a longtime *New Yorker* staff writer and editor, has published many collections of essays on baseball, including *Late Innings* and *Five Seasons*.

Blake Bailey, the winner of the National Book Critics Circle Award for his biography of John Cheever, has also written biographies of the writers Richard Yates and Charles Jackson.

Carlos Baker, the author of biographies of Ernest Hemingway and Percy Bysshe Shelley, died in 1987.

Milton G. Baker founded the Valley Forge Military Academy in 1928 and was its superintendent until 1971. He died in 1976.

Hanson W. Baldwin was the longtime military affairs editor of the *New York Times* and wrote more than a dozen books on military and naval history and policy. He died in 1991.

Joseph Balkoski is the command historian of the Maryland National Guard and the author of several books on D-Day, including *Omaha Beach*.

Donald Barr taught at Columbia University and was headmaster of the Dalton School in New York City. He was literary editor of *Tomorrow* and a frequent contributor to the *New York Times Book Review*, *Saturday Review*, and *Commonweal*. He died in 2004.

James Barron has been a reporter for the *New York Times* for many years.

John B. Beach was a lieutenant in the 1st Infantry Division during World War II and leader of the 1st Platoon.

Jim Bellows was the editor of the *New York Herald Tribune* from 1961 to 1967, then became managing editor of *Entertainment Tonight* and executive editor of *ABC News: World News Tonight*. Author of *The Last Editor*, he died in 2009.

Edward Jackson Bennett was a newspaper publisher and editor.

A. Scott Berg is the author of biographies of Maxwell Perkins (for which he won a National Book Award), Charles Lindbergh (for which he won a Pulitzer Prize), Sam Goldwyn, and, most recently, Woodrow Wilson.

Tony Bill is the Academy Award–winning producer of *The Sting*, *Taxi Driver*, and other films.

Sven Birkerts, a literary critic and essayist, is the author of several books of literary criticism, including *The Gutenberg Elegies*.

H. W. Blakeley, a division commander in World War II and commander of the 4th Infantry Division from 1944 to 1946, was made a major general in 1945. He died in 1966.

Shirlie Blaney was a reporter for the Windsor High School newspaper; her interview with J. D. Salinger appeared in the *Daily Eagle* of Claremont, New Hampshire, in 1953.

Eleanor Blau covered arts, culture, and film for the *New York Times* for many years.

Joseph L. Blotner is the coauthor of *The Fiction of J. D. Salinger.*

Ashley Blum recently graduated from Dartmouth College.

Louise Bogan was a poet and, for many years, an editor and poetry critic at the *New Yorker*; she received several submissions of poems from J. D. Salinger during World War II. Bogan died in 1970.

Susan J. Boutwell was a reporter for the West Lebanon, New Hampshire, *Valley News*; she is now senior public affairs officer for strategic communication at Dartmouth College.

Robert Boynton, director of New York University's literary reportage concentration, is the author of *The New Journalism.*

Thomas F. Brady was a journalist.

Stephen Braun who won a Pulitzer Prize as a national correspondent for the *Los Angeles Times*, is now a reporter and editor for Associated Press.

Richard Brooks writes for the *Guardian.*

Andreas Brown was the owner of the Gotham Book Mart.

Himan Brown was a radio and television producer who created *CBS Radio Mystery Theater.* He rented to Salinger the Westport, Connecticut, house in which *The Catcher in the Rye* was written. Brown died in 2010.

Frank P. Burk commanded the Infantry from Utah Beach to the end of World War II. He died in 1978.

Nash K. Burger was on the editorial staff of the *New York Times Book Review* for thirty years and wrote *The Road to West 43rd Street.* He died in 1996.

Whit Burnett, who taught J. D. Salinger in a Columbia University Extension Division short-story writing course, cofounded *Story* magazine in 1931 and coedited the magazine until its demise in 1967 (the magazine was later resurrected). He died in 1973.

Robert Callagy was an attorney with and chairman of the New York law firm Satterlee, Stephens, Burke & Burke. He served as lead counsel on several landmark First Amendment and copyright law cases, including Ian Hamilton's defense against a J. D. Salinger lawsuit. He died in 2006.

Glenn Gordon Caron was the creator of the television shows *Moonlighting* and *Medium*; he has worked as a producer and director of a number of other shows, including *Remington Steele*.

Doreen Carvajal, a journalist for the *New York Times* and other publications, is the author of *The Forgetting River*.

Subhash Chandra is a literary critic and the author of *The Fiction of J. D. Salinger: A Study in the Concept of Man*.

Charlie Chaplin, who died in 1977, was a world-famous actor, director, and screenwriter.

Jane Chaplin, the daughter of Oona O'Neill and Charlie Chaplin, was born in 1957.

Patrice Chaplin is the former daughter-in-law of Charlie and Oona Chaplin and the author of *Hidden Star*, a biography of Oona Chaplin.

Mark David Chapman is serving a life sentence for the murder of John Lennon.

Thomas Childers is the author of many books on World War II, including *In the Shadows of War*.

Marcia Clark served as lead prosecutor in the O. J. Simpson murder trial and the trial of Robert Bardo, the killer of Rebecca Schaeffer.

Michael Clarkson is an author specializing in the topics of fear and stress.

Annabelle Cone teaches French at Dartmouth College.

Paul Corkery wrote for *People* magazine.

Donald Costello, professor emeritus of English at Notre Dame, is the author of the influential essay "The Language of 'The Catcher in the Rye.'"

Catherine Crawford is a literary agent and the editor of *If You Really Want to Hear About It: Writers on J. D. Salinger and His Work*.

Lindsay Crouse is an actress who has starred in *House of Games*, *Places in the Heart*, and numerous other films and plays.

John Curran was an Associated Press reporter. He died in 2011.

John Dean was White House counsel from July 1970 to April 1973 and the key witness in the Watergate hearings. Since then, he has worked as an investment banker and written *Conservatives Without Conscience*, *Blind Ambition*, and other books.

Richard Deitzler was a classmate of J. D. Salinger at Ursinus College, in Collegeville, Pennsylavania.

Don DeLillo is the author of more than a dozen novels, including *Underworld*, *White Noise*, and *Mao II*.

Peter De Vries worked as a staff writer for the *New Yorker* from 1944 to 1967 and wrote numerous comic novels, including *But Who Wakes the Bugler?*, *The Blood of the Lamb*, and *Madder Music*. He died in 1993.

Joan Didion is a novelist, nonfiction writer, literary critic, and frequent contributor to the *New York Review of Books*. Her works include *Slouching Towards Bethlehem*, *Play It As It Lays*, *The White Album*, and *The Year of Magical Thinking*, which won the National Book Award in 2005.

E. L. Doctorow is the author of many novels, including *Billy Bathgate*, *Ragtime*, and *The Book of Daniel*. The recipient of a National Book Award, two PEN/Faulkner Awards, and three National Book Critics Circle Awards, he teaches at New York University.

Claire Douglas, a clinical psychologist and Jungian analyst, has been a training and supervisory analyst with the C. G. Jung Institute of Los Angeles since 1992. The author of *Translate This Darkness: The Life of Christiana Morgan*, she lectures and writes books and articles on Jung and on women's psychology. She was J. D. Salinger's second wife, from 1953 to 1967, and is the mother of his two children.

Maureen Dowd is a Pulitzer Prize–winning editorial page columnist for the *New York Times*.

John Dryfhout is the author of *The Work of Augustus Saint-Gaudens*.

Helen Dudar was a cultural critic and journalist for many newspapers, including the *Chicago Tribune*. She died in 2002.

Dave Eggers is the author of *A Heartbreaking Work of Staggering Genius*; he is the founder and editor of the independent publishing house McSweeney's.

Mel Elfin was *Newsweek*'s Washington bureau chief from 1965 to 1985 and an editor at *U.S. News & World Report* from 1985 to 1998.

Michael Ellison is an actor who has appeared on *Law & Order: Criminal Intent* and *Crutch*.

Betty Eppes, was a reporter for the *Morning Advocate* in Baton Rouge, Louisiana, from 1976 to 1990. In 1980 she interviewed J. D. Salinger.

Leslie Epstein is a professor at Boston University and the author of such novels as *King of the Jews*, *Pandaemonium*, and *San Remo Drive*.

Clifton Fadiman was the editor of the *New Yorker*'s book reviews from 1933 to 1943, when he became an editor for the Book-of-the-Month Club. He died in 1999.

William Faulkner is the author of such novels as *The Sound and the Fury*, *As I Lay Dying*, *Light in August*, and *Absalom, Absalom!* He also wrote the screenplays for *The Big Sleep* and *To Have and Have Not*. A recipient of the Nobel Prize for Literature, he died in 1962.

John Fitzgerald is the son of Paul Fitzgerald, who served with J. D. Salinger during World War II.

Paul Fitzgerald served with Salinger in the Counter Intelligence Corps (CIC) during World War II; the two men maintained a friendship over the next sixty years.

Fred Fogo is the author of *I Read the News Today: The Social Drama of John Lennon's Death*. He is a communications professor at Westminster College in Salt Lake City.

Lacey Fosburgh worked as a staff reporter for the *New York Times* from 1968 to 1973 and, in that role, interviewed J. D. Salinger. She died in 1993.

Will Fowler is the author of over a dozen books on military history, including *D-Day: The Normandy Landings of June 6, 1944*.

Elizabeth Frank, a professor at Bard College, is the author of a Pulitzer Prize–winning biography of the poet and critic Louise Bogan.

Paul Fussell, a professor at the University of Pennsylvania, wrote many books on war and literature, including *The Great War and Modern Memory*. He died in 2012.

Gerard L. Gaudrault was a psychiatrist in New Hampshire.

David Geffen created Asylum Records in 1970 and Geffen Records in 1980; he was one of the three founders of the film production company Dream Works SKG.

Maxwell Geismar was a critic and the author of *American Moderns: From Rebellion to Conformity, a Mid-Century View of Contemporary Fiction* and *Reluctant Radical: A Memoir*. He died in 1979.

Martha Gellhorn was a longtime war correspondent and the author of many books, including *The Heart of Another*. Married to Ernest Hemingway during the early 1940s, she died in 1998.

Rudolf Christoph von Gersdorff was the chief of staff for the German Seventh Army during World War II. He died in 1980.

Elizabeth Gleick is a former book reviewer for *Time* magazine who is now an executive editor at *People*.

Sanford Goldstein is a translator of Japanese literature and the author of numerous articles on J. D. Salinger.

Richard Gonder was a roommate of J. D. Salinger at Valley Forge Military Academy.

Anne Goodman was a writer and book reviewer for various publications, including *Harper's* and the *New Republic*, where she wrote an influential essay on *The Catcher in the Rye* called "Mad About Children."

Adam Gopnik is the author of *Paris to the Moon*, among other books, and a staff writer for the *New Yorker*.

Barbara Graustark, an editor at the *New York Times*, is a former journalist with *Newsweek*.

George Dawes Green is a writer and actor. He wrote the novel *The Juror* and appeared in the TV series *The Moth*.

Lawrence Grobel is the author of books on Truman Capote, Al Pacino, John Huston, and Marlon Brando.

Gerold Gross, publisher and agent, has worked at Harcourt, Brace and Pantheon Books, and served as senior vice president of Macmillan Company.

Henry Grunwald was managing editor of *Time* magazine. He died in 2005.

John Guare is the author of more than two dozen plays, including *Six Degrees of Separation*, which won an Obie Award, and *The House of Blue Leaves*, which won four Tony awards. He was awarded the 2003 PEN/Laura Pels Foundation Award for drama.

Stephen Guirgis is the author of several plays, including *Jesus Hopped the A Train* and *The Motherfucker with the Hat*, which was nominated for six Tony Awards. He has written for such television shows as *NYPD Blue* and *The Sopranos*.

Frederick L. Gwynn is the coauthor of *The Fiction of J. D. Salinger*.

Doug Hackett is the manager of the police department of Cornish, New Hampshire.

Bart Hagerman served in the 17th Airborne Division during World War II and is the author of such books as *War Stories: The Men of the Airborne.*

Richard Haitch writes for the *Nation.*

Jack Hallett served in the U.S. military during World War II.

Ian Hamilton was a founder of the influential British poetry magazines the *Review* and the *New Review.* The author of several books of poetry, including *The Visit* and *Sixty Poems,* he wrote biographies of Robert Lowell, Matthew Arnold, and J. D. Salinger, as well as *Against Oblivion: Some Lives of the Twentieth-Century Poets.* He died in 2001.

Alex Hanson is a reporter for the West Lebanon, New Hampshire, *Valley News.*

Howard M. Harper, the author of *Desperate Faith: A Study of Bellow, Salinger, Mailer, Baldwin, and Updike,* died in 1991.

David Victor Harris was a leader of Students for a Democratic Society during the 1960s. Married to Lacey Fosburgh from 1975 until her death in 1993, he is the author of the books *Dreams Die Hard* and *Our War: What We Did in Vietnam and What It Did to Us.*

Ihab Hassan, a professor at the University of Wisconsin at Milwaukee, is the author of *Radical Innocence: Studies in the Contemporary American Novel* and *The Dismemberment of Orpheus: Toward a Postmodern Literature.*

Ernest Havemann was a journalist for such publications as *Life* magazine and the author of several books on psychology and society. He died in 1995.

Ernest Hemingway, winner of the Nobel Prize in Literature, is the author of numerous novels and stories, including *A Farewell to Arms* and *The Sun Also Rises.* He committed suicide in 1961.

Seán Hemingway, the grandson of Ernest Hemingway, is the Greek and Roman art curator at the Metropolitan Museum of Art. He is the editor of *Hemingway on Hunting* and *Hemingway on War.*

Anabel Heyen was a classmate of J. D. Salinger at Ursinus College, during the 1938–39 academic year.

Granville Hicks, a literary critic, was the author of *The Great Tradition: An Interpretation of American Literature Since the Civil War* and the novel *Behold*

Trouble. He wrote for a variety of publications, including the *New Republic* and the *Nation*. He died in 1982.

Phoebe Hoban, named after the J. D. Salinger character Phoebe Caulfield, is the author of *Basquiat: A Quick Killing in Art* and a contributor to the *New York Times* and *New York* magazine.

Russell Hoban was an illustrator and the author of a series of children's and young adult books, including *The Mouse and the Child*, and the novel *Riddley Walker*. He died in 2011.

Will Hochman is the co-editor of *Letters to J .D. Salinger*.

William H. Honan, a longtime reporter for the *New York Times,* is the author of *Treasure Hunt*.

A. E. Hotchner, a friend of J. D. Salinger in the late 1940s and longtime friend of Ernest Hemingway, is the author of *Papa Hemingway*, *King of the Hill*, and many other books.

Irving Howe, a literary and cultural critic, is the author of numerous books, including *World of Our Fathers*. He died in 1993.

Mark Howland is a teacher at the Tabor Academy in Massachusetts.

David Huddle is a professor and fiction writer who served in the United States Army from 1964 to 1967.

Hillel Italie is an Associated Press reporter.

Harvey Jason is a co-owner of Mystery Pier Books, a rare books store in West Hollywood.

Burnace Fitch Johnson is the former town clerk of Cornish, New Hampshire.

Elliot Johnson was a lieutenant in the 4th Infantry Division during World War II.

Colonel Gerden F. Johnson wrote the history of the U.S. Army's 12th Infantry Regiment in World War II.

Charisse Jones is a national correspondent for *USA Today*.

Jack Jones, the author of *Let Me Take You Down*, a biography of Mark David Chapman, is a journalist.

Michiko Kakutani is the lead book critic for the *New York Times*; she won the 1998 Pulitzer Prize in Criticism.

Isa Kapp was a literary critic.

Alfred Kazin was an influential New York literary critic and author of many books, including *New York Jew*, *A Writer's America*, and *Writing Was Everything*. He died in 1998.

John Keenan, who served with Salinger in the Counter Intelligence Corps (CIC) during World War II, was chief of New York City detectives until his retirement in 1978.

Alex Kershaw is the author of three books on World War II—*The Bedford Boys*, *The Longest Winter*, and *The Few: The American "Knights of the Air" Who Risked Everything to Fight in the Battle of Britain*—as well as biographies of Robert Capa and Jack London.

Werner Kleeman served with J. D. Salinger in World War II. He is the author of *From Dachau to D-Day*.

Seymour Krim was an author and critic. He wrote the books *Views of a Near-sighted Cannoneer*, *Manhattan, Stories of a Great City*, and *Maugham the Artist*. He died in 1989.

Chris Kubica is the co-editor of *Letters to J. D. Salinger*.

Thomas Kunkel is the author of *Genius in Disguise: Harold Ross of the New Yorker* and *Letters from the Editor: The New Yorker's Harold Ross*.

Richard Lacayo is a writer for *Time*.

Roger Lathbury is a professor at George Mason University and proprietor of Orchises Press, which was scheduled, several times during the late 1990s, to publish "Hapworth 16, 1924" as a book.

John Leggett is the author of *Ross and Tom: Two American Tragedies* and a biography of William Saroyan. He was an editor and publicity director at Houghton Mifflin from 1950 to 1960 and an editor at Harper & Row from 1960 to 1967.

John Lennon was a member of the Beatles who went on to release several solo albums before being assassinated in 1980.

Pierre N. Leval was a judge on the U.S. Court of Appeals for the Second Circuit.

Paul Levine was a literary critic.

Jon E. Lewis is a historian and author whose books include *The Mammoth Book of Eyewitness World War II: Over 200 First-Hand Accounts from the Six Years That Tore the World Apart*.

Gordon Lish is a novelist, former book editor at Knopf, and former fiction editor at *Esquire;* he wrote a story in 1977 initially rumored to be by J. D. Salinger.

Gus Lobrano was a fiction editor at the *New Yorker* who edited many of Salinger's short stories that appeared in the magazine.

T. Morris Longstreth was a critic at the *Christian Science Monitor* and a novelist. He wrote a series of novels on the Adirondack region, including *Mac of Placid.*

Arnold H. Lubasch was a reporter for the *New York Times.*

Leila Hadley Luce was a travel writer, journalist, and philanthropist; her books include *A Journey with Elsa Cloud* and *Give Me the World.* A onetime girlfriend of J. D. Salinger, she died in 2009.

James Lundquist is the author of *J. D. Salinger*, a work of literary criticism.

Stephan Lynn operated on John Lennon following his shooting by Mark David Chapman. He is the emergency room director at St. Luke's–Roosevelt Hospital in New York City.

John McCarten was a writer for the *New Yorker* during the 1930s.

Mary McCarthy wrote novels, memoirs, and literary criticism, including, in 1962, the influential "J. D. Salinger's Closed Circuit." She died in 1989.

Michael McDermott is a photographer who twice photographed J. D. Salinger.

Julie McDermott resides in Cornish, New Hampshire, and works at a grocery store in Hanover, New Hampshire.

Edwin McDowell was a reporter for the *New York Times.* He died in 2007.

Bradley R. McDuffie is the author of the essay "For Ernest, with Love and Squalor: the Influence of Ernest Hemingway on J. D. Salinger."

Robert D. McFadden, winner of the Pulitzer Prize, is a longtime reporter for the *New York Times.*

Geraldine McGowan is a freelance writer and editor living in Boston.

Charles McGrath, a former editor of the *New Yorker*, is a writer for the *New York Times.*

Cathleen McGuigan is a senior editor and writer at *Newsweek.*

Jesse McKinley is a writer on culture for the *New York Times.*

John C. McManus, a military consultant to this book, is a professor of U.S. military history at Missouri University of Science and Technology. The official historian for the U.S. Army's 7th Infantry Regiment, he is the author of many books on military history, including *The Americans at Normandy* and, most recently, *Grunts: Inside the American Infantry Combat Experience, World War II Through Iraq*.

Larissa MacFarquhar is a staff writer for the *New Yorker*.

Norman Mailer is the author of many books, including *Executioner's Song* and *Armies of the Night*, both of which won the Pulitzer Prize. He died in 2007.

Janet Malcolm is a staff writer for the *New Yorker* and the author of several books.

Marsha Malinowski is an expert in the books and manuscripts department of Sotheby's.

Jay Martin, a professor at Claremont McKenna University, is the author of *Who Am I This Time: Uncovering the Fictive Personality*.

Anne Marple was a literary critic, writing for such publications as the *New Republic*.

Sergeant Ralph G. Martin served in World War II, writing for *Stars and Stripes* and *Yank*.

Carol Matthau, a childhood friend of Oona O'Neill, was married to William Saroyan, then to Walter Matthau. The author of the memoir *Among the Porcupines*, she died in 1978.

Herbert Mayes, an editor at *Good Housekeeping* and *McCall's*, died in 1987.

William Maxwell was a fiction editor at the *New Yorker* from 1936 to 1976 and author of several works of fiction, including the National Book Award-winning novel *So Long See You Tomorrow*. He died in 2000.

Joyce Maynard, who lived with J. D. Salinger in the early 1970s, is the author of many novels, including *To Die For*, and a memoir, *At Home in the World*.

Ved Mehta was a staff writer at the *New Yorker* for more than thirty years. He has written numerous books about India.

Ib Melchior is a Danish writer and filmmaker.

J. Reid Meloy is a forensic psychologist specializing in stalkers and assassins.

Louis Menand is a professor at Harvard University, a critic at the *New Yorker*, and the author of *The Metaphysical Club*, which received the Pulitzer Prize.

Robert E. Merriam was an army captain during World War II and later became a politician who served in various government positions. He wrote *Dark December: The Full Account of the Battle of the Bulge.*

Stephen Metcalf is a writer for *Slate* magazine.

Nicholas Meyer is the writer/director of three *Star Trek* films; he also wrote and directed *Time After Time.*

Charles Meyers served in the Counter Intelligence Corps during World War II.

Edward G. Miller served in the army from 1980 to 2000. He is the author of *A Dark and Bloody Ground: The Hürtgen Forest and the Roer River Dams, 1944–1945.*

Jean Miller met J. D. Salinger in 1949 and had a relationship with him for the next six years.

Michael Mitchell designed the original cover of *The Catcher in the Rye.*

Paul L. Montgomery was a reporter for the *New York Times.*

Rick Moody is the author of several novels, including *The Ice Storm.*

David Moore was an official at the YMCA who served with Mark David Chapman at an Arkansas camp for the resettlement of Vietnamese refugees in the late 1970s.

Deborah Dash Moore is the author of *G.I. Jews* and other books and articles on Jewish culture and history. She teaches at the University of Michigan, where she serves as director of the Frankel Center for Judaic Studies.

Dinty Moore is a writer, the editor of *Creative Nonfiction*, and an English professor at Ohio University. His books include *Between Panic and Desire.*

George Morgan was a sergeant in the 22nd Infantry Regiment during the battle of Hürtgen Forest.

Mack Morriss was an army sergeant and war correspondent for *Yank* magazine during World War II.

Joe Moses was a lieutenant in the United States Army during World War II.

John Mosher was a longtime writer and editor at the *New Yorker.*

Bruce F. Mueller, who lives in San Francisco, is a Salinger scholar.

Elizabeth Murray, whose brother was a classmate of J. D. Salinger at Valley Forge Military Academy, was an early encourager of Salinger's literary ambitions.

Gloria Murray is the daughter of Elizabeth Murray and the author of a biography of Oona O'Neill.

Debs Myers was a war correspondent during World War II.

Ethel Nelson, who resides in Cornish, New Hampshire, was nanny to J. D. Salinger's children; she met him while attending Windsor High School in the early 1950s. Nelson and Salinger knew each other over many decades.

Jay Neugeboren is the author of over a dozen books, including *Imagining Robert*, *The Stolen Jew*, and *Before My Life Began*.

Jon O. Newman is an American Federal Appeals Court judge. He has served on the U.S Second Circuit Court of Appeals since 1979.

Sarah Norris's great-grandmother was Elizabeth Murray, who befriended Salinger; Norris is now a writer who lives in Nashville.

Edward Norton is a film and stage actor, writer, and director, known for roles in films such as *American History X*, *Fight Club*, and *The Bourne Legacy*.

Peter Norton is a computer programmer.

Cyrus Nowrasteh is the writer/director of *The Day Reagan Was Shot* and the writer of *The Path to 9/11* and other TV miniseries.

Ken Oakley was a British naval commando who landed on Sword Beach in the first wave on D-Day and later chaired the Royal Naval Commando Association. He died on October 25, 2007.

Joyce Carol Oates is the author of more than forty novels; her novel *them* won the National Book Award.

Dorothy Olding was Salinger's literary agent for fifty years.

Colleen O'Neill, a nurse and award-winning quilter, was married to J. D. Salinger from 1988 until his death in 2010.

Oona O'Neill, the daughter of Eugene O'Neill, dated J. D. Salinger until his entry into the U.S. Army. She married Charlie Chaplin, had eight children, and died in 1991.

Cynthia Ozick is an essayist, short story writer, and novelist. Her books include *The Messiah of Stockholm*, *The Blue Shawl*, *What Henry James Knew*, and *The Din in the Head: Essays*.

Arthur J. Pais is a New York–based freelance writer, editor, and journalism teacher. He writes regularly for *India Today*, *Economic Times*, and *Far Eastern Economic Review*.

Alton Pearson served as a corporal in the 12th Regiment of the 4th Infantry Division during World War II.

S. J. Perelman was a humorist, screenwriter, longtime contributor to the *New Yorker*, and author of over twenty books. He died in 1979.

Marc Peyser is the author of *First Cousins: The Untold Story of Eleanor Roosevelt and Alice Roosevelt Longworth*.

Gina Piccalo is a reporter with the *Los Angeles Times*.

Joyce Burrington Pierce is a resident of Windsor, Vermont.

Jose de M. Platanopez was a resident of Houston, Texas, who wrote a letter to the *New York Times Book Review* criticizing J. D. Salinger's *Raise High the Roof Beam, Carpenters and Seymour: An Introduction*.

George Plimpton was the editor of the *Paris Review* until his death in 2003. He published an account of Betty Eppes's 1980 interview with J. D. Salinger.

Katha Pollitt is an American poet, essayist, and critic. She writes the "Subject to Debate" column for the *Nation* and is the author of *Antarctic Traveller*, a poetry collection that won the National Book Critics Circle Award in 1983.

Charles Poore was a book critic for the *New York Times*.

Vincent Powell was a sergeant in the 237th Engineer Combat Battalion during World War II.

Orville Prescott was a book critic for the *New York Times*. He died in 1996.

Ernie Pyle was a correspondent during World War II who died in Okinawa in April 1945.

Judy Quinn is an artist from Kenya who now lives in the United Sates.

Nancy Ralston was a literary critic.

Sri Ramakrishna was a Hindu guru in India who was born in 1836 and died in 1886.

Russell Reeder served as a colonel and commander of the 12th Infantry Regiment in World War II at the time of the D-Day invasion. After being severely wounded, he wrote many books on the military and war. He died in 1998.

David Remnick is the editor of the *New Yorker*. He is the author of *Lenin's Tomb: The Last Days of the Soviet Empire*, which won the 1994 Pulitzer Prize.

Mordecai Richler was a Canadian novelist, screenwriter, and essayist. His books include *The Apprenticeship of Duddy Kravitz*, for which he wrote the Academy Award–nominated screenplay, and *Barney's Version*. He died in 2001.

General Matthew Ridgway commanded U.S. paratroopers during World War II and later commanded Allied troops in the Korean War.

David Roderick, who was a staff sergeant in the 4th Infantry Division, became a teacher and high school football coach. The author of *Deeds Not Words*, an unpublished history of the 22nd Infantry Regiment, he died in 2007.

John Romano is a screenwriter.

Franklin D. Roosevelt was the thirty-second president of the United States.

Ron Rosenbaum is a writer for the *New York Observer* and the author of *Explaining Hitler* and *The Secret Parts of Fortune: Three Decades of Intense Investigations and Edgy Enthusiasms*.

Noah Rosenberg is a reporter for the *Queens* (N.Y.) *Courier*.

Lillian Ross is an American journalist and author who has been a staff writer at the *New Yorker* since 1949. She was a longtime friend of J. D. Salinger.

Philip Roth, an American novelist, is the author of such novels as *Portnoy's Complaint*, *The Human Stain*, and *American Pastoral*, He has received the National Book Critics Circle Award, the National Book Award, and the Pulitzer Prize.

Louise Roug is a reporter with the *Los Angeles Times*.

S. J. Rowland was a columnist at the *Christian Science Monitor*.

Howard Ruppel, a World War II veteran, is the chancellor and academic dean of the Institute for Advanced Study of Human Sexuality.

Ted Russell is a former photographer for *Life*.

Doris Salinger, J. D. Salinger's sister and a longtime buyer at Bloomingdale's, died in 2001.

Margaret Salinger, the daughter of J. D. Salinger, is the author of a memoir, *Dream Catcher*. A Phi Beta Kappa graduate of Brandeis University, she received a master's degree in Management Studies from Oxford University and studied at the Harvard University Divinity School.

Matthew Salinger, the son of J. D. Salinger, is an actor and theater producer. He appeared in *What Dreams May Come* and on episodes of *Law & Order: Special Victims Unit.* He produced the award-winning play *The Syringa Tree* in 2000.

Aram Saroyan is a poet, novelist, biographer, memoirist, and playwright. His books include *Trio: Portrait of an Intimate Friendship—Oona Chaplin, Carol Matthau, Gloria Vanderbilt.*

Jennifer Schuessler is a staff editor at the *New York Times Book Review.*

Jonathan Schwartz is a radio host on WYNC and Sirius.

Jane Scovell is the author of *Oona: Living in the Shadows*, a biography of Oona O'Neill.

Walter Scott writes a column for *Parade* magazine.

John Seabrook is a staff writer at the *New Yorker.*

John Seelye is an American literature professor at the University of Florida,

Laurence Shames is an American writer of crime fiction and the author of *Boss of Bosses*, a bestselling book about the Mafia.

Ian Shapiro is a reporter for the *Washington Post.*

William Shawn was the editor of the *New Yorker* from 1952 until 1987. He edited the later stories of J. D. Salinger that appeared in the magazine. He died in 1998.

Michael Silverblatt is the host of the nationally syndicated radio show *Bookworm.*

William L. Shirer is the author of *The Rise and Fall of the Third Reich.* He died in 1993.

Judith Shulevitz is a contributor to *Slate* and the *New York Times.*

Franklin Sibert was a lieutenant colonel in the 12th Infantry Regiment of the 4th Infantry Division during World War II. He commanded the Second Battalion.

John Sim served as a captain in the 12th Parachute Battalion in World War II.

Dean Simonton is a professor of psychology at the University of California, Davis; his research focuses on genius and psychological history.

Mona Simpson's novels include *Anywhere But Here* and *The Lost Father.* She teaches at UCLA.

John Skow was a longtime staff writer for *Time* magazine.

Dinitia Smith is a national cultural correspondent for the *New York Times*. She is the author of three novels, including *The Illusionist.*

Albert Sohl was a private in the 12th Infantry Regiment during World War II.

Stephen Spiro served in the New York Police Department for decades before retiring. He arrested Mark David Chapman following Chapman's shooting of John Lennon.

Alessandra Stanley is the chief television critic for the *New York Times.*

Richard Stayton is the editor of *Written By*, the magazine of the Writers Guild of America, West.

Sharon Steel is a senior editor at *Artizia.*

George Steiner is a literary critic.

Pamela Hunt Steinle is a professor of American Studies at California State University, Fullerton, and the author of *In Cold Fear:* The Catcher in the Rye *Censorship Controversies and Postwar American Character.*

Charles Steinmetz was a classmate of J. D. Salinger at Ursinus College.

James Stern was a literary critic, translator, and author of such short-story collections as *The Man Who Was Loved.* He died in 1993.

Clyde Stodghill served in the 4th Infantry Division in World War II.

David Streitfeld had been a reporter for the *Washington Post* and is now a reporter for the *New York Times*

Harvey Swados was an essayist and novelist who wrote *Out Went the Candle* and *Nights in the Gardens of Brooklyn.* He died in 1972.

Gay Talese is the author of eleven books, including *The Kingdom and the Power* and *Thy Neighbor's Wife.*

Michael Tannenbaum has written on J. D. Salinger.

Cielle Tewksbury teaches workshops in Mythology, Movement, and Symbolism.

Gwen Tetirick was a neighbor of J. D. Salinger.

Frances Thierolf was a classmate of J. D. Salinger at Ursinus College; her married name, Frances Glassmoyer, was the inspiration for the name "Franny Glass."

John Toland was a historian and author whose books include *Battle: The Story of the Bulge* and *Adolf Hitler: The Definitive Biography*. He died in 2004.

Michael Tosta was a literary critic and professor at Johnson College.

Robert Towne wrote the screenplays for *Chinatown* and *Shampoo*, directed *Without Limits*, and has served as a script doctor for numerous films including, most famously, *The Godfather*.

Joseph B. Treaster is a veteran reporter and former foreign correspondent for the *New York Times*.

John C. Unrue is a professor at the University of Nevada, Las Vegas, and the author of *J. D. Salinger's "The Catcher in the Rye."*

John Updike, who died in 2009, was the author of more than fifty books, including the Pulitzer Prize–winning *Rabbit Is Rich* and *Rabbit at Rest*.

Gloria Vanderbilt, a childhood friend of Oona O'Neill, is an American heiress and socialite.

Gore Vidal, a novelist, essayist, playwright, and journalist, is the author of such books as *Burr*, *Myra Breckinridge*, *Lincoln*, and *Palimpsest*. His essay collection, *United States*, received the National Book Award. He died in 2012.

John Wain, who died in 1994, was an English writer and critic.

Jerry Wald was a screenwriter and movie producer.

Michael Walzer is a professor emeritus of political science at Princeton. His books include *What It Means to Be an American* and *The Company of Critics*.

Bob Wandesforde served in the 4th Infantry Division during World War II and later became a commercial illustrator. He died in 1990.

Donald A. Warner was a first lieutenant in the 22nd Infantry Regiment of the 4th Infantry Division during World War II.

Juliet Waters is a journalist at the *Montreal Mirror*.

Myles Weber is a professor at Ashland University in Ohio. He is the author of *Consuming Silences: How We Read Nonpublication* and *Middlebrow Annoyances: American Drama in the 21st Century*.

Marc Weingarten is the author of *The Gang That Wouldn't Write Straight* and *From Hipsters to Gonzo*.

John Wenke, a professor at Salisbury State University in Maryland, is the author of *J. D. Salinger: A Study of the Short Fiction*.

Lawrence Weschler is the author of many books, including *Everything That Rises: A Book of Convergences.*

Leslie Aldridge Westoff was a reporter for the *New York Times.*

E. B. White was an American writer and journalist at the *New Yorker* best known for his children's books *Charlotte's Web* and *Stuart Little.* He died in 1985.

Steven Whitfield is a professor of American studies at Brandeis University. His books include *In Search of American Jewish Culture* and *The Culture of the Cold War.*

William Wiegand was a book critic and professor of English at San Francisco State College.

Jon Wiener, a professor of history at University of California, Irvine, is the author of *Come Together: John Lennon in His Time* and *Gimme Some Truth: The John Lennon FBI Files.*

Billy Wilder was the director of numerous movies, including *Sunset Boulevard* and *The Apartment.*

George Wilson was a lieutenant in Company F of the 4th Infantry Division who landed on D-Day. His books include *If You Survive.*

John M. Wilson is a journalist at the *Los Angeles Times.*

Tom Wolfe, a key figure in the development of New Journalism, is the author of *The Electric Kool-Aid Acid Test*, *The Right Stuff*, and several novels, including *The Bonfire of the Vanities.*

John Worthman served as a medic in the 22nd Regiment of the 4th Infantry Division during World War II.

David Yaffe is a professor at City University of New York and the author of *Fascinating Rhythm: Reading Jazz in American Writing.*

Ben Yagoda, the author of *About Town: The New Yorker and the World It Made,* is the director of the University of Delaware's journalism department.

Jonathan Yardley is a Pulitzer Prize–winning book critic for the *Washington Post.*

Bertrand Yeaton was an artist and friend of J. D. Salinger.

Pat York is a photographer.

James Yuenger was a reporter for the *Chicago Tribune.*

Katie Zezima, formerly a reporter for the *New York Times,* is now a supervisory correspondent for the Associated Press.

NOTES

This book consists primarily of interviews with more than 200 people, dozens of whom are authors who not only spoke to us at length about their subjects of expertise but also read aloud on camera passages from their work. As a result, certain passages in this book are, with the authors' permission, combinations of oral testimony and written source.

In order to provide the reader with as complete account as possible, we also quoted from published sources in cases where the individual either was deceased or did not consent to an interview. In a number of these cases, we obtained special permission from the copyright holder.

1: WE'RE GOING TO START THE WAR FROM RIGHT HERE

3 "I landed on Utah Beach": J. D. Salinger, "Backstage with *Esquire*," *Esquire*, October 1945.

3 "I landed on D-Day": Margaret Salinger, *Dream Catcher: A Memoir*, p. 53.

3 "On the evening prior": Able Seaman Ken Oakley, quoted in Max Arthur, *Forgotten Voices of World War II*, p. 304.

4 "Jerry was just a nice": Werner Kleeman, quoted in Richard Firstman, "Werner Kleeman's Private War," *The New York Times*, November 11, 2007.

4 "I guess about 3 a.m.": John Keenan, quoted in "Voices from the Battlefront: [Nassau and Suffolk Edition 1]," *Newsday*, May 29, 1994.

5 "Shells were flying over our": Werner Kleeman, quoted in *D-Day Plus 40 Years*, anchored by Tom Brokaw, 1984.

6 "The battleships were firing at": John Keenan, quoted in "Voices from the Battlefront: [Nassau and Suffolk Edition 1]" *Newsday*, May 29, 1994.

6 "The waves were pitching the": Stephen E. Ambrose, *D-Day*, p. 285.

6 "The boats were going round": Private Ralph Della-Volpe, quoted in Stephen E. Ambrose, *D-Day*, p. 285.

6 "So did many others": Stephen E. Ambrose, *D-Day*, p. 285.

6 "The beach at Utah Beach": Staff Sergeant David Roderick, *Utah Beach Normandy June 6, 1944.*

7 " 'Get ready!' the coxswain shouted": Private Albert Sohl, quoted in "From Utah Beach to the Hedgerows," *Military History*, June 2004.

7 "The men felt their": Colonel Gerden F. Johnson, *History of the Twelfth Infantry Regiment in World War II*, p. 58.

7 "For the first time I": General Matthew Ridgway, quoted in Clay Blair, *Ridgway's Paratroopers*, p. 62.

8 "Never before in my life": Captain George Mayberry, quoted in Russell Miller, *Nothing Less Than Victory: The Oral History of D-Day*, p. 365.

9 "Once we were on the": Werner Kleeman and Elizabeth Uhlig, *From Dachau to D-Day*, Marble House Editions, 2006, p. 90.

9 "The 4th Division's entire": Joseph Balkoski, *Utah Beach: The Amphibious Landing and Airborne Operations on D-Day, June 6, 1944*, p. 184.

11 "We come in twenty minutes": J. D. Salinger, "The Magic Foxhole," unpublished story, *Story* magazine archive, Firestone Library, Princeton University.

12 "Our team rushed out of": Private Ray A. Mann, quoted in Peter Liddle, *D-Day, by Those Who Were There*, 2004.

13 "I had seen many terrible": John Clark, quoted in Robert O. Babcock, *War Stories: Utah Beach to Pleiku*, p. 123.

14 "Following the breakout": Colonel Gerden F. Johnson, *History of the Twelfth Infantry Regiment in World War II*, p. 151.

15 "Colonel Russell 'Red' Reeder": Stephen E. Ambrose, *D-Day*, p. 286.

15 "The Germans had flooded": Colonel Russell "Red" Reeder, quoted in Joseph Balkoski, *Utah Beach*, p. 236.

16 "In choosing their [defensive] positions": Colonel Gerden F. Johnson, *History of the Twelfth Infantry Regiment in World War II*, p. 120.

17 "Bodies were lying in a": Clyde Stodghill, quoted in Robert O. Babcock, *War Stories: Utah Beach to Pleiku*, p. 205.

17 "We ran into elements": Colonel Gerden F. Johnson, *History of the Twelfth Infantry Regiment in World War II*, p. 62.

18 "Happy Birthday to me, 22": David Roderick, *Utah Beach Normandy June 6, 1944.*

18 "During the days that followed": Bill Garvin, quoted in Robert O. Babcock, *War Stories: Utah Beach to Pleiku*, p. 123.

18 "It was at the hedgerows": Private Albert Sohl, quoted in "From Utah Beach to the Hedgerows" *Military History*, June 2004.

19 "While we were in our position": Corporal Alton Pearson, quoted in John C. McManus, *The Deadly Brotherhood: The American Combat Soliders in World War II*, p. 134.

19 "During the bombing, some German": Paul Fussell, *The Boys' Crusade: The American Infantry in Northwestern Europe, 1944–1945*, p. 51.

20 "We were surrounded": Lieutenant Elliot Johnson, quoted in Studs Terkel, *The Good War*, p. 259.

20 "While we were being mortared": Captain John Sim, quoted in Max Arthur, *Forgotten Voices of World War II*, p. 327.

23 "The Air Corps finally smartened": J. D. Salinger, "The Magic Foxhole" unpublished story, *Story* magazine archive, Firestone Library, Princeton University.

24 "After much discussion Lt. Everett": Lieutenant Joe Moses, letter to Colonel Russell "Red" Reeder, November 1945.

24 "[They] made the enemy pay": Captain Frank P. Burk, 4th Infantry Division combat interview.

24 "As we went into": Colonel Gerden F. Johnson, *History of the Twelfth Infantry Regiment in World War II*, p. 82.

26 "Our job was support for": John Keenan, quoted in "Voices from the Battlefront: [Nassau and Suffolk Edition 1]," *Newsday*, May 29, 1994.

27 "The point of the whole operation": Paul Fussell, *The Boys' Crusade: The American Infantry in Northwestern Europe, 1944-1945*, pp. 40–41.

29 "Following the bombing and": Clyde Stodghill, quoted in Robert O. Babcock, *War Stories: Utah Beach to Pleiku*, p. 206.

2: SLIGHT REBELLION OFF PARK AVENUE

30 "His father, Sol Salinger": Ian Hamilton, *In Search of J. D. Salinger*, p. 13.

31 "So far as the present": William Maxwell, *Book-of-the-Month Club News*, midsummer 1953.

32 "Did mother ever tell you": Doris Salinger, quoted in Margaret Salinger, *Dream Catcher: A Memoir*, pp. 17–18.

33 "Salinger was vice-president": Shane Salerno, discussing "FTC Bans Price Fixing by Cheese Companies," *The New York Times*, October 5, 1940; "15 Named in Fixing of Cheese Prices," *The New York Times*, July 2, 1941; *The New York Times*, September 7, 1944.

34 "He wanted to do unconventional": childhood friend, quoted in *Salinger: A Critical and Personal Portrait*, ed. Henry Grunwald, p. 11.

34 "[Salinger] was anything but a": Ernest Havemann, "The Search for the Mysterious J. D. Salinger: The Recluse in Rye," *Life*, November 3, 1961.

35 "Unlike Zooey and the rest": John Skow, "Sonny: An Introduction," *Time*, September 15, 1961.

35 "He was interested in dramatics": Ernest Havemann, "The Search for the Mysterious J. D. Salinger: The Recluse in Rye," *Life*, November 3, 1961.

35 "In 1932, Sol Salinger set": Paul Alexander, *Salinger: A Biography*, p. 36.

35 "His record as a freshman": Ernest Havemann, "The Search for the Mysterious J. D. Salinger: The Recluse in Rye," *Life*, November 3, 1961.

37 "At the age of fifteen": William Maxwell, *Book-of-the-Month Club News*, midsummer 1953.

38 "Miss Doris Jane Salinger, daughter": *The New York Times*, May 19, 1935.

40 "Jerry's conversation was frequently laced": Richard Gonder, quoted in Paul Alexander, *Salinger: A Biography*, p. 43.

42 "One of his classmates at": James Lundquist, *J. D. Salinger*, p. 8.

42 "As literary editor of *Crossed*": James Lundquist, *J. D. Salinger*, p. 8.

42 "The last parade, our hearts": J. D. Salinger, 1936 Valley Forge Class Yearbook.

42 "Salinger spent two years at": Subhash Chandra, *The Fiction of J. D. Salinger*, p. 35.

43 "At Valley Forge": Shane Salerno, discussing Brett E. Weaver, *Annotated Bibliography (1982–2002) of J. D. Salinger*, p. 54; and David W. Berry, "Salinger Slept Here," *Philadelphia* magazine, October 1991.

45 "Spent a year in Europe": J. D. Salinger, S*tory*, November-December 1944, p. 1.

45 "He lived in Vienna, with": William Maxwell, *Book-of-the-Month Club News*, July 1951.

46 "Leah was the daughter in": J. D. Salinger, "A Girl I Knew," *Good Housekeeping*, February 1948.

47 "When this handsome, suave, and": Frances Thierolf, quoted in "Biography of J. D. Salinger," *Bloom's BioCritiques: J. D. Salinger*, ed. Harold Bloom, p. 13.

47 "He felt he had come": Anabel Heyen, quoted in Paul Alexander, *Salinger: A Biography*, p. 50.

47 "Salinger found an outlet"" Ian Hamilton, In Search of *J. D. Salinger*, pp. 46–47.

47 "On returning to America, he": J. D. Salinger, contributor's note, "Heart of a Broken Story," *Esquire*, September 1941.

48 "Letter: Dear Mother—You and": J. D. Salinger, "The Skipped Diploma," *Ursinus Weekly*, October 10, 1938 .

48 "Act One: Franklin:—I hate": J. D. Salinger, "The Skipped Diploma," *Ursinus Weekly*, October 17, 1938 .

48 "Mr. X: College feller?": "The Skipped Diploma," *Ursinus Weekly*, December 12, 1938.

49 "Early one evening, not too": Paul Alexander, *Salinger: A Biography*, p. 50.

49 "He wasn't what I'd call": Richard Deitzler, quoted in Paul Alexander, *Salinger: A Biography*, p. 50.

49 "I was in the same": Charles Steinmetz, quoted in Paul Alexander, *Salinger: A Biography*, p. 52.

50 "He didn't say goodbye to": Richard Deitzler, quoted in Paul Alexander, *Salinger: A Biography*, p. 53.

52 "There was one dark-eyed": Whit Burnett, quoted in Ernest Havemann, "The Search for the Mysterious J. D. Salinger: The Recluse in the Rye," *Life*, November 3, 1961.

52 "Mr. Burnett simply and very": J. D. Salinger, "A Salute to Whit Burnett," *Fiction Writer's Handbook*, pp. 187-188.

53 "He was a silent fellow": Whit Burnett, quoted in Ernest Havemann, "The Search for the Mysterious J. D. Salinger: The Recluse in Rye," *Life*, November 3, 1961".

54 "In class, one evening, Mr.": J. D. Salinger, "A Salute to Whit Burnett," Hallie and Whit Burnett, *Fiction Writer's Handbook*, pp. 187–88.

54 "He suddenly came to life": Hallie and Whit Burnett, *Fiction Writer's Handbook*, p. 105.

55 "What do you do most": J. D. Salinger, "The Young Folks," *Story*, March-April 1940.

56 "Edna shifted her position": J. D. Salinger, "The Young Folks," *Story*, March-April 1940.

57 "In a letter to a friend": Ian Hamilton, *In Search of J. D. Salinger*, p. 66.

57 " 'Hey, Carl,' Holden said": J. D. Salinger, "Slight Rebellion Off Madison," *The New Yorker*, December 21, 1946.

58 "I knew he'd be a writer": Oona O'Neill quoted in Patrice Chaplin, *Hidden Star: Oona O'Neill Chaplin*, p. 175.

64 "The show consists": Stork Club regular, quoted in David W. Stowe, "The Politics of Café Society," *The Journal of American History* 84, no. 4 (March 1998), pp. 1384–1406.

65 "Last year I made a rule": J. D. Salinger, *The Catcher in the Rye*, p. 63.

66 "Girls. Jesus Christ": J. D. Salinger, *The Catcher in the Rye*, p. 73.

67 "Dear Mr. Salinger, I'm sorry": John Mosher, letter to J. D. Salinger regarding "Fisherman," March 21, 1941.

67 "I'll try a couple more": J. D. Salinger, letter to Marjorie Sheard, November 18, 1941.

68 "The United States of America was suddenly": Franklin Delano Roosevelt, address to Congress, December 8, 1941.

70 "The young man": J. D. Salinger, "A Young Girl in 1941 with No Waist At All," *Mademoiselle*, May 1947.

71 "Oona O'Neill, No. 1 deb": Bettmann Archive, photograph caption, 1942.

71 "Not 'Glamour Girl No.'": Associated Press, photograph caption, 1942.

72 "There isn't any night club": J. D. Salinger, *The Catcher in the Rye*, p. 76.

73 "That winter Lois did her best": J. D. Salinger, "The Long Debut of Lois Taggett," *Story*, September-October 1942.

74 "I want to kill": J. D. Salinger, "Last Day of the Last Furlough," *Saturday Evening Post*, July 15, 1944.

75 "I am of the opinion": Colonel Milton G. Baker, quoted in Paul Alexander, *Salinger: A Biography*, p. 80.

75 "I have known Jerry Salinger": Whit Burnett, letter to Colonel Collins, July 1, 1942.

76 "The sarge almost had an attack": J. D. Salinger, "The Hang of It," *Collier's*, July 12, 1941.

78 "I am inside the truck": J. D. Salinger, "This Sandwich Has No Mayonnaise," *Esquire*, October 1945.

83 "Charlie Chaplin was the first": Lillian Ross, "Moments from Chaplin," *The New Yorker*, May 22, 1978.

84 "I arrived early and on": Charlie Chaplin, *My Autobiography*, p. 414.

84 "Just met Charlie Chaplin": Oona O'Neill, quoted in "Charlie Chaplin & Oona O'Neill," *People* magazine, February 12, 1996.

87 "At first I was afraid": Charlie Chaplin, *My Autobiography*, p. 414.

87 "It was a great, great love-affair": Carol Matthau, quoted in "Charlie Chaplin & Oona O'Neill," *People*, February 12, 1996.

87 "Salinger said terrible things about my being": Oona O'Neill, quoted in Patrice Chaplin, *Hidden Star: Oona O'Neill Chaplin*, p. 175.

89 "Burke, he didn't stay": J. D. Salinger, "Soft-Boiled Sergeant," *Saturday Evening Post,* April 15, 1944.

90 "Laughter is one of Charlie's": Oona O'Neill, quoted in *Time*, June 27, 1960.

91 "[Charlie] made me more mature": Ibid.

CONVERSATION WITH SALINGER #1

94 Shane Salerno interview with Michael Clarkson.

3: SIX-FEET-TWO OF MUSCLE AND TYPEWRITER RIBBON IN A FOXHOLE

104 "As was standard operating": Ib Melchior, *Case by Case*, p. 83.

106 "You may be 'baldheaded and'": J. D. Salinger, letter to Paul Fitzgerald, February 10, 1979.

109 "As long as I live": Sergeant Ralph G. Martin quoted in *Yank: The Story of World War II as Written by the Soldiers*, p. 51.

110 "The people cheered and laughed": John Worthman, quoted in Robert O. Babcock, *War Stories: Utah Beach to Pleiku*, p. 255.

110 "Another of Ernest's visitors at": Carlos Baker, *Ernest Hemingway: A Life Story*, p. 420.

111 "He found Hemingway": Ibid.

111 "Vincent smiled": J. D. Salinger, "Last Day of the Last Furlough," *The Saturday Evening Post*, July 15, 1944 .

112 "Salinger returned to his unit": Carlos Baker, *Ernest Hemingway: A Life Story*, p. 420.

112 "In her memoir *Running with*": Bradley R. McDuffie, "When Papa Met Salinger," *Edmonton Journal*, July 23, 2010.

112 "He shared with me a": Lillian Ross, "The JD Salinger I Knew," *Guardian* (UK), December 12, 2010.

113 "All writers—no matter how": J. D. Salinger, contributor's notes for "Down at the Dinghy," *Harper's*, April 1949 [note published in *Harper's*, February 1959].

113 "X threaded his fingers": J. D. Salinger, "For Esmé—with Love and Squalor," *The New Yorker*, April 8, 1950.

114 "In the years that followed": Bradley R. McDuffie, "When Papa Met Salinger," *Edmonton Journal*, July 23, 2010.

115 "I'm twenty-five, was born in": J. D. Salinger, contributor's note to *Story*, November–December 1944.

116 "In those days": Werner Kleeman, quoted in Noah Rosenberg, "Lifelong Pal Remembers J. D. Salinger," *Queens Courier*, February 2, 2010.

116 "I can't remember very acutely": J. D. Salinger, letter to Elizabeth Murray, August 1944.

116 "I met and have had": J. D. Salinger, letter to Frances Glassmoyer, August 9, 1944.

116 "You never saw six-feet-two": Salinger, letter to Whit Burnett, in Jack R. Sublette, *J. D. Salinger: An Annotated Bibliography, 1938–1981.*

CONVERSATION WITH SALINGER #2

119 Shane Salerno interview with Michael McDermott and Ted Russell.

4: INVERTED FOREST

123 "Just south of Aachen": Stephen E. Ambrose, *Citizen Soldiers: The U.S. Army from the Normandy Beaches to the Bulge to the Surrender of Germany*, p. 167.

125 "My opinion was, it was": Werner Kleeman, interview with Bobby Allen Wintermute, Queens College WWII Alumni Veterans Project, March 31, 2009.

125 "The country was obstacle enough": Lieutenant George Wilson, *If You Survive: From Normandy to the Battle of the Bulge to the End of World War II*, 1987, p. 132.

125 "Added to the natural obstacles": Major General Raymond G. Barton, 4th Infantry Division combat interview.

125 "The companies moved through": Lieutenant Colonel William Gayle, 4th Infantry Division combat interview.

126 "Higher commanders had regarded": Colonel Gerden F. Johnson, *History of the Twelfth Infantry Regiment in World War II*, p. 217.

126 "He [D.B., Holden Caulfield's": J. D. Salinger, *The Catcher in the Rye*, p. 140.

127 "I was a forward observer": Lieutenant Elliot Johnson, quoted in Studs Terkel, *The Good War*, p. 246.

128 "In Hürtgen Forest the 4th": Lieutenant Colonel William Gayle, 4th Infantry Division combat interview.

128 "At 1400 hours the battalion commander": Colonel Gerden F. Johnson, *History of the Twelfth Infantry Regiment in World War II*, p. 203.

130 "Uh, he [Vincent Caulfield]": J. D. Salinger, "The Stranger," *Collier's*, December 1, 1945.

130 "I send you another of": Louise Bogan, letter to William Maxwell, 1944.

131 "Dear M, I send": Ibid.

132 "On a November night": Werner Kleeman and Elizabeth Uhlig, *From Dachau to D-Day*, pp. 97–98.

132 "Winter brought the conditions": Margaret Salinger, *Dream Catcher: A Memoir*, p. 64.

132 "One dreary evening": Werner Kleeman and Elizabeth Uhlig, *From Dachau to D-Day*, pp. 285–86 .

133 "To this day, Kleeman": Noah Rosenberg, "Lifelong Pal Remembers J. D. Salinger," *Queens Courier*, February 2, 2010.

133 "I have the feeling you": J. D. Salinger, letter to Werner Kleeman, 1961.

135 "We flushed three krauts out": Colonel Gerden F. Johnson, *History of the Twelfth Infantry Regiment in World War II*, p. 213.

136 "There were dead bodies all": First Lieutenant John B. Beach, quoted in Edward G. Miller, *A Dark and Bloody Ground: The Hürtgen Forest and the Roer River Dams, 1944-1945*, p. 100.

136 "God, it was cold": Lieutenant Colonel Franklin Sibert, quoted in Edward G. Miller, *A Dark and Bloody Ground: The Hürtgen Forest and the Roer River Dams, 1944-45*, p. 87.

136 "During the night": Colonel Gerden F. Johnson, *History of the Twelfth Infantry Regiment in World War II*, p. 221.

137 "Ernest Hemingway was a correspondent": Edward G. Miller, 4th Infantry Division combat interview.

137 "I hadn't washed or shaved": Bob Wandesforde, quoted in John McManus, *The Deadly Brotherhood*, p. 67.

137 "For those in the know": Paul Fussell, *The Boys' Crusade: The American Infantry in Northwestern Europe, 1944–1945*, p. 84.

138 "Behind them they left": Sergeant Mack Moriss, *Yank: the GI Story of the War*, ed. Deb Meyers, p.12.

CONVERSATION WITH SALINGER #3

139 Barbara Graustark, "Newsmakers," *Newsweek*, July 17, 1978.

5: DEAD MEN IN WINTER

142 "There was a film on": J. D. Salinger, letter to Paul Fitzgerald, February 3, 1960.

142 "They all said it was": Martha Gellhorn, *The Face of War*, p. 145.

142 "Hitler knew Germany": Stephen E. Ambrose, *Citizen Soldiers: The U.S. Army from the Normandy Beaches to the Bulge to the Surrender of Germany*, p. 184.

142 "Hitler realized that by remaining": William L. Shirer, *The Rise and Fall of the Third Reich*, p. 1090.

143 "[The 4th] Division": U.S. Army Historical Division.

143 "In the first frantic days": Sergeant Ed Cunningham, quoted in *Yank: The Story of World War II as Written by the Soldiers*, p. 71.

144 "The enemy's plan was simple": Colonel Gerden F. Johnson, *History of the Twelfth Infantry Regiment in World War II*, p. 231.

144 "There's been a complete breakthrough": Ernest Hemingway, quoted in Stanley Weintraub, *11 Days in December: Christmas at the Bulge, 1944*, p. 55.

144 "The front ran for nearly": Colonel Gerden F. Johnson, *History of the Twelfth Infantry Regiment in World War II*, p. 230.

144 "Roaring cannons along an 80-mile front": Robert E. Merriam, *Dark December: The Full Account of the Battle of the Bulge*, p. 106.

145 "It was dark and it": Paul Fussell, *The Boys' Crusade: The American Infantry in Northwestern Europe, 1944–1945*, pp. 128–29.

145 "The initial German attacks rolled": Colonel Richard Marr, 4th Infantry Division combat interview.

145 "The experienced German infantry": Danny S. Parker, *The Battle of the Bulge: Hitler's Ardennes Offensive, 1944-1945*, p. 86.

146 "The Battle of the Bulge": John Toland, *Battle: The Story of the Bulge*, p. xvii.

146 "To provide the will": Stephen E. Ambrose, *Citizen Soldiers: The U.S. Army from the Normandy Beaches to the Bulge to the Surrender of Germany*, p. 184.

147 "The Germans had infiltrated to": Colonel Gerden F. Johnson, *History of the Twelfth Infantry Regiment in World War II*, p. 94.

148 "My father said that no": Margaret Salinger, *Dream Catcher: A Memoir*, p. 65.

149 "[A G.I. named] Gordon got ripped": Private Bob Conroy, quoted in Paul Fussell, *Boys' Crusade: The American Infantry in Northwestern Europe, 1944–1945*, p. 132.

149 "The casualties had been hit": William Montgomery, quoted in Robert O. Babcock, *War Stories: Utah Beach to Pleiku*, p. 357.

149 "The enemy hoped to break up": Colonel Gerden F. Johnson, *History of the Twelfth Infantry Regiment in World War II*, pp. 233–34.

149 "The Americans used desperate methods": Stephen E. Ambrose, *Citizen Soldiers: The U.S. Army from the Normandy Beaches to the Bulge to the Surrender of Germany*, p. 201.

150 "On Christmas of '44, in": George Knapp, quoted in Robert O. Babcock, *War Stories: Utah Beach to Pleiku*, p. 355.

150 "On those days": Colonel Gerden F. Johnson, *History of the Twelfth Infantry Regiment in World War II*, p. 309.

150 "There were half-tracks and": Martha Gellhorn, *The Face of War*, p. 146.

151 "The fundamental reason": Hanson W. Baldwin, *Battles Lost and Won: Great Campaigns of World War II*, p. 352.

151 "The Fighting Fourth Division": Paul Fitzgerald, unpublished poem.

151 "The 12th Infantry held": Colonel Richard Marr 4th Infantry Division combat interview.

151 "There were many dead and": Martha Gellhorn, *The Face of War*, 1988, p. 152.

152 "The will of the German soldier": John Toland, *Battle: The Story of the Bulge*, p. 377.

153 "I was in the Counter": Charles Meyers, quoted in Bradley R. McDuffie, "For Ernest, with Love and Squalor: The Influence of Ernest Hemingway on J. D. Salinger," *Hemingway Review*, March 22, 2011.

153 "[When Hemingway took a hotel": Leicester Hemingway, *My Brother, Ernest Hemingway*, 4th ed., p. 264.

153 "Every time it snows": Bart Hagerman, quoted in John C. McManus, *The Deadly Brotherhood: The American Combat Soldiers in World War II*, p. 346.

153 "There are many of the living": Ernie Pyle, "On Victory in Europe," draft of a column found on Pyle's body after he was killed in Ie Shima, reprinted at http://journalism.indiana.edu/resources/erniepyle/wartime-columns

/on-victory-in-europe/ and http://wwpbs.org/weta/reportingamericaatwar/reporters/pyle/europe.html.

154 "I remember standing next to": Margaret Salinger, *Dream Catcher: A Memoir*, p. 59.

6: STILL BURNING

155 "Exhausted at war's end, Salinger": United States Holocaust Memorial Museum, *Holocaust Encyclopedia,* "The Fourth Infantry Division," http://www.ushmm.org/wlc/en/article.php?ModuleId=10006134.

158 "As a counter-intelligence officer": Margaret Salinger, *Dream Catcher: A Memoir*, p. 55.

158 "You never really get the": J. D. Salinger, quoted in Margaret Salinger, *Dream Catcher: A Memoir*, p. 55; Jean Miller interview with Shane Salerno.

160 "The first thing I saw": Jack Hallett, quoted in *The Holocaust Chronicle*, p. 609, http://www.holocaustchronicle.org/staticpages/609.html.

161 "Paul Fitzgerald, Salinger's close friend": Shane Salerno, discussing Paul Fitzgerald, letter to the Holocaust Library and Research Center of San Francisco, July 25, 1980; Holocaust Library and Research Center of San Francisco, letter to Paul Fitzgerald, November 14, 1980; Holocaust Library and Research Center of San Francisco, letter to Paul Fitzgerald, February 24, 1981 (letters given to the authors by the Fitzgerald family).

164 "Salinger told [Whit] Burnett he": Paul Alexander, *Salinger: A Biography*, p. 96.

165 "But now—the sudden vast": J. D. Salinger, "Elaine," *Story*, March–April 1945.

7: VICTIM AND PERPETRATOR

168 "The National Broadcasting Company delays": NBC broadcast, May 8, 1945.

168 "I didn't want to rehash": Howard Ruppel, quoted in John C. McManus, *The Deadly Brotherhood: The American Combat Soldiers in World War II*, p. 346.

169 "Salinger wound up receiving five": Eberhard Alsen, discussing Ernest Havemann, "The Recluse in the Rye," *Life* magazine, November 3, 1961; Margaret Salinger *Dream Catcher: A Memoir*, p. 66; "Enlisted Record and Report of Separation Honorable Discharge, Jerome D. Salinger," 1945.

170 "Dear Poppa, I'm writing from": J. D. Salinger, letter to Ernest Hemingway, undated, 1945.

172 "To Whom It May Concern": First Lieutenant A. Raymond Boudreau, CIC letter of recommendation upon honorable discharge, 1945.

176 "My Aunt [Doris] described Sylvia": Margaret Salinger, *Dream Catcher: A Memoir*, p. 71.

183 "The trip over was hell": J. D. Salinger, letter to Paul Fitzgerald, May 24, 1946.

185 "Sylvia and I separated less": J. D. Salinger letter to Paul Fitzgerald, November 23, 1946.

187 "Well. In the first place": Salinger, "A Perfect Day for Bananafish," *The New Yorker*, January 31, 1948.

8: MEASURING UP

196 "In January 1947": Paul Alexander, *Salinger: A Biography*, p. 121.

196 "We like parts of 'The Bananafish'": William Maxwell, letter from William Maxwell to Harold Ober, January 22, 1947.

197 "Did he keep calling you": J. D. Salinger, "A Perfect Day for Bananafish," *The New Yorker*, January 31, 1948.

198 "It really seemed to be": Gay Talese, "Talese on Salinger," *The New York Observer*, February 3, 2010.

199 " 'Listen,' Corinne said": J. D. Salinger, "The Inverted Forest," *Cosmopolitan*, December 1947.

199 "Half a dozen of [Salinger's": Frederick L. Gwynn and Joseph L. Blotner, *The Fiction of J. D. Salinger*, p. 9.

200 "He must have known the": Gloria Murray, quoted in Paul Alexander, *Salinger: A Biography*, p. 132.

200 "I don't know what upset Salinger": Herbert Mayes, quoted in Ian Hamilton, *In Search of J. D. Salinger*, p. 104.

201 "As for me, I signed": J. D. Salinger, letter to Paul Fitzgerald, April 29, 1948.

202 " 'Stop that,' Eloise said": J. D. Salinger, "Uncle Wiggily in Connecticut," *The New Yorker*, March 20, 1948.

202 "My work goes along pretty": J. D. Salinger, letter to Paul Fitzgerald, October 19, 1948.

203 "Dear Miss Olding": Gus Lobrano, letter to Dorothy Olding, December 10, 1948.

204 "Samuel Goldwyn has borrowed": Thomas Brady, "Miss Hayward Set for Goldwyn Film," *The New York Times*, April 2, 1949.

206 "Goldwyn's team": Paul Alexander, *Salinger: A Biography*, p. 140.

207 "All of a sudden he [Walt Glass]": J. D. Salinger, "Uncle Wiggily in Connecticut," *The New Yorker*, March 28, 1948.

207 "Eloise (to Walt)": *My Foolish Heart*, 1949.

208 "If you're interested in movies": J. D. Salinger, letter to Paul Fitzgerald, August 26, 1949.

208 "Eloise: The important thing, Lou": *My Foolish Heart*, 1949.

208 "Full of soap opera clichés": John McCarten, "The Current Cinema," *The New Yorker*, January 28, 1950, p. 75, quoted in Paul Alexander, *Salinger: A Biography*, p. 141.

210 "Dear Swanie: as you know": Jerry Wald, letter to H. L. Swanson, January 25, 1957.

211 "About halfway to the bathroom": J. D. Salinger, *The Catcher in the Rye*, pp. 103–4.

211 "When my college friend Matt": John Seabrook, "A Night at the Movies," *The New Yorker*, February 8, 2010 .

CONVERSATION WITH SALINGER #4

217 Shane Salerno interview with Myles Weber, Paul Alexander, and Michael Silverblatt.

9: THE ORIGIN OF ESMÉ

222 "He won't take his bathrobe": J. D. Salinger, "A Perfect Day for Bananafish," *The New Yorker*, January 31, 1948.

225 "You say you still feel": J. D. Salinger, letter to Jean Miller, undated.

228 "Dear Jean, I arrived in": J. D. Salinger, letter to Jean Miller, March 19, 1949.

229 "Dear Jean, Yours is the": J. D. Salinger, letter to Jean Miller, March 28, 1949.

230 "Over on third base, Mary": J. D. Salinger, "The Laughing Man," *Nine Stories*, 1953.

230 "I've been working steadily": J. D. Salinger, letter to Jean Miller, April 16, 1949.

231 "I grew up in this": J. D. Salinger, letter to Jean Miller, June 3, 1949.

232 "I planted some vegetables yesterday": J. D. Salinger, letter to Jean Miller, April 30, 1953.

232 "You don't think you'll": Ibid.

234 "What a good girl you are": J. D. Salinger, letter to Jean Miller, October 5, 1953.

234 "I was oddly touched": J. D. Salinger, letter to Jean Miller, undated.

235 "It still seems completely": J. D. Salinger, letter to Jean Miller, October 1953.

238 "[In a letter to Michael": Sharon Steel, *TimeOut New York*, March 8, 2010.

10: IS THE KID IN THIS BOOK CRAZY?

244 "My boyhood was very much": J. D. Salinger, interview by Shirlie Blaney, *Daily Eagle* (Claremont, NH), November 13, 1953.

244 "I'd rather be the catcher": J. D. Salinger, *The Catcher in the Rye*, p. 173.

244 "longer, autobiographical piece": J. D. Salinger, letter to Whit Burnett, 1940.

245 "I stood there—boy I": J .D. Salinger, "I'm Crazy," *Collier's*, December 22, 1945.

248 "I've taken a small place": J. D. Salinger, letter to Gus Lobrano, October 12, 1949.

248 "During Salinger's brief stay": Peter De Vries, quoted in Paul Alexander, *Salinger: A Biography* (New York: St. Martin's Griffin, 1999), p. 137.

248 "He'd come over and express": Jon De Vries, quoted in Timothy Dumas, "The Return of Peter De Vries," *Westport Magazine*, April 2006.

248 "I was eating a sandwich": Robert Giroux, "The Art of Publishing No. 3," interview by George Plimpton, *Paris Review*, no. 155 (Summer 2000).

248 "'Mr. Salinger is here,'": Robert Giroux, ibid.

249 "Possibly by now you've": Gus Lobrano, letter to J. D. Salinger, January 25, 1951.

249 "Imprisoned": Gus Lobrano, January 25, 1951.

250 "Tactless": Robert Giroux, "The Art of Publishing No. 3," interview by George Plimpton, *Paris Review*, no. 155 (Summer 2000).

250 "He didn't like it,": Robert Giroux, quoted in Al Silverman, *The Time of Their Lives: The Golden Age of Great American Publishers, Their Editors and Authors* (New York: St. Martin's Press, 2008), p. 27.

251 "Was evidently prudent enough": Louis Menand, "Holden at Fifty," *The New Yorker*, October 1, 2001.

253 "I can't explain what I": J. D. Salinger, *The Catcher in the Rye*, p. 122.

253 "It means a great deal": William Maxwell, *Book-of-The-Month-Club News*, 1951.

253 "I think writing is a": J. D. Salinger, *Book-of-the-Month-Club News*, 1951.

254 "Anyone who has read": J. D. Salinger, dust jacket copy, *The Catcher in the Rye*, 1951.

254 "J. D. Salinger was born in": J. D. Salinger, author's note, *The Catcher in the Rye*, 1951.

255 "I seldom care to know": J. D. Salinger, contributor's note for "Down at the Dinghy," *Harper's*, April 1949 [note published in *Harper's*, February 1959].

255 "I think, even if I": J. D. Salinger, *The Catcher in the Rye*, p. 204.

255 "Here is a novel about": Paul Engle, *Chicago Daily Tribune*, July 15, 1951.

255 "So real it hurts": Irene Elwood, *Los Angeles Times*.

256 "Sponsoring a brilliant, new young": Clifton Fadiman, , *Book-of-the-Month-Club News*, July 1951, quoted in James Lundquist, *J. D. Salinger*, p. 54 .

258 "short story guy": James Stern, "Aw, the World's a Crumby Place," *The New York Times Book Review*, July 15, 1951.

258 "The strange, wonderful language": Nash K. Burger, "Books of the Times; Adolescence Speaking for Itself," *The New York Times*, July 16, 1951.

258 "I was impressed by": William Faulkner, quoted in *Faulkner in the University*, ed. Frederick L. Gwynn and Joseph L. Blotner, pp. 246–47.

259 "Have you read *The Catcher*": Samuel Beckett, letter to Loly Rosset, November 20, 1953.

259 "People are always ruining things": J. D. Salinger, *The Catcher in the Rye*, p. 87.

259 "I fought alongside him in": Werner Kleeman, "Lifelong Pal Remembers J. D. Salinger," *The Queens Courier*, February 2, 2010.

260 "I may give [*The Catcher*": J. D. Salinger, *The New Yorker*, December 1951.

260 "If the teenager as we": Geoff Pevere, "J. D. Salinger, 91: Literary Giant Lived as Recluse," *The Toronto Star*, January 29, 2010.

261 "Holden Caulfield is the Malcolm": Jake Gyllenhaal, interviewed by Chelsea Clinton, *Interview* magazine, February 2003.

261 "Holden Caulfield": Andy Rogers, *The Veteran Who Is, the Boy Who Is No More*.

261 "The mental health professionals": Andy Rogers, *The Veteran Who Is, the Boy Who Is No More*.

262 "If you sat around there": J. D. Salinger, *The Catcher in the Rye*, p. 142.

262 "Salinger's quarrel": Andy Rogers, *The Veteran Who Is, the Boy Who Is No More*.

262 "When I was *really* drunk": J. D. Salinger, *The Catcher in the Rye*, p. 150.

264 "I'm aware": J. D. Salinger, unpublished jacket statement, *The Catcher in the Rye*, 1951.

264 "Among other things you'll find": J. D. Salinger, *The Catcher in the Rye*, p. 189.

265 "If a body catch a": J. D. Salinger, *The Catcher in the Rye*, p. 173.

265 "If a body meet a": Robert Burns, "Comin thro' the Rye," *The Catcher in the Rye*, p. 178.

265 "I can be quite sarcastic": J. D. Salinger, *The Catcher in the Rye*, p. 21.

265 "One day": Billy Wilder quoted in *Conversations with Salinger*, p. 299.

266 "The goddam movies": J. D. Salinger, *The Catcher in the Rye*, p. 104.

267 "Holden Caulfield is not likely": Nancy C. Ralston, quoted in Peter G. Beidler, *A Reader's Companion to J. D. Salinger's* The Catcher in the Rye, p. 62.

11: WE CAN STILL RUN AWAY

271 "First published in mid-July": Pamela Hunt Steinle, *In Cold Fear:* The Catcher in the Rye *Censorship Controversies and Postwar American Character*, p. 15.

272 "In the fall of 1951": Paul Alexander, *Salinger: A Biography*, p. 157.

273 "I was not prepared for": The wife of an editor, quoted in Ian Hamilton, *In Search of J. D. Salinger*, p. 124.

274 "If you want to know": J. D. Salinger, *The Catcher in the Rye*, p. 134.

278 "That fall [of 1951], Salinger": Paul Alexander, *Salinger: A Biography*, pp. 167–68.

278 "Dear Mr. Ross, Just to": J. D. Salinger, letter to Harold Ross, October 6, 1951.

278 "He escaped some of the publicity": James Lundquist, *J. D. Salinger*, p. 27.

278 "Celebrity is a mask that": John Updike, *Self-Consciousness*, p. 252.

280 "I know he and his sister": Margaret Salinger interview with WBUR Radio show "The Connection," September 14, 2000.

281 "[Salinger's] 90-acre tract of land": Paul Alexander, "Cornish, New Hampshire: J. D. Salinger Country," *Travel & Leisure Magazine*, April 1999.

282 "Salinger had bought a small gambrel-roofed cottage": Paul Alexander, *Salinger: A Biography*, p. 168.

282 "That winter [of 1953]": John Skow, "Sonny: An Introduction," *Time*, September 15, 1961.

284 "We have a date": S. J. Perelman, *Don't Tread on Me: Selected Letters*, p. 144.

286 "I knew all about him": Shirlie Blaney, quoted in Ernest Havemann, "The Search for the Mysterious J. D. Salinger: The Recluse in Rye," *Life*, November 3, 1961.

287 "He seemed to be delighted": Shirlie Blaney, quoted ibid.

287 "[Joyce Burrington] Pierce was a": Susan J. Boutwell and Alex Hanson, "J. D. Salinger, Recluse of Cornish, Dies," *Valley News*, January 29, 2010.

287 "My father was a bit leery": Joyce Burrington Pierce, quoted ibid.

287 "Finally I decided": Shirlie Blaney, quoted in Ernest Havemann, "The Search for the Mysterious J. D. Salinger: The Recluse in Rye," *Life*, November 3, 1961.

288 "[Salinger] seems to understand children": John Wain, "Holden and Huck," *The Observer* (London), June 8, 1958, p. 17.

288 "The best thing, though, in": J. D. Salinger, *The Catcher in the Rye*, p. 121.

288 "Leah's knock on my door": J. D. Salinger, "A Girl I Knew," *Good Housekeeping*, February 1948.

289 "Our page came out once": Shirlie Blaney, quoted in Ernest Havemann, "The Search for the Mysterious J. D. Salinger: The Recluse in Rye," *Life*, November 3, 1961.

289 "The Windsor High School [paper] came out": Ernest Havemann, "The Search for the Mysterious J. D. Salinger: The Recluse in Rye," *Life*, November 3, 1961.

289 "During the preparation of": *Claremont Daily Eagle*, November 13, 1953.

CONVERSATION WITH SALINGER #5

293 "Betty Eppes is a reporter": George Plimpton, quoted in "What I Did Last Summer," *The Paris Review*, Summer 1981.

295 "In her letter to Mr.": Edwin McDowell, "Publishing: Visit with J. D. Salinger," *The New York Times*, September 11, 1981.

298 "I've been writing seriously": J. D. Salinger, contributor's note for "Down at the Dinghy," *Harper's*, April 1949 [note published in *Harper's*, February 1959].

298 "I will state this: it": J. D. Salinger, quoted in Betty Eppes, "What I Did Last Summer," *Paris Review*, Summer 1981.

12: FOLLOW THE BULLET: *NINE STORIES*

303 "So far the novels of this war": J. D. Salinger, "Backstage with Esquire," *Esquire*, October 24, 1945, p. 34.

303 "there is a thin": George Highet, "New Books: Always Roaming with a Hungry Heart," *Harper's*, June 1953.

304 "You get off": J. D. Salinger, "A Perfect Day for Bananafish," p. 26.

305 "the only great": Ibid., pp. 7–8.

305 "lose control of" to "see more glass.": Ibid., pp. 8–10, 14.

305 "They're very ordinary-looking" to "through the door": Ibid., p. 23.

305 "raving maniac": Ibid., p. 13.

305 "the belt" to "Sybil's hand": Ibid., p. 19.

305 "Sybil's ankles" to "my love": Ibid., p. 24.

306 "regiment" to "steady it": J. D. Salinger, "Uncle Wiggily in Connecticut," pp. 48-49.

306 "the g.d. war is over": J. D. Salinger, "For Esmé—with Love and Squalor," p. 160.

307 "Why don't you boys": J. D. Salinger, "Uncle Wiggily in Connecticut," p. 52.

307 "husband was stationed" to "something": Ibid., pp. 33–34.

307 "air-minded" to "M.P.": Ibid., pp. 27–28.

307 "Trenton to New York": Ibid., pp. 43–44.

307 "You know what": Ibid., pp. 44–45.

307 "Ever cut your" to "*cute*": J. D. Salinger, "Just Before the War with the Eskimos," pp. 62–71.

307 "bleedin' like mad": Ibid., p. 65.

308 "draft board" to "or something": Ibid., pp. 72–73.

308 "lovely—the first": Ibid., p. 77.

308 "A few years earlier": Ibid., p. 82.

308 "carpenter's vise": J. D. Salinger, "The Laughing Man," p. 87.

309 "face covered with a": Ibid., p. 88.

309 "around the countryside": Ibid., p. 89.

309 "deep but pleasantly" to "escape method": Ibid., pp. 89–90.

309 "the largest personal" to "face": Ibid., pp. 90–91.

310 "best friend": Ibid., pp. 100–2.

310 "two and two together" to "hideous features": Ibid., pp. 102, 108–10.

310 "beloved Black Wing" to "mask": Ibid., pp. 109–10.

310 "in terms of permanently" to "decorously": J. D. Salinger, "Down at the Dinghy," pp. 119, 120–24, 130.

311 "itching imperceptibly" to "lightning": J. D. Salinger, "For Esmé—with Love and Squalor," pp. 133–34.

311 "experience levitation" to "camp": Ibid., pp. 133–35, 137.

311 "military-looking" to "sentimental way of life": Ibid., p. 140, epigraph, pp. 149, 153–55.

312 "getting better acquainted" to "all over the place": Ibid., 156–58, 165.

312 "Home sweet home" to "animal": J. D. Salinger, "Pretty Mouth and Green My Eyes," pp. 178, 180, 186, 188, 181, 182.

313 "at best a" to "enamel flowers": J. D. Salinger, "De Daumier-Smith's Blue Period," pp. 241, 249–50.

313 "wear them whenever" to "thousands of times": J. D. Salinger, "Teddy," pp. 274, 276, 284, 287, 294.

314 "in this world" to "fictional characters": Announcement of Salinger's death, released by Harold Ober Associates, January 28, 2010.

CONVERSATION WITH SALINGER #6

315 "In 1966 I was invited": Pat York, "Catching J. D. Salinger," *The Huffington Post*, February 2, 2010, http://www.huffingtonpost.com/pat-york/catching-jd-salinger_b_446863.html.

13: HIS LONG DARK NIGHT

320 "She arrived at the party": Margaret Salinger, *Dream Catcher: A Memoir*, p. 7.

321 "Her childhood was not one": Margaret Salinger, "Biographer Margaret Salinger Discusses Her Book on Her Father Author J. D. Salinger," *NBC News Today*, September 7, 2000.

322 "The black sheets and the": Claire Douglas, quoted in Margaret Salinger, *Dream Catcher: A Memoir*, p. 12.

323 "I've had two invitations": Letter from Salinger to Miller, undated, 1953.

324 "Uncharacteristically, Salinger threw a party": John Skow, "Sonny: An Introduction," *Time*, September 15, 1961.

326 "As in any good Scott Fitzgerald tale": Maxwell Geismar, "The Wise Child and the *New Yorker* School of Fiction," in *Salinger: A Critical and Personal Portrait*, ed. Henry Grunwald, p. 103.

327 "Lane had sampled his": J. D. Salinger, "Franny," *The New Yorker*, January 29, 1955.

327 "Alienated from her Ivy League boy friend": Paul Levine, "J. D. Salinger: The Development of the Misfit Hero," in *J. D. Salinger and the Critics*, ed. William F. Belcher and James W. Lee, p. 111.

327 " 'Franny' is an indictment": Paul Alexander, *Salinger: A Biography*, p. 185.

327 "*The Way of a Pilgrim*": James Lundquist, *J. D. Salinger*, p. 123.

328 "We must pray unceasingly": *The Way of a Pilgrim*, p. 9.

328 "Lord Jesus Christ, have mercy": *The Way of a Pilgrim*, p. 10.

328 "Stories about his wife": Henry Grunwald, ed., *Salinger: A Critical and Personal Portrait*, p. 21.

329 "Claire Salinger was attracted": Arthur J. Pais, *Rediff*, October 27, 2000.

329 "'You have been chosen'": Paramhansa Yogananda, *Autobiography of a Yogi*, p. 355.

329 "On the train home to Cornish": Claire Douglas, quoted in Margaret Salinger, *Dream Catcher: A Memoir*, p. 91.

330 "A man may live": *The Gospel of Sri Ramakrishna*, translated by Swami Nikhilananda, chapter 20, "Rules for Householders and Monks," (Ramakrishna Math and Ramakrishna Mission, Belur Math, West Bengal, India, 1942 and 2006), http://www.belurmath.org/gospel/.

331 "We did not make love very often": Claire Douglas, quoted in Margaret Salinger, *Dream Catcher: A Memoir*, p. 91.

331 "Between extreme indifference": J. D. Salinger, letter to Swami Nikhilananda, 1972 .

335 "The importance of 'Raise High' ": Bruce Mueller and Will Hochman, *Critical Companion to J. D. Salinger*, p. 279.

335 "["Raise High the Roof Beam, Carpenters"]": James Lundquist, *J. D. Salinger*, p. 137.

336 "[It is] the best": John Updike, "Anxious Days for the Glass Family," *The New York Times Book Review*, September 17, 1961.

336 "I read a bit from the": J. D. Salinger, letter to Swami Adiswarananda, 1975.

336 "'We were up at the Lake": J. D. Salinger, "Raise High the Roof Beam, Carpenters," *The New Yorker*, November 19, 1955.

337 "In the story of his wedding": Ihab Hassan, "J. D. Salinger: Rare Quixotic Gesture," *Western Review*, Summer 1957.

337 "Salinger kills Seymour": Subhash Chandra, *The Fiction of J. D. Salinger*, p. 144.

338 "He has learned to live": Philip Roth, "Writing American Fiction," *Commentary*, March 1961, pp. 223–33.

338 "When he first came": Roger Angell, quoted in Paul Alexander, *Salinger: A Biography*, p. 189.

340 "Imagine the most phobic man": Lawrence Weschler, "Mr. Shawn's *New Yorker*: For Nearly Forty Years William Shawn Was a World Traveler—of Sorts," *Columbia Journalism Review*, March–April 1993.

342 " 'Zooey' is an interminable,": Maxwell Geismar, "The Wise Child and the *New Yorker* School of Fiction," in *Salinger: A Critical and Personal Portrait*, ed. Henry Grunwald, p. 105.

343 "Near the end": Ernest Havemann, "The Search for the Mysterious J. D. Salinger: The Recluse in Rye," *Life*, November 3, 1961.

344 "In each story": Alfred Kazin, "J. D. Salinger: Everybody's Favorite," *The Atlantic Monthly*, August 1961.

344 "The cumulative effect is bright": S. J. Rowland, "Love Parable," *The Christian Century*, October 6, 1961, p. 1464.

345 "During 1958, Salinger had": Paul Alexander, *Salinger: A Biography*, p. 202.

345 "In letters, he reported": Phoebe Hoban, "The Salinger File," *New York* Magazine, June 15, 1987.

345 "He was in New York, working": *New Yorker* intern quoted in Edward Kosner, "The Private World of J. D. Salinger," *New York Post Magazine*, April 30, 1961.

346 "In 'Seymour,' Buddy takes up": William Wiegand, "The Knighthood of J. D. Salinger," *The New Republic*, October 19, 1959.

346 "It is the idea of compromise": James Lundquist, *J. D. Salinger*, p. 142.

346 "Self-consciousness gives the story": Granville Hicks, "J. D. Salinger: Search for Wisdom," *Saturday Review*, July 25, 1959.

347 "There are one or two more": J. D. Salinger, "Seymour: An Introduction," *The New Yorker*, June 6, 1959.

347 "[Since *The Catcher in the Rye*] Salinger has": Michael Walzer, "In Place of a Hero," *Dissent*, Spring 1960.

349 "Yet when I first read": J. D. Salinger, "Seymour: An Introduction," *The New Yorker*, June 6, 1959.

349 "It is 'woman and gold' ": *The Gospel of Sri Ramakrishna*, translated by Swami Nikhilananda, chapter 7, "The Master and Vijay Goswami," http://www.belurmath.org/gospel.

350 "In February 1962 the telephone": Gordon Lish, "A Fool for Salinger," *Antioch Review*, 1986, pp. 408–15, quoted in Paul Alexander, *Salinger: A Biography*, p. 221.

14: A TERRIBLE, TERRIBLE FALL

352 "Ever since Jerome David Salinger": Mel Elfin, "The Mysterious J. D. Salinger. . . His Woodsy, Secluded Life," *Newsweek*, May 30, 1960.

353 "For Salinger, writing": Ibid.

353 "Jerry works like a dog": Bertrand Yeaton, quoted ibid.

355 "It is sunny at the": John Skow, "Sonny: An Introduction," *Time*, September 15, 1961.

358 "At one side of the road": Ernest Havemann, "The Search for the Mysterious J. D. Salinger: The Recluse in Rye," *Life*, November 3, 1961.

360 "He has adopted a T. E.": George Steiner, "The Salinger Industry," *The Nation*, November 14, 1959.

360 "As nearly as possible": J. D. Salinger, dedication to *Franny and Zooey*.

361 " 'Franny' came out in *The New Yorker*": J. D. Salinger, flap copy for *Franny and Zooey*.

362 "There are, I am convinced": Granville Hicks, "J. D. Salinger: Search for Wisdom," *Saturday Review*, July 25, 1959.

363 "Salinger has suffered": Ernest Havemann, "The Search for the Mysterious J. D. Salinger: The Recluse in Rye," *Life*, November 3, 1961.

364 "The characters of Salinger's": John Skow, "Sonny: An Introduction," *Time*, September 15, 1961.

364 "*Franny and Zooey* is better than anything": Charles Poore, "Books of The Times," *The New York Times*, September 14, 1961.

365 "Salinger, it bears repeating": Blake Bailey, *Cheever*, pp. 300-301.

365 "Not the least dismaying": John Updike, "Anxious Days for the Glass Family," *The New York Times Book Review*, September 17, 1961.

367 "What gives": Joan Didion, "Finally (Fashionably) Spurious," *National Review*, November 18, 1961.

367 "I am sorry to have": Alfred Kazin, "J. D. Salinger: 'Everybody's Favorite,'" *The Atlantic Monthly*, August 1961.

367 "[Salinger's] stories read like": Seymour Krim, "Stung by an Exquisite Gadfly," *The Washington Post*, September 17, 1961.

367 "In spite of the intellectual sponginess": Isa Kapp, "Salinger's Easy Victory," *The New Leader*, January 8, 1962.

367 "In Hemingway's work": Mary McCarthy, "J. D. Salinger's Closed Circuit," *Harper's*, October 1962.

369 "This 'prose home movie'": Anne Marple, "Salinger's Oasis of Innocence," *New Republic*, September 18, 1961.

369 "Salinger's skillful use": Howard M. Harper Jr., *Desperate Faith: A Study of Bellow, Salinger, Mailer, Baldwin, and Updike*, p. 94.

370 "'Seymour: An Introduction'": Orville Prescott, "Books of the Times," *The New York Times*, January 28, 1963.

370 "Both of these stories": Irving Howe, "More Reflections in the Glass Mirror," *The New York Times Book Review*, April 7, 1963.

370 "I have just finished reading": Jose de M. Platanopez, "Salinger," letter to the editor, *The New York Times Book Review*, May 26, 1963.

370 "It is necessary to say": Norman Mailer, "Some Childern of the Goddess: Further Evaluations of the Talent in the Room," *Esquire*, July 1963.

378 "I sent over Shawn's letter": Jim Bellows, *The Last Editor*, pp. 7, 10.

380 "When J. D. Salinger's": Janet Malcolm, "Justice to J. D. Salinger," *New York Review of Books*, June 21, 2001.

381 "It was suddenly borne in": J. D. Salinger, "Hapworth 16, 1924," *The New Yorker*, June 19, 1965.

383 "Nobody writes about suicide": Ian Hamilton, *In Search of J. D. Salinger*, p. 273.

384 "Mrs. Claire Salinger has been treated": Gerard L. Gaudrault, M.D., statement in petition for divorce of Claire Douglas and J. D. Salinger, quoted in Paul Alexander, *Salinger: A Biography*, p. 236.

385 "No one said": Margaret Salinger, "Biographer Margaret Salinger Discusses Her Book on Her Father Author J. D. Salinger," *NBC News Today*, September 7, 2000.

385 "The libelee, wholly regardless": Claire Douglas, quoted in Paul Alexander, *Salinger: A Biography*, p. 236.

386 "Divorced: J. D. Salinger": *Time*, November 24, 1967.

386 "You have the right to": *The Bhagavad-Gita* 2, 47.

387 "I had moved to Cornish": Edward Jackson Bennett, "Encounter with Salinger," *New Hampshire* magazine, August 2009.

CONVERSATION WITH SALINGER #7

391 Salerno interview with Tom Wolfe.

CONVERSATION WITH SALINGER #8

392 Salerno interview with Ethel Nelson.

15: SEYMOUR'S SECOND SUICIDE

395 "He explored Scientology": Margaret Salinger, *Dream Catcher: A Memoir*, p. 95.

395 "For some years": Ian Hamilton, *In Search of J. D. Salinger*, p. 92.

396 "In our research": Eberhard Alsen, "J. D. Salinger, Somerset Maugham, and Vedanta Hinduism," unpublished essay.

396 "D. T. Suzuki": Margaret Salinger, *Dream Catcher: A Memoir*, p. 9.

396 "After *Catcher*, Salinger became": Donald Simons, "J. D. Salinger and Vedanta," (blog post), December 2, 2012.

396 Information about the four stages: Eberhard Alsen, "J. D. Salinger and Vedanta: The Four Stages and the Four Paths of Life," unpublished essay.

397 "I never saw such a bunch of apple-eaters": J. D. Salinger, "Teddy," *Nine Stories*, p. 191.

397 "experienced a transformation": Donald Simons, "J. D. Salinger and Vedanta" (blog post), December 2, 2012.

397 "according to the Center": Press release from Ramakrishna-Vivekananda Center of New York, April 3, 2013, http://www.pr.com/press-release/482721.

397 "A man may live": *The Gospel of Sri Ramakrishna*, pp. 180, 557.

398 "Swami Premananda": Margaret Salinger, *Dream Catcher: A Memoir*, pp. 89–90.

398 "*New York Post*": J. D. Salinger, "Man-Forsaken Men," *New York Post Magazine*, December 9, 1959, p. 48.

398 "Also, in 1959": Ian Hamilton, *In Search of J. D. Salinger*, p. 123.

399 "In 1967 he wrote": J. D. Salinger, letter to Swami Nikhilananda, May 1, 1967.

399 "In *The Influence of*": Sumitra Paniker, "The Influence of Eastern Thoughts on 'Teddy' and the Seymour Glass Stories of J. D. Salinger," Ph.D. thesis, 1971, University of Texas at Austin.

399 "In 1972 Salinger wrote": J. D. Salinger, letter to Swami Nikhilananda, January 19, 1972.

400 "Later in 1972": A. L. Bardach, "What Did J. D. Salinger, Leo Tolstoy, and Sarah Bernhardt Have in Common?" *Wall Street Journal*, March 30, 2012.

400 "in a letter he wrote in 1973": J. D. Salinger, letter to Swami Adiswarananda, December 7, 1973.

400 "In 1975 Salinger wrote again": J. D. Salinger, letter to Swami Adiswarananda, December 26, 1975.

400 "He is in this world": Announcement of Salinger's death, released by Harold Ober Associates, January 28, 2010.

401 "For the last five decades": Press release from Ramakrishna-Vivekananda Center of New York, April 3, 2013, http://www.pr.com/press-release/482721.

401 "On April 12, 2013": Ibid.

401 "Ramakrishna died in 1886": A. L. Bardach,"What Did J. D. Salinger, Leo Tolstoy, and Sarah Bernhardt Have in Common?" *Wall Street Journal*, March 30, 2012.

402 "There isn't anyone *anywhere*": *Franny and Zooey*, pp. 201–2 .

402 "Vedanta: 'The goal is' ": A. L. Bardach, "What Did J. D. Salinger, Leo Tolstoy, and Sarah Bernhardt Have in Common?" *Wall Street Journal*, March 30, 2012.

402 "Vedanta: 'As soon as'": Ibid.

402 "Buddy: 'An unknown boy'": J. D. Salinger, *Raise High the Roof Beam, Carpenters and Seymour: An Introduction*, pp. 205–6.

403 "nutcase": Margaret Salinger, *Dream Catcher: A Memoir*, p. 44.

403 "a condition, not a man": J. D. Salinger, letter to Frances Glassmoyer, August 7, 1944.

403 "As the author A. L. Bardarch": A. L. Bardach, "What Did J. D. Salinger, Leo Tolstoy, and Sarah Bernhardt Have in Common?" *Wall Street Journal*, March 30, 2012.

403 "The trouble is": "Teddy," *Nine Stories*, pp. 191, 188.

404 "I'm sick to death of just liking people"; "I'm just sick of ego, ego, ego."; "I mean all these really advanced": J. D. Salinger, "Franny," *Franny and Zooey*, pp. 20, 29, 39.

404 "flatting": J. D. Salinger, "For Esmé—with Love and Squalor," *Nine Stories*, p. 87.

404 "I've been reading": "Raise High the Roof Beam, Carpenters," *Raise High the Roof Beam, Carpenters and Seymour: An Introduction*, p. 91.

404 "One thing I *know*": J. D. Salinger, "Zooey," *Franny and Zooey*, p. 196.

405 "I tend to regard myself": J. D. Salinger, "Seymour: An Introduction," *Raise High the Roof Beam, Carpenters and Seymour: An Introduction*, p. 208.

405 "*Raja-Yoga* and *Bhakti-Yoga*": J. D. Salinger, "Hapworth 16, 1924," *The New Yorker*, June 19, 1965.

405 "As Som P. Ranchan": Som P. Ranchan, *An Adventure in Vedanta: J. D. Salinger's The Glass Family*, pp. 106–7.

406 "In 'The Holy Refusal'": Dipti R. Pattanaik, "'The Holy Refusal': A Vedantic Interpretation of J. D. Salinger's Silence," *MELUS* 23, no. 2 (Summer 1998), p. 119.

407 "Three key Vedantic concepts": A.L. Bardach, "What Did J. D. Salinger, Leo Tolstoy, and Sarah Bernhardt Have in Common?" *Wall Street Journal*, March 30, 2012.

CONVERSATION WITH SALINGER #9

408 Shane Salerno interview with A. Scott Berg.

16: DEAR MISS MAYNARD

409 J. D. Salinger letters to Joyce Maynard.

17: DEAR MR. SALINGER

420 Joyce Maynard.

CONVERSATION WITH SALINGER #10

444 Shane Salerno interview with David Victor Harris as well as Stayton, Alexander, and Howland.

CONVERSATION WITH SALINGER #11

451 Shane Salerno interview with Michael McDermott.

453 "Two shitty literary kids": J. D. Salinger letter to Michael Mitchell, August 31, 1979.

CONVERSATION WITH SALINGER #12

454 Paul Corkery, "Solitude May Be Bliss for Author J. D. Salinger, but to Son Matt, All the World's a Stage," *People* magazine, October 31, 1983.

457 "Matt Salinger: Into the Spotlight," by David Remnick, *The Washington Post*, December 28, 1984.

460 J. D Salinger, letter to Michael Mitchell, December 16, 1992.

18: ASSASSINS

462 "Paul: A substitute teacher out": John Guare, *Six Degrees of Separation*, pp. 24–25.

464 "Chapman was graduated from high": James Yuenger, "Tormented Man Who Thought He Was Lennon," *Chicago Tribune*, December 14, 1980.

464 "[I remember] a guy down on": Tony Adams, quoted in Jack Jones, *Let Me Take You Down*, p. 124.

464 "Too unsettled to continue in": James Yuenger, "Tormented Man Who Thought He Was Lennon," *Chicago Tribune*, December 14, 1980.

464 "Chapman and another young volunteer": Jack Jones, *Let Me Take You Down*, pp. 125–26.

464 "Chapman returned from Lebanon": James Yuenger, "Tormented Man Who Thought He Was Lennon," *Chicago Tribune*, December 14, 1980.

464 "I had come off the": Mark David Chapman, quoted in Jack Jones, *Let Me Take You Down*, p. 131.

464 "Paul Tharp, community relations director": Paul L. Montgomery, "Police Trace Tangled Path Leading to Lennon's Slaying at the Dakota," *The New York Times*, December 10, 1980.

464 "On Oct. 27, Mr. Chapman": Ibid.

467 "Well, he, he's a phony": Mark David Chapman, speaking on *Larry King Live*, September 30, 2000.

468 "Returning to Reeves's apartment": Jack Jones, *Let Me Take You Down*, p. 198.

469 "On December 8, 1980, Mark": Mark David Chapman, speaking on *Larry King Live*, September 30, 2000.

470 "The adult and the child": Mark David Chapman, quoted in Jack Jones, *Let Me Take You Down*, p. 44.

470 "About 5 p.m.": Paul L. Montgomery, "Police Trace Tangled Path Leading to Lennon's Slaying at the Dakota," *The New York Times*, December 10, 1980.

470 "I left the hotel room": Mark David Chapman, speaking on *Larry King Live*, September 30, 2000.

470 "A newspaper reproduction": Paul L. Montgomery, "Police Trace Tangled Path Leading to Lennon's Slaying at the Dakota," *The New York Times*, December 10, 1980.

471 "The Lennons returned": Ibid.

472 "John came out, and he": Mark David Chapman, speaking on *Larry King Live*, September 30, 2000.

472 "As the couple walked by": Paul L. Montgomery, "Police Trace Tangled Path Leading to Lennon's Slaying at the Dakota," *The New York Times*, December 10, 1980.

472 "Afterwards, it was like the": Mark David Chapman, speaking on *Larry King Live*, September 30, 2000.

473 "Officer Moran said": Paul L. Montgomery, "Police Trace Tangled Path Leading to Lennon's Slaying at the Dakota," *The New York Times*, December 10, 1980.

476 "I never wanted to hurt": Mark David Chapman, written statement to the police, quoted in Jack Jones, *Let Me Take You Down*, pp. 65–66.

478 "The reason I wanted": Mark David Chapman, letter from jail to officer Steven Spiro, January 28, 1983, Steven Spiro reading letter to Shane Salerno in interview.

480 "Have you read *The Catcher*": Mark David Chapman, letter to Steven Spiro, January 15, 1983.

480 "So it didn't end with": Mark David Chapman, speaking on *Larry King Live*, September 30, 2000.

481 "Across from the Dakota": Dinty W. Moore, *Between Panic and Desire*, p. 61.

482 "The list of ingredients": Jack Jones, *Let Me Take You Down*, pp. 242–43.

482 "Hinckley settled on assassination": Dinty W. Moore, *Between Panic and Desire*, p. 61.

483 "A teacher's aide": Robert D. McFadden, "Hostages at L.I. School Are Freed, and Gunman Then Kills Himself," *The New York Times*, May 17, 1983.

483 "Mr. Wickes was calm": James Barron, "Last Hostage Recounts the Violent End of Siege at L.I. School," *The New York Times*, May 18, 1983.

485 "From his parents' house in a treeless": Stephen Braun and Charisse Jones, "Victim, Suspect from Different Worlds," *Los Angeles Times*, July 23, 1989.

485 "The star of the television series": Associated Press, July 22, 1989.

485 "Later, acting on information": Stephen Braun and Charisse Jones, *The Los Angeles Times*, July 23, 1989.

487 "I'm not blaming a book": Mark David Chapman, speaking on *Larry King Live*, September 30, 2000.

19: A PRIVATE CITIZEN

491 "For the past two decades": J. D. Salinger, quoted in court documents in Ian Hamilton, *In Search of J. D. Salinger*, p. 199.

492 "[After a visit to Martha's Vineyard in August,] I ended up": S. J. Perelman, *Don't Tread on Me: Selected Letters*, p. 320.

492 "Through the years, Salinger would": Andreas Brown, quoted in Paul Alexander, *Salinger: A Biography*, p. 239.

493 "The more I age": J. D. Salinger, letter to Janet Eagleson, August 9, 1982.

494 "I'm in the middle": J. D. Salinger, letter to Janet Eagleson, August 9, 1982.

494 "According to the suit": "J. D. Salinger Files Impersonation Lawsuit," *The New York Times*, October 14, 1982.

494 "A settlement has been reached": "J. D. Salinger in Accord on Impersonation Suit," Associated Press, November 6, 1982.

495 "Four years ago [in 1983],": Ian Hamilton, *In Search of J. D. Salinger, p.* 3.

495 "Dear Sir: You say you've": J. D. Salinger, letter to Ian Hamilton, quoted in Phoebe Hoban, "The Salinger File," *New York*, June 15, 1987.

497 "[In a letter Michael Mitchell]": Sharon Steel, *TimeOut New York*, March 8, 2010.

498 "That terrible ordeal": Lillian Ross, quoted in Paul Alexander, *Salinger: A Biography*, p. 285.

498 "'At any time during the past'": deposition of J. D. Salinger, October 7, 1986.

499 "My thought is that": Robert Callagy, quoted in Paul Alexander, *Salinger: A Biography*, p. 286.

499 "There is an overexcited, wound-up": Ian Hamilton, "In Search of J. D. Salinger," *People* magazine, June 6, 1988.

499 "The letters are also": Mordecai Richler, "Summer Reading, Rises at Dawn, Writes, Then Retires," *The New York Times Book Review*, June 5, 1988.

500 "At one point": Robert Callagy, quoted in Paul Alexander, *Salinger: A Biography*, p. 287.

501 "It is my view": Pierre N. Leval, New York District Court Judge, November 5, 1986, judgment, quoted in Ian Hamilton, *In Search of J. D. Salinger*, p. 203.

501 "In July 1983": United States Court of Appeals, Second Circuit, January 29, 1987.

503 "Public awareness": Ian Hamilton, *In Search of J. D. Salinger*, p. 208.

503 "A biography of J. D. Salinger": Arnold H. Lubasch, "Salinger Biography Is Blocked," *The New York Times*, January 30, 1987.

504 "If you take this opinion": Robert Callagy, quoted in Phoebe Hoban, "The Salinger File," *New York* magazine, June 15, 1987, p. 42.

504 "The Supreme Court yesterday": Eleanor Blau, "High Court Refuses to Review Salinger Book Ruling," *The New York Times*, October 6, 1987.

506 "Mr. Hamilton's biography": Mordecai Richler, "Summer Reading; Rises at Dawn, Writes, Then Retires," *The New York Times Book Review*, June 5, 1988.

507 "In the spring of 1988": David Remnick, "Exile on Main Street: Don DeLillo's Undisclosed Underworld," *The New Yorker*, September 15, 1997.

507 "One day in April 1988": Paul Alexander, *Salinger: A Biography*, p. 288.

508 "The withheld work of art": Don DeLillo, *Mao II*, p. 67.

509 "Mr. Salinger's modest house": William H. Honan, "Fire Fails to Shake Salinger's Seclusion," *The New York Times*, October 24, 1992.

509 "He liked living in New": Lillian Ross, "My Long Friendship with J. D. Salinger," *The New Yorker*, February 8, 2010.

509 "I'm impressed, mightily, at": J. D Salinger, letter to Paul Fitzgerald, July 27, 1990.

510 "Windsor, Vermont/Cornish": Paul Fitzgerald, diary entry, September 26, 1991.

511 "Called on Salinger": Paul Fitzgerald, diary entry, September 27, 1991.

511 "J. D. Salinger's home was heavily": "J. D. Salinger's House Burns," Associated Press, October 21, 1992.

511 "Jerry used to come": Burnace Fitch Johnson, quoted in Paul Alexander, "J. D. Salinger's Women," *New York* magazine, February 9, 1998.

511 "Not even a fire": William H. Honan, "Fire Fails to Shake Salinger's Seclusion," *The New York Times*, October 24, 1992.

512 "Thanks, too, for your concern": J. D. Salinger, postcard to Paul Fitzgerald, December 1993.

513 "A fire ravaged Salinger's home": Sharon Steel, "Letters by J. D. Salinger," *Time Out*, December 16, 1992.

513 "His search for landsmen led": Margaret Salinger, quoted in Linton Weeks, "The Driven Character of J. D. Salinger," *The Los Angeles Times*, September 6, 2000.

517 "In 1988, Roger Lathbury": Ian Shapiro, "Publisher Roger Lathbury Recalls Book Deal with J. D. Salinger That Went Sour," *The Washington Post*, January 29, 2010.

517 "Here was the voice": Roger Lathbury, quoted ibid.

518 "I was a bit nervous": Ibid.

518 "Salinger insisted on": Ibid.

518 "I foolishly gave an interview": Roger Lathbury quoted ibid.

518 "J. D. Salinger, whose life": David Streitfeld, "Salinger Book to Break Long Silence," *The Washington Post*, January 17, 1997.

519 "This is a book meant for readers": Roger Lathbury, quoted in David Streitfeld, "Salinger Book to Break Long Silence," *The Washington Post*, January 17, 1997.

519 "Seymour was the one": Michiko Kakutani, "From Salinger, a New Dash of Mystery," *The New York Times*, February 20, 1997.

520 "My general feeling is anguish": Roger Lathbury, quoted in Ian Shapiro, "Publisher Roger Lathbury Recalls Book Deal with J. D. Salinger That Went Sour," *The Washington Post*, January 29, 2010.

520 ["Hapworth" is] like the *Dead Sea Scrolls*": Ron Rosenbaum, quoted in David Streitfeld, "Salinger Book to Break Long Silence," *The Washington Post*, January 20, 1997.

526 "In the 25 intervening years": Larissa MacFarquhar, "The Cult of Joyce Maynard," *The New York Times Magazine*, September 6, 1998.

527 "Flatly written, with detail": Elizabeth Gleick, "Ah, Dull Revenge," *Time*, September 7, 1998 .

527 "What we have is two celebrities": Cynthia Ozick, quoted in Peter Applebome, "Love Letters in the Wind," *The New York Times*, May 12, 1999.

527 "[*At Home in the World* is] smarmy": Jonathan Yardley, "Avert Your Eyes! (But Read This First)," *The Washington Post*, August 24, 1998 .

527 "I wonder, why you are": Joyce Maynard, posting on her website, quoted in Paul Alexander, "J. D. Salinger's Women," *New York* magazine, February 9, 1998.

528 "The intensity of the literary catfight": Juliet Waters, "Critiquing the Catfight over Joyce Maynard's Biography," *Montreal Mirror*, October 8, 1998.

528 "Although many readers will": Michiko Kakutani, "More of Her Life, and Love, to Look Back On," *The New York Times*, September 8, 1998.

528 "Defiant, taunting, score-settling": Lisa Schwarzbaum, review of *At Home in the World*, by Joyce Maynard, *Entertainment Weekly*, September 18, 1998.

528 "It's easy to make fun": Katha Pollitt, "With Love and Squalor," *The New York Times Book Review*, September 13, 1998.

529 "Fifteen minutes into our first date": man quoted in Paul Alexander, "J. D. Salinger's Women," *New York*, February 9, 1998.

529 "Paul, old friend, No real news": J. D. Salinger, card to Paul Fitzgerald, December 1998.

530 "Now, 27 years later": Cathleen McGuigan, "Whose Life Is It Anyway?" *Newsweek*, May 24, 1999.

530 "What of the letter-writer's": Joyce Carol Oates, "Words of Love, Priced to Sell," *The New York Times*, May 18, 1999.

531 "I went to Sotheby's": Maureen Dowd, "Leech Women in Love!" *The New York Times*, May 19, 1999.

531 "Peter Norton, a software millionaire": Marc Peyser, "Open Season on Salinger," *Newsweek*, July 5, 1999.

532 "My intention is to do": Peter Norton, quoted in Dinitia Smith, "J. D. Salinger's Love Letters Sold to Entrepreneur Who Says He Will Return Them," *The New York Times*, June 23, 1999.

532 "The daughter of the obsessively": Doreen Carvajal, "Salinger's Daughter Plans to Publish a Memoir," *The New York Times*, June 24, 1999.

532 "It turned out that I": Margaret Salinger interview with Diane Rehm, *The Diane Rehm Show*, NPR, September 13, 2000, http://thedianerehmshow.org/shows/2000-09-13/margaret-salinger-dream-catcher-washington-square-press.

533 "The Plaza [Hotel in New York]": Dinitia Smith, "Salinger's Daughter's Truths as Mesmerizing as His Fiction," *The New York Times*, August 30, 2000.

534 "Certainly, in my family, [writing]": Margaret Salinger interview with Diane Rehm, *The Diane Rehm Show*, NPR, September 13, 2000, http://thedianerehmshow.org/shows/2000-09-13/margaret-salinger-dream-catcher-washington-square-press.

535 "She says she wrote it": Ron Rosenbaum, "The Flight from Fortress Salinger," *New York Times Book Review*, October 8, 2000.

536 "One woman, responding to a": Thomas Childers, *Soldier from the War, Returning*, p. 10.

536 "Of all the private documents": Benjamin Anastas, "An Unexamined Life," in *With Love and Squalor*, ed. Kip Kotzen and Thomas Beller, pp. 150–51.

537 "It seems to me that": Sven Birkerts, "Margaret Invades J. D.'s Studio; She Should Have Let Daddy Work," *The Observer*, September 18, 2000.

537 "*Dream Catcher* is indeed": Jonathan Yardley, "Punching Salinger Below the Belt," *The Washington Post*, September 1, 2000.

538 "Ladies and gentlemen": Judith Shulevitz, "Salinger on Trial," *Slate.com*, September 21, 2000.

539 "Gosh, I wish": Margaret Salinger, CNN.com interview, September 7, 2000, http://www.cnn.com/chat/transcripts/2000/9/7/salinger.

540 "I really would like to": Margaret Salinger, speaking in *CNN* interview with Bill Hemmer, September 7, 2000, http://transcripts.cnn.com/TRANSCRIPTS/0009/07/mn.08.html.

542 "I love my father very much": Matthew Salinger, quoted in Leslie Aldridge Westoff.

542 "I would prefer not to speak": Margaret Salinger, CNN.com interview, September 7, 2000.

542 "Of course, I can't say": Matthew Salinger, letter to *The New York Observer*, September 25, 2000.

20: A MILLION MILES AWAY IN HIS TOWER

546 "Salinger had invited me for": Renata Adler, *Gone: The Last Days of The New Yorker*, June 2000, pp. 98–99.

546 "Salinger has been seen": Walter Scott, "Walter Scott's Personality Parade," *Parade*, May 23, 1971.

546 "He's just working": Richard Haitch, *The New York Times*, February 12, 1978.

546 "Another friend, Jonathan Schwarz, tells": Richard Brooks, *London Sunday Times*, "J. D. Salinger 'Has 15 New Books in Safe,'" March 21, 1999.

547 "My sister and I": Matthew Salinger, quoted in David Remnick, "Matt Salinger: Into the Spotlight," *The Washington Post*, December 28, 1984.

547 "At one point during the more than half century": Lillian Ross, "Bearable," *The New Yorker*, February 8, 2010.

547 "Salinger's place in Cornish history": Hillel Italie, "J. D. Salinger's New Hampshire Hometown Has a Rich Artistic History," *USA Today*, February 7, 2010.

547 "Mr. Salinger was a regular": Katie Zezima, "J. D. Salinger a Recluse? Well, Not to His Neighbors," *The New York Times*, January 31, 2010.

548 "Salinger would occasionally take in": John Curran, Associated Press, January 29, 2010.

548 "He would, until recent years": Katie Zezima, "J. D. Salinger a Recluse? Well, Not to His Neighbors," *The New York Times*, January 31, 2010.

549 "Gwen Tetirick, one of Salinger's": Ashley Blum, "Town Shielded Salinger from Visitors," *The Dartmouth*, February 4, 2010.

549 "We all just say 'J. D.": Gwen Tetirick, quoted ibid.

549 "In order to be accepted": Annabelle Cone, quoted by Ashley Blum, "Town Shielded Salinger from Visitors," *The Dartmouth*, February 4, 2010.

549 "[Salinger] was like the Batman": Mike Ackerman, quoted by Katie Zezima, "J. D. Salinger a Recluse? Well, Not to His Neighbors," *The New York Times*, January 31, 2010.

549 "Locals concur that Salinger": Tom Leonard, "What I Heard at J. D. Salinger's Doorstep," *The Spectator*, April 1, 2009.

549 "During the last two years": Ashley Blum, "Town Shielded Salinger from Visitors," *The Dartmouth*, February 4, 2010.

549 "His wife stopped by the last two Saturdays": Susan J. Boutwell and Alex Hanson, "J. D. Salinger, Recluse of Cornish, Dies" *Valley News*, January 29, 2010.

550 "J. D. Salinger, who was thought": Charles McGrath, "J. D. Salinger, Literary Recluse, Dies at 91," *The New York Times*, January 28, 2010.

550 "In keeping with his lifelong": Harold Ober Associates statement, quoted in Charles McGrath, "J. D. Salinger, Literary Recluse, Dies at 91," *The New York Times*, January 28, 2010.

551 "Cornish is a truly remarkable place": Colleen O'Neill, quoted in Susan J. Boutwell and Alex Hanson, "J. D. Salinger, Recluse of Cornish, Dies," *Valley News*, January 29, 2010.

551 "Obviously, we're prepared": Doug Hackett, quoted in, Susan J. Boutwell and Alex Hanson, "Salinger's Neighbors Protected Him," *Rutland Herald*, January 29, 2010.

551 "No one else could make": Lillian Ross, "Bearable," *The New Yorker*, February 8, 2010.

551 "Matt Salinger answered the doorbell": John Curran, Associated Press, January 29, 2010.

551 "J. D. Salinger, who died last month at 91": Jennifer Schuessler, "Inside the List," *The New York Times Book Review*, February 4, 2010.

551 "There are lots of good": Adam Gopnik, "What Salinger Means to Me," *All Things Considered*, NPR, January 28, 2010.

552 "Ernest Hemingway famously said": Rick Moody, "Salinger: An Influential Voice, Even in 'Silence,'" NPR, January 28, 2010.

552 "Some critics dismissed the easy": Michiko Kakutani, "Of Teen Angst and an Author's Alienation," *The New York Times*, January 28, 2010.

553 "Lost along the way, much": Stephen Metcalf, "Salinger's Genius: He Was the Great Poet of Post-Traumatic Stress," *Slate*, January 28, 2010.

554 "I have never been bothered by": Michael Tannenbaum, "Twice Dead," *Johns Hopkins Newsletter*, February 4, 2010.

554 "Everyone is trying to keep": Annabelle Cone, quoted in Ashley Blum, "Town Shielded Salinger from Visitors," *The Dartmouth*, February 4, 2010.

554 "Depending on one's point of view": Charles McGrath, "J. D. Salinger, Literary Recluse, Dies at 91," *The New York Times*, January 28, 2010.

555 "My own pet theory is": Dave Eggers, "Remembering Salinger: Dave Eggers," *The New Yorker* blog, January 29, 2010, http://www.newyorker.com/online/blogs/books/2010/01/remembering-salinger-dave-eggers.html.

556 "Jay McInerney, a young star": Hillel Italie, Associated Press, February 7, 2010.

558 "My father on many occasions": Margaret Salinger, *Dream Catcher: A Memoir*, p. 47.

558 "Boy, when you're dead, they": J. D. Salinger, *The Catcher in the Rye*, July 1951.

559 "I am in this world": J. D. Salinger, Harold Ober Associates statement, quoted in Charles McGrath, "J. D. Salinger, Literary Recluse, Dies at 91," *The New York Times*, January 28, 2010 .

21: JEROME DAVID SALINGER: A CONCLUSION

560 "meeting up with those he loves": Harold Ober Associates statement, quoted in Charles McGrath, "J. D. Salinger, Literary Recluse, Dies at 91," *The New York Times*, January 28, 2010.

562 "I'm a condition, not a man": J. D. Salinger, letter to Frances Glassmoyer, August 7, 1944.

562 "avoid woman and gold": *The Gospel of Sri Ramakrishna*, translated by Swami Nikhilananda, Chapter 7, "The Master and Vijay Goswami," http://www.belurmath.org/gospel.

563 "in this world": Harold Ober Associates statement, quoted in Charles McGrath, "J. D. Salinger, Literary Recluse, Dies at 91," *The New York Times*, January 28, 2010.

563 "little Oona is in love": J. D. Salinger, letter to Elizabeth Murray, undated.

563 "just not right for us": William Maxwell, letter to Dorothy Olding, February 4, 1944.

BIBLIOGRAPHY

Adler, Renata. *Gone: The Last Days of the New Yorker.* New York: Simon & Schuster, 1999.

Alexander, Paul. "Biography of J. D. Salinger." In *J. D. Salinger*, edited by Harold Bloom. Bloom's BioCritiques. Philadelphia: Chelsea House, 2000.

———. "J. D. Salinger's Women." *New York*, February 9, 1998.

———. *Salinger: A Biography.* Los Angeles: Renaissance Books, 1999.

Alighieri, Dante. *The Inferno.* Translated by John Ciardi. New York: New American Library, 1954.

Alsen, Eberhard. "New Light on the Nervous Breakdowns of Salinger's Sergeant X and Seymour Glass." *CLA Journal* 45, no. 3 (2000): 379–87.

———. "'Raise High the Roof Beam, Carpenters' and the Amateur Reader." *Studies in Short Fiction* 17 (Winter 1980): 39–47.

———. *A Reader's Guide to J. D. Salinger.* Westport, CT: Greenwood Press, 2002.

———. "The Role of Vedanta Hinduism in Salinger's Seymour Novel." *Renascence* 33, no. 2 (1981): 99–116.

———. *Salinger's Glass Stories as a Composite Novel.* Troy, NY: Whitston, 1983.

———. "Seymour: A Chronology." *English Record* 29, no. 4 (1978): 28–30.

Ambrose, Steven E. *Citizen Soldiers: The U.S. Army from the Normandy Beaches to the Bulge to the Surrender of Germany.* New York: Simon & Schuster, 1997.

———. *D-Day, June 6, 1944: The Climactic Battle of World War II.* New York: Simon & Schuster, 1994.

———. *The Victors: Eisenhower and His Boys: The Men of World War II.* New York: Simon & Schuster, 1999.

Amur, G. S. "Theme, Structure, and Symbol in *The Catcher in the Rye.*" *Indian Journal of American Studies* 1 (1969): 11–24.

Antico, John. "The Parody of J. D. Salinger: Esmé and the Fat Lady Exposed." *Modern Fiction Studies* 12, no. 3 (1966): 325–40.

Antonio, Eugene Dale. "The Fiction of J. D. Salinger: A Search through Taoism." Ph.D. diss., Florida State University, 1991.

Arthur, Max. *Forgotten Voices of World War II: A New History of World War II in the Words of the Men and Women Who Were There.* Guilford, CT: Lyons Press, 2004.

Babcock, Robert O. *War Stories: Utah Beach to Pleiku.* St. John's Press, 2001.

"Backstage with *Esquire.*" *Esquire*, September 1941, 24.

"Backstage with *Esquire*," *Esquire*, October 1945.

Bailey, Blake. *Cheever: A Life.* New York: Knopf, 2009.

Baldwin, Hanson W. *Battles Lost and Won: Great Campaigns of World War II.* Old Saybrook, CT: Konecky & Konecky, 2000.

Balkoski, Joseph. *Utah Beach: The Amphibious Landing and Airborne Operations on D-Day, June 6, 1944.* Mechanicsburg, PA: Stackpole Book, 2004.

Baro, Gene. "Some Suave and Impressive Slices of Life." *New York Herald Tribune Book Review*, April 12, 1953, 6.

Barr, Donald. "Ah, Buddy: Salinger." In *The Creative Present*, edited by Nona Balakian and Charles Simmons, 27–62. New York: Gordian Press, 1973.

———. "Saints, Pilgrims and Artists." *Commonweal*, October 25, 1957, 88–90.

———. "The Talent of J. D. Salinger." *Commonweal*, October 30, 1959, 165, 167.

Barron, Cynthia M. "The Catcher and the Soldier: Hemingway's 'Soldier's Home' and Salinger's *The Catcher in the Rye.*" *Hemingway Review* 2, no. 1 (1982) 70–73.

Barrows, R. M., and E. X. Pastor. *The Kit Book for Soldiers, Sailors, and Marines.* Chicago: Consolidated, 1943.

Baskett, Sam S. "The Splendid/Squalid World of J. D. Salinger." *Wisconsin Studies in Contemporary Literature* 4, no. 1 (1963): 48–61.

Baumbach, Jonathan, Jr. "The Saint as a Young Man: A Reappraisal of *The Catcher in the Rye.*" *Modern Language Quarterly* 25 (December 1964): 461–72.

Bawer, Bruce. "Salinger Redux." *New Criterion* 6, no. 10 (1988): 92–96.

———. "Salinger's Arrested Development." *New Criterion* 5, no. 1 (1986): 34–47.

Beckers, Marion, and Elisabeth Moortgat. *Atelier Lotte Jacobi: Berlin, New York.* Berlin: Nicolai, 1998.

Beckett, Samuel. "Letters to Barney Rosset." *Review of Contemporary Fiction* 10, no. 3 (): 64–71.

Beebe, Maurice, and Jennifer Sperry. "Criticism of J. D. Salinger: A Selected Checklist." *Modern Fiction Studies* 12, no. 3 (1966): 377–90.

Behrman, S. N. "The Vision of the Innocent." *New Yorker*, August 11, 1951, 71–76.

Beidler, Peter G. *A Reader's Companion to J. D. Salinger's* The Catcher in the Rye. Seattle: Coffeetown Press, 2009.

———. "What Holden Looks Like and Who 'Whosis' Is: A Newly Identified Movie

Allusion in *The Catcher in the Rye.*" *ANQ: A Quarterly Journal of Short Articles, Notes, and Reviews* 20, no. 1 (2007): 52–57.

Belcher, William F., and James W. Lee, eds. *J. D. Salinger and the Critics*. Belmont, CA: Wadsworth, 1962.

Bellman, Samuel Irving. "New Light on Seymour's Suicide: Salinger's 'Hapworth 16, 1942.'" *Studies in Short Fiction* 3 (Spring 1966): 348–51.

Bellows, Jim. *The Last Editor.* Kansas City: Andrews McMeel, 2002.

Berg, A. Scott. *Goldwyn: A Biography*. New York: Knopf, 1989.

Bernstein, Richard, ed. *Radical Evil: A Philosophical Investigation.* Cambridge, UK: Polity Press, 2002.

Berry, David W. "Salinger Slept Here." *Philadelphia Magazine* 82, no. 10 (1991): 53–56.

Bhaerman, Robert D. "Rebuttal: Holden in the Rye." *College English* 23, no. 6 (1962): 508.

Bidney, Martin."The Aestheticist Epiphanies of J. D. Salinger: Bright-Hued Circles, Spheres, and Patches: 'Elemental' Joy and Pain." *Style* 34, no. 1 (2000): 117–31.

Bishop, Elizabeth. *One Art: Letters.* New York: Farrar, Straus & Giroux, 1994.

Bishop, John. "A Study of the Religious Dimensions in the Fiction of J. D. Salinger." Master's thesis, McMaster University, 1976.

Bixby, George. "J. D. Salinger: A Biographical Checklist." *American Book Collector* n.s. 2 (May–June 1981): 29–32.

Blair, Clay. *Ridgway's Paratroopers: The American Airborne in World War II.* New York: Dial Press, 1985.

Blaney, Shirlie. "Twin State Telescope: Interview with an Author." *Daily Eagle* (Claremont, N.H.), November 13, 1953, editorial page.

Bloom, Harold, ed. *Holden Caulfield.* Major Literary Characters. New York: Chelsea House 1990.———. *Holden Caulfield.* New ed. Bloom's Major Literary Characters. Philadelphia: Chelsea House, 2005.

———. *J. D. Salinger.* Modern Critical Views. New York: Chelsea House, 1987.

———. *J. D. Salinger.* Bloom's Major Short Story Writers. Broomall, PA: Chelsea House, 1999.

———. *J. D. Salinger.* Bloom's BioCritiques. Philadelphia: Chelsea House, 2000.

———. *J. D. Salinger.* New ed. Bloom's Modern Critical Views. New York: Chelsea House, 2008.

———. *J. D. Salinger's The Catcher in the Rye.* Bloom's Notes. New York: Chelsea House, 1996.

———. *J. D. Salinger's The Catcher in the Rye.* Modern Critical Interpretations. Philadelphia: Chelsea House, 2000.

———. *J. D. Salinger's The Catcher in the Rye*. Bloom's Guides. New York: Chelsea House, 2007.

———. *J. D. Salinger's The Catcher in the Rye*. New ed. Bloom's Modern Critical Interpretations. New York: Chelsea House, 2009.

Blotner, Joseph L. "Salinger Now: An Appraisal." *Wisconsin Studies in Contemporary Literature* 4, no. 1 (1963): 100–108.

Blyth, R. H. *Haiku*. 4 vols. Tokyo: Hokuseido Press, 1949–52.

———. *Zen in English Literature and Oriental Classics*. Tokyo: Hokuseido Press, 1942.

Blythe, Hal, and Charlie Sweet. "The Caulfield Family of Writers in *The Catcher in the Rye*." *Notes on Contemporary Literature* 32, no. 5 (2002): 6–7.

Blythe, Hal, and Charlie Sweet. "Falling in Salinger's *Catcher in the Rye*." *Notes on Contemporary Literature* 32, no. 4 (2002): 5–7.

Blythe, Hal, and Charlie Sweet. "Holden, the Bomb, and Dr. Strangelove." *Notes on Contemporary Literature* 34, no. 3 (2004): 11–12.

Blythe, Hal, and Charlie Sweet. "Holden's Mysterious Hat." *Notes on Contemporary Literature* 32, no. 4 (2002): 7–8.

Boe, Alfred F. "Salinger and Sport." *Arete* 2, no. 2 (1985): 17–22.

Bonetti, Kay. "An Interview with William Maxwell." *Missouri Review* 19 (1996): 83–95.

Booth, Wayne C. "Censorship and the Values of Fiction." *English Journal* 53 (March 1964): 155–64.

———. *The Rhetoric of Fiction*. Chicago: University of Chicago Press, 1961.

Bostwick, Sally. "Reality, Compassion, and Mysticism in the World of J. D. Salinger." *Midwest Review* 5 (1963): 30–43.

Bourke, Joanna. *An Intimate History of Killing: Face to Face Killing in Twentieth Century Warfare*. New York: Basic Books, 1999.

Bowen, Elizabeth. "Books of 1951: Some Personal Choices." *Observer (London)*, December 30, 1951, 71.

Bowen, Robert O. "The Salinger Syndrome: Charity against Whom?" *Ramparts*, May 1962, 52–60.

Boyle, Robert S. "Teaching 'Dirty Books' in College." *America*, December 13, 1958, 337–39.

Bradbury, Malcolm. "Other New Novels: Franny and Zooey." *Punch*, June 27, 1962, 989–90.

Bradley, Omar N. *A Soldier's Story*. New York: Modern Library, 1999.

Branch, Edgar. "Mark Twain and J. D. Salinger: A Study in Literary Continuity." *American Quarterly* 9 (Summer 1958): 144–58.

Brandon, Henry. "A Conversation with Edmund Wilson: 'We Don't Know Where We Are.'" *New Republic*, March 30, 1959, 13–15.

Bratman, Fred. "Holden, 50, Still Catches." *New York Times*, December 21, 1979, A-35.

Breit, Harvey. "Reader's Choice." *Atlantic*, August 1951, 82–85.

Brenna, Duff. "Secondary Educations: An Interview with Greg Herriges." *South Carolina Review* 38, no. 2 (2006): 33–45.

Brinkley, Thomas Edwin. "J. D. Salinger: A Study of His Eclecticism—Zooey as Existential Zen Therapist." Ph.D. diss., Ohio State University, 1976.

Brod, Max, ed. *The Diaries of Franz Kafka 1910–1913*. New York: Schocken Books, 1948.

———. *The Diaries of Franz Kafka 1914–1923*. New York: Schocken Books, 1949.

Brookeman, Christopher. "Pencey Preppy: Cultural Codes in *The Catcher in the Rye*." In *New Essays on* The Catcher in the Rye, edited by Jack Salzman, 57–76. Cambridge: Cambridge University Press, 1991.

Brooks, Richard. "J. D. Salinger 'Has 15 New Books in Safe.'" *Sunday Times (London)*, March 21, 1999, 3.

Brown, Scott. "Literary Lotte." *OP Magazine* 2 (2004): 4–7.

Browne, Robert M. "In Defense of Esmé." *College English* 22, no. 8 (1961): 584–85.

Brozan, Nadine. "J. D. Salinger Receives an Apology for an Award." *New York Times*, April 27, 1991, 9, 26.

Bruccoli, Matthew. "States of Salinger Book." *American Notes & Queries* 2 (October 1963): 21–22.

Bryan, James. "The Admiral and Her Sailor in Salinger's 'Down at the Dinghy.'" *Studies in Short Fiction* 17 (Spring 1980): 174–78.

———. "J. D. Salinger: The Fat Lady and the Chicken Sandwich." *College English* 23, no. 3 (1961): 226–29.

———. "The Psychological Structure of *The Catcher in the Rye*." *PMLA* 89, no. 5 (1974): 1065–74.

———. "A Reading of Salinger's 'For Esmé—with Love and Squalor,'" *Criticism* 9 (Summer 1967): 275–88.

———. "A Reading of Salinger's 'Teddy.'" *American Literature* 40, no. 3 (1968): 352–69.

———. "Salinger and His Short Fiction." Ph.D. diss., University of Virginia, 1968.

———. "Salinger's Seymour's Suicide." *College English* 24, no. 3 (1962): 226–29.

———. "Sherwood Anderson and *The Catcher in the Rye*: A Possible Influence." *Notes on Contemporary Literature* 1, no. 5 (1971): 2–6.

Bryden, Ronald. "Living Dolls." *Spectator*, June 8, 1962, 755–56.

Bryfonski, Dedria, ed. *Depression in J. D. Salinger's* The Catcher in the Rye. Detroit: Greenhaven Press, 2009.

Buchan, John. "Skule Skerry." In *The Far Islands and Other Tales of Fantasy*, 75–92. West Kingston, RI: Donald M. Grant, 1984.

Bufithis, Philip. "J. D. Salinger and the Psychiatrist." *West Virginia University Bulletin: Philological Papers* 21 (December 1974): 67–77.

Burger, Nash K. "Books of the Times." *New York Times*, July 16, 1951, 19.

Burke, Brother Fidelian. "Salinger's 'Esmé': Some Matters of Balance." *Modern Fiction Studies* 12, no. 3 (1966): 341–47.

Burnett, Hallie, and Whit Burnett. *Fiction Writers' Handbook*. New York: Harper & Row, 1975.

Burnett, Whit, and John Pen. "Immortal Bachelor: The Love Story of Robert Burns." *Story*, November–December 1942.

Burrows, David J. "Allie and Phoebe: Death and Love in J. D. Salinger's 'The Catcher in the Rye.'" In *Private Dealings: Modern American Writers in Search of Integrity*, edited by David J. Burrows et al., 106–14. Rockville, MD: New Perspectives, 1974.

Burt, Daniel S., ed. *The Chronology of American Literature: America's Literary Achievements from the Colonial Era to Modern Times*. Boston: Houghton Mifflin, 2004.

Cagle, Charles. "*The Catcher in the Rye* Revisited." *Midwest Quarterly* 4 (Summer 1963): 343–51.

Cahill, Robert. "J. D. Salinger's Tin Bell." *Cadence* 14 (Autumn 1959): 20–22.

California, John David [Fredrik Colting]. *60 Years Later: Coming through the Rye*. London: Windupbird, 2009.

Carpenter, Frederic I. "The Adolescent in American Fiction." *English Journal* 46 (September 1957): 313–19.

Carvajal, Doreen. "Salinger's Daughter Plans to Publish a Memoir." *New York Times*, June 24, 1999, E-10.

Carver, Michael. Introduction to *D-Day As They Saw It*, by Jon E. Lewis. New York: Avalon.

Castronovo, David. "Holden Caulfield's Legacy." *New England Review* 22, no. 2 (2001): 180–86.

"The Catcher on the Hill." *Newsweek*, November 18, 1974, 17.

Cawelti, John G. "The Writer as a Celebrity: Some Aspects of American Literature as Popular Culture." *Studies in American Fiction* 5 (1977): 161–74.

Chambers, Andrea. "In Search of J. D. Salinger, Biographer Ian Hamilton Discovers a Subject Who Didn't Want to Be Found." *People*, June 6, 1988, 51–53.

Chandra, Subhash. *The Fiction of J. D. Salinger: A Study in the Concept of Man*. New Delhi: Prestige, 2000.

Chaplin, Patrice. *Hidden Star: Oona O'Neill Chaplin*. London: Richard Cohen Books, 1995.

Cheatham, George, and Edwin Arnaudin. "Salinger's Allusions to *My Foolish Heart*—The Salinger Movie." *ANQ: A Quarterly Journal of Short Articles, Notes, and Reviews* 20, no. 2 (2007): 39–43.

Chester, Alfred. "Salinger: How to Love without Love." *Commentary* 35 (June 1963): 467–74.

Childers, Thomas. *Soldier from the War Returning: The Greatest Generation's Troubled Homecoming from World War II.* New York: Houghton Mifflin Harcourt, 2009.

Clarkson, Michael. "Catching the 'Catcher in the Rye,' J. D. Salinger." In *If You Really Want to Hear about It: Writers on J. D. Salinger and His Work*, edited by Catherine Crawford, 49–62. New York: Thunder's Mouth Press, 2006. Originally published in *Niagara Falls Review*, November 1979.

Cohen, David S. *Screen Plays: How 25 Screenwriters Made It to a Theater Near You—for Better or Worse.* New York: HarperCollins, 2008.

Cohen, Hubert I. '"A Woeful Agony Which Forced Me to Begin My Tale': *The Catcher in the Rye.*" *Modern Fiction Studies* 12, no. 3 (1966): 355–66.

Coles, Robert. "Anna Freud and J. D. Salinger's Holden Caulfield." *Virginia Quarterly Review* 76, no. 2 (2000): 214–24.

———. "Reconsideration: J. D. Salinger." *New Republic*, April 28, 1973, 30–32.

"Contributors." *Story* 16 (March–April 1940): 2.

"Controversial Story Not by J. D. Salinger." *New Orleans Times Picayune*, February 27, 1977, 18.

Corbett, Edward P. "Raise High the Barriers, Censors." *America*, January 7, 1961, 441–43.

Costello, Donald P. "The Language of 'The Catcher in the Rye.'" *American Speech* 34, no. 3 (1959): 172–81.

———. "Salinger and His Critics." *Commonweal*, October 25, 1963, 132–35.

Cotter, James Finn. "Religious Symbols in Salinger's Shorter Fiction." *Studies in Short Fiction* 15 (Spring 1978): 121–32.

———. "A Source for Seymour's Suicide: Rilke's 'Voices' and Salinger's *Nine Stories.*" *Papers on Language and Literature* 25, no. 1 (1989): 83–89.

Cowan, Alison Leigh, "To a Dear Buddyroo: Salinger Letters Unleashed." *New York Times*, February 12, 2010, C-23, C-28.

Cowan, Michael. "Holden's Museum Pieces: Narrator and Nominal Audience in *The Catcher in the Rye.*" In *New Essays on* The Catcher in the Rye, edited by Jack Salzman, 35–55. Cambridge: Cambridge University Press, 1991.

Cox, James M. "Toward Vernacular Humor." *Virginia Quarterly Review* 46 (Spring 1970): 311–30.

Crawford, Catherine, ed. *If You Really Want to Hear about It: Writers on J. D. Salinger and His Work.* New York: Thunder's Mouth Press, 2006.

Creeger, George R. *"Treacherous Desertion": Salinger's* The Catcher in the Rye. Middletown, CT: Wesleyan University Press, 1961.

Cronin, Gloria, and Ben Siegel, eds. *Conversations with Saul Bellow.* Jackson: University of Mississippi Press, 1994.

Cullen, Frank. *Vaudeville, Old and New.* New York: Routledge, 2007.

Cunningham, Ed. *Yank: The Story of World War II as Written by the Soldiers.* Brassey's, 1991.

Curry, Renee R. "Holden Caulfield Is Not a Person of Colour." In *J. D. Salinger's* The Catcher in the Rye, edited by Sarah Graham, 78–88. London: Routledge, 2007.

Cutchins, Dennis. "*Catcher* in the Corn: J. D. Salinger and *Shoeless Joe.*" In The Catcher in the Rye: *New Essays*, edited by J. P. Steed, 53–77. New York: Peter Lang, 2002.

Dahl, James. "What *about* Antolini?" *Notes on Contemporary Literature* 13, no. 2 (1983): 9–10.

Dann, Sam. *Dachau 29 April 1945: The Rainbow Liberation Memoirs.* Lubbock: Texas Tech University Press, 1998.

"A Dark Horse." *Virginia Kirkus' Bookshop Service*, May 15, 1951, 247.

Daughtry, Vivian F. "A Novel Worth Teaching: Salinger's *The Catcher in the Rye.*" *Virginia English Bulletin* 36, no. 2 (1986): 88–94.

Davis, Kenneth C. *Two-Bit Culture: The Paperbacking of America.* Boston: Houghton Mifflin, 1984.

Davis, Tom. "J. D. Salinger: A Checklist." *Papers of the Bibliographical Society of America* 53 (January–March 1959): 69–71.

———. "J. D. Salinger: 'Some Crazy Cliff' Indeed." *Western Humanities Review* 14 (Winter 1960): 97–99.

———. "J. D. Salinger: 'The Sound of One Hand Clapping.'" *Wisconsin Studies in Contemporary Literature* 4, no. 1 (1963): 41–47.

———. "J. D. Salinger: The Identity of Sergeant X." *Western Humanities Review* 16 (Spring 1962): 181–83.

Davison, Richard Allan. "Salinger Criticism and 'The Laughing Man': A Case of Arrested Development." *Studies in Short Fiction* 18 (Winter 1981): 1–15.

D-Day Plus 40 Years. Television documentary, NBC Television Network, 1984.

Deer, Irving, and John H. Randall III. "J. D. Salinger and the Reality beyond Words." *Lock Haven Review* 6 (1964): 14–29.

DeLillo, Don. *Mao II.* New York: Viking Penguin, 1991.

Dempsey, David. "Ten Best-Selling Authors Make Their Holiday Choices." *New York Times Book Review*, December 2, 1951, 244.

"Depositions Yield J. D. Salinger Details." *New York Times*, December 12, 1986, C-27.

Dev, Jai. "Franny and Flaubert." *Journal of American Studies* 25, no. 1 (1991): 81–85.

———. "Strategies of Self-Defence: Self-Reflexivity in *Franny and Zooey.*" *Panjab University Research Bulletin* 21, no. 1 (1990): 17–41.

Dickstein, Morris. *Leopards in the Temple: The Transformation of American Fiction 1945–1970.* Cambridge, MA: Harvard University Press, 2002.

Didion, Joan. "Finally (Fashionably) Spurious." In *Salinger: A Critical and Personal Por-*

trait, edited by Henry Anatole Grunwald, 77–79. New York: Harper & Row, 1962. Originally published in *National Review*, November 18, 1961.

Dodge, Stewart. "The Theme of Quest: In Search of 'The Fat Lady.'" *English Record* 8 (Winter 1957): 10–13.

Dolbier, Maurice. "Franny and Zooey." *New York Herald Tribune*, September 14, 1961, 19.

Douglas, Claire. *Translate This Darkness.* Princeton: Princeton University Press, 1993.

Drake, Robert Y. "Two Old Juveniles." *Georgia Review* 13 (Winter 1959): 10–13.

Ducharme, Edward R. "J.D., D.B., Sonny, Sunny, and Holden." *English Record* 19, no. 2 (1968): 54–58.

Dudar, Helen. "In Search of J. D. Salinger, Publishing's Invisible Man." *Chicago Tribune*, June 19, 1979, 2: 1, 6.

Dudley, Robin. "J. D. Salinger's Uncollected Stories and the Development of Aesthetic and Moral Themes in *The Catcher in the Rye*." Master's thesis, Idaho State University, 2004.

Dugan, Lawrence. "Holden and the Lunts." *Notes and Queries* 52, no. 4 (2005): 510–11.

Edwards, Duane. "Holden Caulfield: 'Don't Ever Tell Anybody Anything.'" *Journal of English Literary History* 44, no. 3 (1977): 554–65.

Eisman, Gregory Dwight. "The Importance of Being Seymour: The Dramatic Function of Seymour Glass in the Works of J. D. Salinger." Master's thesis, Florida Atlantic University, 1974.

Elfin, Mel. "The Mysterious J. D. Salinger . . . His Woodsy, Secluded Life." *Newsweek*, May 30, 1960, 92–94.

Eliason, Marcus. "Conspiracy of Silence Guards Private World of J. D. Salinger." *New Orleans Times Picayune*, December 21, 1975, 3: 15.

Eliot, T. S. *Collected Poems 1909–1962.* New York: Harcourt Brace, 1963.

Elmen, Paul. "Twice-Blessed Enamel Flowers: Reality in Contemporary Fiction." In *The Climate of Faith in Modern Literature*, edited by Nathan A. Scott Jr., 84–101. New York: Seabury Press, 1964.

Engle, Paul. "Brilliantly Detailed Glimpses of the Glass Family." *Chicago Tribune*, September 24, 1961, 3.

Engel, Steven, ed. *Readings on* The Catcher in the Rye. San Diego: Greenhaven Press, 1998.

Eppes, Betty. "What I Did Last Summer." *Paris Review* 23 (Summer 1981): 221–39.

Erwin, Kenneth J. "An Analysis of the Dramatic and Semantic Use of Altruism in the Writings of J. D. Salinger." Ph.D. diss., University of Texas at Austin, 1968.

Everston, Matt. "Love, Loss, and Growing Up in J. D. Salinger and Cormac McCarthy." In The Catcher in the Rye: *New Essays*, edited by J. P. Steed, 101–42. New York: Peter Lang, 2002.

Fadiman, Clifton. *Book-of-the-Month Club News*, July 1951, 1–4.

Faris, Christiane Brandt. "The Pattern of Withdrawal in J. D. Salinger and R. M. Rilke." Master's thesis, Bucknell University, 1969.

Faulkner, William. "A Word to Young Writers." In *Faulkner in the University: Class Conferences at the University of Virginia 1957–1958,* edited by Frederick L. Gwynn and Joseph L. Blotner, 244–48. Charlottesville: University of Virginia Press, 1959.

Fiedler, Leslie. "The Eye of Innocence." In *Salinger: A Critical and Personal Portrait,* edited by Henry Anatole Grunwald, 218–45. New York: Harper & Row, 1962.

———. "Up from Adolescence." *Partisan Review* 29 (Winter 1962): 127–31.

Field, Michele. "In Pursuit of J. D. Salinger." *Publishers Weekly,* June 27, 1986, 63–64.

Fiene, Donald M. "A Bibliographical Study of J. D. Salinger: Life, Work and Reputation." Master's thesis, University of Louisville, 1961.

———. "From a Study of Salinger: Controversy in *The Catcher.*" *The Realist* 1 (December 1961): 23–25.

———. "J. D. Salinger: A Bibliography." *Wisconsin Studies in Contemporary Literature* 4, no. 1 (1963): 109–49.

———. "Rye on the Rocks." *Time,* May 30, 1960, 2.

Fitzgerald, F. Scott. *The Great Gatsby.* New York: Scribner, 2004.

———. *Tales of the Jazz Age.* In *Novels and Stories 1920–1922.* New York: Library of America, 2000.

Fleissner, Robert F. "Salinger's Caulfield: A Refraction of Copperfield and His Caul." *Notes of Contemporary Literature* 3, no. 3 (1973): 5–7.

Flogel, Amy. "Where the Ducks Go: *The Catcher in the Rye.*" *Ball State Teacher's College Forum* 3 (Spring 1962): 75–79.

Foley, Martha J., ed. *The Best American Short Stories and The Yearbook of the American Short Story.* Boston: Houghton Mifflin, 1948–66.

Foran, Donald J. "A Doubletake on Holden Caulfield." *English Journal* 57 (October 1968): 977–79.

Fosburgh, Lacey. "J. D. Salinger Speaks about His Silence." *New York Times,* November 3, 1974, 1, 69.

———. "Salinger Books Stir F.B.I. Search." *New York Times,* November 10, 1974, 75.

Fowler, Albert. "Alien in the Rye." *Modern Age* 1 (Fall 1957): 193–97.

Fowler, Will. *D-Day: The Normandy Landings of June 6, 1944.* New York: Barnes and Noble, 2006.

Frank, Jeffrey. "Riches of Embarrassment." *New Yorker,* May 24, 2004, 46–55.

Freedman, Carl. "Memories of Holden Caulfield and of Miss Greenwood." *Southern Review* 39, no. 2 (2003): 401–17.

Freedman, Ralph. *Life of a Poet: Rainer Maria Rilke.* New York: Farrar, Straus & Giroux, 1996.

Freeman, Fred B., Jr. "Who Was Salinger's Sergeant X?" *American Notes and Queries* 11 (September 1972): 6.

Fremont-Smith, Eliot. "Franny and Zooey." *Village Voice*, March 8, 1962, 5–6.

French, Warren. "The Age of Salinger." In *The Fifties: Fiction, Poetry, Drama,* edited by Warren French, 1–39. Deland, FL: Everett/Edwards, 1970.

———. "Holden's Fall." *Modern Fiction Studies* 10 (Winter 1964–65): 389.

———. "J. D. Salinger." In *American Novelists since World War II*, edited by Jeffrey Helterman and Richard Layman, 434–44. Detroit: Gale, 1978.

———. *J. D. Salinger.* New York: Twayne, 1963.

———. *J. D. Salinger.* Rev. ed. Boston: G. K. Hall, 1976.

———. *J. D. Salinger, Revisited.* New York: Twayne, 1988.

———. "The Phony World and the Nice World." *Wisconsin Studies in Contemporary Literature* 4, no. 1 (1963): 21–30.

———. "An Unnoticed Salinger Story." *College English* 26, no. 5 (1965): 394–95.

Friedrich, Jörg. *The Fire: The Bombing of Germany, 1940–1945.* New York: Columbia University Press, 2006.

"From Utah Beach to the Hedgerows," *Military History*, June 2004.

Fry, John R. "Skill Is the Word." *Christian Century*, February 6, 1963, 175–76.

Frye, Northrup. *The Critical Path.* Bloomington: Indiana University Press, 1971.

Fulford, Robert. "Newsstand: Seymour Glass at 7." *Toronto Star*, June 21, 1965, 16.

Furst, Lilian R. "Dostoyevsky's *Notes from the Underground* and Salinger's *The Catcher in the Rye.*" *Canadian Review of Comparative Literature* 5 (Winter 1978): 72–85.

Fussell, Paul. *The Boys' Crusade.* New York: Modern Library, 2003.

———. *Wartime: Understanding and Behavior in the Second World War.* Oxford: Oxford University Press, 1989.

Galloway, David D. *The Absurd Hero in American Fiction.* Austin: University of Texas Press, 1966.

Gehman, Richard. Introduction to *The Best from Cosmopolitan,* edited by Richard Gehman, xiii–xxvii. New York: Avon Books, 1961.

Geismar, Maxwell. "J. D. Salinger: The Wise Child and *The New Yorker* School of Fiction." In *American Moderns: From Rebellion to Conformity*, edited by Maxwell Geismar, 195–209. New York: Hill and Wang, 1958.

Gellhorn, Martha. *The Face of War.* New York: Simon & Schuster, 1959.

Genthe, Charles V. "Six, Sex, Sick: Seymour, Some Comments." *Twentieth Century Literature* 10, no. 4 (1965): 170–71.

Giles, Barbara. "The Lonely War of J. D. Salinger." *Mainstream* 12, no. 2 (1959): 2–13.

Giles, Lionel, trans. *Taoist Teachings from the Book of Lieh Tzu.* London: John Murray, 1925.

Gill, Brendan. *Here at* The New Yorker. New York: Random House, 1975.

Gilman, Richard. "Salinger Considered." *Jubilee* 9 (October 1961): 38–41.

"The Glass House Gang." *Time,* February 8, 1963, 86.

Glasser, William. "The Catcher in the Rye." *Michigan Quarterly Review* 15 (Fall 1976): 432–57.

Glazier, Lyle. "The Glass Family Saga: Argument and Epiphany." *College English* 27, no. 3 (1965): 248–51.

Gold, Arthur R. "J. D. Salinger: Through a Glass Darkly." *New York Herald Tribune Books,* April 7, 1963, 8.

Goldhurst, William. "The Hyphenated Ham Sandwich of Ernest Hemingway and J. D. Salinger." In *Fitzgerald/Hemingway Annual 1970,* edited by Matthew J. Bruccoli and C. E. Frazer Clark Jr., 136–50. Washington, D.C.: NCR, 1970.

Goldstein, Bernice, and Sanford Goldstein. "Bunnies and Cobras: Zen Enlightenment in Salinger." *Discourse* 13 (Winter 1970): 98–106.

Goldstein, Bernice, and Sanford Goldstein. "Ego and 'Hapworth 16, 1924.'" *Renascence* 24 (Spring 1972): 159–256.

Goldstein, Bernice, and Sanford Goldstein. "'Seymour: An Introduction'—Writing as Discovery." *Studies in Short Fiction* 7 (Spring 1970): 248–56.

Goldstein, Bernice, and Sanford Goldstein. "Seymour's Poems." *Literature East and West* 17 (June–December 1973): 335–48.

Goldstein, Bernice, and Sanford Goldstein. "Some Zen References in Salinger." *Literature East and West* 25 (1971): 83–95.

Goldstein, Bernice, and Sanford Goldstein. "Zen and *Nine Stories.*" *Renascence* 22 (Summer 1970): 171–82.

Goldstein, Bernice, and Sanford Goldstein. "Zen and Salinger." *Modern Fiction Studies* 12, no. 3 (1966): 313–24.

Goodman, Anne L. "Mad about Children." *New Republic,* July 16, 1951, 20–21.

Gopnik, Adam. "J. D. Salinger." *New Yorker,* February 8, 2010, 20–21.

The Gospel of Sri Ramakrishna. Transcribed by Mahendranath Gupta. Translated and introductory biography by Swami Nikhilananda. New York: Ramakrishna-Vivekananda Center, 1942.

Graham, Sarah. *J. D. Salinger's* The Catcher in the Rye. London: Routledge, 2007.

———. *Salinger's* The Catcher in the Rye. London: Continuum, 2007.

Graustark, Barbara. "Newsmakers." *Newsweek*, July 17, 1978, 57.

Green, Martin Burgess. "American Rococo: Salinger and Nabokov." In *Re-appraisals: Some Common-sense Readings in American Literature*, 211–19. New York: Norton, 1965.

———. "Amis and Salinger: The Latitude of Private Conscience." *Chicago Review* 11 (Winter 1958): 20–25.

———. "Cultural Images in England and America." In *A Mirror for Anglo-Saxons: A Discovery of America, a Rediscovery of England*, 69–88. New York: Harper & Brothers, 1960.

———. "Franny and Zooey." In *Re-appraisals: Some Common-sense Readings in American Literature,* 197–210. New York: Norton, 1965.

Greiner, Donald J. "Updike and Salinger: A Literary Incident." *Critique: Studies in Contemporary Fiction* 47, no. 2 (2006): 115–30.

Gross, Theodore L. "J. D. Salinger: Suicide and Survival in the Modern World." *South Atlantic Quarterly* 68 (Autumn 1969): 454–62.

Grunwald, Henry Anatole. "He Touches Something Deep in Us." *Horizon* 4 (May 1962): 100–107.

———, ed. *Salinger: A Critical and Personal Portrait.* New York: Harper & Row, 1962.

Guare, John. *Six Degrees of Separation*. New York: Vintage, 1990.

Gutwillig, Robert. "Everybody's Caught 'The Catcher in the Rye.'" *New York Times Book Review*, January 15, 1961, 38–39.

Gwynn, Frederick L., and Joseph L. Blotner. *The Fiction of J. D. Salinger*. Pittsburgh: University of Pittsburgh Press, 1958.

Haberman, Clyde. "Notes on People: A Muted Singer." *New York Times*, November 29, 1978, C-18.

———. "A Recluse Meets His Match." *New York Times*, June 18, 1999, B-1.

Hackett, Alice Payne, and James Henry Burke. *80 Years of Best Sellers, 1895–1975.* New York: R. R. Bowker, 1977.

Hagopian, John V. "'Pretty Mouth and Green My Eyes': Salinger's Paolo and Francesca in New York." *Modern Fiction Studies* 12, no. 3 (1966): 349–54.

Hainsworth, J. D. "Maturity in J. D. Salinger's 'The Catcher in the Rye.'" *English Studies* 48 (October 1967): 426–31.

Haitch, Richard. "Follow-Up in the News: J. D. Salinger." *New York Times*, February 12, 1978, 41.

Hale, John K. "Salinger's *The Catcher in the Rye*." *Explicator* 60, no. 4 (2002): 220–21.

Hamilton, Ian. "A Biographer's Misgivings." In *Walking Possession: Essays and Reviews, 1968–1993*, 5–21. New York: Addison-Wesley, 1996.

———. *In Search of J. D. Salinger*. New York: Random House, 1988.

———. *J. D. Salinger: A Writing Life*. New York: Random House, 1986. Bound galleys; book publication blocked by Salinger.

Hamilton, Kenneth. "Hell in New York: J. D. Salinger's 'Pretty Mouth and Green My Eyes.'" *Dalhousie Review* 47 (Autumn 1967): 394–99.

———. "J. D. Salinger's Happy Family." *Queen's Quarterly* 71 (Summer 1964): 176–87.

———. *Jerome David Salinger: A Critical Essay*. Grand Rapids, MI: Eerdmans, 1967.

———. "One Way to Use the Bible: The Example of J. D. Salinger." *Christian Scholar* 47 (Fall 1964): 243–51.

Harper, Howard M., Jr. *Desperate Faith: A Study of Bellow, Salinger, Mailer, Baldwin, and Updike*. Chapel Hill: University of North Carolina Press, 1967.

———. "J. D. Salinger—Through the Glasses Darkly." In *Desperate Faith: A Study of Bellow, Salinger, Mailer, Baldwin, and Updike*, 65–95. Chapel Hill: University of North Carolina Press, 1967.

Hart, James D. *The Oxford Companion to American Literature*. 3rd ed. New York: Oxford University Press, 1956.

———. *The Oxford Companion to American Literature*. 4th ed. New York: Oxford University Press, 1965.

Hassan, Ihab. "Almost the Voice of Silence: The Later Novelettes of J. D. Salinger." *Wisconsin Studies in Contemporary Literature* 4, no. 1 (1963): 5–20.

———. "The Casino of Silence." *Saturday Review*, January 26, 1963, 38.

———. "The Character of Post-war Fiction in America." *English Journal* 51 (January 1962): 1–8.

———. *The Dismemberment of Orpheus: Toward a Postmodern Literature*. New York: Oxford University Press, 1971.

———. "The Idea of Adolescence in American Fiction." *American Quarterly* 10 (Fall 1958): 312–24.

———. "J. D. Salinger: Rare Quixotic Gesture." *Western Review*, Summer 1957.

———. *Radical Innocence: Studies in the Contemporary American Novel*. Princeton: Princeton University Press, 1961.

———. "Rare Quixotic Gesture: The Fiction of J. D. Salinger." *Western Review* 21 (Summer 1957): 261–80.

Hastings, Max. *Armageddon: The Battle for Germany, 1944–1945*. New York: Knopf, 2004.

———. *Overlord: D-Day and the Battle for Normandy*. New York: Vintage Books, 1984.

Havemann, Ernest. "The Search for the Mysterious J. D. Salinger." *Life*, November 3, 1961, 129–30, 132, 135, 137–38, 141–42, 144.

Hazard, Eloise P. "Eight Fiction Finds." *Saturday Review*, February 16, 1952, 16–18.

Hedges, Chris. *War Is a Force That Gives Us Meaning.* New York: Public Affairs, 2002.

Heiserman, Arthur, and James E. Miller Jr. "J. D. Salinger: Some Crazy Cliff." *Western Humanities Review* 10 (Spring 1956): 129–37.

Hekanaho, Pia Livia. "Queering *Catcher*: Flits, Straights, and Other Morons." In *J. D. Salinger's* The Catcher in the Rye, edited by Sarah Graham, 90–97. London: Routledge, 2007.

Hemingway, Ernest. *Across the River and into the Trees.* New York: Charles Scribner and Sons, 1950.

Hemingway, Seán. *Ernest Hemingway on War.* New York: Scribner, 2003.

Hermann, John. "J. D. Salinger: Hello Hello Hello." *College English* 22, no. 4 (1961): 262–64.

Herriges, Greg. *JD: A Memoir of a Time and a Journey.* Le Grande, OR: Wordcraft of Oregon, 2006.

———. "Ten Minutes with J. D. Salinger." *Oui*, January 1979, 86–88, 126–30.

Hicks, Granville. "Another Look at the Deserving." *Saturday Review*, December 23, 1961, 18.

———. "A Glass Menagerie." *Saturday Review*, January 26, 1963, 37–38.

———. "J. D. Salinger: Search for Wisdom." *Saturday Review*, July 25, 1959, 13, 30.

———. "Sisters, Sons, and Lovers." *Saturday Review*, September 16, 1961, 26.

Highet, Gilbert. "New Books: Always Roaming with a Hungry Heart." *Harper's*, June 1953, 100–109.

Hoban, Phoebe. "The Salinger File." *New York*, June 15, 1987, 36–42.

Hochman, Will. "Strategies of Critical Response to the Fiction of J. D. Salinger." Ph.D. diss., New York University, 1994.

———. "Swimming with Bananafish: The Literary Suicides of Seymour Glass and J. D. Salinger." In *The Image of Violence in Literature, the Media, and Society*, edited by Will Wright and Steven Kaplan, 458–62. Pueblo: Society for the Interdisciplinary Study of Society Imagery, University of Southern Colorado, 1995.

Honan, William H. "Fire Fails to Shake Salinger's Seclusion." *New York Times*, October 24, 1992, 13.

Hotchner, A. E. *Choice People.* New York: William Morrow, 1984.

Howe, Irving. "More Reflections in the Glass Mirror." *New York Times Book Review*, April 7, 1963, 4–5, 34.

Howell, John M. "Salinger in the Waste Land." *Modern Fiction Studies* 12, no. 3 (1966): 367–75.

Hugh-Jones, Siriol. "The Salinger Puzzle." *Tatler and Bystander*, June 20, 1962, 748.

Hughes, Riley. "New Novels: *The Catcher in the Rye*." *Catholic World* 174 (November 1951): 154.

———. *Catholic World* 178 (June 1953): 233.

Hutchens, John K. "On an Author." *New York Herald Tribune Book Review*, August 19, 1951, 2.

James Alvin Huston, *Across the Face of France*

Hyman, Stanley Edgar. "J. D. Salinger's House of Glass." In *Standards: A Chronicle of Books of Our Time,* 123–27. New York: Horizon Press, 1966.

"In Place of the New, a Reissue of the Old." *Newsweek*, January 28, 1963, 90, 92.

Jacobs, Robert G. "J. D. Salinger's *The Catcher in the Rye*: Holden Caulfield's 'Goddam Autobiography.'" *Iowa English Yearbook* 4 (Fall 1959): 9–14.

Jacobsen, Josephine. "The Felicity of J. D. Salinger." *Commonweal*, February 26, 1960, 589–91.

J. D. Salinger Doesn't Want to Talk. VHS and DVD. Directed by Sarah Aspinall. London: BBC, 1999.

"J. D. Salinger Files Impersonation Lawsuit." *New York Times*, October 14, 1982, C-13.

"J. D. Salinger Sues to Bar a Bibliography." *New York Times*, October 4, 1986, 8.

Johannson, Ernest J. "Salinger's Seymour." *Carolina Quarterly* 12 (Winter 1959): 51–54.

Johnson, Gerden F. *History of the Twelfth Infantry Regiment in World War II.* St. Peters, MO: National 4th Infantry Division Association, 1947.

Johnson, James W. "The Adolescent Hero: A Trend in Modern Fiction." *Twentieth Century Literature* 5 (April 1959): 3–11.

Johnson, Laurie. "Carrousel Burns in Central Park." *New York Times*, November 8, 1950, 35.

Jones, Ernest. "Case History of All of Us." *Nation*, September 1, 1951, 176.

Jones, Jack. *Let Me Take You Down: Inside the Mind of Mark David Chapman, the Man Who Shot John Lennon.* New York: Villard, 1992.

Jonnes, Denis. "Trauma, Mourning and Self-(Re)fashioning in *The Catcher in the Rye.*" In *J. D. Salinger's* The Catcher in the Rye, edited by Sarah Graham, 98–108, London: Routledge, 2007.

Jordan, Joseph William. "J. D. Salinger as a Writer of Fiction for Students in Senior High School." Ph.D. diss., Ohio State University, 1962.

Kafka, Franz. *Dearest Father: Stories and Other Writings.* New York: Schocken Books, 1954.

———. *Letters to Felice.* New York: Schocken Books, 1973.

Kakutani, Michiko. "From Salinger, a New Dash of Mystery." *New York Times*, February 20, 1997, C-15, C-19.

———. "More of Her Life, and Love, to Look Back On." *New York Times*, September 8, 1998.

Kaplan, Charles. "Holden and Huck: The Odysseys of Youth." *College English* 18, no. 2 (1956): 76–80.

Kapp, Isa. "Salinger's Easy Victory." *New Leader*, January 8, 1962, 27–28.

Karlstetter, Klaus. "J. D. Salinger, R. W. Emerson and the Perennial Philosophy." *Moderna Sprak* 63, no. 3 (1969): 224–36.

Kaufman, Anthony. "'Along This Road Goes No One': Salinger's 'Teddy' and the Failure of Love." *Studies in Short Fiction* 35 (Spring 1998): 129–40.

Kaufman, King. "When Books Kill," Salon.com, December 15, 2003.

Kazin, Alfred. *Bright Book of Life: American Novelties and Storytellers from Hemingway to Mailer.* Boston: Little, Brown, 1973.

———. *Contemporaries.* Boston: Little, Brown, 1962.

———. "J. D. Salinger: 'Everybody's Favorite.'" In *If You Really Want to Hear about It: Writers on J. D. Salinger and His Work*, edited by Catherine Crawford, 109–19. New York: Thunder's Mouth Press, 2006. Originally published in *Atlantic Monthly*, August 1961.

Kearns, Francs E. "Salinger and Golding: Conflict on Campus." *America*, January 26, 1963, 136–39.

Keating, Edward M. "Salinger: The Murky Mirror." *Ramparts* 1 (May 1962): 61–66.

Keerdoja, E., and P. E. Simons. "The Dodger in the Rye." *Newsweek*, July 30, 1979, 11, 13.

Kegel, Charles H. "Incommunicability in Salinger's *The Catcher in the Rye.*" *Western Humanities Review* 11 (Spring 1957): 188–90.

Kennedy, Sighle. "New Books: Franny and Zooey." *Catholic World* 194 (February 1962): 312–13.

Kermode, Frank. "The Glass Menagerie." *New Statesman*, March 15, 1963, 388.

———. "J. D. Salinger: One Hand Clapping." *New Statesman*, June 8, 1962, 831.

Kilicci, Esra. "J. D. Salinger's Characters as Existential Heroes: Encountering 1950s America." Ph.D. diss., Indiana University of Pennsylvania, 2008.

Kingston, Anne. "Lolita Writes Back." *Saturday Night*, October 1998, 64–72, 111.

Kinney, Arthur F. "J. D. Salinger and the Search for Love." *Texas Studies in Literature and Language* 5 (Spring 1963): 111–26.

———. "The Theme of Charity in *The Catcher in the Rye.*" *Papers of the Michigan Academy of Science, Arts, and Letters* 48 (1963): 691–702.

Kinnick, Bernard C. "Holden Caulfield: Adolescents' Enduring Model." *High School Journal* 53 (May 1970): 440–43.

Kinsella, W. P. *Shoeless Joe.* Boston: Houghton Mifflin, 1982.

Kirschner, Paul. "Salinger and His Society: The Pattern of *Nine Stories.*" *London Review* 6 (Winter 1969–70): 34–54.

———. "Salinger and Scott Fitzgerald: Complementary American Voices." *Dutch Quarterly Review of Anglo-American Letters* 17 (1987): 53–73.

Kleban, Barbara. "Young Writer Brings the World a Message from J. D. Salinger: 'Go Away.'" *People*, February 25, 1980, 43–44.

Kleeman, Werner, and Elizabeth Uhlig. *From Dachau to D-Day: A Memoir.* Rego Park, N.Y.: Marble House Editions, 2006.

Kosner, Edward. "The Private World of J. D. Salinger." *New York Post Magazine*, April 30, 1961, 5.

Kotzen, Kip, and Thomas Beller, eds. *With Love and Squalor: 14 Writers Respond to the Work of J. D. Salinger*. New York: Broadway Books, 2001.

Kranidas, Thomas. "Point of View in Salinger's 'Teddy.'" *Studies in Short Fiction* 2 (Fall 1964): 89–91.

Krassner, Paul. "An Impolite Interview with Alan Watts." *Realist* 14 (December 1960): 1, 8–11.

Krim, Seymour. "Surface and Substance in a Major Talent." *Commonweal*, April 24, 1953, 78.

Kubica, Chris, and Will Hochman, eds. *Letters to J. D. Salinger*. Madison: University of Wisconsin Press, 2002.

Kukil, Karen V., ed. *The Unabridged Journals of Sylvia Plath*. New York: Anchor Books, 2000.

Kunitz, Stanley J., and Vineta Colby, eds. *Twentieth Century Authors.* New York: H. W. Wilson, 1955.

Kurian, Elisabeth N. *A Religious Response to the Existential Dilemma in the Fiction of J. D. Salinger.* New Delhi: Intellectual Publishing House, 1992.

Lacy, Robert. "Sing a Song of Sonny." *Sewanee Review* 113 (2005): 309–16.

Lane, Gary. "Seymour's Suicide Again: A New Reading of J. D. Salinger's 'A Perfect Day for Bananafish.'" *Studies in Short Fiction* 10 (Winter 1973): 27–33.

Larner, Jeremy. "Salinger's Audience: An Explanation." *Partisan Review* 29 (Fall 1962): 594–98.

Larrabee, C. X. "Nine Short Stories by a Writer with an Extraordinary Talent." *San Francisco Chronicle*, May 3, 1953, 13.

Laser, Marvin. "Character Names in *The Catcher in the Rye*." *California English Journal* 1 (Winter 1965): 29–40.

Laser, Marvin, and Norman Fruman, eds. *Studies in J. D. Salinger: Reviews, Essays, Critiques of "The Catcher in the Rye" and Other Fiction.* New York: Odyssey Press, 1963.

Lee, Robert A. "'Flunking Everything Else Except English Anyway': Holden Caulfield, Author." In *Critical Essays on Salinger's* The Catcher in the Rye, edited by Joel Salzberg, 185–97. Boston: G. K. Hall, 1990.

Leitch, David. "The Salinger Myth." *Twentieth Century* 168 (November 1960): 428–35.

Lerman, Leo. "It Takes 4." *Mademoiselle*, October 1961, 108–11.

Lerner, Paul. *Hysterical Men: War, Psychiatry, and the Politics of Trauma in Germany, 1890–1930.* Ithaca, NY: Cornell University Press, 2003.

Lerner, Paul, and Mark S. Micale, eds. *Traumatic Pasts: History, Psychiatry, and Trauma in the Modern Age, 1870–1930.* Cambridge: Cambridge University Press, 2001.

Lettis, Richard. "Holden Caulfield: Salinger's 'Ironic Amalgam.'" *American Notes & Queries* 15 (November 1976): 43–45.

Levin, Beatrice. "J. D. Salinger in Oklahoma." *Chicago Jewish Forum* 19 (Spring 1961): 231–33.

Levine, Paul. "J. D. Salinger: The Development of the Misfit Hero." *Twentieth Century Literature* 4, no. 3 (1958): 92–99.

Lewis, Jon E., ed. *The Mammoth Book of Eyewitness World War II: Over 200 First-Hand Accounts from the Six Years That Tore the World Apart.* New York: Carroll & Graf, 2002.

Lewis, Jonathan P. "'All That David Copperfield Kind of Crap': Holden Caulfield's Rejection of Grand Narratives." *Notes on Contemporary Literature* 32, no. 4 (2002): 3–5.

Lewis, Roger. "Textual Variants in J. D. Salinger's *Nine Stories.*" *Resources for American Literary Study* 10 (Spring 1980): 79–83.

Liddle, Peter. *D-Day: By Those Who Were There.* Barnsley, UK: Pen & Sword Military, 2004.

Light, James F. "Salinger's *The Catcher in the Rye.*" *Explicator* 18 (June 1960): item 59.

Limmer, Ruth, ed. *What the Woman Lived: Selected Letters of Louise Bogan, 1920–1970.* New York: Harcourt, Brace, Jovanovich, 1973.

Lipstadt, Deborah. *Denying the Holocaust: The Growing Assault on Truth and Memory.* New York: Free Press, 1993.

Lish, Gordon. "A Fool for Salinger." *Antioch Review* 44, no. 4 (1986): 408–15.

———. "For Jeromé—with Love and Kisses." In *What I Know So Far*, 153–225. New York: Four Walls Eight Windows, 1996.

———. "For Rupert—with No Promises." In *What I Know So Far*, 85–104. New York: Four Walls Eight Windows, 1996. Originally published anonymously in *Esquire*, February 1977.

Livingston, James T. "J. D. Salinger: The Artist's Struggle to Stand on Holy Ground." In *Adversity and Grace,* edited by Nathan A. Scott Jr., 113–32. Chicago: University of Chicago Press, 1968.

Lodge, David. "Family Romances." *Times Literary Supplement*, June 13, 1975, 642.

———. *The Modes of Modern Writing*. Ithaca, NY: Cornell University Press, 1979.

———. *The Novelist at the Crossroads and Other Essays on Fiction and Criticism.* Ithaca, NY: Cornell University Press, 1971.

Longstreth, T. Morris. "New Novels in the News." *Christian Science Monitor*, July 19, 1951, 11.

Lorch, Thomas M. "J. D. Salinger: The Artist, the Audience, and the Popular Arts." *South Dakota Review* 5, no. 4 (1967–68): 3–13.

Lowrey, Burling. "Salinger and the House of Glass." *New Republic*, October 26, 1959, 23–24.

Lubasch, Arnold H. "Salinger Biography Is Blocked." *New York Times*, January 30, 1987, A-1, C-26.

Luedtke, Luther S. "J. D. Salinger and Robert Burns: *The Catcher in the Rye.*" *Modern Fiction Studies* 16, no. 2 (1970): 198–201.

Lundquist, James. *J. D. Salinger.* New York: Ungar, 1979.

Luscher, Robert M. "Textual Variants in J. D. Salinger's 'De Daumier-Smith's Blue Period.'" *Resources for American Literary Study* 18 (1992): 53–57.

Lutz, Norma Jean. "Biography of J. D. Salinger." In *J. D. Salinger*, edited by Harold Bloom, 3–44. Bloom's BioCritiques. Philadelphia: Chelsea House, 2002.

Lyman, Rick. "Dorothy Olding, Loyal Literary Agent, Dies at 87." *New York Times*, May 20, 1997, D-23.

Lyons, John O. "The Romantic Style of Salinger's 'Seymour: An Introduction.'" *Wisconsin Studies in Contemporary Literature* 4, no. 1 (1963): 62–69.

Mahon, Gigi. *The Last Days of* The New Yorker. New York: McGraw Hill, 1988.

Mailer, Norman. *Advertisements for Myself.* New York: G. P. Putnam's Sons, 1959.

———. "Evaluations—Further Quick and Expensive Comments on the Talent in the Room." *Esquire*, July 1963.

———. "Some Children of the Goddess." *Esquire*, July 1963, 64–69,105.

Malcolm, Janet. "Justice to J. D. Salinger." *New York Review of Books*, June 21, 2001, 16, 18–22.

Mandel, Siegfried. "Salinger in Continental Jeans: The Liberation of Boll and Other Germans." In *Critical Essays on Salinger's* The Catcher in the Rye, edited by Joel Salzberg, 214–26. Boston: G. K. Hall, 1990.

Maple, Anne. "Salinger's Oasis of Innocence." *New Republic*, September 18, 1961, 22–23.

Marcus, Fred H. "*The Catcher in the Rye:* A Live Circuit." *English Journal* 52 (January 1963): 1–8.

Margolis, John D. "Salinger's *The Catcher in the Rye.*" *Explicator* 22 (November 1963): item 23.

Marie Cecile, Sister. "J. D. Salinger's Circle of Privacy." *Catholic World* 194 (February 1962): 296–301.

Marsden, Malcolm M. *If You Really Want to Know: A Catcher Casebook.* Glenview, IL: Scott, Foresman and Company, 1963.

Martin, Augustine. "A Note on J. D. Salinger." *Studies: An Irish Quarterly Review* 48 (Fall 1959): 336–45.

Martin, Douglas. "Ian Hamilton, 63, Whose Salinger Book Caused a Stir, Dies." *New York Times*, January 7, 2002, B-6.

Martin, Hansford. "The American Problem of Direct Address." *Western Review* 16 (Winter 1952): 101–14.

———. "Four Volumes of Short Stories: An Irreverent Review." *Western Review* 18 (Winter 1954): 172–74.

Martin, John S. "Copperfield and Caulfield: Dickens in the Rye." *Notes on Modern American Literature* 4 (1980): item 29.

Martin, Robert A. "Remembering Jane in *The Catcher in the Rye*." *Notes on Contemporary Literature* 28, no. 4 (1998): 2–3.

Matis, Jim. "'The Catcher in the Rye': Controversy on Novel in Texas Is Just One in Long List of Episodes." *Houston Post*, May 4, 1961, 7:6.

Matthews, James F. "J. D. Salinger: An Appraisal." *University of Virginia Magazine* 1 (Spring 1956): 52–60.

Matthews, Marsha Caddell. "Death and Humor in the Fifties: The Ignition of Barth, Heller, Nabokov, O'Connor, Salinger and Vonnegut." Ph.D. diss., Florida State University, 1987.

Maxwell, William. "J. D. Salinger." *Book-of-the-Month Club News*, July 1951, 5–6.

Mayhew, Alice Ellen. "Salinger's Fabulous Glass Family." *Commonweal*, October 6, 1961, 48–50.

Maynard, Joyce. Afterword. In *At Home in the World: A Memoir*, 349–54. New York: Picador, 1999. Paperback edition only.

———. *At Home in the World: A Memoir*. New York: Picador, 1998.

———. *Looking Back*. New York: Doubleday, 1973.

McCarthy, Mary. "J. D. Salinger's Closed Circuit." In *If You Really Want to Hear about It: Writers on J. D. Salinger and His Work,* edited by Catherine Crawford, 127–33. New York: Thunder's Mouth Press, 2006. Originally published in *Harper's,* October 1962.

McCort, Dennis. "Hyakujo's Geese, Amban's Doughnuts, and Rilke's Carrousel: Sources East and West for Salinger's Catcher." *Comparative Literature Studies* 34 (1997): 260–78.

McDaniel, Sean. *A Catcher's Companion: The World of Holden Caulfield.* Santa Monica, CA: Lit. Happens, 2009.

McDowell, Edwin. "154 at *The New Yorker* Protest Choice of Editor." *New York Times*, January 15, 1987, C-22.

McGrath, Charles. "J. D. Salinger, Author Who Fled Fame, Dies at 91." *New York Times*, January 29, 2010, A-1, A-16, A-17.

———. "Still Paging Mr. Salinger." *New York Times*, December 31, 2008, C-1.

McIntyre, John P. "A Preface for 'Franny and Zooey.'" *Critic* 20 (February–March 1962): 25–28.

McKinley, Jesse. "Iranian Film Is Canceled after Protest by Salinger." *New York Times*, November 21, 1998, B-9.

McManus, John C. *The American at Normandy: The Summer of 1944—The American War from the Normandy Beaches to Falaise*. New York: Tom Doherty Associates, 2004.

———. *The Deadly Brotherhood: The American Combat Soldiers in World War II*. New York: Presidio Press, 1998.

McNamara, Eugene. "Holden as Novelist." *English Journal* 54, no. 3 (1965): 166–70.

McSweeny, Kerry. "Salinger Revisited." *Critical Survey* 20, no. 1 (1978): 61–68.

Mehta, Ved. *Remembering Mr. Shawn's* New Yorker: *The Invisible Art of Editing*. New York: Overlook Press, 1998.

Melchior, Ib. *Case by Case*. New York: Presidio, 1993.

Mellard, James M. "The Disappearing Subject: A Lacanian Reading of *The Catcher in the Rye*." In *Critical Essays on Salinger's* The Catcher in the Rye, edited by Joel Salzberg, 197–214. Boston: G. K. Hall, 1990.

Menand, Louis. "Holden at Fifty: 'The Catcher in the Rye' and What It Spawned." *New Yorker*, October 1, 2001, 82–87.

Meral, Jean. "The Ambiguous Mr. Antolini in Salinger's *The Catcher in the Rye*." *Caliban* 7 (1970): 55–58.

Merriam, Robert. *Dark December: The Full Account of the Battle of the Bulge*. Chicago: Ziff-Davis, 1947.

Metcalf, Frank. "The Suicide of Salinger's Seymour Glass." *Studies in Short Fiction* 9 (Summer 1972): 243–46.

Miller, Edward G. *A Dark and Bloody Ground: The Hürtgen Forest and the Roer River Dams, 1944–1945*. College Station: Texas A&M University Press, 1995.

Miller, Edwin Haviland. "In Memoriam: Allie Caulfield in *The Catcher in the Rye*." *Mosaic: A Journal for the Interdisciplinary Study of Literature* 15, no. 1 (1982): 129–40.

Miller, James E., Jr. "*Catcher* in and out of History." *Critical Inquiry* 3, no. 3 (1977): 599–603.

———. *J. D. Salinger*. Minneapolis: University of Minnesota Press, 1965.

Miltner, Robert. "Mentor Mori; or, Sibling Society and the Catcher in the Bly." In The Catcher in the Rye: *New Essays*, edited by J. P. Steed, 33–52. New York: Peter Lang, 2002.

Mirza, Humayun A. "The Influence of Hindu-Buddhist Psychology and Philosophy on J. D. Salinger's Fiction." Ph.D. diss., State University of New York at Binghamton, 1976.

Mizener, Arthur. "The American Hero as Poet: Seymour Glass." In *The Sense of Life in the Modern Novel*, 227–46. Boston: Houghton Mifflin, 1964.

———. "In Genteel Traditions." *New Republic*, May 25, 1953, 19–20.

———. "The Love Song of J. D. Salinger." *Harper's*, February 1959, 83–90.

"Mlle Passports." *Mademoiselle*, May 1947, 34.

Monas, Sidney. "Fiction Chronicle: 'No Mommy and No Daddy.'" *Hudson Review* 6 (Autumn 1953): 466–70.

Montgomery, Paul L. "Lennon Murder Suspect Preparing Insanity Defense." *New York Times*, February 9, 1981, B-12.

———. "Police Trace Tangled Path Leading to Lennon's Slaying at the Dakota." *New York Times*, December 10, 1980.

Moore, Deborah Dash. *GI Jews: How World War II Changed a Generation*. Cambridge, MA: Belknap Press of Harvard University Press, 2004.

Moore, Dinty. *Between Panic and Desire*. Lincoln: University of Nebraska Press, 2008.

Moore, Robert P. "The World of Holden." *English Journal* 54 (March 1965): 159–65.

Moss, Adam. "Catcher Comes of Age." *Esquire*, December 1981, 56–58, 60.

Mueller, Bruce, and Will Hochman. *Critical Companion to J. D. Salinger*. New York: Facts on File, 2010.

Murray, James G. "Franny and Zooey." *Critic* 20 (October–November 1961): 72–73.

Nabokov, Dmitri, and Matthew Bruccoli, eds. *Vladimir Nabokov: Selected Letters*. New York: Harcourt, Brace and Jovanovich, 1989.

Nabokov, Vladimir. *Strong Opinions*. New York: McGraw-Hill, 1973.

Nadel, Alan. "Rhetoric, Sanity, and the Cold War: The Significance of Holden Caulfield's Testimony." *Centennial Review* 32, no. 4 (1988): 351–71.

Naparsteck, Martin. "Collecting J. D. Salinger." *Firsts: The Book Collector's Magazine* 19, no. 1 (2009): 28–37.

Newlove, Donald. "'Hapworth 16, 1924.'" *Village Voice*, August 22, 1974, 27.

Nieman, Susan. *Evil in Modern Thought: An Alternative History of Philosophy*. Princeton: Princeton University Press, 2002.

Nikhilananda, Swami. *Hinduism: Its Meaning for the Liberation of the Spirit*. New York: Harper and Brothers, 1958.

Noland, Richard W. "The Novel of Personal Formula: J. D. Salinger." *University Review* 33 (Autumn 1966): 19–24.

"The No-Nonsense Kids." *Time*, November 18, 1957, 51–52, 54.

Nordell, Rod. "The Salinger Phenomenon." *Christian Science Monitor*, September 14, 1961, 7.

"Notes on People: J. D. Salinger Privately Passes a Milestone." *New York Times*, January 1, 1979, 22.

Oates, Joyce Carol. "Words of Love, Priced to Sell." *New York Times*, May 18, 1999, A-23.

O'Connor, Dennis L. "J. D. Salinger: Writing as Religion." *Wilson Quarterly* 4 (Spring 1980): 182–90.

———. "J. D. Salinger's Religious Pluralism: The Example of 'Raise High the Roof Beam, Carpenters.'" *Southern Review* 20, no. 2 (1984): 316–32.

O'Connor, Flannery. *Collected Works.* New York: Library of America, 1988.

O'Hara, J. D. "No Catcher in the Rye." *Modern Fiction Studies* 9 (Winter 1963–64): 370–76.

O'Hearn, Sheila. "The Development of Seymour Glass as a Figure of Hope in the Fiction of J. D. Salinger." Master's thesis, McMaster University, 1982.

Ohmann, Carol, and Richard Ohmann. "Reviewers, Critics, and *The Catcher in the Rye.*" *Critical Inquiry* 3, no. 1 (1976): 15–37.

Ohmann, Carol, and Richard Ohmann. "Universals and the Historically Particular." *Critical Inquiry* 3, no. 4 (1977): 773–77.

Olan, Levi A. "The Voice of the Lonesome: Alienation from Huck Finn to Holden Caulfield." *Southwest Review* 48 (Spring 1963): 143–50.

Oldsey, Bernard S. "The Movies in the Rye." *College English* 23, no. 3 (1961): 209–15.

———. "Salinger and Golding: Resurrection or Response." *College Literature* 6 (Spring 1979): 136–44.

Pace, Eric. "William Shawn, 85, Is Dead: *New Yorker*'s Gentle Despot." *New York Times,* December 9, 1992, A-1, B-15.

Panichas, George A. "J. D. Salinger and the Russian Pilgrim." In *The Reverent Discipline: Essays in Literary Criticism and Culture,* 292–305. Knoxville: University of Tennessee Press, 1974.

Paniker, Sumitra. "The Influence of Eastern Thought on 'Teddy' and the Seymour Glass Stories of J. D. Salinger." Ph.D. diss., University of Texas at Austin, 1971.

Panova, Vera. "On J. D. Salinger's Novel." In *Soviet Criticism of American Literature in the Sixties,* edited and translated by Carl R. Proffer, 4–10. Ann Arbor, MI: Ardis, 1972.

Parker, Christopher. "'Why the Hell *Not* Smash All the Windows?'" In *Salinger: A Critical and Personal Portrait,* edited by Henry Anatole Grunwald, 254–58. New York: Harper & Row, 1962.

Parker, Danny S. *The Battle of the Bulge: Hitler's Ardennes Offensive, 1944–1945.* Philadelphia: Combined Books, 1991.

Pattanaik, Dipti R. "'The Holy Refusal': A Vedantic Interpretation of J. D. Salinger's Silence." *MELUS* 23, no. 2 (1998): 113–27.

Patterson, Charles. *Eternal Treblinka.* New York: Lantern Books, 2002.

Paul, Marcia B., and Kevan Choset. Complaint: J. D. Salinger, individually and as Trustee of the J. D. Salinger Literary Trust, Plaintiff, v. John Doe, writing under the name John David California, [et al.]. Filed in United States District Court, Southern District of New York, June 1, 2009.

Pawel, Ernst. *The Nightmare of Reason: A Life of Franz Kafka.* New York: Farrar, Straus & Giroux, 1984.

Peavy, Charles D. "'Did You Ever Have a Sister?' Holden, Quentin and Sexual Innocence." *Florida Quarterly* 1, no. 3 (1968): 82–95.

Peden, William. "Esthetics of the Story." *Saturday Review*, April 11, 1953, 43–44.

"People." *Time*, June 25, 1965, 52.

Perelman, S. J. *Don't Tread on Me*. Edited by Prudence Crowther. New York: Penguin, 1987.

Perrine, Laurence. "Teddy? Booper? Or Blooper?" *Studies in Short Fiction* 4 (Spring 1967): 217–24.

"Personal and Otherwise." *Harper's*, April 1949, 9–10.

Phelps, Robert. "The Difference Is Qualitative." *Freeman*, August 24, 1953, 857.

———. "Salinger: A Man of Fierce Privacy." *New York Herald Tribune Books*, September 17, 1961, 3.

———. "A Writer Who Talks to and of the Young." *New York Herald Tribune Books*, September 17, 1961, 3, 14.

Phillips, Mark. "J. D. Salinger: A Hidden Hand?" *Saturday Review*, November–December 1985, 39–45.

Phillips, Paul. "Salinger's *Franny and Zooey*." *Mainstream* 15 (January 1962): 32–39.

Pickering, John Kenneth. "J. D. Salinger: Portraits of Alienation." Ph.D. diss., Case Western Reserve University, 1968.

Pickrel, Paul. "Outstanding Novels." *Yale Review* 42 (Summer 1953): vi–xvi.

The Pilgrim Continues His Way. London: Society for Promoting Christian Knowledge, 1943.

Pilkington, John. "About This Madman Stuff." *University of Mississippi Studies in English* 7 (1966): 67–75.

Pillsbury, Frederick. "Mysterious J. D. Salinger: The Untold Chapter of the Famous Writer's Years as a Valley Forge Cadet." *Sunday Bulletin Magazine*, October 29, 1961, 23–24.

Pinsker, Sanford. The Catcher in the Rye: *Innocence under Pressure*. New York: Twayne, 1993.

———. "*The Catcher in the Rye* and All: Is the Age of Formative Books Over?" *Georgia Review* 40, no. 4 (1986): 953–67.

Pinsker, Sanford, and Ann Pinsker. *Understanding* The Catcher in the Rye: *A Student Casebook to Issues, Sources, and Historical Documents*. Westport, CT: Greenwood Press, 1999.

Piwinski, David J. "Salinger's 'De Daumier-Smith's Blue Period': Pseudonym as Cryptogram." *Notes on Contemporary Literature* 15, no. 5 (1985): 3–4.

Pokrovsky, Gleb, trans. *The Way of a Pilgrim*. Woodstock, VT: Skylight Paths, 2001.

Poore, Charles. "Books of the Times." *New York Times*, April 9, 1953, 25.

———. "Books of the Times." *New York Times*, September 14, 1961, 29.

Poster, William. "Tomorrow's Children." *Commentary* 13 (January 1952): 90–92.

Prescott, Orville. "Books of the Times." *New York Times*, January 28, 1963, 9.

Prigozy Ruth. "*Nine Stories:* J. D. Salinger's Linked Mysteries." In *Modern America Short Story Sequences: Composite Fictions and Fictive Communities*, edited by J. Gerald Kennedy, 114–32. Cambridge: Cambridge University Press, 1995.

Pugsley, Alexander Hunt. "'The Secret Goldfish': A Study of J. D. Salinger's Short Fiction." Master's thesis, University of Toronto, 1990.

Purcell, William F. "From Half-Shot to Half-Assed: J. D. Salinger and the Evolution of a *Skaz.*" *Studies in American Literature* 35 (February 1999): 109–23.

———. "Narrative Voice in J. D. Salinger's 'Both Parties Concerned' and 'I'm Crazy.'" *Studies in Short Fiction* 33 (Spring 1996): 278–80.

———. "Waker Glass: Salinger's Carthusian Doppelganger." *Literature and Belief* 20 (2000): 153–68.

———. "World War II and the Early Fiction of J. D. Salinger." *Studies in American Literature* 28 (1991): 77–93.

Quagliano, Anthony. "Hapworth 16, 1924: A Problem in Hagiography." *University of Dayton Review* 8, no. 2 (1971): 35–43.

Quinn, Judy. "Is It Possible? A J. D. Salinger for Spring." *Publishers Weekly*, January 27, 1997, 10.

———. "A Spotlight on Salinger." *Publishers Weekly*, July 12, 1999, 26–27.

Rachels, David. "Holden Caulfield: A Hero for All the Ages." *Chronicle of Higher Education,* March 30, 2001, B-5.

Raeburn, Ben, ed. *Treasury for the Free World.* New York: Arco, 1946.

Ralston, Nancy C. "Holden Caulfield: Super-Adolescent." *Adolescence* 6 (Winter 1971): 429–32.

Ranchan, Som P. *An Adventure in Vedanta: J. D. Salinger's The Glass Family*. Delhi: Ajanta, 1989.

———. "Echoes of the Gita in Salinger's 'Franny and Zooey.'" In *The Gita in World Literature*, edited by C. D. Verma, 214–19. New Delhi: Sterling, 1990.

Ranly, Ernest W. "Journey to the East." *Commonweal*, February 23, 1973, 465–69.

Raymond, John. "The Salinger Situation." *Sunday Times (London)*, June 3, 1962, 33.

Razdan, Brij M. "From Unreality to Reality: *Franny and Zooey*—A Reinterpretation." *Panjab University Research Bulletin 9*, nos. 1–2 (1978): 3–15.

Rees, Richard. "The Salinger Situation." In *Contemporary American Novelists*, edited by Henry T. Moore, 95–105. Carbondale: Southern Illinois University Press, 1964.

Reiff, Raychel Haugrud. *J. D. Salinger:* The Catcher in the Rye *and Other Works*. Tarrytown, NY: Marshall Cavendish Benchmark, 2008.

Reiman, Donald H. "Salinger's *The Catcher in the Rye*, Chapters 22–26." *Explicator* 21 (March 1963): item 58.

Remnick, David. "Exile on Main Street: Don DeLillo's Undisclosed Underworld." *New Yorker*, September 15, 1997.

———. "Matt Salinger: Into the Spotlight." *Washington Post*, December 28, 1984, C-1, C-2.

Rilke, Rainer Maria. *Duino Elegies*. New York: Norton, 1939.

———. *The Notebooks of Malte Laurids Brigge.* New York: Norton, 1949.

———. *Poems 1906 to 1926*. Introduction by J. B. Leishman. New York: New Directions, 1957.

———. *Translations from the Poetry of Rainer Maria Rilke*. New York: Norton, 1938.

Roberts, Preston Thomas, Jr. "*The Catcher in the Rye* Revisited." *Cresset* 40 (November–December 1976): 6–10.

Robinson, Sally. "Masculine Protest in *The Catcher in the Rye*." In *J. D. Salinger's* The Catcher in the Rye, edited by Sarah Graham, 70–76. London: Routledge, 2007.

Roemer, Danielle M. "The Personal Narrative and Salinger's *The Catcher in the Rye*." *Western Folklore* 51, no. 1 (1992): 5–10.

Rogers, Lydia. "The Psychoanalyst and the Fetishist: Wilhelm Stekel and Mr. Antolini in *The Catcher in the Rye*." *Notes on Contemporary Literature* 32, no. 4 (2002): 2–3.

Romano, John. "Salinger Was Playing Our Song." *New York Times Book Review*, June 3, 1979, 11, 48–49.

Roper, Pamela E. "Holden's Hat." *Notes on Contemporary Literature* 7, no. 3 (1977): 8–9.

Rose, Kenneth D. *Myth and the Greatest Generation.* New York: Routledge, 2008.

Rosen, Gerald. "A Retrospective Look at *The Catcher in the Rye*." *American Quarterly* 29 (Winter 1977): 547–62.

———. *Zen in the Art of J. D. Salinger*. Berkeley, CA: Creative Arts, 1977.

Rosenbaum, Ron. "The Catcher in the Driveway." In *If You Really Want to Hear about It: Writers on J. D. Salinger and His Work*, edited by Catherine Crawford, 63–87. New York: Thunder's Mouth Press, 2006. Originally published as "The Man in the Glass House," *Esquire*, June 1997.

Rosenthal, Edward H., et al. Brief for Defendants-Appellants Fredrik Colting, writing under the name John David California, [et al.] v. J. D. Salinger, individually and as Trustee of the J. D. Salinger Literary Trust. Filed in the United States Court of Appeals for the Second Circuit, July 23, 2009.

Ross, Lillian. "Bearable." *New Yorker*, February 8, 2010, 22–23.

———. *Here but Not Here: A Love Story*. New York: Random House, 1998.

Ross, Theodore J. "Notes on J. D. Salinger." *Chicago Jewish Forum* 22 (Winter 1963–64): 149–53.

Rot, Sandor. "J. D. Salinger's Oeuvre in the Light of Decoding Stylistics and Information-Theory." *Studies in English and American* 4 (1978): 85–129.

Roth, Philip. *My Life as a Man.* In *Novels 1973–1977.* New York: Library of America, 2006.

———. "Writing American Fiction." In *Reading Myself and Others*, 117–35. New York: Farrar, Straus & Giroux, 1975.

Rowe, Joyce. "Holden Caulfield and American Protest." In *New Essays on* The Catcher in the Rye, edited by Jack Salzman, 77–95. Cambridge: Cambridge University Press, 1991.

Rowland, Stanley J., Jr. "Love Parable." *Christian Century*, December 6, 1961, 1464–65.

Rupp, Richard H. "J. D. Salinger: A Solitary Liturgy." In *Celebration of Postwar American Fiction, 1945–1967*, 113–31. Coral Gables, FL: University of Miami Press, 1970.

Rush, Robert Sterling. *Hell in Hürtgen Forest: The Ordeal and Triumph of an American Infantry Regiment.* Lawrence: University Press of Kansas, 2001.

Russell, John. "Salinger, from Daumier to Smith." *Wisconsin Studies in Contemporary Literature* 4, no. 1 (1963): 70–87.

———. "Salinger's Feat." *Modern Fiction Studies* 12, no. 3 (1966): 299–311.

Saha, Winifred M. "J. D. Salinger: The Younger Writer and Society." Ph.D. diss., University of Chicago, 1957.

"Saint or Slob?" *Times Literary Supplement*, March 8, 1963, 165.

Salinger, J. D. *The Catcher in the Rye.* Boston: Little, Brown, 1951.

———. *Franny and Zooey.* Boston: Little, Brown, 1961.

———. "Hapworth 16, 1924." *New Yorker*, June 19, 1965.

———. *Nine Stories.* Boston: Little, Brown, 1953.

———. *Raise High the Roof Beam, Carpenters and Seymour: An Introduction.* Boston: Little, Brown, 1963.

Salinger, Margaret A. Afterword. In *Dream Catcher: A Memoir,* 435–47. New York: Pocket Books, 2001. Paperback edition only.

———. *Dream Catcher: A Memoir.* New York: Washington Square Press, 2000.

Salzberg, Joel, ed. *Critical Essays on Salinger's* The Catcher in the Rye. Boston: G. K. Hall, 1990.

Salzman, Jack, ed. *New Essays on* The Catcher in the Rye. Cambridge: Cambridge University Press, 1991.

Schiff, Stacy. *Vera: Mrs. Vladimir Nabokov.* New York: Random House, 1999.

Schrader, Allen. "Emerson to Salinger to Parker." *Saturday Review*, April 11, 1959, 52, 58.

Schriber, Mary Suzanne. "Holden Caulfield, C'est Moi." In *Critical Essays on Salinger's* The Catcher in the Rye, edited by Joel Salzberg, 226–38. Boston: G. K. Hall, 1990.

Schulz, Max F. "Epilogue to 'Seymour: An Introduction': Salinger and the Crisis of Consciousness." *Studies in Short Fiction* 5 (Winter 1968): 128–38.

Schwartz, Arthur. "For Seymour—with Love and Judgment." *Wisconsin Studies in Contemporary Literature* 4, no. 1 (1963): 88–99.

Scott, Walter. "Personality Parade." *St. Louis Post-Dispatch Parade*, May 23, 1971, 4.

Seabrook, John. "A Night at the Movies." *New Yorker*, February 8, 2010, 23.

Searles, George J., ed. *Conversations with Philip Roth.* Jackson: University Press of Mississippi, 1992.

———. "Salinger Redux via Roth: An Echo of *Franny and Zooey* in *My Life as a Man.*" *Notes on Contemporary Literature* 16, no. 2 (March 1986): 7.

Seed, David. "Keeping It in the Family: The Novellas of J. D. Salinger." In *The Modern American Novella*, edited by A. Robert Lee, 139–61. New York: St. Martin's Press, 1989.

Seelye, John. "Holden in the Museum." In *New Essays on* The Catcher in the Rye, edited by Jack Salzman, 23–33. Cambridge: Cambridge University Press, 1991.

Seitzman, Daniel. "Salinger's 'Franny': Homoerotic Imagery." *American Imago* 22 (Spring–Summer 1965): 57–76.

———. "Therapy and Antitherapy in Salinger's 'Zooey.'" *American Imago* 25 (Summer 1968): 140–62.

Seng, Peter J. "The Fallen Idol: The Immature World of Holden Caulfield." *College English* 23, no. 3 (1961): 203–9.

Senzaki, Nyogen, and Paul Reps. *101 Zen Stories.* Philadelphia: David McKay, 1940.

Shames, Laurence. "John Lennon, Where Are You?" *Esquire*, November 1980.

Shapira, Ian. "For a Very Brief While, J. D. Salinger Returned His Calls." *Washington Post*, January 29, 2010, C-1.

Shaw, Peter. "Love and Death in *The Catcher in the Rye.*" In *New Essays on* The Catcher in the Rye, edited by Jack Salzman, 97–114. Cambridge" Cambridge University Press, 1991.

Shay, Jonathan. *Achilles in Vietnam: Combat Trauma and the Undoing of Character.* New York: Scribner, 1994.

Sheed, Wilfred. "J. D. Salinger, Humorist." In *Essays in Disguise*, 3–25. New York: Knopf, 1990. Originally published in *New York Review of Books*, October 27, 1988.

———. "Raise High the Roof Beam, Carpenters and Seymour: An Introduction." *Jubilee* 10 (April 1963): 51, 53–54.

Shepard, Ben. *A War of Nerves: Soldiers and Psychiatrist in the Twentieth Century.* Cambridge, MA: Harvard University Press, 2001.

Sherr, Paul C. "'The Catcher in the Rye' and the Boarding School." *Independent School Bulletin* 26 (December 1966): 42–44.

Shirer, William L. *The Rise and Fall of the Third Reich.* New York: Simon & Schuster, 1998.

Silverberg, Mark. "A Bouquet of Empty Brackets: Author-Function and the Search for J. D. Salinger." *Dalhousie Review* 75 (Summer–Fall 1995): 222–46.

———. "'You Must Change Your Life': Formative Responses to *The Catcher in the Rye.*" In The Catcher in the Rye: *New Essays,* edited by J. P. Steed, 7–32. New York: Peter Lang, 2002.

Silverman, Al, ed. *The Book of the Month: Sixty Years of Books in American Life.* Boston: Little, Brown, 1986.

———. *The Time of Their Lives: The Golden Age of Great American Book Publishers, Their Editors and Authors.* New York: St. Martin's Press, 2008.

Simms, L. Moody, Jr. "Seymour Glass: The Salingerian Hero as Vulgarian." *Notes on Contemporary Literature*, no. 5 (November 1975): 6–8.

Simonson, Harold P., and Phillip E. Hager, eds. *Salinger's "Catcher in the Rye": Clamor vs. Criticism.* Lexington, MA: D. C. Heath, 1963.

Skow, Jack. "Sonny: An Introduction." *Time*, September 15, 1961, 84–90.

Slabey, Jack M. "*The Catcher in the Rye:* Christian Theme and Symbol." *College Language Association Journal* 6 (March 1963): 170–83.

———. "Salinger's 'Casino': Wayfarers and Spiritual Acrobats." *English Record* 14 (February 1964): 16–20.

———. "Sergeant X and Seymour Glass." *Western Humanities Review* 16 (Autumn 1962): 376–77.

Slethaug, G. E. "Form in Salinger's Short Fiction." *Canadian Review of American Studies* 3, no.1 (1972): 50–59.

———. "Seymour: A Clarification." *Renascence* 23 (Spring 1971): 115–28.

Slide, Anthony. *The Encyclopedia of Vaudeville.* Westport, CT: Greenwood Press, 1994.

Sloan, Robin Adams. "The Gossip Column." *Washington Post*, October 17, 1982, A-1.

Smith, Dinitia. "Salinger Letters Are Sold and May Return to Sender." *New York Times*, June 23, 1999, B-1.

Smith, Dominic. "Salinger's *Nine Stories*: Fifty Years Later." *Antioch Review* 61, no. 4 (2003): 639–49.

Smith, Harrison. "Manhattan Ulysses, Junior." *Saturday Review*, July 14, 1951, 12–13.

Spanier, Sandra Wipple. "Hemingway's 'The Last Good Country' and *The Catcher in the Rye:* More Than a Family Resemblance." *Studies in Short Fiction* 19 (1982): 35–43.

Stannard, Richard M. *Infantry: An Oral History of a World War II Battalion*. New York: Macmillan, 1993.

Starosciak, Kenneth. *J. D. Salinger: A Thirty-Year Bibliography 1938–1968.* St. Paul, MN: Croixide Press, 1971.

Steed, J. P., ed. The Catcher in the Rye: *New Essays.* New York: Peter Lang, 2002.

Stein, William Bysshe. "Salinger's 'Teddy': *Tat Tvam Asi* or That Thou Art." *Arizona Quarterly* 29 (Autumn 1973): 253–65.

Steiner, George. "The Salinger Industry." *Nation,* November 14, 1959, 360–63.

Steinle, Pamela Hunt. *In Cold Fear:* The Catcher in the Rye *Censorship Controversies and Postwar American Character.* Columbus: Ohio State University Press, 2002.

Stern, James. "Aw, the World's a Crumby Place." *New York Times Book Review,* July 15, 1951, 5.

Stevenson, David L. "J. D. Salinger: The Mirror of Crisis." *Nation,* March 9, 1957, 215–17.

Stoltz, Craig. "J. D. Salinger's Tribute to Whit Burnett." *Twentieth Century Literature* 27, no. 4 (1981): 325–30.

Stone, Edward. "De Daumier-Smith's Blue Period." In *A Certain Morbidness: A View of American Literature,* 121–39. Carbondale: Southern Illinois University Press, 1969.

———. "Naming in Salinger." *Notes on Contemporary Literature* 1 (March 1971): 2–3.

———. "Salinger's Carrousel." *Modern Fiction Studies* 13, no. 4 (1967–68): 520–23.

Strauch, Carl F. "Kings in the Back Row: Meaning through Structure—A Reading of Salinger's *The Catcher in the Rye.*" *Wisconsin Studies in Contemporary Literature* 2, no. 1 (1961): 5–30.

———. "Salinger: The Romantic Background." *Wisconsin Studies in Contemporary Literature* 4, no. 1 (1963): 31–40.

Streitfeld, David. "Salinger Book to Break Long Silence." *Washington Post,* January 17, 1997, D-1.

Strong, Paul. "Black Wing, Black Heart—Betrayal in J. D. Salinger's 'The Laughing Man.'" *West Virginia University Philological Papers* 31 (1986): 91–96.

Sublette, Jack R. *J. D. Salinger: An Annotated Bibliography, 1938–1981.* New York: Garland, 1984.

Surace, Peter Carl. "Round Trips in the Fiction of Salinger, Bellow and Barth during the Nineteen Fifties." Ph.D. diss., Case Western Reserve University, 1996.

Suzuki, D. T. *Manual of Zen Buddhism.* London: Rider, 1950.

Swados, Harvey. "Must Writers Be Characters?" *Saturday Review,* October 1, 1960, 12–14, 50.

Swinton, John. "A Case Study of an 'Academic Bum': Salinger Once Stayed at Ursinus." *Ursinus Weekly,* December 12, 1960, 2, 4.

Symula, James Francis. "Censorship of High School Literature: A Study of the Incidents of Censorship Involving J. D. Salinger's 'The Catcher in the Rye.'" Ph.D. diss., State University of New York at Buffalo, 1969.

Tae, Yasuhiro. "Between Suicide and Enlightenment." *Kyushu American Literature* 26 (1985): 21–27.

Takeuchi, Yashiro. "The Burning Carousel and the Carnivalesque: Subversion and Transcendence at the Close of *The Catcher in the Rye*." *Studies in the Novel* 34, no. 3 (2002): 320–36.

———. "Salinger's *The Catcher in the Rye*." *Explicator* 60, no. 3 (2002): 164–66.

———. "The Zen Archery of Holden Caulfield." *English Language Notes* 42, no. 1 (2004): 55–63.

Teachout, Terry. "Salinger Then and Now." *Commentary* 84, no. 3 (1987): 61–64.

Terkel, Studs. *The Good War*

Theweleit, Klaus. *Male Fantasies,* vol. 1: *Women, Bodies, Floods, History.* Minneapolis: University of Minnesota Press, 1987.

Thorp, Willard. "Whit Burnett and *Story* Magazine." *Princeton University Library Chronicle* 27 (Autumn 1965): 107–12.

Thurber, James. *The Years with Ross.* Boston: Little, Brown, 1959.

Tierce, Mike. "Salinger's 'De Daumier-Smith's Blue Period.'" *Explicator* 42, no. 1 (1983): 56–58.

———. "Salinger's 'For Esmé—with Love and Squalor.'" *Explicator* 42, no. 3 (1984): 56–57.

Toland, John. *Battle: The Story of the Bulge.* New York: Random House, 1959.

Tosta, Michael R. "Will the Real Sergeant X Please Stand Up?" *Western Humanities Review* 16 (Autumn 1962): 376.

Toynbee, Philip. "Voice of America." *Observer (London)*, June 14, 1953, 9.

Travis, Mildred K. "Salinger's *The Catcher in the Rye*." *Explicator* 21 (December 1962): item 36.

Trombetta, Jim. "On the Untimely Demise of J. D. Salinger." *Crawdaddy*, March 1975, 34–38.

Trowbridge, Clinton W. "Hamlet and Holden." *English Journal* 57 (January 1968): 26–29.

———. "Salinger's Symbolic Use of Character and Detail in *The Catcher in the Rye*." *Cimarron Review* 4 (June 1968): 5–11.

———. "The Symbolic Structure of *The Catcher in the Rye*." *Sewanee Review* 74 (July–September 1966): 681–93.

Turner, Decherd, Jr. "The Salinger Pilgrim." In *Seventeenth Annual Conference: American Theological Library Association*, 59–69. Austin, TX: Episcopal Theological Seminary of the Southwest, 1963.

Unrue, John C. *J. D. Salinger*. Detroit: Gale, 2002.

———. *J. D. Salinger's* The Catcher in the Rye. Detroit: Gale, 2001.

Updike, John. "Anxious Days for the Glass Family." *New York Times Book Review*, September 17, 1961, 1, 52.

———. Foreword to *Franz Kafka: The Complete Stories*, edited by Nahum N. Glatzer, ix–xxi. New York: Schocken Books, 1983.

Vail, Dennis. "Holden and Psychoanalysis." *PMLA* 91, no. 1 (1976): 120–21.

Vanderbilt, Kermit. "Symbolic Resolution in *The Catcher in the Rye:* The Cap, the Carrousel, and the American West." *Western Humanities Review* 17 (Summer 1963): 271–77.

Vivekananda, Swami. *Vivekananda: The Yogas and Other Works*, complied and with a biography by Swami Nikhilananda. New York: Ramakrishna-Vivekananda Center, 1953.

Vogel, Albert W. "J. D. Salinger on Education." *School and Society* 91 (Summer 1963): 240–42.

Wain, John. "Go Home, Buddy Glass." *New Republic*, February 16, 1963, 21–22.

Wakefield, Dan. "Salinger and the Search for Love." In *Salinger: A Critical and Personal Portrait*, edited by Henry Anatole Grunwald, 176–91. New York: Harper & Row, 1962. Originally published in *New World Writing*, no. 14 (1958).

Walker, Gerald. "Salinger and the Purity of Spirit." *Cosmopolitan*, September 1961, 36.

Walker, Joseph S. "The Catcher Takes the Field: Holden, Hollywood, and the Making of a Man." In The Catcher in the Rye: *New Essays*, edited by J. P. Steed, 79–99. New York: Peter Lang, 2002.

Walter, Eugene. "A Rainy Afternoon with Truman Capote." *Intro Bulletin* 2 (December 1957): 1–2.

Waters, Juliet. "Critiquing the Catfight over Joyce Maynard's Biography." *Montreal Mirror*, October 8, 1998.

Way, Brian. "'Franny and Zooey' and J. D. Salinger." *New Left Review* 15 (May–June 1962): 72–82.

The Way of a Pilgrim. London: Society for Promoting Christian Knowledge, 1941.

Weatherby, W. J. "J.D." *Guardian (London)*, January 15, 1960, 8.

Weaver, Brett E. *An Annotated Bibliography (1982–2002) of J. D. Salinger.* Lewiston, NY: Edwin Mellen Press, 2002.

Weber, Myles. "Augmenting the Salinger Oeuvre by Any Means." In *Consuming Silences: How We Read Authors Who Don't Publish*, 88–116. Athens: University of Georgia Press, 2005.

———. *Consuming Silences: How We Read Authors Who Don't Publish.* Athens: University of Georgia Press, 2005.

Weinberg, Helen. "J. D. Salinger's Holden and Seymour and the Spiritual Activist Hero." In *The New Novel in America: The Kafkan Mode in Contemporary Fiction*, 141–64. Ithaca, NY: Cornell University Press, 1970.

Weintraub, Stanley. *11 Days in December*. New York: NAL Caliber, 2007.

Wells, Arvin R. "Huck Finn and Holden Caulfield: The Situation of the Hero." *Ohio University Review* 2 (1960): 31–42.

Welty, Eudora. "Threads of Innocence." *New York Times Book Review*, April 5, 1953, 4.

Wenke, John. *J. D. Salinger: A Study of the Short Fiction*. Boston: Twayne, 1991.

———. "Sergeant X, Esmé, and the Meaning of Words." *Studies in Short Fiction* 18 (Summer 1981): 251–59.

Wexellblatt, Robert. "Chekhov, Salinger, and Epictetus." *Midwest Quarterly* 28 (Autumn 1986): 50–76.

Whissen, Thomas Reed. *Classic Cult Fiction: A Companion to Popular Cult Literature*. Westport, CT: Greenwood Press, 1992.

White, William. *By-Line: Ernest Hemingway*. New York: Charles Scribner's Sons, 1967.

Whitfield, Stephen J. "Cherished and Cursed: Toward a Social History of *The Catcher in the Rye*." *New England Quarterly* 70, no. 4 (1997): 567–600.

Wieb, Dallas E. "Salinger's 'A Perfect Day for Bananafish.'" *Explicator* 23 (September 1964): item 3.

Wiegand, William. "J. D. Salinger's Seventy-eight Bananas." *Chicago Review* 11, no. 4 (1958): 3–19.

———. "The Knighthood of J. D. Salinger." *New Republic*, October 19, 1959, 19–21.

———. "Salinger and Kierkegaard." *Minnesota Review* 5 (May–July 1965): 137–56.

Wilkinson, Alec. *My Mentor: A Young Man's Friendship with William Maxwell*. Boston: Houghton Mifflin, 2002.

Willbern, David. *The American Popular Novel after World War II: A Study of 25 Best Sellers, 1947–2000*. Jefferson, NC: McFarland, 2013.

Wilson, Edmund. *Letters on Literature and Politics*. New York: Farrar, Straus & Giroux, 1977.

Wilson, George. *If You Survive: From Normandy to the Battle of the Bulge to the End of World War II, One American Officer's Riveting True Story*. New York: Ballantine Books, 1987.

Wiseman, Mary B. "Identifying with Characters in Literature." *Journal of Comparative Literature and Aesthetics* 4, nos. 1–2 (1981): 47–57.

"With Love & 20-20 Vision." *Time*, July 16, 1951, 97.

Wolfe, Tom. *Hooking Up*. New York: Farrar, Straus & Giroux, 2000.

———. "The *New Yorker* Affair." In *Hooking Up*, 247–93. New York: Farrar, Straus & Giroux, 2000.

"Writers' Writers." *New York Times Book Review*, December 4, 1977, 3, 58, 62, 68, 74.

Yagoda, Ben. *About Town: The* New Yorker *and the World It Made*. Cambridge, MA: Da Capo Press, 2001.

Yardley, Jonathan. *Ring: A Biography of Ring Lardner*. New York: Random House, 1977.

Yogananda, Paramahansa. *Autobiography of a Yogi*. Los Angeles: Self-Realization Fellowship, 1979.

"Young Authors: Twelve Whose First Novels Make Their Appearances This Fall." *Glamour*, September 1951, 202–5.

"Youthful Horror." *Nation*, April 18, 1953, 332.

ACKNOWLEDGMENTS

SHANE SALERNO:

This book had its origins on a rare rainy day in Los Angeles when I saw two photographs of J. D. Salinger, one superimposed over the other in a used bookstore known as much for its dust as its books. The first photograph was the iconic image of Salinger from the 1951 back jacket of *The Catcher in the Rye*. The second was taken many years later and depicted a haunted man in the winter of a difficult life. I spent nine years working on this book, trying to reconcile those two photographs and tell as complete a story as possible about Jerome David Salinger.

This book initially grew out of a documentary film I directed called *Salinger,* which was released theatrically in 2013 by The Weinstein Company and is forthcoming in 2014 from *American Masters* on PBS. While the origin of this book can be found in many of the interviews I conducted for that film, the book took on a life of its own when David Shields and I began studying the thousands of pages of interview transcripts, organizing and editing the interview passages into sections and chapters, conducting important new research, and adding our own analyses and commentaries.

Most biographies include photographs of and letters to and from the biographical subject, but in the case of someone as secretive as Salinger, photographs of Salinger and letters from him were extremely difficult to come by. For nearly a decade, I conducted a worldwide search for information that would help to unravel the enigma that is Salinger. I am honored to present it here and extremely grateful to everyone who provided photographs and letters; without this material, this book would not have been possible, and it would certainly not be anywhere nearly as complete an account as it is now.

I would like to thank:

Jonathan Karp, my publisher, for believing in this project from the very beginning and for pursuing it with incredible passion and conviction;

Jofie Ferrari-Adler, my editor, for his thoughtful suggestions, spirited debates, and intelligent criticisms on issues that mattered;

A. Scott Berg, the late (great) Gore Vidal, and Ben Yagoda for the kind advice they gave me during many phone calls when I thought I would never complete this project;

military historian John McManus for his careful review of the World War II sections of this book and historian Robert Abzug for his detailed review of the material that formed the basis for the chapter on Kaufering, the subcamp of Dachau that Salinger walked into in 1945 and as these pages argue, never walked out of;

the Fitzgerald family for allowing me to publish, for the first time, the extraordinary photos of J. D. Salinger taken by Paul Fitzgerald from 1945 to 1991 and Salinger's letters to Paul from 1945 to 2008. For more than sixty years Paul Fitzgerald never spoke of his relationship with J. D. Salinger, and his name cannot be found in any previous article or book about Salinger. I want to thank his family for trusting me with telling this important part of Salinger's story. The Fitzgerald photos and letters were invaluable to gaining a full understanding of J. D. Salinger's complex life and I cannot imagine this book without them;

Jean Miller for sharing—in these pages for the first time—her story and portions of Salinger's letters. Jean has a remarkable story to tell, beginning when she met Salinger at the age of fourteen, that could not be fully contained in these pages. I look forward to her memoir on her relationship with Salinger;

Eberhard Alsen for his many research trips to Germany, which I directed and funded over a six-year period. His commitment led to important new information and documents on Sylvia Welter, Salinger's first wife, his stay in a mental hospital, and other aspects of Salinger's service in World War II;

I want to express my deep gratitude to my sources, the great majority of whom spoke to me on the record. I personally interviewed more than two hundred people over nine years, and while not everyone appears by name, their important contributions are reflected on every page. I am particularly indebted to the residents of Cornish, New Hampshire, and Windsor, Vermont, for answering my questions in person and over the phone and directing me to others who *might* do the same. I am also grateful to former colleagues of Salinger's at the *New Yorker* who agreed to speak with me off the record. In every case where information was used from a source who would not go on the record, the information was confirmed by at least one additional independent source before appearing in these pages;

the gifted and generous Don Winslow for keeping the "anytime, anywhere" promise that he made to me in the dedication of *The Kings of Cool*. You are a great writer and an extraordinary friend;

Russell David Harper, revising editor of the 16th edition of the *Chicago Manual of Style*, for his careful vetting of this manuscript;

Alonzo Wickers at Davis Wright Tremaine and Michael Donaldson at Donaldson and Callif for their intelligent, methodical, and truly exhaustive (and exhausting) legal vetting on this complex project, which spreads across three different mediums: publishing (Simon & Schuster), film (The Weinstein Company), and television (*American Masters*). I also want to thank Robert Offer and Shelby Weiser and Toni Boim of Sloane, Offer, Weber & Dern who worked on this project daily for years, litigation counsel Max Sprecher and Emily Remes at Simon & Schuster.

Despite the project's consuming nine long years, critical information was still coming in during the final weeks (and even the final days) before going to print and I frustrated many with my insistence on writing and revising until the alarm bells rang. This certainly made for a better book but was a daily challenge for the hardworking men and women behind the scenes. I want to extend a very special thanks to Irene Kheradi for her unwavering support and enormous tolerance and her entire team at Simon & Schuster for their dedication, hard work, and long hours. Additionally I want to thank Nancy Singer for her tireless work and vision and Christopher Lin for his creative design. Everyone at Simon & Schuster worked under enormous time constraints in the closing months and this book would not have been possible without the commitment shown by every single department.

Also, Deborah Randall for her extraordinary producing efforts over nine years. I simply could not have made *Salinger* without her counsel and many remarkable contributions.

Anyone who writes about J. D. Salinger's life owes a debt to the many writers and reporters who have covered him. I want to acknowledge two previous Salinger biographers, Ian Hamilton and, of course, Paul Alexander, the latter of whom gave countless hours of assistance, support, and counsel to this project for nearly a decade. I also want to acknowledge Joyce Maynard's and Margaret Salinger's memoirs. Readers can debate the complicated motivations behind these books, but they have made an important contribution to our understanding of the life and work of J. D. Salinger. I was also helped by the work of John Skow, Ron Rosenbaum, Ernest Havemann, James Lundquist, Warren French, Eberhard Alsen, Harold Bloom, John Updike, Mary McCarthy, Alfred Kazin, Joan Didion, Frederick L. Gwynn, Joseph L. Blotner, William F. Belcher, and James W. Lee. Each of these writers valuably assisted my efforts to unravel the mystery of J. D. Salinger;

Cary Goldstein, Richard Rhorer, and their teams for their hard work behind the scenes;

Jonathan Harr for *A Civil Action* and Steven Bach for *Final Cut*, two books that proved extremely helpful to me during this process despite having nothing whatsoever to do with J. D. Salinger;

I want to give special thanks to Bonnie Rowan for nine years of extremely challenging research work in Washington, D.C., Maryland, Missouri, and other locations where she found material that shaped this project;

Natalie Mann for her extraordinary dedication and the countless contributions she made;

at The Weinstein Company, I want to thank Harvey Weinstein, David Glasser, Jennifer Malloy, Mark Gooder, Stephen Bruno, Erik Lomis, and Dani Weinstein;

at *American Masters,* Susan Lacy for being the first believer in this project and Stephen Segaller for being there on the day it really counted;

Carolyn K. Reidy;

Jim and Ann Gianopulos;

David Ellison;

Jim Cameron and Jon Landau;

Michael Mann for being both friend and mentor. Since I was nine years old I have aspired to the standard that you have set. I am incredibly grateful for the lessons you have passed onto me during years of collaboration;

J.C. for support, encouragement, and laughter;

Jean, Thomas, and Ottis Winslow, Buddy Squires, Betty Eppes, Michael Clarkson, David Victor Harris, Seán Hemingway, Brian Lipson, Jeffrey Doe, Ethel Nelson, Leila Hadley Luce, Alex Kershaw, Arne Schmidt, A. E. Hotchner, Joe Lee, Lois Lee and Braden Peter Lee, Ana Castillo, Regis Kimble, Langdon F. Page, Lorne Balfe, Craig and Stephanie Fanning, Michael McDermott and the McDermott family for their counsel, contributions, and friendship;

My deepest gratitude to Kristen for encouraging me nine long years ago to take this journey, knowing full well how relentlessly I would pursue it.

David Shields for his commitment to this project, particularly in the closing months, and for steadfastly believing it would happen years before there was a publishing, film, or television deal. I also want to thank the Shields family and Natalie Shields for her creative design work behind the scenes;

Finally, I want to thank Jerome David Salinger for living such an extraordinary life and one that I devoted nearly a decade to telling honestly. As do millions of others around the world, I look forward with great anticipation to reading the work Salinger diligently produced from 1965 until his death in 2010.

DAVID SHIELDS:

I would like to thank Laurie and Natalie for keeping all my faculties intact.

PHOTO CREDITS

Page 2: Courtesy of National Archives Still Pictures Division.
Page 5: Photo courtesy of Denise Fitzgerald.
Page 9: Courtesy of National Archives Still Pictures Division.
Page 10: Courtesy of National Archives Still Pictures Division.
Page 11: Courtesy of National Archives Still Pictures Division.
Page 13: Courtesy of National Archives Still Pictures Division.
Page 14: Courtesy of National Archives Still Pictures Division.
Page 17: Photo by Charles E. Rotkin.
Page 19: Courtesy of National Archives Still Pictures Division.
Page 21: Nancy McManus.
Page 22: Nancy McManus.
Page 23: Nancy McManus.
Page 25: Photo courtesy of Denise Fitzgerald.
Page 26: Courtesy of National Archives Still Pictures Division.
Page 28: Courtesy of Denise Fitzgerald.
Page 36: Yearbook photo, 1932.
Page 37: Yearbook photo, 1934.
Page 39: 1935 Valley Forge yearbook, 1935.
Page 41: Yearbook photo, 1935.
Page 43: Yearbook photo, 1936.
Page 51: Courtesy of Library of Congress.
Page 55: Courtesy of Library of Congress.
Page 59: © Bettmann/CORBIS.
Page 60: Hulton Archive/Stringer.
Page 61: Courtesy of Library of Congress.
Page 63: Photo by R. Gates.
Page 65: Courtesy of Library of Congress.
Page 67: Courtesy of Ben Yagoda.
Page 69, top: AP Photo/Robert Kradin.

Page 69, bottom: Photo by Weegee (Arthur Fellig)/International Center of Photography/Getty Images.
Page 72: © Bettmann/CORBIS.
Page 73: © Bettmann/CORBIS.
Page 77: Courtesy of Air Corps.
Page 82: Courtesy of Ben Yagoda.
Page 83: Courtesy of Library of Congress.
Page 84: © Bettmann/CORBIS.
Page 85: © Bettmann/CORBIS.
Page 86: Courtesy of *Ladies' Home Journal.*
Page 88, top: Courtesy of The Story Factory
Page 88, bottom: © Bettmann/CORBIS.
Page 92: Courtesy of Library of Congress.
Page 94: Courtesy of Michael Clarkson.
Page 99: Photo by Michael McDermott.
Page 103: Photo courtesy of Denise Fitzgerald.
Page 106: Photo courtesy of Denise Fitzgerald.
Page 108: Courtesy of Denise Fitzgerald.
Page 109: Photo courtesy of Denise Fitzgerald.
Page 119: Photo by Ted Russell.
Page 122: Photo by Ted Russell.
Page 124: Courtesy of National Archives Still Pictures Division.
Page 126: Courtesy of Library of Congress.
Page 131, left: © Bettmann/CORBIS.
Page 131, right: Courtesy of Library of Congress.
Page 141: Courtesy of National Archives Still Pictures Division.
Page 143: Courtesy of National Archives Still Pictures Division.
Page 146: Courtesy of Library of Congress.
Page 148: Courtesy of National Archives Still Pictures Division.
Page 152: Courtesy of Library of Congress.
Page 155: Courtesy of National Archives Still Pictures Division.
Page 156: Courtesy of Library of Congress.
Page 157: Courtesy of Library of Congress.
Page 159: Courtesy of Library of Congress.
Page 162: Courtesy of Library of Congress.
Page 166: Courtesy of Library of Congress.
Page 174: Courtesy of The Story Factory.
Page 177: Photo courtesy of Denise Fitzgerald.
Page 178: Photo courtesy of Denise Fitzgerald.

Page 179: Courtesy of relatives of Sylvia Welter.
Page 180: Photo courtesy of Denise Fitzgerald.
Page 181: Photo courtesy of Denise Fitzgerald.
Page 182: Courtesy of relatives of Sylvia Welter.
Page 183: Courtesy of The Story Factory.
Page 189: Illustration by Thomas Lea.
Page 190: Photo by Cary Hazlegrove.
Page 205: Pictorial Parade/Staff.
Page 206: Courtesy Leslie Epstein.
Page 214: Photo by Antony Di Gesu.
Page 215: Photos by Antony Di Gesu.
Page 216: Photo by Antony Di Gesu.
Page 219: Photo courtesy of Jean Miller.
Page 221: Photo by Katherine Huber.
Page 222: Photo courtesy of Jean Miller.
Page 223: Courtesy of The Story Factory.
Page 225: Courtesy of The Story Factory.
Page 228: Photo courtesy of Jean Miller.
Page 233: Photo courtesy of Jean Miller.
Page 237: Photo courtesy of Jean Miller.
Page 247: Photo courtesy of Denise Fitzgerald.
Page 252: Courtesy of The Story Factory.
Page 253: Photo by Antony Di Gesu.
Page 256: Photo by Lotte Jacobi.
Page 257: Time & Life Pictures/Getty Images.
Page 266: Photo by Gordon Parks//Time Life Pictures/Getty Images.
Page 267: Photo by Evening Standard/Getty Images.
Page 270: Photo by Antony Di Gesu.
Page 271: Photo by Antony Di Gesu.
Page 272: Photos by Antony Di Gesu.
Page 275: Photo by Antony Di Gesu.
Page 281: Photo courtesy of Jean Miller.
Page 286: Courtesy of Ethel Nelson.
Page 290: Courtesy of Ethel Nelson.
Page 293: Courtesy of Betty Eppes.
Page 296: Courtesy of Betty Eppes.
Page 301: Photo by Betty Eppes.
Page 304: Courtesy of Bantam.
Page 320: Yearbook photo.

Page 325: Courtesy of The Story Factory.
Page 330: Illustration by Xiaonan Sun.
Page 339: Illustration by Xiaonan Sun.
Page 353: Photo by Ted Russell.
Page 354: Photo by Ted Russell.
Page 356: Courtesy of *Time* magazine.
Page 358: *Life* magazine photo by Ted Russell.
Page 366, top: Photo by Ted Streshinsky.
Page 366, middle right: © Bettmann/CORBIS.
Page 366, middle left: Photo by Oscar White.
Page 366, bottom: Photo by Sylvia Salmi.
Page 368: Photo by Gisele Freund.
Page 376: Photo by Bernard Gotfryd/Getty Images.
Page 385: Courtesy of The Story Factory
Page 388: Photos by Bob Nelson.
Page 390: Copyright 2010 The Story Factory.
Page 410: Illustration by Xiaonan Sun.
Page 421: Photo by Bernard Gotfryd.
Page 422: Photo by Rick Maiman.
Page 423: Courtesy of Joyce Maynard.
Page 425: Courtesy of Joyce Maynard.
Page 426: Courtesy of Joyce Maynard.
Page 428: Photo by Bob Nelson.
Page 430: Courtesy of Joyce Maynard.
Page 431: Courtesy of Ballantine Books.
Page 432: Photo by Ted Russell.
Page 434: Courtesy of Joyce Maynard.
Page 436: Illustration by Xiaonan Sun.
Page 437: Illustration by Xiaonan Sun.
Page 442: Courtesy of Doubleday.
Page 443: Courtesy of Joyce Maynard.
Page 444: Courtesy of David Victor Harris.
Page 445: Courtesy of David Victor Harris.
Page 447: Courtesy of *New York Times*.
Page 452: Photos by Michael McDermott.
Page 453: Photos by Michael McDermott.
Page 454: Courtesy of CBS.
Page 456: Yearbook photo.
Page 462: © MC CLENDON JEAN/CORBIS SYGMA.

Page 471: Courtesy of New York Police Department.
Page 474: Photo by Andrew Lopez.
Page 476: © KEITH BEDFORD/Reuters/CORBIS.
Page 478: © Bettmann/CORBIS.
Page 481: AP photo.
Page 484: Photo by Jim Ruymen.
Page 496: © Bettmann/CORBIS.
Page 510: Photo courtesy of Denise Fitzgerald.
Page 516: Courtesy of Joyce Maynard.
Page 521: Courtesy of *Esquire* Magazine.
Page 525, left: Photo courtesy of Jean Miller.
Page 525, right: Courtesy of Doubleday.
Page 526: Courtesy of Joyce Maynard.
Page 533: Photo by Rick Friedman.
Page 550: Photo by Michael McDermott.
Page 561: Photo by Michael McDermott.

PERMISSIONS

Mel Elfin, "The Mysterious J. D. Salinger," was originally published in *Newsweek*, May 30, 1960. All rights reserved. Used by permission and protected by the Copyright Laws of the United States. The printing, copying, redistribution, or retransmission of this content without express written permission is prohibited.

John Skow, "Sonny: An Introduction," was originally published in *Time* magazine, September 15, 1961. Reprinted with permission.

Ernest Havemann, "The Search for the Mysterious J. D. Salinger," was originally published in *Life* magazine, November 3, 1961. Reprinted courtesy of Joel Havemann.

Lacey Fosburgh, "J. D. Salinger Speaks About His Silence," was originally published in the *New York Times*, November 3, 1974. Reprinted with permission.

Paul L. Montgomery, "Police Trace Tangled Path Leading to Lennon's Slaying at the Dakota; Police Trace Road to Lennon's Slaying; Celebrity-Seekers Common; A Moaning Response," was originally published in the *New York Times*, December 10, 1980. Reprinted with permission.

Paul Corkery, "Solitude May Be Bliss for Author J. D. Salinger, but to Son Matt, All the World's a Stage," was originally published in *People* magazine, October 31, 1983. All rights reserved. Reprinted/Translated from *People* magazine and published with permission of Time Inc. Reproduction in any manner in any language in whole or in part without written permission is prohibited.

David Remnick, "Matt Salinger: Into the Spotlight," was originally published in the *Washington Post*, December 28, 1984. Reprinted with permission.

James Brady, "In Step With: Matt Salinger," was originally published in *Parade* magazine, July 31, 1994. All rights reserved.

"Charlie Chaplin & Oona O'Neill" was originally published in *People* magazine, February 12, 1996. Reprinted with permission.

"Author Margaret Salinger and 'Dream Catcher'" was originally published on CNN.com, September 7, 2000. © 2000, Cable News Network, Inc. All rights reserved. Used by permission and protected by the Copyright Laws of the United States. The printing, copying, redistribution, or retransmission of this content without express written permission is prohibited.

Ron Rosenbaum, "The Flight from Fortress Salinger," was originally published in the *New York Times*, October 8, 2000. All rights reserved. Used by permission and protected by the Copyright Laws of the United States. The printing, copying, redistribution, or retransmission of this content without express written permission is prohibited.

Andrew Rogers, *The Veteran Who Is, the Boy Who Is No More: The Casualty of Identity in War Fiction*, was originally published by VDM Verlag Dr. Müller Aktiengesellschaft & Co. KG. © 2008 by VDM Verlag Dr. Müller Aktiengesellschaft & Co. KG and licensors. All rights reserved. Reprinted with permission.

Sharon Steel, "Letters by J. D. Salinger," was originally published in *Time Out New York*, March 8, 2010. Reprinted with permission.

ABOUT THE AUTHORS

DAVID SHIELDS is the author of fifteen books, including the *New York Times* bestseller *The Thing About Life Is That One Day You'll Be Dead*; *Reality Hunger*, named one of the best books of 2010 by more than thirty publications; *Black Planet*, a finalist for the National Book Critics Circle Award; and *Remote*, winner of the PEN/Revson Award. His work has been translated into twenty languages.

SHANE SALERNO is the director, producer, and writer of *Salinger*, the acclaimed documentary film about Salinger that premiered in September 2013 from the Weinstein Company and debuts as the 200th episode of *American Masters* on PBS in January 2014. In addition to *Salinger*, Salerno has written and produced a number of successful films and TV series. He most recently co-wrote and served as an executive producer of the highly praised film *Savages*, directed by Oliver Stone.